Wolters Kluwer

2016
Guidebook to
MICHIGAN
TAXES

Wayne D. Roberts, JD, MST, CPA.

Marjorie Gell, BA, JD, LLM.

Contributing Editors

Wolters Kluwer Editorial Staff Publication

Editor .... Amber Harker, Laura Leelun, Jennifer Troyer

Production Coordinator .... Govardhan. L

Production .... Dinesh Kumar R, M Sagar Subudhi

ISBN 978-0-8080-4179-5

4025 W. Peterson Ave.
Chicago, IL 60646-6085
800 248 3248
CCHGroup.com

Printed in the United States of America

PREFACE

This *Guidebook* gives a general picture of the taxes imposed by the state of Michigan and the general property tax levied by the local governments. All 2015 legislative amendments received as of press time are reflected, and references to Michigan and federal laws are to the laws as of the date of publication of this book.

The emphasis is on the law applicable to the filing of income tax returns in 2016 for the 2015 tax year. However, if legislation has made changes effective after 2015, we have tried to note this also, with an indication of the effective date to avoid confusion.

The taxes of major interest—income and sales and use—are discussed in detail. Other Michigan taxes, including intangibles and estate or inheritance taxes, are summarized, with particular emphasis on application, exemptions, returns, and payment.

Throughout the *Guidebook,* tax tips are highlighted to help practitioners avoid pitfalls and use the tax laws to their best advantage.

The *Guidebook* is designed as a quick reference work, describing the general provisions of the various tax laws, rules, and administrative practices. It is useful to tax practitioners, businesspersons, and others who prepare or file Michigan returns or who are required to deal with Michigan taxes.

The *Guidebook* is not designed to eliminate the necessity of referring to the law and rules for answers to complicated problems, nor is it intended to take the place of detailed reference works such as the CCH MICHIGAN TAX REPORTS. With this in mind, specific references to the publisher's Michigan and federal tax products are inserted in most paragraphs. By assuming some knowledge of federal taxes, the *Guidebook* is able to provide a concise, readable treatment of Michigan taxes that will supply a complete answer to most questions and will serve as a time-saving aid where it does not provide the complete answer.

SCOPE OF THE BOOK

This *Guidebook* is designed to do three things:

1. Give a general picture of the impact and pattern of all taxes levied by the state of Michigan and the general property tax levied by local governmental units.

2. Provide a readable, quick-reference work for the personal income tax and the single business tax. As such, it explains briefly what the Michigan law provides and indicates whether the Michigan provision is the same as federal law.

3. Analyze and explain the differences, in most cases, between Michigan and federal law.

HIGHLIGHTS OF 2015 MICHIGAN TAX CHANGES

The most important 2015 Michigan tax changes received by press time are noted in the "Highlights of 2015 Michigan Tax Changes" section of the *Guidebook,* beginning on page 11. This useful reference gives the practitioner up-to-the-minute information on changes in tax legislation.

LOCAL TAXES

Because Michigan cities may impose income taxes by adopting a uniform ordinance prescribed by the legislature, the *Guidebook* features a chapter (Chapter 23) on city income taxes that illustrates the nature and application of the taxes and the manner of their administration.

FINDERS

The practitioner may find the information wanted by consulting the general Table of Contents at the beginning of the *Guidebook*, the Table of Contents at the beginning of each chapter, the Topical Index, or the Law and Rule Locator.

The Topical Index is a useful tool. Specific taxes and information on rates, allocation, credits, exemptions, returns, payments, collection, penalties, and remedies are thoroughly indexed and cross-referenced to paragraph numbers in the *Guidebook*.

The Law and Rule Locator is an equally useful finders tool. Beginning on page 397, this finding list shows where sections of Michigan statutory law and administrative rules referred to in the *Guidebook* are discussed.

November 2015

ABOUT THE EDITORS

Wayne D. Roberts, JD, MST, CPA

Wayne D. Roberts is a tax attorney with more than twenty years of federal and state tax planning and litigation experience. He is a past Chair of the State Bar of Michigan – Taxation Section, and currently is Chair of the Taxation Section's Past Chairs Committee. Mr. Roberts also is a member of: the Executive Committee of the National Association of State Bar Taxation Sections ("NASBTS"); the Michigan Association of CPAs ("MICPA"), and both the Michigan and Grand Rapids Chamber of Commerce Taxation Committees. Mr. Roberts is a prolific writer and presenter on tax topics. Mr. Roberts currently serves as Chair of the Annual Michigan Tax Conference (sponsored jointly by the MICPA, the Taxation Section of the State Bar of Michigan, and the Michigan Department of Treasury), he is a co-author of the *Practical Guide to the Michigan Business Tax* (CCH 2009), and a co-Contributing Editor to the 2012, 2013, 2014, and 2015 editions of the *Guidebook to Michigan Taxes* (CCH).

Mr. Roberts earned his law degree, with honors, Order of the Coif, from the Ohio State University Michael E. Mortiz College of Law, his MS in Taxation, with distinction, from Grand Valley State University, and his BBA in Accountancy, Summa Cum Laude, from Western Michigan University. He is a member of the Taxation Practice Group at Varnum, LLP and can be reached at wdroberts@varnumlaw.com or (616) 336-6892.

Marjorie Gell, BA, JD, LLM

Marjorie Gell is a tax professor at Western Michigan University Cooley Law School's Grand Rapids campus where she teaches federal income tax and wills, estate and trusts at the J.D. level, as well as federal tax research in Cooley's LL.M. program.

Past Chair of the Taxation Section of the State Bar of Michigan, Professor Gell has served on Tax Council, the governing board of the Taxation Section of the State Bar of Michigan, since 2005. On behalf of the Taxation Section, she has authored and co-authored *amicus* briefs for submission to the Michigan Supreme Court and Michigan Court of Appeals. Professor Gell served for several years as a member of the State Bar of Michigan Standing Committee on Libraries, Legal Research, and Legal Publications. Professor Gell is the founder and active member of the Michigan Women's Tax Association, an organization of women accountants, attorneys, tax professors, students and members of Michigan industry. She is also a past member of the Grand Rapids Chamber of Commerce Tax and Regulatory Policy Committee. Professor Gell currently serves as a board member of the Grandville Avenue Arts and Humanities in Grand Rapids, and previously served on both the Board of Trustees as well as the Advisory Board of the Arts Council of Greater Grand Rapids.

Professor Gell was co-editor of *Guidebook to Michigan Taxes* (CCH 2012, 2013, 2014, and 2015), and was co-author of the *Practical Guide to the Michigan Business Tax* (CCH 2009). Professor Gell has written numerous articles in national and state tax journals, including the Pittsburgh Tax Review, State Tax Notes, Michigan Tax Lawyer and the Michigan Bar Journal. Her column "As a Matter of Tax" appeared in RIA State Tax Notes from 2009-2011.

CONTENTS

HIGHLIGHTS OF 2015 MICHIGAN TAX CHANGES

The most important tax changes received by press time that affect 2015 taxes are noted below.

Michigan Business Tax; Corporate Income Tax

• *Multistate Tax Compact repealed*

The state's adoption of the MTC (codified at M.C.L. 205.581 through M.C.L. 205.589) is repealed retroactively to January 1, 2008. See ¶1471. (Act 282 (S.B. 156), Laws 2014)

• *Retroactive repeal of MTC provisions was valid and constitutional*

The Michigan Court of Appeals has ruled that S.B. 156 (P.A. 282) that retroactively repealed the state's Multistate Tax Compact (MTC) provisions, including the MTC three-factor apportionment formula, effective January 1, 2008, was a valid act by the state Legislature and did not violate the U.S. or Michigan Constitution because the law provided clarity to taxpayers concerning the Legislature's original intent of the Michigan Business Tax (MBT) Act to require the use of a single sales-factor apportionment formula. See ¶1471. (*Gillette Commercial Operations North America & Subsidiaries, et al. v. Department of Treasury,* Michigan Court of Appeals, No. 325258, September 29, 2015, CCH MICHIGAN TAX REPORTS, ¶402-005)

• *"Affiliated groups" allowed to file combined returns*

Applicable to tax years that begin after 2012, "affiliated groups" are allowed to elect to file combined returns under the Michigan corporate income tax law. See ¶1567. (Act 266 (S.B. 367), Laws 2013)

• *Combined reporting calculation revised*

Applicable to tax years beginning after 2013, for the purposes of determining Michigan corporate income tax exemptions, credits, and the filing threshold, all transactions between persons included in a unitary business group are eliminated. See ¶1567. (Act 14 (H.B. 5009), Laws 2014)

Personal Income Tax

• *Rate reduction bill enacted*

Michigan Gov. Rick Snyder has approved an act that would decrease the personal income tax rate for any tax year beginning on or after January 1, 2023, when certain circumstances apply. See ¶102. (Act 180 (S.B. 414), Laws 2015)

Sales and Use Taxes

• *Affiliate and click-through nexus provisions added*

As of October 1, 2015, a seller is presumed to be engaged in business in Michigan if it or an affiliated person, other than a common carrier, engaged in certain specified activities. A seller is also presumed to be engaged in business in Michigan if the seller enters into an agreement with one or more residents under which the resident, for a commission or other consideration, directly or indirectly, refers potential customers, by a link on an Internet website, in-person oral presentation, or otherwise, to the seller. The presumption requires that the cumulative gross receipts from sales by the seller to customers in this state who are referred to the seller be greater than $10,000 during the immediately preceding 12 months and that the seller's total cumulative gross receipts from sales to customers in Michigan be greater than $50,000 during the immediately preceding 12 months. Both presumptions are rebuttable. See ¶1604. (Act 553 (S.B. 658) and Act 554 (S.B. 659, Laws 2015))

• *Cloud computing transactions were not taxable*

The Michigan Court of Appeals has affirmed a Court of Claims decision that held that a taxpayer's purchases of cloud computing services were not taxable because transactions involving the remote access to a third-party provider's technology infrastructure did not involve the delivery of prewritten software. The taxpayer, a property and casualty insurance provider, engaged third parties to provide services, including web-conferencing, web-hosting, payment processing, and online legal research, and information such as risk analyses and property valuations. The court determined that these transactions did not qualify as the sale of prewritten software because the third-party providers did not surrender possession and control of the code to the taxpayer. In regards to transactions where prewritten software was installed onto the taxpayer's computers, the taxpayer did exercise a right or power over tangible personal property. However, applying the factors in *Catalina Marketing Sales Corp. v. Department of Treasury*, 470 Mich 13 (2004), the court concluded that the transfer of such property was incidental to the rendition of nontaxable professional services. See ¶1704. (*Auto-owners Insurance Company v. Department of Treasury*, Michigan Court of Appeals, No. 321505, October 27, 2015)

• *Over-the-counter drugs exempt from use tax*

An exemption from use tax has been enacted, effective retroactively to March 14, 2014, for the sale of over-the-counter drugs for human use legally dispensed by prescription to correspond to the current sales tax exemption. An "over-the-counter drug" is defined as a drug labeled in accordance with the format and content requirements for labeling over-the-counter drugs under CFR 201.66. In addition, the sales tax exemption for prescription drugs for human use has been amended to exempt drugs that can only be legally dispensed by prescription. See ¶1703. (Act 171 (H.B. 4464) and Act 172 (H.B. 4465), Laws 2015)

• *Electric utility equipment used to alter voltage partially exempt under industrial processing exemption*

The Michigan Supreme Court has held that an electric utility was entitled to an industrial processing exemption from use tax on equipment located outside its generation plants because altering the voltage of the electricity constitutes "converting or conditioning [electricity] by changing the form, composition, quality, combination, or character... for ultimate sale at retail." However, the property was also used simultaneously for nonexempt distribution and shipping activities, and, consequently, the exemption is limited to the percentage of exempt use to total use as determined by a reasonable formula approved by the Michigan Department of Treasury. See ¶1705. (*Detroit Edison Company v. Department of Treasury*, Michigan Supreme Court, No. 148753, July 22, 2015)

• *Exemption for property used in a qualified convention facility expires*

The exemption for tangible personal property used in the construction or renovation of a qualified convention facility and affixed to that facility, terminates January 1, 2016. See ¶1704. (Act 53 (S.B. 711) and Act 54 (S.B. 735), Laws 2014)

• *Tax extended to use of motor fuel and alternative fuel by interstate motor carriers*

Effective January 1, 2017, a 6% tax is imposed on interstate motor carriers for the privilege of using or consuming "motor fuel" and "alternative fuel" as defined in Motor Fuel Tax Act. The interstate motor carrier may claim a credit for the payment of such tax on its international fuel tax returns. See ¶1604. (Act 177 (H.B. 4614), Laws 2015)

Property Taxes

- *Delinquent property tax installment payment plan enacted*

Michigan has enacted legislation regarding property taxes that would allow certain financially distressed taxpayers to enter into a delinquent property tax installment payment plan and avoid a tax foreclosure. Under the legislation, taxpayers must use the property as their principal residence and meet financial hardship qualifications. If the taxpayer successfully completes the payment plan, additional interest that is applied to tax-delinquent property would be waived. (Act 499 (H.B. 4882), Laws 2015, effective January 10, 2015)

- *Certain personal property exemption provisions modified*

Enacted Michigan legislation revises exemption requirements for new personal property owned or leased by an eligible business in an eligible local assessing district, for new eligible manufacturing personal property, and for previously existing eligible manufacturing personal property. For the exemption for new personal property owned or leased by an eligible business in an eligible local assessing district, the enacted law requires an eligible business to file an affidavit with the township or city assessor by February 20 in the first year that personal property was eligible personal property. "New personal property" does not include eligible manufacturing personal property for exemptions subject to local resolutions adopted after December 31, 2014. (Act 119 (H.B. 4553), Laws 2015, effective July 10, 2015)

Motor Fuel Taxes

- *Fuel tax increase, other changes enacted*

Michigan legislation enacted as part of a Road Funding Package increases the tax rate on motor fuels from $0.19 per gallon to $0.263 per gallon, and the tax rate on diesel fuel from $0.15 per gallon to $0.263 per gallon, effective January 1, 2017. Beginning with the rate effective January 1, 2022, and January 1 of each year thereafter, the fuel tax rates will be adjusted based on the lesser of 5% or the inflation rate, rounding up to the nearest 1/10 of a cent. The enacted legislation also applies the motor fuel tax to alternative fuels (based on the per-gallon energy equivalent to motor fuels), effective for alternative fuel commercial users beginning January 1, 2017, and for persons other than alternative fuel commercial users or alternative fuel dealers beginning January 1, 2018. Additionally, the legislation makes complementary amendments to the Motor Carrier Fuel Tax Act. (Act 176 (H.B. 4738), Laws 2015, and Act 178 (H.B. 4616), Laws 2015, effective as noted)

Administration

- *Tax appeal procedures revised*

Michigan has enacted legislation that deletes the requirement that a taxpayer first pay the disputed portion of a tax, including penalties and interest, under protest and claim a refund as part of an appeal to the Court of Claims. The law also allows a taxpayer 60 days to appeal to the Tax Tribunal (formerly, 35 days). See ¶2508. (Act 79 (S.B. 100), Laws 2015, effective 91 days following adjournment)

TAX CALENDAR

The following table lists significant dates of interest to Michigan taxpayers and tax practitioners.

January

10th—Property taxes in fourth class cities become delinquent
Natural resources or improvements may no longer be removed if tax on land is not paid by this date

15th—Final estimated income tax and business tax return and payment of estimated tax due for calendar-year taxpayers for preceding year (due date for fiscal-year taxpayers must correspond to calendar year)

31st—Employers' annual statement of wages paid and taxes withheld due

February

15th—Property taxes draw collection fees and late penalty charges

20th—Personal property statements due

28th—Annual reconciliation of personal income tax withheld due

Last Day—Commercial vehicle registration plates expire
Annual sales and use tax return due
Trailer or semitrailer registration plates expire
Pole trailer registrations expire
Insurance company retaliatory tax statement due

March

1st—Delinquent property taxes draw interest and administrative fees
Insurers' annual reports due

Second Monday—Township boards review assessment rolls

15th—Property tax reports due for public service companies whose gross receipts do not exceed $1 million

31st—Property tax reports due for public service companies whose annual gross receipts exceed $1 million
Sleeping car companies' property tax reports due

April

15th—Income tax returns and payments due for calendar-year individuals, estates, and trusts (fiscal-year taxpayer's return and tax due by 15th day of the fourth month following close of taxable year)
Estimated business tax return and payment of estimated tax due for taxpayers on a calendar-year basis (due dates for fiscal-year taxpayers must correspond to calendar year)
Annual payment of estimated income tax due for individuals on calendar-year basis (fiscal-year taxpayers must file annual estimated tax return and pay tax at the same time the income tax return for the previous year is filed)

30th—Intangibles tax return and payment due for calendar-year taxpayer
Annual Michigan business tax return and corporate income tax return for taxpayers on a calendar-year basis (due dates for fiscal-year taxpayers must correspond to calendar year)

May

1st—Personal residence and agricultural property tax exemption claims due

First Tuesday—Annual tax sale for the collection of property taxes

15th—Annual corporation tax reports due
Foreign corporations' statements upon increase of capital stock due
Third Monday—State Board of Assessors reviews assessment roll for public service companies

June

15th—Estimated income tax return and payment of estimated tax due for calendar-year taxpayers (due date for fiscal-year taxpayers must correspond o calendar year)
30th—Cigarette licenses expire
Tobacco products licenses expire

July

1st—School taxes become lien against property
City property taxes due in fourth-class cities
Public service companies' property tax due
Village property taxes become a lien against the property assessed
15th—Estimated business tax return and payment of estimated tax due for calendar-year taxpayers (due date for fiscal-year taxpayers must correspond to calendar year)
31st—First half of public service companies' property taxes due to avoid interest

August

1st—Public service companies' property taxes bear interest if not paid before this day

September

15th—Property taxes in fourth class cities on July roll become delinquent
Estimated income tax return and payment of estimated tax due for calendar-year taxpayers (due date for fiscal-year taxpayers must correspond to calendar year)
Village property taxes collected on or after the 15th bear interest
30th—Claim for home heating credit against personal income tax due
Sales tax licenses expire

October

1st—Delinquent property taxes draw additional charge for expense of preparing delinquent land lists for sale
15th—Estimated business tax return and payment of estimated tax due for calendar-year taxpayers (due date for fiscal-year taxpayers must correspond to calendar year)

November

15th—Property taxes in fourth class cities on July roll draw interest if not paid by this day
30th—Second half of public service companies' property tax due

December

1st—Property taxes become a lien
31st—Property tax assessment date
Public service companies' property tax assessment date

Monthly Requirements

5th—Trailer coach parks' reports and tax payments due
10th—Prepayment of gasoline tax and diesel fuel tax received after the 15th and before the end of the preceding month due
20th—Sales and use tax returns and tax payments due
Income withholding tax returns due
Gasoline suppliers' reports and tax payments due
Diesel motor fuel suppliers' reports and tax payments due

Liquefied petroleum gas dealers' reports and tax payments due
Recreational fuel tax reports and tax payments due
Cigarette or other tobacco products tax licensees' returns and tax payments due

25th—Severance tax returns and tax payments due
Prepayment of gasoline tax and diesel fuel tax received after the end of the preceding month and before the 16th of the current month

Quarterly Requirements

20th of month following the end of the calendar quarter—Sales tax returns and payments for quarterly filers due
Withholding tax returns and payments for quarterly filers due

20th of the month following the end of the calendar quarter—Motor fuel reports and payments due

Last day of the month following the end of the calendar quarter—Motor carrier returns and payments due

PART I

TABLES

TAX RATES

¶1 Income Tax

The personal income tax rate is 4.25% (see ¶102).

• *Personal exemptions*

Michigan provides a personal exemption for 2014 of $4,000 times the number of personal or dependency exemptions allowable on the taxpayer's federal income tax return. The personal exemption amount is adjusted annually for inflation. For 2014, an additional exemption of $2,500 is allowed for taxpayers who are disabled, deaf, or blind. An individual who has taxable income and is claimed as a dependent on the federal return of another taxpayer is allowed a $1,500 personal exemption. An additional personal exemption of $400 is available for taxpayers and their dependents who are qualified disabled veterans.

Nonresidents or part-year residents receive appropriately proportioned exemptions (¶205).

¶8 Michigan Business Tax

Applicable to all business activity occurring after December 31, 2007, the general Michigan business tax (MBT) is comprised of an income tax component and a modified gross receipts tax component. The business income tax is imposed at a rate of 4.95%. The modified gross receipts tax is imposed at a rate of 0.8% (¶1452). A taxpayer that elects to claim the small business tax credit (¶1484) and that is not required to reduce the credit as a result of excess compensation paid to shareholders, members, partners, or self-employed individuals, may compute the tax utilizing an alternative tax rate of 1.8%.

Surcharge.—There is an annual surcharge based on a percentage of the taxpayer's MBT liability before credits. For all other taxpayers other than financial institutions, the surcharge is 21.99%. The surcharge is capped at $6 million per taxpayer per year.

• *Financial institutions*

The Michigan financial institutions' franchise tax, applicable to financial institution's business activities occurring after 2007, is imposed at a rate of 0.235%. The surcharge applied to financial institutions is 23.4% (see ¶1455).

• *Insurance companies*

The insurance companies' tax is equal to 1.25% of gross direct premiums. The surcharge applicable to other taxpayers does not apply to insurance companies subject to the gross direct premiums tax (see ¶1456).

¶9 Corporate Income Tax

Effective January 1, 2012, the corporate income tax is imposed at a rate of 6%. A taxpayer that elects to claim the small business tax credit (¶1551) and that is not required to reduce the credit as a result of excess compensation paid to shareholders, members, partners, or self-employed individuals, may compute the tax utilizing an alternative tax rate of 1.8%.

• *Financial institutions*

Effective January 1, 2012, and applicable to financial institutions, the franchise tax rate is 0.29% (see ¶1514).

• *Insurance companies*

The insurance companies' tax is equal to 1.25% of gross direct premiums (see ¶1515).

¶10 Sales and Use Taxes

The state sales and use taxes are levied at the rate of 6% of the gross proceeds (sales tax) or price (use tax). However, the sale or consumption for residential use of electricity, natural gas, or home heating fuel are subject to sales or use tax at the rate of 4%.

¶15 Estate Tax

Estates of persons who die between December 31, 2004 and January 1, 2011 are not subject to a Michigan inheritance or estate tax.

FEDERAL/STATE KEY FEATURE COMPARISONS

¶40 Personal Income Tax Comparison of Federal/State Key Features

The following is a comparison of key features of federal income tax laws that have been enacted as of December 19, 2014, and Michigan personal income tax laws. Michigan taxable income is based on federal adjusted gross income (see ¶203). Michigan adopts the Internal Revenue Code (IRC) as in effect on January 1, 1996, or at the taxpayer's option, in effect for the tax year (see ¶201). State modifications to federal adjusted gross income required by law differences are discussed beginning at ¶203.

CCH Caution: Using Current IRC

The following information assumes that the taxpayer is electing to follow the IRC in effect for the tax year.

Nonresidents and part-year residents.—Nonresidents and part-year residents are subject to Michigan income tax only on taxable income attributable to Michigan sources (see ¶103). Exemptions (see ¶205) and deductions (see ¶203) that relate to income included in Michigan gross income must be prorated.

• *Alternative minimum tax (IRC Sec. 55—IRC Sec. 59)*

There is no Michigan equivalent to the federal alternative minimum tax on tax preference items (IRC Sec. 55—IRC Sec. 59).

• *Asset expense election (IRC Sec. 179)*

The same as federal (IRC Sec. 179) because the starting point for Michigan taxable income is federal adjusted gross income (see ¶203).

• *Bad debts (IRC Sec. 166)*

The same as federal (IRC Sec. 166) because the starting point for Michigan taxable income is federal adjusted gross income (see ¶203).

• *Capital gains and capital losses (IRC Sec. 1(h), IRC Sec. 1202, IRC Sec. 1211, IRC Sec. 1212, and IRC Sec. 1221)*

Generally, capital gains and losses are determined in the same manner as federal (IRC Sec. 1(h), IRC Sec. 1202, IRC Sec. 1211, IRC Sec. 1212, and IRC Sec. 1221) because the starting point for Michigan taxable income is federal adjusted gross income (see ¶203) However, Michigan allows an adjustment to the taxable income base for capital gains or capital losses attributable to property acquired prior to October 1, 1967. Michigan does not have a special tax rate for capital gains (see ¶211).

• *Charitable contributions (IRC Sec. 170)*

Michigan does not incorporate the federal itemized deduction for charitable contributions, but allowed a modified version of the IRC Sec. 170 deduction as a subtraction adjustment through 2011 (see ¶203). In addition, Michigan allowed a partial credit through 2011 for charitable contributions to qualifying Michigan public institutions, community foundations, food banks and homeless shelters (see ¶306) and a credit through 2011 for automobiles donated to qualified recipients (see ¶317).

• *Child care credit (IRC Sec. 45F)*

Michigan has no equivalent to the federal employer-provided child care credit (IRC Sec. 45F).

• *Civil rights deduction (IRC Sec. 62)*

The same as federal (IRC Sec. 62) because the starting point for Michigan taxable income is federal adjusted gross income (see ¶203).

• *Dependents (IRC Sec. 152)*

Michigan conforms to the federal definition of "dependent" (IRC Sec. 152) (see ¶201).

• *Depreciation (IRC Sec. 167, IRC Sec. 168, and IRC Sec. 1400N)*

The same as federal (IRC Sec. 167, IRC Sec. 168, and IRC Sec. 1400N) because the starting point for Michigan taxable income is federal adjusted gross income (see ¶203).

• *Earned income credit (IRC Sec. 32)*

Michigan allows a percentage of the federal earned income tax credit (IRC Sec. 32) to be claimed against the state personal income tax (see ¶320).

• *Educational benefits and deductions (IRC Sec. 62(a)(2)(D), IRC Sec. 127, IRC Sec. 221, IRC Sec. 222, IRC. Sec. 529)*

The same as federal (IRC Sec. 62(a)(2)(D), IRC Sec. 127, IRC Sec. 221, IRC Sec. 222, IRC. Sec. 529) because the starting point for Michigan taxable income is federal adjusted gross income (see ¶203).

• *Foreign earned income (IRC Sec. 911 and IRC Sec. 912)*

The same as federal (IRC Sec. 911 and IRC Sec. 912) because the starting point for Michigan taxable income is federal adjusted gross income (see ¶203).

• *Health insurance and health savings accounts (HSAs) (IRC Sec. 106(e), IRC Sec. 139C, IRC Sec. 139D, IRC Sec. 162(l), IRC Sec. 223)*

The same as federal (IRC Sec. 106(e), IRC Sec. 139C, IRC Sec. 139D, IRC Sec. 162(l), IRC Sec. 223) because the starting point for Michigan taxable income is federal adjusted gross income (see ¶203). Because Michigan does not allow itemized deductions, the state has not increased the medical expense itemized deduction threshold from 7.5% to 10% for post-2012 tax years.

• *Indebtedness (IRC Sec. 108 and IRC Sec. 163)*

The same as federal (IRC Sec. 108 and IRC Sec. 163) because the starting point for Michigan taxable income is federal adjusted gross income (see ¶203).

• *Interest on federal obligations (IRC Sec. 61)*

Interest on federal obligations, net of related expenses, are exempt from Michigan income tax and may be subtracted from federal adjusted gross income in computing Michigan taxable income; however, interest on federal obligations that are secondary, indirect, or contingent are not exempt (see ¶203). Distributions from a mutual fund, investment fund, or regulated investment company that are attributable to federal obligations are also exempt from Michigan income tax. However, mutual fund income derived from repurchase agreements is not exempt.

• *Interest on state and local obligations (IRC Sec. 103)*

Interest on non-Michigan state or local obligations must be added to federal adjusted gross income in computing Michigan taxable income. However, Michigan allows a subtraction for related expenses that are not deductible in computing federal adjusted gross income (see ¶203).

• *Losses not otherwise compensated (IRC Sec. 165)*

The same as federal (IRC Sec. 165) because the starting point for Michigan taxable income is federal adjusted gross income (see ¶203). However, Michigan does not adopt federal itemized deductions, including nonbusiness casualty losses.

• *Net operating loss (IRC Sec. 172 and IRC Sec. 1400N)*

The federal net operating loss (IRC Sec. 172 and IRC Sec. 1400N) is disallowed for Michigan purposes and must be added back to federal adjusted gross income. A subtraction from federal adjusted gross income is allowed for net operating losses that are apportioned and allocated to Michigan. The carryforward and carryback period for the Michigan NOL is the same as federal (see ¶203).

• *Personal residence (IRC Sec. 121, IRC Sec. 132(n), IRC Sec. 163, and IRC Sec. 1033)*

The same as federal (IRC Sec. 121, IRC Sec. 132(n), IRC Sec. 163, and IRC Sec. 1033) because the starting point for Michigan taxable income is federal adjusted gross income (see ¶203).

• *Retirement plans (IRC Sec. 401—IRC Sec. 424, IRC Sec. 457A, and IRC Sec. 1400Q)*

Michigan generally conforms to federal provisions regarding retirement plans (IRC Sec. 401—IRC Sec. 424, IRC Sec. 457A, and IRC Sec. 1400Q).

Michigan allows a subtraction from federal adjusted gross income for qualifying retirement and pension benefits included in the federal return. The subtraction for retirement and pension benefits received from a qualified retirement plan or other private source is subject to various limitations. Pension benefits received from a federal or state public retirement system may be subtracted from federal adjusted gross income in certain circumstances. Pension benefits received from another state's public retirement system may be subtracted only if the other state permits a similar deduction for Michigan pension benefits (see ¶203).

• *Start-up expenses (IRC Sec. 195)*

The same as federal (IRC Sec. 195) because the starting point for Michigan taxable income is federal adjusted gross income (see ¶203).

• *Taxes paid (IRC Sec. 63(c)(1), IRC Sec. 164)*

Michigan requires an addition to federal adjusted gross income for self-employment tax or other income taxes, such as a distributive share of state or city income taxes, taken as a federal deduction. Also, because Michigan does not adopt federal itemized deductions, the state does not conform to the optional sales tax deduction. Although Michigan requires an addback of income taxes, the requirement applies only to income taxes deducted to arrive at federal adjusted gross income, not those taken as itemized deductions (see ¶203). Furthermore, because Michigan does not allow a standard deduction it does not allow nonitemizers to take an additional standard deduction for real estate taxes paid. State and local income tax refunds included in federal adjusted gross income may be subtracted from the taxable income base for Michigan purposes (see ¶203). A credit against Michigan personal income tax is also allowed for income taxes paid to non-Michigan government units (see ¶301).

• *Unemployment compensation (IRC Sec. 85)*

The same as federal (IRC Sec. 85) because the starting point for Michigan taxable income is federal adjusted gross income (see ¶203). However, through 2011, Michigan allows an additional exemption if a certain percentage of the adjusted gross income is from unemployment compensation (see ¶205).

¶45 Michigan Business Tax/Corporate Income Tax Comparison of Federal/State Key Features

The following is a comparison of key features of federal income tax laws that have been enacted as of December 19, 2014, the corporate income tax and the Michigan business tax laws.

CCH Caution: Using Current IRC

The following information assumes that the taxpayer is electing to follow the IRC in effect for the tax year.

The starting point for computing the business income component of the Michigan business tax (MBT) is federal taxable income. For purposes of the MBT, applicable to business activities occurring after 2007, Michigan adopts the IRC as in effect on January 1, 2008, or at the option of the taxpayer, as in effect for the tax year (see

¶1462). State modifications to federal taxable income are discussed beginning at ¶1463. The following information assumes that the taxpayer is electing to follow the IRC in effect for the tax year.

The starting point for computing the corporate income tax is federal taxable income. For purposes of the corporate income tax, Michigan adopts the IRC as in effect on January 1, 2012, or at the option of the taxpayer, as in effect for the tax year (see ¶1521). State modifications to federal taxable income are discussed beginning at ¶1522. The following information assumes that the taxpayer is electing to follow the IRC in effect for the tax year.

• *IRC Sec. 27 foreign tax credit*

The corporate income tax and the MBT have no equivalent to the federal foreign tax credit (IRC Sec. 27) and do not allow a deduction for foreign taxes on, or measured by, income regardless of whether the federal foreign tax credit was taken. (¶1463d, ¶1526)

• *IRC Sec. 40 alcohol fuels credit*

The corporate income tax and the MBT have no equivalent to the federal alcohol fuels credit (IRC Sec. 40).

• *IRC Sec. 41 incremental research expenditures credit*

The corporate income tax has no equivalent to the federal research expenditures credit (IRC Sec. 41). Taxpayers may claim a credit against the MBT for research and development (IRC Sec. 41) (see ¶1478). In addition, qualified start-up businesses may claim a credit against the MBT equal to their tax liability if, among other criteria, they spend at least a portion of their business expenses on qualified research and development. Taxpayers also may claim a credit against the MBT for research and development activities conducted in an alternative energy zone (see ¶1488).

• *IRC Sec. 42 low-income housing credit*

The corporate income tax and the MBT have no equivalent to the federal low-income housing credit (IRC Sec. 42). The MBT does allow a qualified affordable housing project to deduct income received from residential rental units in Michigan for purposes of computing the tax (see ¶1464e and ¶1465).

• *IRC Sec. 44 disabled access credit*

The corporate income tax and the MBT have no equivalent to the federal disabled access credit (IRC Sec. 44).

• *IRC Sec. 45A Indian employment credit*

The corporate income tax and the MBT have no equivalent to the federal Indian employment credit (IRC Sec. 45A).

• *IRC Sec. 45B employer social security credit*

The corporate income tax and the MBT have no equivalent to the federal employer social security credit (IRC Sec. 45B).

• *IRC Sec. 45C orphan drug credit*

The corporate income tax and the MBT have no equivalent to the federal orphan drug credit (IRC Sec. 45C).

• *IRC Sec. 45D new markets credit*

The corporate income tax and the MBT have no equivalent to the federal new markets credit (IRC Sec. 45D).

• *IRC Sec. 45E small business pension start-up costs credit*

The corporate income tax and the MBT have no equivalent to the federal small business pension start-up costs credit (IRC Sec. 45E), although small businesses are entitled to a credit against the MBT if they have gross receipts under a specified amount (see ¶1481). This credit is not available against the corporate income tax.

• *IRC Sec. 45F employer-provided child care credit*

The corporate income tax and the MBT have no equivalent to the federal employer-provided child care credit (IRC Sec. 45F).

• *IRC Sec. 45K fuel from nonconventional source credit*

The corporate income tax and the MBT have no equivalent to the federal fuel from nonconventional source credit (IRC Sec. 45K). However, Michigan allows a credit against the MBT based on qualified alternative energy business activity (see ¶1488). This credit is not available against the corporate income tax.

• *IRC Sec. 45L new energy-efficient homes credit*

The corporate income tax has no equivalent to the federal new energy-efficient homes credit (IRC Sec. 45L). The MBT has no equivalent to the federal new energy-efficient homes credit.

• *IRC Sec. 45M energy efficient appliance credit*

The corporate income tax has no equivalent to the federal energy efficient appliance credit (IRC Sec. 45M). The MBT has no equivalent to the federal energy efficient appliance credit.

• *IRC Sec. 46—IRC Sec. 49 investment credit (former law)*

Michigan has no equivalent to the former federal investment credit (repealed effective for property placed in service after 1985) or to the current federal investment credits (IRC Sec. 48, IRC Sec. 48A, IRC Sec. 48B, and IRC Sec. 48C). However, Michigan allows a credit similar to the federal rehabilitation credit (IRC Sec. 47); if the taxpayer's expenditures are eligible for the federal credit, the taxpayer must claim the federal credit in order to claim the state credit and the state credit must be reduced by the amount of the federal credit received (see ¶1489b). In addition, Michigan provides an investment tax credit (see ¶1477), a small business credit (see ¶1484), and a start-up businesses credit (see ¶1483). Although the credits are available against the MBT, they are not available against the corporate income tax.

• *IRC Sec. 51—IRC Sec. 52 (and IRC Sec. 1396) wage credits*

The corporate income tax and the MBT have no equivalent to the federal work opportunity credit (IRC Sec. 51—IRC Sec. 52), or the empowerment zone employment credit (IRC Sec. 1396). Certain businesses authorized by the Michigan Economic Growth Authority (MEGA) are allowed a credit against the MBT for the creation of new jobs (see ¶1489). The credit for creating new jobs is not available against the corporate income tax.

• *IRC Sec. 55—IRC Sec. 59 tax preferences*

There is no corporate income tax or MBT equivalent to the federal alternative minimum tax on tax preference items (IRC Sec. 55—IRC Sec. 59).

• *IRC Sec. 78 deemed dividends*

Any foreign dividend gross-up under IRC Sec. 78 may be subtracted from federal taxable income for corporate income tax and for MBT purposes (see ¶1464a, ¶1536).

• *Interest on federal obligations*

Michigan excludes most interest income received, including interest on federal obligations, from the tax base; any such interest included in federal taxable income may be subtracted from the corporate income tax and from the MBT (see ¶1464b, ¶1537).

• *IRC Sec. 103 interest on state obligations*

Interest income received on state or local obligations, other than those of Michigan and its political subdivisions, must be added back to federal taxable income for the corporate income tax and for the MBT (see ¶1463a, ¶1523).

• *IRC Sec. 108 discharge of indebtedness*

The same as federal (IRC Sec. 108) because the IRC is incorporated by reference for the corporate income tax and the MBT (see ¶1462 and ¶1521).

• *IRC Sec. 163 interest on indebtedness*

The same as federal (IRC Sec. 163) because the IRC is incorporated by reference for the corporate income tax and the MBT (see ¶1462 and ¶1521).

• *IRC Sec. 164 income and franchise tax deductions*

State, local, and foreign taxes on, or measured by, net income are not deductible for purposes of the corporate income tax and the MBT and must be added back to federal taxable income (see ¶1463d, ¶1526).

• *IRC Sec. 165 losses*

The same as federal (IRC Sec. 165) because the IRC is incorporated by reference for the corporate income tax and the MBT (see ¶1462, ¶1521).

• *IRC Sec. 166 bad debts*

The same as federal (IRC Sec. 166) because the IRC is incorporated by reference for the corporate income tax and the MBT (see ¶1462, ¶1521).

• *IRC Sec. 167 and Sec. 168 (and Sec. 1400N) depreciation*

For corporate income tax purposes, the same as federal (IRC Sec. 167, IRC Sec. 168 and IRC Sec. 1400N) because the IRC is incorporated by reference (see ¶1521). However, Michigan does not conform to the bonus depreciation deduction for corporate income tax purposes (see ¶1527). For MBT purposes, the same as federal because the IRC is incorporated by reference (see ¶1462). However, Michigan does not conform to the bonus depreciation deduction for MBT purposes (see ¶1463e). Also, Michigan allows an investment credit against the MBT in addition to the federal deduction for depreciation, amortization, or immediate or accelerated write-off of the cost of tangible assets (see ¶1477). However, this credit is not available against the corporate income tax.

• *IRC Sec. 168(f) safe harbor leasing (pre-1984 leases)*

No adjustments are required for the corporate income tax or for the MBT.

• *IRC Sec. 169 pollution control facilities amortization*

For corporate income tax and MBT purposes, the same as federal (IRC Sec. 169) because the IRC is incorporated by reference (see ¶1462, ¶1521). Michigan allows an investment credit against the MBT in addition to depreciation (see ¶1477). However, this credit is not available against the corporate income tax.

• *IRC Sec. 170 charitable contributions*

Generally the same as federal (IRC Sec. 170) because the IRC is incorporated by reference for the corporate income tax and the MBT (see ¶1462 and ¶1521). In addition, Michigan provides a public contributions credit, a credit for contributions to community foundations, and a credit for contributions to homeless shelters, food kitchens, and food banks. The credits are available against the MBT (see ¶1486). The credits are not available the corporate income tax.

• *IRC Sec. 171 amortizable bond premium*

The same as federal (IRC Sec. 171) because the IRC is incorporated by reference for the corporate income tax and the MBT (see ¶1462, ¶1521).

• *IRC Sec. 172 (and IRC Sec. 1400N) net operating loss*

In lieu of the federal net operating loss deduction (IRC Sec. 172 and IRC Sec. 1400N), Michigan permits a deduction for "business loss" for the corporate income tax and for the MBT (see ¶1464, ¶1535). Any federal net operating loss deduction claimed on the federal return must be added back to federal taxable income for corporate income tax and for MBT purposes (see ¶1463c, ¶1525).

• *IRC Sec. 174 research and experimental expenditures*

For corporate income tax and for MBT purposes, the same as federal (IRC Sec. 174) because the IRC is incorporated by reference (see ¶1462, ¶1521).

• *IRC Sec. 179 asset expense election*

For corporate income tax and for MBT purposes, the same as federal (IRC Sec. 179) because the IRC is incorporated by reference (see ¶1462, ¶1521). Also, Michigan allows an investment credit against the MBT in addition to depreciation (see ¶1477). This credit is not available against the corporate income tax.

• *IRC Sec. 179D energy efficient commercial buildings deduction*

The same as federal (IRC Sec. 179D) because the IRC is incorporated by reference for the corporate income tax and the MBT (see ¶1462, ¶1521).

• *IRC Sec. 190 deduction for barriers removal*

For corporate income tax and for MBT purposes, the same as federal (IRC Sec. 190) because the IRC is incorporated by reference (see ¶1462, ¶1521). The investment credit is available against the MBT, in addition to depreciation. However, this credit is not available against the corporate income tax.

• *IRC Sec. 195 start-up expenditures*

The same as the federal (IRC Sec. 195) because the IRC is incorporated by reference for the corporate income tax and the MBT (see ¶1462, and ¶1521). Michigan also allows a credit against the MBT for qualified start-up businesses (see ¶1483). This credit is not available against the corporate income tax.

• *IRC Sec. 197 amortization of intangibles*

The same as federal (IRC Sec. 197) because the IRC is incorporated by reference for the corporate income tax and the MBT (see ¶1462, ¶1521).

• *IRC Sec. 199 domestic production activities deduction*

Michigan does not conform to the domestic production activities deduction (IRC Sec. 199); an addback is required for the corporate income tax and for the MBT (see ¶1463f, ¶1528).

• *IRC Sec. 243—IRC Sec. 245 dividends-received deduction*

Michigan excludes all dividends received from the tax base for the corporate income tax and the MBT (IRC Sec. 243—IRC Sec. 245) (see ¶1464a, ¶1536) whether or not such dividends qualify for the current federal dividends received deduction.

• *IRC Sec. 248 organizational expenditures*

For corporate income tax and for MBT purposes, the same as federal (IRC Sec. 248) because the IRC is incorporated by reference (see ¶1462, ¶1521). The investment credit is available against the MBT, in addition to depreciation. This credit is not available against the corporate income tax.

• *IRC Sec. 301—IRC Sec. 385 corporate distributions and adjustments*

The same as federal (IRC Sec. 301—IRC Sec. 385) because the IRC is incorporated by reference for the corporate income tax and the MBT (see ¶1462 and ¶1521).

• *IRC Sec. 441—IRC Sec. 483 accounting periods and methods*

The same as federal (IRC Sec. 441—IRC Sec. 483) because the IRC is incorporated by reference for the corporate income tax and the MBT (see ¶1462 and ¶1521). Under the corporate income tax and the MBT, unitary business groups must file combined returns (see ¶1493, ¶1567).

• *IRC Sec. 501—IRC Sec. 530 exempt organization*

Generally, most organizations that are exempt from federal income tax (IRC Sec. 501—IRC Sec. 530) are exempt from the corporate income tax and the MBT except on their unrelated taxable business income (see ¶1454, ¶1513).

• *IRC Sec. 531—IRC Sec. 547 corporations used to avoid shareholder taxation*

Michigan has no provisions regarding corporations used to avoid shareholder taxation (IRC Sec. 531—IRC Sec. 547). Michigan does not impose a tax on accumulated earnings or an additional tax on the undistributed income of personal holding companies (IRC Sec. 541) under the corporate income tax or the MBT.

• *IRC Sec. 581—IRC Sec. 597 banking institutions*

The corporate income tax and the MBT have no special provisions regarding financial institutions (IRC Sec. 581—IRC Sec. 597). Financial institutions are subject to a franchise tax (see ¶1455, ¶1514).

• *IRC Sec. 611—IRC Sec. 638 natural resources*

The same as federal (IRC Sec. 611—IRC Sec. 638) because the IRC is incorporated by reference for the corporate income tax and the MBT (see ¶1462, ¶1521).

• *IRC Sec. 801—IRC Sec. 848 insurance companies*

The corporate income tax and the MBT have no equivalent to the federal provisions relating to insurance companies (IRC Sec. 801—IRC Sec. 848). Insurance companies are subject to a gross direct premiums tax (see ¶1456, ¶1515).

• *IRC Sec. 851—IRC Sec. 860L RICs, REITs, REMICs, and FASITs*

Generally, the corporate income tax has no specific provisions regarding the taxation of RICs, REITs, REMICs, and FASITs. Generally, RICs, REITs, and FASITs are subject to the MBT (see ¶1453). Generally, FASITs were repealed, effective after 2004.

• *IRC Sec. 861—IRC Sec. 865 foreign source income*

Michigan follows the federal foreign sourcing rules for the corporate income tax and the MBT (IRC Sec. 861—IRC Sec. 865). Multistate and international businesses that conduct business both inside and outside Michigan utilize the state's allocation and apportionment rules for determining whether income is attributable to state sources (see ¶1471, ¶1472, ¶1547).

• *IRC Sec. 901—IRC Sec. 908 foreign tax credit*

The corporate income tax and the MBT have no equivalent to the federal foreign tax credit (IRC Sec. 901—IRC Sec. 908) and do not allow a deduction for foreign taxes on, or measured by, income regardless of whether the federal foreign tax credit was taken (see ¶1463d, ¶1526).

• *IRC Sec. 1001—IRC Sec. 1092 gain or loss on disposition of property*

The same as federal (IRC Sec. 1001—IRC Sec. 1092) because the IRC is incorporated by reference for the corporate income tax and the MBT (see ¶1462, ¶1521).

• *IRC Sec. 1201 alternative capital gains tax*

Michigan does not provide for an alternative tax rate for capital gains under the corporate income tax or the MBT (IRC Sec. 1201).

• *IRC Sec. 1211 and IRC Sec. 1212 capital losses*

The same as federal (IRC Sec. 1211 and IRC Sec. 1212) because the IRC is incorporated by reference for the corporate income tax and the MBT (see ¶1462, ¶1521).

• *IRC Sec. 1221—IRC Sec. 1260 determining capital gains and losses*

The same as federal (IRC Sec. 1221—IRC Sec. 1260) because the IRC is incorporated by reference for the corporate income tax and the MBT (see ¶1462 and ¶1521).

• *IRC Sec. 1361—IRC Sec. 1379 S corporations*

For the corporate income tax, Michigan follows the federal tax treatment of S corporations (IRC Sec. 1361—IRC Sec. 1379) (see ¶853). However, S corporations are subject to the MBT and are treated in the same manner as other corporations (see ¶1462).

• *IRC Sec. 1391—IRC Sec. 1397F and IRC Sec. 1400E—IRC Sec. 1400J empowerment zones and renewal communities*

The same as federal (IRC Sec. 1391—IRC Sec. 1397F and IRC Sec. 1400E—IRC Sec. 1400J) because the IRC is incorporated by reference for the corporate income tax and the MBT (see ¶1462, ¶1521). Michigan has MEGA tax credits against the MBT available to businesses located in federally designated empowerment zones (see ¶1489). Michigan also allows various credits against the MBT for businesses located in enterprise zones (see ¶1489a). None of these credits are available against the corporate income tax.

• *IRC Sec. 1501—IRC Sec. 1504 consolidated returns*

Combined reporting is required for all unitary groups under the corporate income tax and the MBT (see ¶1493, ¶1567).

BUSINESS INCENTIVES AND CREDITS

¶50 Introduction

Michigan has created a number of tax incentives designed to attract business to the state, stimulate expansion, and/or encourage certain economic activity. These incentives are listed below, by tax, with a brief description and a cross-reference to the paragraph at which they are discussed in greater detail. Most exemptions and deductions that might also be considered business incentives, which are too numerous to be fully included below, are discussed under the taxes to which they apply (see the Table of Contents or the Topical Index).

¶57 Michigan Business Tax

The Michigan business tax applies to business activities that occur after 2007.

• *Compensation credit*

A credit against the MBT may be claimed for a percentage of a taxpayer's Michigan compensation paid (¶1476).

• *MEGA credits*

The MBT provisions contain a Michigan Economic Growth Authority credit for "certified amounts" based on new jobs and employment and a modified version of the additional credit based on capital investment and new jobs (¶1489).

• *Renaissance zone credits*

Businesses operating in a designated renaissance zone (RZ) are eligible for various MBT credits. There are also credits available to specific industries within RZs, such as pharmaceuticals, agriculture, and tool and die (¶1489a).

• *Investment credit*

A taxpayer may claim an investment tax credit against the MBT. The credit is equal to 2.9% of the taxpayer's net capital assets (¶1477).

• *Research and development credit*

Taxpayers may claim a credit against MBT equal to 1.9% of the taxpayer's research and development expense incurred in Michigan (¶1478).

• *Small business credit*

Businesses whose gross receipts do not exceed $20 million, and whose adjusted business income, minus any loss adjustment, does not exceed $1.3 million are allowed a credit against the MBT. The credit is the greater of the amount by which the tax exceeds 1.8% of the adjusted business income (¶1484).

• *Credit for businesses with low gross receipts*

A credit against the MBT is available to a taxpayer that has Michigan gross receipts that are greater than $350,000 but less than $700,000 (¶1481).

• *Alternative energy credits*

A taxpayer that is certified under the Michigan Next Energy Authority Act as an eligible taxpayer may claim a nonrefundable credit based on qualified business activity. A taxpayer that is a qualified alternative energy entity may also claim a credit for the taxpayer's qualified payroll amount (¶1488).

• *Start-up businesses credit*

A qualified start-up business that does not have business income for two consecutive tax years is eligible to claim a credit equal to its MBT liability for the second of the those two consecutive years and for each subsequent year in which a taxpayer does not have business income (¶1483).

• *Venture capital investment credit*

A taxpayer that is an investor in the Early Stage Venture Capital Investment Fund may claim a tax credit against either the MBT or the personal income tax (¶1485).

• *Credits for property taxes paid*

A taxpayer may claim a refundable credit against the MBT equal to a percentage of the amount of property taxes paid. The percentage ranges from 10% for personal property taxes on natural gas pipeline property to 35% of personal property taxes paid on industrial personal property (see ¶1482).

• *Brownfield credit*

A taxpayer may claim a credit against the MBT for the redevelopment or improvement of a facility (contaminated property), or functionally obsolete or blighted property, provided that certain conditions are met including obtaining a preapproval letter for the project issued prior to 2013 and unless specified exceptions apply, the completing the project within five years after the preapproval letter is issued (see ¶1489c).

• *Entrepreneurial credit*

Qualified taxpayers that create Michigan jobs or transfer jobs to Michigan and satisfy a capital investment threshold may claim a credit for the increased employment (see ¶1489e).

• *Grocery store credits*

Credits are available to qualified grocery stores headquartered in Michigan (see ¶1489f).

• *Federal procurement credit*

Taxpayers that create at least 25 new jobs may claim a credit for the employee payroll attributed to new jobs created as a result of being awarded a federal procurement contract with either the departments of Defense, Energy, or Homeland Security (see ¶1489o).

• *Photovoltaic energy manufacturer credit*

A qualified taxpayer may claim a credit for the development and manufacturing of photovoltaic energy, photovoltaic systems, or other photovoltaic technology (see ¶1489m).

• *Historic rehabilitation credit*

The historic rehabilitation credit has been expanded and enhanced. In addition to the existing MBT credit, two additional historic rehabilitation credits are created (see ¶315 and ¶1489b).

• *Credit for converting fuel delivery systems*

Applicable to tax years that begin after 2008 and end before 2012, a taxpayer that was an owner of a service station may claim a credit for a portion of the costs incurred to convert existing fuel delivery systems. The credit was equal to 30% of the costs incurred to convert existing systems to provide E85 fuel or qualified biodiesel blends or to create new fuel delivery systems for those fuels (see ¶1489s).

• *Credit for development account contributions*

A taxpayer, including a qualified financial institution, may claim a credit equal to a portion of the contributions made in a tax year to a fiduciary organization's reserve fund pursuant to the Individual or Family Development Account Program Act. The amount of the credit is equal to 75% of the contributions made (see ¶1489t).

• *Bonus depreciation credit*

Taxpayers may claim a credit to mitigate the effects of decoupling from bonus depreciation under IRC Sec. 168(k) (see ¶1489u).

• *Public exhibition credit*

A qualified taxpayer may claim a credit, provided that it meets certain conditions for a public exhibition. The amount of the credit is the lesser of the taxpayer's tax liability or $250,000 (see ¶1489v).

• *Automobile alternative power credits*

Four new credits for automobile alternative power may be claimed. The credits are for (1) the manufacturing of plug-in traction battery packs (applicable to tax years beginning after 2009 and ending before 2015), (2) expenses for vehicle engineering (applicable to tax years beginning after 2011), (3) engineering activities for advanced automotive battery technologies (applicable to tax years beginning after 2011 and ending before 2015), and (4) the construction of an integrative cell manufacturing facility (credit cannot be claimed for tax years beginning before 2012) (see ¶1489w, ¶1489x, ¶1489y, ¶1489z).

• *Construction of large scale battery facility credit*

A credit for the construction of a large scale battery facility may be claimed. The credit is 25% of capital investment expenses for any tax year for the construction of a facility that will produce large scale batteries and manufacture integrated power management, smart control, and storage systems from 500 kilowatts to 100 megawatts (see ¶1489aa).

• *Lithium ion battery pack credit*

Applicable to tax years beginning after 2011 and ending before 2017, a taxpayer that manufactures advanced lithium ion battery packs in Michigan may claim a credit. A taxpayer must enter into an agreement with the Michigan Economic Growth Authority (MEGA) and meet certain requirements (see ¶1489ab).

• *Sourcing program credit*

Applicable to tax years beginning after 2014 and ending before 2017, a taxpayer may claim a credit for a portion of the costs incurred to implement a sourcing program to use battery cells from a business that has agreed to construct an integrative cell manufacturing facility. The amount of the credit is equal to 75% of the costs incurred to implement a sourcing program to use battery cells (see ¶1489ac).

• *Film industry credits*

A taxpayer may claim a credit against the Michigan business tax for a portion of the base investment made in qualified film and digital media infrastructure projects. In addition, a taxpayer may claim a credit against the MBT for a portion of direct production and personnel expenditures incurred in Michigan. Finally, a taxpayer may claim a credit against the MBT for a portion of qualified job training expenditures (see ¶1489l, ¶1489p, ¶1489ae).

• *Cigarette dealers credit*

A taxpayer that is a wholesale dealer, retail dealer, distributor, manufacturer, or seller that had receipts from the sale of cigarettes or tobacco products may claim a credit, provided that the taxpayer paid federal and state excise taxes on the tobacco products during the 2008 and 2009 tax years (see ¶1489ad).

¶58 Corporate Income Tax

The corporate income tax is effective January 1, 2012.

• *Small business credit*

Businesses whose gross receipts do not exceed $20 million, and whose adjusted business income, minus any loss adjustment, does not exceed $1.3 million are allowed a credit against the corporate income tax. The credit is the greater of the amount by which the tax exceeds 1.8% of the adjusted business income (¶1551).

¶60 Sales and Use Taxes

• *Manufacturing exemption*

A sales and use tax exemption is available for tangible personal property sold to industrial processors and other purchasers. The property is exempt only to the extent that it is used for the exempt purposes provided in the statute. The exemption is limited to the percentage of exempt use to total use determined by a reasonable formula or method approved by the Department of Treasury (¶1705).

• *Pollution control equipment exemption*

Property installed as a component part of an air or water pollution control facility is exempt from sales and use tax. Air pollution control facilities do not include air conditioners or dust collectors used for the benefit of personnel (¶1705).

¶65 Property Taxes

• *Industrial facilities*

Certified industrial facilities are exempt from real and personal property taxes and subject instead to the industrial facilities tax. Certification is a tax incentive for new or improved facilities in areas in which facilities are obsolete (¶2004).

• *Obsolete property rehabilitation districts*

Qualified local governments may establish obsolete property rehabilitation districts and grant abatements from Michigan property tax, subject to state approval, for rehabilitated commercial property and commercial housing property that is located in these districts. The rehabilitated facilities are subject to an obsolete properties tax in lieu of most general property taxes (¶2004).

• *Telecommunications providers*

Telecommunications providers are allowed a credit against the property tax imposed on public utilities for expenditures for eligible broadband investments and, if tax liability remains, a credit equal to the maintenance fee imposed (¶2209), less the equipment credit (¶2006).

• *Start-up businesses and innovation centers*

Qualified start-up businesses are exempt from real and personal property taxes, the technology park facilities tax, the industrial facility tax, the obsolete property tax, and the lessee-user tax, provided certain conditions are met (¶2004, ¶2005).

The property of an innovations center that is located in a certified technology park and owned or used in the administration of the center by a qualified high-technology business is also exempt from real and personal property taxes (¶2004).

• *Special tools exemption*

Special tools are exempt from taxation. "Special tools" means finished or unfinished devices, such as dies, jigs, fixtures, molds, patterns, and special gauges, used or being prepared for use in the manufacturing function for which they are designed or acquired or made for the production of products or models and are of such specialized nature that their utility and amortization cease with the discontinuance of such products or models (¶2004).

• *Exemption for pollution control facilities*

Water and air pollution control facilities are exempt from real and personal property taxes (¶2004).

¶70 Renaissance and Enterprise Zones

• *Renaissance zones*

Michigan has designated certain areas of the state as tax-free Renaissance Zones (RZ). In a RZ, each of the following state and local taxes are waived: Michigan Business Tax; Local Personal Property Tax; Local Real Property Tax; Michigan 6 mill State Education Tax; State Personal Income Tax (must be permanent resident within the RZ); Local Personal Income Tax; and Utility Users Tax (applies only to the Detroit RZ) (¶1489, ¶2004).

• *Enterprise zones*

Businesses located in an enterprise zone are eligible for tax incentives relating to business conducted in the zone including property tax exemptions for locating within an enterprise zone (¶2003, ¶2004).

PART II

INCOME TAX

CHAPTER 1

RATES, PERSONS SUBJECT

¶101 Overview

The Michigan Income Tax Act was enacted in 1967, and took effect October 1, 1967, for individuals, estates, and trusts.

The Michigan income tax is a flat tax on the net adjusted incomes of resident individuals, trusts, and estates and on the income earned in Michigan of nonresidents. Partnerships are required to file information returns.

Computation of the tax is discussed in Chapter 2, and information on credits is found in Chapter 3. Allocation and apportionment of income is treated in Chapter 4. Returns and payment are discussed in Chapter 5, and withholding is discussed in Chapter 6. Administration, assessment of tax, collection of tax, and appeals are treated in Chapter 7, while refunds, penalties, and recordkeeping requirements are found in Chapter 8. Income taxes imposed by Michigan cities are discussed in Chapter 23.

Chapter 14.5 begins the discussion of the Michigan business tax on business entities.

Chapter 15.1 begins the discussion of the Michigan corporate income tax.

¶102 Rates of Tax

Law: Sec. 206.51, M.C.L. (CCH MICHIGAN TAX REPORTS, ¶ 15-355).

Comparable Federal: Secs. 1—5 (CCH U.S. MASTER TAX GUIDE ¶ 11).

The personal income tax rate is 4.25%. (Sec. 206.51(1), M.C.L., Instructions, MI-1040, Michigan Individual Income Tax Return).

Beginning on or after January 1, 2023, the personal income tax rate for a tax year may decrease when certain circumstances apply. The tax rate will be reduced when the percentage increase in the total general fund/general purpose revenue from the immediately preceding fiscal year is greater than the positive inflation rate. The amount of the reduction is dependent upon a formula, based upon the current tax rate multiplied by a fraction, the numerator of which is the difference between the general fund/general purpose revenue for the preceding fiscal year and the capped general fund/general purpose revenue, and the denominator of which is the total personal income tax collected in the preceding fiscal year.

¶103 Tax Imposed on Individuals, Estates, and Trusts

Law: Secs. 206.51, 450.4101—450.5200, M.C.L. (CCH MICHIGAN TAX REPORTS, ¶15-010, 15-110, 15-115, 15-205).

Comparable Federal: Secs. 1—5, 641 (CCH U.S. MASTER TAX GUIDE ¶11, 501, et seq.).

The tax is imposed on income received by resident and nonresident individuals, partners, beneficiaries of trusts and estates, and estates and trusts, having a source in, or attributable to, Michigan under the allocation and apportionment rules discussed in Chapter 4.

A taxpayer whose income-producing activities are confined solely to Michigan will have his or her entire taxable income allocated to, and taxable by, Michigan, unless the income is otherwise nontaxable. A taxpayer having income from a business activity that is taxable both within and without Michigan, other than from the rendering of personal services by an individual, will allocate and apportion taxable income within and without the state under the allocation and apportionment provisions of the law.

Resident estates and resident trusts are subject to tax on all income from any source, except for income that is attributable to another state. Nonresident estates and trusts are subject to personal income tax on income sourced to Michigan. Beneficiaries who are Michigan residents are subject to personal income tax on all sources of income distributed from an estate or trust (after adjustments). Nonresident beneficiaries are subject to Michigan personal income tax on income distributed by an estate or trust if the income is allocated to or apportioned to Michigan. The allocation of Michigan income additions and subtractions must be in proportion to the beneficiary's share of distributable net income of the estate or trust. (*Revenue Administrative Bulletin 2015-15*, Michigan Department of Treasury, August 20, 2015, CCH MICHIGAN TAX REPORTS ¶401-998)

¶104 "Resident" and "Nonresident" Defined

Law: Secs. 206.14, 206.18, M.C.L. (CCH MICHIGAN TAX REPORTS, ¶15-110, 15-115).

"Resident" is defined to include the following:

— an individual domiciled in Michigan;

— the estate of a decedent who, at death, was domiciled in Michigan; and

— any trust created by will of a decedent domiciled in Michigan at the time of death and any trust created by, or consisting of property of, a person domiciled in Michigan at the time the trust becomes irrevocable.

"Domicile" means the place where a person has his or her true, fixed, and permanent home and principal establishment to which, whenever absent, the person intends to return. Domicile continues until another permanent home is established. If an individual changes residence during a taxable year, taxable income is determined separately for income received while in each status as resident and nonresident. An individual who lives in Michigan at least 183 days during the tax year (or more than one-half the days during a taxable year of less than 12 months) is considered a resident individual domiciled in Michigan.

For the purpose of the definition of "resident", a taxable year is considered terminated at the date of death.

A "nonresident" individual, estate, or trust is any person not included in the definition of "resident".

• *Filing status*

For filing status, Michigan recognizes the "single","married, filing jointly", and "married, filing separately" for the personal income tax. (Instructions, Form MI-1040)

Practice Note: Same-sex couples

Same-sex married couples must file as "married filing jointly" or "married filing separately" on Michigan personal income tax returns. This is in response to the United States Supreme Court's decision in *Obergefell et al. v. Hodges* on June 26, 2015. Taxpayers may file amended returns within the statute of limitations, but the amended returns are not required. (*Notice: Michigan Income Tax Filing Status for Married Same-Sex Couples*, Michigan Department of Treasury, July 1, 2015, CCH MICHIGAN TAX REPORTS ¶401-983) For tax years before 2015, taxpayers may seek refunds for personal income tax paid on same-sex spousal employee benefits that were included in Michigan taxable income. (*Notice: Michigan Income Tax Treatment of Employee Benefits for Same-Sex Spouses*, Michigan Department of Treasury, July 16, 2015, CCH MICHIGAN TAX REPORTS ¶401-988)

Practitioner Comment: Same Sex Couple Filing Jointly: Amended Returns and Refund of Overpayments

Michigan now allows same-sex married couples to file state returns using the married filing jointly or married filing separately status.

On June 26, 2015, the U.S. Supreme Court in *Obergefell v. Hodges*, 135 S. Ct. 2584, 192 L. Ed. 2d 609 (2015) ruled that a state ban on same-sex marriage is a constitutional violation of the Equal Protection Clause of the Fourteenth Amendment to the U.S. Constitution. Prior to the ruling, Michigan did not recognize same-sex marriage and, therefore, same-sex couples could not file Michigan returns using the married filing jointly or married filing separately status. As a result of the decision, Michigan now permits same-sex married couples to file their state tax returns using the married filing jointly or married filing separately status. If the spouses file a joint federal income tax return, they must also file a joint Michigan return. However, if the spouses do not file a joint federal return, they may still choose to file separately or jointly. Same-sex married couples living in Michigan may, but are not required to, amend state income tax returns for the years 2012, 2013 or 2014 and obtain a refund of any overpayment. Amended returns must be filed within four years of the date that the original return was due. *Michigan Department of Treasury Notice, Michigan Income Tax Filing Status for Married Same-Sex Couples* (July 1, 2015).

Wayne D. Roberts, Varnum, LLP and Marjorie B. Gell, Western Michigan University Cooley Law School

¶105 Persons Exempt Under Federal Law Exempt from Michigan Tax

Law: Sec. 206.201, M.C.L. (CCH MICHIGAN TAX REPORTS, ¶15-110, 15-530).

Comparable Federal: Secs. 501—528 (CCH U.S. MASTER TAX GUIDE, ¶601, et seq.).

Persons who are exempt from federal income tax are also exempt from Michigan income tax. However, the unrelated taxable income of an exempt person, as determined under the federal law, is taxable.

Tax-exempt entities, however, are not exempt from tax withholding (Chapter 6) and information return (¶510) requirements.

¶106 Common Trust Funds Exempt

Law: Sec. 206.91, M.C.L. (CCH MICHIGAN TAX REPORTS, ¶15-530).

Comparable Federal: Sec. 584 (CCH U.S. MASTER TAX GUIDE ¶595, 2389).

A common trust fund that meets the requirements of IRC Sec. 584 is not subject to the income tax. However, each participant in such a fund must include in his or her taxable income his or her proportionate share of the taxable income from the fund, whether or not distributed or distributable.

¶107 Shareholders of S Corporations

(CCH MICHIGAN TAX REPORTS, ¶15-185).

For a detailed discussion of S corporations and their shareholders, see ¶853 and ¶854.

¶108 Taxpayers with Limited Sales Activities—Optional Tax

Law: Sec. 206.191, M.C.L. (CCH MICHIGAN TAX REPORTS, ¶15-355).

Alternate methods of computing the tax of taxpayers with limited sales activity in Michigan are not reflected on the income tax forms although the provisions have not been repealed.

¶109 Military Personnel

Law: (Sec. 206.301(1)(e), M.C.L.; R206.10, Mich. Admin. Code (CCH MICHIGAN TAX REPORTS, ¶15-175).

Comparable Federal: Secs. 112, 121(9), 132(n), 134, 692 (U.S. MASTER TAX GUIDE ¶889—896, 1078, 2609, 2533).

For taxpayers that elect to use the Internal Revenue Code as in effect for the tax year, Michigan's taxation of pay and benefits received by members of the U.S. Armed Forces is generally the same as federal because the starting point for Michigan taxable income is federal adjusted gross income (¶203). Military provisions apply to all regular and reserve components of the uniformed services subject to the jurisdiction of the Secretaries of Defense, Army, Navy, or Air Force, including members of the Marines and Coast Guard. Members of the National Oceanic and Atmospheric Administration also are included, but not members of the Merchant Marine.

The following income of military personnel is subject to both federal and Michigan income taxes:

— active duty and reserve training pay;

— enlistment and reenlistment bonuses;

— incentive pay;

— lump-sum payments for accrued leave;

— severance, separation, or release pay;

— readjustment pay;

— travel and per diem allowances;

— personal allowances for high-ranking officers;

— military retirement pay based on age or length of service; and

— scholarships and student loan repayments.

• *Residency and domicile*

Under the provisions of the federal Servicemembers' Civil Relief Act, a member of the Armed Forces retains, while in service, the same domicile as when entering military service. Military personnel (usually career personnel) may change their domicile from Michigan to another state just as any other individual. Conclusive evidence must be submitted showing that their Michigan domicile has been abandoned and a new domicile established in another state.

Military personnel temporarily assigned and living in Michigan are not subject to tax on their income or compensation for military service unless they have changed their domicile with intent to establish a Michigan residence (50 U.S.C. §574). However, income from nonmilitary Michigan sources is subject to Michigan income tax and must be reported on a nonresident return.

CCH Comment: Military Spouses

Applicable to state or local income tax returns for tax years beginning after 2008, the Military Residency Relief Act of 2009 (P.L. 111-97) prohibits a servicemember's spouse from either losing or acquiring a residence or domicile for purposes of taxation because he or she is absent or present in any U.S. tax jurisdiction solely to be with the servicemember in compliance with the servicemember's military orders, if the residence or domicile is the same for the servicemember and the spouse. P.L. 111-97 also prohibits a spouse's income from being considered income earned in a tax jurisdiction if the spouse is not a resident or domiciliary of such jurisdiction when the spouse is in that jurisdiction solely to be with a servicemember serving under military orders.

• *Combat pay exclusion*

Members of the Armed Forces may exclude combat pay and hostile fire pay for any month for which such pay is received. However, the exclusion for a commissioned officer is limited to the highest rate of enlisted pay for each month.

Hospitalization: The monthly exclusion also applies if the service member is hospitalized anywhere as the result of wounds, disease, or injury sustained while serving in a combat zone, but is limited to two years after the termination of combatant activities in the combat zone. Payments for leave accrued during service in a combat zone are also excluded.

Practice Note: Michigan Exempts All Military Compensation

Compensation paid from federal appropriations, including retirement benefits, for military services in the armed forces is exempt from Michigan income tax, and is deductible from adjusted gross income by the recipient to the extent it is included in federal adjusted gross income. However, the subtraction must be reduced by employee business expenses attributable to military income. If the expenses exceed the military income, there can be no subtraction for military income.

• *Tax forgiveness for decedents*

Income tax is forgiven for members of the Armed Forces who die as the result of wounds, disease, or injury incurred in a combat zone or as a result of wounds or injuries sustained in terroristic or military action. Forgiveness includes the entire taxable year in which the death occurs, not just the shortened tax year, and extends to any earlier year ending on or after the first day of service in a combat zone. Taxes for those years are abated, credited, or refunded. However, refunds are subject to the statute of limitations.

Practice Note: Spouse of Deceased Member

The tax forgiveness applies only to the deceased person, not to the spouse.

• *Other nontaxable items*

Miscellaneous items of income received by service members are nontaxable, as follows:

— living allowances, including Basic Allowance for Quarters (BAQ), Basic Allowance for Subsistence (BAS), Variable Housing Allowance (VHA), and housing and cost-of-living allowances abroad;

— family allowances, including those for emergencies, evacuation, separation, and certain educational expenses for dependents;

— death allowances, including those for burial services, travel of dependents, and the death gratuity payment to eligible survivors.

• *Sale of residence*

Two important benefits are available to members of the military who sell their homes.

Homeowner's Assistance Program (HAP): The HAP reimburses military homeowners for losses incurred on the private sale of their homes after a base closure or reduction in operations. The HAP payment is the difference between 95% of the home's fair market value before the closure or reduction announcement and the greater of the home's fair market value at the time of sale or the actual sale price.

HAP payments are excludable from gross income.

Capital gains: All homeowners may exclude up to $250,000 ($500,000 on a joint return) of gain on the sale of a home if they have owned and used the home as their personal residence for two of the five years preceding the date of sale (a prorated amount is excluded if the home is used for a nonqualified use). Because members of the military, Public Health Service officers, and Foreign Service officers may be required to move frequently, the five-year testing period may be suspended for up to 10 years. The suspension applies whenever the person is on qualified official extended duty for more than 90 days and is stationed at least 50 miles from the person's residence or is under orders to reside in government quarters.

• *Moving expenses*

Armed forces members, their spouses and dependents may deduct moving expenses without regard to the distance and time requirements that otherwise would apply. The move must be pursuant to a military order that results in a permanent change of station.

• *Filing requirements*

Members of the military are generally subject to the same filing requirements as other taxpayers (¶501), but for service members stationed outside the U.S. or Puerto Rico, the due date is automatically extended to June 15th. However, interest accrues on any unpaid tax liability from April 15th, regardless of any extensions.

Members in combat zones: For service members in designated combat zones, hazardous duty areas, hospitalized outside the U.S. due to a combat injury, or deployed in contingency operations, the due date is postponed without interest or penalties until 180 days after the member's return to the U.S. The extended due date also applies to filing amended returns.

• *Veterans*

Payments to veterans for benefits administered by the Veterans Administration are tax-free. Such items include education, training, or subsistence allowances; veterans' pensions, insurance proceeds, and dividends paid to veterans or their families or beneficiaries; grants to disabled veterans for motor vehicles or homes with disability accommodations; and disability compensation.

INCOME TAX

CHAPTER 2

COMPUTATION OF INCOME

¶201 In General—Michigan Taxable Income Based on Federal Law

Law: Secs. 206.12, 206.28, M.C.L. (CCH MICHIGAN TAX REPORTS, ¶15-220, 15-230).

Michigan taxable income is computed by starting with a federal base and making adjustments. Michigan law terms have the same meaning when used in a comparable context as in the federal income tax law unless a different meaning is clearly required.

"Internal Revenue Code" is defined to mean the Code as in effect on January 1, 1996, or at the option of the taxpayer, the Code in effect for the tax year. For taxpayers that make the election to incorporate the IRC as in effect for the tax year amendments enacted by the following post-2006 federal Acts are applicable for purposes of computing the Michigan individual income tax to the extent applicable to the 2014 taxable year:

— the Small Business and Work Opportunity Tax Act of 2007;

— the U.S. Troop Readiness, Veterans' Care, Katrina Recovery, and Iraq Accountability Appropriations Act of 2007;

— the Energy Independence & Security Act of 2007;

— the Mortgage Forgiveness Debt Relief Act of 2007;

— the Tax Increase Prevention Act of 2007;

— the Tax Technical Corrections Act of 2007;

— the Economic Stimulus Act of 2008;

— the Heartland, Habitat, Harvest, and Horticulture Act of 2008;

— the Heroes Earnings Assistance and Relief Tax Act of 2008;

— the Housing Assistance Tax Act of 2008;

— the Emergency Economic Stabilization Act of 2008;

— the Worker, Retiree, and Employer Recovery Act of 2008;

— the American Recovery and Reinvestment Act of 2009;

— the Worker, Homeownership, and Business Assistance Act of 2009;

— Hiring Incentives to Restore Employment Act of 2010;

— Patient Protection and Affordable Care Act, as amended by the Health Care and Education Reconciliation Act of 2010;

— Education Jobs and Medicaid Assistance Act of 2010;

— Small Business Jobs Act of 2010;

— Tax Relief, Unemployment Insurance Reauthorization, and Job Creation Act of 2010;

— Regulated Investment Company Modernization Act of 2010; and

— American Taxpayer Relief Act of 2012.

¶202 Charts of Relationship of Federal Base to Michigan Taxable Income

Because Michigan adopts federal base as the starting point for computation of Michigan taxable income, the items that constitute gross income and the items allowed as business deductions are the same as under the federal law. However, Michigan provides for various adjustments to the federal base.

The charts on the following pages show how to arrive at Michigan taxable income for individuals, using federal adjusted gross income as a starting point.

COMPUTATION OF FEDERAL TAXABLE INCOME — INDIVIDUALS

	Commissions, Bonuses, Tips, Fees, Certain Fringe Benefits
	Wages, Salaries, other compensation
	Annuities, Pensions
	Interest Received
	State and Local Income Tax Refunds
	Prizes
	Farm Income
GROSS INCOME	Social Security
	Alimony Received
	Dividends Received
	Gross Business Profits
	Unemployment Compensation
	Gains on Sales or Exchanges
	Rents and Royalties
minus	
	Trade or Business Expenses
	Performing Artists Expenses
	Employee's Reimbursed Expenses
	Losses from Sales or Exchanges
DEDUCTIONS FROM GROSS INCOME	Expenses of Producing Rental or Royalty Income
	Self-Employed Retirement Plan Contributions
	Alimony Paid
	Contributions to IRAs
	Interest Forfeited upon Premature Withdrawal from Time Savings Account
	Repayment of Supplemental Unemployment Compensation Benefits
	Jury Duty Pay Remitted to Employer
	Employment-Related Moving Expenses
	Medical Savings Account Contributions
	Health Savings Account Contributions
equals	
ADJUSTED GROSS INCOME	
	(Not allowed for Michigan Purposes)
minus	Nonbusiness Taxes Paid
	Nonbusiness Interest Paid

ITEMIZED DEDUCTIONS OR STANDARD DEDUCTIONS	Nonbusiness Casualty or Theft Losses Medical Expenses Investor's Expenses Unreimbursed Employee Business Expenses Unreimbursed Employee Educational Expenses Charitable Contributions
and minus	
EXEMPTIONS	Taxpayer Spouse Dependents
equals	
FEDERAL TAXABLE INCOME	To which the applicable federal tax rate is applied. Federal credits are then subtracted from the resulting tax.

COMPUTATION OF MICHIGAN TAXABLE INCOME—INDIVIDUALS

Plus (¶ 203)		Minus (¶ 203)
	FEDERAL ADJUSTED GROSS INCOME	
	with	
Income from State Bonds of Other States Losses from Federal Obligations Capital Loss Adjustment (¶ 211) Certain Income Taxes Out-of-State Business Losses Federal Net Operating Loss Deduction Refunds of Advance Tuition Contract Payments State Payment of Defaulted Loans	MICHIGAN ADJUSTMENTS	Income from Federal Obligations Military Pay Retirement or Pension Benefits Capital Gain Adjustment (¶ 211) Political Contributions Michigan Net Operating Loss Deduction Social Security Benefits Amounts Related to Federal Credit for Elderly/Disabled Wages Not Deductible Under Federal Jobs Credit Advance Tuition Contract Payments State Income Tax Refunds Included in Federal Income Out-of-State Business Gains Discriminatory Self-Insured Medical Plan Payments Regulated Bingo Prizes Interest from Local Obligations Dividends and Interest Received by Senior Citizens Income Received by RZ Residents (¶ 204) Deduction for Child Dependent Holocaust Victim Settlement Payments Education Savings Account Interest and Contributions Charitable Distributions Equity Investment Gain
	equals	
	MICHIGAN INCOME	
	subject to	
	ALLOCATION AND APPORTIONMENT	Nonbusiness Income (¶ 406—411) Business Income (¶ 412—416)
	minus	
	MICHIGAN EXEMPTIONS	Taxpayer, Spouse, Dependents, Over 65, Blind, Disabled, Deaf, Partially Unemployed
	equals	
	MICHIGAN TAXABLE INCOME	To Which is Applied the Tax Rate (¶ 102) And From the Resulting Tax Subtract Various Credits (¶ 301—316) Withheld Taxes and Estimated Tax Payments (¶ 308, 309)

¶203 Individuals—Taxable Income—Federal Adjusted Gross Income

Law: Secs. 206.30, 206.30b, 206.30c, 206.30d, 206.30f, 206.30bb, 211.87c, M.C.L.; R206.7, Mich. Admin. Code (CCH MICHIGAN TAX REPORTS, ¶15-505—¶16-370).

Comparable Federal: Secs. 62, 170, 221 (CCH U.S. MASTER TAX GUIDE ¶1005, 927—931, 1058—1071, 1082).

Taxable income for individuals is federal adjusted gross income as defined in the Internal Revenue Code (¶201), with adjustments.

Neither standard nor itemized deductions are provided for in the Michigan personal income tax law. The only deductions permitted are those allowed in the computation of adjusted gross income under the Internal Revenue Code or those that are specifically provided as Michigan adjustment modifications to federal adjusted gross income. Taxpayers who itemize for federal reporting will have different taxable incomes for Michigan and federal income tax purposes.

Practice Note: Federal Tax Benefit Rule Incorporated

The Michigan Court of Appeals has held that the federal tax benefit rule is incorporated into personal income tax law. According to the federal tax benefit rule, gross income does not include income attributable to the recovery during the taxable year of any amount deducted in any prior taxable year to the extent that such amount did not reduce the amount of tax imposed. (*Sturrus v. Department of Treasury*, Michigan Court of Appeals, No. 295403, Unpublished February 8, 2011, Approved for Publication May 19, 2011, CCH MICHIGAN TAX REPORTS, ¶401-559)

A nonresident or part-year resident is allowed that proportion of a deduction that the taxpayer's portion of adjusted gross income from Michigan sources bears to the taxpayer's total adjusted gross income.

The adjustments to federal adjusted gross income to obtain Michigan taxable income are discussed in the following paragraphs.

- *Interest and dividends from state obligations*

Interest and dividends from obligations or securities of states other than Michigan must be added to the federal base in the amount excluded from federal adjusted gross income. However, taxpayers may deduct from the income any related expenses that are not deductible in computing federal adjusted gross income.

- *Taxes*

Taxes on or measured by income are added to the federal base to the extent that they were deducted from federal gross income. State or local income taxes not attributable to a trade or business are not added back to the federal base, however, because these taxes are deductible only as itemized deductions, and not in the computation of federal adjusted gross income.

Practice Note: Taxes Paid by Pass-Through Entity

An addback could be required if the taxpayer receives income from a conduit entity, such as an estate, trust, partnership, or S corporation, that has paid income tax at the entity level (R206.7, Mich. Admin. Code; CCH MICHIGAN TAX REPORTS, ¶19-039).

• *Losses from sales of U.S. obligations*

Losses from the sale of U.S. obligations must be added back to the federal base to the extent deducted in computing federal adjusted gross income. Losses reported through a mutual fund are treated as having been received directly by the taxpayer (*Revenue Administrative Bulletin 86-3;* CCH MICHIGAN TAX REPORTS, ¶319-002).

• *Losses from out-of-state business property*

Losses from a business or property located outside Michigan are added back to the federal base.

• *Income from U.S. obligations*

Income from U.S. obligations or from the sale or exchange of U.S. obligations is exempt from state income taxes and may be subtracted from the federal base. The amount subtracted is reduced by any attributable indebtedness interest or expenses incurred to the extent that such expenses were deducted in arriving at federal adjusted gross income.

• *Military compensation*

Compensation, including retirement benefits, received for service in the U.S. Armed Forces may be subtracted to the extent included in federal adjusted gross income. Beginning January 1, 2012, retirement or pension benefits received for services in the Michigan National Guard may be deducted.

• *Retirement benefits*

Social security benefits: To the extent included in adjusted gross income, social security benefits may be subtracted. (Sec. 206.30(1)(f), M.C.L.)

Public pension plans: To the extent included in adjusted gross income, federal retirement benefits and all retirement and pension benefits received from a public retirement system of Michigan or any of its political subdivisions may be subtracted. (Sec. 206.30(1)(f), M.C.L.) The Teachers Insurance and Annuity Association/College Retirement Equities Fund (TIAA/CREF) is considered a public retirement plan for purposes of the exemption. (*Revenue Administrative Bulletin 1988-30,* CCH MICHIGAN TAX REPORTS, ¶319-059)

CCH Caution: Deduction Limitations

See Caution Note below discussing deduction limitations, effective January 1, 2012.

The statute providing the state employee exemption was held to be discriminatory by the U.S. Supreme Court in 1989 in the *Davis* case because it exempted retirement income of state and local employees while taxing that of federal employees (1989, US SCt), 489 US 803, 109 SCt 1500; CCH MICHIGAN TAX REPORTS, ¶15-310.35). On remand, the Michigan Court of Appeals extended the exemption to federal employees as well. Federal law (4 U.S.C. 114) limits a state's ability to impose an income tax on any retirement income of an individual who is not a resident of the state. H.R. 4019 (P.L. 109-264), clarifies that the prohibition against state taxation of retirement income applies to the retirement income of partners, as well as that of employees.

To the extent included in adjusted gross income, retirement or pension benefits received from public retirement systems of other states or their subdivisions may also be subtracted if the income tax laws of the other jurisdictions permit a reciprocal deduction or exemption for benefits from public retirement systems of Michigan and its subdivisions. (Sec. 206.30(1)(f), M.C.L.) The deduction is limited to the smaller of (1) the amount allowed by the other state to residents receiving Michigan public pension income, or (2) the amount included in federal adjusted gross income. (*Revenue Administrative Bulletin 1988-25,* CCH MICHIGAN TAX REPORTS, ¶319-054)

Private pension plans: Certain retirement and pension benefits or benefits from retirement annuity policies in which payments are made for life to senior citizens are deductible from adjusted gross income within certain maximum amounts. However, the maximum amount of any such deduction must be reduced by the amount of any deduction that is allowed for retirement income received from the Armed Forces or from public retirement systems. (Sec. 206.30(1)(f)(iv), M.C.L.) For 2014, the maximum private pension deduction is $49,027 on a single return and $98,054 on a joint return. (Instructions, Form MI-1040, Individual Income Tax Return)

CCH Caution: Deduction Limitations

Effective January 1, 2012, for persons born before 1946, the deduction for pension benefits is unchanged. However, for persons born in 1946 through 1952, the deduction for pension benefits is limited to $20,000 for a single return and $40,000 for a joint return, and after that person reaches age 67, the pension benefits deduction is no longer applicable, but the taxpayer is eligible for a deduction of $20,000 for a single return and $40,000 for a joint return against all types of income. For persons born after 1952, when the person reaches age 67, the taxpayer may elect to take the deduction of $20,000 for a single return and $40,000 for a joint return against all types of income, and forgo the deduction for social security and the personal exemption. Or, persons born after 1952 (after reaching age 67) may elect the social security deduction and the personal exemption. (Sec. 206.30(9), M.C.L.)

The private pension plan deduction must be reduced by the amount of any deduction claimed by a senior citizen for interest, dividends, or capital gains.

In response to the governor's request, the Michigan Supreme Court issued an advisory opinion regarding the constitutionality of several of the personal income tax changes enacted earlier in 2011. This way the statute's validity could be decided before the law took effect on January 1, 2012. In its opinion, the Michigan Supreme Court held that (1) reducing or eliminating the personal income tax statutory exemption for public pension income does not impair accrued financial benefits of a pension plan or retirement system of Michigan or its political subdivisions under the state constitution; (2) reducing or eliminating the statutory exemption for pension income does not impair a contract obligation in violation of the federal or state constitutions; and (3) determining eligibility for exemptions on the basis of date of birth does not violate equal protection under the federal or state constitutions. (*In Re Request for Advisory Opinion Regarding Constitutionality of 2011 PA 38*, Michigan Supreme Court, Docket No. 143157, Nov. 18, 2011; CCH MICHIGAN TAX REPORTS, ¶401-617)

Pension benefits that qualify for the subtraction include (1) plans for self-employed persons, commonly known as Keogh or HR10 plans; (2) individual retirement accounts that qualify under IRC Sec. 408 if the distributions are not made until the participant has reached 59-1/2 years of age, except in certain cases; (3) employee annuities or tax-sheltered annuities purchased under IRC Sec. 403(b); (4) distributions from a 401(k) plan attributable to employee contributions mandated by the plan or attributable to employer contributions; (5) other unqualified pension plans that prescribe eligibility for retirement and predetermine contributions and benefits if the distributions are made from a pension trust; and (6) retirement or pension benefits received by a surviving spouse if those benefits qualified for a deduction prior to the decedent's death. However, pension benefits that do not qualify for the subtraction include (1) benefits received from certain deferred compensation plans, including IRC Sec. 457 plans and distributions from certain IRC Sec. 401(k) and Sec. 403(b) plans, (2) certain premature distributions paid on separation, withdrawal, or discontinuance of a plan, and (3) payments received as an early retirement incentive unless the distributions are from a pension trust. (Sec. 206.30(8), M.C.L.; *Revenue Administrative Bulletin 1988-22*, CCH MICHIGAN TAX REPORTS, ¶319-051)

Planning Note: Distributions From a Private IRA

The Michigan Court of Appeals has held that the distributions from a private IRA whose principal wholly originated in a nontaxable 403(b) retirement account were not subject to the personal income tax. The Department of Treasury argued that because the distributions came directly from a private IRA the distributions must be taxed regardless of the fact that the IRA principal came from a tax-free retirement plan. Private IRAs were not normally tax-free, but rather tax-deferred. At retirement, state retirees received tax-free benefits in the form of periodic annuity payments or in a single lump-sum payment. The lump sum could be deposited into an investment account or a bank account, but the amount deposited was not taxable when it was withdrawn. In this case, the income placed in the IRA was not state tax-deferred income but, rather, state nontaxable income. Obtaining deferral on the applicable tax by rolling the money over into an IRA did not create a deferred obligation to pay state income tax on the money that was not subject to personal income tax to start with. (*Magen v. Department of Treasury*, Michigan Court of Appeals, No. 302771, February 21, 2013, CCH MICHIGAN TAX REPORTS, ¶401-771)

Military retirement benefits: To the extent included in adjusted gross income, retirement benefits received for services in the armed forces of the United States may be subtracted. Beginning January 1, 2012, retirement or pension benefits received for services in the Michigan National Guard may be deducted. (Sec. 206.30(1)(e), M.C.L.)

Railroad retirement benefits: To the extent included in adjusted gross income, Tier 2 railroad retirement benefits may be subtracted. Also, if Tier 1 railroad retirement benefits were subject to federal income tax, then those benefits may be subtracted on the Michigan return. (Sec. 206.30(1)(e), M.C.L.; Instructions, Form MI-1040, Individual Income Tax Return)

Benefits from government agency not covered by federal Social Security Act: Beginning January 1, 2013, for a person born in 1946 through 1952 who receives retirement or pension benefits from employment with a government agency not covered by the federal Social Security Act, the deduction for public retirement or pension benefits is limited to $35,000 for single returns or $55,000 for joint returns. If both spouses receive such public retirement or pension benefits, the deduction is increased to $70,000 for joint returns. After the taxpayer reaches age 67, this deduction does not apply. Instead, the taxpayer is eligible for a deduction of $35,000 for single returns or $55,000 for joint returns (or $70,000 for joint returns, if applicable); this deduction is available against all types of income. However, the deduction against all types of income is not available for persons who claimed the deduction of compensation for services in the U.S. Armed Forces, Railroad Retirement Act benefits or pension benefits from Michigan National Guard services. (Sec. 206.30(9)(c), M.C.L.)

For a person born after 1952 who has reached age 62 through 66 and who receives retirement or pension benefits from employment with a government agency not covered by the federal Social Security Act, the deduction for public retirement or pension benefits is limited to $15,000 for a single return or $15,000 for a joint return. However, if both spouses receive such income, then the deduction is $30,000 for a joint return. (Sec. 206.30(9)(d), M.C.L.)

Planning Note: Claiming the Subtraction

The Michigan Department of Treasury has provided guidance discussing the personal income tax subtraction for pension or retirement income from governmental agencies not covered by the Social Security Act (SSA) for individuals born on January 1, 1953. Taxpayers who reach age 62 and receive a pension or retirement income from employment with a government agency that was not covered by the SSA, are eligible to receive a pension or retirement deduction of up to $15,000 ($30,000 on a jointly filed return provided that both spouses receive pension or retirement benefits from employment that was not covered by the SSA). Taxpayers should complete only page 1 of Form 4884 and write "born January 1, 1953" at the top of the form. Also, taxpayers should claim this pension or retirement income subtraction on Schedule 1, line 22 as a miscellaneous subtraction and write "born January 1, 1953" as the description. (*E-mail,* Michigan Department of Treasury, January 20, 2015)

• *Political contributions*

Individuals may deduct from federal adjusted gross income political contributions in amounts up to $50, or $100 in the case of a joint return. However, this deduction is not available to taxpayers after January 1, 2012.

• *Net operating losses*

The amount of a federal net operating loss is added back to federal AGI. After allocation and apportionment, the resulting Michigan net operating loss is then deducted from federal taxable income. Michigan follows the federal NOL carryback and carryforward provisions.

CCH Advisory: Michigan NOL Deduction May be Claimed Even if No Federal NOL Claimed

A taxpayer may claim a Michigan NOL deduction even if no federal NOL deduction is claimed (*Preston v. Department of Treasury,* 190 MichApp 491, 476 NW2d 455, lv den 439 Mich 980; CCH MICHIGAN TAX REPORTS [1989—1993 Transfer Binder], ¶400-148) and may claim a Michigan NOL deduction that exceeds the taxpayer's federal modified taxable income (*Beznos v. Department of Treasury* (1997, Ct App), 224 MichApp 717, 569 NW2d 908; CCH MICHIGAN TAX REPORTS, ¶400-669).

Computation of the Michigan deduction is discussed in *Revenue Administrative Bulletin 98-3;* CCH MICHIGAN TAX REPORTS, ¶319-277. An NOL adjustment is also required for income and losses pertaining to certain oil and gas royalties; see the discussion of oil and gas royalties below.

• *Amounts eligible for the federal credit for the elderly and disabled*

Amounts eligible for the federal credit for the elderly or disabled under IRC Sec. 22 that have been included in federal taxable income may be subtracted from the federal base.

• *Federal tax credit wages*

Wages that are not deductible as a business expense on a taxpayer's federal income tax return because of the operation of IRC Sec. 280C, relating to expenses for which separate federal credits are allowable, may be subtracted from the federal base in determining Michigan taxable income. However, this deduction is not available after January 1, 2012. Accordingly, it would appear Michigan taxpayers may deduct wages that were not deducted on their federal returns but that were used to compute the following federal credits:

— the work opportunity credit under IRC Sec. 51;

— the clinical testing (orphan drug) credit under IRC Sec. 45C;

— the research credit under IRC Sec. 41;

— the Indian employment credit under IRC Sec. 45A;

— the empowerment zone credit under IRC Sec. 1396;

— the employer wage credit for employees who are active duty members of the uniformed services under IRC Sec. 45P;

— the credit for production of low sulfur diesel fuel under IRC Sec. 45H;

— the mine rescue team training credit under IRC Sec. 45N; and

— the agricultural chemicals security credit under IRC Sec. 45).

• *Miscellaneous adjustments*

Any adjustments resulting from the application of Sec. 206.271, relating to the treatment of capital gains or losses on assets acquired prior to October 1, 1967 (¶211); any adjustments with respect to estate or trust income under Sec. 206.36 (¶208); and any adjustments resulting from the allocation and apportionment of income (Chapter 4) are added or subtracted, as applicable.

• *Advance tuition contract payments*

Payments made for advance tuition contracts under the Michigan Education Trust Act (MET) are deductible from the federal base. If a purchaser is unable to open up a trust account with the MET because the Trust's board of director's determines that it can not accept an unlimited number of enrollees, the amount of payment made under a contract with a private sector investment manager may also be deducted if the contract:

— receives certification by the MET's board of directors;

— applies only for a state institution of higher education or a Michigan community or junior college; and

— requires that the qualified beneficiary to be enrolled in not less than 4 years after the date on which the contract is entered into.

The total purchase price of a Michigan Education Trust contract may be deducted in the year in which the contract is purchased. In addition, earnings on contributions are tax exempt to beneficiaries if used for qualified higher education expenses. Finally, MET benefits used to pay college tuition and mandatory fees are exempt from federal and state income taxes. (MET Contract Enrollment Booklet, Michigan Department of Treasury)

Under federal law, refunds of tuition made as a result of the termination of a contract are added back for purposes of computing federal adjusted gross income. If a previously deducted advance tuition contract payment is refunded because the qualified beneficiary does not attend an institution of higher learning, the lesser of the amount of the refund or the amount of the deduction must be added to the federal base. However, the taxpayer may then deduct the amount added back if the contract is terminated because the qualified beneficiary attends an institution of postsecondary education other than either a state institution of higher education or an institution of postsecondary education located outside this state with which a state institution of higher education has reciprocity.

The amount paid by Michigan on behalf of a taxpayer to repay the outstanding principal on a defaulted loan used to fund an advance tuition payment contract under the MET is added back to the taxpayer's federal base if the cost of the contract was previously deducted and was financed with a MET-secured loan.

• *State income tax refunds*

Refunds of state income tax that have been included in federal taxable income are deductible from the federal base.

• *Interest from local obligations*

Interest derived from local obligations that has been statutorily declared to be exempt from Michigan tax is subtracted from the federal base to the extent that it has been included in federal taxable income. Examples of such an obligation are notes issued to fund delinquent tax revolving funds.

• *Oil and gas royalty payments*

Oil and gas lease royalty payments are exempt from personal income tax if severance tax has been paid on the royalties (*Bauer et al. v. Department of Treasury* (1993, Ct App) 203 MichApp 97, 512 NW2d 42; CCH MICHIGAN TAX REPORTS, ¶400-306). Generally, a taxpayer must deduct the amount of any interest income and add the amount of any interest losses that were included in federal AGI. A taxpayer with income from oil, gas, and other business activity must allocate its expenses between the oil and gas activity and the other business activity. Oil and gas production expenses and net operating losses may not be deducted when calculating taxable income (*Cook*, (1998 Ct App) 229 MichApp. 653 , 583 NW2d 696; CCH MICHIGAN TAX REPORTS, ¶400-730; *Elenbaas*, (1999 CtApp) 235 MichApp. 372, 597 NW2d 271; CCH MICHIGAN TAX REPORTS, ¶400-778). If oil and gas production assets are sold, the capital gains realized from the sale are subject to Michigan income tax (*Fruehauf*, MTT, No. 233268 and No. 233271, June 9, 1997; CCH MICHIGAN TAX REPORTS, ¶400-659).

• *Out-of-state business income*

Resident taxpayers may subtract net rents and royalties from real property located or used in another state and business income derived solely in other states and included in federal adjusted gross income.

• *Bingo and lottery prizes*

Prizes awarded at regulated bingo games are subtracted from the federal base because they are not taxed. However, lottery prizes are subject to tax. (The constitutionality of the repeal of the statutory exemption for state lottery prize winnings by P.A. 516, Laws 1988, was upheld in *Mooahesh v. Department of Treasury et al.* (1992, Ct App) 195 MichApp 551, 492 NW2d 246; CCH MICHIGAN TAX REPORTS [1989—1993 Transfer Binder], ¶400-227)

Practice Note: Bingo Games and Lottery Prizes

The amount of prizes on in state of Michigan-related bingo may be subtracted, but state lottery winnings may not.

• *Self-insured medical expense benefits*

Benefits from discriminatory self-insured medical expense reimbursement plans are subtracted from the federal base to the extent they have been included in federal adjusted gross income.

• *Senior citizen interest, dividend, and capital gain income*

To the extent included in adjusted gross income, a taxpayer who is a senior citizen may deduct interest, dividends, and capital gains received in the tax year. For the 2014 tax year, the adjustment is limited to a maximum of $10,929 for a single return and $21,857 for a joint return. However, the deduction is reduced by amounts received as retirement benefits from the armed forces or from public or private retirement systems. Effective January 1, 2012, this deduction is not available to a senior citizen born after 1945.

• *Education savings account interest, contributions, and IRA distributions*

Taxpayers may deduct, to the extent not deducted in determining adjusted gross income, the total of all contributions made to Education Savings Accounts (ESAs), not to exceed $5,000 for a single return or $10,000 for a joint return per tax year. Contribution deductions must be decreased by the amount of any qualified withdrawals made during the tax year, calculated on a per savings account basis. The amount of contribution calculated for each education savings account cannot be less than zero.

Interest earned on the account and qualified withdrawals from the account may also be deducted, to the extent not included in adjusted gross income. Taxpayers may also deduct, to the extent included in adjusted gross income, the amount of a distribution from an individual retirement account that is used to pay qualified higher education expenses.

"Qualified withdrawal" means a distribution that is not subject to a penalty or an excise tax under IRC Sec. 529, a penalty under the Michigan education savings program statutes, or taxation under the Michigan income tax statutes, and that meets any of the following:

— A withdrawal from an account to pay the qualified higher education expenses of the designated beneficiary incurred after the account is established;

— A withdrawal made as the result of the death or disability of an account's designated beneficiary;

— A withdrawal made because a beneficiary received a scholarship that paid for all or part of the beneficiary's qualified higher education expenses to the extent the withdrawal amount does not exceed the scholarship amount;

— A withdrawal made because a beneficiary attended a service academy to the extent that the withdrawal amount does not exceed the costs of the advanced education attributable to the beneficiary's attendance in the service academy (a service academy means the U.S. military academy, naval academy, air force academy, coast guard academy, or merchant marine academy);

— A transfer of funds due to the termination of a management contract; or

— A transfer of funds to another education savings account or another account in a qualified tuition program under IRC Sec. 529. (Sec. 390.1472(n), M.C.L.)

Total contributions to all accounts that name one individual as the designated beneficiary must not exceed a maximum of $235,000. Distributions must be made for qualified higher education expenses and must be paid directly to the eligible education institution or to the beneficiary of the account. Distributions that are not qualified withdrawals are added to taxable income. The amount added may not exceed the total amount deducted for ESA contributions in the tax year and all previous tax years. In addition, no addition is required for withdrawals that are less than the sum of all contributions made to an ESA in all previous tax years for which no deduction was claimed, less any withdrawn contributions for which no deduction was claimed in all previous tax years.

If a federal penalty is imposed under IRC Sec. 529, a penalty is not imposed by the state. If a distribution that is not a qualified withdrawal is not subjected to a federal penalty under IRC Sec. 529, the state will withhold 10% of the accumulated earnings attributable to that distribution amount as a penalty. The penalty may be increased or decreased if the treasurer and program manager determine that it is necessary to increase or decrease the penalty to comply with IRC Sec. 529.

• *Holocaust reparation payments*

Holocaust victims may deduct settlement payments, to the extent included in their federal adjusted gross income, from their taxable income subject to Michigan personal income tax.

The deduction applies to amounts received as a result of a settlement of claims for any recovered asset under a German act regulating unresolved property claims, a settlement of a New York action for Holocaust victims, or any similar action. Interest earned on the settlement amount may be deducted, but income and interest must be kept separate from the taxpayer's other funds and assets. The term "Holocaust victim" means a person, or the heir or beneficiary of that person, who was persecuted by Nazi Germany or any Axis regime during any period from 1933 to 1945.

• *Charitable distributions*

To the extent included in adjusted gross income, taxpayers are allowed to subtract qualified charitable distributions made to charitable organizations during the tax year. The amount of the subtraction is equal to the amount deductible under IRC Sec. 170(c), reduced by (1) the amount of the retirement or pension benefits deduction claimed under state law, and (2) two times the total amount of personal income tax credits claimed under state law for charitable contributions (see ¶306). However, this deduction is not available to taxpayers after January 1, 2012.

A qualified charitable contribution is one made within 60 days of receipt of the assets as a distribution from a retirement or pension plan, either to an organization exempt under IRC Sec. 501(c)(3) (except for organizations controlled by a political party, elected official, or candidate for office), or to certain charitable remainder trusts and unitrusts, pooled income funds, or for the issuance of charitable gift annuities.

• *Equity investment gain*

Michigan personal income tax taxpayers are allowed to deduct the gain realized from an initial equity investment made in a qualified business before December 31, 2009. However, the initial investment must be at least $100,000, and the gain must be reinvested within one year. However, this deduction is not available after January 1, 2012. A "qualified business" has the following characteristics:

— it is a seed business;

— it is headquartered or domiciled in Michigan or has a majority of its employees working in Michigan;

— it has a pre-investment valuation of less than $10 million;

— it has existed fewer than five years (unless the business is a charitable organization or a university research facility);

— it has engaged only in competitive edge technology; and

— it is certified as meeting these requirements by the Michigan Strategic Fund for each investment.

• *Claim of right doctrine*

A tax liability recomputed under the claim of right doctrine is not allowed as an adjustment in determining Michigan income tax liability (*Revenue Administrative Bulletin 94-9;* CCH MICHIGAN TAX REPORTS, ¶319-250). However, a credit is available (¶312).

• *Child's income claimed on parent's return*

A parent of a child with income only from interest and dividends who elects under federal law to include the child's income on his or her return must include the child's income in his or her Michigan taxable income and household income (*Revenue Administrative Bulletin 90-22;* CCH MICHIGAN TAX REPORTS, ¶319-178).

Practice Note: Children Under 19 Years of Age

Through 2011, Michigan allows an additional deduction for each child dependent who is claimed as an exemption and who is under 19 years of age (¶205).

• *Michigan residents working abroad*

For Michigan residents who are engaged in foreign employment, the Michigan Department of Treasury has issued guidelines regarding the income tax consequences of working abroad. In general, an individual domiciled in Michigan who has made an election under IRC Sec. 911 to exclude certain income will be allowed to exclude that income from the Michigan tax base. The individual must report and pay the Michigan income tax upon all other taxable income from any source whatsoever. (*Revenue Administration Bulletin 2002-5*; CCH MICHIGAN TAX REPORTS, ¶319-315)

• *Certain charitable contributions*

The amount of a charitable contribution made to an advance tuition payment fund may be subtracted from the federal base.

• *Depletion*

For the 2013 tax year and beyond, personal income taxpayers can eliminate income derived from a mineral, as well as eliminate expenses related to this income, to the extent included in adjusted gross income. (Sec. 206.31b, M.C.L.)

• *Oil and gas*

For tax years beginning after 2011, personal income taxpayers are required to add back the gross expenses of producing oil and gas (subject to the Michigan severance tax) to the extent deducted from adjusted gross income. In addition, taxpayers may subtract the gross income from producing oil and gas to the extent included in adjusted gross income. (Sec. 206.30(1)(w), M.C.L.)

¶204 Renaissance Zone Residents—Income Tax Deductions

Law: Secs. 125.2689, 125.2690, 206.31, 206.31a, M.C.L. (CCH MICHIGAN TAX REPORTS, ¶16-350).

A qualified taxpayer may deduct from adjusted gross income the income earned or received while the taxpayer was a resident of a designated Renaissance Zone (RZ). Interest and dividends are deductible, as are capital gains prorated on the basis of the percentage of time that the asset was held by the qualified taxpayer while the qualified taxpayer was a resident of the RZ. Lottery winnings are also deductible (see below). Taxable income derived from an illegal activity is not deductible.

A "qualified taxpayer" is an RZ resident with $1 million or less in gross income for any applicable year. Generally, an RZ "resident" is an individual who has been domiciled in a designated RZ for a period of 183 consecutive days.

Individuals are ineligible for the incentives if they are delinquent in the payment of taxes. In addition, residential rental property located in an RZ is ineligible for the incentives if it is not in substantial compliance with state and local zoning, building, and housing laws. An individual who is a resident of an RZ is ineligible for the incentives if the Department of Treasury determines that the incentives granted that person have resulted in $10 million in forgone revenue.

For the most current list of renaissance zones and information concerning local contacts, see the Michigan Economic Development Corporation's website at: **http://www.michigan.org/medc/services/sitedevelopment/renzone/index.asp**.

A taxpayer is required to file a return in order to be eligible for the RZ deductions. A taxpayer's income is characterized separately whenever the taxpayer acquires or relinquishes status as a "qualified" taxpayer.

• *Tool and die renaissance recovery zones*

The Michigan Strategic Fund is authorized to designate tool and die renaissance recovery zones in the state. Such recovery zones will have renaissance zone status, and qualified tool and die businesses will be entitled to the tax exemptions described above, for a period determined by the Strategic Fund.

For details about tool and die renaissance zones, see ¶1489a.

For details concerning the tool and die recovery program and the application process, see the Michigan Economic Development Corporation's website at http://medc.michigan.org/services/sitedevelopment/renzone/toolanddierecovery.

Practice Note: Interplay with Other Deductions

In addition, income used to calculate a deduction under any other section of the Michigan Income Tax Act may not be used to calculate an RZ deduction, and the Michigan net operating loss deduction is determined without regard to the RZ deductions.

• *Residency issues*

If a qualified taxpayer completes the RZ residency requirements before the end of the tax year in which the taxpayer first resided in the zone, the taxpayer may claim the deductions for that year. Also, if a taxpayer completes the residency requirements in the tax year subsequent to the year in which the taxpayer first resided in the RZ and *before* the date for filing an annual return for the preceding year, the taxpayer may claim the deductions for the tax year in which the taxpayer first resided in the RZ. However, if a taxpayer completes the residency requirements in the subsequent tax year and *after* the date for filing an annual return for the preceding year, the taxpayer may claim the deductions for the tax year in which the residency requirements were completed on an annual return for that year, and may also claim the deductions for the tax year in which the taxpayer first resided in an RZ by filing an amended return for that year.

• *Lottery winnings*

Income received by a qualified taxpayer from winning an on-line lottery game is deductible only if the drawing date is after the date that the taxpayer became an RZ resident. Income received by a qualified taxpayer from winning an instant lottery game is deductible only if the taxpayer was an RZ resident on the validation date of the ticket.

• *Reduction of incentives*

During its last three years of designation, an RZ's tax breaks are reduced by the following percentages: (1) 25% for the tax year that is two years before the final year of designation; (2) 50% for the tax year immediately preceding the final year of designation; and (3) 75% for the tax year that is the final year of designation.

• *Other tax incentives*

Exemptions or deductions from, or credits against, Michigan business tax, city income tax, or city utility users tax are available under certain circumstances to taxpayers doing business in RZs (¶1489a, ¶1613). In addition, property located in an RZ is exempt from many types of property tax (¶2004, ¶2005).

¶205 Personal Exemptions and Dependent Deductions

Law: Secs. 206.30(2), 206.30a, 206.30d, 206.504, 206.522(e)(4), M.C.L. (CCH MICHIGAN TAX REPORTS, ¶15-130, 15-535).

Comparable Federal: Secs. 151—152 (CCH U.S. MASTER TAX GUIDE ¶133—149).

Michigan provides a personal exemption for 2014 of $4,000 times the number of personal or dependency exemptions allowable on the taxpayer's federal income tax return. The personal exemption amount is adjusted annually for inflation. For the 2014 tax year, an additional exemption of $2,500 is allowed for taxpayers who are disabled, deaf, or blind effective January 1, 2012, senior citizens and partially employed taxpayers are no longer eligible for the addition exemption.

Practice Note: Claiming Exemptions for Both Age and Disability Prohibited

Michigan, like federal law, reclassifies disabled individuals as senior citizens upon reaching age 65. Consequently, taxpayers are precluded from claiming exemptions for both age and disability.

A personal income exemption of $400 may be claimed by taxpayers and each of their dependents who are qualified disabled veterans. (Sec. 206.30(3)(d), M.C.L.)

• *Dependent exemptions*

An additional $600 deduction may be claimed for each dependent child for whom the taxpayer claimed an exemption and who is younger than 19 years of age on the last day of the tax year. Effective January 1, 2012, this deduction is no longer available.

An individual who has taxable income and is claimed as a dependent on the federal return of another taxpayer is allowed a $1,500 personal exemption.

• *Nonresidents and part-year residents*

Nonresidents or part-year residents receive appropriately proportioned exemptions.

¶206 Reciprocal Agreement Exemption for Nonresidents

Law: Sec. 206.256, M.C.L. (CCH MICHIGAN TAX REPORTS, ¶15-115).

Nonresidents from states that have entered into reciprocal agreements with Michigan are exempt from Michigan income tax on salaries, wages, and other employee compensation earned from work performed in Michigan; however, they do have to pay Michigan tax on business income derived from business activity in Michigan. Conversely, Michigan residents pay only Michigan income tax on their salaries and wages earned in any of these states. Michigan residents may be required to make estimated income tax payments on this income.

To date, the states that have entered into reciprocal agreements with Michigan are Illinois, Indiana, Kentucky, Minnesota, Ohio, and Wisconsin.

¶207 Trust Income Taxed to Grantor Under Federal Law

Law: Sec. 206.51, M.C.L. (CCH MICHIGAN TAX REPORTS, ¶15-205).

Comparable Federal: Secs. 671—678 (CCH U.S. MASTER TAX GUIDE ¶571—588).

Taxable income of a resident who is required to include income from a trust in his or her federal income tax return (under provisions treating the grantor or another person as the owner of a portion of any trust) must include all items of income and deductions from the trust to the same extent as is required with respect to property owned outright by such resident.

¶208 Estates and Trusts—Taxable Income Based on Federal Taxable Income

Law: Sec. 206.36, M.C.L. (CCH MICHIGAN TAX REPORTS, ¶15-215).

Comparable Federal: Sec. 63 (CCH U.S. MASTER TAX GUIDE ¶126, 701, et seq.).

Taxable income for estates and trusts is federal taxable income as defined in the Internal Revenue Code (¶201), with adjustments.

The following adjustments to federal taxable income are made by estates and trusts in computing Michigan taxable income:

— Interest and dividends from obligations or securities of states other than Michigan must be added to the federal base in the amount excluded from federal taxable income. However, taxpayers may deduct any related expenses that are not deductible in computing federal taxable income.

— Any income taxes, or taxes measured by net income, deducted in arriving at federal taxable income must be added back.

— Any loss on the sale or exchange of U.S. obligations (the income from which the state is prohibited from taxing) must be added back to the federal base to the extent deducted in computing federal taxable income.

— Income from U.S. obligations or from the sale or exchange of U.S. obligations must be subtracted from the federal base. The amount of the income to be subtracted should be reduced by any interest on indebtedness incurred in carrying the obligations and by any expenses incurred in the production of the income to the extent that the expenses, including amortizable bond premiums, were deducted in arriving at federal taxable income.

— Any adjustment resulting from the application of Sec. 206.271, relating to capital gains or losses on assets acquired prior to October 1, 1967 (¶211), and any adjustment resulting from the allocation and apportionment of income (Chapter 4) are added or subtracted as appropriate.

¶209 Allocation of Shares of an Estate or Trust

Law: Sec. 206.36, M.C.L. (CCH MICHIGAN TAX REPORTS, ¶15-235).

Comparable Federal: Sec. 662 (CCH U.S. MASTER TAX GUIDE ¶556).

The respective shares of an estate or trust and its beneficiaries (including, for this purpose, nonresident beneficiaries) in the addition and subtraction modifications are in proportion to their respective shares of distributable net income of the estate or trust as defined in the Internal Revenue Code. If the estate or trust has no distributable net income for the taxable year, the share of each beneficiary in the additions and subtractions is in proportion to each individual's share of the estate or trust income for the year (under local law or the terms of the estate or trust instrument) required to be distributed currently and any other amounts of income distributed during the year. Any balance of the additions and subtractions is allocated to the estate or trust.

If capital gains and losses are distributed or distributable to a beneficiary under the Internal Revenue Code, the fiduciary must advise each beneficiary of the share of any adjustment resulting from the application of the provisions relating to capital gains or losses on assets acquired prior to October 1, 1967 (¶211). The election to make an adjustment or the failure to make the election with respect to capital gains or losses taxable to the estate or trust will not affect a beneficiary's right to make or not make the election.

¶210 Residents and Nonresidents—Taxable Income Computed in Same Manner

Law: Sec. 206.51, M.C.L. (CCH MICHIGAN TAX REPORTS, ¶15-105, 15-115).

Taxable income of a nonresident is computed in the same manner as taxable income of a resident, subject to allocation and apportionment of income derived from sources outside Michigan. Allocation and apportionment provisions are discussed in Chapter 4.

Michigan is prohibited by federal law from taxing distributions of deferred compensation made to nonresidents who earned the deferred compensation in Michigan. The prohibition applies to the retirement income of a nonresident retired partner, as well as a nonresident retired employee. Distributions of deferred compensation to Michigan residents are subject to Michigan income tax regardless of where the deferred compensation was earned (*Revenue Administrative Bulletin 97-2;* CCH MICHIGAN TAX REPORTS, 319-272).

A nonresident is any person who is not a resident. "Resident" is defined at ¶104.

¶211 Income from Disposition of Asset Acquired Prior to Effective Date of Income Tax

Law: Secs. 206.30, 206.36, 206.271, M.C.L.; R206.19, Mich. Admin. Code (CCH MICHIGAN TAX REPORTS, ¶15-620, 16-070).

Generally, Michigan follows the federal treatment of capital gains and losses. However, taxpayers may elect to adjust taxable income when they have capital gains or losses resulting from dispositions of property acquired prior to the effective date of the Michigan income tax, October 1, 1967. Thus, capital gains attributable to holding periods prior to October 1, 1967, may be subtracted from the federal base, and the proportion of the loss represented by the holding period prior to October 1, 1967, is added to income.

A taxpayer whose capital transactions involving property acquired before October 1, 1967, resulted wholly or primarily in losses would generally not elect the adjustment, because it would increase Michigan taxable income. The law requires, however, that all relevant capital items be included in a given year; consequently, losses must be added if gains are adjusted. To compute the adjustment, a fraction is applied to the loss (R206.19, Mich. Admin. Code; CCH MICHIGAN TAX REPORTS, ¶19-100). The denominator is the total months held, and the numerator is the number of months held before October 1, 1967. The resulting figure is added to the federal base.

¶212 "Taxable Year" Defined

Law: Sec. 206.24, M.C.L. (CCH MICHIGAN TAX REPORTS, ¶15-455).

Comparable Federal: Secs. 441, 7701 (CCH U.S. MASTER TAX GUIDE ¶211, 1501—1511, 2451).

"Taxable year" or "tax year" means the calendar year, or the fiscal year ending during the calendar year, used as the basis for computing taxable income under the Michigan income tax law. A taxpayer's tax year for Michigan purposes must be the same as the tax year for federal purposes.

If a return is made for a fractional part of a year, "tax year" or "taxable year" means the period for which the return is made.

INCOME TAX

CHAPTER 3

CREDITS

¶301 Credit for Income Taxes Paid Other States

Law: Secs. 206.20, 206.255, 206.256, M.C.L. (CCH MICHIGAN TAX REPORTS, ¶16-825).

Comparable Federal: Secs. 901—906 (CCH U.S. MASTER TAX GUIDE ¶2475—2485).

Forms: MI-1040, Individual Income Tax Return.

Individuals, estates, and trusts are allowed credits against the Michigan income tax for income taxes paid to other taxing jurisdictions, as discussed below.

• *Residents*

A resident individual, estate, or trust is allowed a credit for income tax imposed on the taxpayer for the taxable year by another state or a political subdivision thereof, the District of Columbia, or a Canadian province on income that is derived from sources outside of Michigan and that is also subject to Michigan tax.

The amount of the credit is the lesser of the following:

— the amount of tax imposed by the other jurisdiction on income derived from sources outside Michigan that is also subject to state personal income tax; or

— an amount determined by dividing income subject to taxation both in Michigan and in another jurisdiction by taxable income and multiplying the result by the taxpayer's tax liability before any credits are deducted.

• *Nonresidents*

Although Michigan does not provide a tax credit for nonresidents, the State Treasurer is authorized to enter into reciprocal agreements with other states to provide personal income tax exemptions for income earned for personal services in Michigan by nonresidents if the laws of the state of residence provide a similar exemption for Michigan residents (¶206, ¶508, ¶605).

• *Forms*

The credit is claimed on MI-1040, Michigan Individual Income Tax Return, and a copy of the other state's tax return must be attached.

Practice Tip: Canadian Taxes

The credit for taxes paid to Canadian provinces is limited to any amounts of provincial tax not claimed as a credit on a taxpayer's federal return, with the presumption that Canadian federal income tax is claimed first. (Sec. 206.255(1), M.C.L; LR 87-66, Commissioner of Revenue, ¶250-383) If the credit for Canadian provincial tax is claimed, Michigan Form 777, Resident Credit for Tax Imposed by a Canadian Province must be filed. Required attachments are: Canadian Form T-1, Federal Individual Tax Return; Canadian Form T-4, Statement of Remuneration Paid; federal Form 1116, Foreign Tax Credit; and federal Form 1040, Individual Income Tax Return. (Instructions, Form MI-1040, Individual Income Tax Return)

¶302 Michigan City Income Taxes Credit

Law: Sec. 206.257, M.C.L.; R206.17, Mich. Admin. Code (CCH MICHIGAN TAX REPORTS, ¶15-826).

Comparable Federal: Secs. 164, 275 (CCH U.S. MASTER TAX GUIDE ¶1021—1027).

Forms: MI-1040, Michigan Individual Income Tax Return.

Individuals, estates, and trusts are allowed a credit for city income taxes paid (Chapter 23), computed as follows:

If the total city income tax is:	The credit is:
Not over $100.00	20% of the city income taxes
Over $100.00 but not over $150.00	$20.00 plus 10% of the excess over $100.00
Over $150.00	$25.00 plus 5% of the excess over $150.00 but the total credit shall not exceed $10,000.00

CCH Caution: Credit Repealed

Effective January 1, 2012, this credit is repealed.

The amount of city income tax on which the credit is based is the amount of city income taxes that are deductible for federal income tax purposes or the amount that would have been deductible if the standard deduction had not been taken. Penalties or interest paid in relation to city taxes are not includible in the amount of tax subject to credit (R206.17, Mich. Admin. Code; CCH MICHIGAN TAX REPORTS, ¶19-089).

The tax amount used as the basis for the credit is that amount paid by the taxpayer in the tax year, reduced by any refund of overpaid taxes of a prior year. If a taxpayer is assessed and pays additional city income taxes applicable to prior years, the additional taxes paid are added to the city tax of the year in which they are paid for purposes of computation of the credit.

The credit is claimed on MI-1040, Michigan Individual Income Tax Return.

¶303 Homestead Property Tax Credit

Law: Secs. 206.30, 206.501—206.526, 206.530, 206.532, M.C.L. (CCH MICHIGAN TAX REPORTS, ¶16-827).

Forms: MI-1040, Individual Income Tax Return, MI-1040CR; Homestead Property Tax Credit Claim; MI-1040CR-2, Homestead Property Tax Credit Claim for Veterans and Blind People.

A Michigan resident who paid property tax or rent on a Michigan homestead may claim a refundable property tax credit against income tax. A claimant must have been domiciled in Michigan for at least six months of the calendar year preceding the year in which the claim is filed and must occupy the homestead or dwelling. Special rules apply to certain welfare recipients, servicepersons, veterans, senior citizens, paraplegics, hemiplegics, and quadriplegics, blind persons, and disabled individuals. Beginning January 1, 2012, a person is not eligible for this credit if the taxable value of his homestead is more than $135,000; however, the portion of real property that is unoccupied and classified as agricultural for real property tax purposes is excluded from the taxable value of the homestead.

Practice Note: "Homestead" Changed to "Principal Residence"

Most references to the term "homestead" in Michigan law were amended to refer instead to a taxpayer's "principal residence". However, the provision of the Income Tax Law governing the homestead property tax credit has not been amended to change this terminology.

• *Basis of credit*

The credit is based on property taxes that were billed for the taxable year. To qualify for the credit, the property tax must exceed 3.5% of the taxpayer's household income or total household resources; however, this limitation is reduced or eliminated for special taxpayers. Effective January 1, 2012, for senior citizens, the credit ranges from 100% to 60% of the difference between the homestead property taxes (or the rental credit) and 3.5% of total household resources when household resources range from $21,000 or less to $30,000 or more. (Sec. 206.522(1)(b), M.C.L.) For renters, 20% of the gross rent paid is considered property tax eligible for the credit, or 10% of the gross rent paid if the person renting or leasing a homestead is subject to a service charge in lieu of property taxes.

Certain special assessments paid by the taxpayer qualify as property taxes for purposes of computing the credit base. A special assessment may not be included in the base unless it:

(1) was levied using a uniform millage rate on all real property that is not exempt by state law from the levy;

(2) was levied and based on State Equalized Value (SEV) or taxable value; and

(3) complied with one of the following: (a) the assessment was levied in an entire city, village, or township; or (b) the assessment was levied for police, fire, or advanced life support and levied in an entire township excluding all or a portion of a village within the township.

• *Amount of credit*

For ordinary taxpayers, the credit is 60% of the amount by which the homestead property tax for the year exceeds 3.5% of the claimant's total household income or total household resources for the taxable year.

Senior citizens and disabled individuals: For senior citizens, paraplegics, hemiplegics, quadriplegics, and totally and permanently disabled individuals the credit is 100% of the homestead property tax in excess of the percentage of household income specified below. For tax years that begin after 2012, blind taxpayers are eligible to calculate the credit under this subsection.

Household income	Percentage
Not over $3,000.00	0%
Over $3,000.00 but not over $4,000.00	1.0%
Over $4,000.00 but not over $5,000.00	2.0%
Over $5,000.00 but not over $6,000.00	3.0%
Over $6,000.00	3.5%

A senior citizen whose total household income for the tax year is $6,000 or less and who received a senior citizen's property tax homestead exemption for 1973 (this exemption, for homesteads to the amount of $2,500 equalized value, was repealed after 1973) may compute the income tax credit for a percentage of homestead taxes paid as follows: (a) if the taxable value of the homestead is $2,500 or less, 100% of the property taxes; or (b) if the taxable value is more than $2,500, the percentage that $2,500 bears to the taxable value of the homestead.

Servicepersons: An eligible serviceperson, veteran, or veteran's widow or widower is entitled to a credit against the income tax for a percentage of the property taxes not in excess of 100% on the homestead for the taxable year, computed by (1) dividing the taxable value allowance by the taxable value of the homestead or, for renters, 20% of the total annual rent paid on the property divided by the property tax rate on the rented property, and (2) multiplying the property taxes on the homestead by the percentage obtained by step (1).

Blind persons: A claimant who is blind is entitled to a homestead property tax credit computed as follows: (1) if the taxable value of the homestead is $3,500 or less, 100% of the property taxes; or (2) if the taxable value of the homestead is more than $3,500, the percentage that $3,500 bears to the taxable value of the homestead. If both the husband and wife filing a joint return are blind, each is considered a claimant.

Welfare recipients: Generally, the homestead property tax credit is reduced for persons who received state family assistance or state disability assistance. The amount of the reduction may not exceed the sum of the aid provided in a tax year.

• *Limitations*

Only one claimant per household for a tax year is entitled to the credit unless both the husband and wife filing a joint return are blind, in which case each is considered a claimant.

The credit is reduced by 10% for each $1,000 increment by which the total household resources exceed $41,000, beginning in 2012 (previously, if household income exceeded $73,650). Thus, taxpayers with household income over $82,650 are not eligible for the credit before 2012. The amount of the credit may not exceed $1,200.

Unmarried taxpayers: For taxpayers who are not a husband and wife and who share a homestead, the homestead property tax credit may be limited. Non-married taxpayers who own a home and who jointly own and occupy the same dwelling, must file separate claims on their prorated share of their taxes. For taxpayers who jointly rent property, the rental payments must be the amount the renter or lessee contracts to pay the landlord. If the individual does not have a contract to rent or cannot establish that an arm's length transaction exists between himself or herself and the landlord, the taxpayer will be ineligible to claim the homestead property tax credit. (*Revenue Administrative Bulletin 2002-4;* CCH MICHIGAN TAX REPORTS, ¶319-314)

Use in trade or business: Taxpayers who use their homestead as the site of a trade or business may also have their homestead property tax credit limited. Property taxes that may be claimed for a homestead property tax credit must be prorated when a claimant used a portion of his or her homestead for business purposes or to produce income during the year. Thus, taxpayers who conduct a trade or business from their home, must prorate the property taxespaid or the gross rent paid between homestead use and business use to properly calculate the homestead property tax credit. (*Revenue Administrative Bulletin 2002-3;* CCH MICHIGAN TAX REPORTS, ¶319-313)

Nursing home residents: Taxpayers who are permanent residents of a nursing home and have substantially all or a part of the charges for rent, food, nursing or other services paid directly to the nursing home by agencies of the state or federal government are not allowed a full homestead property tax credit. The resident of the nursing home is only allowed a homestead property tax credit for his or her allocable share of the charges paid to the nursing home. (*Revenue Administrative Bulletin 2002-2;* CCH MICHIGAN TAX REPORTS, ¶319-312)

• *Household income*

"Household income" means all income received by all persons of a household in a tax year while members of a household. "Household income" includes military pay (*Revenue Administrative Bulletin 91-2;* CCH MICHIGAN TAX REPORTS, ¶319-195). Because all income is includible, household income includes those items deductible or excludible from federal Adjusted Gross Income (AGI) and consequently may be a larger figure than federal AGI.

"Income" means federal AGI plus all income specifically excluded or exempt from the computation of federal AGI. Net operating loss deductions are subtracted except that such deductions may not exceed federal modified taxable income as defined by federal law. The term does not include the following:

— the first $300 of gifts in cash or kind from nongovernmental sources;

— the first $300 of income from awards, prizes, lottery, bingo, or gambling winnings;

— surplus food or relief in kind supplied by a governmental agency;

— payments or credits under the Michigan Income Tax Act;

— homestead rehabilitation grants;

— stipends received by a person 60 years of age or older who is acting as a foster grandparent or as a senior companion;

— medicare premiums deducted from social security or railroad retirement payments;

— employer-provided life, accident, or health insurance plans payments;

— energy assistance grants and tax credits; and

— family accident or health insurance plan premiums paid for by the filer.

CCH Comment: Health Insurance Premiums

The premiums paid for the following health insurance plans may be deducted from household income:

— medical insurance plans;

— dental insurance plans;

— vision insurance plans;

— prescription drug plans;

— automobile insurance premiums for medical coverage;

— Medicare Parts A—D; and

— premiums paid for the types of plans that are deducted to arrive at federal adjusted gross income. (*Internal Policy Directive 2009-1,* Michigan Department of Treasury, March 30, 2009, CCH MICHIGAN TAX REPORTS, ¶401-415)

"Taxable value" is discussed at ¶2007 in Chapter 20, "Property Taxes".

Practice Note: Money Was Rebate of Taxes Paid, Not Income

The Michigan Court of Appeals has held that the money a personal income taxpayer received through the homestead property tax credit was a rebate of property taxes paid and was not income for purposes of the property tax poverty exemption. A tax refund was not income because a refund returned money to the taxpayer that need not have been paid. A tax credit can function like a tax refund in some cases, such as here. The homestead property tax credit does not confer income nor is it a program to transfer new monies to an individual; rather, it is to rebate a portion of property taxes already paid. The amount of money received and the basis upon which it was received was identical whether it was received as a decrease in income taxes due or as a payment of the rebate amount that exceeded the individual's income tax liability. Accordingly, the homestead property tax credit money the taxpayer received did not count as income for the property tax poverty exemption. (*Ferrero v. Township of Walton*, Michigan Court of Appeals, No. 302221, February 23, 2012; CCH MICHIGAN TAX REPORTS, ¶401-643) Property tax exemptions are discussed at ¶2004 in Chapter 20, "Property Taxes".

Practice Note: Refundable Homestead Credit May Be Garnished

A taxpayer's Michigan homestead property tax credit was not exempt from garnishment, because the funds debt collector sought to garnish, although arguably originally deriving from exempt Social Security benefits, did not retain their exempt status. The taxpayer argued that when, as here, a source of funds itself exempt from garnishment was used to pay rent, which rent subsequently resulted in a tax credit, then the tax credit should also be exempt from garnishment. Although Social Security funds deposited in the bank retained their exempt status, once paid to the landlord, the rent money was in the landlord's control and became entirely the landlord's property and was no longer subject to the taxpayer's use. (*Asset Acceptance Corp. v. Hughes*, (2005 CtApp) 268 Mich. App. 57, 706 N.W.2d 446; CCH MICHIGAN TAX REPORTS, ¶401-183).

• *"Total household resources"*

Applicable January 1, 2012, "total household resources" is defined as all income received by all persons of a household in a tax year while members of a household. To calculate this figure, taxpayers must include (add back) any net business loss, any net rental or royalty loss, and any deduction from federal adjusted gross income for a net operating loss carryback or carryforward. (Sec. 206.508(4), M.C.L.)

Effective for tax years beginning after 2011, a revenue administrative bulletin defines "total household resources" and provides examples of taxable and nontaxable income included in "total household resources" as well as examples of items not included. (*Revenue Administrative Bulletin 2015-18*, CCH MICHIGAN TAX REPORTS, ¶402-007)

• *Forms*

The credit is claimed on Form MI-1040, line 26. Also, the taxpayer must complete and attached Form MI-1040CR. Veterans and blind taxpayers complete MI-1040CR-2.

Michigan personal income taxpayers who file electronically and report property taxes on their homes may include an attachment for the property tax statement. The attachment is optional. The attachment may be included when completing (1) line 10 on Form MI-1040CR, Homestead Property Tax Credit Claim; (2) line 10 on Form MI-1040CR-2, Homestead Property Tax Credit Claim for Veterans and Blind People; or (3) Form MI-1040CR-5, Farmland Preservation Tax Credit Claim. (*Email*, Michigan Department of Treasury, May 15, 2015)

¶304 Credit for Homestead Heating Costs

Law: Sec. 206.527a, M.C.L. (CCH MICHIGAN TAX REPORTS, ¶16-905).

Form: MI-1040CR-7, Home Heating Credit.

A credit for homestead heating costs is available to assist low-income people who own or rent their homes.

Practice Note: Renters/Shared Housing

People who share a home or apartment and who are not on the lease or rental contract are ineligible to claim the credit. A renter who is share a home/apartment may divide the credit based on his or her household income and his or her share of the standard allowance. For example, if 3 people are sharing an apartment, and all of them are on the lease. The standard allowance for 3 in 2014 is $763. Each person must use a standard allowance of $251 to compute his or her credit (Instructions to MI-1040CR-7).

The claimant's homestead must be in Michigan and the claimant's income must be below an income ceiling that is indexed for inflation; the ceilings are shown each year on the claim form, Form MI-1040CR-7. Part-year residents prorate the credit on the basis of the number of days they owned or rented and occupied a Michigan homestead.

The credit is not claimed as a credit against personal income tax but is claimed as a separate refundable credit (usually paid as an energy draft made out to the heating provider) on Form MI-1040CR-7. Form MI-1040CR-7 must be filed by September 30th immediately following the tax year for which the credit is claimed. The filing of an extension for income taxes does not extend the due date for the homestead heating credit.

Full-time students who are claimed as dependents on another person's income tax return are not eligible for the credit. Similarly, residents of "licensed care facilities" who live in the facility for the entire year are not eligible for the credit. "Licensed care facilities" include adult foster care homes, nursing homes, and substance abuse treatment centers. However, if a person lives in a licensed care facility for only part of the year, the person may qualify for a partial credit for the period that the person lived outside the facility. The credit is available to persons when one spouse lives in a licensed care facility and the other spouse lives at home.

Generally, certain recipients of public assistance, including recipients of Family Independent Assistance, are also eligible for the credit. However, for anyone who receives assistance from the Michigan Family Independence Agency and whose heat is directly vended, the Department of Treasury will send the credit directly to the heat provider.

The credit is allowed only if there is a federal appropriation of federal Low-Income Home Energy Assistance Program block grant funds of any amount for the federal fiscal year that began in that tax year. If the amount available for the credit is less than the full home heating credit amount, each individual credit is reduced by multiplying the credit by a fraction, the numerator of which is the amount available for the credit and the denominator of which is the full home heating credit amount.

• *Computation*

A claimant is entitled to receive the greater amount of credit figured as follows:

— Subtract 3.5% of the claimant's household income from the standard allowance that corresponds with the applicable number of exemptions allowed a claimant. Standard allowances are shown on the claim form, Form MI-1040CR-7. Claimant's whose heating costs are included in the rent, may only claim 50% of this amount. Applicable January 1, 2012, household income is replaced with total household resources.

— Alternatively, if a claimant's household income does not exceed a specified maximum, as adjusted, subtract 11% of the claimant's household income from the total cost of heating during the 12 consecutive months ending October 31 of the tax year or $2,642 (for 2013), whichever is less, and multiply the result by 70%. "Household income" is defined at ¶ 303.

A credit claimed on a return for less than 12 months must be calculated using the first method and prorated accordingly.

The standard allowance (and income ceiling) amounts for 2014 for the standard home heating credit are $4503 ($12,842) for zero or one exemption; $607 ($17,329) for two exemptions; $763 ($21,786) for three exemptions; $919 ($26,243) for four exemptions; $1,076 ($30,728) for five exemptions; and $1,232 ($35,186) for six exemptions. For each exemption over six, add $156 to the standard allowance and $4,457 to the income ceiling.

The maximum income for the alternate home heating credit is $13,727 for 2014 for zero or one exemption. For two exemptions, the maximum income for the alternative home heating credit is $18,472, and for three exemptions, the maximum income amount is $23,222, and for four or more exemptions the maximum income amount is $24,018.

Practice Note: Exemptions for Children

For purposes of the credit an exemption may only be claimed for a child for children living with the taxpayer. Thus, if the taxpayer does not have custody of the child, he or she may not claim an exemption for purposes of the credit even though the taxpayer may claim an exemption for the child on the taxpayer's MI-1040 (Michigan Individual Income Tax Return) (Instructions to MI-1040CR-7).

• *Proration of credit*

The home heating fuel credit is allowed only if there is a federal appropriation for the affected fiscal year of federal low income home energy assistance block grant funds of any amount. If the amount available for the credit is less than the full home heating credit amount, each individual credit is reduced by multiplying the credit by a fraction, the numerator of which is the full amount available for the credit and the denominator of which is the full home heating credit amount.

¶305 Farmland Preservation Credit

Law: Sec. 324.36109, M.C.L. (CCH MICHIGAN TAX REPORTS, ¶16-900).

Form: MI-1040, Individual Income Tax Return; MI-1040CR-5, Farmland Preservation Tax Credit.

An owner of farmland and related buildings covered by an agricultural conservation easement or a development rights agreement under the Farmland and Open Space Preservation Act, who is eligible or required to file an individual income tax return, is eligible for an income tax credit for property taxes paid on the farmland. The credit is equal to the amount by which the property taxes on land and structures used in the farming operation (including the homestead) and restricted by the development agreement or agricultural conservation easement exceed 3.5% of household income, excluding any deduction taken under IRC Sec. 613 (percentage depletion deduction). "Household income" is defined at ¶303.

A partner in a partnership, an S corporation shareholder, or a limited liability company member will be considered to have paid a proportion of the property taxes on such property equal to the partner's share of ownership of capital or distributive share of ordinary income, the shareholder's percentage of stock ownership for the tax year, or the member's ownership interest or distributive share of ordinary income. A beneficiary of an estate or trust is entitled to the same percentage of the credit as that person's percentage of all other distributions of the estate or trust.

Both the farmland credit and the homestead property tax credit may be claimed; however, the total credits allowable cannot exceed the total property tax due. A refund will be allowed if the farmland credit exceeds the income tax due or if there is no income tax due.

The credit must be repaid if a development rights agreement is relinquished unless the farmland becomes subject to an agricultural conservation easement or purchase of development rights.

Persons not subject to income tax are allowed a credit against the Michigan business tax (¶1114).

• *Forms*

Individuals, partners, joint owners, most S corporation shareholders, and specified trusts claim the credit on MI-1040CR-5. All federal forms and schedules demonstrating the taxpayer's farm income must be attached, see the Instructions to MI-1040CR-5 for details.

Michigan personal income taxpayers who file electronically and report property taxes on their homes may include an attachment for the property tax statement. The attachment is optional. The attachment may be included when completing (1) line 10 on Form MI-1040CR, Homestead Property Tax Credit Claim; (2) line 10 on Form MI-1040CR-2, Homestead Property Tax Credit Claim for Veterans and Blind People; or (3) Form MI-1040CR-5, Farmland Preservation Tax Credit Claim. (*Email*, Michigan Department of Treasury, May 15, 2015)

¶306 Credit for Certain Charitable Contributions

Law: Secs. 206.260, 206.261, M.C.L. (CCH MICHIGAN TAX REPORTS, ¶16-950—¶16-952).

Comparable Federal: Sec. 170 (CCH U.S. MASTER TAX GUIDE ¶1058—1071).

Form: MI-1040, Individual Income Tax Form.

A limited credit is allowed equal to 50% of the aggregate charitable contributions made by the taxpayer during the year to any of the following:

— Michigan or a Michigan municipality, of certain artwork created by the taxpayer for display in a public place;

— the State Art in Public Places Fund;

— either a municipality or a nonprofit corporation affiliated with both a municipality and an art institute located in the municipality, of money or artwork, whether or not created by the taxpayer, if for the purpose of benefitting an art institute located in that municipality;

— a public library;

— a public broadcast station that is not affiliated with an institution of higher learning and that is located in Michigan;

— an institution of higher learning located in Michigan;

— the Michigan Colleges Foundation;

— the Michigan Museum;

— the Department of State for the Preservation of the State Archives; or

— a nonprofit corporation, fund, foundation, trust, or association organized and operated exclusively for the benefit of institutions of higher learning within Michigan.

Direct donations to public broadcasting stations and institutions of higher learning that meet the statutory qualifications are eligible for the credit regardless of religious affiliation or orientation; donations paid to a church and designated to the church-owned station or institution will not qualify for the credit (*Letter to CCH*, Department of Treasury, July 26, 1991; CCH MICHIGAN TAX REPORTS, ¶15-650.20).

The credit allowed a taxpayer other than a resident estate or trust may not exceed $100 ($200 on a joint return). The credit allowed a resident estate or trust may not exceed the lesser of (a) 10% of the tax liability for the year, determined without regard to this credit, or (b) $5,000. The sum of this credit and that for city income taxes (¶ 302) may not exceed the taxpayer's tax liability.

An identical credit is provided for contributions to endowment funds of community foundations, as defined in the law. The credit is also available for cash contributions to shelters for the homeless, food kitchens, food banks, or other entities whose primary purpose is to provide overnight accommodation, food, or meals to indigent persons, if such contribution is tax deductible as a charitable contribution under the Internal Revenue Code. Beginning with the 2008 taxable year, the credit may also be claimed for food items donated to homeless shelters, food kitchens, and food banks if the food items are contributed in conjunction with a program in which a vendor makes a matching contribution of similar items. The credit is equal to the value of the food items contributed up to the $100 ($200 for joint returns) limitation discussed above. Lists of certified community foundations are provided in *Revenue Administrative Bulletin 2011-5*, Michigan Department of Treasury, CCH MICHIGAN TAX REPORTS, ¶ 401-623. Guidelines regarding the credit for contributions to homeless shelters, food kitchens or food banks, and similar entities have been established by the Department of Treasury (*Revenue Administrative Bulletin 1992-10;* CCH MICHIGAN TAX REPORTS, ¶ 319-223).

CCH Caution: Credit Repealed

Effective January 1, 2012, these credits are repealed.

• *Forms*

All three credits may be claimed on MI-1040, Michigan Individual Income Tax Return.

¶ 307 Shareholders of S Corporations

Law: Secs. 206.257, 206.260, 206.263, 206.520, 324.36109, M.C.L. (CCH MICHIGAN TAX REPORTS, ¶ 16-825, 16-900).

The applicability of various credits to shareholders of S corporations is as follows:

— *Income taxes paid to other states:* Resident shareholders are eligible for credit when an out-of-state S corporation income is taxed by the other state (*Chocola v. Department of Treasury* (1985, SCt) 369 NW2d 843; CCH MICHIGAN TAX REPORTS, ¶ 15-145.25).

— *Farmland credit:* The provision granting a credit against income tax for certain property taxes on farmland covered by a development rights agreement (¶ 305) allows a shareholder of an S corporation to take the same percentage of the farmland credit allowed the corporation as the shareholder's percentage of all other distributions of the corporation.

¶ 308 Withheld Taxes

Law: Sec. 206.251, M.C.L. (CCH MICHIGAN TAX REPORTS, ¶ 16-805).

Tax withheld by an employer from wages is allowed as a credit against tax due. The amount withheld during any calendar year is allowed as a credit for the taxable year beginning in the calendar year. If more than one taxable year begins in a calendar year, the withheld tax will be allowed as a credit for the last taxable year.

¶309 Estimated Taxes

Law: Sec. 206.301, M.C.L. (CCH MICHIGAN TAX REPORTS, ¶16-805).

Comparable Federal: Sec. 6315 (CCH U.S. MASTER TAX GUIDE ¶2679—2691).

Amounts of estimated tax paid are allowed as credits against Michigan income tax due. See Chapter 5 for provisions relating to declarations and payments of estimated tax.

¶310 Resident Beneficiary of Trust—Accumulation Distribution Credit

Law: Sec. 206.51, M.C.L. (CCH MICHIGAN TAX REPORTS, ¶15-230).

Comparable Federal: Sec. 665—667 (CCH U.S. MASTER TAX GUIDE ¶567).

A resident beneficiary of a trust whose taxable income includes all or part of an accumulation distribution by a trust is allowed a credit against the tax otherwise due. The credit allowed is all or a proportionate part of any Michigan income tax paid by the trust for any preceding taxable year that would not have been payable if the trust had made distribution to its beneficiaries during the preceding five years, as provided in the Internal Revenue Code. The credit may not reduce the tax otherwise due from the beneficiary to an amount less than would have been due if the accumulation distribution were excluded from taxable income.

¶312 Claim-of-Right Credit

Law: Sec. 206.265, M.C.L. (CCH MICHIGAN TAX REPORTS, ¶16-955).

Comparable Federal: Sec. 1341 (CCH U.S. MASTER TAX GUIDE ¶1543).

Forms: MI-1040, Individual Income Tax Return.

A taxpayer may claim a refundable credit equal to the tax paid in any prior tax year that is attributable to income received in the prior tax year and repaid during the tax year if the taxpayer is eligible for a deduction or credit against his or her federal tax liability under IRC Sec. 1341, the claim-of-right statute, based on the repayment. However, the credit is allowed only if the repayment is not deducted when calculating the taxpayer's adjusted gross income for the tax year. The calculation of the credit is discussed in *Revenue Administrative Bulletin 1994-09;* CCH MICHIGAN TAX REPORTS, ¶319-250.

• *Reporting the credit*

The credit is added to Michigan income tax withheld and reported on the Michigan Income Tax Withheld line of the MI-1040. A statement that the amount of withholding includes a credit for repayments made under the claim of right must be included on the withholding line. Verification of the amount repaid, a copy of the federal return and schedules, and a schedule showing the calculation of the credit must be attached to the Michigan income tax return. Amended Michigan income tax returns can be submitted for amounts repaid during the 1991 and subsequent tax years. (*Revenue Administrative Bulletin 1994-09;* CCH MICHIGAN TAX REPORTS, ¶319-250)

¶314 Credit for Higher Education Costs

Law: Sec. 206.274, M.C.L. (CCH MICHIGAN TAX REPORTS, ¶16-915).

Forms: Schedule CT, Michigan College Tuition and Fees Credit.

A Michigan taxpayer with an adjusted gross income of $200,000 or less may claim a personal income tax credit for 8% of all uniformally-required fees and tuition paid to a qualified institution of higher learning, not to exceed $375 per undergraduate student for each tax year. The credit may not be claimed for more than four years for any one student. The Department of Treasury may require reasonable proof of payment and the credit must be claimed on a separate income tax form (Schedule CT).

CCH Caution: Credit Repealed

Effective January 1, 2012, this credit is repealed.

The student must attend a public Michigan institution of higher education that certifies that tuition will not increase in the ensuing academic year by more than the preceding year's rate of inflation. A list of qualified institutions is provided in the Instructions to Schedule CT.

Practice Note: Credit for Higher Education Costs

A taxpayer may not take a credit for tuition paid to a college or university unless the institution is located in Michigan.

Although costs covered by student loans are eligible for the credit, costs paid by Michigan Education Trust Act (MET) contracts (see ¶204), scholarships, and grants are ineligible. In addition, amounts paid into a MET contract are not eligible for the credit. (Instructions, Schedule CT, Michigan College Tuition and Fees Credit.)

"Fees" mean fees required of and uniformly paid by all students and that have been promulgated and published in the catalog of the qualified institution of higher learning and "tuition" means in-state tuition less any applicable refunds received by the credit claimant or the student.

¶315 Credit for Rehabilitation of Historic Resources

Law: Sec. 206.266, M.C.L. (CCH MICHIGAN TAX REPORTS, ¶16-895).

Form: MI-3581, Michigan Historic Preservation Tax Credit.

A qualified taxpayer with a certified rehabilitation plan which is certified before 2012 may claim a credit against the personal income tax based on the qualified expenditures for the rehabilitation of a historic resource. An income tax credit may be claimed for 25% of a qualified taxpayer's qualified expenditures to rehabilitate a historic resource. Rehabilitation must be done in accordance with a rehabilitation plan certified by the Michigan Historical Center after 1998. The credit is claimed on Form MI-3581.

The credit may be claimed for the rehabilitation of an historic resource in the year the certification of completed rehabilitation is issued, provided that the certificate is issued within five years after certification of the rehabilitation plan by the Michigan Historical Center.

Definitions and qualifications: "Qualified expenditures" are capital expenditures that:

— qualify either for the federal income tax credit under IRC Sec. 47(a)(2) for qualified rehabilitation expenditures for a certified historic structure or for the Michigan income tax credit for rehabilitating historic resources;

— are paid within five years after the initial certification of the rehabilitation plan that includes those expenditures approved by the Michigan Historical Center; and

— that are paid after 1998 for the rehabilitation of a historic resource.

Qualified expenditures do not include capital expenditures for nonhistoric additions to a resource, except for additions required by state or federal regulations that relate to historic preservation, safety, or accessibility.

To qualify for the state credit, the taxpayer must claim the federal credit if the taxpayer's expenditures are eligible for the federal credit and the state credit must be reduced by the amount of the federal credit received.

A "historic resource" is a publicly or privately owned historic building, structure, site, object, feature, or open space located within an historic district designated by the national register of historic places, by the state register of historic sites, or by a local unit acting under the Michigan Local Historic Districts Act, or that is individually listed on the state or national register of historic sites.

A "qualified taxpayer" is a person who either:

— owns the resource to be rehabilitated or who has a long-term lease agreement (at least 27.5 years for a residential resource or 31.5 years for a nonresidential resource) with the owner and who has made qualified expenditures for the rehabilitation of the resource that are equal to at least 10% of the state equalized valuation of the property; or

— is an assignee of a partnership, LLC, or S corporation that is a qualified taxpayer and has assigned the credit to its partners, members, or shareholders.

The credit assignment is irrevocable and must be made in the year in which the certificate of completed rehabilitation is issued.

Limitations and carryovers: If a taxpayer sells an historic resource, or if the certification of rehabilitation is revoked, less than five years after a tax year in which the credit is claimed, a percentage of the credit amount previously claimed for that resource must be added back to the taxpayer's tax liability for the year of sale or revocation. One hundred percent of the previously claimed credit must be added back if the sale or revocation occurs less than one year after the year in which the credit was claimed. For a sale or revocation in the second, third, fourth, or fifth year after the credit is claimed, the recapture percentage is 80%, 60%, 40%, or 20%, respectively. For tax years beginning after 2008, a taxpayer may elect to forgo the credit and transfer the credit and property ownership to a new owner in order to avoid recapture.

Unused credit may be carried forward for up to 10 subsequent tax years.

Effective January 1, 2009, for projects for which a completed rehabilitation certificate is issued for a post 2008 tax year and for which the credit amount is less than $250,0000, taxpayers may claim a refund in lieu of a credit carryover. The refund is limited to 90% of the amount that exceeds the taxpayer's tax liability.

Aggregation of credits: The total of the Michigan income tax credits for rehabilitating historic structures claimed by a taxpayer must be added to the total Michigan business tax credits for rehabilitating historic structures claimed by the taxpayer under the analogous business tax credit (¶1120), and the sum may not exceed the total qualified expenditures for that project.

¶316 Adoption Expenses Credit

Law: Sec. 206.268, M.C.L. (CCH MICHIGAN TAX REPORTS, ¶16-911).

Comparable Federal: Sec. 23 (CCH U.S. MASTER TAX GUIDE ¶1306).

Forms: MI-1040, Individual Income Tax Return; MI-8839, Michigan Qualified Adoption Expenses.

Taxpayers who claim the federal adoption expense credit under IRC Sec. 23 may claim a refundable credit against Michigan personal income tax for qualified adoption expenses paid during the tax year in excess of the federal credit allowed. The amount of the credit is the lesser of the amount of qualified expenses in excess of the federal credit, or $1,200 per child.

CCH Caution: Credit Repealed

Effective January 1, 2012, this credit is repealed.

To claim the credit, taxpayers must attach a copy of MI-8839, Michigan Qualified Adoption Expenses and form US 8839, Qualified Adoption Expenses, to their MI-1040.

¶317 Automobile Donation Credit

Law: Sec. 206.269, M.C.L. (CCH MICHIGAN TAX REPORTS, ¶16-953).

Comparable Federal: None.

Form: MI-1040, Individual Income Tax Return.

A nonrefundable credit is allowed in an amount equal to 50% of the fair market value of an automobile donated by a taxpayer to a qualified organization that intends to provide the automobile to a qualified recipient. The value of the passenger vehicle is the lesser of the value determined by the qualified organization or the value of the automobile in the appropriate guide published by the National Automotive Dealers Association.

CCH Caution: Credit Repealed

Effective January 1, 2012, this credit is repealed.

A list of the qualified organizations is provided in the MI-1040 Instruction Booklet. Donors must receive a Form 4284, Donor Tax Credit Certificate for Donated Vehicle, from the organization and must make it available to the Department of Treasury upon request.

For a taxpayer other than a resident estate or trust, the amount allowable as an income tax credit for a tax year may not exceed $50 ($100 for joint filers).

¶318 Venture Capital Investment Credit

Law: Secs. 206.270, 208.37e, M.C.L. (CCH MICHIGAN TAX REPORTS, ¶16-830).

For tax years beginning after 2008, investors under the Michigan Early Stage Venture Investment may claim a credit against the personal income tax. The agreement must be entered into before 2012. The credit is also allowed against the MBT and is discussed in detail at ¶1485.

¶319 Credit for Stillbirth

Law: Secs. 206.2725, M.C.L. (CCH MICHIGAN TAX REPORTS, ¶16-910).

Comparable Federal: None.

Form: MI-1040, Individual Income Tax Return.

A stillbirth credit is available against the Michigan personal income tax. The refundable credit is equal to 4.5% of the single personal exemption amount, rounded up to the nearest $10 (currently, $150).

CCH Caution: Credit Repealed

Effective January 1, 2012, this credit is repealed.

A certificate of stillbirth from the Michigan Department of Community Health is required to claim the credit. (Sec. 206.275(1), M.C.L.) Taxpayers that do not have a certificate should contact the Michigan Department of Community Health at 517-335-8666. (Instructions, MI-1040, Individual Income Tax Return)

¶320 Earned Income Tax Credit

Law: Secs. 206.272, M.C.L. (CCH MICHIGAN TAX REPORTS, ¶16-820).

Comparable Federal: Sec. 32 (CCH U.S. MASTER TAX GUIDE ¶1375).

Form: MI-1040, Individual Income Tax Return.

The Michigan percentage of the federal earned income tax credit is 6%. (Sec. 206.272, M.C.L.)

¶321 Development Account Contributions Credit

Law: Secs. 206.276, M.C.L. (CCH MICHIGAN TAX REPORTS, ¶16-912).

Taxpayers who are not account holders may claim a credit equal to 75% of the contributions made in a tax year to a fiduciary organization's reserve fund. The contributions must be made pursuant to the Individual or Family Development Account Program Act. The credit is nonrefundable and is capped annually at a cumulative maximum of $1 million. (Sec. 206.276, M.C.L.)

CCH Caution: Credit Repealed

Effective January 1, 2012, this credit is repealed.

¶322 Energy Efficiency Credits

Law: Secs. 206.253, M.C.L. (CCH MICHIGAN TAX REPORTS, ¶16-885, 16-905a).

Taxpayers may claim energy efficiency credits against the personal income tax for (1) a portion of qualified home improvements and (2) a portion of the charges for an electric utility's compliance with renewable energy standards. (Sec. 206.253, M.C.L.)

CCH Caution: Credit Repealed

Effective January 1, 2012, these credits are repealed.

- *Qualified home improvement credit*

For tax years that begin prior to 2012, taxpayers who purchase and install a qualified home improvement for their principal residence during the tax year may claim a refundable credit equal to 10% of the amount paid. The credit is limited to taxpayers with Adjusted Gross Incomes (AGI) equal to or less than $37,500 (or $75,000, for married taxpayers filing a joint return) and is capped at $75 ($150, for a joint return). (Sec. 206.253, M.C.L.)

Taxpayers are limited to one home improvement credit per tax year and must provide documentation. "Qualified home improvements" are the following items intended for residential or noncommercial use that meet or exceed energy star energy efficiency guidelines: insulation, furnaces, water heaters, windows, refrigerators, clothes washers, and dishwashers.

- *Electric utilities renewable energy compliance credit*

For tax years that begin prior to 2012, taxpayers may claim a nonrefundable credit equal to a percentage of the amount authorized and paid for the customer's electric utility's compliance with renewable energy standards (currently, $3 per month per residential customer meter). The credit is expanded to include customer's municipally owned electric utilities. The nonrefundable credit is limited to taxpayers with AGIs equal to or less than $65,000 (130,000, for married taxpayers filing a joint return).

The credit is 25% for tax years that begin after 2008 and before 2010, and is reduced to 20% for tax years that begin after 2009 and before 2012. (Sec. 206.253(2), M.C.L.)

¶323 Venture Investment Credit

Law: Sec. 206.278, M.C.L. (CCH MICHIGAN TAX REPORTS, ¶16-830a).

The venture investment credit may be claimed against the personal income tax by a taxpayer that makes a qualified investment after 2010 and before 2012 in a qualified business. The amount of the credit is equal to 25% of the investment. Up to $1 million in investments may be made in one business. In addition, a taxpayer may not claim a credit of more than $250,000 for investments in one or more businesses in any one year. Credits for all taxpayers are capped at $9 million per calendar year. The credit must be taken in two equal installments. Credits exceeding the taxpayer's tax liability may be carried forward for five years. (Sec. 206.278, M.C.L.)

A taxpayer must request certification from the Michigan Strategic Fund within 60 days of making an investment. The Michigan Strategic Fund will issue a certificate, which must be attached to the taxpayer's tax return. A taxpayer cannot claim the credit if he or she is in a bankruptcy proceeding or if the taxpayer has not paid or entered into an installment agreement regarding a final assessment. (Sec. 206.278, M.C.L.)

"Qualified business" is defined as a business that (1) is a seed or early-stage business; (2) has its headquarters in Michigan, is domiciled in Michigan, and has a majority of its employees working in Michigan; (3) has a preinvestment valuation of less than $10 million and has fewer than 100 full-time employees; (4) has been in existence less than five years, unless it is an institution of higher education or an organization exempt under IRC § 501(c)(3) (then it must have been in existence less than 10 years); and (5) is not a retail establishment. Also, the business must not have claimed the following credits against the Michigan business tax: MEGA employment, film production expenditures, film infrastructure project, and film job training expenses. A "qualified investment" is at least $20,000, and must meet other requirements. (Sec. 206.278, M.C.L.)

INCOME TAX

CHAPTER 4

ALLOCATION AND APPORTIONMENT

¶401 Overview

The problem of allocation or apportionment of income is chiefly one of determining the amount of income taxable by a particular state. To avoid unconstitutional discrimination against interstate commerce, the states have devised methods for dividing the income of businesses operating in more than one state. The main objective of allocating income is to furnish each state with its fair share of the taxpayer's tax payments.

¶402 Application of Allocation and Apportionment Provisions

Law: Secs. 206.102—206.105, M.C.L. (CCH MICHIGAN TAX REPORTS, ¶16-515).

Comparable Federal: Secs. 861—882.

If a taxpayer's income-producing activities are confined solely to Michigan, the entire taxable income is allocated to Michigan, except as otherwise expressly provided (¶406—¶411). A taxpayer having income from business activity that is taxable both within and without Michigan, other than the rendering of personal services by an individual, allocates and apportions net income under the provisions contained in the following paragraphs. A taxpayer is taxable in another state if:

— the taxpayer is subject to a net income tax, a franchise tax measured by net income, a franchise tax for the privilege of doing business, or a corporate stock tax in the other state; or

— the other state has jurisdiction to subject the taxpayer to a net income tax regardless of whether, in fact, the state does or does not impose the tax.

¶403 Resident Individuals, Estates, and Trusts

Law: Secs. 206.110—206.115, M.C.L. (CCH MICHIGAN TAX REPORTS, ¶15-110, 16-530, 16-550, 16-555).

Through 2011, for purposes of the income tax, business income is apportioned within and without the state by means of a three-factor formula (¶412) and nonbusiness income is directly allocated to Michigan or to another state. All income of a resident individual, estate, or trust that is not apportioned or allocated outside Michigan by one of these provisions is allocated to Michigan.

Nonbusiness income of *residents* is allocated as follows:

— net rents and royalties from *real property* are allocated to the state where the property is located, and rents and royalties from *tangible personal property* are allocated to Michigan (¶408);

— capital gains and losses from *real property* are allocated to the state of situs and capital gains and losses from *tangible* and *intangible personal property* are allocated to Michigan (¶409);

— interest and dividends are allocated to Michigan (¶410); and

— patent and copyright royalties are allocated to Michigan (a) if and to the extent the patent or copyright is utilized by the payer in Michigan, or (b) if and to the extent the patent or copyright is utilized by the payer in a state in which the taxpayer is not taxable and the taxpayer is a resident of Michigan (¶411).

"Resident" is defined at ¶104.

¶404 Nonresident Individuals, Estates, and Trusts

Law: Secs. 206.36, 206.110, M.C.L. (CCH MICHIGAN TAX REPORTS, ¶15-115, 16-515, 16-530, 16-550, 16-555, 16-570).

For purposes of the income tax, taxable income of nonresident individuals, estates, or trusts is allocated to Michigan to the extent that it is:

— attributable to personal services rendered in Michigan;

— derived from business activity carried on in Michigan, except as allocated to another state under the provisions relating to rents and royalties (¶408), gains and losses (¶409), interest and dividends (¶410), and income from patents and copyrights (¶411);

— earned as a prize won by the taxpayer under the McCauley-Traxler-Law-Bowman-McNeely lottery act (M.C.L. 432.1-432.27); or

— earned as winnings from a wagering transaction with a casino or as a payoff price on a winning ticket resulting from parimutuel wagering at a licensed race meeting if the casino or race meeting is located in Michigan.

The respective shares of a nonresident estate or trust and its beneficiaries (including, for allocation purposes only, resident and nonresident beneficiaries) in the income attributable to Michigan, are in proportion to their respective shares of distributable net income under the Internal Revenue Code. If the estate or trust has no distributable net income for the taxable year, the share of each beneficiary in the income attributable to Michigan is in proportion to his or her share of the estate or trust income for the year that, under local law or the terms of the trust instrument, is required to be currently distributed and the amounts of the income actually distributed in the year. Any balance of income attributable to Michigan is allocated to the estate or trust.

Michigan lottery prizes won by nonresident individuals, estates, or trusts are allocated to Michigan.

¶405 "Business" and "Nonbusiness" Income Defined

Law: Sec. 206.4, 206.14, M.C.L. (CCH MICHIGAN TAX REPORTS, ¶16-515).

For purposes of the income tax, under the Michigan allocation and apportionment provisions, business income is apportioned and nonbusiness income is directly allocated. "Business income" means all income arising from transactions, activities and sources in the regular course of the taxpayer's trade or business and includes the following:

— all income from tangible and intangible property if the acquisition, rental, management and disposition of the property constitutes integral parts of the taxpayer's regular trade or business operations;

— gains or losses from stock and securities of any foreign or domestic corporation and dividend and interest income;

— income derived from isolated sales, leases, assignment, licenses, divisions, or other infrequently occurring dispositions, transfers, or transactions if the subject property had been used in the taxpayer's trade or business; and:

— income derived from the sale of a business.

"Nonbusiness income" means all income other than business income.

Income from the sale of a limited partnership interest was business income, but was not attributable to Michigan and was not subject to the personal income tax. The taxpayers owned an interest in a partnership, which, in turn, owned a limited partnership interest in an entity that owned and operated properties throughout the United States (but not Michigan) during the relevant time period. The limited partnership interest was liquidated in 2004. On audit, the Department of Treasury asserted that the income received from the sale of the partnership interest was capital gain on the sale of an investment and not business income. The statute provided that business income includes income from the sale of a business or business property. In an earlier decision, the Michigan taxpayers were not permitted to claim a loss from a limited partnership on the Michigan return when the loss arose from an out-of-state apartment building. Thus, the court concluded that the income at issue was business income. However, the income was not attributable to Michigan under the circumstances. (*Aikens v. Department of Treasury*, Michigan Court of Appeals, No. 310528, January 28, 2014, CCH MICHIGAN TAX REPORTS, ¶401-857)

¶406 Nonbusiness Income Directly Allocated

Law: Sec. 206.110, M.C.L. (CCH MICHIGAN TAX REPORTS, ¶16-505, 16-515).

For purposes of the income tax, rents and royalties from real or tangible personal property, capital gains, interest, dividends, and patent or copyright royalties, to the extent that they constitute nonbusiness income, are allocated within or without Michigan on the basis of situs or utilization of the property or residence or commercial domicile of the taxpayer. "Nonbusiness income" is defined at ¶405, "commercial domicile" at ¶407, and "resident" at ¶104.

¶407 "Commercial Domicile" Defined

Law: Sec. 206.6, M.C.L. (CCH MICHIGAN TAX REPORTS, ¶16-515).

"Commercial domicile" means the principal place from which the trade or business of the taxpayer is directed or managed. The phrase "directed or managed" is intended as two words serving the same end, not as two separate concepts.

¶408 Rents and Royalties

Law: Sec. 206.111, M.C.L. (CCH MICHIGAN TAX REPORTS, ¶16-530, 16-550).

For purposes of the income tax, net rents and royalties that constitute nonbusiness income from *real property* are allocated according to the situs of the property. If the real property is located in Michigan, the rents or royalties are allocated to Michigan; if the property is located outside Michigan, the rents or royalties are allocated outside Michigan.

Net rents and royalties from *tangible personal property* are allocated entirely to Michigan if the taxpayer is a resident individual, estate, trust, or partnership or has a commercial domicile in Michigan and is not organized under the laws of, or taxable in, the state in which the property is utilized. Otherwise, rents and royalties from tangible personal property are allocated to Michigan if and to the extent the property is utilized in Michigan.

Rents from mobile tangible personal property are allocated to Michigan according to a fraction based on the number of days in Michigan on the assumption that rents are generally based on time of use. If the physical location of the property during the rental period is unknown, the property is considered utilized in the state in which the property was located at the time the rental or royalty payer obtained possession.

"Commercial domicile" is defined at ¶407.

¶409 Gains and Losses

Law: Sec. 206.112, M.C.L. (CCH MICHIGAN TAX REPORTS, ¶16-555).

For purposes of the income tax, capital gains and losses from sales or exchanges of *real property* that constitute nonbusiness income are allocated according to the location of the real property. Capital gains and losses from sales of real property located in Michigan are allocated to Michigan; gains or losses from sales of property located outside Michigan are allocated outside Michigan.

Capital gains and losses from sales or exchanges of *tangible personal property* are allocated to Michigan if (1) the property has a situs in Michigan at the time of sale, or (2) the taxpayer is a resident individual, estate, trust, or partnership or has a commercial domicile in Michigan and the taxpayer is not taxable in the state in which the property has a situs.

Capital gains and losses from sales of *intangible personal property* are allocated to Michigan if the taxpayer is a resident individual, estate, trust, or partnership or has a commercial domicile in Michigan.

"Commercial domicile" is defined at ¶407.

¶410 Interest and Dividends

Law: Sec. 206.113, M.C.L. (CCH MICHIGAN TAX REPORTS, ¶16-515, 16-530).

Nonbusiness income from interest and dividends is allocated to Michigan if the taxpayer is a resident individual, estate, trust, or partnership or has a commercial domicile in Michigan. If the taxpayer is a nonresident or has a commercial domicile outside of Michigan, the nonbusiness income from interest and dividends is allocated outside of Michigan.

¶411 Income from Patents and Copyrights

Law: Sec. 206.114, M.C.L. (CCH MICHIGAN TAX REPORTS, ¶16-530).

Patent and copyright royalties that constitute nonbusiness income are allocated to Michigan if and to the extent the patent or copyright is utilized by the payer (1) in Michigan or (2) in a state in which the taxpayer is not taxable and the taxpayer is a resident individual, estate, trust, or partnership or has a commercial domicile in Michigan.

A *patent* is utilized in a state to the extent it is employed in production, fabrication, manufacturing, or other processing in the state or to the extent that a patent product is produced in the state. A *copyright* is utilized in a state to the extent that printing or other publication originates in the state. If the basis of receipts from patent or copyright royalties does not permit allocation to states or if the accounting procedures do not reflect states of utilization, the patent or copyright is utilized in Michigan if the taxpayer is a resident individual, estate, trust, or partnership or has a commercial domicile in Michigan.

¶412 Apportionment of Business Income—Three-Factor Formula

Law: Secs. 206.4, 206.115, M.C.L. (CCH MICHIGAN TAX REPORTS, ¶16-515).

Before January 1, 2012, all business income (see ¶405), other than income from transportation services, was apportioned within or without Michigan by means of a three-factor—property, payroll, and sales—formula. The business income was apportioned by multiplying it by a fraction, the numerator of which was the property factor plus the payroll factor plus the sales factor and the denominator of which was three. After December 31, 2011, all business income, other than income from transportation services, is apportioned by means of only the sales factor.

Example: This formula may be illustrated as follows:

$$\text{Business income} \times \frac{\text{Property factor + payroll factor + sales factor}}{3} = \text{Michigan apportioned income}$$

The following practical illustration will show how the apportionment factor is calculated:

Michigan property	$ 10,000		
Total property	$ 300,000	Property factor is	.0333
Michigan payroll	$ 50,000		
Total payroll	$ 600,000	Payroll factor is	.0833
Michigan sales	$ 625,000		
Total sales	$5,900,000	Sales factor is	.1059
		Total factors	.2225
Number of factors	3	Percentage of income attributable to Michigan is	.0742

CCH Comment: Combined Reporting Permitted for Unitary Flow-Through Businesses, Even If Foreign

The Michigan Supreme Court has ruled that (1) the personal income tax law does not prohibit individual taxpayers from combining profits and losses from unitary flow-through businesses and then apportioning that income on the basis of the business's combined apportionment factors and (2) for the years at issue, combined reporting could include foreign entities to the extent that the foreign entity and the individual taxpayers in the state were a unitary business. In the consolidated cases, the Department of Treasury required the income of each entity to be apportioned separately.

By law, Michigan has formulary apportionment, which can be calculated on a separate entity basis or with combined reporting. The court examined the applicable statutory sections to determine that the law does not prohibit individual taxpayers from using combined reporting. The department argued that combined reporting was prohibited because it was not expressly authorized. However, the court noted that neither method was expressly authorized. Furthermore, the department has not promulgated a rule to require separate entity reporting for individual taxpayers. Thus, in the absence of a policy choice by the Legislature, the statute permitted either method. Combined reporting was allowed because it satisfied the statutory requirement that "all business income be apportioned to the state".

With respect to foreign entities, the court again turned to the statutory language to decide that apportionment was not limited to the domestic entities of a unitary business. To determine if a business is unitary, the totality of the circumstances, especially the economic realities, functional integration, centralized management, economies of scale, and substantial mutual interdependence, should be considered. Michigan law in effect for the tax years at issue did not contain any limiting language to indicate that combined reporting was appropriate for domestic entities only.

As such, the court reversed the appellate decision in *Malpass,* which held that taxpayers were not permitted to combine business income from separate entities for personal income tax purposes. The court affirmed the appellate decision in *Wheeler,* which held that an S corporation and a lower-tier general partnership were unitary, so that the shareholders/taxpayers properly apportioned their income to Michigan under the personal income tax laws; however, the court vacated the portion of the opinion that relied on *Malpass.* (*Malpass et al. v. Department of Treasury,* Michigan Supreme Court, Nos. 144430, 144431, 144432, 145367, 145368, 145369, 145370, June 24, 2013, CCH MICHIGAN TAX REPORTS, ¶401-800)

CCH Comment: Combination Not Allowed If Entities Are Not Unitary

The Michigan Court of Appeals held that the taxpayers were not permitted to combine business income from separate entities for personal income tax purposes because the entities were not unitary. As an individual, the husband-taxpayer was the sole shareholder in several S corporations, some of which had multistate operations. On remand from the Michigan Supreme Court, the appellate court affirmed the Tax Tribunal, which had determined that the taxpayers should calculate and apply separate apportionment percentages to each S corporation. The state supreme court had vacated the earlier appellate court decision. The taxpayers argued that apportionment may be calculated by adding the property, payroll, and sales of multiple S corporations to establish a single property factor, a single payroll factor, and a single sales factor. The court acknowledged that this apportionment method was valid, but only if the multistate businesses were unitary. In *Malpass et al. v. Department of Treasury,* the Michigan Supreme Court answered the question of whether the income tax act prohibited individual taxpayers from using combined reporting; however, the court did not eliminate the requirement that the businesses be unitary in order to apportion income. In this case, because there were no facts supporting a conclusion that the entities were unitary, combined reporting was not allowed. (*Winget v. Department of Treasury,* Michigan Court of Appeals, No. 302190, unpublished December 5, 2013, MICHIGAN TAX REPORTS, ¶401-843, approved for publication March 11, 2014, MICHIGAN TAX REPORTS, ¶401-875, Michigan Supreme Court, No. 148879, application for leave to appeal denied, order issued June 24, 2014)

Practitioner Comment: Reporting Options for Business Income of Flow-Through Entities: Individual Taxpayers May Combine Income and Apportionment Factors from Unitary Flow-Through Businesses

Application of the unitary business principle to the Michigan Income Tax was clarified by the Michigan Supreme Court in *Estate of Wheeler et al. v. Department of Treasury* and *Malpass v. Dep't of Treasury,* 494 Mich. 237; 833 N.W.2d 272 (2013). In its holding, the Court found that the apportionment language of the Michigan Income Tax Act is broad enough to allow an individual income tax taxpayer (i.e., an individual) to use either the separate-entity or combined reporting methods of formulary apportionment for business income derived from flow-through entities. Because neither reporting method is specifically required under either the statute or promulgated rules, individuals with interests in unitary flow through entities that apportion business income to Michigan presumably have the option of reporting on a separate or combined basis. In contrast, corporate owners of flow-through entities that for apportionment purposes are unitary with the corporate taxpayer are required to apportion income from the flow-through entity based on a combination of corporation and flow-through entity factors. (Sec.

661(2), M.C.L.; Sec. 663(1), M.C.L.). Amended returns should be considered for individual taxpayers with business income from unitary flow-through entities. Pending any anticipated statutory changes or promulgated rules, planning opportunities should also be considered for individual taxpayers with business income from unitary flow-through entities.

Wayne D. Roberts, Varnum, LLP and Marjorie B. Gell, Western Michigan University Cooley Law School.

The means of arriving at the various factors are discussed in ¶413—¶415.

¶413 Apportionment of Business Income—Property Factor

Law: Secs. 206.116—206.118, M.C.L. (CCH MICHIGAN TAX REPORTS, ¶16-515).

CCH Caution: Apportionment Provision Repealed

These provisions are repealed, effective January 1, 2012.

The property factor was a fraction, the numerator of which is the average value of the taxpayer's real and tangible personal property owned or rented and used in Michigan during the taxable year and the denominator of which was the average value of all the taxpayer's real and tangible personal property owned or rented and used during the taxable year. The property to be included in the numerator and denominator was property producing the net income to be apportioned. Net income from rents and royalties, capital gains and losses, interest and dividends, and patent and copyright royalties that was directly allocated (¶408— ¶411) should be excluded in computing the property factor.

Property owned by the taxpayer was valued at its original cost rather than depreciated cost. The use of original cost obviates any differences due to varying methods of depreciation and had the advantage that the basic figure was readily ascertainable from the taxpayer's books.

Property rented by the taxpayer was valued at eight times the net annual rental rate. The net annual rental rate was the annual rental paid less any subrentals received by the taxpayer.

The average value of the property was determined by averaging the values at the beginning and end of the tax year. However, the Michigan Department of Treasury may require the averaging of monthly values during the tax year if necessary to reflect average values.

¶414 Apportionment of Business Income—Payroll Factor

Law: Secs. 206.6, 206.119, 206.120, M.C.L. (CCH MICHIGAN TAX REPORTS, ¶16-515).

CCH Caution: Apportionment Provision Repealed

These provisions are repealed, effective January 1, 2012.

The payroll factor was a fraction, the numerator of which was the total amount of compensation paid in Michigan during the taxable year and the denominator of which was the total compensation paid everywhere during the taxable year. Payroll attributable to management or maintenance or otherwise allocable to nonbusiness property should be excluded from the factor. Payroll paid was determined by the normal accounting methods of the business so that if the taxpayer accrued such items the payroll should be treated as "paid" for this factor.

"Compensation" meant any form of remuneration as defined by federal laws defining wages for withholding purposes.

Compensation was paid in Michigan if:

— the individual's service was performed entirely in Michigan;

— the individual's service was performed both within and outside Michigan, but the service performed outside Michigan was incidental to the service within Michigan; or

— some part of the service was performed in Michigan and (a) the base of operations, or if there was no base of operations, the place from which the service was directed or controlled was in Michigan, or (b) the base of operations or the place from which the service was directed or controlled was not in any state in which some part of the service was performed, but the individual's residence was in Michigan.

¶415 Apportionment of Business Income—Sales Factor

Law: Secs. 206.20, 206.121—206.123, M.C.L. (CCH MICHIGAN TAX REPORTS, ¶16-515).

The sales factor is a fraction, the numerator of which is the total sales of the taxpayer in Michigan during the taxable year, and the denominator of which is the total sales of the taxpayer everywhere during the taxable year. The "sales" to be included in the fraction are only sales that produce business income. Sales that produce "capital gains" are to be allocated rather than apportioned (¶409). "Total sales" means "total net sales" after discounts and returns.

CCH Practice Tip: Business Income Apportionment

Effective January 1, 2012, all business income is apportioned only by the sales factor.

Destination test: A determination of which sales are attributed to Michigan for the purpose of computing the numerator of the sales factor is made on the basis of the destination of the personal property sold. Sales of such property are in Michigan if:

— the property is delivered or shipped to a purchaser, other than the U.S. Government, within Michigan, regardless of the f.o.b. point or other condition of the sale; or

— the property is shipped from an office, warehouse, factory, or other place of storage in Michigan and the purchaser is the U.S. government, or the taxpayer is not taxable in the state of the purchaser.

Personal services: Payments for personal services are considered to be in Michigan if:

— the income-producing activity is performed in Michigan; or

— the income-producing activity is performed both within and outside Michigan and a greater proportion of the income-producing activity is performed in Michigan than in any other state, based on costs of performance.

"Sales" means all gross receipts of the taxpayer not allocated under ¶408—¶411.

¶416 Apportionment of Income from Transportation Services

Law: Secs. 206.131—206.134, M.C.L. (CCH MICHIGAN TAX REPORTS, ¶16-515).

Special methods are provided for the apportionment of taxable income derived from transportation services rendered partly within and partly without Michigan, as discussed below.

• *Transportation of oil by pipeline*

Taxable income derived from the transportation of oil by pipeline is apportioned to Michigan according to the ratio of barrel miles transported in Michigan to barrel miles transported everywhere.

• *Transportation of gas by pipeline*

Taxable income derived from the transportation of gas by pipeline is apportioned to Michigan according to the ratio of thousand-cubic-foot miles transported in Michigan to thousand-cubic-foot miles transported everywhere.

• *Other transportation services*

Taxable income derived from transportation services other than the transportation of oil or gas by pipeline is apportioned to Michigan according to the ratio of revenue miles in Michigan to revenue miles everywhere. A "revenue mile" is the transportation, for consideration, of one net ton in weight or one passenger the distance of one mile. If a taxpayer is engaged in the transportation of both passengers and freight, taxable income attributable to Michigan is that portion of net income that is equal to the average of passenger miles and ton mile fractions, separately computed and individually weighted by the ratio of gross receipts from passenger transportation to total gross receipts from all transportation and by the ratio of gross receipts from freight transportation to total gross receipts from all transportation, respectively.

If the information necessary for the above computations is unavailable or cannot be obtained without unreasonable expense to the taxpayer, the Michigan Department of Treasury may use other available data which, in its opinion, will result in an equitable apportionment.

¶417 Alternate Allocation and Apportionment Methods

Law: Sec. 206.195, M.C.L. (CCH MICHIGAN TAX REPORTS, ¶16-515).

If allocation and apportionment methods do not fairly represent the extent of the taxpayer's business activity in Michigan, the taxpayer may request or the Michigan Department of Treasury may require the following:

— separate accounting;

— the exclusion of any factor in the apportionment formula or the inclusion of additional factors; or

— the use of any other method to effectuate an equitable allocation and apportionment of the taxpayer's income.

INCOME TAX

CHAPTER 5

RETURNS AND PAYMENT

¶501 Annual Returns and Payments Required

Law: Secs. 206.51a, 206.311, 206.315, M.C.L. (CCH MICHIGAN TAX REPORTS, ¶89-102).

Comparable Federal: Secs. 6001—6012 (CCH U.S. MASTER TAX GUIDE ¶2501, *et seq.*).

Annual returns, due on or before April 15 for calendar-year taxpayers and on or before the 15th day of the fourth month following the close of the taxable year for fiscal-year taxpayers, are required of every individual, estate, or trust required to make a return for any taxable period under the federal income tax law. However, an individual does not have to file a Michigan return if his or her Michigan personal exemptions exceed his or her federal adjusted gross income, unless a refund of Michigan withheld taxes is sought.

In the case of an individual who could be claimed as a dependent by another taxpayer on the federal return, a return is not required unless adjusted gross income is more than $1500.

Payment of tax is due at the same time as the return.

Personal income tax payments, quarterly estimated payments, and extension payments may be made by direct debit, credit card, or debit card. (*New Developments for Tax Year 2014*, Michigan Department of Treasury, December 2014)

• *Electronic filing*

Tax preparers who complete 11 or more Michigan income tax returns are required to e-file all returns that are supported by their software. An MI-1040 may be filed electronically, even if a taxpayer is filing an MI-1045, Application for Michigan Net Operating Loss Refund, or Form 4, Application for Extension of Time to File Michigan Tax Returns. However, the latter two forms must be mailed to the address included on the form. (*Michigan E-File*, Michigan Department of Treasury)

• *"No-form" option*

Eligible taxpayers may elect to pay their Michigan personal income tax under a "no-form" option. Under this option, no annual return is required to be filed and the taxpayer's tax is calculated by multiplying taxable compensation, less the standard personal and dependency exemptions, by the current income tax rate (¶102). All other exemption, dependency, and credit claims are prohibited, except for credit claims for withholding and home heating. A taxpayer who makes the election reserves the right to a file a return and pay the tax due in the usual manner.

Eligible taxpayers are Michigan residents who elect the "no-form" option on their withholding exemption certificates (¶608) and have taxable compensation of less than $100 for a single return or $200 for a joint return. For purposes of the "no-form" option, "taxable compensation" means compensation from which tax is commonly withheld, except for (1) compensation for service in the U.S. Armed Forces or certain retirement and pension benefits received from Michigan or federal public retirement systems, (2) IRC Sec. 86 social security benefits, and (3) certain other retirement or pension benefits.

• *Entity-level composite returns*

Nonresident members, partners, or shareholders of flow-through entities having income in Michigan from one or more such entities may elect to be included in the composite income tax return of the entity (Form 807, Michigan Composite Individual Income Tax Return). A flow-through entity is permitted to file a composite return on behalf of electing nonresident members, partners, and shareholders (hereinafter referred to as "member") and report and pay tax due based on such nonresidents' shares of income available for distribution from the flow-through entity for doing business in, or deriving income from, Michigan sources. For purposes of these provisions, a nonresident member includes an individual who is not domiciled in Michigan, a nonresident estate or trust, or a flow-through entity with a nonresident member.

Practice Note: Certain Members Ineligible

A member may not participate in a composite return if any of the following apply:

— the member intends to claim the city income tax credit, any of the charitable contributions credits discussed at ¶306, Michigan Historic Preservation Credit, college tuition credit, or the vehicle donation credit;

— the member was a resident during any portion of the tax year;

— the member intends to claim more than one Michigan exemption.

(Instructions, Form 807, Michigan Composite Individual Income Tax Return)

Members of a flow-through entity with income from other Michigan sources may participate in a composite filing if otherwise qualified. The member is required to file a Michigan income tax return to report the additional income and claim a credit on that return for any taxes paid on the member's behalf through the composite filing.

A composite return may be filed by a flow-through entity with two or more nonresident members. Entities that file a composite nonresident return are required to withhold on payments made to all nonresident members (whether or not participating). (Instructions, Form 807, Michigan Composite Individual Income Tax Return)

A composite return must be filed by April 15 of the immediately succeeding tax year. For flow-through entities who file fiscal year federal returns, the due date of the composite return will be April 15 of the year following the entity's fiscal year end. This provision places the due date for composite filers in conformity with the calendar year due date for members not participating in the composite filing. (*Revenue Administrative Bulletin 2004-1,* Michigan Department of Treasury, April 5, 2004, CCH MICHIGAN TAX REPORTS, ¶319-336)

¶502 Annual Returns—Extension of Time for Filing

Law: Sec. 206.311, M.C.L. (CCH MICHIGAN TAX REPORTS, ¶89-102).

Comparable Federal: Sec. 6081 (CCH U.S. MASTER TAX GUIDE ¶2537).

An extension to file a return may be granted for good cause upon the filing of Form 4, Application for Extension of Time to File Michigan Tax Returns. Also, if a taxpayer has been granted an extension of time for filing his or her final federal return, filing a copy of the federal extension will automatically extend the due date for the Michigan return for an equivalent period. An extension need not be filed if the taxpayer will be claiming a refund.

The extension, however, applies only to the filing. Payment not made by the due date is subject to interest and penalties (¶802).

• *Military personnel serving in combat zones*

A taxpayer who has an automatic extension for the federal return based on service in a combat zone is allowed an automatic filing extension for the Michigan personal income tax return. The state due date for a return or a payment of estimated tax would be extended for a period of time equivalent to the federal extension. The taxpayer is not required to file a copy of the federal extension but must print the words "Combat Zone" in red ink at the top of the return when filing. The taxpayer is not required to pay the tax due by the date of the normal filing deadline, and the Department of Treasury cannot impose any interest or penalties for the unpaid tax for the period of the extension.

¶503 Copies of Federal Return

Law: Sec. 206.325, M.C.L. (CCH MICHIGAN TAX REPORTS, ¶89-102).

Taxpayers required to file Michigan returns may be required, at the request of the Department of Treasury, to furnish copies of any return or schedules filed under federal income tax law.

The Instructions to MI-1040, Michigan Individual Income Tax Return, provides a list of the federal schedules that must be attached to the Michigan return if the taxpayer filed the schedule for federal purposes.

¶504 Status of Return—Joint or Separate

Law: Sec. 206.311, M.C.L. (CCH MICHIGAN TAX REPORTS, ¶15-310).

Comparable Federal: Sec. 6013 (CCH U.S. MASTER TAX GUIDE ¶154—168, 711).

Married persons filing a joint federal return must file a joint Michigan return. Spouses filing separate federal returns may file joint or separate Michigan returns. (Instructions, Form MI-1040)

¶505 Annual Return Forms—Ordering and Reproduction

All individuals required to file an income tax return use Form MI-1040. Fiduciaries use Form MI-1041. Form MI-1040CR, Homestead Property Tax Credit Claim Form, must be filed to claim a homestead credit.

• *Ordering forms*

Generally, forms can be obtained from the Michigan Department of Treasury, Lansing, Michigan 48922, 800-827-4000. Many tax forms are available for downloading from the Department of Treasury's website at http://www.michigan.gov/incometax.

• *Reproduction of forms*

The Michigan Department of Treasury will accept reproductions of official income tax returns for filing. Forms printed on colored paper may be reproduced on white paper. Reproductions must be made in the same size as the original form and on the same weight paper as the official form. (*Policy Statement ET-03066,* Department of Treasury, effective September 1, 2004; CCH MICHIGAN TAX REPORTS, ¶16-720.20)

¶506 Payments of Estimated Tax

Law: Sec. 206.301, M.C.L. (CCH MICHIGAN TAX REPORTS, ¶89-104).

Comparable Federal: Sec. 6654 (CCH U.S. MASTER TAX GUIDE ¶2679—2682).

Individuals required to declare and pay estimated federal income tax are also required to file returns of estimated tax with Michigan if annual Michigan tax can reasonably be expected to exceed the amount withheld and certain credits by more than $500. Exceptions to the requirement occur if:

— withholding for the current tax year will exceed tax owed for the previous tax year;

— withholding for the current tax year will be at least 90% of tax owed for the current tax year (qualified farmers, fishermen, and seafarers use 66 2/3%); or

— 110% of the taxpayer's tax liability for the previous tax year if the taxpayer's adjusted gross income for the previous tax year was more than $150,000 ($75,000 for married, filing separately).

• *Due dates*

Declarations and payment of estimated tax of calendar-year individuals, filed on Form MI-1040ES, are due on or before April 15, June 15, and September 15 of the tax year, and January 15 of the following year, depending on when the requirements for filing are met. Fiscal-year taxpayers substitute the appropriate due dates in the fiscal year that correspond to the calendar-year dates. See ¶502 for a discussion of the extensions available to taxpayers affected by presidential declared disasters and to military personnel serving in combat zones.

In lieu of filing and paying estimated taxes quarterly, a taxpayer may elect to make an annual estimated tax payment for the succeeding year. The return is due at the same time the annual return for the previous full tax year is filed.

• *Farmers, fishermen, seafarers*

Farmers, fishermen, and seafarers, as qualified under federal law, who elect to file federal income tax returns under an alternative schedule may file for state tax purposes in the same manner. Federal law permits these taxpayers to make only one installment payment of estimated tax equal to two-thirds of the tax liability, due January 15 of the following taxable year, or to file the return and pay the tax in full by March 1 of the following year without penalty for failure to pay installments.

Practice Note: Penalty Relief

The Michigan Department of Treasury has announced that farmers and fishermen are not subject to the penalty and interest for the underpayment of estimated personal income tax if the 2012 tax return is filed and the entire tax due is paid by April 15, 2013. Due to the delayed start for filing the federal 2012 tax year returns, the IRS is granting a filing extension to April 15 and Michigan is following the federal extension.

(*Press Release*, Michigan Department of Treasury, March 2013)

• *Estates and trusts*

Estates and trusts are required to file declarations and make payments of estimated tax. A bank or financial institution that acts as a fiduciary for 200 or more taxable trusts and that submits federal quarterly estimated tax payment information through the federal tax deposit system on magnetic tape is also required to submit Michigan quarterly estimated income tax payment information to the Department of Treasury on magnetic tape.

• *Amended estimates*

If estimated tax changes after the original return is filed, the estimate is amended on the next quarterly return. However, if the annual return is filed and the balance of tax paid by January 31 of the year following the tax year, a taxpayer need not file the January voucher. Taxpayers who were not paying estimated taxes and who met requirements for doing so after September 1 may file the return by January 31 in lieu of filing Form MI-1040 ES.

¶507 Tax Return Preparers

Law: R206.33, Mich. Admin. Code (CCH MICHIGAN TAX REPORTS, ¶89-238).

Although tax preparers are not specifically regulated under Michigan law, a rule sets forth standards of performance (R206.33, Mich. Admin. Code; CCH MICHIGAN TAX REPORTS ¶19-167). The requirements, for which no specific sanctions are indicated, include the following:

— a completed return or refund claim is to be presented to the taxpayer for signing; and

— a copy of the return (or list that includes name, social security number, and taxable year) is to be retained for three years during which time it must be made available for inspection by the Department of Treasury.

"Income tax return preparer" is defined as any person who, for compensation, prepares any return of income tax or claim for refund of income tax.

¶508 Reciprocal Agreements on Nonresidents

Michigan has entered into reciprocal agreements with Illinois, Indiana, Kentucky, Minnesota, Ohio, and Wisconsin, under which a resident of Michigan who performs personal services in one or more of those states is not required to file a nonresident income tax return in the state in which he is employed if his or her only income from the state is from personal services. Michigan grants a similar privilege to persons resident in those states and working in Michigan.

The agreements also provide that no withholding is required on the wages of nonresidents (¶605).

¶509 Notice of Change in Federal Return

Law: Sec. 206.325, M.C.L. (CCH MICHIGAN TAX REPORTS, ¶89-102).

A taxpayer must file an amended return with the Department of Treasury showing any alteration in, or modification of, his or her federal income tax return that affects taxable income under Michigan law, or any related recomputation of tax or determination of deficiency under the provisions of the Internal Revenue Code. The requirement does not apply if the increase in federal tax is less than $500. The amended return must be filed within 120 days after the alteration, modification, recomputation, or determination of deficiency.

¶510 Information Returns

Law: Sec. 206.331, M.C.L. (CCH MICHIGAN TAX REPORTS, ¶89-104).

Comparable Federal: Secs. 6031—6049 (CCH U.S. MASTER TAX GUIDE ¶2565).

Every corporation, voluntary association, joint venture, partnership, estate, or trust, at the request of the Department of Treasury, must file a copy of any tax return or portion of any tax return filed under the Internal Revenue Code.

At the request of the Department, every person required by the Internal Revenue Code to file or submit an information return of income paid to others is required at the same time to file the information with the Department, in form and content as prescribed by the Department, to the extent the information is applicable to residents of Michigan.

• *Publicly-traded partnerships*

Every publicly trade partnership (as defined under IRC Sec. 7704) that has equity securities registered with the federal Securities and Exchange Commission is required to file, on or before August 31 each year all unitholder information from its schedule K-1 for the immediately preceding calendar year on forms to be prescribed by the Department.

• *Form 1099-MISC*

Individuals must file a copy of federal form 1099-MISC with the Michigan Department of Treasury if they are required under the Internal Revenue Code to file that form for a tax year. An individual also must file a copy of form 1099-MISC with the city reported as the payee's address on the form, if the city imposes a personal income tax.

The form 1099-MISC is for miscellaneous income paid to a taxpayer, including business payments to nonemployees such as subcontractors. An individual who fails to comply with the filing requirement is liable for a penalty of $50 for each form that should have been filed. The form must be filed by January 31 each year, or by the day required for filing the form under the Internal Revenue Code, whichever date is later.

INCOME TAX

CHAPTER 6

WITHHOLDING

¶601 Withholding Required

Law: Secs. 206.6, 206.8, 206.351, 206.703, M.C.L. (CCH MICHIGAN TAX REPORTS, ¶16-615).

Comparable Federal: Secs. 3401—3402 (CCH U.S. MASTER TAX GUIDE ¶2601, *et seq.*).

Every employer in Michigan who is required to withhold tax under the federal income tax law is required to withhold Michigan income tax at the statutory rate (¶102) from salaries or wages after deducting personal and dependency exemptions.

Michigan reporting and withholding on fringe benefits (e.g., 401K plans, deferred compensation, profit sharing, and cafeteria benefit plans) follow federal guidelines as provided in the Federal Employer's Tax Guide, Circular E. (*Michigan Income Tax Withholding Guide*)

Out-of-state employers that have employees who work in Michigan are required to withhold from such individuals in the same manner as are Michigan employers. However, see ¶605 relating to reciprocal agreements between Michigan and Illinois, Indiana, Kentucky, Minnesota, Ohio, and Wisconsin regarding withholding and tax liability of persons resident in one state and performing services in another, and see ¶606 for a discussion of the exemption of nonresidents in general.

"Employee" and "employer" are given the same meanings as those given in the Internal Revenue Code.

Flow-through entities: Any entity, whether or not recognized for federal income tax purposes, that is an employer under federal law is also an employer for state personal income tax withholding purposes and is required to be registered for income tax withholding. As a result, the Michigan withholding taxpayer may be different from the taxpayer for federal tax purposes. A disregarded entity that is not required to have a federal employer identification number because of its disregarded status will be issued a Michigan Department of Treasury number for Michigan withholding purposes. Upon request, the Department of Treasury also is authorized to enter into an agreement allowing a disregarded single-member entity to file a combined withholding tax return with its owner.

For further discussion of flow-through entity withholding, see ¶857.

Pensions: Effective January 1, 2012, income tax withholding is required for persons who disburse pension or annuity payments. Qualified pension and retirement benefits include most payments reported on Form 1099-R for federal tax purposes. For example, defined benefit pensions, IRA distributions, and most payments from defined contribution plans are included. However, on the other hand, payments received before the recipient could retire under plan provisions or benefits from 401(k), 457, or 403(b) plans attributable to employee contributions alone are not considered pension and retirement benefits. (*2012 Pension Withholding Guide*, Michigan Department of Treasury)

Gambling licensees: Casino licensees are required to withhold Michigan income tax at the statutory rate from the winnings of nonresidents that are reportable under the Internal Revenue Code. Similarly, race meeting and track licensees must withhold tax by applying the requisite rate to a payoff price on a winning ticket held by a nonresident reportable by the licensee under the IRC that is a result of pari-mutuel wagering at a licensed race meeting. Finally, with respect to resident winnings, casino licensees, race meeting licensees, and track licensees are required to report winnings of a Michigan resident reportable to the IRS to the Michigan Department of Treasury in the same format and manner as provided under the Internal Revenue Code.

¶602 Withholding for Temporary or Part-Time Employees

(CCH MICHIGAN TAX REPORTS, ¶16-615).

Comparable Federal: Sec. 3402 (CCH U.S. MASTER TAX GUIDE ¶2601).

The filing of an Employee's Michigan Withholding Exemption Certificate (Form MI-W4) enables an employee to claim an exemption from Michigan withholding if the employee does not anticipate a Michigan income tax liability for the current year because the employment is less than full time and the personal and dependency exemptions exceed annual compensation ("Employer's Withholding Tax Guide"; CCH MICHIGAN TAX REPORTS, ¶16-120).

¶603 Withholding on Supplemental Unemployment Benefits and Annuities

(CCH MICHIGAN TAX REPORTS, ¶16-615).

Comparable Federal: Secs. 3402 and 3405 (CCH U.S. MASTER TAX GUIDE ¶2611, 2643).

Employers required to withhold federal tax from supplemental unemployment compensation benefits are also required to withhold Michigan income tax. ("Employer's Withholding Tax Guide"; CCH MICHIGAN TAX REPORTS, ¶16-120)

¶604 Methods of Withholding

(CCH MICHIGAN TAX REPORTS, ¶16-615).

Comparable Federal: Sec. 3402 (CCH U.S. MASTER TAX GUIDE ¶2614—2629).

The amount of tax withheld may be determined by a direct percentage computation or by use of withholding tables prescribed by the state. The withholding formula, exemption allowances, and withholding tables are found in the "Employer's Withholding Tax Guide" reproduced at CCH MICHIGAN TAX REPORTS, ¶16-120.

¶605 Reciprocal Withholding Agreements

Michigan has entered into agreements with Illinois, Indiana, Kentucky, Minnesota, Ohio, and Wisconsin to avoid the possibility of double withholding on compensation of persons resident in those states. Under the agreements, each state will not require withholding from compensation paid residents of the other state working in Michigan, and vice versa, if the nonresident employees file certificates of nonresidence with their employers.

The reciprocal agreements also exempt nonresidents from the requirement of filing returns in the state of nonresidence, if all income from sources in the state of nonresidence is from wages (¶508). See ¶206 for a discussion of the exemption available to nonresidents in these states.

¶606 Exemption for Nonresidents

Law: Sec. 206.351, 206.703, M.C.L. (CCH MICHIGAN TAX REPORTS, ¶16-635).

Employers are not required to withhold Michigan income tax from wages paid a nonresident employee whose credit for income taxes paid another state equals or exceeds the Michigan income tax estimated to be due, or who is exempt from Michigan tax. Annually, each nonresident employee must give his or her employer a verified statement of nonresidency.

¶607 Returns and Remittance of Withheld Taxes

Law: Secs. 205.19, 206.351, 206.355, 206.703, 206.705, 206.711, M.C.L. (CCH MICHIGAN TAX REPORTS, ¶89-102).

Comparable Federal: Sec. 3501 (CCH U.S. MASTER TAX GUIDE ¶2650—2658).

Generally, withheld taxes must be returned and paid to the state within 20 days after the end of any month in which the taxes are withheld. However, the Michigan Department of Treasury is authorized to provide for other than monthly withholding, in order to provide more efficient administration of the income tax.

A taxpayer other than a city or county that paid in the immediately preceding calendar year an average of $40,000 or more per month in withheld income taxes must deposit the withheld taxes either in the same manner and according to the same schedule as is used to make deposits of federal income taxes withheld or in another manner approved by the Department of Treasury.

Responsible corporate officers, or responsible members, managers, or partners of flow-through entities are personally liable for failure to file returns or pay tax due in the event of failure to perform by the corporation or flow-through entity.

Effective January 1, 2012, a flow-through entity that has withheld Michigan personal income taxes on distributive shares of business income reasonably expected to accrue is required to file an annual reconciliation return no later than the last day of the second month following the end of the flow-through entity's federal tax year (i.e., February 28 for calendar year taxpayers). The Department of Treasury may require the flow-through entity to file an annual business income information return on the due date, including extensions, of its annual federal information return. (Sec. 206.711, M.C.L.)

¶608 Withholding Certificates

Law: Secs. 206.351, 206.365, 206.703, 206.711, M.C.L. (CCH MICHIGAN TAX REPORTS, ¶16-615).

Comparable Federal: Sec. 3402 (CCH U.S. MASTER TAX GUIDE ¶2634).

Employees, nonresident members of flow-through entities, and winnings holders of casino and race track licensees are required to furnish their employers, entities, or licensees with information needed to make an accurate withholding.

They must notify the appropriate party, within 10 days, of any decrease in the number of withholding exemptions or a change of status from nonresident to resident. In addition, employees are required to notify their employers within 10 days after satisfying renaissance zone (RZ) residency requirements and when changing their status from resident to nonresident of a such a zone (RZs are discussed at ¶204).

The employer, flow-through entity, casino licensee, or race track licensee is required to rely on this information for withholding purposes unless directed by the Department of Treasury to withhold on another basis. If an employee, nonresident member, or winnings holder fails to furnish the required information (Form MI-W4), the employer will withhold the full rate of tax from the employee's total compensation, the nonresident member's share of income available for distribution, or the winnings holder's total winnings.

Employers, flow-through entities, casino licensees, and race track licensees must provide the Department of Treasury with a copy of any exemption certificate on which an employee claims more than nine personal exemptions, claims a status exempt from income tax withholding, or elects to pay the tax due under the "no-form" option (¶501). The copy is due by the 15th of the month following the employee's claim.

Employers are responsible for obtaining a MI-W4 exemption certificate from each employee. The federal Form W-4 cannot be used in place of the Michigan Form MI-W4 ("Employer's Withholding Tax Guide"; CCH MICHIGAN TAX REPORTS, ¶16-120).

Practice Note: Reporting Information About New Hires

Employers must report to the Michigan Department of Treasury the name, address, and social security number of each newly hired employee within 20 days of the hiring date. The information may be submitted on-line at **www.mi-newhire.com** or mailed on Form MI-W4, which must also include the employer's name, address, and federal identification number.

¶609 Annual Statements of Wages, Distributions, or Winnings Paid

Law: Sec. 206.365, 206.711, M.C.L. (CCH MICHIGAN TAX REPORTS, ¶89-102).

Comparable Federal: Sec. 6051 (CCH U.S. MASTER TAX GUIDE ¶2655).

Employers, flow-through entities, casino licensees, and race track licensees must provide employees, on or before January 31 of the succeeding year, with a statement, in duplicate, of the total salary or wages paid, share of income available for distribution, winnings, or payoff on a winning ticket during the preceding year and the amount of tax deducted or withheld. Employers may use one of the Internal Revenue Service's approved Combined W-2 Forms, which are commercially available, for both federal and state purposes ("Employer's Withholding Tax Guide"; CCH MICHIGAN TAX REPORTS, ¶16-120).

Michigan follows federal guidelines regarding the number of W-2 forms to be filed for each taxpayer. Thus, only one Form W-2 is provided to an employee who works in more than one branch office of the same corporation or to an employee who is paid, in addition to but separate from his or her regular salary, a bonus or incentive under a corporation's executive bonus plan (*Letter,* Department of Treasury, January 29, 1990; CCH MICHIGAN TAX REPORTS, ¶16-090).

If employment is terminated by an employer going out of business or ceasing to be an employer in the state during the year, or a flow-through entity, casino licensee, race meeting licensee, or track licensee goes out of business or permanently ceases to be a flow-through entity, casino licensee, race meeting licensee, or track licensee before the close of a calendar year, the statement must be provided within 30 days after the last compensation, share of income available for distribution, winnings, or payoff of a winning ticket is paid.

¶610 Annual Reconciliation of Tax Withheld Required

Law: Sec. 206.365, 206.711, M.C.L. (CCH MICHIGAN TAX REPORTS, ¶89-102).

Comparable Federal: Sec. 6011 (CCH U.S. MASTER TAX GUIDE ¶2650).

An annual reconciliation of income tax withheld must be filed by employers, flow-through entities, casino licensees, race meeting licensees, or track licensees by February 28 of the succeeding year for the preceding tax year.

¶611 Taxpayers Required to Keep Records of Withholding

Law: Secs. 206.408, 206.455, M.C.L. (CCH MICHIGAN TAX REPORTS, ¶89-142).

Comparable Federal: Sec. 6001 (CCH U.S. MASTER TAX GUIDE ¶2523).

Employers, flow-through entities, casino licensees, race meeting licensees, and track licensees are required to keep all records relating to withholding available for inspection by the Department of Treasury. For employers, the records should include:

— the amounts and dates of all wage payments reported subject to withholding;

— names, addresses and occupations of employees receiving the payments;

— the periods of employment of the employees;

— periods for which wages are paid while employees are absent due to sickness or personal injuries and the amount and weekly rate of such payments;

— employees' social security numbers;

— employees' withholding exemption certificates;

— the employers' identification numbers; and

— duplicate copies of returns filed.

Records should be kept for at least six years after the date the tax to which they relate becomes due, or the date the tax is paid, whichever is later ("Employer's Withholding Tax Guide"; CCH MICHIGAN TAX REPORTS, ¶16-120). See ¶804 for other information about recordkeeping.

¶612 Credits

Law: Sec. 206.367, M.C.L. (CCH MICHIGAN TAX REPORTS, ¶16-890).

A film production expenditures credit against withholding taxes may be claimed by an eligible production company for a state certified qualified production. The credit is similar to the Michigan business tax credit discussed at ¶14891, however, the credit against withholding taxes is not refundable. This provision is repealed, effective January 1, 2012. (Sec. 206.367, M.C.L)

INCOME TAX

CHAPTER 7

ADMINISTRATION, ASSESSMENT, COLLECTION

¶701 Tax Administered by Department of Treasury

Law: Sec. 206.471, M.C.L. (CCH MICHIGAN TAX REPORTS, ¶15-030).

Comparable Federal: Secs. 7801—7805 (CCH U.S. MASTER TAX GUIDE ¶2701).

The Michigan income tax law is administered by the Department of Treasury. The Department is required to prescribe forms and promulgate rules regarding computation of the tax, maintenance of books and records, manner and time of changing or electing accounting methods and exercising the various options provided in the law, making of returns, payment of tax, and assessment and collection of tax.

Rules issued by the Michigan Department of Treasury are to follow the rulings of the Internal Revenue Service so far as possible without being inconsistent with the provisions of Michigan law. The adoption of portions of the Internal Revenue Code or rulings is authorized. For a general discussion of administrative provisions, including taxpayer remedies, see Chapters 24 and 25.

¶702 Taxpayer Bill of Rights

Law: Secs. 205.4, 205.5, M.C.L.; R205.1001—R205.1013. Mich. Admin. Code (CCH MICHIGAN TAX REPORTS, ¶89-222).

A series of rules known as the Taxpayer Bill of Rights (R205.1001—R205.1013, Mich. Admin. Code; CCH MICHIGAN TAX REPORTS, ¶89-700—89-700*l*) address standards for treatment of the public, confidentiality of information, representation before the Department, informal conferences (¶704), and the penalties for negligence and failure to file a return or pay the tax owed (¶802). The rules apply to all taxes administered by the Department. See also ¶2501.

¶703 Assessment

Law: Secs. 205.21, 205.23, M.C.L. (CCH MICHIGAN TAX REPORTS, ¶89-162, 89-164).

Comparable Federal: Secs. 6201—6204 (CCH U.S. MASTER TAX GUIDE ¶2711—2724).

Michigan income tax, like other income taxes, is normally self-assessed by taxpayers. However, if any person fails or refuses to make a return or pay the tax or if the Department of Treasury has reason to believe that a refund claim is excessive or that any return made does not supply sufficient information for an accurate determination of the tax due, the Department may obtain information on which to base an assessment of the tax due. The Department is authorized to examine the books, records, and papers of the taxpayer and to audit the taxpayer's accounts. The Department will assess the tax due, and notify the taxpayer as soon as possible after obtaining the necessary information.

¶704 Notice and Hearing on Assessment

Law: Secs. 205.21, 205.28, M.C.L. (CCH MICHIGAN TAX REPORTS, ¶89-164).

Comparable Federal: Sec. 6212 (CCH U.S. MASTER TAX GUIDE ¶2711).

After determining the amount of tax due from a taxpayer, the Department of Treasury must give notice to the taxpayer of its intent to levy the tax. The taxpayer may request an informal conference on the question of his or her liability for the assessment by serving notice on the Department within 60 days after receipt of the notice of intent to levy the tax. Upon receipt of a request for a conference, the Department will set a time and place for the conference and give the taxpayer reasonable notice not less than 20 days before the conference.

At the conference, the taxpayer is entitled to appear or to be represented before the Department and to present testimony and argument. After the conference, the Department issues its decision and order of determination in writing, setting forth the reasons and authority, and issues a final assessment, levying any tax, interest, and penalty found to be due and payable.

See Chapters 24 and 25 for more details concerning assessments and appeal procedures.

¶705 Limitations of Time

Law: Secs. 205.27a, 206.411, M.C.L. (CCH MICHIGAN TAX REPORTS, ¶89-164).

Comparable Federal: Sec. 6501 (CCH U.S. MASTER TAX GUIDE ¶2726—2736).

No deficiency, interest, or penalty may be assessed after the expiration of four years from the later of (a) the due date for the filing of the annual return, or (b) the date the return was filed. However, in the event of fraudulent concealment of liability, an assessment may be made within two years after the discovery of the fraud.

The statute of limitations is suspended for the period pending final determination of litigation or a hearing on the taxpayer's federal or state income tax return, or if notice is required of a change in the federal return that will affect the state return, and for one year following. (Sec. 205.27(a)(3), M.C.L.)

Practice Note: Suspension Period for Audits

Applicable to audit confirmation letters with a commencement date on or after January 1, 2009, the Department of Treasury has clarified the suspension period in situations in which an audit is conducted. In those instances in which an audit is conducted prior to the date the four year statute of limitations otherwise would have run, the limitations period is extended to a date one year after the conclusion of the audit or one year after the conclusion of an appeal if the audit is appealed, plus any days remaining from the four year limitations period that had not run prior to the audit commencement date. The running of the four year general statute of limitations recommences when the audit determination that was appealed has been finalized. Under this statutory authority, waivers are not required. (*Revenue Administrative Bulletin 2008-8;* CCH MICHIGAN TAX REPORTS, ¶401-398)

The taxpayer and the Department of Treasury may agree to extend the statute of limitations for any period.

The statute of limitations is suspended for any taxable year for which no return has been filed.

¶706 Appeals

Law: Sec. 205.22, M.C.L. (CCH MICHIGAN TAX REPORTS, ¶89-234—89-240).

Comparable Federal: Sec. 7422 (CCH U.S. MASTER TAX GUIDE ¶2776—2798).

Appeals from determinations of tax by the Department of Treasury must be filed with the Michigan Tax Tribunal (MTT) within 35 days or to the Court of Claims within 90 days of the Department's assessment, decision, or order.

When the appeal is taken to the Court of Claims, the tax, including any penalties and interest, must be paid under protest and a refund claimed as a part of the appeal. Only the uncontested portion of the assessment must be paid before an appeal to the MTT. An appeal from the decision of the MTT or the Court of Claims may be taken to the Court of Appeals as of right. Further appeal may be taken to the Supreme Court only by leave.

See also ¶2501—2511.

¶707 Jeopardy Assessments

Law: Secs. 205.26, 206.355, 206.705, M.C.L. (CCH MICHIGAN TAX REPORTS, ¶89-168).

Comparable Federal: Secs. 6861, 6863 (CCH U.S. MASTER TAX GUIDE ¶2713).

When the Department of Treasury finds that a person liable for income tax is planning to leave the state, remove his or her property from the state, conceal property, or take other action to evade collection of the tax, the Department may give notice to the taxpayer of such findings, and make a demand for an immediate return and payment of the tax. A warrant may be issued immediately upon issuance of a jeopardy assessment, and the tax becomes immediately due and payable.

However, if the person is not in default in making any return or payment of tax and if the person can furnish satisfactory evidence that he or she will file a timely return and make payment of tax, the tax will not be payable prior to the time otherwise fixed for payment.

Similarly, if there is reason to believe that an employer, flow-through entity, casino licensee, race meeting licensee, or track licensee will not pay over withheld taxes as prescribed, the Department may require the employer to make the return and pay tax at any time, or may require the employer to deposit the tax in a separate account in a bank approved by the Department, in trust for the Department.

¶708 Collection of Unpaid Tax

Law: Secs. 205.25, 205.28, 205.29, M.C.L. (CCH MICHIGAN TAX REPORTS, ¶89-162 and following).

Comparable Federal: Secs. 6321—6344 (CCH U.S. MASTER TAX GUIDE ¶2751—2755).

The Department of Treasury may make a demand on a delinquent taxpayer for payment if the income tax due is not paid at the time required. If the tax remains unpaid for ten days after demand and the taxpayer has not sought review of the tax, the Department may issue a warrant and, through any state officer authorized to serve process, levy upon and sell the real and personal property of the delinquent taxpayer within the state for the payment of the tax, including interest, penalties, and the cost of executing the warrant.

In addition to the above method of collection, the Department may institute an action at law to collect the tax in any county in which the taxpayer resides or transacts business.

The income tax, together with interest and penalties, is a lien in favor of the state against all property and rights of the taxpayer to secure the payment of tax. The lien attaches to the property from and after the date that any report or return is required to be filed, continues for seven years, and may be refiled for an additional seven years.

Property exempt from levy includes that enumerated in IRC Sec. 6334 for an unpaid tax or disposable earnings as provided by Sec. 303 of the Consumer Protection Act for amounts due the state other than unpaid tax.

The lien takes precedence over all other liens, other than bona fide liens recorded before the date the income tax lien attaches, but the income tax lien will not be valid against any mortgagee, pledgee, purchaser (including contract purchaser) or judgment creditor until notice of the lien has been recorded in the office of the register of deeds of the county in which the property subject to the income tax lien is located.

• *Innocent spouse relief*

Michigan has adopted the federal innocent spouse relief provisions. Among other things, these amendments allow relief for all erroneous tax understatements, allow apportionment of relief, enable a taxpayer to elect innocent spouse relief within two years from assessment, and authorize certain legally separated couples to elect separate tax liability even if they filed jointly. Taxpayers who are relieved from, or who are eligible for relief from, federal tax liability are entitled to relief from Michigan personal income tax liability.

The Department of Treasury may issue a refund of payments made by a spouse who has been granted relief under the federal guidelines for innocent spouse and equitable relief only, but will not issue a refund for relief granted under the separate liability provisions (*Revenue Administrative Bulletin 2000-9;* CCH MICHIGAN TAX REPORTS, ¶319-303).

Practice Note: Requesting Relief

A request for relief must be in writing and include documentation supporting the criteria for relief and a copy of any federal relief that was granted. A taxpayer may request relief from joint and several liability at any time upon learning of a joint debt but no later than two years after the Department begins collection activity against the requesting spouse. In determining this date, collection activity includes an offset of the electing spouse's tax refund or other money owed by the state, garnishment of the electing spouse's wages, and notice of levy against the electing spouse's property. However, collection activity does not include a final assessment or final demand letter addressed to both spouses (*Revenue Administrative Bulletin 2000-9;* CCH MICHIGAN TAX REPORTS, ¶319-303).

INCOME TAX

CHAPTER 8

REFUNDS, PENALTIES, RECORDS

¶801 Refunds

Law: Secs. 205.27a, 205.30, 206.352, 206.473, M.C.L. (CCH MICHIGAN TAX REPORTS, ¶89-224).

Comparable Federal: Secs. 6401, 6511, 6611 (CCH U.S. MASTER TAX GUIDE ¶2759—2773).

Overpayments of tax and erroneous and unjust assessments, penalties, and interest are credited or refunded; however, refunds of less than $1 will not be made. Claims for refund must be filed within four years from the due date set for filing the original return; however, claims for refund based on the unconstitutionality of a tax law must be filed within 90 days after the date set for filing the return.

The general four-year statute of limitations is suspended during the period pending a final determination of federal or Michigan tax and for one year thereafter. Even though another statute (Sec. 206.325(2), M.C.L.) provided that an amended return must be filed within 120 days after the final alternation, modification, recomputation or determination of a deficiency, this was a filing requirement and did not supercede the four-year statute of limitations. (Sec. 205.27a(3), M.C.L.; *Fegert v. Department of Treasury*, Michigan Court of Appeals, No. 270236, December 19, 2006, CCH MICHIGAN TAX REPORTS, ¶401-265; *Krueger v. Department of Treasury*, Michigan Court of Appeals, No. 302246, May 29, 2012, CCH MICHIGAN TAX REPORTS, ¶401-682)

Practice Note: Suspension Period for Audits

Applicable to audit confirmation letters with a commencement date on or after January 1, 2009, the Department of Treasury has clarified the suspension period in situations in which an audit is conducted. In those instances in which an audit is conducted prior to the date the four year statute of limitations otherwise would have run, the limitations period is extended to a date one year after the conclusion of the audit or one year after the conclusion of an appeal if the audit is appealed, plus any days remaining from the four year limitations period that had not run prior to the audit commencement date. The running of the four year general statute of limitations recommences when the audit determination that was appealed has been finalized. Under this statutory authority, waivers are not required. (*Revenue Administrative Bulletin 2008-8;* CCH MICHIGAN TAX REPORTS, ¶401-398)

The period to claim a refund is extended when a taxpayer obtains an extension of time to file the original return or when the refund claim period is otherwise extended by law. (*Revenue Administrative Bulletin 96-4*, Department of Treasury, May 13, 1996)

If a tax return reflects an overpayment or credits in excess of tax due, the declaration of the overpayment or credit on the return constitutes a claim for refund.

If the Department of Treasury agrees that the taxpayer's claim for refund is valid, the overpayment, penalties, and interest must first be applied against any known liability and the excess, if any, may be refunded or credited, at the taxpayer's request, against any current or subsequent liability.

Interest at the rate calculated for deficiencies (¶802) must be added to the refund, commencing 45 days after the claim is filed or 45 days after the required date for the filing of returns, whichever is later.

Whether a taxpayer elects to receive an overpayment as a cash refund or to apply it to the following year's income tax liability, the taxpayer is deemed to have received a refund, either actual or constructive, which must be reported by Michigan for federal income tax purposes on federal Form 1099-G.

Taxpayers may request that a refund be directly deposited with a financial institution of the taxpayer's choice. A request for direct deposit is made on Form 3174, Michigan Direct Deposit of Refund.

CCH Advisory: Refunds Applied to Federal Tax Liabilities

The IRS and the Michigan Department of Treasury have entered into an agreement that allows the state to turn over state income tax refunds to the IRS to satisfy a taxpayer's federal tax balance due (*IRS News Release No. MI-2004-15,* May 21, 2004).

¶802 Penalties and Interest

Law: Sec. 205.23, M.C.L. (CCH MICHIGAN TAX REPORTS, ¶89-202 and following).

Comparable Federal: Sec. 6601 and following (CCH U.S. MASTER TAX GUIDE ¶2801, *et seq.*).

Interest on tax deficiencies and refunds is charged at 1% above the adjusted prime rate charged by banks. The rate is administratively determined twice per year, and the rate so determined becomes effective on January 1 and July 1 of each year. See ¶2404 for further details.

Penalties are discussed at ¶2404.

¶803 Criminal Penalties

Criminal penalties are discussed at ¶2404.

¶804 Records

Law: Secs. 206.408, 206.455, M.C.L. (CCH MICHIGAN TAX REPORTS, ¶89-142).

Comparable Federal: Sec. 6001 (CCH U.S. MASTER TAX GUIDE ¶2523).

Every person is required to keep whatever records, books, and accounts necessary to allow a determination of the amount of tax for which he or she is liable. Records must be kept for a period of six years, and must be available for examination by the Department of Treasury at any time during regular business hours of the taxpayer.

Failure to comply with the recordkeeping provisions is punishable by a fine of not more than $1,000 or imprisonment for not more than one year, or both.

¶805 Closing of Estate

Law: Sec. 206.451, M.C.L.

No estate of a person subject to the Michigan income tax may be closed without the payment of any income tax due, both in respect to the liability of the estate and the liability of the decedent prior to death.

PART II.5

PASS-THROUGH ENTITIES

CHAPTER 8.5

INCOME TAX TREATMENT OF PASS-THROUGH ENTITIES

¶850 Introduction

Under federal law, S corporations, limited liability companies (LLCs), and partnerships are treated for income tax purposes as "pass-through" entities, because they are not taxed at the entity level and income is passed through to the shareholders, members, or partners of the entity. Michigan does not adopt the federal income tax treatment of S corporations, limited liability companies (LLCs), partnerships, or other pass-through entities. In general, all pass-through entities with business activity in the state are subject to the Michigan business tax to the same extent as C corporations (see Part III.5, Michigan Business Tax ¶1450—¶1505).

CCH Practice Tip: Pass-Through Entities Exempt

Effective January 1, 2012, the corporate income tax is generally imposed only on C corporations. Pass-through entities are not required to file and pay the tax (see ¶1510). The corporate income tax follows the federal check-the-box regulations. (Michigan Department of Treasury, FAQs Filing Requirements #8)

This chapter covers the various types of pass-through entities, the treatment of the pass-through entity at the entity level, the tax treatment of pass-through entity owners, reporting requirements, unified reporting options for nonresidents, and penalties.

¶851 Limited Liability Companies

Law: Secs. 205.27a (8), (9), 206.699, 208.1512, 450.4101, *et seq.*, M.C.L. (CCH MICHIGAN TAX REPORTS, ¶10-240)

Comparable Federal: Treas. Reg. Secs. 301.7701-1 through 301.7701-3. (U.S. MASTER TAX GUIDE ¶402B)

An LLC is a business entity that shares characteristics of both partnerships and corporations. Like a partnership, an LLC is a pass-through entity in which the profits and losses are passed through to its members. However, unlike a limited partnership in which the individual partners are personally liable for amounts up to and including the amount of their contributions to the partnership, or a general partnership in which all members are liable for the partnership obligations, members of an LLC incur no personal liability. The characteristics of an LLC are also similar to those of an S corporation, but LLCs are not subject to the many restrictions placed on S corporations, such as the limitations on the number and types of shareholders, the allowable classes of stock, and the flow through of losses.

Michigan adopts the federal income tax treatment and entity classification of a limited liability company (LLC). (Sec. 450.4101, M.C.L., *et seq.; Revenue Administrative Bulletin 1999-9*, Michigan Department of Treasury, CCH MICHIGAN TAX REPORTS, ¶319-291) The applicable Michigan statutes and regulations permit an LLC to elect tax classification as either a corporation, partnership, or "disregarded entity," unless the entity meets certain specifications requiring classification as a corporation.

CCH Practice Tip: Pass-Through Entities Exempt

Effective January 1, 2012, the corporate income tax is generally imposed only on C corporations. Pass-through entities are not required to file and pay the tax (see ¶1510).

Single-member LLCs.—A person that is a disregarded entity for federal income tax purposes is classified as a disregarded entity for the corporate income tax. (Sec. 206.699, M.C.L.)

However, unlike federal law, under which LLCs are not taxed at the entity level, LLCs are subject to the Michigan business tax (MBT), to the same extent and in the same manner as corporations (see Part III.5, Michigan Business Tax ¶1450—¶1505).

CCH Advisory: Federally Disregarded Entities Required to File MBT Returns

Retroactive and effective for taxes levied on or after January 1, 2008, a person that is a disregarded entity for federal income tax purposes is classified as a disregarded entity for the MBT. A person that is a disregarded entity for federal income tax that before 2012 in an originally filed return was treated as a person separate from its owner or before December 1, 2011 in an amended return was treated as a person separate from its owner for a tax year that begins after 2007 is not required to file an amended return with the owner as a disregarded entity. In addition, a person that is a disregarded entity for federal income tax that before 2012 in an originally filed return was treated as a person separate from its owner or before December 1, 2011 in an amended return was treated as a person separate from its owner for the first tax year that begins after 2009 may be treated as a person separate from its owner under the MBT for its tax year that begins after 2010 and ends before 2012. (Sec. 208.1512, M.C.L.)

The Michigan Department of Treasury has issued a notice explaining the MBT filing requirements for federally disregarded entities. In general, an entity that is disregarded for federal income tax purposes is classified as a disregarded entity for MBT purposes. There are two exceptions:

— An entity disregarded for federal income tax purposes that filed separate from its owner for the 2008, 2009, and 2010 tax years in original returns filed before 2012 or in amended returns filed before December 1, 2011, is not required to amend those returns.

— An entity disregarded for federal income tax purposes that filed separate from its owner for the 2010 MBT tax year in an original return filed before 2012 or in an amended return filed before December 1, 2011, may file separate from its owner for the 2011 tax year.

Therefore, if a federally disregarded entity did not file as a separate entity, then it may not file as a separate entity for the 2008—2011 MBT tax years. However, if the federally disregarded entity did file as a separate entity for the 2008—2010 MBT tax years, it may file an amended MBT return as a disregarded entity if the return is within the statute of limitations.

If a disregarded entity is eligible to file as a separate entity for the 2011 MBT tax year and does file separately, it must file all required forms and schedules. The disregarded entity must select the organization type under which the parent filed its tax return. Both the disregarded entity and the parent must prepare corresponding pro forma federal returns and attach them to the MBT returns. (*Notice to Taxpayers Regarding Federally Disregarded Entities and the Michigan Business Tax*, Michigan Department of Treasury, January 26, 2012)

The LLC's entity classification for federal income tax purposes is also effective on the Michigan personal income tax return of a resident or nonresident individual, shareholder, partner, or member. Because Michigan's personal income tax is based on federal adjusted gross income, the Michigan income tax return must conform to the entity reported on the federal return. (*Revenue Administrative Bulletin 1999-9*, Michigan Department of Treasury, CCH MICHIGAN TAX REPORTS, ¶319-291)

¶852 Partnerships

Law: Sec. 449.44, *et seq.* M.C.L. (CCH MICHIGAN TAX REPORTS, ¶10-220 through 10-235)

Comparable Federal: Secs. 701—761, 7704. (U.S. MASTER TAX GUIDE ¶401—481)

Michigan does not adopt the federal income tax treatment of a general partnership and its partners. A Michigan general partnership is subject to the Michigan business tax (MBT). (Sec. 208.1113(3), M.C.L., Sec. 208.1117(5), M.C.L.)

Although, Michigan recognizes both limited partnerships and limited liability partnerships (LLPs) as business entities (Sec. 449.44, M.C.L., *et seq.*), those entities are subject to the MBT.

CCH Practice Tip: Pass-Through Entities Exempt

Effective January 1, 2012, the corporate income tax is generally imposed only on C corporations. Pass-through entities are not required to file and pay the tax (see ¶1510).

Michigan does not incorporate the federal income tax provisions that authorize the election of large partnership status.

¶853 S Corporations

Law: Secs. 206.699, 208.1512, M.C.L. (CCH MICHIGAN TAX REPORTS, ¶10-215)

Comparable Federal: Secs. 1361—1379. (U.S. MASTER TAX GUIDE ¶305—349)

S corporations are taxable persons under the Michigan business tax (MBT), and are generally treated in the same manner as other corporations.

CCH Practice Tip: Pass-Through Entities Exempt

Effective January 1, 2012, the corporate income tax is generally imposed only on C corporations. Pass-through entities are not required to file and pay the tax (see ¶1510).

• *Q-Subs*

Because federal law treats a QSub's assets, liabilities, and items of income, deduction, and credit as those of the parent S corporation, the parent or subsidiary has nexus with Michigan for personal income tax purposes by virtue of the property and activities of either. (*Revenue Administrative Bulletin 2000-5*, Department of Treasury, CCH MICHIGAN TAX REPORTS, ¶319-299)

CCH Advisory: Federally Disregarded Entities Required to File MBT Returns

Retroactive and effective for taxes levied on or after January 1, 2008, a person that is a disregarded entity for federal income tax purposes is classified as a disregarded entity for the MBT. A person that is a disregarded entity for federal income tax that before 2012 in an originally filed return was treated as a person separate from its owner or before December 1, 2011 in an amended return was treated as a person separate from its owner for a tax year that begins after 2007 is not required to file an amended return with the owner as a disregarded entity. In addition, a person that is a disregarded entity for federal income tax that before 2012 in an originally filed return was treated as a person separate from its owner or before December 1, 2011 in an amended return was treated as a person separate from its owner for the first tax year that begins after 2009 may be treated as a person separate from its owner under the MBT for its tax year that begins after 2010 and ends before 2012. (Sec. 208.1512, M.C.L.)

The Michigan Department of Treasury has issued a notice explaining the MBT filing requirements for federally disregarded entities. In general, an entity that is disregarded for federal income tax purposes is classified as a disregarded entity for MBT purposes. There are two exceptions:

— An entity disregarded for federal income tax purposes that filed separate from its owner for the 2008, 2009, and 2010 tax years in original returns filed before 2012 or in amended returns filed before December 1, 2011, is not required to amend those returns.

— An entity disregarded for federal income tax purposes that filed separate from its owner for the 2010 MBT tax year in an original return filed before 2012 or in an amended return filed before December 1, 2011, may file separate from its owner for the 2011 tax year.

Therefore, if a federally disregarded entity did not file as a separate entity, then it may not file as a separate entity for the 2008—2011 MBT tax years. However, if the federally disregarded entity did file as a separate entity for the 2008—2010 MBT tax years, it may file an amended MBT return as a disregarded entity if the return is within the statute of limitations.

If a disregarded entity is eligible to file as a separate entity for the 2011 MBT tax year and does file separately, it must file all required forms and schedules. The disregarded entity must select the organization type under which the parent filed its tax return. Both the disregarded entity and the parent must prepare corresponding pro forma federal returns and attach them to the MBT returns. (*Notice to Taxpayers Regarding Federally Disregarded Entities and the Michigan Business Tax,* Michigan Department of Treasury, January 26, 2012)

Under the MBT, a taxpayer includes a unitary group. A unitary group has nexus with Michigan if any of its members have nexus with Michigan (see ¶1493).

A person that is a disregarded entity for federal income tax purposes is classified as a disregarded entity for the corporate income tax. (Sec. 206.699, M.C.L.)

¶854 Tax Treatment of Pass-Through Entities

Law: (CCH MICHIGAN TAX REPORTS, ¶10-215, 10-220, 10-240, 10-525)

Comparable Federal: Secs. 701—761, 1361—1379. (U.S. MASTER TAX GUIDE ¶305—349, 401—481)

Generally, S corporations, partnerships, and limited liability companies (LLCs) are taxed in the same manner as corporations for purposes of Michigan business tax (MBT). Deviations from the general rules for corporations are discussed below.

CCH Practice Tip: Pass-Through Entities Exempt

Effective January 1, 2012, the corporate income tax is generally imposed only on C corporations. Pass-through entities are not required to file and pay the tax (see ¶1510).

• *Allocation and apportionment*

S corporations: The property, payroll, and sales of the combined entities are used to determine the apportionment factors for personal income tax of an S corporation and its QSub. Special apportionment formulas are used for certain types of businesses. The QSub treatment applies to an S corporation and its QSub even when they are not subject to the same tax base or apportionment calculations. However, the special tax base and apportionment provisions that apply to one, but not all, must be applied on a separate entity basis. (*Revenue Administrative Bulletin 2000-5,* Department of Treasury, CCH MICHIGAN TAX REPORTS, ¶319-299)

For MBT apportionment purposes, the sales of all members of a unitary group are included in both the numerator and the denominator of the single sales factor (see ¶1472).

• *Accounting periods and methods*

The Michigan Business Tax Annual Return must be filed for the same period as the federal income tax return. (Form 4600, Instruction Booklet for Standard Taxpayers) Presumably, the same accounting method used for federal purposes must also be used for Michigan MBT purposes because the starting point for computing the MBT base is federal taxable income.

• *Taxable income computation*

Business income subject to the MBT is that part of federal taxable income derived from business activity. For a partnership or S corporation, business income includes payments and items of income and expense that are attributable to the business activity of the partnership or S corporation and separately reported to the partners or shareholders. This would include both capital gain and cancellation of debt (COD) income that are excluded from the calculation of partnership taxable income on the federal 1065 form, and separately reported to the partners or shareholders on the K-1 forms. (*Frequently Asked Questions, B.21,* Michigan Department of Treasury) For a discussion of the taxable income computation for MBT purposes, see ¶1461 *et seq.*

Partnerships:

IRC Sec. 199 Domestic production activities deduction.—Pass-through entities are not entitled to take the IRC Sec. 199 deduction, although the partners, members, or shareholders may claim the deduction on the Michigan personal income tax returns. The domestic production activities deduction, by its express terms, does not apply to the entity level and is not included in the federal taxable income of the entity. Thus, pass-through entities must report the information needed to calculate the IRC Sec. 199 deduction to their partners, members, or shareholders so that they may claim the deduction on personal income tax returns. (*Internal Policy Directive 2006-7,* Michigan Department of Treasury, September 29, 2006, CCH MICHIGAN TAX REPORTS, ¶380-026) The IRC Sec. 199 deduction is not allowed for the MBT. (*Frequently Asked Questions, B.44,* Michigan Department of Treasury)

• *Credits*

Because they are subject to the MBT to the same extent as corporations, pass-through entities generally may claim the credits against the MBT allowed to C corporations (see Ch. 14.75).

A partnership or S corporation may be disqualified from claiming the small business credit if a partner or shareholder receives more than a specified level of distributive shares of adjusted business income, see ¶1484.

¶855 Treatment of Owners' Income

Law: Secs. 206.110, M.C.L.; Reg. 206.12, Mich. Adm. Code. (CCH MICHIGAN TAX REPORTS, ¶15-505, 16-505)

Comparable Federal: Secs. 701-761, 1366, 1367. (U.S. MASTER TAX GUIDE ¶309—322, 401—488)

Because Michigan taxable income for individuals, estates, and trusts is based on federal adjusted gross income, with adjustments, if income from an S corporation is included in the federal tax base, it will also be included in the Michigan tax base. Income distributed from S corporations has been classified as business income subject to apportionment (*Chocola v. Department of Treasury* (1985, SCt) 369 NW2d 843; CCH MICHIGAN TAX REPORTS, ¶201-178, overruling *Wilson v. Department of Treasury*, CCH MICHIGAN TAX REPORTS, ¶200-968).

CCH Practice Tip: Pass-Through Entities Exempt

Effective January 1, 2012, the corporate income tax is generally imposed only on C corporations. Pass-through entities are not required to file and pay the tax (see ¶1510).

CCH Advisory: Qualified Subchapter S Subsidiaries

The election of qualified subchapter S subsidiary (QSub) status for federal income tax purposes is effective on the Michigan personal income tax return of both resident and nonresident individual shareholders. Because Michigan's personal income tax is based on federal adjusted gross income, which reflects the QSub election, the state personal income tax return must conform to the QSub election reported on the federal return. Taxpayers choosing to use the Internal Revenue Code in effect in 1996, which did not include the QSub election, that have an S corporation or subsidiary with business activity outside Michigan must separately account for the S corporation and subsidiary and determine apportionment factors based on the separate entities (*Revenue Administrative Bulletin 2000-5*, Michigan Department of Treasury, CCH MICHIGAN TAX REPORTS, ¶319-299).

• *Nexus*

Michigan business tax.—If a flow through entity has business income tax nexus with Michigan for MBT, the individual partners or shareholders will be subject to apportionment under the Income Tax Act (ITA) on their distributive or pro-rata share of the flow through entity's (partnership or S corporation) income. If a flow through entity has nexus with Michigan under the MBT nexus standards, but the business activity of the flow through entity is afforded immunity under Public Law (P.L.) 86-272, the individual partners or shareholders will not be subject to apportionment on their share of profits from the flow through entity. Conversely, if a Michigan flow through entity has nexus with another state or states as described above, and the activity of the flow through entity is not protected under PL 86-272, the individual partners or shareholders, whether residents or nonresidents of Michigan, would be able to apportion income from the flow through entity to other states under the apportionment provisions of the ITA. Michigan's Income Tax Act does not apply to gross receipts. (*Frequently Asked Questions, N.3,* Michigan Department of Treasury)

If the only activity a corporate partner has in Michigan is an ownership interest in a Michigan partnership, it would not have nexus in this state under either the physical presence or actively solicits standards because it would have no property or employees in Michigan and does not actively solicit sales in Michigan. (*Frequently Asked Questions, B.11,* Michigan Department of Treasury)

• *Taxable income computation*

Michigan business tax.—Both residents and nonresidents of Michigan are subject to Michigan income tax on their share of income from partnerships and S corporations to the extent the income is attributable to Michigan under the Michigan Income Tax Act allocation and apportionment provisions and included in adjusted gross income on the partner or shareholder's federal income tax return. The imposition of the Michigan business income tax on a flow through entity does not affect the imposition of the Michigan personal income tax on the individual partners or shareholders of the flow through entity. (*Frequently Asked Questions, B.3,* Michigan Department of Treasury)

Pass-through entity owners are only subject to the MBT on business income from the entity. Gains from the sale of personal assets, and other income received by an individual not specifically derived from a trade or business are not included in the MBT tax base. (*Frequently Asked Questions, B.9,* Michigan Department of Treasury)

For an individual, the sale of an ownership interest in a corporation, partnership, or limited liability company will generally not constitute business income or gross receipts to that individual so long as such investment does not constitute the trade or business of the individual. This is true even if the shareholder, partner, or member is an active rather than passive investor. (*Frequently Asked Questions, B.15,* Michigan Department of Treasury)

Partnerships: As discussed in more detail at ¶1464d, a deduction for self-employment income is available to partners for their distributive share of the partnership income. (Sec. 208.1201(2)(h), M.C.L.) The distributive share of a partnership to a partner that is an individual does not constitute business income or gross receipts to that individual. This deduction is not available to S corporation shareholders. (*Frequently Asked Questions, B.15,* Michigan Department of Treasury)

Limited liability companies: Single member LLCs are treated as sole proprietorships. Therefore, the LLC owner is considered the MBT taxpayer. (*Frequently Asked Questions, B.17,* Michigan Department of Treasury)

• *Apportionment*

For MBT apportionment purposes, the sales of all members of a unitary group are included in both the numerator and the denominator of the single sales factor (see ¶1472). If the entity and the owner(s) are not unitary, then the apportionment factors are determined separately.

• *Credits*

Shareholders of S corporations may be eligible for the credit for income taxes paid to other states and for the farmland credit (see ¶307).

A shareholder in an S corporation is not entitled to make claim credits on his individual income tax return: for city income taxes (¶302), homestead property taxes paid (¶303), or for contributions to colleges or libraries (¶306).

¶856 Nonresident Owners

Law: Sec. 206.110(2), 206.315, M.C.L. (CCH MICHIGAN TAX REPORTS, ¶89-104)

Nonresidents who receive distributions from Michigan S corporations are required to file Michigan returns and pay tax on the distributive income. The statute of limitations is suspended during any period for which a return has not been filed. (Sec. 206.110(2), M.C.L.; *Revenue Administrative Bulletin 1988-16,* Department of Treasury, CCH MICHIGAN TAX REPORTS, ¶319-045)

• *Composite nonresident return*

Nonresident members having income in Michigan from one or more flow-through entities may elect to be included in the composite income tax return of the entity. (Sec. 206.315(2)) A flow-through entity is permitted to file a composite return on behalf of electing nonresident members and report and pay tax due based on such members' shares of income available for distribution from the flow-through entity for doing business in, or deriving income from, Michigan sources. (Sec. 206.315(3), M.C.L.)

A nonresident member who is included in a composite return and also files an individual income tax return for the same period may claim a credit against the tax imposed on their individual return for the amount paid on their behalf by the flow-through entity on the composite return. (Sec. 206.315(4), M.C.L.) Composite returns are due on or before April 15 each year, and each such return must report information required by the Department for the immediately preceding calendar year. (Sec. 206.315(5), M.C.L.)

A Revenue Administrative Bulletin describes in detail the procedures required for composite filing by flow-throughs, including when such returns are authorized, due dates, eligible members, and other requirements. (*Revenue Administrative Bulletin 2004-1*, Michigan Department of Treasury, CCH MICHIGAN TAX REPORTS, ¶319-336)

• *Estimated tax payments*

Because pass-through entities, referred to by Michigan as "flow-through" entities, are required to withhold tax on distributions to nonresident owners (see ¶857), there are no specific estimated tax payment requirements for nonresident owners.

¶857 Withholding

Law: Secs. 206.12, 206.351, 206.703, M.C.L. (CCH MICHIGAN TAX REPORTS, ¶16-655)

All flow-through entities are required to withhold Michigan income tax at the statutory rate from taxable income distributed to nonresident members of the entity, after deducting personal and dependency exemptions. If a flow-through entity is a nonresident member of a separate flow-through entity in Michigan, the Michigan flow-through entity is required to withhold taxes as described above on behalf of the nonresident flow-through entity member and all of its individual members. Effective January 1, 2012, every flow-through entity with business activity in Michigan that has more than $200,000 in business income after apportionment is required to withhold on the share of business income for each member that is a corporation. To calculate the $200,000 withholding threshold for flow-through entities, taxpayers should apportion business income to Michigan with the flow-through entity's sales factor. The sales factor's numerator is total sales in Michigan during the tax year, and the sales factor's denominator is total sales everywhere during the tax year. (Sec. 206.351(2), 206.703, M.C.L.)

Michigan personal income tax withholding by flow-through entities accrues to Michigan on April 15, July 15, October 15, and January 15 for calendar year taxpayers. Fiscal year taxpayers should use corresponding dates. Withholding for each period should be equal to 25% of the total withholding calculated on the distributive share that is reasonably expected to accrue during the tax year. However, publicly traded partnerships are not subject to withholding requirements. (Sec. 206.703, M.C.L.; *Withholding for Flow-Through Entities*, Michigan Department of Treasury)

Practice Note: Separate Registration Required

Flow-through entities must register with the Michigan Department of Treasury separately for flow-through entity withholding tax and employee withholding tax. (*Revenue Administrative Bulletin 2010-8*, Michigan Department of Treasury, CCH MICHIGAN TAX REPORTS, ¶401-540)

Income available for distribution of flow-through entities with business activities will be exempt from the withholding requirements if any of the following circumstances are present:

— the income available for distribution consists entirely of income exempt from Michigan personal income tax (i.e., income from U.S. obligations or income from oil and gas production);

— the member is a resident individual, estate, or trust, or an entity exempt from income tax (i.e., a nonprofit organization or C corporation); or

— the aggregate income available for distribution of all nonresident members subject to withholding is less than $1,000 per quarter.

Finally, a flow-through entity's compliance with the withholding requirements does not relieve its nonresident members from the obligation to file a Michigan personal income tax return. Such members must file a return, and claim the amount withheld from the flow-through as a credit against tax due on the return. Flow-through entity withholding tax is computed and credited on a calendar year basis, even when the flow-through entity files a federal return and reports income to members on a fiscal year basis. Thus, income and payments may not match and may be on different annual year composite returns. (*Revenue Administrative Bulletin 2010-7*, Michigan Department of Treasury, CCH MICHIGAN TAX REPORTS, ¶401-539; *Revenue Administrative Bulletin 2010-8*, Michigan Department of Treasury, CCH MICHIGAN TAX REPORTS, ¶401-540)

Effective June 28, 2012, flow-through entities are not required to withhold for a member that voluntarily elects to file a return and pay the tax. (Sec. 206.703(18), M.C.L.)

Effective September 30, 2014, a flow-through entity is not required to comply with the income tax withholding requirements to the extent that the withholding would violate:

— distribution restrictions for housing assistance payment programs;

— rural housing service return on investment restrictions; or

— articles of incorporation or other documents of organization adopted pursuant to the state Housing Development Authority Act.

(Sec. 206.703(19), M.C.L.)

Practice Note: No Withholding Required

Federally disregarded entities are not required to withhold under the corporate income tax. (Michigan Department of Treasury, FAQs Filing Requirements #20)

A "flow-through entity" includes S corporations, partnerships, limited partnerships (LPs), limited liability partnerships (LLPs), and limited liability companies (LLCs), but not publicly traded partnerships. (Sec. 206.12(1), M.C.L.) "Member of a flow-through entity" means a shareholder in an S corporation, a partner in a partnership, LP, or LLP, or a member of an LLC. (Sec. 206.12(4), M.C.L.) Finally, a "nonresident member" is defined to include any of the following members of a flow-through entity:

— individuals not domiciled in Michigan;

— a nonresident estate or trust; or

— a flow-through entity with a nonresident member. (Sec. 206.12(5), M.C.L.)

A flow-through entity that has one or more members that are other flow-through entities is a tiered entity. Only the flow-through entity with business activity in Michigan is liable for the withholding tax. A flow-through entity that includes a member that is another flow-through entity with nonresident individual owners must withhold Michigan income tax from the share of income available for distribution of the member flow-through entity without regard to any allowances for personal dependency exemptions of the member flow-through entity's individual owners. Since the taxable share of income available for distribution is computed by reference to the combined income of the disregarded entity and its owner, and reported by the owner to its members on federal Form K-1, an owner that is another flow-through entity, such as a partnership or S corporation, is responsible for any flow-through entity reporting and payment requirements that may arise through the activity of the QSUB or single-member LLC. (*Revenue Administrative Bulletin 2010-7*, Michigan Department of Treasury, CCH MICHIGAN TAX REPORTS, ¶401-539)

• *Exemption certificate*

Effective June 28, 2012, a member other than a nonresident individual (before 2013, corporation) may give a flow-through entity an exemption certificate. In this case, the flow-through entity is not required to withhold tax on the distributive share of that member's (before 2013, corporation's) business income, provided that these conditions are met:

— the exemption certificate is completed and certifies that the member (before 2013, corporation) will file required tax returns, pay the tax on the distributive share of business income received from any flow-through entity in which the member (before 2013, corporation is a member or in which the corporation) has an ownership or beneficial interest, and submit to Michigan's taxing jurisdiction;

— the corporation may (before 2013, must) file the exemption certificate with the Department of Treasury and include a copy to the flow-through entity;

— the flow-through entity may (before 2013, must) attach a copy of the exemption certificate to its annual reconciliation return; and

— the member (before 2013, corporation) and the flow-through entity must keep a copy of the exemption certificate.

The department may revoke the election to use an exemption certificate if the member (before 2013, corporation) or flow-through entity is not abiding by the certificate's terms. (Sec. 206.703(16), (17), M.C.L.) To claim the exemption, taxpayers should complete Form 4912, Certificate of Exemption for Flow-Through Withholding Payments. The member and the flow-through entity must each keep a copy of the exemption certificate, but not file it with the department. (*Notice to Taxpayers Regarding Available Opt-Out From Flow-Through Withholding*, Michigan Department of Treasury, June 2013)

¶858 Returns

Law: (CCH MICHIGAN TAX REPORTS, ¶89-102)

Comparable Federal: Secs. 6063, 6072(b) 6081. (U.S. MASTER TAX GUIDE ¶301, 406)

The same provisions that apply to general corporations, which relate to due dates, forms required to be filed, extension requests, consolidated returns, and amended returns apply equally to returns filed by flow-through entities. (See Chapter 14.9, Returns and Payments, for Michigan business tax returns)

¶859 Penalties

Law: (CCH MICHIGAN TAX REPORTS, ¶89-206, 89-208)

Comparable Federal: Sec. 6721. (U.S. MASTER TAX GUIDE ¶2814, 2816)

For details about penalties and interest, see ¶2404.

PART III

SINGLE BUSINESS TAX

CHAPTER 9

HISTORICAL OVERVIEW

¶901 Historical Overview

Law: Former Secs. 208.1—208.145, M.C.L.

From 1976 through 2007, the Michigan Single Business Tax (SBT) was levied and imposed on the privilege of doing business in the state (it was not imposed upon income). The SBT was characterized as a modified consumption-type value-added tax. It was imposed at the rate of 1.9%. (Former Sec. 208.31, M.C.L.; *Mobile Oil v. Department of Treasury*, Michigan Supreme Court, (373 NW2d 730) No. 70388, Sept. 6, 1985, CCH MICHIGAN TAX REPORTS, ¶201-186)

• *Nexus*

In *Gillette v. Department of Treasury*, the state appellate court held that, because the SBT was not a tax on net income, P.L. 86-272 did not apply. (Michigan Court of Appeals, (198 Mich. App. 303) No. 118660, March 1, 1993, CCH MICHIGAN TAX REPORTS, ¶400-243) Accordingly, the Department issued Revenue Administrative Bulletin 1998-1 (CCH MICHIGAN TAX REPORTS, ¶319-375) describing activities that would subject out-of-state persons, including corporations, to the SBT. Physical presence was required, but could be supplied by employees or agents visiting Michigan to perform solicitation-type activities.

• *Adjustments*

The SBT's tax base was business income, even if zero or negative, subject to various adjustments. Required additions included:

— Interest income and dividends derived from state obligations (other than Michigan), in the same amount that was excluded from federal taxable income;

— Taxes on or measured by net income and the SBT;

— Carryback or carryover of a net operating loss;

— Carryback or carryover of a capital loss;

— Deduction for depreciation, amortization, or immediate or accelerated write-off related to the cost of tangible assets;

— Dividends paid or accrued;

— Deduction or exclusion by a taxpayer due to classification as a domestic international sales corporation;

— Interest;

— Royalties (with certain exceptions);

— Deduction for rent attributable to a lease back under former IRC Sec. 168(f)(8);

— Compensation;

— Capital gain related to business activity of individuals.

(Former Sec. 208.9, M.C.L.)

Certain subtractions from the tax base were allowed, including subtractions for:

— Dividends received;

— Interest;

— Certain royalties;

— Rent attributable to a lease back under former IRC Sec. 168(f)(8);

— Capital loss;

— Small business innovation research grants and small business technology transfer programs.

(Former Sec. 208.9, M.C.L.) In lieu of the federal net operating loss, a deduction for any available business loss was allowed. (Former Sec. 208.23b, M.C.L.) Before 2000, a capital acquisition deduction (CAD) was permitted. (Former Sec. 208.23, M.C.L.)

Taxpayers could choose an alternate method to compute the SBT, which subjected 50% of the adjusted gross receipts (instead of the adjusted tax base) to the tax rate. (See Form C-8044, Single Business Tax Simplified Return)

Special provisions applied to financial organizations and insurance companies. (Former Secs. 208.21, 208.22a, M.C.L.)

• *Apportionment*

For the 2007 tax year, the tax base was apportioned to Michigan using a three-factor formula: 3.75% for property, 3.75% for payroll, and 92.5% for sales. (Former Sec. 208.45a, M.C.L.) Taxpayers who conducted business entirely within Michigan allocated the whole tax base to Michigan. (Former Sec. 208.40, M.C.L.)

Practitioner Comment: Election of an Equally Weighted, Three-Factor Apportionment Formula Under the Multistate Tax Compact Not Available in Michigan Under the SBT Act

The Multistate Tax Compact election to use an equally weighted, three-factor formula consisting of property, payroll, and sales factors is not available to taxpayers under the SBT Act. In *Emco Enterprises, Inc. v. Department of Treasury* (April 21, 2015) No. 12-000152-MT, the Michigan Court of Claims held that an SBT taxpayer had no authority to depart from the equally weighted, three-factor apportionment formula under the former SBT Act for the 2005-2007 tax years. The court held that to the extent the SBTA conflicted with the election and apportionment provisions of the Compact the Legislature repealed the earlier enacted statute (the Compact) by implication. The decision has been appealed and is currently pending in the Michigan Court of Appeals. The SBT is not covered under the Michigan Legislature's retroactively repeal of the compact made through Public Act 282. Taxpayers with open SBT years continue to pursue protective claims for refunds based on the MTC election.

Wayne D. Roberts, Varnum, LLP and Marjorie B. Gell, Western Michigan University Cooley Law School

---

• *Credits*

Various credits were available against the SBT, including the small business credit, credit for business activity in an Enterprise Zone, brownfield properties credit, the Renaissance Zone credit, credit for the rehabilitation of historic resources, the investment tax credit, among others. (Former Secs. 208.35a, 208.35e, 208.36, 208.37a, 208.39b, 208.39c, M.C.L.)

PART III.5

MICHIGAN BUSINESS TAX

CHAPTER 14.5

RATES, TAXABLE AND EXEMPT ENTITIES

¶ 1451 Overview of Michigan Business Tax

CCH Caution: Corporate Income Tax Enacted

Only for the first tax year ending after 2011, taxpayers with certificated credits may elect to pay the Michigan business tax. All other taxpayers are required to file and pay the corporate income tax (see ¶ 1510). (Sec. 206.680, M.C.L.)

In 2007, the 94th Michigan Legislature enacted the Michigan Business Tax (MBT) Act, 2007 Public Act 36. The MBT replaces the Michigan Single Business Tax (SBT), effective January 1, 2008, but only applies to business activities occurring after 2007. Taxpayers filing 2007 tax returns computed their taxes based on the SBT, but they were required to compute and report all 2008 estimated tax installment payments made in 2007 based on the MBT.

Practice Note: Registration

Taxpayers who were registered for the SBT are automatically registered for the MBT. (*Frequently Asked Questions*, Michigan Department of Treasury, November 28, 2007)

The general MBT is comprised of two separate taxes: a tax on business income (¶ 1462) and a tax on modified gross receipts (¶ 1465). Financial institutions and insurance companies are exempt from these taxes but are subject to special taxes based on net capital (¶ 1455) or gross direct premiums (¶ 1466), respectively.

Aside from the differences in the tax base and the tax credit, key differences between the MBT and the SBT include:

—the use of a single sales factor apportionment formula (¶ 1472);

—the treatment of a unitary group as a taxable entity and the requirement that such entities file a combined return (¶ 1453, ¶ 1493);

—although the MBT retains a $350,000 filing threshold for purposes of the tax on business income, it also contains a credit that phases in tax liability for businesses with gross receipts of less than $700,000 (¶ 1454 and ¶ 1481);

—exemptions based on federal exemptions are limited to those organizations exempt under IRC Sec. 501(a) (¶ 1454);

—the MBT retains the alternative rate for small businesses, but reduces the rate from 2.0% to 1.8%, and increases the limits on owner income, gross receipts, and business income (¶1452 and ¶1484);

—while retaining many of the SBT credits, including the current economic development credits, such as those related to the Michigan Economic Growth Authority (¶1489), brownfield redevelopment (¶1489c), and historic preservation (¶1489b), the MBT provides new credits such as a compensation credit (¶1476), research and development credits (¶1478 and ¶1478a), and a revised investment credit (¶1477);

—the MBT narrows the definition of "gross receipts" by excluding amounts reflecting the principal of various financial transactions for brokers and dealers, thereby reducing their liability under the MBT Act.

The tax base for the tax on business income and modified gross receipts is discussed in Ch. 14.6. Chapter 14.7 addresses apportionment and the various credits against the MBT are discussed in Chapter 14.75. Return and payment requirements are discussed at Ch. 14.9.

¶1452 Tax Rates

Law: Secs. 208.1201, 208.1203, 208.1281, 208.1417 (CCH MICHIGAN TAX REPORTS, ¶10-380).

CCH Caution: Corporate Income Tax Enacted

Only for the first tax year ending after 2011, taxpayers with certificated credits may elect to pay the Michigan business tax. All other taxpayers are required to file and pay the corporate income tax (see ¶1510). (Sec. 206.680, M.C.L.)

Applicable to all business activity occurring after December 31, 2007, the general Michigan Business Tax (MBT) contains an income tax portion and a modified gross receipts tax portion. The business income tax is imposed at a rate of 4.95%. (Sec. 208.1201(1), M.C.L.) The modified gross receipts tax is imposed at a rate of 0.8%. (Sec. 208.1203(1), M.C.L.)

A taxpayer that elects to claim the small business tax credit (¶1484) and that is not required to reduce the credit as a result of excess compensation paid to shareholders, members, partners, or self-employed individuals, may compute the tax utilizing an alternative tax rate of 1.8%. (Sec. 208.1417(7), M.C.L.)

Surcharge.—There is an annual surcharge based on a percentage of the taxpayer's MBT liability before credits. The surcharge is inapplicable to insurance companies subject to the direct premiums tax (¶1456) and to financial institutions that are authorized to exercise only trust powers (¶1455). For all other taxpayers other than financial institutions (see ¶1455), the surcharge is 21.99%. The surcharge is capped at $6 million per taxpayer per year. (Sec. 208.1281, M.C.L.)

The surcharge is scheduled to sunset after 2016 if the Michigan personal income growth exceeds 0% in either calendar 2014, 2015, or 2016. (Sec. 208.1281(2), M.C.L.)

¶1453 Entities Subject To Tax

Law: Secs. 208.1105, 208.1113, 208.1115, 108.1200, 208.1201, 208.1203, M.C.L. (CCH MICHIGAN TAX REPORTS, ¶10-075).

CCH Caution: Corporate Income Tax Enacted

Only for the first tax year ending after 2011, taxpayers with certificated credits may elect to pay the Michigan business tax. All other taxpayers are required to file and pay the corporate income tax (see ¶1510). (Sec. 206.680, M.C.L.)

The Michigan Business Tax (MBT) is imposed against individual persons as well as a unitary group that meet the appropriate nexus standard discussed below. (Sec. 208.1115(5), M.C.L.) For MBT purposes, a person is defined as an individual, firm, bank, financial institution, insurance company, limited partnership, limited liability partnership, copartnership, partnership, joint venture, association, corporation, subchapter S corporation, limited liability company, receiver, estate, trust, or any other group or combination of groups acting as a unit. Although technically subject to the MBT, financial institutions and insurance companies are exempt from the general MBT based on business income and modified gross receipts, but are subject to an MBT based on net capital and direct gross premiums respectively, see ¶1455 and ¶1456.

• *Nexus*

The MBT is imposed on every taxpayer with substantial Michigan nexus. Substantial nexus occurs if: (1) the taxpayer has physical presence in Michigan for more than one day; or (2) the taxpayer actively solicits sales in Michigan and has $350,000 or more of gross receipts attributable to state sources. Physical presence may be established by independent contractors. However, physical presence does not include professional services, provided that those services are not significantly associated with the taxpayer's ability to establish and maintain a market in Michigan. (Sec. 208.1200(1), M.C.L.; Sec. 208.1200(3), M.C.L.)

The business income tax portion of the MBT is imposed on every taxpayer with business activity in the state. (Sec. 208.1201(1), M.C.L.) "Business activity" is defined broadly to include the transfer of title to any property (including intangible property), or the performance of services, or a combination of both. It applies to an activity that is conducted with the object of gain, benefit, or advantage to the taxpayer, whether in intrastate, interstate, or foreign commerce. However, it does not include the services performed by an employee to his or her employer or services as a director of a corporation. (Sec. 208.1105(1), M.C.L.) P.L. 86-272 may protect taxpayers from the business income tax portion of the MBT, but not the modified gross receipts tax portion. The modified gross receipts tax portion of the MBT is imposed on every taxpayer with substantial nexus. (Sec. 208.1203(1), M.C.L.) Unlike the former Michigan Single Business Tax, there is no "casual transaction" exemption (see ¶904).

CCH Comment: Nexus Guidelines Issued

The Michigan Department of Treasury has issued guidance, effective retroactively to January 1, 2008, regarding the nexus standards under the Michigan Business Tax (MBT) described above. Once nexus is established, nexus lasts for the entire tax year. Furthermore, if one member of a unitary business group has nexus with Michigan, all group members must be included to calculate the tax bases and apportionment formulas.

A taxpayer has physical presence in Michigan if it conducts business activities in Michigan, owns, rents, or leases tangible personal or real property, or delivers goods to Michigan in its own (or leased) vehicles. Nexus may be created, depending on the facts and circumstances, with the following activities:

— meeting with suppliers or government officials;

— attending occasional meetings;

— holding hiring events;

— advertising;

— renting to or from a customer list; and

— attending trade shows.

Corporations incorporated in Michigan have a physical presence in the state. Also, physical presence for a portion of a day establishes physical presence for the entire day. Active solicitation is the purposeful solicitation of persons in Michigan. The quality, nature, and magnitude of the activities are examined on a facts and circumstances basis to determine if active solicitation has been established.

P.L. 86-272 protects taxpayers from the imposition of the business income tax portion of the MBT, but not the modified gross receipts tax portion. Only the solicitation to sell tangible personal property is immune. Therefore, leasing activities and activities regarding intangible property are not protected. Protection by P.L. 86-272 is determined on a tax year by tax year basis. Examples of protected and unprotected activities are provided. De minimis activities establish only a trivial connection. However, if they are conducted on a regular or systematic basis or pursuant to company policy, then the activities are not trivial. (*Revenue Administrative Bulletin 2008-4*, Michigan Department of Treasury, October 21, 2008, ¶401-392)

¶1454 Exempt Entities and Activities

Law: Secs. 208.1117, 208.1207, M.C.L. (CCH MICHIGAN TAX REPORTS, ¶10-245).

CCH Caution: Corporate Income Tax Enacted

Only for the first tax year ending after 2011, taxpayers with certificated credits may elect to pay the Michigan business tax. All other taxpayers are required to file and pay the corporate income tax (see ¶1510). (Sec. 206.680, M.C.L.)

Exempt organizations are generally subject to the Michigan Business Tax (MBT) only on their unrelated business income. Financial institutions and insurance companies are exempt from the general MBT tax based on business income and gross receipts, but are subject to an MBT based on net capital and direct gross premiums, see ¶1455 and ¶1456.

The United States, Michigan, other states, and the agencies, political subdivisions, and enterprises of each of these governmental entities, are exempt from the MBT. (Sec. 208.1207(1)(a), (b), M.C.L.)

Generally, most organizations that are exempt from the federal income tax under IRC Sec. 501(c) and (d), which encompasses charitable, educational, and religious organizations, are exempt from the MBT, except on the organizations' unrelated taxable business income. (Sec. 208.1117(8), M.C.L.; Sec. 208.1207(1)(b), M.C.L.; IRC Sec. 512(a)) However, the following federally-exempt organizations are subject to the MBT:

— local benevolent life insurance associations, mutual ditch or irrigation companies, and mutual or cooperative telephone companies included under IRC Sec. 501(c)(12);

— farmers' cooperative corporations included in IRC Sec. 501(c)(16) that are organized to finance ordinary crop operations; or

— organizations exempt under IRC Sec. 501(c)(4) *i.e.*, certain civic leagues, nonprofit organizations, and local associations of employees] that would be exempt from taxation under IRC Sec. 501(c)(12) but for their failure to meet the requirement that 85% or more of their income consist of amounts collected from members.

(Sec. 208.1207(1)(b), M.C.L.)

The exemption is available even if the taxpayer is organized as a pass-through entity, provided that the taxpayer's partners or members are exempt from federal income tax. (Sec. 208.1207(1)(b), M.C.L.)

Also exempt are the following:

—nonprofit cooperative housing corporations but only as relates to the housing services provided to its stockholders and members (Sec. 208.1207(1)(c), M.C.L.);

—commercial farmers to the extent of their tax base from the production of agricultural goods (Sec. 208.1207(1)(d), M.C.L.);

—farmer's cooperative activities that meet specified criteria and activities under the Agricultural Commodities Marketing Act (Sec. 208.1207(1)(e) and (2), (f) M.C.L.);

—attorney-in-fact services provided to a reciprocal insurer (Sec. 208.12071(g));

—multiple employer welfare arrangements that provide dental benefits only and that have a certificate of authority under the Michigan Insurance Code.

CCH Comment: Exemptions Narrower Than SBT Exemptions

Unlike the SBT exemptions (see ¶902), which exempt all organizations exempt under the Internal Revenue Code, the MBT tax exemptions are limited to those organizations exempt under IRC Sec. 501(a), which generally applies to charitable, educational, and religious organizations, plus those organizations specifically listed, such as the commercial farming activities, farmer's cooperatives, and nonprofit housing corporations.

¶1455 Financial Institutions

Law: Secs. 208.1200, 208.1261, 208.1263, 208.1265, 208.1267, 208.1281, 208.1403, 208.1431, 208.1437, M.C.L. (CCH MICHIGAN TAX REPORTS, ¶10-340).

CCH Caution: Corporate Income Tax Enacted

Only for the first tax year ending after 2011, taxpayers with certificated credits may elect to pay the Michigan business tax. All other taxpayers are required to file and pay the corporate income tax (see ¶1510). (Sec. 206.680, M.C.L.)

A Michigan franchise tax is levied on the net capital of financial institutions with Michigan nexus. The franchise tax is in lieu of the Michigan business tax imposed on general business corporations and other entities' business income or gross receipts. (Sec. 208.1263, M.C.L.) Business activities undertaken by financial institutions prior to 2008 were subject to the Single Business Tax, see ¶1005.

The discussion below addresses all issues regarding the MBT tax on financial institutions, including entities subject to tax, nexus, tax base, and credits. Report filing and payment requirements are discussed in Ch. 14.9.

• *Financial institutions defined*

Financial institutions include the following:

— a bank holding company, a national bank, a state chartered bank, an office of thrift supervision chartered bank or thrift institution, a savings and loan holding company other than a diversified savings and loan holding company as defined in 12 USC 1467a(a)(F), or a federally chartered farm credit system institution;

— any person, other than a person subject to the insurance premiums tax, who is directly or indirectly owned by an entity described above and is a member of the unitary business group;

— a unitary business group of entities described above.

(Sec. 208.1261(f), M.C.L.)

• *Unitary business groups*

The Michigan Department of Treasury has provided franchise tax guidance for financial institutions on unitary filing and reporting eliminations under the Michigan Business Tax (MBT) and the Corporate Income Tax (CIT). According to Generally Accepted Accounting Principles (GAAP), equity is residual interest in assets after deducting liabilities. If the financial institution does not have positive equity capital, then the equity deficit is presented as zero on the MBT and CIT returns. (*Notice to Taxpayers Regarding Financial Institution Unitary Filing and Reporting of Eliminations for the MBT and CIT*, Department of Treasury, September 20, 2013, ¶401-822)

For a unitary business group of financial institutions, each member is required to calculate the net capital tax base in accordance with GAAP. The unitary business group member may eliminate investment in positive equity capital of the other members of the same group at the member level. Eliminations are not separately presented on a member's unitary return. Thus, the member's equity capital line may be a negative number after eliminations, even when the member has positive or zero equity capital before eliminations. (*Notice to Taxpayers Regarding Financial Institution Unitary Filing and Reporting of Eliminations for the MBT and CIT*, Department of Treasury, September 20, 2013, ¶401-822)

For the 2008-2012 MBT returns and the 2012 CIT return, the inability to separately present eliminations on the required return resulted in incorrect computations of liability for some taxpayers. Beginning October 1, 2013, all affected taxpayers should file original or amended returns for all affected tax years. The guidance provides examples regarding how to present negative numbers on the equity capital line and the net capital line of the unitary reporting schedule after eliminations and deductions. (*Notice to Taxpayers Regarding Financial Institution Unitary Filing and Reporting of Eliminations for the MBT and CIT*, Department of Treasury, September 20, 2013, ¶401-822)

Unitary business groups are covered in more detail at ¶1567, Combined Returns.

Unitary business groups are covered in more detail at ¶1493, Combined Returns.

• *Nexus*

In order to be subject to the franchise tax, the financial institution must have substantial nexus with Michigan. Substantial nexus occurs if: (1) the taxpayer has physical presence in Michigan for more than one day; or (2) the taxpayer actively solicits sales in Michigan and has $350,000 or more of gross receipts attributable to state sources. Physical presence may be established by independent contractors. However, physical presence does not include professional services, provided that those services are not significantly associated with the taxpayer's ability to establish and maintain a market in Michigan. (Sec. 208.1263(1), M.C.L.; Sec. 208.1200(1), (3), M.C.L.)

• *Rate of tax*

The Michigan franchise tax, applicable to business activities occurring after 2007, is imposed at a rate of 0.235%. (Sec. 208.1263(1), M.C.L.)

Surcharge.—There is an annual surcharge based on a percentage of the taxpayer's franchise tax liability before credits. For financial institutions taxpayers, the surcharge is:

— 27.7% for tax years ending in 2008; and

— 23.4% for tax years ending after 2008.

The surcharge does not apply to financial institutions authorized to exercise only trust powers. (Sec. 208.1281, M.C.L.)

The surcharge is scheduled to sunset after 2016 provided that the Michigan personal income growth exceeds 0% in either calendar year 2014, 2015, or 2016. (Sec. 208.1281(2), M.C.L.)

• *Basis of tax*

The franchise tax is based on a financial institution's net capital. "Net capital" is equity capital as computed in accordance with Generally Accepted Accounting Principles (GAAP). If the financial institution does not maintain its books and records in accordance with GAAP, net capital is computed in accordance with the financial institution's books and records, so long as the method fairly reflects the financial institution's net capital. Net capital does not include:

— goodwill arising from purchase accounting adjustments for transactions that occurred after July 1, 2007;

— the average daily book value of U.S. and Michigan obligations;

— up to 125% of the minimum regulatory capitalization requirements of a person subject to the insurance premiums tax.

(Sec. 208.1265(1), M.C.L.) Also, when a unitary business group of financial institutions calculates the tax, net capital does not include the investment of one member of a unitary business group in another member of that same group. (Sec. 208.1265(3), M.C.L.)

To calculate net capital, add the net capital as of the close of the current tax year and the preceding four tax years and divide the sum by five. If the institution has been in existence for less than five years, the number of years the institution has been in existence is substituted. A partial year is treated as a full year for this particular purpose. (Sec. 208.1265(2), M.C.L.)

• *Allocation and apportionment*

A financial institution that has its business activities confined solely to Michigan, allocates its entire franchise tax base to Michigan. (Sec. 208.1267(1), M.C.L.)

A financial institution whose business activities are subject to tax both within and outside Michigan apportions its franchise tax base among the various jurisdictions in which it conducts its business activities by multiplying its tax base by a gross business factor. The numerator of the gross business factor is the financial institution's total gross business in Michigan and the denominator is the financial institution's total gross business everywhere. (Sec. 208.1267(3), M.C.L.)

A financial institution whose business activities are subject to tax within and without Michigan is considered to be subject to tax in another state if:

— the taxpayer is subject to a business privilege tax, a net income tax, a franchise tax measured by net income, a franchise tax for the privilege of doing business, a corporate stock tax, or a tax similar to the Michigan business tax; or

— that state has jurisdiction to subject the taxpayer to one or more of the taxes listed above, regardless of whether that state actually does or not.

CCH Practice Tip: Special Apportionment Factor

Effective December 10, 2009, a taxpayer that restructures as a financial institution on or after January 1, 2008, and that before restructuring qualified to apportion its Michigan business tax base according to the sales factor calculated under M.C.L. 208.1307 (i.e., sales factor for spun-off corporations) may elect to continue to use that same law section to apportion its tax base.

Gross business.—Gross business is the sum of the following transactions:

— fees, commissions, or other compensation for financial services;

— net gains, not less than zero, from the sale of loans and other intangibles;

— net gains, not less than zero, from trading in stocks, bonds, or other securities;

— interest charged to customers for carrying debit balances of margin accounts;

— interest and dividends received; and

— any other gross proceeds resulting from the operation as a financial institution.

(Sec. 208.1261(g), M.C.L.)

Practice Note: Unitary Groups

Gross business of a unitary group includes the gross business in Michigan of every financial institution member in the unitary group whether or not the financial institution has nexus in Michigan. However, gross business between financial institutions included in a unitary business group must be eliminated in calculating the gross business factor. (Sec. 208.1267(4), M.C.L.)

Sourcing rules.—The statute contains many rules for determining when gross business should be assigned to Michigan. Gross business from these activities is determined as follows:

— receipts from credit card receivables (including interest, fees, and penalties) are in Michigan if the billing address of the card holder is in Michigan;

— credit card issuer's reimbursement fees are in Michigan if the billing address of the card holder is in Michigan;

— receipts from merchant discounts are in Michigan if the commercial domicile of the merchant is in Michigan;

— loan servicing fees are in Michigan for a loan secured by real property, if the property is in Michigan;

— loan servicing fees are in Michigan for a loan not secured by real property, if the borrower is located in Michigan;

— receipts from services are in Michigan if the recipient of the services receives all of the benefit of the services in Michigan or if the recipient receives only some of the benefit of the services in the state, the receipts are included in the apportionment factor numerator in proportion to the extent that the recipient receives the benefit of the services in Michigan;

— receipts from investment assets and activities and trading assets and activities, including interest and dividends are in Michigan if the financial institution's customer is in Michigan;

— interest charged to customers for carrying debit balances on margin accounts without deduction of any costs incurred in carrying the accounts is in Michigan if the customer is in Michigan;

— interest from loans secured by real property is in Michigan if the property is in Michigan;

— interest from loans not secured by real property is in Michigan if the borrower is in Michigan;

— net gains from the sale of loans secured by real property or mortgage service rights relating to real property are in Michigan if the property is in Michigan;

— net gains from the sale of loans not secured by real property or any other intangible assets are in Michigan if the depositor or borrower is in Michigan;

— receipts from the lease of real property are in Michigan if the property is in Michigan;

— receipts from the lease of tangible personal property are in Michigan if the property is located in Michigan when it is first placed in service by the lessee; and

— receipts from the lease of transportation tangible personal property are in Michigan if the property is used in Michigan or if the extent of use of the property in Michigan cannot be determined but the property has its principal base of operations in Michigan.

(Sec. 208.1269, M.C.L.)

• *Credits*

Financial institutions are eligible to claim the following credits against the Michigan franchise tax (Secs. 208.1403(2), 208.1431, 208.1433, 208.1435, 208.1437, M.C.L.):

— the compensation credit (see ¶ 1476);

— the brownfield credit (see ¶ 1489c);

— the MEGA employment credits (see ¶ 1489);

— the renaissance zone credit (see ¶ 1489a);

— the historic preservation credit (see ¶ 1489b).

¶1456 Insurance Companies

Law: Secs. 208.1107, 208.1235, 208.1237, 208.1239, 208.1243, 208.1281, 208.1403, 208.1431, 208.1437, 500-476a, M.C.L. (CCH MICHIGAN TAX REPORTS, ¶ 10-335).

CCH Caution: Corporate Income Tax Enacted

Only for the first tax year ending after 2011, taxpayers with certificated credits may elect to pay the Michigan business tax. All other taxpayers are required to file and pay the corporate income tax (see ¶ 1510). (Sec. 206.680, M.C.L.)

Applicable to all business activity occurring after 2007, insurance companies, other than insurance companies authorized as captive insurance companies or as special purpose financial captives, are subject to the lesser of (1) a tax on gross direct premiums written on property or risk located or residing in Michigan or (2) the retaliatory tax. (Sec. 208.1235(2), M.C.L.; Sec. 208.1243(1), M.C.L.) The discussion below addresses all issues regarding the MBT tax on insurance companies, including exemptions, tax base, and credits. Report filing and payment requirements are discussed in Ch. 14.9.

The retaliatory tax on foreign insurers is either the amount due as calculated under the MBT tax on gross direct premiums or the rate imposed on domestic insurers by the laws of the foreign insurer's state, whichever is greater. The State Treasurer may declare that a domestic insurer is an alien or foreign insurer if the insurer fails to comply with certain requirements regarding maintenance of records and personnel in the state. (Sec. 500.476a, M.C.L.)

The gross direct premiums tax is in lieu of all other privilege or franchise fees or taxes, except as otherwise provided in the insurance code, taxes on real and personal property, and sales and use taxes. (Sec. 208.1235(3), M.C.L.)

Practice Note: Sales and Use Taxes

Under the Single Business Tax provisions, insurance companies were only subject to property taxes and the SBT in addition to the insurance tax. However, under the MBT provisions, insurance companies will now be liable for sales and use taxes, effective January 1, 2008.

• *Exemptions*

For purposes of the gross direct premiums tax, the following items are excluded from direct premiums:

— Premiums on policies not taken;

— Returned premiums on canceled policies;

— Receipts from the sale of annuities;

— Receipts on reinsurance premiums if the tax has been paid on the original premiums; and

— The first $190 million of disability insurance premiums written in Michigan, other than credit insurance and disability income insurance premiums.

However, the disability insurance premiums exemption is reduced by $2 for each $1 by which the taxpayer's gross direct premiums from insurance carrier services exceed $280 million. (Sec. 208.1235(2), M.C.L.)

• *Tax rate*

The tax is equal to 1.25% of gross direct premiums (Sec. 208.1235(2), M.C.L.). The surcharge (see ¶1412) applicable to other taxpayers does not apply to insurance companies subject to the gross direct premiums tax. (Sec. 208.1281(4)(a), M.C.L.)

• *Apportionment*

The direct premiums tax base for insurance companies is not subject to apportionment. (*Frequently Asked Questions,* Michigan Department of Treasury, November 28, 2007)

• *Credits*

Insurance companies may claim credits against the gross direct premiums tax for the following:

Insurance company expenditures.—The credit is equal to the assessments paid by the insurance companies to the following entities:

— the Michigan Worker's Compensation Placement Facility;

— the Michigan Basic Property Insurance Association;

— the Michigan Automobile Insurance Placement Facility;

— the Property and Casualty Guaranty Association; and

— the Life and Health Guaranty Association.

(Sec. 208.1237(1), M.C.L.)

Regulatory fees.—The credit is equal to 50% of the examination fees paid by the insurance company during the tax year. (Sec. 208.1239, M.C.L.)

Worker's disability compensation payments.—A refundable credit is available equal to the amount of the workers' disability compensation payments for the tax year. The credit may be applied to the taxpayer's quarterly estimated tax liability. Excess credit must be refunded by the Department within 60 calendar days of the filing of the insurance company's annual return. (Sec. 208.241, M.C.L.)

Compensation.—Insurance companies may claim a credit against the direct gross premiums tax for compensation paid. The credit is equal to 0.296% (0.37% beginning with the 2009 tax year) of the taxpayer's Michigan compensation.

Compensation means all wages, salaries, fees, bonuses, commissions, and other payments made on behalf of or for the benefit of employees, officers, and directors. It includes any net earnings from self-employment as well as payments to a pension or profit sharing plan and payments for insurance for which employees are the beneficiaries. Compensation may be subject to or exempt from federal income tax withholding. (Sec. 208.1107(2), M.C.L.)

The credit is capped at 65% of the gross direct premiums tax liability after claiming other credits. (Sec. 208.1239(2), M.C.L.; Sec. 208.1403, M.C.L.)

Brownfield development.—See ¶1489a.

MEGA employment.—See ¶1489c.

Renaissance zone credit.—See ¶1489a.

Historic preservation credit.—See ¶1489b.

MICHIGAN BUSINESS TAX

CHAPTER 14.6

BASIS OF TAX

¶1461 Computation of Tax—In General

Law: Secs. 208.1201, M.C.L. (CCH MICHIGAN TAX REPORTS, ¶10-820).

CCH Caution: Corporate Income Tax Enacted

Only for the first tax year ending after 2011, taxpayers with certificated credits may elect to pay the Michigan business tax. All other taxpayers are required to file and pay the corporate income tax (see ¶1510). (Sec. 206.680, M.C.L.)

The Michigan Business Tax (MBT) is effective January 1, 2008, and is applicable to all business activity occurring after December 31, 2007. The starting point for computing the income tax portion of the MBT is business income before apportionment or allocation (see Ch. 14.7), subject to addition and subtraction modifications, see ¶1463 and ¶1464, respectively. A business loss deduction (¶1464) is then taken from the adjusted apportioned business income amount. (Sec. 208.1201(1) and (2), M.C.L.) The MBT also has a modified gross receipts portion (Sec. 208.1203, M.C.L.), which is covered at ¶1465. For the tax basis of the MBT portion of the tax imposed on insurance companies, see ¶1456, and for the tax imposed on financial institutions, see ¶1455.

Michigan conforms to the Internal Revenue Code (see ¶1462). Michigan also adopts the federal accounting methods and periods (see ¶1462).

¶1462 Starting Point of Business Income Computation

Law: Secs. 208.1117, 208.1201, 208.1103, 208.1503, M.C.L. (CCH MICHIGAN TAX REPORTS, ¶10-510, 10-515, 10-520).

CCH Caution: Corporate Income Tax Enacted

Only for the first tax year ending after 2011, taxpayers with certificated credits may elect to pay the Michigan business tax. All other taxpayers are required to file and pay the corporate income tax (see ¶1510). (Sec. 206.680, M.C.L.)

Applicable to all business activities occurring after 2007, the income tax portion of the Michigan Business Tax (MBT) is imposed on the business income tax base. (Sec. 208.1201(1), M.C.L.) "Business income" is defined as the portion of federal taxable income derived from business activity (see ¶1453). For a partnership or S corporation, business income includes payments and items of income and expense that are attributable to the business activity of the entity and separately reported to the partners or shareholders. For a tax-exempt person (see ¶1454), business income is limited to the portion of federal taxable income derived from unrelated business activity. (Sec. 208.1105(2), M.C.L.)

For individuals, estates, or person organized for estate or gift planning purposes, and trusts organized exclusively for estate or gift planning purposes, business income is that part of federal taxable income derived from transactions in the regular course of the person's trade or business. Business income includes the following transactions:

— all income from tangible and intangible property if the acquisition, rental, lease, management, or disposition of the property constitutes integral parts of the person's regular trade or business operations;

— gains or losses incurred in the person's trade or business from stock and securities of any foreign or domestic corporation and dividend and interest income;

— income derived from isolated sales, leases, assignments, licenses, divisions, or other infrequently occurring dispositions, transfers or transactions involving tangible, intangible, or real property if the property is or was used in the person's trade or business operation;

— income derived from the sale of an interest in a business that constitutes an integral part of the person's trade or business; and

— income derived from the lease or rental of real property.

Income that is not included in business income or gross receipts for such entities includes personal investment activity and disposition of tangible, intangible, or real property held for personal use. (Sec. 208.1105(2), M.C.L.)

Business income excludes income derived from investment activities unless the activity is in the regular course of the person's trade or business for a person that is organized exclusively to conduct investment activities and that does not conduct investment activities for any person other than the individual or a person related to that individual and for a common trust fund established under the Collective Investments Funds Act. (Sec. 208.1105(2), M.C.L.)

• *Federal conformity*

For purposes of the MBT, Michigan has adopted the provisions of the IRC of 1986 in effect on January 1, 2008, or, at the option of the taxpayer, in effect for the tax year. (Sec. 208.1111(3), M.C.L.) References to the IRC in the Michigan Business Tax Act include other federal laws relating to federal income taxes. (Sec. 208.1103, M.C.L.)

• *Accounting periods and methods*

Computation of tax for short taxable year.—In computing a business's tax for the first taxable year of less than twelve months, a taxpayer may elect either of the following methods:

(1) the tax may be computed as if the MBT were effective on the first day of the taxpayer's annual accounting period and then the amount computed is multiplied by the number of months included on the short-period return and divided by the number of months in the taxpayer's annual accounting period; or

(2) the tax may be computed by determining the business income tax base and the modified gross receipts tax base in the first taxable year in accordance with an accounting method that is satisfactory to the Department of Treasury and that reflects the actual tax bases attributable to the period.

(Sec. 208.1503, M.C.L.)

Effective January 1, 2012, the definition of "tax year" is revised to add that a taxpayer with a fiscal year ending after 2011 has two separate tax years: (1) the fractional part of the fiscal tax year before January 1, 2012, and (2) the fraction part of the fiscal tax year after December 31, 2011. Each short period return filed is considered an annual return. In addition, the method chosen to calculate the tax for a partial tax year should be the same method used for both the MBT and the corporate income tax. (Sec. 208.1117(4), M.C.L.; Sec. 208.1503(2), M.C.L.)

When a taxpayer's allocated or apportioned gross receipts are for a tax year of less than 12 months, the requisite amount is multiplied by a fraction, the numerator of which is the number of months in the tax year and denominator of which is 12. (Sec. 208.1505(2), M.C.L.)

¶1463 Additions to Business Income—Intangible Expenses

Law: Secs. 208.1201(2)(f), (CCH MICHIGAN TAX REPORTS, ¶10-620).

CCH Caution: Corporate Income Tax Enacted

Only for the first tax year ending after 2011, taxpayers with certificated credits may elect to pay the Michigan business tax. All other taxpayers are required to file and pay the corporate income tax (see ¶1510). (Sec. 206.680, M.C.L.)

Beginning with the 2008 tax year, royalties, interest, and other expenses paid to related parties for the use of an intangible asset must be added back to the Michigan business tax base. (Sec. 208.1201(2)(f), M.C.L.)

Practice Note: Unitary Business Groups

The addback is not required if the person is included in the taxpayer's unitary business group.

Exceptions.—The addback is not required if the taxpayer can show that the transaction: (1) has a nontax business purpose other than tax avoidance; (2) is conducted with arm's-length pricing, rates, and terms under IRC Secs. 482 and 1274(d); and (3) meets one of the following requirements:

— Is a pass through of another transaction between a third party and the related person with comparable rates and terms;

— Results in double taxation;

— Is unreasonable as determined by the Department of Treasury; or

— Effective October 1, 2009, the related person recipient of the transaction is organized under the laws of a foreign nation which has a comprehensive income tax treaty with the United States.

(Sec. 208.1201(2)(f), M.C.L.)

¶1463a Additions to Business Income—Interest and Dividend Income from State Bonds

Law: Secs. 208.1115(3), 208.1201(2)(a), M.C.L. (CCH MICHIGAN TAX REPORTS, ¶10-610).

CCH Caution: Corporate Income Tax Enacted

Only for the first tax year ending after 2011, taxpayers with certificated credits may elect to pay the Michigan business tax. All other taxpayers are required to file and pay the corporate income tax (see ¶1510). (Sec. 206.680, M.C.L.)

Taxpayers are required to addback interest income and dividends derived form all state obligations (except Michigan) in the same amount that was excluded from federal taxable income. Such income may be reduced by related expenses not allowed as a deduction by IRC Sec. 265 (expenses and interest relating to tax-exempt income) and IRC Sec. 291 (corporate preference items) in computing federal taxable income. (Sec. 208.1201(2)(a), M.C.L.)

"State" is defined as any state of the United States, the District of Columbia, the Commonwealth of Puerto Rico, any territory or possession of the United States, and any foreign country. Furthermore, it includes political subdivisions. (Sec. 208.1115(3), M.C.L.)

¶1463b Additions to Business Income—Losses Attributable to Pass-Through Entities

Law: Sec. 208.1201(2)(e), M.C.L. (CCH MICHIGAN TAX REPORTS, ¶10-635).

CCH Caution: Corporate Income Tax Enacted

Only for the first tax year ending after 2011, taxpayers with certificated credits may elect to pay the Michigan business tax. All other taxpayers are required to file and pay the corporate income tax (see ¶1510). (Sec. 206.680, M.C.L.)

Losses that are attributable to another entity whose business activities are either taxable under the Michigan business tax or would be taxable if the activities were carried on in Michigan must be added back to federal taxable income to the extent such losses were deducted on the federal return. (Sec. 208.1201(2)(e), M.C.L.)

¶1463c Additions to Business Income—Net Operating Loss

Law: Sec. 208.1201(2)(c), M.C.L. (CCH MICHIGAN TAX REPORTS, ¶10-605).

CCH Caution: Corporate Income Tax Enacted

Only for the first tax year ending after 2011, taxpayers with certificated credits may elect to pay the Michigan business tax. All other taxpayers are required to file and pay the corporate income tax (see ¶1510). (Sec. 206.680, M.C.L.)

The amount of any Net Operating Loss (NOL) carryback or carryover deducted on the federal return must be added back to the MBT base. (Sec. 208.1201(2)(c), M.C.L.) In lieu of the federal NOL, Michigan permits a deduction for any available "business loss" (see ¶1464).

¶1463d Additions to Business Income—Taxes

Law: Sec. 208.1201(2)(b), M.C.L. (CCH MICHIGAN TAX REPORTS, ¶10-615).

CCH Caution: Corporate Income Tax Enacted

Only for the first tax year ending after 2011, taxpayers with certificated credits may elect to pay the Michigan business tax. All other taxpayers are required to file and pay the corporate income tax (see ¶1510). (Sec. 206.680, M.C.L.)

Any state, local, federal environmental, or foreign income taxes on, or measured by, net income, as well as any Michigan business taxes, that were deducted for federal income tax purposes must be added back to federal taxable income in determining the MBT base. (Sec. 208.1201(2)(b), M.C.L.)

¶1463e Additions to Business Income—Depreciation

Law: Secs. 208.1105(2), 208.1109(3), M.C.L. (CCH MICHIGAN TAX REPORTS, ¶10-670).

CCH Caution: Corporate Income Tax Enacted

Only for the first tax year ending after 2011, taxpayers with certificated credits may elect to pay the Michigan business tax. All other taxpayers are required to file and pay the corporate income tax (see ¶1510). (Sec. 206.680, M.C.L.)

Effective January 1, 2008, the MBT requires federal taxable income to be calculated as if IRC Sec. 168(k) (bonus depreciation) were not in effect. (Sec. 208.1109(3), M.C.L.) Federal taxable income is the base used to compute business income for purposes of the Michigan business tax. (Sec. 208.1105(2), M.C.L.) Thus, taxpayers must add back the amount of the federal bonus depreciation deduction for purposes of determining Michigan business income.

Certain taxpayers may be able to claim a credit with respect to the disallowed bonus depreciation (see ¶1489u).

¶1463f Additions to Business Income—Items Related to Federal Deductions or Credits

Law: Secs. 208.1105(2), 208.1109(3), M.C.L. (CCH MICHIGAN TAX REPORTS, ¶10-660).

CCH Caution: Corporate Income Tax Enacted

Only for the first tax year ending after 2011, taxpayers with certificated credits may elect to pay the Michigan business tax. All other taxpayers are required to file and pay the corporate income tax (see ¶1510). (Sec. 206.680, M.C.L.)

Effective January 1, 2008, the Michigan business tax requires federal taxable income to be calculated as if IRC Sec. 199 (domestic production activities deduction) were not in effect. (Sec. 208.1109(3), M.C.L.) Federal taxable income is the base used to compute business income for purposes of the Michigan business tax. (Sec. 208.1105(2), M.C.L.) Thus, taxpayers must add back the amount of the IRC Sec. 199 deduction for purposes of determining Michigan business income.

¶1464 Subtractions from Business Income—Business Losses

Law: Secs. 208.1201(2) and (5), M.C.L. (CCH MICHIGAN TAX REPORTS, ¶10-605).

CCH Caution: Corporate Income Tax Enacted

Only for the first tax year ending after 2011, taxpayers with certificated credits may elect to pay the Michigan business tax. All other taxpayers are required to file and pay the corporate income tax (see ¶1510). (Sec. 206.680, M.C.L.)

Taxpayers subject to the Michigan business tax may subtract any available business loss incurred after December 31, 2007, in computing the tax base. "Business loss" means a negative business income taxable amount after allocation or apportionment. The loss may be carried forward for 10 years, but may not be carried back. (Sec. 208.1201(5), M.C.L.) Unlike the other subtraction adjustments discussed below, this subtraction is taken after allocation and apportionment. (Sec. 208.1201(2), M.C.L.)

This subtraction is in lieu of the federal Net Operating Loss (NOL). The amount of any NOL carryback or carryforward deducted on the federal return must be added back to the MBT base (see ¶1463c).

¶1464a Subtractions from Business Income—Dividends

Law: Secs. 208.1201(2)(d), M.C.L. (CCH MICHIGAN TAX REPORTS, ¶10-810).

CCH Caution: Corporate Income Tax Enacted

Only for the first tax year ending after 2011, taxpayers with certificated credits may elect to pay the Michigan business tax. All other taxpayers are required to file and pay the corporate income tax (see ¶1510). (Sec. 206.680, M.C.L.)

Taxpayers may subtract dividends and royalties received, to the extent included in federal taxable income, in computing the Michigan business tax base. This includes dividends determined under IRC Sec. 78 and under IRC Secs. 951—964 (Subpart F deemed dividends). However, dividends and royalties received from U.S. persons and foreign operating entities may not be deducted. (Sec. 208.1201(2)(d), M.C.L.)

¶1464b Subtractions from Business Income—Interest on U.S. Obligations

Law: Secs. 208.1201(2)(g), M.C.L. (CCH MICHIGAN TAX REPORTS, ¶10-815).

CCH Caution: Corporate Income Tax Enacted

Only for the first tax year ending after 2011, taxpayers with certificated credits may elect to pay the Michigan business tax. All other taxpayers are required to file and pay the corporate income tax (see ¶1510). (Sec. 206.680, M.C.L.)

Michigan taxpayers may deduct interest income derived from U.S. obligations, to the extent included in federal taxable income, when computing their MBT bases. (Sec. 208.1201(2)(g), M.C.L.)

¶1464c Subtractions from Business Income—Pass-Through Entity Income

Law: Secs. 208.1201(2)(e), M.C.L. (CCH MICHIGAN TAX REPORTS, ¶10-914).

CCH Caution: Corporate Income Tax Enacted

Only for the first tax year ending after 2011, taxpayers with certificated credits may elect to pay the Michigan business tax. All other taxpayers are required to file and pay the corporate income tax (see ¶1510). (Sec. 206.680, M.C.L.)

Income that is attributable to another entity whose business activities are either taxable under the MBT or would be taxable if the activities were carried on in Michigan may be subtracted from federal taxable income to the extent such income was included on the federal return. (Sec. 208.1201(2)(e), M.C.L.)

¶1464d Subtractions from Business Income—Self-Employment Income

Law: Secs. 208.1201(2)(h), M.C.L. (CCH MICHIGAN TAX REPORTS, ¶10-911).

CCH Caution: Corporate Income Tax Enacted

Only for the first tax year ending after 2011, taxpayers with certificated credits may elect to pay the Michigan business tax. All other taxpayers are required to file and pay the corporate income tax (see ¶1510). (Sec. 206.680, M.C.L.)

Taxpayers may subtract any earnings that are net earnings from self-employment as defined under IRC Sec. 1402, to the extent included in federal taxable income. For purposes of a taxpayer's partner, the deduction for net earnings from self-employment is the amount properly reported on federal form 1065 schedule K-1 as self-employment earnings for federal income tax purposes. (Sec. 208.1201(2)(h), M.C.L.)

Practice Note: Pass-Through Entity Owners

Under IRC Sec. 1402, the business income of an individual or sole proprietor, and a partner's distributive share of partnership income, whether distributed or not, from any trade or business carried on by the partnership, may be considered self employment income (with certain statutory exceptions), and subject to the federal self employment tax. Therefore, a sole proprietorship or partnership may deduct any income subject to the federal self employment tax when computing the MBT income tax base. Corporations, including S corporations, are not subject to self employment tax, and, as a result, no deduction is allowed for earnings from self employment income for corporate entities. There is no deduction allowed for S corporation distributions that is equivalent to the self employment deduction allowed for partnerships and sole proprietorships under the MBT. (*Frequently Asked Questions*, Michigan Department of Treasury, November 28, 2007)

¶1464e Subtractions from Business Income—Affordable Housing Projects

Law: Secs. 208.1201, M.C.L. (CCH MICHIGAN TAX REPORTS, ¶10-915).

CCH Caution: Corporate Income Tax Enacted

Only for the first tax year ending after 2011, taxpayers with certificated credits may elect to pay the Michigan business tax. All other taxpayers are required to file and pay the corporate income tax (see ¶1510). (Sec. 206.680, M.C.L.)

Effective June 30, 2008, a qualified affordable housing project (project) may deduct an amount equal to the taxable income attributable to its Michigan residential rental units multiplied by a fraction of the tax base when calculating the Michigan business income tax. The fraction's numerator is the number of Michigan rent restricted units owned by the project; the denominator is the number of all Michigan residential rental units owned by the project. (Sec. 208.1201(7), M.C.L.)

A "project" is defined as a person that is organized, qualified, and operated as a limited dividend housing association that has limited the amount of dividends or other distributions that may be distributed to its owners and has received funding through certain sources. (Sec. 208.1201(9), M.C.L.)

The deduction is reduced by the amount of limited dividends and other distributions made to the project's partners, members, or shareholders. Also, taxable income attributable to residential rental units does not include income received by a management, construction, or development company for completion and operation of the project. (Sec. 208.1201(7), M.C.L.)

This deduction is made after allocation and apportionment. (Sec. 208.1201(2), M.C.L.)

¶1464f Subtractions from Business Income—Certain Charitable Contributions

Law: Secs. 208.1201(2)(j), M.C.L. (CCH MICHIGAN TAX REPORTS, ¶10-880).

CCH Caution: Corporate Income Tax Enacted

Only for the first tax year ending after 2011, taxpayers with certificated credits may elect to pay the Michigan business tax. All other taxpayers are required to file and pay the corporate income tax (see ¶1510). (Sec. 206.680, M.C.L.)

Applicable to tax years starting after 2009, the amount of a charitable contribution made to an advance tuition payment fund may be subtracted from the MBT base, to the extent included in federal taxable income. (Sec. 208.1201(2)(j), M.C.L.)

This deduction is made before allocation and apportionment. (Sec. 208.1201(2), M.C.L.)

¶1464g Subtractions from Business Income—Taxes

Law: Secs. 208.1201(2)(i), (3), M.C.L. (CCH MICHIGAN TAX REPORTS, ¶10-840).

CCH Caution: Corporate Income Tax Enacted

Only for the first tax year ending after 2011, taxpayers with certificated credits may elect to pay the Michigan business tax. All other taxpayers are required to file and pay the corporate income tax (see ¶1510). (Sec. 206.680, M.C.L.)

Effective January 1, 2008, Michigan business taxpayers may subtract from the tax base a portion of the book-tax differences if the book-tax difference for the first fiscal period ending after July 12, 2007, resulted in a deferred tax liability. (Sec. 208.1201(2)(i), M.C.L.) The deduction is allowed for the following percentages of the total book-tax difference for each qualifying asset:

— 4%, for the 2015 through 2019 tax years;

— 6%, for the 2020 through 2024 tax years; and

— 10%, for the 2025 through 2029 tax years.

The deduction may be claimed each year. (Sec. 208.1201(2)(i), M.C.L.)

The amount of the deduction cannot exceed the amount needed to offset the net deferred tax liability as computed under generally accepted accounting principles which would otherwise result if the deduction were not allowed. The deduction should be calculated without regard to the federal effect of the deduction. Any unused amounts may be carried forward. Also, the deduction is intended to flow through and reduce the surcharge. (Sec. 208.1201(3), M.C.L.)

¶1465 Modified Gross Receipts Tax Base

Law: Secs. 208.1111, 208.1113, 208.1203, M.C.L. (CCH MICHIGAN TAX REPORTS, ¶10-535).

CCH Caution: Corporate Income Tax Enacted

Only for the first tax year ending after 2011, taxpayers with certificated credits may elect to pay the Michigan business tax. All other taxpayers are required to file and pay the corporate income tax (see ¶1510). (Sec. 206.680, M.C.L.)

Applicable to all business activity occurring after December 31, 2007, the modified gross receipts tax is imposed on every taxpayer with Michigan nexus (see ¶1453). (Sec. 208.1203(1), M.C.L.) The tax is levied on the privilege of doing business. (Sec. 208.1203(2), M.C.L.) However, taxpayers with apportioned or allocated gross receipts of less than $350,000 are exempt. (Sec. 208.1505(1), M.C.L.)

The tax base is a taxpayer's gross receipts less purchases from other firms (before apportionment). (Sec. 208.1203(3), M.C.L.) "Purchases from other firms" include inventory; assets eligible for federal depreciation, amortization, or accelerated capital cost recovery; materials; supplies; and compensation of personnel supplied to customers of staffing companies. The definition also includes film rental or royalty payments paid by a theater owner to a film distributor or producer. Effective July 12, 2011, it includes payments to subcontractors to transport freight by motor vehicle under contract for persons classified under NAICS code 484 that do not qualify for the small business credit (see ¶1484). (Sec. 208.1113(6), M.C.L.)

Practice Note: Construction Contractors

For purposes of general building contractors, heavy construction contractors, and construction special trade contractors that do not qualify for a small business credit (discussed at ¶1484), "purchases from other firms" include (1) payments to subcontractors for a construction project under a contract specific to that project and (2) to the extent not previously deducted as inventory or materials and supplies, payments for materials deducted as purchases in determining the cost of goods sold for the purpose of calculating total income on the taxpayer's federal income tax return. (Sec. 208.1113(6)(e), M.C.L.) Consequently, such amounts are not included in the modified gross receipts subject to tax.

"Gross receipts" are defined as the entire amount received by the taxpayer from any activity in intrastate, interstate, or foreign commerce for the gain, benefit, or advantage to the taxpayer or for others. It includes capital gains from investors and sales taxes collected by a retail business. (*Frequently Asked Questions M.6 and M.10*, Michigan Department of Treasury, November 28, 2007) However, over 30 items are excluded from gross receipts, including the following:

— Proceeds from sales by a principal that the taxpayer collects in an agency capacity solely on behalf of the principal and delivers to the principal;

— Amounts received by the taxpayer as an agent solely on behalf of the principal that are expended by the taxpayer under specified circumstances;

— Amounts excluded from gross income of a foreign corporation engaged in the international operation of aircraft under IRC Sec. 8883(a); (208.1111(1)(c), M.C.L.);

— Amounts received by an advertising agency used to acquire advertising media time, space, production, or talent on behalf of another person. (208.1111(1)(d), M.C.L.);

— Amounts received by a taxpayer that manages real property owned by the taxpayer's client that are deposited into a separate account kept in the name of the taxpayer's client, provided that the amounts are not reimbursements to the taxpayer and are not indirect payments for management services that the taxpayer provides to that client;

— Proceeds from a taxpayer's transfer of an account receivable if the sale that generated the account receivable was included in gross receipts for federal income tax purposes. However, this provision does not apply to a taxpayer that during the tax year both buys and sells any receivables;

— Proceeds from the original issue of stock or equity instruments or debt instruments, refunds from returned merchandise, cash and in-kind discounts, trade discounts, federal, state or local tax refunds, security deposits, payment of the principal portion of loans, and value of property received in a like-kind exchange;

— Proceeds from a sale, transaction, exchange, involuntary conversion, or other disposition of tangible, intangible, or real property that is a capital asset as defined in IRC Sec. 1221(a) or land that qualifies as property used in the trade or business as defined in IRC Sec. 1231(b), less any gain from the disposition to the extent that gain is included in federal taxable income;

— For a professional employer organization, any amount charged that represents the actual cost of wages, salaries, benefits, worker's compensation, payroll taxes, or withholding paid to or on behalf of a covered employee by the professional employer organization;

— Proceeds from a policy of insurance, a settlement of a claim, or a judgment in a civil action less any proceeds under this subdivision that are included in federal taxable income;

— For a sales finance company owned in whole or in part by a motor vehicle manufacturer as of January 1, 2008, and for a broker or dealer or a person included in the unitary business group of that broker or dealer that buys and sells for its own account, contracts that are subject to the commodity exchange act, (1) amounts realized from the repayment, maturity, sale, or redemption of the principal of a loan, bond, or mutual fund, certificate of deposit, or similar marketable instrument, provided such instruments are not held as inventory, and (2) the principal amount received under a repurchase agreement or other transaction properly characterized as a loan;

— For a mortgage company, proceeds representing the principal balance of loans transferred or sold in the tax year;

— Any invoiced items used to provide more favorable floor plan assistance to a person subject to the MBT than to a person not subject to the MBT and paid by a manufacturer, distributor, or supplier;

— For an individual, estate, partnership organized exclusively for estate or gift planning purposes, or trust organized exclusively for estate or gift planning purposes, amounts received other than those from transactions, activities, and sources in the regular course of the taxpayer's trade or business;

— The amount deducted as a bad debt under federal income tax law that corresponds to items included in the modified gross receipts tax base may be subtracted at the rate of 60% in 2009 and 2010 (50% in 2008), 75% in 2011, and 100% in 2012 and beyond;

— Proceeds from the sale less any gain to the extent the gain is included in federal taxable income if the property is (1) a capital asset under IRC Sec. 1221(a), (2) land used in a trade or business under IRC Sec. 1231(b), (3) a hedging transaction, or (4) an investment or trading assets managed as part of a treasury function;

— Amounts attributable to an ownership interest in a pass-through entity, regulated investment company, or a real estate investment trust;

— Amounts attributable to a taxpayer pursuant to a discharge of indebtedness as described under IRC § 61(a)(12), including the forgiveness of a nonrecourse debt, applicable for tax years beginning on or after January 1, 2010.

(Sec. 208.1111(1), M.C.L.)

Practice Note: Inventory

"Inventory" includes freight, shipping, delivery, and engineering charges included in the original contract price. "Supplies" includes repair parts and fuel. Special rules clarify what is included in inventory for purposes of new motor vehicle dealers and other brokers and dealers.

Practice Note: Labor Costs

For taxpayers other than staffing companies and contractors (persons included in SIC codes 15, 16, and 17), labor is not included in "purchases from other firms." For staffing companies, labor may be deductible to the extent that it constitutes compensation of personnel supplied to its customers. However, amounts paid to a staffing company for personnel, may not be deducted by the staffing company's clients. Professional employment organizations exclude wages and the cost of wages from gross receipts. For contractors, labor may be deductible to the extent that it is included in payments made to subcontractors under a contract specific to a project. (*Frequently Asked Questions*, Michigan Department of Treasury, November 28, 2007)

Unitary business group.—The modified gross receipts of a unitary business group is the sum of modified gross receipts of each person (except foreign operating entities, insurance companies, and financial institutions) included in the group *less* any modified gross receipts arising from transactions between persons included in the unitary business group. (Sec. 208.1203(3), M.C.L.)

2008 tax year.—For the 2008 tax year, 65% of any remaining business loss carryforward calculated under the former Michigan single business tax may be deducted provided that the business loss was actually incurred in the 2006 or 2007 tax year. Business loss carryforwards that were incurred prior to 2006 may not be deducted. For unitary business groups, the business loss carryforward may be deducted only against the tax base of the taxpayer included in the group calculated as if the taxpayer were not included in the group. (Sec. 208.1203(4), M.C.L.)

Affordable housing project income deduction.—An affordable housing project income deduction, similar to that applied for purposes of calculating the business income portion of the MBT (see ¶1464e), is also available for purposes of calculating the modified gross receipts tax base. (Sec. 208.1203(4), M.C.L.)

MICHIGAN BUSINESS TAX

CHAPTER 14.7
ALLOCATION AND APPORTIONMENT

¶1470 Overview

Law: Secs. 208.1301, M.C.L. (CCH MICHIGAN TAX REPORTS, ¶ 11-510, ¶ 11-515).

CCH Caution: Corporate Income Tax Enacted

Only for the first tax year ending after 2011, taxpayers with certificated credits may elect to pay the Michigan business tax. All other taxpayers are required to file and pay the corporate income tax (see ¶ 1510). (Sec. 206.680, M.C.L.)

Applicable to business activities that occur after 2007, the Michigan business tax base is either entirely allocable to Michigan or entirely apportionable among states in which taxpayer is doing business. If a taxpayer's business activities are confined solely to Michigan, the entire tax base of the taxpayer is allocated to Michigan. If, however, the taxpayer's business activities are taxable both within and without Michigan, the entire tax base of the taxpayer is subject to apportionment. (Sec. 208.1301(2), M.C.L.)

A taxpayer whose business activities are subject to tax within and without Michigan is considered to be subject to tax in another state if:

— the taxpayer is subject to a business privilege tax, a net income tax, a franchise tax measured by net income, a franchise tax for the privilege of doing business, a corporate stock tax, or a tax similar to the MBT; or

— that state has jurisdiction to subject the taxpayer to one or more of the taxes listed above, regardless of whether that state actually does or not.

(Sec. 208.1301(3), M.C.L.)

Michigan uses a single-factor sales apportionment formula to apportion income to Michigan (see ¶ 1471). Combined reporting is required for unitary businesses (see ¶ 1473).

¶1471 Apportionment

Law: Secs. 208.1301(2), 208.1309, M.C.L. (CCH MICHIGAN TAX REPORTS, ¶ 11-520).

CCH Caution: Corporate Income Tax Enacted

Only for the first tax year ending after 2011, taxpayers with certificated credits may elect to pay the Michigan business tax. All other taxpayers are required to file and pay the corporate income tax (see ¶ 1510). (Sec. 206.680, M.C.L.)

Beginning with the 2008 tax year, the Michigan business tax provides for a single-factor sales apportionment formula (see ¶ 1472). (Sec. 208.1301(2), M.C.L.)

• *Alternate apportionment methods* . If the apportionment provisions do not fairly represent the extent of a taxpayer's business activity in Michigan, the taxpayer may request, or the Department of Treasury may require, the use of the following methods with respect to the taxpayer's business activity:

— separate accounting;

— the inclusion of one or more factors; or

— the employment of any other equitable method.

(Sec. 208.1309(1), M.C.L.) The alternate apportionment method must be approved by the Michigan Department of Treasury. (Sec. 208.1309(2), M.C.L.)

Practice Note: Amended Returns

Filing a tax return (original or amended) is not considered a request to use an alternate apportionment method.

In general, the apportionment provisions are presumed to fairly represent the Michigan business activity of the taxpayer. The taxpayer may rebut this presumption by showing that:

— the Michigan business activity attributed is out of all appropriate proportion to the actual business activity transacted in Michigan and leads to a grossly distorted result; or

— the apportionment provisions would operate unconstitutionally to tax the taxpayer's extraterritorial activity. (Sec. 208.1309(3), M.C.L.)

Practice Note: Multistate Tax Compact Election

The Michigan Supreme Court has held that (1) a taxpayer was allowed to elect to use the three-factor apportionment formula under the Multistate Tax Compact (MTC) for the 2008 Michigan Business Tax (MBT) year and (2) the MTC's apportionment formula could be used to apportion the MBT base subject to the modified gross receipts tax because the modified gross receipts tax qualified as an "income tax" for purposes of the MTC. (*International Business Machines Corp. v. Department of Treasury*, Michigan Supreme Court, No. 146440, July 14, 2014, MICHIGAN TAX REPORTS, ¶401-911)

First, the court considered whether the legislature repealed the MTC's election provision by implication when the MBT was enacted. The court concluded that the MTC's election provision was not repealed by implication. Repeals by implication are disfavored. If the legislature had intended to repeal the law, it could have been explicit. The court noted that statutes claimed to be in conflict should be construed harmoniously to find any other reasonable construction other than a repeal by implication. Thus, the MTC's three-factor apportionment formula election and the MBT's single-sales factor apportionment formula laws were *in pari materia* and had to be construed together.

The court reasoned that the MTC's election provision ("may elect") contemplated a divergence between the party state's mandated apportionment formula and the MTC's own formula, either at the time of the MTC's adoption by the party state or at some point in the future. Accordingly, the taxpayer could choose (1) the MTC and use the three-factor apportionment formula or (2) Michigan tax law and use the single-sales factor apportionment formula. By subsequently repealing the MTC's election provision starting January 1, 2011, the legislature created a window in which it did not expressly preclude the use of the MTC's election provision.

Second, the court considered, for purposes of the MTC, whether the modified gross receipts tax portion of the MBT was an "income tax." The court concluded that the modified gross receipts tax portion of the MBT was an income tax. The MTC election is available to any taxpayer subject to an income tax. Under the MTC's broad definition of "income tax," a tax is an income tax if the tax measures net income by subtracting expenses from gross income, with at least one of the expense deductions not being specifically and directly related to a particular transaction. After examining how the modified gross receipts tax portion of the MBT was calculated, the court determined that the term "gross receipts" in Michigan was similar to "gross income" under the federal income tax law. There was at least one expense deduction allowed under the

MBT that was not specifically and directly related to a particular transaction. As such, the modified gross receipts tax portion of the MBT qualified as an income tax for the MTC. This allowed the three-factor apportionment formula election to be applied to this portion of the MBT as well as the income tax portion of the MBT.

However, Act 282 (S.B. 156), Laws 2014, retroactively repealed the state's adoption of the MTC (codified at M.C.L. 205.581 through M.C.L. 205.589) to January 1, 2008. It is the intent of the Legislature that this repeal express the original intent of the Legislature regarding the application of M.C.L. 208.1301 (requiring apportionment of tax base by 100% sales factor), and the intended effect of that section to eliminate the apportionment formula election provision in the MTC (codified at M.C.L. 205.581), which allows taxpayers the option of apportioning income pursuant to the MTC's equally weighted formula or the Michigan single-sales factor formula contained in M.C.L. 208.1301. The legislation also clarifies that the election provision included in M.C.L. 205.581 is not available under the income tax act (codified at M.C.L. 206.1 through M.C.L. 206.713).

Practitioner Comment: Election of an Equally-Weighted, Three-Factor Apportionment Formula Under the Multistate Tax Compact Not Available in Michigan Under the MBT Act

The Multistate Tax Compact election to use an equally weighted, three-factor formula consisting of property, payroll, and sales factors is not available to taxpayers under the MBT Act, and Michigan taxpayers are required to allocate or apportion income based on a single sales factor.

In 2014, in response to a Michigan Supreme Court decision, *Int'l Business Machines Corp v Dep't of Treasury*, 496 Mich 642; 852 NW2d 865 (2014), Michigan enacted retroactive legislation that retroactively repealed the Multistate Tax Compact's three-factor apportionment election for all taxpayers, beginning January 1, 2008. See 2014 PA 282.

On September 29, 2015, the Michigan Court of Appeals in the consolidated action *Gillette Commercial Operations N. Am. & Subsidiaries v. Dep't of Treasury*, 2015 Mich. App. LEXIS 1818 (Mich. Ct. App. Sept. 29, 2015), upheld the trial court's findings that the retroactive repeal of the Multistate Tax Compact's apportionment election, effective January 1, 2008, was constitutional. See *Yaskawa America Inc. v. Department of Treasury*, (Mich. Ct. Cl), Docket No. 11-000077-MT, and *Ingram Micro Inc. v. Department of Treasury*, (Mich. Ct. Cl), Docket No. 11-000035-MT. The Michigan Court of Appeals' ruling, which is expected to be appealed to the Michigan Supreme Court, is consistent with several recent rulings in similar cases around the country. Pending appeals, many taxpayers continue to pursue MBT refunds based on the MTC election.

Wayne D. Roberts, Varnum, LLP and Marjorie B. Gell, Western Michigan University Cooley Law School

---

Practice Note: Retroactive Repeal of Multistate Tax Compact Was Valid and Constitutional

Affirming the Court of Claims, the Michigan Court of Appeals has held that S.B. 156 (P.A. 282) that retroactively repealed the state's Multistate Tax Compact (MTC) provisions, including the MTC three-factor apportionment formula, effective January 1, 2008, was a valid act by the state Legislature and did not violate the U.S. or Michigan Constitution because the law provided clarity to taxpayers concerning the Legislature's original intent of the Michigan Business Tax (MBT) Act to require the use of a single sales-factor apportionment formula. In the consolidated appeals, the taxpayers claimed an MBT refund based on the election to use the three-factor apportionment formula under the MTC, instead of the single-factor apportionment formula mandated by the MBT. The Michigan Supreme Court approved this filing method in International Business Machines Corp. v. Department of Treasury, No. 146440, July 14, 2014, in which a taxpayer was allowed to elect to use the three-factor apportionment formula under the MTC for the 2008 MBT year. Two months later, the state Legislature enacted S.B. 156, to limit the impact of the IBM decision and prevent the significant fiscal harm to the state that would have resulted if taxpayers had been permitted to elect apportionment provisions under the MTC. (*Gillette Commercial Operations North America & Subsidiaries, et al. v. Department of Treasury*, Michigan Court of Appeals, No. 325258, September 29, 2015, CCH MICHIGAN TAX REPORTS, ¶402-005)

The enactment of S.B. 156 did not violate the Contracts Clause of the federal or state constitution. According to the court, the compact lacked the three "classic indicia" of a binding interstate compact under federal law. The MTC does not: (1) establish a joint regulatory body; (2) require reciprocal action for effectiveness; or (3) prohibit unilateral modification or repeal. Therefore, it was more properly interpreted as a non-binding advisory compact. The court also found that the MTC was not a binding contract under state law because there was no clear indication under the Michigan law that enacted the MTC that the state contracted away its ability to either select an apportionment formula that differed from the MTC or repeal the MTC altogether. The compact even expressly stated that members could withdraw unilaterally without notice to other states. Since no contract was created under federal compact or Michigan law, there was no impairment of contractual obligations and therefore no violation of the Contracts Clause of the federal or state constitution. Consequently, the state Legislature was free to amend or repeal the MTC. Also, the court noted that the taxpayers had no vested interest in the continuation of any tax law.

The court also determined that the retroactive application of S.B. 156 did not violate other provisions of the state or federal constitution. The legislation did not violate due process because the taxpayers had no vested rights in a tax refund based on the continuation of the MTC election provisions, the protection of state revenues provided the Legislature with a legitimate purpose for giving retroactive effect to the legislation, and retroactive application of the legislation was a rational means of furthering the legitimate purpose. Similarly, the steps taken by the state Legislature to correct a mistake made clear in the IBM decision and to retroactively repeal the MTC provisions explicitly, clarifying its original intent in enacting the MBT, did not impinge upon the judiciary's functions in violation of the separations of powers. Furthermore, the legislation did not violate the Commerce Clause because the MBT single-factor apportionment formula was not facially discriminatory and did not have the effect of discriminating against an out-of-state taxpayer. The legislation prevents all taxpayers, whether in-state or out-of-state, from making an election to apply a three-factor apportionment formula for MBT purposes. The retroactive application of the legislation likewise did not violate a taxpayer's First Amendment right to petition the government.

• *Pass-through entities*

S corporations, partnerships, and LLCs are subject to the MBT at the entity level and are subject to the same apportionment provisions as C corporations. (Sec. 208.1113(3), M.C.L; Sec. 208.1301(2), M.C.L.)

¶1472 Sales Factor

Law: Secs. 208.1115, 208.1305, M.C.L. (CCH MICHIGAN TAX REPORTS, ¶11-525).

CCH Caution: Corporate Income Tax Enacted

Only for the first tax year ending after 2011, taxpayers with certificated credits may elect to pay the Michigan business tax. All other taxpayers are required to file and pay the corporate income tax (see ¶1510). (Sec. 206.680, M.C.L.)

The Michigan business tax sales factor is a fraction, the numerator of which is the taxpayer's total sales in Michigan during the tax year and the denominator is the taxpayer's total sales everywhere during the tax year. (Sec. 208.1303(1), M.C.L.)

Practice Note: Unitary Businesses

For unitary business groups, sales include the Michigan sales of every person included in the group, regardless of whether the person has nexus with Michigan. However, sales between persons included in a unitary business group must be eliminated when the sales factor is calculated. (Sec. 208.1303(2), M.C.L.)

• *Definition of "sales"*

Sales include the amounts the taxpayer received as consideration for:

— the transfer of title to (or possession of) inventory held primarily for sale to customers in the ordinary course of trade or business;

— the performance of services that constitute business activities;

— the rental, lease, licensing, or use of tangible or intangible property (including interest) that constitutes business activity;

— for taxpayers not engaged in any other business activities, sales include interest, dividends, and other income from investment assets, activities, and trading.

For intangible property, the amounts received are limited to any gain from the property's disposition. (Sec. 208.1115(1), M.C.L.)

Practice Note: Occasional Sales

A taxpayer's occasional sale of business assets is not considered a "sale," so long as the assets sold are neither stock in trade nor inventory and are not held by the taxpayer for sale to customers in the ordinary course of the taxpayer's business. This determination is made on a facts and circumstances basis. (*Frequently Asked Questions, Ap1*, Michigan Department of Treasury, November 28, 2007)

• *Specific sourcing rules*

Tangible personal property. —Sales of tangible personal property are in Michigan if the property is shipped or delivered to a purchaser in Michigan. Property stored in transit for 60 days or more before receipt by the purchaser, or in the case of a dock sales not picked up for 60 days or more, is deemed to have come to rest at this ultimate destination. Property stored in transit for fewer than 60 days before receipt, or in the case of a dock sale picked up before 60 days, is not deemed to have come to rest at this ultimate destination. (Sec. 208.1305(1)(a), M.C.L.)

Practice Note: Throwback Rule

The Michigan business tax does not have a "throwback" rule. (*Frequently Asked Questions. Ap3*, Michigan Department of Treasury, November 28, 2007)

Real property.—Receipts from the sale or lease of real property are in Michigan if the property is located in Michigan. (Sec. 208.1305(1)(b), M.C.L.) Loan origination receipts, loan servicing fees, interest on loans, and gains from the sale of a loan secured by real property are sourced to Michigan if the property is located in Michigan, or more than 50% of the fair market value of the property is located in this state, or if more than 50% of the real property is not located in any one state, if the borrower is in Michigan. (Sec. 208.1305(3), M.C.L.)

Practice Note: Location of Borrower

A borrower is considered located in Michigan if the borrower's billing address is in Michigan. (Sec. 208.1305(20), M.C.L.)

Lease/use of property.—Receipts from the lease or rental of tangible personal property are Michigan sales to the extent that the property is used in Michigan, based on a fraction, the numerator of which is the number of days the property is located in Michigan during the lease period in the tax year and the denominator of which is the number of days of the property's physical location everywhere during all lease or rental periods in the tax year. If the physical location of the property during the lease or rental period is unknown or cannot be determined, the tangible personal property is considered utilized in the state in which the property was located at the time the lease or rental payer obtained possession. (Sec. 208.1305(1)(c), M.C.L.)

Practice Note: Recordkeeping Requirements

To ensure that the proper amount of receipts from the lease or rental of property is apportioned to Michigan, taxpayers must keep detailed records, including the number of days during the tax year that the property was leased and its location.

Similarly, receipts from the lease or rental of property that is mobile transportation property are Michigan sales to the extent that the property is used in Michigan. The extent an aircraft will be deemed to be used in this state and the amount of receipts that is to be included in the numerator of this state's sales factor is determined by multiplying all the receipts from the lease or rental of the aircraft by a fraction, the numerator of the fraction is the number of landings of the aircraft in this state and the denominator of the fraction is the total number of landings of the aircraft. If the extent of the use of any transportation property within this state cannot be determined, then the receipts are in this state if the property has its principal base of operations in this state. (Sec. 208.1305(1)(d), M.C.L.)

Royalties received for the use of intangible property, such as patents or franchises, are Michigan sales if the property is used in Michigan. If the property is used in more than one state, the income is apportioned to Michigan based on the proportion of the property's use in Michigan. If the portion of Michigan use of the intangible property cannot be determined, then the taxpayer must exclude the royalties from the sales factor numerator and denominator. (Sec. 208.1305(1)(e), M.C.L.)

Performance of services.—All receipts from the performance of services are Michigan sales if the recipient of the services receives all of the benefit of the services in Michigan. However, if the recipient receives only *some* of the benefit of the services in Michigan, then the receipts are Michigan sales (*i.e.*, included in the sales factor numerator) to the extent that the recipient receives the benefit of the services in Michigan. (Sec. 208.1305(2), M.C.L.)

Practice Note: Switch From Cost-of-Performance to Market Based Sourcing Rules

Generally, under the former Single Business Tax Act, for the purposes of calculating the sales apportionment factor, the sales of services and intangible property (i.e. sales other than sales of tangible personal property) were "sourced" to Michigan if a greater proportion of business activity, based on the cost of performance, occurs within Michigan than outside of Michigan. In contrast, the MBT provisions utilize a "market-based" method of sourcing sales to Michigan, in which sales are sourced based on the location of the purchaser or where the good or service is used.

Practice Note: Where Is the Benefit of the Services Received?

The Michigan Department of Treasury has issued guidance to determine where the benefit of services is received for sales factor apportionment purposes. The recipient of the services performed may be someone other than the purchaser. All of the benefit is received in Michigan if one of the following apply:

— The service relates to real property that is located entirely in Michigan.

— The service relates to tangible personal property that (a) is owned or leased by the purchaser and located in Michigan at the time that the service is received, or (b) is delivered to the purchaser in Michigan.

— The service is provided to a purchaser who is an individual physically present in Michigan at the time that the service is received.

— The services are received in Michigan and are in the nature of personal services that are typically conducted or performed first-hand, on a direct, one-to-one or one-to-many basis.

— The service is provided to a purchaser that is engaged in a trade or business in Michigan and relates only to the trade or business of that purchaser in Michigan.

— The service relates to the use of intangible property which is used entirely in Michigan.

— The services provided are professional in nature, such as legal or accounting services, and are provided to a purchaser that is an individual domiciled in Michigan, or to a purchaser with business operations only in Michigan.

In addition, if the recipient of the services receives only a portion of the benefit of the services in Michigan, then the receipts are included in the apportionment factor in proportion to the extent that the benefit of the services is received in Michigan. The method to determine the extent of the benefit received in Michigan must be reasonable in light of the existing facts and circumstances. The method chosen by the taxpayer must be uniformly and consistently applied. (*Revenue Administrative Bulletin 2010-5;* CCH MICHIGAN TAX REPORTS, ¶ 401-504)

Securities brokerage services: Receipts from securities brokerage services are sourced to Michigan on the basis of the location of the brokerage's customers. Receipts from securities brokerage services include the following:

—commissions on transactions;

—the spread earned on principal transactions in which the broker buys or sells from its account;

—total margin interest paid on behalf of brokerage accounts owned by the broker's customers; and

—fees and receipts of all kinds from the underwriting of securities.

If receipts from brokerage services can be associated with a particular customer, but it is impractical to associate the receipts with the customer's address, then the customer's address is presumed to be the address of the branch office that generates the transactions for the customer. (Sec. 208.1305(2), M.C.L.)

Regulated investment companies: Sales of services that are derived from the sale of management, distribution, administration, or securities brokerage services to, or on behalf of, a Regulated Investment Company (RIC) or its beneficial owners are assigned to Michigan to the extent that the RIC shareholders are domiciled in Michigan. A separate computation must be made with respect to the receipts derived from each RIC. The total amount of sales attributable to Michigan is equal to the total receipts received by each RIC multiplied by a fraction, the numerator of which is the average of the sum of the beginning-of-year and end-of-year number of shares owned by the RIC shareholders domiciled in Michigan and the denominator of which is the average of the sum of the beginning-of-year and end-of-year number of shares owned by all shareholders. For purposes of the fraction, the year is the RIC's tax year that ends with or within the taxpayer's tax year. (Sec. 208.1305(2), M.C.L.)

Unsecured loans.—Interest from a loan not secured by real property, gain from the sale of such loan, and loan servicing fees, are in Michigan if the borrower is located in Michigan. (Sec. 208.1305(5), (6), and (9), M.C.L.)

Credit cards.—Receipts from credit card receivables, credit card fees, the sale of credit card or other receivables, and credit card issuer's reimbursement fees are in Michigan if the card holder's billing address is in Michigan. (Sec. 208.1305(7), M.C.L.) Receipts from qualified merchant discounts are in Michigan if the merchant's commercial domicile is in Michigan. (Sec. 208.1305(8) and (6), M.C.L.)

Investment services.—Sales of securities and other assets from investment and trading activities, such as interest dividends and gains, are sourced to Michigan if the person's customer is in Michigan or if the location of the person's customer cannot be determined than to the taxpayer's regular place of business within Michigan if the assets or the average value of the assets, depending on the assets involved, is assigned to taxpayer's regular place of business within Michigan. (Sec. 208.1305(10), M.C.L.)

Telecommunications services.—In general, receipts from the sale of telecommunications services, including mobile services, are in Michigan if the customer's place of primary use of the service is in Michigan. "Place of primary use" is the customer's residential street address or primary business street address. For mobile services, the customer's address is the place of primary use only if it is within the provider's licensed service area. However, special rules apply to telecommunications service sold on an individual call-by-call basis, post-paid and pre-paid telecommunications services, private communication services, services with a channel termination in Michigan and at least two other states; billing and ancillary telecommunications services; network access fess or telecommunication sales for resale. (Sec. 208.1305(13)-(19), M.C.L.)

Media.—Media receipts of taxpayers whose business activities include live radio or television programming or who are involved in radio, television, cable, motion picture production or distribution activities, are sourced to Michigan only if the commercial domicile of the customer is in Michigan, the customer has a contractual relationship with the taxpayer in relation to the media receipts, and the customer receives all the benefit of the media receipts in Michigan. For media receipts from the sale of advertising, the receipts are included in the numerator of the apportionment factor in proportion to the extent the recipient receives benefit of the services in this state. If the recipient of services is a television or radio broadcaster, the benefit of services are proportioned based on the ratio that the broadcaster's viewing or listening audience in the state bears to its total viewing or listening ordinance. (Sec. 208.1305(20), M.C.L.)

Transportation services.—Generally receipts from transportation services rendered by a person subject to tax in another state are sourced to Michigan on the basis of the ratio of Michigan revenue miles over total revenue miles. However, alternative approaches are available if the information is not available or cannot be obtained with reasonable expense. In addition, special apportionment rules apply to the following transportation services:

— *Maritime transportation services:* 50% of receipts are sourced to Michigan if the services either originate or terminate in Michigan; 100% if the service both originates and terminates in Michigan.

— *Services involving the transport of both persons and property:* Receipts sourced separately determined on the basis of the total gross receipts for passenger miles and ton mile fractions, separately computed and individually weighted by the ratio of gross receipts from passenger transportation to total gross receipts from all transportation, and by the ratio of gross receipts from freight transportation to total gross receipts from all transportation, respectively.

— *Oil pipeline transportation services:* Receipts sourced on the basis of the ratio that the gross receipts for the Michigan barrel miles bear to the gross receipts for the total barrel miles transported by the person.

— *Gas pipeline transportation services:* Receipts sourced to Michigan on the basis of the ratio that the gross receipts for the 1,000 cubic feet miles transported in this state bear to the gross receipts for the 1,000 cubic feet miles transported by the person everywhere.

Practice Note: Sourcing vs. Apportionment

Although transportation services are subject to a specific sourcing rule, transportation companies do not—and receipts from transportation services are not—apportioned separately. (*Frequently Asked Questions, U.5,* Michigan Department of Treasury, November 28, 2007)

All other receipts.—All other receipts not otherwise specifically sourced are sourced based on where the benefit to the customer is received or, if that cannot be determined, to the customer's location. (Sec. 208.1311, M.C.L.)

• *Alternate formula for spun-off corporations*

Spun-off corporations that qualified to use an alternative formula for Michigan single business tax purposes under former Sec. 208.228 (see ¶1205) may elect to continue to use the alternative formula for an additional four years (three years if an extension had previously been approved under the SBT provisions). The alternate apportionment formula allows spun-off corporations to exclude from the sales factor any sales made to a purchaser that was a member of a Michigan affiliated group that included the spun-off corporation until the restructuring transaction. (Sec. 208.1307(3), M.C.L.) Department of Treasury approval is required unless the taxpayer had received a previous extension under the SBT, and will only be granted if the corporation meets the following requirements:

— submits a statement that the spun-off corporation qualifies for the election;

— submits a list of all corporations and any other business entities that the spun-off corporation controlled at the time of restructuring; and

— commits to invest (1) at least an additional $200 million of capital investment in Michigan within the additional four years and commits to maintain at least 80% of the full-time equivalent employees in Michigan; (2) an additional $400 million in Michigan within the additional four years; or (3) a total of $1.3 billion Michigan within 11 years beginning with the year in which the restructuring transaction was completed.

(Sec. 208.1307(1), M.C.L.)

A taxpayer that is a buyer of a Michigan plant that was included in the initial restructuring may request the Department to extend the election for an additional four years, if the taxpayer makes an election prior to the end of the 11th year following the initial restructuring. Such an election would enable the spun-off corporation to disregard sales made to the taxpayer's former parent and the sales attributable to the plant will be treated as sales by a spun-off corporation.

The taxes saved as a result of the use of the alternative apportionment formula, plus interest, are subject to recapture if the taxpayer fails to make the requisite investment or maintain the requisite level of employment by the end of the four year period.

MICHIGAN BUSINESS TAX

CHAPTER 14.75

CREDITS

¶1475 Overview

Law: Secs. 208.1401, M.C.L. (CCH MICHIGAN TAX REPORTS, ¶12-001).

CCH Caution: Corporate Income Tax Enacted

Only for the first tax year ending after 2011, taxpayers with certificated credits may elect to pay the Michigan business tax. All other taxpayers are required to file and pay the corporate income tax (see ¶1510). (Sec. 206.680, M.C.L.)

The Michigan Business Tax (MBT) maintains many of the credits available under the SBT but also adds numerous credits.

CCH Practice Note: Single Business Tax Credit Carryovers

With the exception of the Historical Preservation Credit, the Brownfield Credit, and the Hybrid Vehicle Technology Research Credit (see ¶1489b, ¶1489c, and ¶1489i), any unused single business tax credit carry forward can be applied against the MBT during the 2008 and 2009 tax years. Any unused SBT carry forward remaining after 2009 is lost (Sec. 208.1401, M.C.L.). This carry forward provision applies to any unused SBT credit even if the SBT credit was not retained under the MBT and is subject to credit ordering.

The major new credits available against the MBT include:

— the compensation credit (¶1476);

— the investment tax credit (¶1477);

— the research and development credit (¶1478);

— the research and development investment contributions credit (¶1478a);

— the credit for businesses with low gross receipts (¶1481);

— the personal property tax credit (¶1482);

— the entrepreneurial credit (¶1489e);

— the grocery store credits (¶1489g);

— credits for the film industry (¶1489l, ¶1489p, ¶1489ae); and

— credits for advanced automotive technology (¶1489i, ¶1489w, ¶1489x, ¶1489y)

Practitioner Comment: Ordering of Tax Credits Under the Michigan Business Tax Act

An issue pending in the Michigan Court of Appeals is whether unused SBT credit carryforwards and SBT Brownfield rehabilitation credits, just like credits created under the MBT Act, should be applied after the compensation and investment tax credits for purposes of calculating MBT. On May 14, 2014, the Michigan Court of Claims in *Ashley Capital, LLC v Michigan Department of Treasury*, Mich. Ct. Cl.; Docket No. 12-000132-MT, found that unused SBT credit carryforwards and SBT Brownfield rehabilitation credits, just like credits created under the MBT Act, should be applied after the compensation and investment tax credits for purposes of calculating MBT. The court, agreeing with the taxpayer, found that the ordering provision of credits provided under the MBT Act, MCL 208.1403, creates a "super" priority for MBT compensation and investment tax credits, and that credits carried forward from the SBT Act are credited in the same order as those derived under the MBT Act. MBT taxpayers with SBT credit carryforwards and Brownfield tax credits continue to review MBT returns for open tax years and file protective claims for refunds.

Wayne D. Roberts, Varnum, LLP and Marjorie B. Gell, Western Michigan University Cooley Law School

---

Practitioner Comment: Refundability of Excess SBT Brownfield Tax Credits under the Michigan Business Tax Act

The issue of whether an election can be made under the MBT Act to refund excess Brownfield tax credits carried over from the SBT was decided by the Court of Claims in *Vitec v. Department of Treasury*, Mich. Ct. Cl., Docket No. 13-27-MT. Under MCL 208.1437(1), i"f the credit allowed under this section for the tax year exceeds the qualified taxpayer's tax liability for the tax year, the qualified taxpayer may elect to have the excess refunded at a rate equal to 85% of that portion of the credit that exceeds the tax liability of the qualified taxpayer for the tax year and forgo the remaining 15% of the credit and any carryforward credit allowed under this section." The Department of Treasury has taken the position that a "credit under this section" does not include a Brownfield credit carried forward from the SBT and, therefore, such credits are not refundable. The Court of Claims disagreed with this interpretation, finding that SBT excess Brownfield credits are refundable under the MBT Act. The case is currently on appeal in the Michigan Court of Appeals. Protective claims for refunds should be filed for open tax years pending resolution of this issue.

Wayne D. Roberts, Varnum, LLP and Marjorie B. Gell, Western Michigan University Cooley Law School

¶1476 Compensation Credit

Law: Secs. 208.1107(3), 208.1403, M.C.L. (CCH MICHIGAN TAX REPORTS, ¶12-070b).

Forms: Form 4567, Michigan Business Tax Credits for Compensation, Investment, and Research Development; Form 4596, Miscellaneous Credits for Insurance Companies.

CCH Caution: Corporate Income Tax Enacted

Only for the first tax year ending after 2011, taxpayers with certificated credits may elect to pay the Michigan business tax. All other taxpayers are required to file and pay the corporate income tax (see ¶1510). (Sec. 206.680, M.C.L.)

Taxpayers may claim a credit against the Michigan business tax for compensation paid. Insurance companies subject to the gross direct premiums tax as well as financial institutions subject to the franchise tax may claim the credit (see ¶1456 and ¶1455, respectively). (Sec. 208.1403(2), M.C.L.)

Compensation.—Compensation means all wages, salaries, fees, bonuses, commissions, and other payments made on behalf of or for the benefit of employees, officers, and directors. It includes any net earnings from self-employment as well as payments to a pension or profit sharing plan and payments for insurance for which employees are the beneficiaries. Compensation may be subject to or exempt from federal income tax withholding. (Sec. 208.1107(2), M.C.L.)

Unitary business groups.—A taxpayer that is a unitary business group must calculate the credit on the combined Michigan compensation of the unitary group members. Intercompany transactions should not be eliminated for this purposes. (Instructions to Form 4567, Michigan Business Tax Credits for Compensation, Investment, and Research Development)

• *Credit amount and limitations*

The amount of the credit is 0.37% of the taxpayer's Michigan compensation. (Sec. 208.1403(2), M.C.L.)

The combination of this credit and the investment tax credit (see ¶1477) is capped at 52% of the total Michigan business tax liability before the surcharge. (Sec. 208.1403(1), M.C.L.)

However, for taxpayers making investments in electric and gas distribution assets for which a portion of the credit is denied due to the 50% cap, the 50% limitation on the combined credit is increased by the lesser of (1) the amount of denied credit or (2) 50% of the tax increase due to the elimination of the IRC Sec. 168(k) deduction. Regardless, the total combined credit is capped at 80% of the tax liability after the surcharge. (Sec. 208.1403(6), M.C.L.)

• *Planning considerations*

Priority.—This credit and the investment tax credit (see ¶1477) must be claimed before other credits. (Sec. 208.1403(1), M.C.L.)

Professional employer organizations.—Professional employer organizations may not include payments made to a client's officers and employees when the professional employer organization managed the client's employment operations. However, the client may include payments to the client's officers and employees. (Sec. 208.1403(2), M.C.L.)

A professional employer organization is an organization that provides the management and administration of the human resources of another entity by contractually assuming substantial employer rights and responsibilities. (Sec. 208.1113(4), M.C.L.)

Exclusive provisions.—Taxpayers claiming this credit may also claim the research and development credit (see ¶1478), but may not use the same costs and expenses to calculate both credits. (Sec. 208.1403(5), M.C.L.)

Forms.—Standard taxpayers and financial institutions claim the credit on Form 4567, Michigan Business Tax Credits for Compensation, Investment, and Research Development. Insurance companies claim the credit on Form 4596, Miscellaneous Credits for Insurance Companies.

¶1477 Investment Tax Credit

Law: Sec. 208.1403, M.C.L. (CCH MICHIGAN TAX REPORTS, ¶12-055).

Forms: Form 4567, Michigan Business Tax Credits for Compensation, Investment, and Research Development; Form 4596, Miscellaneous Credits for Insurance Companies.

CCH Caution: Corporate Income Tax Enacted

Only for the first tax year ending after 2011, taxpayers with certificated credits may elect to pay the Michigan business tax. All other taxpayers are required to file and pay the corporate income tax (see ¶1510). (Sec. 206.680, M.C.L.)

A taxpayer may claim an investment tax credit against the Michigan business tax for the taxpayer's expenditures on investments in its business. (Sec. 208.1403(3), M.C.L.) A similar credit was available against the former single business tax (see ¶1121).

Unitary business groups.—A taxpayer that is a unitary business group must calculate the credit on the combined Michigan compensation assets of the unitary group members. Intercompany transactions must be eliminated prior to calculating the credit. (Instructions to Form 4567, Michigan Business Tax Credits for Compensation, Investment, and Research Development)

• *Credit amount and limitations*

The amount of the credit is equal to 2.9% of the taxpayer's net capital assets. (Sec. 208.1403(3), M.C.L.)

Net capital assets generally include the following:

— the costs, including fabrication and installation costs, of tangible assets located in Michigan;

— apportioned mobile tangible assets, wherever located; and

— the federal basis for eligible items moved into the state;

less a recapture calculation for like assets for which the MBT investment tax credit or the equivalent single business tax credit was claimed upon their sale, disposition, or removal from the state.

The assets must be of a type that are, or will become, eligible for depreciation, amortization, or accelerated capital cost recovery for federal income tax purposes. (Sec. 208.1403(3), M.C.L.)

CCH Practice Note: Transfer to Out-of-State Unitary Group Member

Moving an asset outside Michigan creates recapture even if the transfer is to a member of a taxpayer's unitary group. (Instructions to Form 4567, Michigan Business Tax Credits for Compensation, Investment, and Research Development)

For a tax year in which the amount determined above is negative, the absolute value of that amount is added to the taxpayer's tax liability for the tax year. (Sec. 208.1403(4), M.C.L.)

The combination of this credit and the compensation credit (see ¶1476) is capped at 52% of the total Michigan business tax liability before the surcharge. (Sec. 208.1403(1), M.C.L.)

However, for taxpayers making investments in electric and gas distribution assets for which a portion of the credit is denied due to the 50% cap, the 50% limitation on the combined credit is increased by the lesser of (1) the amount of denied credit or (2) 50% of the tax increase due to the elimination of the IRC Sec. 168(k) deduction. Regardless, the total combined credit is capped at 80% of the tax liability after the surcharge. (Sec. 208.1403(6), M.C.L.)

• *Planning considerations*

Clawback.—Effective January 1, 2012, if a taxpayer fails to comply with terms in the agreement, then some or all of the credit may be added back to the taxpayer's corporate income tax liability. (Sec. 206.673, M.C.L.)

Priority.—This credit and the compensation credit must be claimed against the MBT before other credits. (Sec. 208.1403(1), M.C.L.)

Exclusive provisions.—Taxpayers claiming this credit may also claim the research and development credit (see ¶1478), but may not use the same costs and expenses to calculate both credits. (Sec. 208.1403(5), M.C.L.)

Forms.—Standard taxpayers and financial institutions claim the credit on Form 4567, Michigan Business Tax Credits for Compensation, Investment, and Research Development. Insurance companies claim the credit on Form 4596, Miscellaneous Credits for Insurance Companies.

Practitioner Comment: Credits From "Closed" Tax Year May Be Carried Forward to Compute the Correct Tax Liability and Affect Tax Liabilities in Future "Open" Tax Years

In *Asahi Kasei Plastics North America, Inc. v. Dep't of Treasury*, Mich Ct App Docket No. 309240 (Jan. 29, 2013), the Michigan Court of Appeals affirmed a Michigan Court of Claims decision holding that non-refundable investment tax credits that, during an audit, were determined to have been generated in a tax year that was "closed" for purposes of obtaining a refund under Sec. 205.27a(2), M.C.L., could be carried forward—under the applicable ITC carryover statute set forth in Sec. 208.35a(4), M.C.L.—to an open tax year to compute the correct amount of net taxes due from the taxpayer in the tax year that was open for purposes of refund and assessment. The court rejected the Department of Treasury's argument that the carryover of non-refundable credits constituted a "refund" that was barred by the applicable statute of limitations. The Michigan holding in *Asahi Kasei* is consistent with parallel federal law as set forth in Rev. Rule 82-49, 1982-1 C.B. 5. Although this was a single business tax case, the reasoning of this "carryover" holding should be considered in connection with analyzing similar factual scenarios that may exist under income tax laws, along with both the MBT Act and the CIT Act.

Wayne D. Roberts, Varnum, LLP and Marjorie B. Gell, Western Michigan University Cooley Law School

---

¶1478 Research and Development Credit

Laws: Sec. 208.1405, M.C.L. (CCH MICHIGAN TAX REPORTS, ¶12-065b).

Forms: Form 4567, Michigan Business Tax Credits for Compensation, Investment, and Research Development.

CCH Caution: Corporate Income Tax Enacted

Only for the first tax year ending after 2011, taxpayers with certificated credits may elect to pay the Michigan business tax. All other taxpayers are required to file and pay the corporate income tax (see ¶1510). (Sec. 206.680, M.C.L.)

Taxpayers may claim a credit against the Michigan business tax for research and development expenses. "Research and development expenses" means qualified research expenses as that term is defined under federal tax law (IRC Sec. 41(b)). (Sec. 208.1405, M.C.L.)

CCH Practice Note: Ineligible Taxpayers

Financial institutions and insurance companies are ineligible for this credit. (Instructions to Form 4567, Michigan Business Tax Credits for Compensation, Investment, and Research Development)

• *Credit amount*

The amount of the credit is 1.9% of the taxpayer's research and development expenses in Michigan.

Unitary business groups.—A taxpayer that is a unitary business group must calculate the credit on the combined research and development expenses of the unitary group members. Intercompany transactions should not be eliminated for this purposes. (Instructions to Form 4567, Michigan Business Tax Credits for Compensation, Investment, and Research Development)

This credit, combined with the compensation credit and the investment tax credit (see ¶1476 and ¶1477), cannot exceed 65% of the total Michigan business tax liability before the surcharge. (Sec. 208.1405, M.C.L.)

¶1478a Research and Development Investment Contributions Credit

Laws: Sec. 208.1407, M.C.L. (CCH MICHIGAN TAX REPORTS, ¶12-102).

Forms: Form 4574, Michigan Business Tax Refundable Credits; Form 4587, MBT Schedule of Recapture of Certain Business Tax Credits and Deductions.

CCH Caution: Corporate Income Tax Enacted

Only for the first tax year ending after 2011, taxpayers with certificated credits may elect to pay the Michigan business tax. All other taxpayers are required to file and pay the corporate income tax (see ¶1510). (Sec. 206.680, M.C.L.)

For the 2008, 2009, and 2010 tax years, a refundable credit against the Michigan business tax is available to taxpayers that contribute at least $350,000 in cash to an eligible business for purposes of research and development and technology innovation. (Sec. 208.1407(1), M.C.L.)

• *Definitions*

Eligible business.—An eligible business is a taxpayer engaged in research and development that employs fewer than 50 full-time employees (including affiliates) or has gross receipts of less than $10 million. In addition, an eligible business must have no prior financial interest in the taxpayer and the taxpayer must have no prior financial interest in the eligible business. (Sec. 208.1407(9)(c), M.C.L.)

• *Credit amount*

The credit is equal to 30% of the taxpayer's eligible contribution, but is capped at $300,000. In addition, a taxpayer may not receive this credit for two consecutive calendar years. (Sec. 208.1407(1), M.C.L.; Sec. 208.1407(9)(d), M.C.L.)

Unitary Business Groups (UBG) may claim the credit for each certificate received by any of its members. The $300,000 limit applies to each certificate, not to the UBG. (Instructions to Form 4574, Michigan Business Tax Refundable Credit)

• *Planning considerations*

Application required.—The taxpayer is required to apply to the Michigan Economic Growth Authority (MEGA) for approval of the credit. Only 20 credits will be approved in a one year period. If the credit is approved, MEGA will issue a certificate to the taxpayer specifying the amount of the credit that may be claimed. The certificate must be attached to the tax return when it is filed. (Sec. 208.1407(2), (4), M.C.L.)

Form.—Standard taxpayers and financial institutions claim the credit on Form 4574, Michigan Business Tax Refundable Credits.

Credit recapture.—The taxpayer and the eligible business must enter an agreement with MEGA requiring the taxpayer and the eligible business to comply with certain application provisions for five years. In the event of noncompliance, the taxpayer is liable for an amount equal to 125% of the total credit received. (Sec. 208.1407(7), M.C.L.) The recapture is reported on Form 4587, MBT Schedule of Recapture of Certain Business Tax Credits and Deductions.

¶1479 Michigan International Speedway Investment Credit

Laws: Secs. 206.673, 208.1409, M.C.L. (CCH MICHIGAN TAX REPORTS, ¶12-055a)

Forms: Form 4574, Michigan Business Tax Refundable Credits.

CCH Caution: Corporate Income Tax Enacted

Only for the first tax year ending after 2011, taxpayers with certificated credits may elect to pay the Michigan business tax. All other taxpayers are required to file and pay the corporate income tax (see ¶1510). (Sec. 206.680, M.C.L.)

For tax years that begin after 2007 and end before 2017, an eligible taxpayer may claim a credit against the Michigan business tax for capital expenditures on infield renovation, grandstand and infrastructure upgrades, and any other construction and upgrades. (Sec. 208.1409(1), M.C.L.) Beginning in the 2009 tax year, an eligible taxpayer may also claim a refundable credit against the Michigan business tax for expenses incurred to ensure traffic and pedestrian safety while hosting motorsports events. (Sec. 208.1409(3), M.C.L.)

A taxpayer must spend at least $30 million on capital expenditures before 2011 to qualify for the credit. Also, a taxpayer must spend at least $32 million on capital expenditures after 2010 and before 2016. (Sec. 208.1409(4), M.C.L.) For purposes of this credit, an "eligible taxpayer" means (1) a person who owns and operates a motorsports entertainment complex and has at least two days of motor sports events each year or (2) a person who is the lessee and operator of a motorsports entertainment complex. (Sec. 208.1409(5)(a), M.C.L.)

• *Credit amount*

The amount of the credit is equal to the amount of capital expenditures, but may not exceed the lesser of the taxpayer's liability for the tax year or:

— $2.1 million for the 2008, 2009, and 2010 tax years;

— $1.58 million for the 2011 and 2012 tax years;

— $1.58 million for tax years after 2012 or the taxpayer's tax liability before the calculation of the credit for professional fees, additional police officers and traffic management devices to ensure traffic and pedestrian safety while hosting motorsports events.

(Sec. 208.1409(1), (2), M.C.L.)

In addition, beginning with the 2009 tax year, an eligible taxpayer may claim a refundable credit equal to 100% of the amount of expenditures incurred including any professional fees, additional police officers, and traffic management devices to ensure traffic and pedestrian safety while hosting motorsports events. (Sec. 208.1409(3), M.C.L.)

MBT Election.—Because this is a certificated credit, taxpayers may choose to claim the credit and pay the MBT in lieu of paying the corporate income tax. (Sec. 206.680, M.C.L.; Sec. 208.1107(1), M.C.L.)

Clawback.—Effective January 1, 2012, if a taxpayer fails to comply with terms in the agreement, then some or all of the credit may be added back to the taxpayer's corporate income tax liability. (Sec. 206.673, M.C.L.)

¶1480 Stadium Investment Credit

Laws: Sec. 208.1410, M.C.L. (CCH MICHIGAN TAX REPORTS, ¶12-138)

Forms: Form 4573, Michigan Business Tax Miscellaneous Nonrefundable Credits.

CCH Caution: Corporate Income Tax Enacted

Only for the first tax year ending after 2011, taxpayers with certificated credits may elect to pay the Michigan business tax. All other taxpayers are required to file and pay the corporate income tax (see ¶1510). (Sec. 206.680, M.C.L.)

For tax years that begin after 2007 and end before 2013, an eligible taxpayer may claim a credit against the Michigan business tax for facility or stadium construction costs. For purposes of this credit, an "eligible taxpayer" is one who:

— is an owner, operator, manager, or tenant of more than one facility or stadium in Michigan that has a capacity of at least 14,000 patrons per facility and is primarily used for professional sporting events or other entertainment;

— has made a capital investment of at least $125 million into the construction cost of a facility or stadium; and

— has not received proceeds from a state appropriation or a public bond issue to assist in the construction or debt retirement of the facility. (Sec. 208.1410, M.C.L.)

Alternatively, a taxpayer may qualify for the credit if it is an owner, operator, manager, or tenant of more than one facility or stadium in Michigan that has a capacity of at least 14,000 patrons per facility and is primarily used for professional sporting events or other entertainment and has made a capital investment of at least $250 million into the construction cost of a facility or stadium. (Sec. 208.1410a, M.C.L.)

• *Credit amount*

The amount of the credit is equal to:

— For the 2008, 2009, and 2010 tax years, 65% of the tax liability, not to exceed $1.7 million;

— For the 2011 tax year, 45% of the tax liability, not to exceed $1.18 million; and

— For the 2012 tax year, 25% of the tax liability, not to exceed $650,000.

(Sec. 208.1410, M.C.L.)

¶1481 Credit for Businesses with Low Gross Receipts

Laws: Sec. 208.1411, M.C.L. (CCH MICHIGAN TAX REPORTS, ¶12-139)

Forms: Form 4571, Michigan Business Tax Common Credits for Small Businesses.

CCH Caution: Corporate Income Tax Enacted

Only for the first tax year ending after 2011, taxpayers with certificated credits may elect to pay the Michigan business tax. All other taxpayers are required to file and pay the corporate income tax (see ¶1510). (Sec. 206.680, M.C.L.)

A credit against the Michigan business tax is available to a taxpayer that has gross receipts allocated or apportioned to Michigan that are greater than $350,000, but less than $700,000. (Sec. 208.1411, M.C.L.)

Gross receipts must be annualized for tax periods of less than 12 months. (Instructions to Form 4571, Michigan Business Tax Common Credits for Small Businesses)

• *Credit amount*

The credit is equal to the taxpayer's tax liability after applying the small business tax credit (see ¶1484) multiplied by a fraction. The fraction's numerator is the difference between the taxpayer's allocated or apportioned gross receipts and $700,000. The fraction's denominator is $350,000. (Sec. 208.1411, M.C.L.)

¶1482 Personal Property Taxes Credit

Laws: Sec. 208.1413, M.C.L. (CCH MICHIGAN TAX REPORTS, ¶12-140)

Forms: Form 4574, Michigan Business Tax Refundable Credits.

CCH Caution: Corporate Income Tax Enacted

Only for the first tax year ending after 2011, taxpayers with certificated credits may elect to pay the Michigan business tax. All other taxpayers are required to file and pay the corporate income tax (see ¶1510). (Sec. 206.680, M.C.L.)

Taxpayers may claim a refundable credit against the Michigan business tax for personal property taxes paid, including the industrial facilities tax, the obsolete property tax, and the tax on certain public utilities. (Sec. 208.1413), M.C.L.)

• *Credit amount*

The amount of the credit is dependent upon the type of personal property involved. The credit is equal to:

— 35% of the amount paid for personal property taxes levied on industrial personal property after 2007;

— 13.5% of the amount paid for personal property taxes on telephone personal property; and

— 10% of the amount paid for personal property taxes on natural gas pipeline property, for property taxes levied after 2007.

(Sec. 208.1413(1), M.C.L.)

CCH Comment: Property Tax Reduction for Industrial Property

With the enactment of the personal property credit for industrial property, together with the exemption from the 6-mill State education tax and the 18-mill local school property tax, industrial personal property would realize an average effective personal property tax reduction of 64.9%. (*Senate Fiscal Analysis*, Enrolled Summary for H.B. 94, June 29, 2007)

• *Planning considerations*

Filing requirement.—In order to qualify for the credit, taxpayers must file, if applicable:

— the statement of assessable personal property required under the property tax law;

— the annual report required by law to identify the telephone personal property; and

— the assessment or bill issued to and paid by the taxpayer.

(Sec. 208.1413(2), M.C.L.)

¶1483 Start-Up Business Credit

Laws: Sec. 208.1415, M.C.L. (CCH MICHIGAN TAX REPORTS, ¶12-135).

Form: Form 4573, Michigan Business Tax Miscellaneous Nonrefundable Credits

---

CCH Caution: Corporate Income Tax Enacted

Only for the first tax year ending after 2011, taxpayers with certificated credits may elect to pay the Michigan business tax. All other taxpayers are required to file and pay the corporate income tax (see ¶1510). (Sec. 206.680, M.C.L.)

A qualified start-up business that does not have business income for two consecutive tax years is eligible to claim a credit against the Michigan business tax. If a taxpayer has business income in any year after the credit is first claimed, the taxpayer must again have no business income for two consecutive years before being eligible to renew its claim for the credit. The credit was available against the former Single Business Tax (SBT). (See ¶1126)

Unitary business groups.—If the taxpayer is a Unitary Business Group (UBG), the credit is based on the eligible member's business activity only. The credit amount is limited to the pro forma tax liability calculated for the eligible taxpayer for that year. The resulting credit amount is then applied against the UBG's tax liability for that tax year. (Instructions to Form 4573, Michigan Business Tax Miscellaneous Nonrefundable Credits)

• *Definitions*

A "qualified start-up business" is defined as a business meeting the following criteria, as certified by the Michigan Economic Development Corporation:

— the business had fewer than 25 full-time employees;

— the business had sales of less than $1 million in the tax year in which the credit was claimed;

— research and development (as defined in IRC Sec. 41(d)) made up at least 15% of the expenses of the business in the credit year;

— the business was not publicly traded; and

— during the immediately preceding seven years, it was in one of the first two years of contribution liability under the Michigan Employment Security Act, or would have been in one of the first two years of contribution liability if (1) it had employees and was liable under the Act or (2) it had not assumed successor liability under the Act.

• *Credit amount*

The credit was equal to the taxpayer's MBT liability for the second of the two consecutive years and for each subsequent year in which a taxpayer did not have business income.

• *Planning considerations*

Limitations: The credit could be claimed for no more than five years.

Maximum amount of compensation, director's fees, distributive shares: For the tax year in which the credit was claimed, any compensation, director's fees, or distributive shares paid to a partner, officer, shareholder, member, or individual owner could not exceed $135,000.

Member of affiliated group, controlled group of corporations, or entity under common control: A member of an affiliated group, a controlled group of corporations under IRC Sec. 1563, or an entity under common control had to determine its number of employees, its sales, and its business income on a consolidated basis for purposes of determining if it qualifies for the credit.

Recapture: If a taxpayer had no business activity in Michigan but had business activity outside the state in any of the first three years following the last year in which it claimed the credit, the total amount of credits previously claimed was subject to recapture pursuant to the following schedule: (1) if the taxpayer had no business activity in Michigan in the tax year immediately following the last year the credit was claimed, 100%; (2) if the taxpayer had no business activity in Michigan in the second year following the last year the credit was claimed, 67%; and (3) if the taxpayer had no business activity in Michigan in the third year following the last year the credit was claimed, 33%.

¶1484 Small Business Credit

Laws: Sec. 208.1417, M.C.L. (CCH MICHIGAN TAX REPORTS, ¶12-142)

Forms: Form 4571, Michigan Business Tax Common Credits for Small Businesses.

CCH Caution: Corporate Income Tax Enacted

Only for the first tax year ending after 2011, taxpayers with certificated credits may elect to pay the Michigan business tax. All other taxpayers are required to file and pay the corporate income tax (see ¶1510). (Sec. 206.680, M.C.L.)

Taxpayers may claim a credit against the Michigan business tax provided that their gross receipts do not exceed $20 million and their adjusted business income minus the loss adjustment (see ¶1464) does not exceed $1.3 million (subject to inflation). (Sec. 208.1417(1), M.C.L.)

The credit is available against the corporate income tax (see ¶1551).

Adjusted business income.—Adjusted business income means business income (see ¶1462) with the following additions:

— compensation and directors' fees of a corporation's active shareholders and officers;

— a carryback or carryover of a net operating loss, to the extent deducted in determining federal taxable income; and

— a capital loss, to the extent deducted in determining federal taxable income.

(Sec. 208.1417(9)(b), M.C.L.)

Loss adjustment.—The loss adjustment is the amount by which adjusted business income was less than zero in any of the five tax years immediately preceding the tax year for which eligibility for this credit is being determined. (Sec. 208.1417(9)(d), M.C.L.)

• *Credit amount*

The credit equals the amount by which the Michigan business tax exceeds 1.8% of the taxpayer's adjusted business income. (Sec. 208.1417(4), M.C.L.)

• *Planning considerations*

Priority.—This credit is taken after the credits for compensation, investment tax, and research and development (see ¶1476, ¶1477, ¶1478). (Sec. 208.1417(1), M.C.L.)

Credit phaseout.—The credit is phased out based on a sliding scale for compensation or distributive shares of adjusted business income ranging from $160,000 to $180,000. For this purpose, the most-highly compensated person is used. (Sec. 208.1417(1)(c), M.C.L.; Sec. 208.1417(3), M.C.L.)

Disqualification.—An individual, partnership, or S corporation is disqualified if the individual or any partner, or shareholder receives more than $180,000 as a distributive share of the adjusted business income. A corporation other than an S corporation is disqualified if the sum of the following exceeds $180,000:

— the compensation and director's fees of a shareholder or officer; and

— the product of the percentage of outstanding ownership or of outstanding stock owned by that shareholder multiplied by the difference between the sum of business income and, to the extent deducted in determining federal taxable income, a carryback or a carryover of a net operating loss or capital loss, minus the loss adjustment. (Sec. 208.1417(1)(a), (b), M.C.L.)

Officers include the chairperson of the board; the president, vice president, secretary, and treasurer of the corporation or board; and any employee, member, manager, partner, or other person performing duties similar to those of chairpersons, presidents, vice presidents, secretaries, and treasurers. (Sec. 208.1417(1)(a), (b), M.C.L.) (*Frequently Asked Questions*, Michigan Department of Treasury, November 28, 2007)

Practice Note: Unitary Businesses

The disqualifiers under MCL 208.1417(1)(a) and (b) and the credit phaseout apply to a taxpayer that is a unitary business group if such disqualifiers apply to any member of that unitary business group. For example, a taxpayer that is a unitary business group is disqualified from taking the alternate credit under MCL 208.1417 if that unitary business group includes a member that is a partnership and any one partner of that partnership receives more than $180,000.00 as a distributive share of the adjusted business income minus loss adjustment of the partnership. (*Frequently Asked Questions*, Michigan Department of Treasury, November 28, 2007)

Practice Note: Irrevocable Trusts

Irrevocable trusts are not subject to the credit's disqualifiers or reduction percentages. However, if a irrevocable trust has gross receipts that exceed $20 million or has adjusted business income minus the loss adjustment that exceeds $1.3 million, then the credit is not available to the trust. (*Letter Ruling No. LR 2013-3*, Michigan Department of Treasury, June 26, 2013, CCH MICHIGAN TAX REPORTS, ¶401-803)

Credit reduction.—If gross receipts exceed $19 million, the credit is reduced by a fraction. The fraction's numerator is the amount of gross receipts over $19 million, and the denominator is $1 million. (Sec. 208.1417(5), M.C.L.)

¶1485 Venture Capital Investment Program

Laws: Secs. 206.673, 208.1419, M.C.L. (CCH MICHIGAN TAX REPORTS, ¶12-101)

CCH Caution: Corporate Income Tax Enacted

Only for the first tax year ending after 2011, taxpayers with certificated credits may elect to pay the Michigan business tax. All other taxpayers are required to file and pay the corporate income tax (see ¶1510). (Sec. 206.680, M.C.L.)

The Michigan Early Stage Venture Capital Investment program establishes the Michigan Early Stage Venture Capital Investment Corporation. (Sec. 125.2231, M.C.L. through Sec. 125.2263, M.C.L.) The corporation is charged with establishing a fund from which monies will be invested in venture capital companies to promote investment in qualified businesses. (Sec. 125.2249, M.C.L.) A similar credit was available against the former single business tax, see ¶1124.

The corporation will enter into agreements with investors that must contain an established investment amount and repayment schedule, a guaranteed negotiated amount or negotiated return on investment over the agreement's term, and a maximum amount of tax credit available to the investor. An investor may claim a credit against the Michigan business tax. (Sec. 125.2247, M.C.L.)

• *Credit amount*

The amount of the credit is equal to the difference between the amount actually repaid and the negotiated return amount set forth in the agreement. (Sec. 125.2247(3), M.C.L.)

Tax voucher certificates issued under Sec. 125.2253, M.C.L. may be used to pay a tax liability for tax years beginning after 2008, and the total amount of certificates is capped at $150 million. However, the total amount of all tax voucher certificates will not exceed an amount sufficient to allow the Michigan early stage venture investment corporation to raise $450 million. The total amount of all tax voucher certificates is capped at $600 million. (Sec. 208.1419(1)-(2), M.C.L.)

• *Planning considerations*

MBT election.—Because this is a certificated credit, taxpayers may choose to claim the credit and pay the MBT in lieu of paying the corporate income tax. (Sec. 206.680, M.C.L.; Sec. 208.1107(1), M.C.L.)

Clawback.—Effective January 1, 2012, if a taxpayer fails to comply with terms in the agreement, then some or all of the credit may be added back to the taxpayer's corporate income tax liability. (Sec. 206.673, M.C.L.)

Limitation on voucher amount.—Only 25% of the vouchers may be approved for use in any one year. (Sec. 208.1419(4), M.C.L.)

Carryforward.—The amount of the voucher that may be used is the lesser of the amount on the voucher, the amount authorized to be used in that tax year, or the taxpayer's tax liability. Excess voucher amounts may be carried forward. (Sec. 208.1419(8), (10), M.C.L.)

Application required.—A taxpayer that is an investor in the Early Stage Venture Capital Investment Fund may apply to the Early Stage Venture Capital Investment Corporation for a tax voucher certificate. The corporation determines which investors are eligible for tax vouchers and the amount of the tax vouchers allowed to each investor, as described under the Michigan Early Stage Venture Investment Act. (Sec. 208.1419(5), (6), M.C.L.)

Sunset.—Tax vouchers may not be approved after 2015. (Sec. 208.1419(3), M.C.L.)

¶1486 Charitable Contributions Credits

Laws: Secs. 208.1421, 208.1422, 208.1425, 208.1427, M.C.L. (CCH MICHIGAN TAX REPORTS, ¶12-127, ¶12-128, ¶12-129, ¶12-141)

Forms: Form 4572, Michigan Business Tax Charitable Contributions Credit.

CCH Caution: Corporate Income Tax Enacted

Only for the first tax year ending after 2011, taxpayers with certificated credits may elect to pay the Michigan business tax. All other taxpayers are required to file and pay the corporate income tax (see ¶1510). (Sec. 206.680, M.C.L.)

Credits are available for contributions to support (1) specified public institutions, (2) the arts, (3) community and education foundations, and (4) shelters for homeless people, food kitchens, food banks, and similar entities.

Unitary business groups.—The credits below are computed on a combined basis. Intercompany transactions are generally not eliminated for the purpose of the credit calculation. (Instructions to Form 4572, Michigan Business Tax Charitable Contributions Credit)

To the extent a qualified taxpayer earning the community and education foundations credit, homeless shelter/food back credit, or public contributions credit, is included in a Unitary Business Group (UBG) for the relevant tax years, the eligible credit amount is limited to the lesser of $5,000, 50% of the contribution, or 5% of the UBG's tax liability.

• *Public contributions credit*

Taxpayers not subject to Michigan income tax are allowed a nonrefundable credit against the MBT for 50% of the aggregate amount of charitable contributions to:

— a public broadcast station not affiliated with an institution of higher education;

— public libraries;

— institutions of higher learning located in Michigan;

— the Michigan colleges foundation;

— any nonprofit corporation, fund, foundation, trust, or association organized and operated exclusively for the benefit of institutions of higher learning; and

— the Michigan housing and community development fund. (Sec. 208.1421, M.C.L.)

The credit equals 50% of the aggregate amount of the charitable contributions. The credit cannot exceed the lesser of 5% of the MBT liability, determined without regard to the credit, or $5,000. A similar credit was available against the former single business tax. (See ¶ 1108)

• *Arts credit*

Taxpayers may claim a nonrefundable credit against the Michigan business tax for charitable contributions of $50,000 or more that are made to either:

— a municipality or a nonprofit corporation affiliated with a municipality and an art, historical, or zoological institute for the purpose of benefiting the art, historical, or zoological institute; or

— an institution devoted to the procurement, care, study, and display of objects of lasting interest or value.

The credit is equal to 50% of the amount by which the aggregate amount of the contributions exceeds $50,000. For example, if a taxpayer contributed $60,000, he or she could claim a $5,000 credit. (Sec. 208.1422(1), M.C.L)

The credit is capped at $100,000 per year. (Sec. 208.1422(2), M.C.L.)

• *Community and education foundation credit*

Taxpayers may claim a credit against the Michigan business tax for contributions to an endowment fund of a community foundation. Contributions to an endowment fund of an education foundation qualify for the credit. (Sec. 208.1425(1), M.C.L.) The credit was available against the former single business tax. (See ¶ 1106)

The credit equals 50% of the amount the taxpayer contributes during the tax year to an endowment fund of a community foundation. However, the credit may not exceed the lesser of 5% of the taxpayer's tax liability for the tax year before claiming any credits or $5,000.

Two Revenue Administrative Bulletins provide a list of the certified community foundations and education endowment fund foundations for the 2014 tax year. (*Revenue Administrative Bulletin 2015-4*, CCH MICHIGAN TAX REPORTS, ¶ 401-965; *Revenue Administrative Bulletin 2015-5*, CCH MICHIGAN TAX REPORTS, ¶ 401-966)

• *Shelters for homeless people, food kitchens, food banks, and similar entities*

Taxpayers may claim a credit against the Michigan business tax for contributions to shelters for homeless people, food kitchens, food banks, and similar entities. The donee's primary purpose must be providing overnight accommodation, food, or meals to indigent people. Also, the contribution must be tax deductible under federal law. (Sec. 208.1427(1), M.C.L.) The credit was available against the former single business tax. (See ¶ 1106)

The credit equals 50% of the cash amount contributed by the taxpayer. However, the credit may not exceed the lesser of 5% of the taxpayer's tax liability for the tax year before claiming any credits or $5,000.

¶ 1487 Credit for Worker's Disability Compensation Payments

Laws: Sec. 208.1423, M.C.L. (CCH MICHIGAN TAX REPORTS, ¶ 12-131).

Forms: Form 4574, Michigan Business Tax Refundable Credits.

CCH Caution: Corporate Income Tax Enacted

Only for the first tax year ending after 2011, taxpayers with certificated credits may elect to pay the Michigan business tax. All other taxpayers are required to file and pay the corporate income tax (see ¶ 1510). (Sec. 206.680, M.C.L.)

A taxpayer that makes workers' disability compensation payments as an insurer or self-insurer may claim a credit against the Michigan business tax. (Sec. 208.1423(1), M.C.L.) The credit was available against the former single business tax. (See ¶1109)

The amount of the credit equals the amount of the workers' disability compensation payments for the tax year. The credit may be applied to the taxpayer's quarterly estimated tax liability.

¶1488 Next Energy Business Credits

Laws: Sec. 208.1429, M.C.L. (CCH MICHIGAN TAX REPORTS, ¶12-060a, ¶12-060b).

Forms: Form 4573, Michigan Business Tax Miscellaneous Nonrefundable Credits.

CCH Caution: Corporate Income Tax Enacted

Only for the first tax year ending after 2011, taxpayers with certificated credits may elect to pay the Michigan business tax. All other taxpayers are required to file and pay the corporate income tax (see ¶1510). (Sec. 206.680, M.C.L.)

A similar credit was available against the former single business tax (see ¶1116).

Unitary business groups.—A credit earned by a member of a Unitary Business Group (UBG) the eligible member's pro forma calculated liability must be used to determine the credit amount certified by the Michigan Economic Development Corporation (MEDC). The supporting pro forma calculation should be attached as a statement to the back of the form. (Instructions to Form 4573, Michigan Business Tax Miscellaneous Nonrefundable Credits)

- *Alternative energy business activity credit*

The credit is equal to the lesser of the following amounts:

— the amount by which the taxpayer's tax liability attributable to qualified business activity for the tax year exceeds the taxpayer's baseline tax liability attributable to qualified business activity; or

— 10% of the amount by which the taxpayer's adjusted qualified business activity performed in the state outside of a renaissance zone for the tax year exceeds the taxpayer's adjusted qualified business activity performed in the state outside of a renaissance zone for the 2001 tax year.

The credit cannot be claimed if the eligible taxpayer's tax liability attributable to qualified business activity for the tax year does not exceed the taxpayer's baseline tax liability attributable to qualified business activity.

The taxpayer's "baseline tax liability attributable to qualified business activity" is the taxpayer's tax liability for the 2001 tax year multiplied by a fraction the numerator of which is the ratio of the value of the taxpayer's property used for qualified business activity and located in Michigan outside of a renaissance zone for the 2001 tax year to the value of all of the taxpayer's property located in Michigan for the 2001 tax year plus the ratio of the taxpayer's payroll for qualified business activity performed outside of a renaissance zone for the 2001 tax year to all of the taxpayer's payroll for the 2001 tax year in Michigan and the denominator of which is two.

A "qualified business activity" is research, development, or manufacturing of an alternative energy marine propulsion system, an alternative energy system, an alternative energy vehicle, alternative energy technology, or renewable fuel. "Renewable fuels" are biodiesel, biodiesel blends containing at least 20% biodiesel, or biomass fuels.

The taxpayer's tax liability attributable to qualified business activity is the taxpayer's tax liability multiplied by a fraction the numerator of which is the ratio of the value of the taxpayer's property used for qualified business activity and located in Michigan outside of a renaissance zone to the value of all of the taxpayer's property located in Michigan plus the ratio of the taxpayer's payroll for qualified business activity performed outside of a renaissance zone to all of the taxpayer's payroll in Michigan and the denominator of which is two.

Practice Note: Attachments to Annual Return Required

A taxpayer that claims this credit must attach a copy of each of the following as issued pursuant to the Michigan Next Energy Authority Act to the annual return for each tax year in which the taxpayer claims the credit: the proof of certification that the taxpayer is an eligible taxpayer for the tax year, the proof of certification of the taxpayer's tax liability attributable to qualified business activity for the tax year, and the proof of certification of the taxpayer's baseline tax liability attributable to qualified business activity.

- *Alternative energy payroll credit*

The credit is equal to the taxpayer's qualified payroll amount. A taxpayer could only claim this credit after all allowable nonrefundable credits. If the credit exceeds the tax liability of the taxpayer for the tax year, that portion of the credit that exceeds the tax liability is refunded.

The "qualified payroll amount" is the amount equal to the payroll of the qualified alternative energy entity attributable to all qualified employees in the tax year of the qualified alternative energy entity for which the credit is being claimed, multiplied by the tax rate for that tax year. For purposes of the credit, "payroll" means the total salaries and wages before deducting any personal or dependency exemptions.

A "qualified alternative energy entity" is a taxpayer located in an alternative energy zone. A "qualified employee" is an individual who is employed by a qualified alternative energy entity, whose job responsibilities are related to the research, development, or manufacturing of activities of the qualified alternative energy entity, and whose regular place of employment is within an alternative energy zone.

¶1489 MEGA Credits

Laws: Secs. 206.673, 208.1431, M.C.L. (CCH MICHIGAN TAX REPORT ¶12-085, ¶12-085b).

Forms: Form 4574, Michigan Business Tax Refundable Credits.

CCH Caution: Corporate Income Tax Enacted

Only for the first tax year ending after 2011, taxpayers with certificated credits may elect to pay the Michigan business tax. All other taxpayers are required to file and pay the corporate income tax (see ¶1510). (Sec. 206.680, M.C.L.)

Authorized businesses that create qualified new jobs in Michigan may claim a credit against the Michigan business tax. The Michigan Economic Growth Authority (MEGA) must issue an initial certification to the taxpayer prior to 2014. In addition, insurance companies and financial organizations may claim this credit. (Sec. 208.1431, M.C.L.) The credit was available against the former single business tax. (See ¶1112)

The MEGA may provide an additional Michigan business tax credit, not to exceed 20 years, to eligible taxpayers that make large capital investments and maintain jobs in Michigan. (Sec. 208.1431, M.C.L.) An eligible taxpayer may not claim this credit unless the MEGA has issued an initial certificate of authority to the taxpayer prior to 2014. (Sec. 208.1431(8), M.C.L.) The credit was available against the former single business tax. (See ¶1112)

• *Credit amount*

The credit amount is certified each year by the MEGA and may not exceed the sum of the payroll and health care benefits of the authorized business attributable to employees who perform qualified new jobs multiplied by the tax rate.

The amount of the credit is determined by the MEGA and is subject to the following limitations. If a taxpayer meets any of the specified criteria, related to businesses relocating in Michigan or businesses meeting specified job retention and investment requirements, the credit amount may not exceed one or both of the following: (1) the payroll attributable to the employees performing retained jobs multiplied by the tax rate, and (2) the tax liability of the taxpayer multiplied by a fraction, the numerator of which is the ratio of the value of new capital investment to all of the taxpayer's property in Michigan plus the ratio of the taxpayer's payroll attributable to retained jobs to all of the taxpayer's payroll in the state, and the denominator of which is two. Beginning with the 2008 taxable year, the credit against the MBT is equal to the payroll attributable to the employees performing retained jobs multiplied by the tax rate. If a taxpayer is located in Michigan on the date of its application, makes new capital investment of $250 million in Michigan, and maintains 500 full-time jobs, the credit amount may not exceed 50% of the credit amount described above. (Sec. 208.1431(1), M.C.L.) For the 2010 calendar year and each year after that, the total amount of credits allowed to be claimed in the first year of all new written agreements approved in that calendar year is capped at $95 million. (Sec. 208.1431(9), M.C.L.)

High-technology business.—High-technology businesses may claim a credit in an amount up to 200% of the sum of payroll and health care benefits attributable to employees who perform new jobs, multiplied by the tax rate, for the first three years of the credit. For the remaining years (the credit may be authorized for a maximum of seven years), the percentage is reduced to 100% from 200%. (Sec. 208.1431(1)(d), M.C.L.)

Historic property.—For businesses creating or retaining at least 15 jobs, occupying a historic resource property, and paying an average wage equal to or greater than 150% of the federal minimum wage, the credit amount is up to 100% of the sum of the payroll and health care benefits attributable to the employees who perform the new or retained jobs, multiplied by the tax rate. (Sec. 208.1431(1)(f), M.C.L.)

Retained jobs.—For businesses retaining at least 50 jobs, making new capital investment equal to $50,000 per retained job, and risking closure without the credit, the credit amount is up to 100% of the sum of the payroll and health care benefits attributable to the employees who perform retained jobs, multiplied by a fraction, and further multiplied by the tax rate. The fraction's numerator is the amount of new capital investment and the denominator is the number of retained jobs times $100,000. (Sec. 208.1431(1)(e), M.C.L.)

• *Planning considerations*

Separate return election.—Effective March 29, 2012, if a Michigan business taxpayer has this certificated credit and is part of a unitary business group, the taxpayer may elect to file a separate MBT return as opposed to a combined return. (Sec. 206.680(3), M.C.L.)

MBT election.—Because this is a certificated credit, taxpayers may choose to claim the credit and pay the MBT in lieu of paying the corporate income tax. (Sec. 206.680, M.C.L.; Sec. 208.1107(1), M.C.L.)

Clawback.—Effective January 1, 2012, if a taxpayer fails to comply with terms in the agreement, then some or all of the credit may be added back to the taxpayer's corporate income tax liability. (Sec. 206.673, M.C.L.)

Length of credit.—The credit may be authorized for up to 20 years. (Sec. 208.1431(1), M.C.L.)

Recapture.—A taxpayer that claims this credit that has an agreement with the MEGA authority based on qualified new jobs and removes from Michigan 51% or more of those qualified new jobs within three years after the first year in which the taxpayer claims the credit must pay the total credit amount to the Department of Treasury within 12 months after those jobs are removed. (Sec. 208.1431(6), M.C.L.)

¶1489a Renaissance Zone Credit

Laws: Secs. 125.2689, 125.2690, 206.673, 208.1433, M.C.L. (CCH MICHIGAN TAX REPORTS, ¶12-061)

Forms: Form 4573, Michigan Business Tax Miscellaneous Nonrefundable Credits; Form 4595, Michigan Business Tax Renaissance Zone Credit Schedule.

CCH Caution: Corporate Income Tax Enacted

Only for the first tax year ending after 2011, taxpayers with certificated credits may elect to pay the Michigan business tax. All other taxpayers are required to file and pay the corporate income tax (see ¶1510). (Sec. 206.680, M.C.L.)

A business located and conducting business activity in a Renaissance Zone (RZ) may claim a Michigan Business Tax (MBT) credit based on the tax liability attributable to business activity conducted within the RZ. (Sec. 208.1433(1), M.C.L.) The credit was available against the former single business tax. (See ¶1118) The credit continues through the tax year in which the renaissance zone designation expires. (Sec. 208.1433(3), M.C.L.)

Individuals or businesses are ineligible for the credit if they are delinquent in paying SBT, property tax, or city income tax. However, a business located in a renaissance zone will not be denied an exemption if the business failed to file an SBT or an MBT return before December 31, provided that the business has no tax liability for that tax year. In addition, residential rental property located in a RZ is ineligible for the incentives if it is not in substantial compliance with state and local zoning, building, and housing laws. RZ incentives do not apply to real property in a RZ on which a casino is operated, personal property of a casino located in a RZ, and all property associated or affiliated with the operation of a casino. (Sec. 125.2690, M.C.L.)

An individual who is a resident of a RZ is ineligible for the incentives when the Department of Treasury determines that the incentives granted that person have resulted in $10 million in forgone revenue. (Sec. 125.2690, M.C.L.)

• *Credit amount*

The amount of the credit is the lesser of:

(1) the tax liability attributable to business activity conducted in a renaissance zone in the tax year, or

(2) 10% of adjusted services performed in a designated renaissance zone; or

(3) for a taxpayer located and conducting business activity in a RZ before December 1, 2002, a credit equal to the greater of: (1) the lesser of the amounts calculated above, or (2) the product of: (a) the credit claimed under the SBT act for the tax year ending in 2007; (b) the ratio of the taxpayer's Michigan payroll in the tax year divided by the taxpayer's Michigan payroll in the tax year ending in

2007; and (c) the ratio of the taxpayer's RZ business activity factor for the tax year divided by the taxpayer's RZ business activity factor for the tax year ending in 2007.

(Sec. 208.1433(1), M.C.L.)

Reduction of credit.—During its last three years, a RZ's tax credit is reduced by the following percentages:

— for the tax year that is two years before the final year of designation, 25%;

— for the tax year immediately preceding the final year of designation, 50%; and

— for the tax year that is the final year of designation, 75%.

(Sec. 125.2689(3), M.C.L.)

• *Planning considerations*

MBT election.—Because this is a certificated credit, taxpayers may choose to claim the credit and pay the MBT in lieu of paying the corporate income tax. (Sec. 206.680, M.C.L.; Sec. 208.1107(1), M.C.L.)

Clawback.—Effective January 1, 2012, if a taxpayer fails to comply with terms in the agreement, then some or all of the credit may be added back to the taxpayer's corporate income tax liability. (Sec. 206.673, M.C.L.)

Unitary business groups.—If the entity located and conducting business activity in the zone is a member of a Unitary Business Group (UBG), the credit must be calculated at the member entity level. If more than one member is eligible for the credit, complete a separate Form 4595 for each member and attach to the UBG's return. (Instructions to Form 4595, Michigan Business Tax Renaissance Zone Credit Schedule)

¶1489b Historic Preservation Credit

Laws: Secs. 206.673, 208.1435, 208.1510, M.C.L. (CCH MICHIGAN TAX REPORTS, ¶12-090)

Forms: Form 3581, Michigan Historic Preservation Credit; Form 3614, Historic Preservation Tax Credit Assignment.

CCH Caution: Corporate Income Tax Enacted

Only for the first tax year ending after 2011, taxpayers with certificated credits may elect to pay the Michigan business tax. All other taxpayers are required to file and pay the corporate income tax (see ¶1510). (Sec. 206.680, M.C.L.)

A similar credit was available against the former single business tax (see ¶1120). Carryforwards of unused credit against the SBT may be claimed against the MBT for the same period that would have been allowed under the SBT provision. Carryovers for both the SBT and MBT credit are limited to 10 years. (Sec. 208.1435(8), M.C.L.)

If a taxpayer has unused carryforward amounts for the historic preservation credit, and an amount of the credit must be added back to the taxpayer's tax liability due to having the certificate of rehabilitation revoked or selling the historic property within certain time limits, then the amount otherwise added back may instead be used to reduce the carryforward amount. (Sec. 208.1435(9), M.C.L.)

• *Credit amount*

The credit is equal to 25% of qualified expenditures. If a taxpayer's expenditures are eligible for the federal credit, the taxpayer must claim the federal credit in order to claim the state credit and the state credit must be reduced by the amount of the federal credit received. (Sec. 208.1435(2), M.C.L.) The total of the credits claimed against the MBT and personal income tax for a rehabilitation project may not exceed 25% of the total qualified expenditures eligible for the MBT credit for that project. (Sec. 208.1435(17), M.C.L.)

Additional credits.—For tax years that begin after 2008, a taxpayer with a preapproval letter issued before 2014 may claim an additional credit against the MBT. At least 25% of these particular credits are reserved for projects with $1 million or less in qualified expenditures. The credit amount is between 10% and 15% of the qualified expenditures; this will be in preapproval letters issued by the State Housing Development Authority. The credit for all taxpayers is capped as follows: $8 million in calendar year 2009, $9 million in 2010, $10 million in 2011, $11 million in 2012, and $12 million in 2013.

For a high community impact rehabilitation plan, the State Housing Development Authority may approve three additional credits during calendar year 2009 and two additional credits during 2010-2013. The amount of the credit may be up to 15% of the taxpayer's qualified expenditures. The credit is capped at $3 million per tax year per taxpayer; unused amounts may be carried forward. These projects will have a significantly greater historic, social, and economic impact than other projects. Other statutory criteria must also be met.

For the 2011, 2012, and 2013 calendar years, the State Housing Development Authority may use one of the additional credits available for a high community impact rehabilitation plan to provide for a combined rehabilitation plan. A "combined rehabilitation plan" means a rehabilitation plan for the rehabilitation of one or more historic resources that are located within the same geographic district. Such a plan is determined to have a greater impact on the community than the rehabilitation of a single larger historic resource would have. The maximum amount of credits available for a combined rehabilitation plan is $24 million, pro rata to each taxpayer. The combined plan is subject to additional statutory requirements.

• *Planning considerations*

MBT election.—Because this is a certificated credit, taxpayers may choose to claim the credit and pay the MBT in lieu of paying the corporate income tax. (Sec. 206.680, M.C.L.; Sec. 208.1107(1), M.C.L.)

Clawback.—Effective January 1, 2012, if a taxpayer fails to comply with terms in the agreement, then some or all of the credit may be added back to the taxpayer's corporate income tax liability. (Sec. 206.673, M.C.L.)

Refund option.—A portion of the credit may be claimed as refundable. (Sec. 208.1510, M.C.L.)

Unitary business groups.—Members of a Unitary Business Group (UBG) calculate the credit at the member entity level and apply it against the UBG's tax liability. If more than one member is eligible for the credit, complete a separate Form 4581 for each member and attach to the UBG's return. (Instructions to Form 3581, Michigan Historic Preservation Credit)

Refund, recapture provisions.—For projects for which a certificate of completed rehabilitation is issued for a tax year beginning after 2008 and for which the credit amount allowed is less than $250,000, a taxpayer may irrevocably elect to receive a refund of the amount that exceeds the taxpayer's tax liability. However, the refund amount is limited to 90% of the amount that exceeds the taxpayer's tax liability. The refund is in lieu of carrying the credit forward. Also, for tax years beginning after 2008, a taxpayer can avoid recapture of the credit if the taxpayer enters a written agreement with the State Historic Preservation Office.

¶1489c Brownfield Credit

Laws: Secs. 206.673, 208.1437, 208.1510, M.C.L. (CCH Michigan Tax Reports, ¶12-080)

Forms: Form 4573; Michigan Business Tax Miscellaneous Nonrefundable Credits, Form 4584, Michigan Business Tax Election of Refund or Carryover of Credits.

CCH Caution: Corporate Income Tax Enacted

Only for the first tax year ending after 2011, taxpayers with certificated credits may elect to pay the Michigan business tax. All other taxpayers are required to file and pay the corporate income tax (see ¶1510). (Sec. 206.680, M.C.L.)

A similar credit was available against the former Single Business Tax (SBT) (see ¶1117).

The Michigan Economic Growth Authority may certify a MBT credit based on an agreement entered into prior to 2008 under the former SBT credit provision. However, the number of years for which the credit may be claimed under the MBT is equal to the maximum number of years designated in the agreement reduced by the number of years for which a credit had been claimed or could have been claimed under the former SBT credit. (Sec. 208.1437(24), M.C.L.) In addition, a credit may be based on an agreement entered into with MEGA after 2007 and before 2013 under the MBT credit provision.

• *Credit amount*

There are two levels of credit. If the total of all credits for a project is $1 million or less, the credit amount equals 10% of the cost of the qualified taxpayer's eligible investment paid or accrued by the qualified taxpayer on an eligible property. If the total of all credits for a project is more than $1 million and less than $30 million and the project is located in a qualified local governmental unit, the credit equals a percentage determined by the MEGA not to exceed 10% of the cost of the qualified taxpayer's eligible investment paid or accrued by the qualified taxpayer on an eligible property. For projects costing either $10 million or less or more than $10 million and $300 million or less (for projects approved on or after January 1, 2010, the $300 million figure is lowered to $100 million), the Michigan Economic Growth Authority (MEGA) may determine the credit amount to be up to 12.5% of the costs of an eligible investment. If the project is designated as an urban development area project, the credit amount may be up to 15% of the costs (or, up to 20% of the costs until December 31, 2010). (Sec. 208.1437(1), M.C.L.)

For projects that will cost $10 million or less, the total of all credits for all projects may not exceed $30 million in any calendar year. For projects that will cost $2 million or less, the total of all credits for all projects may not exceed $10 million in any calendar year. Effective April 8, 2008, the two separate caps are removed; the new cap for such projects is $63 million for the 2008 calendar year, but is reduced to $40 million per year for calendar years after 2008. (Sec. 208.1437(3), (31), M.C.L.)

• *Planning considerations*

MBT election.—Because this is a certificated credit, taxpayers may choose to claim the credit and pay the MBT in lieu of paying the corporate income tax. (Sec. 206.680, M.C.L.; Sec. 208.1107(1), M.C.L.)

Clawback.—Effective January 1, 2012, if a taxpayer fails to comply with terms in the agreement, then some or all of the credit may be added back to the taxpayer's corporate income tax liability. (Sec. 206.673, M.C.L.)

Refund option.—A portion of the credit may be claimed as refundable. (Sec. 208.1510, M.C.L.)

Carryforward provisions.—The credit may be carried forward for up to 10 years. Alternatively, taxpayers may elect to refund the excess credit instead of carrying it forward. If this election is made, the refund amount is equal to 85% of the portion of the credit exceeding the taxpayer's liability; the remaining 15% of the credit is forgone. (Sec. 208.1437(18), M.C.L.)

Recapture.—The credit provides for recapture when personal property is sold or moved. (Sec. 208.1437(19), M.C.L.)

Assignment.—If a qualified taxpayer pays or accrues eligible investment on or to an eligible property that is leased for a minimum of 10 years or sold to another taxpayer for use in a business activity, the qualified taxpayer may assign all or a portion of the credit based on that eligible investment to the lessee or purchaser. A credit may only be assigned to a taxpayer who will be qualified when the assignment is complete. A purchaser may subsequently assign a credit or part of a credit to a lessee. (Sec. 208.1437(20), M.C.L.) A qualified taxpayer that is a partnership, limited liability company, or S corporation may assign all or a portion of its credit to its partners, members, or shareholders based on their proportionate share of ownership or based on an alternative method approved by the Department. (Sec. 208.1437(21), M.C.L.)

¶1489d Credit for Low-Grade Hematite Pellets

Laws: Sec. 208.1439, M.C.L. (CCH MICHIGAN TAX REPORTS, ¶12-134)

Forms: Form 4573, Michigan Business Tax Miscellaneous Nonrefundable Credits.

CCH Caution: Corporate Income Tax Enacted

Only for the first tax year ending after 2011, taxpayers with certificated credits may elect to pay the Michigan business tax. All other taxpayers are required to file and pay the corporate income tax (see ¶1510). (Sec. 206.680, M.C.L.)

A taxpayer may claim a credit against the Michigan business tax based on the amount of qualified low-grade hematite consumed in an industrial or manufacturing process that is the business activity of the taxpayer. A similar credit was available against the former Single Business Tax (SBT). (¶1122)

The credit amount equals $1 per long ton of qualified low-grade hematite consumed in an industrial or manufacturing process. Unused amounts may be carried forward for five years.

Unitary business groups (UBG) calculate the credit on the basis of the aggregate tonnage of the pellets by all members of the UBG in an industrial or manufacturing process.

¶1489e Entrepreneurial Credit

Laws: Sec. 208.1441, M.C.L. (CCH MICHIGAN TAX REPORTS, ¶12-070c)

Forms: Form 4573; Michigan Business Tax Miscellaneous Nonrefundable Credits, Form 4587, Schedule of Recapture of Certain Business Tax Credits and Deductions.

CCH Caution: Corporate Income Tax Enacted

Only for the first tax year ending after 2011, taxpayers with certificated credits may elect to pay the Michigan business tax. All other taxpayers are required to file and pay the corporate income tax (see ¶1510). (Sec. 206.680, M.C.L.)

Eligible taxpayers may claim a credit against the Michigan business tax provided that they meet requirements for new jobs. (Sec. 208.1441, M.C.L.)

For the 2008, 2009, and 2010 tax years, a taxpayer is eligible if all of these conditions are met:

— had less than $25 million (adjusted annually for inflation) in gross receipts in the previous tax year;

— has created or transferred into Michigan at least 20 new jobs in the previous tax year;

— has made a capital investment in Michigan of at least $1.25 million in the previous tax year, excluding the purchase of an existing plant or existing equipment; and

— is not a retail establishment as described in major groups 52—59 and 70 under the standard industrial classification code, other than a new restaurant that is not a franchise or part of a unitary business group.

(Sec. 208.1441(1), M.C.L.)

In addition, a taxpayer may qualify for the credit if it received a research and development capital investment for which another taxpayer claimed the R&D contributions credit (see ¶1478a) and meets the following requirements:

— had less than $25 million in gross receipts in the previous tax year; and

— has increased the number of new jobs in Michigan by at least 20% from the previous tax year.

(Sec. 208.1441(2), M.C.L.)

Unitary business groups.—Members of a Unitary Business Group (UBG) calcualte the credit against the eligible member's business activity only. The resulting credit(s) is then applied against the UBG's tax liability. (Instructions to Form 4573, Michigan Business Tax Miscellaneous Nonrefundable Credits)

• *Credit amount*

The amount of the credit is 100% of the taxpayer's liability attributable to the increased employment. The tax liability attributable to the increased employment is the total liability multiplied by a fraction. The fraction's numerator is the payroll of the increased jobs of the facility; and the denominator is the taxpayer's total Michigan payroll. (Sec. 208.1441, M.C.L.)

• *Planning considerations*

Duration.—The credit may be claimed for three years. (Sec. 208.1441, M.C.L.)

Recapture.—The credit is subject to recapture if the taxpayer relocates the new jobs outside of Michigan within 5 years of claiming the credit or if the taxpayer reduces the employment levels by more than 10%. (Sec. 208.1441(4), M.C.L.)

¶1489f Motor Vehicle Inventory Credit

Laws: Sec. 208.1445, M.C.L. (CCH MICHIGAN TAX REPORTS, ¶12-143)

Forms: Form 4573; Michigan Business Tax Miscellaneous Nonrefundable Credits.

CCH Caution: Corporate Income Tax Enacted

Only for the first tax year ending after 2011, taxpayers with certificated credits may elect to pay the Michigan business tax. All other taxpayers are required to file and pay the corporate income tax (see ¶1510). (Sec. 206.680, M.C.L.)

New motor vehicle dealers may claim a credit against the Michigan business tax for a portion of the costs paid to acquire motor vehicles and motor vehicle parts. (Sec. 208.1445, M.C.L.)

• *Credit amount*

The credit is equal to 0.25% of the amount paid to acquire new motor vehicles and parts in the tax year. (Sec. 208.1445(1), M.C.L.)

• *Planning considerations*

The credit is not refundable and may not be carried forward. (Sec. 208.1445(2), M.C.L.)

¶1489g Grocery Store Credits

Laws: Secs. 208.1447, 208.1449, M.C.L. (CCH MICHIGAN TAX REPORTS, ¶12-144, 12-145)

Forms: Form 4573; Michigan Business Tax Miscellaneous Nonrefundable Credits.

CCH Caution: Corporate Income Tax Enacted

Only for the first tax year ending after 2011, taxpayers with certificated credits may elect to pay the Michigan business tax. All other taxpayers are required to file and pay the corporate income tax (see ¶1510). (Sec. 206.680, M.C.L.)

Two credits against the Michigan business tax are available to qualified Michigan grocery stores.

The first credit is available to a large grocery store that meets the following requirements:

— Operates at least 17 million square feet of enclosed retail space and 2 million square feet of enclosed warehouse space in Michigan;

— Sells fresh or frozen foods, prescriptions, health care products, cosmetics, pet products, carbonated beverages, beer, wine, and liquor at retail;

— Sales of items above account for more than 35% of the taxpayer's total annual sales; and

— Is headquartered in Michigan.

(Sec. 208.1447, M.C.L.)

A small grocer also qualifies for a credit against the MBT if it meets the conditions listed above, except it need only operate at least 2.5 million square feet of enclosed retail space and 1.4 million square feet of enclosed warehouse space, headquarters, and transportation services in Michigan. (Sec. 208.1449, M.C.L.)

• *Credit amounts*

The credit available to large grocery stores is equal to 1% of the taxpayer's Michigan compensation, up to an $8.5 million maximum. (Sec. 208.1447(1), M.C.L.)

The small grocer's credit is equal to 0.125% of the taxpayer's Michigan compensation, up to a $300,000 maximum. (Sec. 208.1449(1), M.C.L.)

• *Planning considerations*

The credits may not be refunded and may not be carried forward. (Secs. 208.1447(2), 208.1449(2), M.C.L.)

Exclusive provision.—The credits are mutually exclusive. (Sec 208.1447(3), M.C.L.)

¶1489h Beverage Container Manufacturer Credit

Laws: Sec. 208.1451, M.C.L. (CCH MICHIGAN TAX REPORTS, ¶12-146)

Forms: Form 4573; Michigan Business Tax Miscellaneous Nonrefundable Credits.

CCH Caution: Corporate Income Tax Enacted

Only for the first tax year ending after 2011, taxpayers with certificated credits may elect to pay the Michigan business tax. All other taxpayers are required to file and pay the corporate income tax (see ¶1510). (Sec. 206.680, M.C.L.)

A distributor or manufacturer who originates a deposit on a beverage container may claim a credit against the Michigan business tax. (Sec. 208.1451, M.C.L.)

• *Credit amount*

If the surcharge is imposed (see ¶1452), the credit amount is equal to 30.5% of the taxpayer's expenses incurred to comply with the beverage container law. If the surcharge is not imposed, the credit rate decreases to 25% of the taxpayer's expenses. (Sec. 208.1451(1), M.C.L.)

• *Planning considerations*

The credit may not be refunded and may not be carried forward. (Sec. 208.1451(2), M.C.L.)

¶1489i Hybrid Vehicle Technology Research Credit

Laws: Secs. 206.673, 208.1450, M.C.L. (CCH MICHIGAN TAX REPORTS, ¶12-065a)

Forms: Form 4574; Michigan Business Tax Refundable Credits.

CCH Caution: Corporate Income Tax Enacted

Only for the first tax year ending after 2011, taxpayers with certificated credits may elect to pay the Michigan business tax. All other taxpayers are required to file and pay the corporate income tax (see ¶1510). (Sec. 206.680, M.C.L.)

Applicable to tax years beginning after 2005 and ending before 2016, a research and development credit against the Michigan business tax is created for qualified technology. "Qualified technology" is defined as a hybrid system to propel a motor vehicle. "Research" has the same meaning as in IRC Sec. 41(d). (Sec. 208.1450, M.C.L.) The credit was available against the former Single Business Tax (SBT). (See ¶1129)

A taxpayer that qualified to claim the hybrid vehicle technology research credit against the SBT may claim the credit against the MBT for the total number of years designated in the agreement with Michigan Economic Growth Authority reduced by the number of years the taxpayer claimed the credit against the SBT, or until January 1, 2016, whichever occurs first. (Sec. 208.1450, M.C.L.)

Practice Note: Relationship to General Research Credit

A taxpayer that claims the hybrid vehicle technology research credit against the SBT is not prohibited from claiming a hybrid vehicle technology research credit against the MBT. However, the taxpayer may not claim both credits based on the same research and development. (Sec. 208.1450a, M.C.L.)

• *Credit amount*

The amount of the credit is equal to 3.9% of compensation paid to employees performing research and development of a qualified technology. The MBT credit is limited to $2 million per year per taxpayer. (Sec. 208.1450(1), (3), M.C.L.)

• *Planning considerations*

MBT election.—Because this is a certificated credit, taxpayers may choose to claim the credit and pay the MBT in lieu of paying the corporate income tax. (Sec. 206.680, M.C.L.; Sec. 208.1107(1), M.C.L.)

Clawback.—Effective January 1, 2012, if a taxpayer fails to comply with terms in the agreement, then some or all of the credit may be added back to the taxpayer's corporate income tax liability. (Sec. 206.673, M.C.L.)

Sunset.—The credit must be claimed in tax years that end before 2016. (Sec. 208.1450(1), M.C.L.)

¶1489j Private Equity Fund Credit

Laws: Sec. 208.1453, M.C.L. (CCH MICHIGAN TAX REPORTS, ¶12-055b)

Forms: Form 4573, Michigan Business Tax Miscellaneous Nonrefundable Credits.

CCH Caution: Corporate Income Tax Enacted

Only for the first tax year ending after 2011, taxpayers with certificated credits may elect to pay the Michigan business tax. All other taxpayers are required to file and pay the corporate income tax (see ¶1510). (Sec. 206.680, M.C.L.)

A nonrefundable credit against the Michigan business tax is available to private equity funds based on the ratio of a fund's activity conducted in the state for the tax year to its total activity conducted everywhere. (Sec. 208.1453, M.C.L.)

The credit is limited to taxpayers that are private equity funds that serve as a conduit for the investment of private securities not listed on a public exchange by "accredited investors" or "qualified purchasers", as defined under the Internal Revenue Code.

• *Credit amount*

The credit is equal to the taxpayer's tax liability for the tax year (after claiming other credits) multiplied by a fraction, the numerator of which is the total activity of the private equity fund manager conducted in Michigan during the tax year and the denominator of which is the total activity of the fund manager conducted everywhere during the tax year. (Sec. 208.1453, M.C.L.)

¶1489k Credit for Property Taxes on Certain Farmland and Buildings

Laws: Secs. 206.673, 324.36101—324.36117, M.C.L. (CCH MICHIGAN TAX REPORTS, ¶12-095)

Forms: Form 4594, Michigan Farmland Preservation Tax Credit; Form 4574, Michigan Business Tax Refundable Credits.

CCH Caution: Corporate Income Tax Enacted

Only for the first tax year ending after 2011, taxpayers with certificated credits may elect to pay the Michigan business tax. All other taxpayers are required to file and pay the corporate income tax (see ¶1510). (Sec. 206.680, M.C.L.)

Owners of farmland and related farm buildings subject to either a development rights agreement, an agricultural conservation easement, or a purchase of development rights under the Michigan farmland and open space preservation provisions (Part 361 of the Natural Resources and Environmental Protection Act) are allowed a credit against the Michigan business tax if they are not allowed a similar personal income tax credit. (Sec. 324.36109(2), M.C.L.) The credit was available against the former Single Business Tax (SBT). (See ¶1114)

• *Credit amount*

The credit equals the amount by which the property taxes on the land and structures used in farming operations restricted by the development rights agreement, easements, or purchases of development rights exceeds 3.5% of business income tax base, plus compensation to shareholders not included in adjusted business income, excluding any deductions taken under IRC Sec. 613. (Sec. 324.36109(2), M.C.L.)

• *Planning considerations*

MBT election.—Because this is a certificated credit, taxpayers may choose to claim the credit and pay the MBT in lieu of paying the corporate income tax. (Sec. 206.680, M.C.L.; Sec. 208.1107(1), M.C.L.)

Clawback.—Effective January 1, 2012, if a taxpayer fails to comply with terms in the agreement, then some or all of the credit may be added back to the taxpayer's corporate income tax liability. (Sec. 206.673, M.C.L.)

Pass-through entities.—A partner in a partnership and a shareholder of an S corporation are considered owners of farmland and related farm buildings subject to an agreement, easement, or purchase and owned by the partnership and S corporation, respectively. A partner or shareholder is deemed to have paid a proportion of the property taxes on such property equal to the partner's or shareholder's percentage of stock ownership for the tax year. A member of a limited Liability Company (LLC) may also claim a credit against income tax for farmland covered by an agreement. A member's share of a credit is proportionate to the member's ownership interest or distributive share of ordinary income in the company. (Sec. 324.36109(1)(a), (f), M.C.L.)

¶1489I Film Production Expenditure Credits

Laws: Secs. 206.673, 208.1455, M.C.L. (CCH MICHIGAN TAX REPORTS, ¶12-085e)

Forms: Form 4574, Michigan Business Tax Refundable Credits; Form 4589, Michigan Film Credit Assignment.

CCH Caution: Corporate Income Tax Enacted

Only for the first tax year ending after 2011, taxpayers with certificated credits may elect to pay the Michigan business tax. All other taxpayers are required to file and pay the corporate income tax (see ¶1510). (Sec. 206.680, M.C.L.)

A taxpayer may claim a refundable credit against the Michigan business tax for a portion of direct production and personnel expenditures incurred in Michigan. A similar credit is available against the personal income withholding tax (see ¶612). To qualify for the credit, a production company must spend at least $50,000 in Michigan for the development, preproduction, production, or postproduction costs of a qualified production. (Sec. 208.1455, M.C.L.) In addition, a taxpayer must produce a product for distribution and is not required to have ownership or control over all the rights necessary to produce the product to qualify for the credit. (*MVW Game, LLC v. Michigan Film Office and Department of Treasury*, Michigan Court of Appeals, No. 304999, October 23, 2012, CCH MICHIGAN TAX REPORTS, ¶401-730)

• *Definitions*

Direct production expenditures.—Direct production expenditures are development, preproduction, production, or postproduction expenditures made in Michigan, including, but not limited to, intellectual property purchases, production software, set design and construction, location fees, catering, and insurance coverage. (Sec. 208.1455(12)(c), M.C.L.)

For a transaction to qualify as a direct production expenditure, two questions to consider are: what is the source within Michigan and what is the nature of the qualified transactions. For a source to be within Michigan, the vendor of property or services must have a non-temporary established level of physical presence in the state (i.e., at least one year of bricks and mortar storefront and at least one full-time employee). Regarding the nature of the transactions, several factors will be considered:

— industry standard markups for individual product categories;

— orders for goods or services to be used by a production company must be placed with suppliers by the seller;

— drop shipment arrangements must be supported by facts and documentation;

— the seller should not be directed or bound by the production company's choice of supplier;

— the seller must have adequate staffing and the staff must have the requisite skill levels to perform the functions attributed to them;

— the seller should bear the risk of the breach of contract; and

— the seller should have taken legal title to the goods before the possession of the goods passes to the production company.

(*Notice to Taxpayers Regarding Michigan Business Tax Film Production Credit Qualified Vendors,* Michigan Department of Treasury, June 22, 2010, CCH MICHIGAN TAX REPORTS, ¶401-508)

Qualified personnel expenditures.—A qualified personnel expenditure is a payment or compensation payable to below the line crew for below the line crew members who were not Michigan residents for at least 60 days before the agreement is approved. The personnel expenditures eligible for the credit are limited to $2 million per person. (Sec. 208.1455(12)(j), M.C.L.)

Qualified production.—Qualified production includes single or multi media entertainment content created in whole or in part in Michigan for distribution or exhibition to the general public in two or more states. Such a production can include a motion picture, documentary, sound recording, commercial, and digital animation, but it does not include live sporting events, political advertising, weather shows, talk or game shows, and obscene matters. (Sec. 208.1455(12)(k), M.C.L.) With respect to commercials, the Michigan Court of Appeals held that the credit is limited to commercials that promote or market other state certified qualified productions. Therefore, commercials that advertise some other product or service are not eligible for the credit. (*Michigan Film Coalition v. State of Michigan, et. al.,* Michigan Court of Appeals, No. 304000, August 21, 2012, CCH MICHIGAN TAX REPORTS, ¶401-704)

• *Credit amount*

The credit is equal up to 42% of direct production expenditures in a core community (up to 40% of direct production expenditures in Michigan other than a core community) and up to 30% of qualified personnel expenditures. (Sec. 208.1455(2), M.C.L.) The credit amount is reduced by a credit application and redemption fee equal to 0.5% of the credit claimed. (Sec. 208.1455(9), M.C.L.)

• *Application process*

An eligible production company must spend at least $50,000 in Michigan and enter an agreement with the Michigan Film Office. The application, along with a $100 fee, to enter an agreement should be submitted before production begins. In general, expenses incurred before the agreement is entered are not eligible for the credit. After production is completed, the taxpayer submits a request to the Film Office for a postproduction certificate. Additional information may be needed, including an independently-audited report of the expenses incurred. The postproduction certificate is then submitted to the Michigan Department of Treasury to claim the credit.

• *Limitations and other planning considerations*

MBT election.—Because this is a certificated credit, taxpayers may choose to claim the credit and pay the MBT in lieu of paying the corporate income tax. (Sec. 206.680, M.C.L.; Sec. 208.1107(1), M.C.L.)

Clawback.—Effective January 1, 2012, if a taxpayer fails to comply with terms in the agreement, then some or all of the credit may be added back to the taxpayer's corporate income tax liability. (Sec. 206.673, M.C.L.)

This credit cannot be claimed for the same expenses for which the film job training expenses credit is claimed. Also, effective May 26, 2011, this credit cannot be claimed for the same expenses for which the film production expenditures credit against the personal income tax is claimed. (Sec. 208.1455(2), M.C.L.)

This credit must be claimed after all other credits. (Sec. 208.1455(7), M.C.L.)

The credit may be irrevocably assigned, in whole or in part, to another taxpayer. (Sec. 208.1455(8), M.C.L.)

¶1489m Photovoltaic Energy Manufacturer

Laws: Secs. 206.673, 208.1430, M.C.L. (CCH MICHIGAN TAX REPORTS, ¶12-085g).

Forms: Form 4574, Michigan Business Tax Refundable Credits.

CCH Caution: Corporate Income Tax Enacted

Only for the first tax year ending after 2011, taxpayers with certificated credits may elect to pay the Michigan business tax. All other taxpayers are required to file and pay the corporate income tax (see ¶1510). (Sec. 206.680, M.C.L.)

Applicable to tax years that begin after 2008, a qualified taxpayer or an eligible taxpayer may claim a credit against the Michigan business tax for the development and manufacturing of photovoltaic energy, photovoltaic systems, or other photovoltaic technology. "Qualified taxpayer" is defined as a taxpayer that has entered an agreement to create at least 500 new jobs and to make at least $50 million in capital investment of which $25 million must be made before a certificate is issued. "Eligible taxpayer" is defined as a taxpayer that has entered into an agreement to create at least 250 new jobs and to make at least $100 million in capital investment of which $25 million must be made before a certificate is issued. (Sec. 208.1430, M.C.L.)

The taxpayer must enter an agreement with the Michigan Economic Growth Authority (MEGA) before 2012. MEGA will issue a certificate, which must be attached to the taxpayer's annual tax return. Failure to comply with requirements, either statutory or negotiated, may result in the credit being reduced, terminated, or added back to the tax liability.

• *Credit amount*

The amount of the credit is equal to 25% of the capital investment made in a new Michigan facility. The total amount of the credit is capped at $15 million per taxpayer. The total amount of the credit for all tax years is capped at $75 million. Generally, the credit should be taken in equal installments over two years. However, a taxpayer with a credit of $15 million or less may claim the entire amount in the same tax year in which the certification was issued. (Sec. 208.1430(1)-(4), M.C.L.)

• *Planning considerations*

MBT election.—Because this is a certificated credit, taxpayers may choose to claim the credit and pay the MBT in lieu of paying the corporate income tax. (Sec. 206.680, M.C.L.; Sec. 208.1107(1), M.C.L.)

Clawback.—Effective January 1, 2012, if a taxpayer fails to comply with terms in the agreement, then some or all of the credit may be added back to the taxpayer's corporate income tax liability. (Sec. 206.673, M.C.L.)

Taxpayers claiming a credit for manufacturers of polycrystalline silicon (see ¶1489n) may not claim this credit. (Sec. 208.1430(7), M.C.L.)

The taxpayer may make an irrevocable assignment of all or a portion of the credit. However, an assignment for each tax year must be made separately. The assignee must attach a completed assignment certificate to the annual tax return. (Sec. 208.1430(6), M.C.L.)

¶1489n Polycrystalline Silicon Manufacturer Credit

Laws: Secs. 206.673, 208.1432, M.C.L. (CCH MICHIGAN TAX REPORTS, ¶12-085f)

CCH Caution: Corporate Income Tax Enacted

Only for the first tax year ending after 2011, taxpayers with certificated credits may elect to pay the Michigan business tax. All other taxpayers are required to file and pay the corporate income tax (see ¶1510). (Sec. 206.680, M.C.L.)

A taxpayer whose Michigan business activity includes the manufacturing of polycrystalline silicon for solar cells and semiconductor microchips may claim a credit against the Michigan business tax based on its consumption of electricity. (Sec. 208.1432, M.C.L.) According to the Governor's Office, this credit is geared towards Dow Corning's Hemlock Semiconductor Corporation, which produces hyper-pure polycrystalline silicon for the semiconductor and solar industries. (*Press Release*, Governor Jennifer M. Granholm, August 6, 2008)

The credit may be claimed for 12 years (2012 through 2023). However, the taxpayer must enter an agreement with the Michigan Economic Growth Authority (MEGA) before November 2, 2008. MEGA will issue a certificate, which must be attached to the taxpayer's annual tax return. At least $25 million must be invested before a certificate is issued. Failure to comply with requirements, either statutory or negotiated, may result in the credit being reduced, terminated, or added back to the tax liability.

• *Credit amount*

The amount of the credit is calculated by multiplying the qualified consumption of electricity by the difference between the projected cost and the guaranteed cost of electricity. For tax years that begin after 2011 and before 2016, the credit may be calculated using the actual delivered price of electricity billed under a tariff rate or the projected cost of electricity, whichever is less. The credit is reduced for the 2022 and 2023 tax years: for the 2022 tax year, the qualified consumption of electricity is cut in half, and for the 2023 tax year, it is multiplied by 25%. (Sec. 208.1432a(1), M.C.L.; Sec. 208.1432b(1), M.C.L.)

• *Planning considerations*

MBT election.—Because this is a certificated credit, taxpayers may choose to claim the credit and pay the MBT in lieu of paying the corporate income tax. (Sec. 206.680, M.C.L.; Sec. 208.1107(1), M.C.L.)

Clawback.—Effective January 1, 2012, if a taxpayer fails to comply with terms in the agreement, then some or all of the credit may be added back to the taxpayer's corporate income tax liability. (Sec. 206.673, M.C.L.)

If the amount of the credit exceeds the taxpayer's liability, the taxpayer may choose a refund or carry forward the unused amount for up to 10 years. (Sec. 208.1432a(2), M.C.L.; Sec. 208.1432b(2), M.C.L.; Sec. 208.1432c(2), M.C.L.; Sec. 208.1432d(2), M.C.L.)

¶1489o Federal Procurement Credit

Laws: Secs. 206.673, 208.1431b, M.C.L. (CCH MICHIGAN TAX REPORTS, ¶12-070e)

Forms: Form 4584, Michigan Business Tax Election of Refund or Carryover of Credits.

CCH Caution: Corporate Income Tax Enacted

Only for the first tax year ending after 2011, taxpayers with certificated credits may elect to pay the Michigan business tax. All other taxpayers are required to file and pay the corporate income tax (see ¶1510). (Sec. 206.680, M.C.L.)

Taxpayers may claim a credit against the Michigan business tax for the employee payroll attributed to new jobs created as a result of being awarded a federal procurement contract from either the departments of Defense, Energy, or Homeland Security. To qualify, a minimum of 25 new full-time jobs must be created. (Sec. 208.1431b, M.C.L.)

• *Credit amount*

The credit is equal to 100% of the payroll attributed to the new jobs, multiplied by the tax rate. (Sec. 208.1431b(3), M.C.L.)

• *Planning considerations*

MBT election.—Because this is a certificated credit, taxpayers may choose to claim the credit and pay the MBT in lieu of paying the corporate income tax. (Sec. 206.680, M.C.L.; Sec. 208.1107(1), M.C.L.)

Clawback.—Effective January 1, 2012, if a taxpayer fails to comply with terms in the agreement, then some or all of the credit may be added back to the taxpayer's corporate income tax liability. (Sec. 206.673, M.C.L.)

Agreement required.—The taxpayer must enter an agreement with the Michigan Economic Growth Authority (MEGA) in order to claim the credit. MEGA will issue a certificate, which must be attached to the taxpayer's return. (Sec. 208.1431b(1) and (4), M.C.L.)

Carryforward or refund.—Unused credit may be refunded or carried forward for up to 10 years. (Sec. 208.1431b(3), M.C.L.)

Length of credit.—The credit may be claimed for up to seven years or the term of the contract, whichever is less, as determined by MEGA. (Sec. 208.1431b(3), M.C.L.)

¶1489p Film Job Training Expenses Credit

Laws: Sec. 208.1459, M.C.L. (CCH MICHIGAN TAX REPORTS, ¶12-075a)

Forms: Form 4573, Michigan Business Tax Miscellaneous Nonrefundable Credits.

CCH Caution: Corporate Income Tax Enacted

Only for the first tax year ending after 2011, taxpayers with certificated credits may elect to pay the Michigan business tax. All other taxpayers are required to file and pay the corporate income tax (see ¶1510). (Sec. 206.680, M.C.L.)

A taxpayer may claim a credit against the Michigan business tax for a portion of the salary and other expenditures paid to provide qualified personnel with on-the-job training as a member of the below the line crew. "Below the line crew" is defined as persons employed by a production company for production expenditures made after production begins and before production is completed, including, among others, the best boy, camera operator, film editor, lighting crew, and music and sound editors. However, below the line crew does not include a producer, director, writer, actor, or other similar personnel. (Sec. 208.1459, M.C.L.)

• *Credit amount*

The credit is equal up to 50% of the qualified job training expenditure, reduced by an application and redemption fee equal to 0.5% of the credit claimed. (Sec. 208.1459(2) and (8), M.C.L.)

• *Planning considerations*

Agreement/certification required.—Until September 30, 2015, the Michigan Film Office can enter an agreement with a taxpayer. To enter an agreement, the taxpayer must submit an application and a $100 application fee. (Sec. 208.1459(1), (3), M.C.L.) The taxpayer submits a request to the Michigan Film Office for job training expenditure certificate. The Office may request additional information, including an expenditure report audited by an independent certified public accountant. (Sec. 208.1459(5), M.C.L.) The certificate must be submitted to the Department of Treasury to claim the credit. (Sec. 208.1459(7), M.C.L.)

Carryforward or refund.—Unused credit may be carried forward for up to 10 years. (Sec. 208.1459(7), M.C.L.)

Exclusivity.—This credit cannot be claimed for the same expenses for which the film production expenditures credit (¶ 1489l) is claimed. (Sec. 208.1459(2), M.C.L.)

¶1489q Anchor Company Payroll Credit

Laws: Secs. 206.673, 208.1431a, M.C.L. (CCH MICHIGAN TAX REPORTS, ¶ 12-070d).

Forms: Form 4573, Michigan Business Tax Miscellaneous Nonrefundable Credits; Form 4584, Michigan Business Tax Election of Refund or Carryover of Credits.

CCH Caution: Corporate Income Tax Enacted

Only for the first tax year ending after 2011, taxpayers with certificated credits may elect to pay the Michigan business tax. All other taxpayers are required to file and pay the corporate income tax (see ¶ 1510). (Sec. 206.680, M.C.L.)

Michigan business taxpayers may claim a credit for a qualified customer's and supplier's payroll attributable to employees who perform qualified new jobs. The taxpayer must be designated as an anchor company, which is a qualified high-technology business that (1) is an integral part of a high-technology activity and (2) has the ability or potential ability to influence business decisions and site location of qualified suppliers and customers. (Sec. 208.1431a, M.C.L.)

A "qualified customer or supplier" is defined as a business that opens a new location in Michigan, a business that locates in Michigan, or an existing business located in Michigan that expands its business within the last year as a result of an anchor company and meets the following requirements:

— has financial transactions with the anchor company;

— sells a critical or unique component or technology necessary for the anchor company to market a finished product or buys a critical or unique component from the anchor company;

— has created more than 10 qualified new jobs; and

— has made an investment of at least $1 million.

(Sec. 208.1431a(6)(g), M.C.L.)

• *Credit amount*

The amount of the credit is up to 100% of the customer's and supplier's payroll attributable to employees who perform new jobs, multiplied by the tax rate. (Sec. 208.1431a(1), M.C.L.)

- *Planning considerations*

MBT election.—Because this is a certificated credit, taxpayers may choose to claim the credit and pay the MBT in lieu of paying the corporate income tax. (Sec. 206.680, M.C.L.; Sec. 208.1107(1), M.C.L.)

Clawback.—Effective January 1, 2012, if a taxpayer fails to comply with terms in the agreement, then some or all of the credit may be added back to the taxpayer's corporate income tax liability. (Sec. 206.673, M.C.L.)

Application/certification required.—The Michigan Economic Growth Authority (MEGA) must approve the taxpayer as an anchor company before the credit may be claimed. MEGA will issue a certificate to the taxpayer; the certificate must be attached to the tax return to claim the credit. (Sec. 208.1431a, M.C.L.)

Refundable/Carryforward.—The taxpayer may elect to have the excess credit refunded or carried forward for up to 10 years. (Sec. 208.1431a(1), M.C.L.)

Priority.—Applicable to tax years that begin after 2008, the credit is taken after all other allowable nonrefundable credits. (Sec. 208.1431a(5), M.C.L.)

Duration.—The credit may be claimed for up to five years. (Sec. 208.1431a(1), M.C.L.)

Credit reduction.—Failure to meet statutory or contractual requirements may result in the credit being reduced, eliminated, or paid back. (Sec. 208.1431a(4), M.C.L.)

¶1489r Anchor Company Taxable Value Credit

Laws: Secs. 206.673, 208.1431c, M.C.L. (CCH MICHIGAN TAX REPORTS, ¶12-085d).

Forms: Form 4573, Michigan Business Tax Miscellaneous Nonrefundable Credits; Form 4584, Michigan Business Tax Election of Refund or Carryover of Credits.

CCH Caution: Corporate Income Tax Enacted

Only for the first tax year ending after 2011, taxpayers with certificated credits may elect to pay the Michigan business tax. All other taxpayers are required to file and pay the corporate income tax (see ¶1510). (Sec. 206.680, M.C.L.)

Qualified taxpayers may claim a credit against the Michigan business tax for a portion of a qualified customer's or supplier's taxable property. The taxpayer must be designated as an anchor company, which is a qualified high-technology business that (1) is an integral part of a high-technology activity and (2) has the ability or potential ability to influence business decisions and site location of qualified suppliers and customers. In addition, the taxpayer must influence at least one customer or supplier to open, locate, or expand its business within a 10-mile radius of the anchor company, or, applicable to tax years that begin after 2008, is located in the same county or the adjacent county to the taxpayer and within an existing industrial site approved by MEGA. (Sec. 208.1431c, M.C.L.)

A "qualified customer or supplier" is defined as a business that opens a new location in Michigan, a business that locates in Michigan, or an existing business located in Michigan that expands its business within the last year as a result of an anchor company and meets the following requirements:

— has financial transactions with the anchor company;

— sells a critical or unique component or technology necessary for the anchor company to market a finished product or buys a critical or unique component from the anchor company;

— has created more than 10 qualified new jobs; and

— has made an investment of at least $1 million.

(Sec. 208.1431c(8)(g), M.C.L.)

• *Credit amount*

The amount of the credit is up to 5% of the taxable value of each qualified supplier's or customer's taxable property that is located within the applicable geographic boundaries of the anchor company. However, the amount of the credit is reduced to a maximum of 2.5% if the supplier's or customer's taxable property that is subject to the tax under the provisions for plant rehabilitation and industrial development districts. (Sec. 208.1431c(1), M.C.L.)

• *Planning considerations*

MBT election.—Because this is a certificated credit, taxpayers may choose to claim the credit and pay the MBT in lieu of paying the corporate income tax. (Sec. 206.680, M.C.L.; Sec. 208.1107(1), M.C.L.)

Clawback.—Effective January 1, 2012, if a taxpayer fails to comply with terms in the agreement, then some or all of the credit may be added back to the taxpayer's corporate income tax liability. (Sec. 206.673, M.C.L.)

Application/certification required.—The Michigan Economic Growth Authority (MEGA) must approve the taxpayer as an anchor company before the credit may be claimed. MEGA will issue a certificate to the taxpayer; the certificate must be attached to the tax return to claim the credit. (Sec. 208.1431a, M.C.L.)

Refundable/carryforward.—The taxpayer may elect to either (1) have the excess credit refunded or (2) have the excess credit carried forward for up to five years. (Sec. 208.1431c(6), M.C.L.)

Duration.—The credit may be claimed for up to five years. (Sec. 208.1431c(1), M.C.L.)

Priority.—Applicable to tax years that begin after 2008, the credit is taken after all other allowable nonrefundable credits. (Sec. 208.1431c(7), M.C.L.)

Credit reduction.—Failure to meet statutory or contractual requirements may result in the credit being reduced, eliminated, or paid back. (Sec. 208.1431c(5), M.C.L.)

¶1489s Fuel Delivery Systems Credit

Laws: Sec. 208.1460, M.C.L. (CCH MICHIGAN TAX REPORTS, ¶12-055d)

Forms: Form 4573, Michigan Business Tax Miscellaneous Nonrefundable Credits.

CCH Caution: Corporate Income Tax Enacted

Only for the first tax year ending after 2011, taxpayers with certificated credits may elect to pay the Michigan business tax. All other taxpayers are required to file and pay the corporate income tax (see ¶1510). (Sec. 206.680, M.C.L.)

Applicable to tax years that begin after 2008 and end before 2012, a taxpayer that is an owner of a service station may claim a credit against the Michigan business tax for a portion of the costs incurred to convert existing fuel delivery systems for E85 fuel or qualified biodiesel blends. (Sec. 208.1460, M.C.L.)

• *Credit amount*

The amount of the credit is equal to 30% of the costs incurred to convert existing systems to provide E85 fuel or qualified biodiesel blends or to create new fuel delivery systems for those fuels. However, costs for which the taxpayer has received a grant may not be included in the credit calculation. The credit is capped at $20,000 per tax year for each taxpayer, and is limited to $1 million per calendar year. (Sec. 208.1460(1)-(3), M.C.L.)

• *Planning considerations*

Nonrefundable.—The credit is not refundable. (Sec. 208.1460(3), M.C.L.)

Certificate.—The Energy Office will issue a certificate that must be attached to the taxpayer's tax return. (Sec. 208.1460(4), M.C.L.)

Recapture.—The credit is subject to possible recapture if the taxpayer stops using the fuel delivery system to provide E85 fuel or qualified biodiesel blends. (Sec. 208.1460(5), M.C.L.)

¶1489t Development Account Contributions Credit

Laws: Sec. 208.1426, M.C.L. (CCH MICHIGAN TAX REPORTS, ¶12-110)

Forms: Form 4573, Michigan Business Tax Miscellaneous Nonrefundable Credits.

CCH Caution: Corporate Income Tax Enacted

Only for the first tax year ending after 2011, taxpayers with certificated credits may elect to pay the Michigan business tax. All other taxpayers are required to file and pay the corporate income tax (see ¶1510). (Sec. 206.680, M.C.L.)

Applicable to the 2009 tax year and beyond, a taxpayer, including a qualified financial institution, may claim a credit against the Michigan business tax equal to a portion of the contributions made in a tax year to a fiduciary organization's reserve fund pursuant to the Individual or Family Development Account Program Act. (Sec. 208.1426, M.C.L.)

• *Credit amount*

The amount of the credit is equal to 75% of the contributions made. This credit and a similar credit against the personal income tax cannot exceed an annual cumulative maximum of $1 million. (Sec. 208.1426(1), (3), M.C.L.)

• *Planning considerations*

Carryforward.—Unused credit amounts may be carried forward for up to 10 years. (Sec. 208.1426(2), M.C.L.)

¶1489u Bonus Depreciation Credit

Laws: Sec. 208.1461, M.C.L. (CCH MICHIGAN TAX REPORTS, ¶12-055i)

Forms: Form 4573, Michigan Business Tax Miscellaneous Nonrefundable Credits.

CCH Caution: Corporate Income Tax Enacted

Only for the first tax year ending after 2011, taxpayers with certificated credits may elect to pay the Michigan business tax. All other taxpayers are required to file and pay the corporate income tax (see ¶1510). (Sec. 206.680, M.C.L.)

For tax years that begin after 2008 and end before 2011, taxpayers may claim a credit against the Michigan business tax for a portion of the 2008 tax year bonus depreciation amount deducted under IRC Sec. 168(k). The bonus depreciation deduction amount must be apportioned as the tax base is apportioned. Taxpayers that are regulated utilities do not qualify for the credit. (Sec. 208.1461, M.C.L.)

• *Credit amount*

The amount of the credit is 0.42% of the deduction amount claimed for the 2008 tax year for bonus depreciation under IRC Sec. 168(k). (Sec. 208.1461, M.C.L.)

• *Planning considerations*

Carryforward.—The credit may be carried forward for 10 years. (Sec. 208.1461, M.C.L.)

¶1489v Public Exhibitions Credit

Laws: Sec. 208.1446, M.C.L. (CCH MICHIGAN TAX REPORTS, ¶12-147).

CCH Caution: Corporate Income Tax Enacted

Only for the first tax year ending after 2011, taxpayers with certificated credits may elect to pay the Michigan business tax. All other taxpayers are required to file and pay the corporate income tax (see ¶1510). (Sec. 206.680, M.C.L.)

A qualified taxpayer may claim a credit against the Michigan business tax, provided that it meets certain conditions for a public exhibition. (Sec. 208.1446(1), M.C.L.) A "qualified taxpayer" is defined as a taxpayer that owns, operates, or controls an exhibition in Michigan that is open to the public and:

— promotes or displays the design or the concept of products that are designed, manufactured, or produced, in whole or in part, in Michigan and are available for sale to the general public;

— the exhibition uses more than 100,000 square feet of floor space;

— the exhibition is open to the general public at least seven consecutive days in a calendar year;

— attendance during the entire exhibition exceeds 500,000; and

— the exhibition has more than 3,000 credentialed journalists, including international ones, attend the exhibition.

(Sec. 208.1446(2), M.C.L.)

• *Credit amount*

In 2009, the amount of the credit is the taxpayer's tax liability or $500,000, whichever is less. In 2010 and beyond, the amount of the credit is decreased to the lesser of the taxpayer's tax liability or $250,000. (Sec. 208.1446(1), M.C.L.)

¶1489w Plug-in Traction Battery Packs Credit

Laws: Secs. 206.673, 208.1434, M.C.L. (CCH MICHIGAN TAX REPORTS, ¶12-055e).

Forms: Form 4574, Michigan Business Tax Refundable Credits.

CCH Caution: Corporate Income Tax Enacted

Only for the first tax year ending after 2011, taxpayers with certificated credits may elect to pay the Michigan business tax. All other taxpayers are required to file and pay the corporate income tax (see ¶1510). (Sec. 206.680, M.C.L.)

Applicable to tax years beginning after 2009 and ending before 2015, a taxpayer may claim a credit against the Michigan business tax for the manufacturing of plug-in traction battery packs in Michigan. To claim the credit, a taxpayer must enter into an agreement with the Michigan Economic Growth Authority (MEGA). At least one taxpayer must make a capital investment of $200 million by the end of 2012. (Sec. 208.1434(2), M.C.L.)

• *Credit amount*

The amount of the credit is as follows:

— For tax years that begin after 2010 and end before 2012, $500 for four kilowatt hours of battery capacity, plus $125 for each kilowatt hour of capacity over four hours. The credit is capped at $2,000 for each battery pack. The total number of battery packs eligible for the credit is capped at 20,000, and the potential total credit is capped at $40 million.

— For tax years that begin after 2011 and end before 2013, $375 for four kilowatt hours of battery capacity, plus $93.75 for each kilowatt hour of capacity over four hours. The credit is capped at $1,500 for each battery pack. The total number of battery packs eligible for the credit is capped at 40,000, and the potential total credit is capped at $43 million. A single taxpayer may not claim the credit for more than 25,000 battery packs.

— For tax years that begin after 2012 and end before 2014, $375 for four kilowatt hours of battery capacity, plus $93.75 for each kilowatt hour of capacity over four hours. The credit is capped at $1,500 for each battery pack. The total number of battery packs eligible for the credit is capped at 40,000, and the potential total credit is capped at $43 million. A single taxpayer may not claim the credit for more than 25,000 battery packs.

— For tax years that begin after 2013 and end before 2015, $375 for four kilowatt hours of battery capacity, plus $93.75 for each kilowatt hour of capacity over four hours. The credit is capped at $1,500 for each battery pack. The total number of battery packs eligible for the credit is capped at 25,000, and the potential total credit is capped at $9 million.

The credit may not be claimed for more than three years. (Sec. 208.1434(2), M.C.L.)

• *Planning considerations*

Separate return election.—Effective March 29, 2012, if a Michigan business taxpayer has this certificated credit and is part of a unitary business group, the taxpayer may elect to file a separate MBT return as opposed to a combined return. (Sec. 206.680(3), M.C.L.)

MBT election.—Because this is a certificated credit, taxpayers may choose to claim the credit and pay the MBT in lieu of paying the corporate income tax. (Sec. 206.680, M.C.L.; Sec. 208.1107(1), M.C.L.)

Clawback.—Effective January 1, 2012, if a taxpayer fails to comply with terms in the agreement, then some or all of the credit may be added back to the taxpayer's corporate income tax liability. (Sec. 206.673, M.C.L.)

Carryforward or refund.—The taxpayer may elect to have any excess credit carried forward for up to 10 years or have it refunded. (Sec. 208.1434(12), M.C.L.)

Priority.—This credit is claimed after nonrefundable credits. (Sec. 208.1434(12), M.C.L.)

Certificate required.—MEGA will issue a certificate, which must be attached to the annual tax return. (Sec. 208.1434(14), M.C.L.)

¶1489x Vehicle Engineering Credit

Laws: Secs. 206.673, 208.1434, M.C.L. (CCH MICHIGAN TAX REPORTS, ¶12-055f).

CCH Caution: Corporate Income Tax Enacted

Only for the first tax year ending after 2011, taxpayers with certificated credits may elect to pay the Michigan business tax. All other taxpayers are required to file and pay the corporate income tax (see ¶1510). (Sec. 206.680, M.C.L.)

Applicable to tax years beginning after 2011, a taxpayer may claim a credit against the Michigan business tax for a portion of the qualified expenses for vehicle engineering in Michigan to support battery integration. The expenses must be incurred for tax years beginning after 2008 and ending before 2014. (Sec. 208.1434(3), M.C.L.)

• *Credit amount*

The amount of the credit is up to 75% of the qualified expenses for vehicle engineering. The portion of annual expenses allowed for the credit depends on the number of motor vehicles manufactured as follows:

— at least 1,000 motor vehicles and fewer than 2,000 vehicles that would qualify for the IRC Sec. 30D credit, 20% of authorized annual expenses;

— at least 2,000 motor vehicles and fewer than 3,000 vehicles that would qualify for the IRC Sec. 30D credit, 40% of authorized annual expenses;

— at least 3,000 motor vehicles and fewer than 4,000 vehicles that would qualify for the IRC Sec. 30D credit, 60% of authorized annual expenses;

— at least 4,000 motor vehicles and fewer than 5,000 vehicles that would qualify for the IRC Sec. 30D credit, 80% of authorized annual expenses; and

— at least 5,000 motor vehicles that would qualify for the IRC Sec. 30D credit, 100% of authorized annual expenses.

(Sec. 208.1434(3), M.C.L.)

The credit is capped at $15 million per year per taxpayer, and at $135 million for all taxpayers. (Sec. 208.1434(3), M.C.L.)

• *Planning considerations*

MBT election.—Because this is a certificated credit, taxpayers may choose to claim the credit and pay the MBT in lieu of paying the corporate income tax. (Sec. 206.680, M.C.L.; Sec. 208.1107(1), M.C.L.)

Clawback.—Effective January 1, 2012, if a taxpayer fails to comply with terms in the agreement, then some or all of the credit may be added back to the taxpayer's corporate income tax liability. (Sec. 206.673, M.C.L.)

Carryforward or refund.—The taxpayer may elect to have any excess credit carried forward for up to 10 years or have it refunded. (Sec. 208.1434(12), M.C.L.)

Priority.—This credit is claimed after nonrefundable credits. (Sec. 208.1434(12), M.C.L.)

Certificate required.—MEGA will issue a certificate, which must be attached to the annual tax return. (Sec. 208.1434(14), M.C.L.)

Exclusive provisions.—Expenses used to calculate and claim this credit may not be used to calculate and claim the compensation credit, the investment tax credit, or the research and development credit. (Sec. 208.1434(3), M.C.L.)

¶1489y Engineering for Automotive Battery Technologies Credit

Laws: Secs. 206.673, 208.1434, M.C.L. (CCH MICHIGAN TAX REPORTS, ¶12-055g)

CCH Caution: Corporate Income Tax Enacted

Only for the first tax year ending after 2011, taxpayers with certificated credits may elect to pay the Michigan business tax. All other taxpayers are required to file and pay the corporate income tax (see ¶1510). (Sec. 206.680, M.C.L.)

Applicable to tax years beginning after 2011 and ending before 2015, a taxpayer may claim a credit against the Michigan business tax for engineering activities in Michigan for advanced automotive battery technologies. The taxpayer must enter into an agreement with the Michigan Economic Growth Authority (MEGA) that provides that the taxpayer will increase those particular engineering activities. In order to qualify, the taxpayer's advanced battery engineering expenses must exceed those expenses for the taxpayer's 2008 fiscal year. (Sec. 208.1434(4), M.C.L.)

• *Credit amount*

The amount of the credit is up to 75% of the total amount of qualified advanced battery engineering expenses incurred during tax years beginning after 2008 and ending before 2014. The credit is capped at $10 million per year per taxpayer and at $30 million for all credits. (Sec. 208.1434(4), M.C.L.)

• *Planning considerations*

MBT election.—Because this is a certificated credit, taxpayers may choose to claim the credit and pay the MBT in lieu of paying the corporate income tax. (Sec. 206.680, M.C.L.; Sec. 208.1107(1), M.C.L.)

Clawback.—Effective January 1, 2012, if a taxpayer fails to comply with terms in the agreement, then some or all of the credit may be added back to the taxpayer's corporate income tax liability. (Sec. 206.673, M.C.L.)

Carryforward or refund.—The taxpayer may elect to have any excess credit carried forward for up to 10 years or have it refunded. (Sec. 208.1434(12), M.C.L.)

Priority.—This credit is claimed after nonrefundable credits. (Sec. 208.1434(12), M.C.L.)

Certificate required.—MEGA will issue a certificate, which must be attached to the annual tax return. (Sec. 208.1434(14), M.C.L.)

Exclusive provisions.—Expenses used to calculate and claim this credit may not be used to calculate and claim the compensation credit, the investment tax credit, or the research and development credit. However, this credit may be in addition to other credits authorized under MEGA. (Sec. 208.1434(4), M.C.L.)

This credit may not be claimed if the credit for plug-in traction battery packs is claimed. (Sec. 208.1434(4), M.C.L.)

¶1489z Construction of Cell Manufacturing Facility Credit

Laws: Secs. 206.673, 208.1434, 208.1500(7), M.C.L. (CCH MICHIGAN TAX REPORTS, ¶12-055h)

CCH Caution: Corporate Income Tax Enacted

Only for the first tax year ending after 2011, taxpayers with certificated credits may elect to pay the Michigan business tax. All other taxpayers are required to file and pay the corporate income tax (see ¶1510). (Sec. 206.680, M.C.L.)

A taxpayer may claim a credit against the Michigan business tax equal to a portion of the capital investment expenses for the construction of an integrative cell manufacturing facility. The facility must include anode and cathode manufacturing and cell assembly. To claim the credit, the taxpayer must enter into an agreement with the Michigan Economic Growth Authority (MEGA), and create at least 300 Michigan jobs. If the taxpayer is part of a unitary business group, the taxpayer may elect to file a separate return. If a separate return is filed, the taxpayer must create an additional 100 new jobs for a total of 400 jobs in Michigan. MEGA cannot adopt a resolution authorizing the agreement to provide the credit after March 1, 2010. However, the credit cannot be claimed for tax years beginning before 2012. (Sec. 208.1434(5), M.C.L.)

• *Credit amount*

The amount of the credit is equal to 50% of the capital investment expenses for any tax year for the construction of an integrative cell manufacturing facility. The credit is capped at $25 million per year for no more than three years. (Sec. 208.1434(5), M.C.L.)

• *Planning considerations*

Separate return election.—Effective March 29, 2012, if a Michigan business taxpayer has this certificated credit and is part of a unitary business group, the taxpayer may elect to file a separate MBT return as opposed to a combined return. (Sec. 206.680(3), M.C.L.)

MBT election.—Because this is a certificated credit, taxpayers may choose to claim the credit and pay the MBT in lieu of paying the corporate income tax. (Sec. 206.680, M.C.L.; Sec. 208.1107(1), M.C.L.)

Clawback.—Effective January 1, 2012, if a taxpayer fails to comply with terms in the agreement, then some or all of the credit may be added back to the taxpayer's corporate income tax liability. (Sec. 206.673, M.C.L.)

Carryforward or refund.—The taxpayer may elect to have any excess credit carried forward for up to 10 years or have it refunded. (Sec. 208.1434(12), M.C.L.)

Priority.—This credit is claimed after nonrefundable credits. (Sec. 208.1434(12), M.C.L.)

Certificate required.—MEGA will issue a certificate, which must be attached to the annual tax return. (Sec. 208.1434(14), M.C.L.)

Exclusivity.—Taxpayers claiming this credit cannot claim the MEGA employment credit (see ¶1489) or the plug-in traction battery packs credit (see ¶1489w). (Sec. 208.1500(7), M.C.L.)

¶1489aa Construction of Large Scale Battery Facility Credit

Laws: Secs. 206.673, 208.1434, M.C.L. (CCH MICHIGAN TAX REPORTS, ¶12-055j)

CCH Caution: Corporate Income Tax Enacted

Only for the first tax year ending after 2011, taxpayers with certificated credits may elect to pay the Michigan business tax. All other taxpayers are required to file and pay the corporate income tax (see ¶1510). (Sec. 206.680, M.C.L.)

A taxpayer may claim a credit against the Michigan business tax equal to a portion of the capital investment expenses for the construction of a facility that will produce at least one or more of batteries, battery components, storage systems, battery thermal and management components or systems, AC or DC power supplies, power electronics, battery formation and test equipment or energy conversion devices including components related to such products of various sizes and capacities. To claim the credit, the taxpayer must enter into an agreement with the Michigan Economic Growth Authority (MEGA), and create at least 750 Michigan jobs. MEGA cannot adopt a resolution authorizing the agreement to provide the credit after June 30, 2012. However, the credit cannot be claimed for tax years beginning before 2012. The agreement with MEGA will provide for repayment if the taxpayer fails to meet the statutory requirements, among other things. (Sec. 208.1434(6), M.C.L.)

• *Credit amount*

The amount of the credit is equal to 25% of capital investment expenses for any tax year for the construction of the facility. The credit is capped at $50 million over four years. (Sec. 208.1434(6), M.C.L.)

• *Planning considerations*

MBT election.—Because this is a certificated credit, taxpayers may choose to claim the credit and pay the MBT in lieu of paying the corporate income tax. (Sec. 206.680, M.C.L.; Sec. 208.1107(1), M.C.L.)

Clawback.—Effective January 1, 2012, if a taxpayer fails to comply with terms in the agreement, then some or all of the credit may be added back to the taxpayer's corporate income tax liability. (Sec. 206.673, M.C.L.)

Carryforward or refund.—The taxpayer may elect to have any excess credit carried forward for up to 10 years or have it refunded. (Sec. 208.1434(12), M.C.L.)

Priority.—This credit is claimed after nonrefundable credits. (Sec. 208.1434(12), M.C.L.)

Certificate required.—MEGA will issue a certificate, which must be attached to the annual tax return. (Sec. 208.1434(14), M.C.L.)

Potential repayment.—The agreement with MEGA will provide for repayment if the taxpayer fails to meet the statutory requirements, among other things. (Sec. 208.1434(13)(e), M.C.L.)

¶1489ab Lithium Ion Battery Pack Credit

Laws: Secs. 206.673, 208.1434, M.C.L. (CCH MICHIGAN TAX REPORTS,¶ 12-055k)

CCH Caution: Corporate Income Tax Enacted

Only for the first tax year ending after 2011, taxpayers with certificated credits may elect to pay the Michigan business tax. All other taxpayers are required to file and pay the corporate income tax (see ¶ 1510). (Sec. 206.680, M.C.L.)

Applicable to tax years beginning after 2011 and ending before 2017, a taxpayer that manufactures advanced lithium ion battery packs in Michigan may claim a credit against the Michigan business tax. (Sec. 208.1434(7), M.C.L.)

• *Credit amount*

A taxpayer must enter into an agreement with the Michigan Economic Growth Authority (MEGA) and meet one of the two following requirements:

— The taxpayer must agree to make capital investments in Michigan of at least $250 million, to create at least 1,000 new jobs (including jobs transferred from a foreign country), and to manufacture at least 225,000 battery packs in Michigan. If these requirements are met, then a credit of up to $26 million per year, for three years may be claimed.

— Alternatively, the taxpayer must agree to make capital investments in Michigan of at least $200 million, and to create at least 300 new jobs. If these requirements are met, a credit of up to $42 million over four consecutive tax years may be claimed.

(Sec. 208.1434(7), M.C.L.)

• *Planning considerations*

MBT election.—Because this is a certificated credit, taxpayers may choose to claim the credit and pay the MBT in lieu of paying the corporate income tax. (Sec. 206.680, M.C.L.; Sec. 208.1107(1), M.C.L.)

Clawback.—Effective January 1, 2012, if a taxpayer fails to comply with terms in the agreement, then some or all of the credit may be added back to the taxpayer's corporate income tax liability. (Sec. 206.673, M.C.L.)

Carryforward or refund.—The taxpayer may elect to have any excess credit carried forward for up to 10 years or have it refunded. (Sec. 208.1434(12), M.C.L.)

Priority.—This credit is claimed after nonrefundable credits. (Sec. 208.1434(12), M.C.L.)

Certificate required.—MEGA will issue a certificate, which must be attached to the annual tax return. (Sec. 208.1434(14), M.C.L.)

Potential repayment.—The agreement with MEGA will provide for repayment if the taxpayer fails to meet the statutory requirements, among other things. (Sec. 208.1434(13)(f), M.C.L.)

Exclusive provisions.—If the first credit above is claimed, then the taxpayer cannot claim the second credit. Capital investments, new jobs, and expenses for this credit cannot also be used to claim these other credits: plug-in traction battery packs, vehicle engineering, engineering for automotive battery technologies, construction of cell manufacturing facility, construction of large scale battery facility, and sourcing program. (Sec. 208.1434(8), M.C.L.)

¶1489ac Sourcing Program Credit

Laws: Secs. 206.673, 208.1434, M.C.L. (CCH MICHIGAN TAX REPORTS, ¶12-0551).

CCH Caution: Corporate Income Tax Enacted

Only for the first tax year ending after 2011, taxpayers with certificated credits may elect to pay the Michigan business tax. All other taxpayers are required to file and pay the corporate income tax (see ¶1510). (Sec. 206.680, M.C.L.)

Applicable to tax years beginning after 2014 and ending before 2017, a taxpayer may claim a credit against the Michigan business tax for a portion of the costs incurred to implement a sourcing program to use battery cells from a business that has agreed to construct an integrative cell manufacturing facility. A taxpayer must manufacture at least 10,000 motor vehicles in each year a credit is claimed at a Michigan facility. Also, some of the costs eligible for the credit must be incurred at the facility where the motor vehicles are manufactured. (Sec. 208.1434(9), M.C.L.)

The costs must be incurred during tax years that begin after 2012 and end before 2016. Eligible costs include payments for the battery packs, vehicle engineering or integration, vehicle regulatory certification, direct labor, purchases of capital equipment at cost, intellectual property licensing, and financing. (Sec. 208.1434(9), M.C.L.)

Planning Note: MEGA Credit Coordination

For this credit to be available, the Michigan Economic Growth Authority (MEGA) must determine that there are previously issued credits authorized for the construction of large scale battery facilities available.

• *Credit amount*

The amount of the credit is equal to 75% of the costs incurred to implement a sourcing program to use battery cells. A single taxpayer cannot claim a credit of more than $12.5 million per year for more than two years. (Sec. 208.1434(9), M.C.L.)

• *Planning considerations*

MBT election.—Because this is a certificated credit, taxpayers may choose to claim the credit and pay the MBT in lieu of paying the corporate income tax. (Sec. 206.680, M.C.L.; Sec. 208.1107(1), M.C.L.)

Clawback.—Effective January 1, 2012, if a taxpayer fails to comply with terms in the agreement, then some or all of the credit may be added back to the taxpayer's corporate income tax liability. (Sec. 206.673, M.C.L.)

Carryforward or refund.—The taxpayer may elect to have any excess credit carried forward for up to 10 years or have it refunded. (Sec. 208.1434(12), M.C.L.)

Priority.—This credit is claimed after nonrefundable credits. (Sec. 208.1434(12), M.C.L.)

Certificate required.—MEGA will issue a certificate, which must be attached to the annual tax return. (Sec. 208.1434(14), M.C.L.)

Potential repayment.—The credit must be repaid if the battery pack assembly facility if relocated outside of Michigan. (Sec. 208.1434(9), M.C.L.)

Exclusive provisions.—Expenses used to calculate and claim this credit may not be used to calculate and claim the compensation credit, the investment tax credit, or the research and development credit. (Sec. 208.1434(9), M.C.L.)

¶1489ad Cigarette Dealers Credit

Laws: Sec. 208.1471, M.C.L. (CCH MICHIGAN TAX REPORTS, ¶12-148).

Forms: Form 4574, Michigan Business Tax Refundable Credits.

CCH Caution: Corporate Income Tax Enacted

Only for the first tax year ending after 2011, taxpayers with certificated credits may elect to pay the Michigan business tax. All other taxpayers are required to file and pay the corporate income tax (see ¶1510). (Sec. 206.680, M.C.L.)

A taxpayer that is a wholesale dealer, retail dealer, distributor, manufacturer, or seller that had receipts from the sale of cigarettes or tobacco products may claim a credit against the Michigan business tax, provided that the taxpayer paid federal and state excise taxes on the tobacco products during the 2008 and 2009 tax years. The refundable credit is only available for the taxpayer's first tax year that begins after 2010. (Sec. 208.1471, M.C.L.)

• *Credit amount*

The credit is equal to the sum of:

— the difference between the taxpayer's modified gross receipts tax liability for the 2008 tax year and the taxpayer's modified gross receipts tax liability if the taxpayer had been allowed to deduct 100% of the federal and state excise taxes instead of 60% of those taxes; and

— the difference between the taxpayer's modified gross receipts tax liability for the 2009 tax year and the taxpayer's modified gross receipts tax liability if the taxpayer had been allowed to deduct 100% of the federal and state excise taxes instead of 75% of those taxes. (Sec. 208.1471, M.C.L.)

¶1489ae Film Infrastructure Projects Credit

Laws: Secs. 206.673, 208.1455, M.C.L. (CCH MICHIGAN TAX REPORTS, ¶12-055c).

Forms: Form 4573, Michigan Business Tax Miscellaneous Nonrefundable Credits.

CCH Caution: Corporate Income Tax Enacted

Only for the first tax year ending after 2011, taxpayers with certificated credits may elect to pay the Michigan business tax. All other taxpayers are required to file and pay the corporate income tax (see ¶1510). (Sec. 206.680, M.C.L.)

A taxpayer may claim a credit against the Michigan business tax for a portion of the base investment made in qualified film and digital media infrastructure projects. "Base investment" is defined as the cost paid or accrued for tangible assets that are eligible for depreciation, amortization, or accelerated capital cost recovery for federal income tax purposes. The assets must be physically located in Michigan for use in a Michigan business activity. Base investment does not include expenditures eligible for the film production expenditures credit (see ¶1489l). (Sec. 208.1455, M.C.L.)

"Qualified film and digital media infrastructure project" is defined as a film, video, television, or digital media production and postproduction facility located in Michigan, as well as movable and immovable property and equipment related to the facility. However, it does not include a movie theater or other commercial exhibition facility. (Sec. 208.1457(11)(d), M.C.L.)

• *Credit amount*

The amount of the credit is equal to 25% (effective July 12, 2011, up to 25%) of the taxpayer's base investment. The credit is capped at $20 million per tax year for all taxpayers. (Sec. 208.1457(2), M.C.L.)

Application and redemption fee.—The amount of the credit is reduced by credit application and redemption fee equal to 0.5% of the credit claimed. (Sec. 208.1457(9), M.C.L.)

• *Planning considerations*

MBT election.—Because this is a certificated credit, taxpayers may choose to claim the credit and pay the MBT in lieu of paying the corporate income tax. (Sec. 206.680, M.C.L.; Sec. 208.1107(1), M.C.L.)

Clawback.—Effective January 1, 2012, if a taxpayer fails to comply with terms in the agreement, then some or all of the credit may be added back to the taxpayer's corporate income tax liability. (Sec. 206.673, M.C.L.)

Agreement required.—Until September 30, 2015, the Michigan Film Office can enter an agreement with a taxpayer. The taxpayer must agree to invest at least $100,000 for a project before January 1, 2009, or at least $250,000 after December 31, 2008. To enter an agreement, the taxpayer must submit an application and a $100 application fee. (Sec. 208.1457(1), (3), M.C.L.)

Credit reduced.—This credit is reduced by any brownfield plan credit (see ¶1489c) for the same base investment. (Sec. 208.1457(2), M.C.L.)

Certificate issued.—The taxpayer submits a request to the Michigan Film Office for an investment expenditure certificate. The Office may request additional information, including an expenditure report audited by an independent certified public accountant. (Sec. 208.1457(5), M.C.L.) The certificate must be submitted to the Department of Treasury to claim the credit. (Sec. 208.1457(7), M.C.L.)

Carryforward.—The credit may be carried forward for up to 10 years. (Sec. 208.1457(7), M.C.L.)

Priority.—This credit must be claimed after all other credits. (Sec. 208.1457(8), M.C.L.)

Assignment.—The credit may be irrevocably assigned, in whole or in part, to another taxpayer. (Sec. 208.1457(8), M.C.L.)

Related incentives.—Credits are available for film job training expenses and for film production expenditures (see ¶1489l and ¶1489p).

MICHIGAN BUSINESS TAX

CHAPTER 14.9

RETURNS, PAYMENTS, AND ADMINISTRATION

¶1491 Returns and Payments

Laws: Sec. 208.1503-1509, M.C.L. (CCH MICHIGAN TAX REPORTS, ¶89-102, 89-104)

CCH Caution: Corporate Income Tax Enacted

Only for the first tax year ending after 2011, taxpayers with certificated credits may elect to pay the Michigan business tax. All other taxpayers are required to file and pay the corporate income tax (see ¶1510). (Sec. 206.680, M.C.L.)

Michigan business tax returns are required for taxpayers having allocated or apportioned gross receipts of $350,000 or more. However, the $350,000 threshold does not apply to insurance companies and financial organizations (see below). In general, returns are due, and any final tax liability paid, on or before the last day of the fourth month after the end of the tax year (*i.e.*, April 30 for calendar-year taxpayers). (Sec. 208.1505(1), M.C.L.)

Standard taxpayers, which are those taxpayers that are not financial institutions or insurance companies, file either Form 4567, Michigan Business Tax Annual Return, or Form 4583, Michigan Business Tax Simplified Return. However, standard taxpayers that are owned by and unitary with financial institutions should file the Form 4590, Annual Return for Financial Institutions.

Beginning January 1, 2015, certain Michigan business tax refunds that are not paid within 90 days after the claim is approved or 90 days after the date established by law for filing the return, whichever is later, are eligible for an additional 3% interest. Required statutory conditions include the following: the refund is claimed on a timely-filed original return and the refund is not claimed by a unitary business group, among other things. (Sec. 205.30, M.C.L.)

• *Combined returns.*

Unitary business groups are required to file combined returns (see ¶1493). (Sec. 208.1511, M.C.L.)

• *E-filing*

Michigan participates in the federal MeF electronic filing program. E-filing is required. See www.MIfastfile.org for additional information.

• *Federal attachments.*

The Department may require taxpayers to submit copies of federal returns or portions of federal returns. (Sec. 208.1507(1), M.C.L.)

• *Filing extensions*

The Department may grant an extension if the taxpayer files an application for extension on Form 4, Application for Extension to File Michigan Returns, and shows good cause. The extension does not apply to payment of the tax. (Sec. 208.1505(3), M.C.L.)

CCH Practice Note: Application for Extension

According to a Michigan statute, if the taxpayer has a federal extension, the taxpayer may file a copy of the federal extension request, a tentative return, and tax payment to receive an automatic extension until the last day of the eighth month following the original due date (*i.e.*, December 31 for calendar-year taxpayers). (Sec. 208.1505(4), M.C.L.) However, the instructions to Form 4, Application for Extension to File Michigan Returns, states that Form 4 must be filed, even if the taxpayer has a valid federal extension.

The Department will grant an automatic extension to the last day of the eighth month beyond the original due date if the taxpayer submits a timely application for extension that establishes good cause. In addition, the taxpayer must have satisfied its estimated tax payment requirements.

There is no need to request an extension to avoid penalty and interest if no tax will be due on the MBT annual return. (*Frequently Asked Questions, A.7*, Michigan Department of Treasury, November 28, 2007)

• *Amended returns*

Taxpayers must file an amended return within 120 days of the issuance of an IRS final determination. (Sec. 208.1507(2), M.C.L.)

• *Information returns*

At the request of the Department, taxpayers who are required to submit a federal information return of income paid to others are required at the same time to file the information with the Department, in form and content as prescribed by the Department, to the extent the information is applicable to residents of Michigan. Also, every corporation, voluntary association, joint venture, partnership, estate, or trust, at the request of the Department, must file a copy of any tax return or portion of any tax return filed under the IRC. (Sec. 208.509, M.C.L.)

• *Short-period returns*

In computing tax for the first taxable year of less than twelve months, a taxpayer may elect either of the following methods:

(1) the tax may be computed as if the MBT were effective on the first day of the taxpayer's annual accounting period and then the amount computed is multiplied by the number of months included on the short-period return and divided by twelve; or

(2) the tax may be computed by determining the business income tax base and the modified gross receipts tax base in the first taxable year in accordance with an accounting method that is satisfactory to the Department and that reflects the actual tax bases attributable to the period.

(Sec. 208.1503, M.C.L.)

CCH Practice Note: Accounting Methods for Fiscal-Year Filers

The Michigan Court of Appeals allowed a fiscal-year taxpayer to file its final single business tax return using the "actual method" and its initial Michigan business tax return using the "annual method." The statute did not require taxpayers to use the same method for the final short year SBT return and the initial MBT return. The purpose behind providing alternative methods of tax computation was to create ease of administration. (*P&M Holding Group, LLP v. Department of Treasury*, Michigan Court of Appeals, No. 307037, November 15, 2012, CCH MICHIGAN TAX REPORTS, ¶401-738)

When a taxpayer's allocated or apportioned gross receipts are for a tax year of less than 12 months, the requisite amount is multiplied by a fraction, the numerator of which is the number of months in the tax year and denominator of which is 12. (Sec. 208.1505(2), M.C.L.)

• *Insurance company returns*

Insurance companies are subject to a gross direct premiums tax (see ¶ 1456) and must file annual tax returns on Form 4588, Insurance Company Annual Return for Michigan Business and Retaliatory Taxes, before March 2 after the end of the tax year. The tax year for an insurance company is the calendar year. Automatic extensions are not available. (Sec. 208.1243(3), M.C.L.)

• *Retaliatory tax statement*

Before March 1 of each year, each insurer liable for the retaliatory tax must file a statement with the Commissioner showing all data necessary for the computation of its tax due. This is completed on Form 4588, Insurance Company Annual Return for Michigan Business and Retaliatory Taxes. Any additional tax owed for the preceding calendar year must accompany the statement. (Sec. 500.443(2), M.C.L.)

• *Financial institution franchise tax returns*

The financial franchise tax return (Form 1490, MBT Annual Return for Financial Institutions) is due on the last day of the fourth month after the financial institution's tax year end. For calendar year taxpayers, this is April 30. (Sec. 208.1505(1), M.C.L.) The same extension provision available to standard taxpayers applies to financial institutions as well. (Instructions, Form 1490, MBT Annual Return for Financial Institutions)

¶1492 Estimated Tax Returns and Payments

Laws: Sec. 208.1501, M.C.L. (CCH MICHIGAN TAX REPORTS, ¶ 89-104)

CCH Caution: Corporate Income Tax Enacted

Only for the first tax year ending after 2011, taxpayers with certificated credits may elect to pay the Michigan business tax. All other taxpayers are required to file and pay the corporate income tax (see ¶ 1510). (Sec. 206.680, M.C.L.)

Generally, a taxpayer who expects its Michigan Business Tax (MBT) liability to exceed $800 is required to file an estimated tax return and pay an estimated tax on a quarterly basis. (Sec. 208.1501(1), M.C.L.) The estimated payments should equal (1) the estimated business income tax base and the modified gross receipts tax base for the quarter or (2) 25% of the estimated annual liability. Quarterly estimates must be calculated to take into account the surcharge. (*Frequently Asked Questions, A.23,* Michigan Department of Treasury) Estimated payments for quarters other than the first quarter must include adjustments for overpayments or underpayments for pervious quarters if needed. (Sec. 208.1501(3), M.C.L.)

MBT payments may be made with either Form 4548, Michigan Business Tax Quarterly Return, or Form 160, Combined Return for Michigan Taxes.

Taxpayers that calculate and pay federal income estimated tax payments pursuant to IRC § 6655(e) may use the same methodology as used to calculate the annualized income installment or the adjusted seasonal installment to calculate quarterly estimated tax payments for the MBT. The penalty for the underpayment of estimated tax will not be assessed for a tax year that ends before December 1, 2009, provided that the taxpayer paid 75% of the MBT due for the tax year. (Sec. 208.1501(3), M.C.L.)

• *Due dates*

Calendar year taxpayers must file the quarterly estimated tax returns and pay the estimated tax by April 15, July 15, October 15, and January 15. For fiscal year taxpayers, returns are due on the corresponding date for the taxpayer's fiscal year end. (Sec. 208.1501(2), M.C.L.)

If filing monthly using Form 160, Combined Return for Michigan Taxes, and not making remittances by electronic funds transfer, monthly payments may be filed on the 20th day of the month. For example, a calendar year taxpayer may file monthly MBT estimates using Form 160 on February 20th, March 20th and on April 20th rather than April 15 for the first quarter. However, for taxpayers required to make remittances by electronic funds transfer or otherwise not using Form 160, MBT estimates remain due on the 15th day of the month following the final month of the quarter. (*Frequently Asked Questions, A.15,* Michigan Department of Treasury)

• *Estimates for short tax years*

The amount paid with each quarterly estimated return by a taxpayer filing an estimate for its first tax year of less than 12 months must be proportional to the number of payments to be made in the first tax year. (Sec. 208.1501(6), M.C.L.)

• *Farmers and fishermen*

The special federal estimated tax provisions available to farmers and fishermen apply for MBT purposes as well. (Sec. 208.1501(9), M.C.L.)

• *Interest on underpayments*

Interest on underpayments will not be imposed if:

— the sum of the estimated payments equals at least 85% of the liability and the amount of each estimated payment reasonably approximates the tax liability incurred during the quarter for which the estimated payment was made; or

— beginning with the 2009 tax year, the preceding year's tax liability was $20,000 or less and the taxpayer submitted four equal installments that equaled the immediately preceding tax year's tax liability.

(Sec. 208.1501(4), M.C.L.)

¶1493 Combined Returns

Laws: Secs. 208.1117(6), 208.1511, M.C.L. (CCH MICHIGAN TAX REPORTS, ¶11-550)

CCH Caution: Corporate Income Tax Enacted

Only for the first tax year ending after 2011, taxpayers with certificated credits may elect to pay the Michigan business tax. All other taxpayers are required to file and pay the corporate income tax (see ¶1510). (Sec. 206.680, M.C.L.)

Beginning with the 2008 tax year, unitary business groups are required to file combined returns for Michigan Business Tax (MBT) purposes. The combined return includes U.S. persons, but not foreign operating entities. (Sec. 208.1511, M.C.L.)

Practice Note: No Intragroup Allocations

Because a taxpayer for MBT purposes includes a unitary group, there is no allocation of the apportioned income between the group members. The group files one combined return. (*Frequently Asked Questions,* Michigan Department of Treasury, November 28, 2007)

• *Unitary business group*

A unitary business group means a group of U.S. persons, other than a foreign operating entity, one of which owns or controls, directly or indirectly, more than 50% of the ownership interest with voting rights. In addition, the group must have business activities or operations which result in a flow of value between or among persons included in the group. Alternatively, the group must have business activities or operations that are integrated with, are dependent upon, or contribute to each other. (Sec. 208.1117(6), M.C.L.)

Practice Note: Control Test

The control test is satisfied when one taxpayer owns or controls, directly or indirectly, more than 50% of the ownership interests with voting (or comparable) rights of the other taxpayer(s). A taxpayer owns or controls more than 50% of the ownership interests with voting rights (or ownership interests that confer comparable rights to voting rights) of another taxpayer if that taxpayer owns or controls, directly or indirectly, (1) more than 50% of the total combined voting power of all ownership interests with voting (or comparable) rights or (2) more than 50% of the total value of all ownership interests with voting (or comparable) rights. (*Revenue Administrative Bulletin 2010-1*, Michigan Department of Treasury, February 5, 2010)

In addition to meeting the control test, a group of taxpayers must meet one of two relationship tests. The two relationship tests are the flow of value test and the contribution/dependency test.

An UBG is a group of persons that have business activities or operations that result in a flow of value between or among the persons in the group. Flow of value is established when members of the group demonstrate one or more of functional integration, centralized management, and economies of scale. An unitary business is functionally integrated, and the parts are mutually interdependent. Functional integration refers to transfers between, or pooling among, business activities that significantly affect the entities' operations. There is no requirement that a specific type exist (*i.e.*,. it may be horizontal or vertical). Centralized management is involvement or oversight by management in operational decisions. However, mere decentralization of day-to-day management responsibility and accountability will not preclude a finding that centralized management exists. Economies of scale are the relationship between business activities that result in a significant decrease in cost of operations or administrative functions for entities due to an increase in operational size.

The contribution/dependency test determines if business activities are integrated with, dependent upon, or contribute to each other. If business activities contribute to income or the value of the whole enterprise, this indicates it is an unitary business. Also, if the facts indicate that the business activities are managed under one central system, there is evidence that the entities are dependent upon each other or that they contribute to each other and thus are an UBG. (*Revenue Administrative Bulletin 2010-2*, Michigan Department of Treasury, February 24, 2010)

Practice Note: Ownership Determination

For purposes of determining the existence of a unitary group the Department will use as guidance attribution rules expressed in IRC § 318 or analogous authority to determine indirect or constructive ownership and control. While IRC § 318 specifically pertains to corporate stock ownership, the Department will apply its principles to all forms of entities subject to the MBT. (*Frequently Asked Questions*, Michigan Department of Treasury, November 28, 2007)

If a husband and wife have difference businesses, each spouse (other than a spouse who is legally separated from the individual under a decree of divorce or separate maintenance) is deemed to own the ownership interest of the other and vice versa. Under these facts and circumstances the more than 50% ownership interest is met as each taxpayer business is deemed to own 100% of the other. However, they must also satisfy the "relationship" tests above to determine whether the businesses are actually unitary. (*Frequently Asked Questions*, Michigan Department of Treasury, November 28, 2007)

Practice Note: Controlled Group vs. Unitary Group

The ownership tests for controlled groups under the Single Business Tax (SBT) differ from that under the MBT. The MBT requires members of a unitary business group to meet a relationship test not found in the SBT. Therefore, while there might be some overlap between affiliated groups under the SBT and unitary business groups under the MBT, an affiliated group under the SBT will not necessarily be a unitary business group under the MBT. All facts and circumstances related to business activities and operations should be reviewed when determining whether a unitary group exits and who the members of the group are. (*Frequently Asked Questions,* Michigan Department of Treasury, November 28, 2007)

• *U.S. person.* The definition under IRC Sec. 7701(a)(30) is adopted. (Sec. 208.1117(7), M.C.L.)

• *Computation of tax*

Each U.S. person is treated as a single person. This means that all transactions between those persons included in the unitary business group are eliminated from the business income tax base, the modified gross receipts tax base, and the sales factor apportionment formula. This includes any transactions attributable to insurance companies and financial organizations. (Sec. 208.1511, M.C.L.)

The business income of a unitary business group is the sum of the business income of each member of the group, except foreign operating persons and insurance companies and financial institutions, less any items of income and related deductions arising from transactions between group members. (Sec. 208.1201, M.C.L). Similarly, the modified gross receipts of a unitary business group is the sum of the modified gross receipts of each member of the group except a foreign operating person, insurance company, or financial institution, less any modified gross receipts arising from transactions between group members. (Sec. 208.1201, M.C.L).

For apportionment purposes, the sales of all members of the unitary group are included in both the numerator and the denominator. This is true even if a particular member does not have nexus with Michigan (see ¶1472).

• *Designated member.* The designated member of a unitary business group must register with the Department for the MBT and is responsible for filing a UBG's returns. "Designated member" means a member of a unitary business group that has nexus with Michigan under MCL 208.1200 and that will file the combined return required under MCL 208.1511 for the unitary business group.

If the member that owns or controls the other members of the unitary business group has nexus with Michigan, then that controlling member must be the designated member. Otherwise, the designated member can be any member of the unitary business group with nexus. The designated member must remain the same every year unless the designated member ceases to be a member of the unitary business group or the controlling member engages in activity in Michigan that subjects that member to nexus.

If the designated member was registered under the SBT, then it will automatically be registered under the MBT. If the designated member was not registered under the SBT, the designated member must register with the Department using Form 518, Complete Registration Booklet, or online at www.michigan.gov/businesstaxes.

MBT returns must be filed under the designated member's FEIN. All members of the unitary group must be listed on the group's annual return. Only the designated member may file an application for extension.

PART III.75

CORPORATE INCOME TAX

CHAPTER 15.1

RATES, TAXABLE AND EXEMPT ENTITIES

¶1510 Overview of Corporate Income Tax

In 2011, the 96th Michigan Legislature enacted the Corporate Income Tax Act, 2011 Public Act 38. The corporate income tax is effective January 1, 2012, and replaces the Michigan business tax. Certain taxpayers, those with "certificated credits," may for the taxpayer's first tax year ending after December 31, 2011 only, elect to file a return and pay the Michigan business tax in lieu of the corporate income tax. If the taxpayer chooses to pay the MBT, then the taxpayer must continue to do so until the credit and any carryforward are exhausted.

The general corporate income tax is a tax on business income (¶1520). Financial institutions and insurance companies are exempt from the general corporate income tax but are subject to a franchise tax (¶1514) or gross direct premiums tax (¶1515), respectively.

Practitioner Comment: Michigan is an "income tax" State

Effective January 1, 2012, Michigan enacted a 6% Corporate Income Tax (CIT). Many aspects of Michigan's prior business tax were retained, including a unitary approach to taxation, single sales factor apportionment with market sourcing (including the "Finnigan" approach) and a broad nexus standard. Nexus for CIT purposes is established by physical presence of an out-of-state company that has physical presence in Michigan for more than one day, or by economic presence if an out-of-state company (1) actively solicits sales in Michigan and (2) has Michigan gross receipts of $350,000 or more. The CIT expands upon Michigan's prior nexus standard by providing that nexus also is established by an ownership or beneficial interest in a flow through entity (with no minimum or de minimis exception). The CIT retains a separate gross direct premiums tax applicable to insurance companies and a separate franchise tax based on net capital applicable to financial institutions. For taxpayers with unused "certificated" credits such as brownfield redevelopment, battery, film, and MEGA credits, an election can be made to remain subject to the MBT as a way of utilizing such credits. This election must be made starting with the taxpayer's first tax year ending after December 31, 2011.

Wayne D. Roberts, Varnum, LLP and Marjorie B. Gell, Western Michigan University Cooley Law School

Some highlights of the corporate income tax include:

— pass-through entities (or flow-through entities), such as S corporations, partnerships, and limited liability companies, are not subject to the corporate income tax (¶1512);

— a single sales factor apportionment formula is used (¶1547);

— a unitary business group is treated as a taxable entity and is required to file a combined return (¶1567);

— the nexus standard is similar to the MBT's standard, except that an ownership interest in a flow-through entity may create nexus under certain circumstances (¶1512); and

— the corporate income tax has only one credit for small businesses (¶1551).

The corporate income tax does not include a modified gross receipts tax component, as the MBT does. The corporate income tax also does not retain the MBT surcharge.

The tax base for the corporate income tax is discussed in Ch. 15.2. Chapter 15.3 addresses apportionment and credits are discussed in Chapter 15.4. Return and payment requirements are discussed at Ch. 15.5.

Practitioner Comment: Changes from the MBT

The CIT incorporates numerous changes from Michigan's prior MBT, including the elimination of the MBT's Modified Gross Receipts Tax component and most tax credits (except for Michigan's longstanding "Small Business Credit"). In addition, flow-through entities are no longer taxed at the entity level. However, new withholding obligations are imposed on flow-through entities with more than $200,000 of post-apportionment business income. Flow through entities must withhold on the distributive share of their members. The withholding is done at the CIT rate of 6% for members that are corporations. The tax rate applicable to other members of flow through entities is the Michigan Individual Tax rate of 4.25% for 2014.

Wayne D. Roberts, Varnum, LLP and Marjorie B. Gell, Western Michigan University Cooley Law School

---

¶1511 Tax Rates

Law: Secs. 206.623, 206.671, M.C.L. (CCH MICHIGAN TAX REPORTS, ¶10-380).

Effective January 1, 2012, the corporate income tax is imposed at a rate of 6%. (Sec. 206.623(1), M.C.L.)

A taxpayer that elects to claim the small business tax credit (¶1551) and that is not required to reduce the credit as a result of excess compensation paid to shareholders, members, partners, or self-employed individuals, may compute the tax utilizing an alternative tax rate of 1.8%. (Sec. 206.671, M.C.L.)

¶1512 Entities Subject To Tax

Law: Secs. 206.603, 206.611, 206.621, 206.623, M.C.L. (CCH MICHIGAN TAX REPORTS, ¶10-075).

The corporate income tax is imposed on taxpayers with business activity in Michigan or with an ownership interest in a flow-through entity that has business activity in Michigan. (Sec. 206.623(1), M.C.L.) For corporate income tax purposes, a taxpayer is defined as a corporation, insurance company, financial institution, or unitary business group. (Sec. 206.611(5), M.C.L.) Although technically subject to the corporate income tax, financial institutions and insurance companies are exempt from the general tax based on business income, but are subject to a franchise tax and direct gross premiums respectively, see ¶1514 and ¶1515.

CCH Comment: Flow-Through Entities Exempt

Unlike the MBT, the corporate income tax is not applicable to flow-through entities such as S corporations, partnerships, limited liability partnerships, and limited liability companies.

Practitioner Comment: The Unitary Business Principle Under the CIT Differs from the Individual Income Tax Treatment of Unitary Business Under the Individual Income Tax

Application of the unitary business principle to the Michigan Income Tax was clarified by the Michigan Supreme Court in *Estate of Wheeler et al. v. Department of Treasury* and *Malpass v. Dep't of Treasury*, 494 Mich. 237; 833 N.W.2d 272 (2013). In its holding, the Court found that the apportionment language of the Michigan Income Tax Act is broad enough to allow an individual income tax taxpayer (i.e., an individual) to use either the separate-entity or combined reporting methods of formulary apportionment for business income derived from flow-through entities. Because neither reporting method is specifically required under either the statute or promulgated rules, individuals with interests in unitary flow through entities that apportion business income to Michigan presumably have the option of reporting on a separate or combined basis. In contrast, corporate owners of flow-through entities that for apportionment purposes are unitary with the corporate taxpayer are required to apportion income from the flow-through entity based on a combination of corporation and flow-through entity factors. (Sec. 661(2), M.C.L.; Sec. 663(1), M.C.L.)

Wayne D. Roberts, Varnum, LLP and Marjorie B. Gell, Western Michigan University Cooley Law School

• *Nexus*

Effective January 1, 2012, the corporate income tax is levied on every taxpayer with business activity in Michigan or ownership interest in a flow-through entity with business activity in Michigan unless prohibited by P.L. 86-272. (Sec. 206.623(1), M.C.L.) A taxpayer has substantial nexus in Michigan if the taxpayer:

— has a physical presence in Michigan for more than 1 day during the tax year,

— actively solicits sales in Michigan and has gross receipts $350,000 or more sourced to Michigan, or

— has an ownership interest or beneficial interest in a flow-through entity, directly or indirectly, that has substantial nexus in Michigan.

Physical presence may be established by independent contractors. However, physical presence does not include professional services, provided that those services are not significantly associated with the taxpayer's ability to establish and maintain a market in Michigan. (Sec. 206.621(1), M.C.L.) "Business activity" is defined broadly to include the transfer of title to any property (including intangible), or the performance of services, or a combination of both. It applies to activity that is conducted with the object of gain, benefit, or advantage to the taxpayer, whether in intrastate, interstate, or foreign commerce. However, it does not include the services performed by an employee to his employer or services as a director of a corporation. (Sec. 206.603(1), M.C.L.) "Actively solicits" is defined as:

— speech, conduct, or activity that is purposefully directed at or intended to reach persons within Michigan and that explicitly or implicitly invites an order for a purchase or sale; or

— speech, conduct, or activity that is purposefully directed at or intended to reach persons within Michigan that neither explicitly or implicitly invites an order, but is entirely ancillary to requests for an order for a purchase or sale.

(Sec. 206.621(2), M.C.L.)

CCH Practice Tip

There is no minimum ownership percentage or degree of control threshold that a taxpayer-owner of a flow-through entity must have in order for nexus with Michigan to exist. (*Revenue Administrative Bulletin 2014-5*, Michigan Department of Treasury, January 29, 2014, CCH MICHIGAN TAX REPORTS, ¶ 401-863)

Active solicitation on its own does not necessarily create nexus. Active solicitation includes, but is not limited to, solicitation through the use of mail, telephone, and email, advertising (including print, radio, Internet, television, and other media), and maintenance of an Internet site through which sales transactions occur with persons in Michigan. Examples include sending mail order catalogs, sending credit applications, maintaining Internet sites offering online shopping, services or subscriptions, and soliciting through media advertising. The same standards used to determine nexus for out-of-state taxpayers are applied to decide if a taxpayer is taxable in another state for apportionment purposes. (*Revenue Administrative Bulletin 2013-9*, Michigan Department of Treasury, June 5, 2013, CCH MICHIGAN TAX REPORTS, ¶ 401-796)

Once nexus is established, nexus lasts for the entire tax year. Furthermore, if one member of a unitary business group has nexus with Michigan, all group members must be included to calculate the tax bases and apportionment formulas. (*Revenue Administrative Bulletin 2014-5*, Michigan Department of Treasury, January 29, 2014, CCH MICHIGAN TAX REPORTS, ¶ 401-863)

CCH Comment: Non-U.S. Corporations

For purposes of the corporate income tax, Michigan recognizes the protection of P.L. 86-272 for non-U.S. corporations. (Michigan Department of Treasury, FAQs Nexus & Apportionment #9)

Practitioner Comment: Deemed Receipts and CIT Gross Receipts

Under Michigan tax laws, there had been an issue regarding whether "deemed" amounts (e.g., deemed amounts attributed to a taxpayer as cancellation of indebtedness or discharge of nonrecourse debt under federal income tax laws) that are attributable to a taxpayer under federal law will be treated by the Department as gross receipts for CIT purposes. However, practitioners should note that the Michigan Court of Appeals has considered the issue of whether deemed receipts were gross receipts under Michigan's prior Single Business Tax Act (the SBT) and held that deemed receipts were not gross receipts. *See Ford Credit International v Department of Treasury*, 270 Mich App 530; 716 NW2d 593 (2006) (stating that the Legislature's use of the term "receipts" indicated an intent to include only amounts actually received and not amounts "deemed" received). The statutory definitions of "gross receipts" under the SBT and Michigan's subsequent tax laws, including the CIT, are not identical, but any differences in the respective definitions do not clearly alter the legal reasoning set forth in the Michigan Court of Appeals decision in *Ford Credit International*. Moreover, the recently created law, SB 156, further clarified that deemed COD amounts that are attributed to a taxpayer pursuant to Code § 61(a)(12) are not MBT gross receipts—because nothing in fact is "received" and there is no "receipt." This clarifying legislation, although it is an MBT amendment (generally effective for tax years after 2010), should provide additional guidance regarding certain aspects of the "deemed receipts" issue for CIT purposes.

Wayne D. Roberts, Varnum, LLP and Marjorie B. Gell, Western Michigan University Cooley Law School

¶1513 Exempt Entities and Activities

Law: Secs. 206.611, 206.625, M.C.L. (CCH MICHIGAN TAX REPORTS, ¶10-245).

Exempt organizations are generally subject to the corporate income tax only on their unrelated business income. Financial institutions and insurance companies are exempt from the general corporate income tax, but are subject to franchise tax and a direct gross premiums tax, see ¶1514 and ¶1515.

The United States, Michigan, other states, and the agencies, political subdivisions, and enterprises of each of these governmental entities, are exempt from the corporate income tax. (Sec. 206.625(1), M.C.L.)

Generally, most organizations that are exempt from the federal income tax under IRC Sec. 501(c) and (d), which encompasses charitable, educational, and religious organizations, are exempt from the corporate income tax, except on the organizations' unrelated taxable business income. (Sec. 206.611(8), M.C.L.; Sec. 206.625(1), M.C.L.; IRC Sec. 512(a)) However, the following federally-exempt organizations are subject to the corporate income tax:

— local benevolent life insurance associations, mutual ditch or irrigation companies, and mutual or cooperative telephone companies included under IRC Sec. 501(c)(12);

— farmers' cooperative corporations included in IRC Sec. 501(c)(16) that are organized to finance ordinary crop operations; or

— organizations exempt under IRC Sec. 501(c)(4) *i.e.*, certain civic leagues, nonprofit organizations, and local associations of employees] that would be exempt from taxation under IRC Sec. 501(c)(12) but for their failure to meet the requirement that 85% or more of their income consist of amounts collected from members.

(Sec. 206.625(1)(b), M.C.L.)

A person that qualifies as a DISC (domestic international sales corporation) as defined in IRC Sec. 992 for a portion of the year that it has in effect a valid election to be treated as a DISC is exempt from the corporate income tax. (Sec. 206.625(1), M.C.L.)

CCH Comment: Exemptions Narrower Than MBT Exemptions

Unlike the MBT exemptions (see ¶1454), which exempts those organizations exempt under IRC Sec. 501(a), which generally applies to charitable, educational, and religious organizations, plus those organizations specifically listed, the corporate income tax exemptions are limited to those discussed above.

¶1514 Financial Institutions

Law: Secs. 206.621, 206.651, 206.653, 206.655, 206.657, 206.659, 208.1107, 208.1500, M.C.L. (CCH MICHIGAN TAX REPORTS, ¶10-340).

Effective January 1, 2012, a Michigan franchise tax is levied on the net capital of financial institutions with Michigan nexus. The franchise tax is in lieu of the corporate income tax imposed on general business corporations. (Sec. 206.653, M.C.L.)

The discussion below addresses all issues regarding the franchise tax on financial institutions, including entities subject to tax, nexus, tax base, and credits. Report filing and payment requirements are discussed in Ch. 15.5.

• *Financial institutions defined*

Financial institutions include the following:

— a bank holding company, a national bank, a state chartered bank, a state chartered savings bank, a federally chartered savings association, or a federally chartered farm credit system institution;

— any person, other than a person subject to the insurance premiums tax, who is directly or indirectly owned by an entity described above and is a member of the unitary business group;

— a unitary business group of entities described above.

(Sec. 206.651(f), M.C.L.)

Practitioner Comment: Financial Institutions no Longer Allowed a Deduction for Goodwill

The franchise tax applicable to financial institutions under the CIT is very similar to the tax applicable to financial institutions under the prior MBT. One notable exception is that, unlike the MBT, the CIT does not allow a deduction for goodwill. Therefore, for financial institutions that possess goodwill, or that may be considering an acquisition that could create or increase goodwill, there likely will be a higher net capital tax base under the CIT than under Michigan's prior business tax.

Wayne D. Roberts, Varnum, LLP and Marjorie B. Gell, Western Michigan University Cooley Law School

---

• *Unitary business groups*

The Michigan Department of Treasury has provided franchise tax guidance for financial institutions on unitary filing and reporting eliminations under the Michigan Business Tax (MBT) and the Corporate Income Tax (CIT). According to Generally Accepted Accounting Principles (GAAP), equity is residual interest in assets after deducting liabilities. If the financial institution does not have positive equity capital, then the equity deficit is presented as zero on the MBT and CIT returns. (*Notice to Taxpayers Regarding Financial Institution Unitary Filing and Reporting of Eliminations for the MBT and CIT*, Department of Treasury, September 20, 2013, CCH MICHIGAN TAX REPORTS, ¶401-822)

For a unitary business group of financial institutions, each member is required to calculate the net capital tax base in accordance with GAAP. The unitary business group member may eliminate investment in positive equity capital of the other members of the same group at the member level. Eliminations are not separately presented on a member's unitary return. Thus, the member's equity capital line may be a negative number after eliminations, even when the member has positive or zero equity capital before eliminations. (*Notice to Taxpayers Regarding Financial Institution Unitary Filing and Reporting of Eliminations for the MBT and CIT*, Department of Treasury, September 20, 2013, CCH MICHIGAN TAX REPORTS, ¶401-822)

For the 2008-2012 MBT returns and the 2012 CIT return, the inability to separately present eliminations on the required return resulted in incorrect computations of liability for some taxpayers. Beginning October 1, 2013, all affected taxpayers should file original or amended returns for all affected tax years. The guidance provides examples regarding how to present negative numbers on the equity capital line and the net capital line of the unitary reporting schedule after eliminations and deductions. (*Notice to Taxpayers Regarding Financial Institution Unitary Filing and Reporting of Eliminations for the MBT and CIT*, Department of Treasury, September 20, 2013, CCH MICHIGAN TAX REPORTS, ¶401-822)

Practitioner Comment: Unitary Financial Institutions Must Report Negative Equity Capital After Certain Eliminations, and May be Required to File Amended MBT and CIT Returns for 2008-2012

On Sept. 20, 2013, the Michigan Department of Treasury issued guidance to unitary financial institution filers under the MBT and CIT regarding the proper reporting of consolidated equity where certain intercompany eliminations create an equity deficit. While it was previously unclear whether the elimination for investment in subsidiaries should be reported, the Department of Treasury now requires Michigan financial institutions to report net capital as a negative amount on original or amended returns for the 2008-2012 tax years (beginning October 1, 2013). Such taxpayers are required to file amended returns for 2008-2012 reflecting the equity deficit, even where there is no change to tax liability. (*See Notice to Taxpayers Regarding Financial Institution Unitary Filing and Reporting of Eliminations for the MBT and CIT*, Department of Treasury, September 20, 2013). The department has also clarified that reported equity capital prior to eliminations cannot be less than zero. Unitary financial institutions should carefully consider whether amended returns need to be filed for the impacted years, and going forward should properly report negative equity capital resulting from intercompany investment in the positive equity of unitary members. Taxpayers should note that the Revenue Act four year period of limitations is an issue for filings related to past years.

Wayne D. Roberts, Varnum, LLP and Marjorie B. Gell, Western Michigan University Cooley Law School

Unitary business groups are covered in more detail at ¶1567, Combined Returns.

• *Nexus*

In order to be subject to the franchise tax, the financial institution must have substantial nexus with Michigan. Substantial nexus occurs if: (1) the taxpayer has physical presence in Michigan for more than one day; (2) the taxpayer actively solicits sales in Michigan and has $350,000 or more of gross receipts attributable to state sources; or (3) the taxpayer has an ownership interest or a beneficial interest in a flow-through entity that has substantial nexus with Michigan. Physical presence may be established by independent contractors. However, physical presence does not include professional services, provided that those services are not significantly associated with the taxpayer's ability to establish and maintain a market in Michigan. (Sec. 206.653(1), M.C.L.; Sec. 206.621(2)(b), M.C.L.)

Practitioner Comment: Nexus for a Financial Institution

Under the CIT, a financial institution is subject to broad nexus standards applicable to other taxpayers. Such standards create a nexus for a financial institution if the financial institution:

a. has physical presence in Michigan for more than one day;

b. engages in active solicitation in Michigan and realizes $350,000 in gross receipts apportioned to Michigan; or

c. has an ownership interest or a beneficial interest in a flow through entity with business activity in Michigan. MCL 206.653(2).

Based on this broad nexus standard, a non-Michigan financial institution, which generally would be subject only to a franchise tax based on the net capital, could conceivably have nexus for corporate income tax purposes through ownership of an interest in a flow through entity that is not a financial institution and that has non-financial business activity in Michigan. Without guidance from the Michigan Department of Treasury, practitioners may need to analyze the different reporting options for such a financial/ non-financial institution scenario.

Wayne D. Roberts, Varnum, LLP and Marjorie B. Gell, Western Michigan University Cooley Law School

• *Rate of tax*

Effective January 1, 2012, the franchise tax rate is 0.29%. (previously, 0.235%) (Sec. 206.653(1), M.C.L.)

• *Basis of tax*

The franchise tax is based on a financial institution's net capital. "Net capital" is equity capital as computed in accordance with Generally Accepted Accounting Principles (GAAP). If the financial institution does not maintain its books and records in accordance with GAAP, net capital is computed in accordance with the financial institution's books and records, so long as the method fairly reflects the financial institution's net capital. Net capital does not include:

— the average daily book value of U.S. and Michigan obligations;

— up to 125% of the minimum regulatory capitalization requirements of a person subject to the insurance premiums tax.

(Sec. 206.655(1), M.C.L.) Also, when a unitary business group of financial institutions calculates the tax, net capital does not include the investment of one member of a unitary business group in another member of that same group. (Sec. 206.655(3), M.C.L.)

To calculate net capital, add the net capital as of the close of the current tax year and the preceding four tax years and divide the sum by five. If the institution has been in existence for less than five years, the number of years the institution has been in existence is substituted. A partial year is treated as a full year for this particular purpose. (Sec. 206.655(2), M.C.L.)

• *Allocation and apportionment*

A financial institution that has its business activities confined solely to Michigan, allocates its entire franchise tax base to Michigan. (Sec. 206.657(1), M.C.L.)

A financial institution whose business activities are subject to tax both within and outside Michigan apportions its franchise tax base among the various jurisdictions in which it conducts its business activities by multiplying its tax base by a gross business factor. The numerator of the gross business factor is the financial institution's total gross business in Michigan and the denominator is the financial institution's total gross business everywhere. (Sec. 206.657(3), M.C.L.)

A financial institution whose business activities are subject to tax within and without Michigan is considered to be subject to tax in another state if:

— the taxpayer is subject to a business privilege tax, a net income tax, a franchise tax measured by net income, a franchise tax for the privilege of doing business, a corporate stock tax, or a tax similar to the corporate income or Michigan business tax; or

— that state has jurisdiction to subject the taxpayer to one or more of the taxes listed above, regardless of whether that state actually does or not.

Gross business.—Gross business is the sum of the following transactions:

— fees, commissions, or other compensation for financial services;

— net gains, not less than zero, from the sale of loans and other intangibles;

— net gains, not less than zero, from trading in stocks, bonds, or other securities;

— interest charged to customers for carrying debit balances of margin accounts;

— interest and dividends received; and

— any other gross proceeds resulting from the operation as a financial institution.

(Sec. 206.651(g), M.C.L.)

Practice Note: Unitary Groups

Gross business of a unitary group includes the gross business in Michigan of every financial institution member in the unitary group whether or not the financial institution has nexus in Michigan. However, gross business between financial institutions included in a unitary business group must be eliminated in calculating the gross business factor. (Sec. 206.657(4), M.C.L.)

Sourcing rules.—The statute contains many rules for determining when gross business should be assigned to Michigan. Gross business from these activities is determined as follows:

— receipts from credit card receivables (including interest, fees, and penalties) are in Michigan if the billing address of the card holder is in Michigan;

— credit card issuer's reimbursement fees are in Michigan if the billing address of the card holder is in Michigan;

— receipts from merchant discounts are in Michigan if the commercial domicile of the merchant is in Michigan;

— loan servicing fees are in Michigan for a loan secured by real property, if the property is in Michigan;

— loan servicing fees are in Michigan for a loan not secured by real property, if the borrower is located in Michigan;

— receipts from services are in Michigan if the recipient of the services receives all of the benefit of the services in Michigan or if the recipient receives only some of the benefit of the services in the state, the receipts are included in the apportionment factor numerator in proportion to the extent that the recipient receives the benefit of the services in Michigan;

— receipts from investment assets and activities and trading assets and activities, including interest and dividends are in Michigan if the financial institution's customer is in Michigan;

— interest charged to customers for carrying debit balances on margin accounts without deduction of any costs incurred in carrying the accounts is in Michigan if the customer is in Michigan;

— interest from loans secured by real property is in Michigan if the property is in Michigan;

— interest from loans not secured by real property is in Michigan if the borrower is in Michigan;

— net gains from the sale of loans secured by real property or mortgage service rights relating to real property are in Michigan if the property is in Michigan;

— net gains from the sale of loans not secured by real property or any other intangible assets are in Michigan if the depositor or borrower is in Michigan;

— receipts from the lease of real property are in Michigan if the property is in Michigan;

— receipts from the lease of tangible personal property are in Michigan if the property is located in Michigan when it is first placed in service by the lessee; and

— receipts from the lease of transportation tangible personal property are in Michigan if the property is used in Michigan or if the extent of use of the property in Michigan cannot be determined but the property has its principal base of operations in Michigan.

(Sec. 206.659, M.C.L.)

• *Credits*

Practice Note: MBT Election

To be claimed after 2011, the credit must be "certificated" and the taxpayer must elect, starting with the taxpayer's first tax year ending after December 31, 2011, to pay the tax under the Michigan business tax law. (Sec. 208.1107(1), M.C.L.; Sec. 208.1500, M.C.L.)

If financial institutions elect to pay the MBT, they are eligible to claim the following credits:

— the brownfield credit (see ¶1489c);

— the MEGA employment credits (see ¶1489);

— the renaissance zone credit (see ¶1489a);

— the historic preservation credit (see ¶1489b).

¶1515 Insurance Companies

Law: Secs. 206.635, 206.637, 206.639, 206.643, 500.476a, M.C.L. (CCH MICHIGAN TAX REPORTS, ¶10-335).

Effective January 1, 2012, insurance companies, other than insurance companies authorized as captive insurance companies or as special purpose financial captives, are subject to the lesser of (1) a tax on gross direct premiums written on property or risk located or residing in Michigan or (2) the retaliatory tax. (Sec. 206.635(2), M.C.L; Sec. 206.643(1), M.C.L.) The discussion below addresses all issues regarding the tax on insurance companies, including exemptions, tax base, and credits. Report filing and payment requirements are discussed in Ch. 15.5.

The retaliatory tax on foreign insurers is either the amount due as calculated under the corporate income tax on gross direct premiums or the rate imposed on domestic insurers by the laws of the foreign insurer's state, whichever is greater. The State Treasurer may declare that a domestic insurer is an alien or foreign insurer if the insurer fails to comply with certain requirements regarding maintenance of records and personnel in the state. (Sec. 500.476a, M.C.L.)

The gross direct premiums tax is in lieu of all other privilege or franchise fees or taxes, except as otherwise provided in the insurance code, taxes on real and personal property, and sales and use taxes. (Sec. 206.635(3), M.C.L.)

Practice Note: Sales and Use Taxes

Similar to the MBT provisions, under the corporate income tax provisions, insurance companies will now be liable for sales and use taxes, effective January 1, 2012.

• *Exemptions*

For purposes of the gross direct premiums tax, the following items are excluded from direct premiums:

— Premiums on policies not taken;

— Returned premiums on canceled policies;

— Receipts from the sale of annuities;

— Receipts on reinsurance premiums if the tax has been paid on the original premiums; and

— The first $190 million of disability insurance premiums written in Michigan, other than credit insurance and disability income insurance premiums.

However, the disability insurance premiums exemption is reduced by $2 for each $1 by which the taxpayer's gross direct premiums from insurance carrier services exceed $280 million. (Sec. 206.635(2), M.C.L.)

• *Tax rate*

The tax is equal to 1.25% of gross direct premiums. (Sec. 206.635(2), M.C.L.)

• *Credits*

Insurance companies may claim credits against the gross direct premiums tax for the following:

Insurance company expenditures.—The credit is equal to the assessments paid by the insurance companies to the following entities:

— the Michigan Worker's Compensation Placement Facility;

— the Michigan Basic Property Insurance Association;

— the Michigan Automobile Insurance Placement Facility;

— the Property and Casualty Guaranty Association; and

— the Life and Health Guaranty Association.

(Sec. 206.637(1), M.C.L.)

Regulatory fees.—The credit is equal to 50% of the examination fees paid by the insurance company during the tax year. (Sec. 206.639, M.C.L.)

CORPORATE INCOME TAX

CHAPTER 15.2

BASIS OF TAX

¶1520 Computation of Tax—In General

Law: Secs. 206.623, M.C.L. (CCH MICHIGAN TAX REPORTS, ¶10-505).

The corporate income tax is effective January 1, 2012. The starting point for computing the tax is business income before apportionment or allocation (see Ch. 15.3), subject to addition and subtraction modifications, see ¶1522 and ¶1535, respectively. A business loss deduction (¶1535) is then taken from the adjusted apportioned business income amount. (Sec. 206.623(4), M.C.L.) For the tax basis of the tax imposed on insurance companies, see ¶1515, and for the tax imposed on financial institutions, see ¶1514.

Michigan conforms to the Internal Revenue Code (see ¶1521). Michigan also adopts the federal accounting methods and periods (see ¶1521).

¶1521 Starting Point of Business Income Computation

Law: Secs. 206.601, 206.603, 206.607, 206.623, 206.625, 206.683, M.C.L. (CCH MICHIGAN TAX REPORTS, ¶10-510, 10-515, 10-520).

Effective January 1, 2012, the corporate income tax is imposed on the corporate income tax base. The corporate income tax base means a taxpayer's business income. (Sec. 206.623(1), (2), M.C.L.) "Business income" is defined as federal taxable income. For a tax-exempt person, business income is limited to the portion of federal taxable income derived from unrelated business activity. (Sec. 206.603(2), M.C.L.)

The corporate income tax is reported on Form 4891, Corporate Income Tax Annual Return.

Practitioner Comment: Definition of Michigan Taxable Income Is Based on Federal Taxable Income

Historically, in tax form instructions, the Michigan Department of Treasury has taken the position that business income for both SBT and MBT purposes starts with federal taxable income as reported in a federal income tax return. However, the Federal bankruptcy court held that "business income" under the governing statutes may not necessarily be equal to federal taxable income as reported in a federal income tax return as filed with the IRS. See *In Re Matter of Delphi Corporation*, Bankruptcy Ct Order No. 05-44481; Adversary Case No. 06-01902 (SDNY 2008) (SBT business income held not required to equal federal taxable income reported in a filed federal income tax return. This distinction was, at least in part, based on the fact that the statutory definition of the term business income incorporates a definition of "Internal Revenue Code" that allows taxpayers to elect to calculate federal taxable income using alternative versions of the Internal Revenue Code. Recently, in *Lear Corporation v Dep't of Treasury*, Mich Ct Cl No. 10-62-MT; appeal pending, Mich Ct App No 309445, the Michigan Court of Appeals agreed with the Department and required the taxpayer to use the federal taxable income—including Code § 59e elections—that was reported in its Federal income tax taxable income. These decisions should provide guidance to both the MBT and CIT because the MBT and CIT definitions of "business income" and "Internal Revenue Code" are similar to the prior SBT definitions with respect to allowing taxpayers to elect to calculate federal taxable income (and their respective MBT and CIT "business income") using alternative versions of the Internal Revenue Code. Taxpayers should exercise caution, however, because although the *Lear Corporation* decision required that federal taxable income as reported to be used, it is unclear how this ruling would apply to a Michigan unitary business group that is not identical to a federal consolidated filing group.

Wayne D. Roberts, Varnum, LLP and Marjorie B. Gell, Western Michigan University Cooley Law School

Foreign persons.—If a foreign person is domiciled in a subnational jurisdiction that does not impose an income tax (or some other type of subnational business tax) on a similarly situated person domiciled in Michigan whose presence in the foreign country is the same as the foreign person's presence in the United States, then the foreign person is exempt from the corporate income tax. (Sec. 206.625(1)(c), M.C.L.) However, if a foreign person is subject to the corporate income tax, then certain rules apply:

— The corporate income tax base does not include proceeds from sales where title passes outside the United States;

— A foreign person's corporate income tax base includes the sum of business income and statutory adjustments that are related to U.S. business activity; and

— The sales factor numerator is the taxpayer's total sales in Michigan during the tax year and the sales factor denominator is the taxpayer's total sales in the United States during the tax year. For sales of tangible personal property, only those sales where the title passes in the United States are included in the sales factor. For sales of property other than tangible personal property, those sales are subject to apportionment.

(Sec. 206.625(2)-(4), M.C.L.) "Foreign person" is defined as a person formed under the laws of a foreign country, regardless of whether the person is subject to tax under federal law. (Sec. 206.625(5)(c), M.C.L.)

• *Federal conformity*

For purposes of the corporate income tax, Michigan has adopted the provisions of the IRC of 1986 in effect on January 1, 2012 or, at the option of the taxpayer, in effect for the tax year. (Sec. 206.607(6), M.C.L.) References to the IRC in the corporate income tax provisions include other federal laws relating to federal income taxes. (Sec. 206.601, M.C.L.)

• *Accounting periods and methods*

Computation of tax for short taxable year.—In computing its tax for the first taxable year of less than twelve months, a taxpayer may elect either of the following methods:

(1) the tax may be computed as if the corporate income tax were effective on the first day of the taxpayer's annual accounting period and then the amount computed is multiplied by the number of months included on the short-period return and divided by the number of months in the taxpayer's annual accounting period; or

(2) the tax may be computed by determining the corporate income tax base in the first taxable year in accordance with an accounting method that is satisfactory to the Department of Treasury and that reflects the actual tax bases attributable to the period.

(Sec. 206.683, M.C.L.)

¶1522 Additions to Business Income—Intangible Expenses

Law: Secs. 206.623, (CCH MICHIGAN TAX REPORTS, ¶10-620).

Effective January 1, 2012, royalties, interest, and other expenses paid to related parties for the use of an intangible asset must be added back to the corporate income tax base. (Sec. 206.623(2)(e), M.C.L.)

Practice Note: Unitary Business Groups

The addback is not required if the person is included in the taxpayer's unitary business group.

Exceptions.—The addback is not required if the taxpayer can show that the transaction: (1) has a nontax business purpose other than tax avoidance; (2) is conducted with arm's-length pricing, rates, and terms under IRC Secs. 482 and 1274(d); and (3) meets one of the following requirements:

— Is a pass through of another transaction between a third party and the related person with comparable rates and terms;

— Results in double taxation;

— Is unreasonable as determined by the Department of Treasury; or

— The related person recipient of the transaction is organized under the laws of a foreign nation which has a comprehensive income tax treaty with the United States.

(Sec. 206.623(2)(e), M.C.L.)

Practitioner Comment: No FAS 109 Relief from Deferred Tax Financial Statement Adjustments Under the CIT

Unlike the MBT, which included a FAS 109 "fix," the CIT provides no transitional relief for financial reporting consequences. The MBT provided a deduction for years 2015-2029 to offset the adverse financial statement impact that resulted when companies were required under FAS 109 to account for deferred income taxes based on the new MBT. Because the CIT provides no such relief, taxpayers, particularly those with significant Michigan deferred tax assets, should assess how the CIT may have affected financial statement reporting requirements.

Wayne D. Roberts, Varnum, LLP and Marjorie B. Gell, Western Michigan University Cooley Law School

---

¶1523 Additions to Business Income—Interest and Dividend Income from State Bonds

Law: Secs. 206.609, 206.623, M.C.L. (CCH MICHIGAN TAX REPORTS, ¶10-610).

Effective January 1, 2012, taxpayers are required to addback interest income and dividends derived form all state obligations (except Michigan) in the same amount that was excluded from federal taxable income. Such income may be reduced by related expenses not allowed as a deduction by IRC Sec. 265 (expenses and interest relating to tax-exempt income) and IRC Sec. 291 (corporate preference items) in computing federal taxable income. (Sec. 206.623(2)(a), M.C.L.)

"State" is defined as any state of the United States, the District of Columbia, the Commonwealth of Puerto Rico, any territory or possession of the United States, and any foreign country. Furthermore, it includes political subdivisions. (Sec. 206.609(6), M.C.L.)

¶1524 Additions to Business Income—Expense Items

Law: Sec. 206.623, M.C.L. (CCH MICHIGAN TAX REPORTS, ¶10-645).

Effective January 1, 2012, the expenses of producing oil and gas are required to be added back to the corporate income tax base, to the extent deducted in calculating federal taxable income. (Sec. 206.623(2)(g), M.C.L.)

¶1525 Additions to Business Income—Net Operating Loss

Law: Sec. 206.623, M.C.L. (CCH MICHIGAN TAX REPORTS, ¶10-605).

The amount of any Net Operating Loss (NOL) carryback or carryover deducted on the federal return must be added back to the corporate income tax base. (Sec. 206.623(2)(c), M.C.L.) In lieu of the federal NOL, Michigan permits a deduction for any available "business loss." (see ¶1535)

¶1526 Additions to Business Income—Taxes

Law: Sec. 206.623, M.C.L. (CCH MICHIGAN TAX REPORTS, ¶10-615).

Effective January 1, 2012, any state, local, federal environmental, or foreign income taxes on, or measured by, net income, as well as the corporate income tax, that were deducted for federal income tax purposes must be added back to federal taxable income in determining the corporate income tax base. (Sec. 206.623(2)(b), M.C.L.)

¶1527 Additions to Business Income—Depreciation

Law: Secs. 206.603, 206.607, M.C.L. (CCH MICHIGAN TAX REPORTS, ¶10-670).

Effective January 1, 2012, the corporate income tax requires federal taxable income to be calculated as if IRC Sec. 168(k) (bonus depreciation) were not in effect. (Sec. 206.607(1), M.C.L.) Federal taxable income is required in order to compute business income. (Sec. 206.603(2), M.C.L.) Thus, taxpayers are essentially required to add back the amount of the IRC Sec. 168(k) deduction claimed for federal income tax purposes.

Taxpayers should re-compute corporate income tax depreciation using a federally accepted depreciation method that computes a depreciation amount as if IRC Sec. 168(k) was not in effect. This depreciation method must be used consistently over the life of the asset until retired or disposed of when computing corporate income tax business income. The federal depreciation expense that is calculated as if Sec. 168(k) was not in effect is the deduction used in calculating corporate income tax business income. A taxpayer must keep sufficient records to track the basis of the asset and depreciation deduction claimed for purposes of the corporate income tax. (Michigan Department of Treasury, FAQs Corporate Tax Base #2)

¶1528 Additions to Business Income—Items Related to Federal Deductions or Credits

Law: Secs. 206.603, 206.607, M.C.L. (CCH MICHIGAN TAX REPORTS, ¶10-660).

Effective January 1, 2012, the corporate income tax requires federal taxable income to be calculated as if IRC Sec. 199 (domestic production activities deduction) were not in effect. (Sec. 206.607(1), M.C.L.) Federal taxable income is required in order to compute business income. (Sec. 206.603(2), M.C.L.) Thus, taxpayers are essentially required to add back the amount of the IRC Sec. 199 deduction claimed for federal income tax purposes.

¶1535 Subtractions from Business Income—Business Losses

Law: Secs. 206.623, M.C.L. (CCH MICHIGAN TAX REPORTS, ¶10-805).

Effective January 1, 2012, taxpayers subject to the corporate income tax may subtract any available business loss incurred after December 31, 2011, in computing the tax base. A taxpayer that acquires the assets of another corporation in a transaction described in IRC Sec. 381(a)(1) or (2) may deduct any business loss attributable to that distributor or transferor corporation. "Business loss" means a negative business income taxable amount after allocation or apportionment. The loss may be carried forward for 10 years, but may not be carried back. (Sec. 206.623(4), M.C.L.) This subtraction may be taken after allocation and apportionment. (Sec. 206.623(2), M.C.L.)

This subtraction is in lieu of the federal Net Operating Loss (NOL). The amount of any NOL carryback or carryforward deducted on the federal return must be added back to the corporate income tax base (see ¶1525).

¶1536 Subtractions from Business Income—Dividends

Law: Secs. 206.623, M.C.L. (CCH MICHIGAN TAX REPORTS, ¶10-810).

Effective January 1, 2012, taxpayers may subtract dividends and royalties received, to the extent included in federal taxable income, in computing the corporate income tax base. This includes dividends determined under IRC Sec. 78 and under IRC Secs. 951—964. However, dividends and royalties received from United States persons and foreign operating entities may not be deducted. (Sec. 206.623(2)(d), M.C.L.)

¶1537 Subtractions from Business Income—Interest on U.S. Obligations

Law: Secs. 206.623, M.C.L. (CCH MICHIGAN TAX REPORTS, ¶10-815).

Effective January 1, 2012, Michigan taxpayers may deduct interest income derived from United States obligations, to the extent included in federal taxable income, when computing their corporate income tax bases. (Sec. 206.623(2)(f), M.C.L.)

¶1538 Subtractions from Business Income—Targeted Business Activity or Zones

Law: Secs. 206.623, M.C.L. (CCH MICHIGAN TAX REPORTS, ¶10-845).

Effective January 1, 2012, the income from producing oil and gas may be subtracted from the corporate income tax base, to the extent included in calculating federal taxable income. (Sec. 206.623(2)(g), M.C.L.)

¶1539 Subtractions from Business Income—Depletion

Law: Secs. 206.623, M.C.L. (CCH MICHIGAN TAX REPORTS, ¶10-850).

For tax years beginning after 2012, corporate income taxpayers can eliminate income derived from a mineral, as well as eliminate expenses related to this income, to the extent included in federal taxable income. (Sec. 206.623(2)(h), M.C.L.)

CORPORATE INCOME TAX

CHAPTER 15.3
ALLOCATION AND APPORTIONMENT

¶1545 Overview

Law: Secs. 206.661, M.C.L. (CCH MICHIGAN TAX REPORTS, ¶ 11-510, 11-515).

Effective January 1, 2012, for corporate income tax purposes, the tax base is either entirely allocable to Michigan or entirely apportionable among states in which taxpayer is doing business. If a taxpayer's business activities are confined solely to Michigan, the entire tax base of the taxpayer is allocated to Michigan. If, however, the taxpayer's business activities are taxable both within and without Michigan, the entire tax base of the taxpayer is subject to apportionment. (Sec. 206.661(2), M.C.L.)

A taxpayer whose business activities are subject to tax within and without Michigan is considered to be subject to tax in another state if:

— the taxpayer is subject to a business privilege tax, a net income tax, a franchise tax measured by net income, a franchise tax for the privilege of doing business, a corporate stock tax; or

— that state has jurisdiction to subject the taxpayer to one or more of the taxes listed above, regardless of whether that state actually does or not.

(Sec. 206.661(3), M.C.L.)

Michigan uses a single-factor sales apportionment formula to apportion income to Michigan. Combined reporting is required for unitary businesses.

• *Relationship to UDITPA*

Michigan has not adopted the Uniform Division of Income for Tax Purposes Act (UDITPA). As a result, taxpayers subject to the corporate income tax may not use the UDITPA allocation and apportionment provisions to determine their corporate income tax base.

Practitioner Comment: Potential Danger in Relying Solely on Economic Nexus to Qualify for Apportionment

Whether a taxpayer is "subject to" tax in another state, and therefore qualifies to apportion income, is based on application of the Michigan nexus standards. (Sec. 206.661(2), M.C.L.). Under the CIT, a taxpayer can be found to have nexus with Michigan under a physical presence standard, an economic nexus standard, and an attributional nexus standard. (Sec. 206.621(2), M.C.L.). The *physical presence* standard is satisfied by physical presence in Michigan for more than 1 day during the tax year. The *economic presence* standard is satisfied by active solicitation of sales in Michigan if Michigan gross receipts are $350,000 or more. The new *"attributional nexus"* standard is satisfied by ownership of an interest or a beneficial interest in a flow-through entity (directly or indirectly through one or more flow-through entities) that has nexus with Michigan. Because the economic presence test – in the absence of any physical presence – has not been fully evaluated in a precedential court decision, a taxpayer attempting to qualify for apportionment should evaluate the propriety of relying solely on the economic presence test to establish that it is "subject to" tax in another state. Such a taxpayer may benefit from creating and documenting physical presence of at least 2 days in another state (or country).

Wayne D. Roberts, Varnum, LLP and Marjorie B. Gell, Western Michigan University Cooley Law School

---

¶1546 Apportionment

Law: Secs. 206.661, 206.667, M.C.L. (CCH MICHIGAN TAX REPORTS, ¶11-520).

Effective January 1, 2012, the corporate income tax provides for a single-factor sales apportionment formula. (Sec. 206.661(2), M.C.L.)

Practitioner Comment: Multistate Tax Compact Election

Under the Michigan Income Tax Act, Sec. 206.1, et seq., Michigan taxpayers are required to allocate or apportion income based on a single sales factor. Under Sec. 206.663(3), M.C.L., taxpayers are specifically precluded from electing to apportion income based on the provisions of the Multistate Tax Compact (MTC), which provide for an equally weighted, three-factor formula consisting of property, payroll and sales factors.

For tax years prior to 2011, the Michigan Supreme Court has ruled that taxpayers can elect to apportion the two MBT tax bases using the MTC three factor formula. *International Business Machines (IBM) v. Department of Treasury*, ___ Mich. ___, ___ N.W.2d ___ (2014). A motion for rehearing is currently pending in the Michigan Supreme Court. In the meantime, Michigan has enacted retroactive legislation that retroactively repeals the MTC three-factor apportionment election for all taxpayers, beginning January 1, 2008. While the constitutionality of the repeal is in question, many taxpayers continue to pursue MBT refunds based on the MTC election.

Wayne D. Roberts, Varnum, LLP and Marjorie B. Gell, Western Michigan University Cooley Law School

---

• *Alternate apportionment methods.* If the apportionment provisions do not fairly represent the extent of a taxpayer's business activity in Michigan, the taxpayer may request, or the Department of Treasury may require, the use of the following methods with respect to the taxpayer's business activity:

— separate accounting;

— the inclusion of one or more factors; or

— the employment of any other equitable method.

(Sec. 206.667(1), M.C.L.) The alternate apportionment method must be approved by the Michigan Department of Treasury. (Sec. 206.667(2), M.C.L.)

Practice Note: Amended Returns

Filing a tax return (original or amended) is not considered a request to use an alternate apportionment method.

In general, the apportionment provisions are presumed to fairly represent the Michigan business activity of the taxpayer. The taxpayer may rebut this presumption by showing that:

— the Michigan business activity attributed is out of all appropriate proportion to the actual business activity transacted in Michigan and leads to a grossly distorted result; or

— the apportionment provisions would operate unconstitutionally to tax the taxpayer's extraterritorial activity.

(Sec. 206.667(3), M.C.L.)

• *Pass-through entities*

S corporations, partnerships, and LLCs are not subject to the corporate income tax at the entity level. (Sec. 206.611(5), M.C.L.; Sec. 206.623(1), M.C.L.)

¶1547 Sales Factor

Law: Secs. 206.609, 206.661, 206.663, 206.665, 206.669, M.C.L. (CCH MICHIGAN TAX REPORTS, ¶11-525).

Effective January 1, 2012, for corporate income tax purposes, the sales factor is a fraction. The numerator is the taxpayer's total sales in Michigan during the tax year and the denominator is the taxpayer's total sales everywhere during the tax year. (Sec. 206.663(1), M.C.L.)

Practice Note: Unitary Businesses

For unitary business groups, sales include the Michigan sales of every person included in the group, regardless of whether the person has nexus with Michigan. However, sales between persons included in a unitary business group must be eliminated when the sales factor is calculated. (Sec. 206.663(2), M.C.L.)

Practitioner Comment: Planning Based on the Statutory Definition of Unitary Business Group

Under the CIT, certain businesses with a unitary relationship are required to file combined tax returns. (Sec. 206.291, M.C.L.). A CIT unitary business group is a group of U.S. persons that are corporations, insurance companies, or financial institutions, other than a foreign operating entity, one of which owns or controls more than 50% of the ownership interest of the other U.S. persons and has business activities that result in a flow of value between the persons in the group. (Sec. 206.611(6), M.C.L.). The unitary business group definition does not include LLCs, LLPs or other flow-through entities. Because regarded LLCs – other than an LLC that elects to be taxed as a C corporation for federal income tax purposes – are not included in unitary groups under the CIT, a planning opportunity may exist based on operating business lines through LLCs that are treated as regarded entities, thereby removing the operations from the unitary business group. Also note that, although disregarded entities are not included in unitary business groups, disregarded entity income and factors will be included in the respective member's CIT return by operation of law. In addition, these factors should be evaluated in connection with the recent amendments that allow taxpayers to elect to file a unitary group based on an existing federal consolidated group.

Wayne D. Roberts, Varnum, LLP and Marjorie B. Gell, Western Michigan University Cooley Law School

---

• *Definition of "sales"*

Sales include the amounts the taxpayer received as consideration for:

— the transfer of title to (or possession of) inventory held primarily for sale to customers in the ordinary course of trade or business;

— the performance of services that constitute business activities;

— the rental, lease, licensing, or use of tangible or intangible property (including interest) that constitutes business activity;

— for taxpayers not engaged in any other business activities, sales include interest, dividends, and other income from investment assets, activities, and trading.

Practice Note: Occasional Sales

The occasional sale of assets by a taxpayer is not a sale for apportionment purposes so long as the assets sold are neither stock in trade nor inventory and are not held by the taxpayer for sale to customers in the ordinary course of the taxpayer's business. The determination is made on a facts and circumstances basis. (Michigan Department of Treasury, FAQs Nexus and Apportionment #1)

For intangible property, the amounts received are limited to any gain from the property's disposition. (Sec. 206.609(4), M.C.L.)

Practitioner Comment: Activities of Professionals Providing Services

Nexus can be created by activities conducted by an employee, agent or independent contractor acting in representative capacity. However, for nexus purposes "physical presence" statutorily does not include the activities of professionals providing services in a professional capacity or other service providers, so long as such activities are not "significantly associated with the taxpayer's ability to establish and maintain a market in this state." (Sec. 206.621(2), M.C.L.). As an illustration, hiring a Michigan attorney or accountant will not normally, by itself, create nexus for an out of state company for CIT purposes. However, practitioners are well-advised to consider whether a particular professional service might or might not be "significantly associated with the taxpayer's ability to establish and maintain a market in Michigan." In this analysis, consider Michigan's "not significantly associated with" test, along with the U.S. Supreme Court's statement that activities affirmatively must be "significantly associated with" establishing and maintaining a market before such activities will create nexus. *See Tyler Pipe v Wash Dept of Revenue*, 483 US 232 (1987).

Wayne D. Roberts, Varnum, LLP and Marjorie B. Gell, Western Michigan University Cooley Law School

• *Flow-through entities*

The sales factor numerator must include the proportionate share of total sales in Michigan of the flow-through entity that is unitary with the taxpayer, and the denominator must include the proportionate share of the total sales everywhere of the flow-through entity that is unitary with the taxpayer. A flow-through entity is unitary with a taxpayer when the taxpayer owns or controls, directly or indirectly, more than 50% of the ownership interest with voting rights of the flow-through entity and that has business activities which result in the flow of value between the taxpayer and the flow-through entity (or between the flow-through entity and another flow-through entity unitary with the taxpayer) or has business activities that are integrated with, dependent upon or contribute to each other. (Sec. 206.663(1), M.C.L.) If a taxpayer has an ownership or beneficial interest in a flow-through entity, the taxpayer's business income attributable to business activities of the flow-through entity is apportioned to Michigan using the sales factor based on the business activities of the flow-through entity unless a flow-through entity is unitary with a taxpayer for apportionment purposes. (Sec. 206.661(2), M.C.L.)

Sales between persons included in a unitary business group must be eliminated in calculating the sales factor. Sales between a taxpayer and the flow-through entity unitary with that taxpayer will, to the extent of the taxpayer's interest in the flow-through entity, be eliminated in calculating the sales factor. Sales between the flow-through entity unitary with a taxpayer and another flow-through entity unitary with that same taxpayer will, to the extent of the taxpayer's interest in the selling flow-through entity, be eliminated in figuring the sales factor. (Sec. 206.663(2), M.C.L.)

Practitioner Comment: Apportionment Methodology for Corporate Owners of Unitary Flow Through Entities

Corporate owners of flow through entities that for apportionment purposes are "unitary" with the corporate taxpayer are required to apportion income from the flow-through entity based on a combination of the flow through entity's factors and the factors of the corporation. (Sec. 661(2), M.C.L.; Sec. 663(1), M.C.L.). A flow through entity generally will be found to be unitary with the corporate taxpayer where (1) the corporation directly or indirectly owns more than 50% of the ownership interests with voting rights; (2) business operations of the taxpayer and the flow through entity create a flow of value between them, and (3) the activities are integrated with, dependent upon or contribute to each other. (Sec. 661(1), M.C.L.) This "pure" apportionment methodology generally prevents a corporation from shifting income to a flow through entity that has a flow Michigan sales factor.

Wayne D. Roberts, Varnum, LLP and Marjorie B. Gell, Western Michigan University Cooley Law School

Example of Apportionment of Income from Unitary Flow Through Entity

Table 1

X Corp owns a 60% interest in the Y Partnership. X Corp is unitary with Y Partnership.

Taxable Income	**X Corp**	**Y Partnership (distributive share)**	**Total**
		5,000,000	
		60.00%	
	3,000,000	2,000,000	5,000,000

Sales Numerator	**X Corp**	**Y Partnership**	**Total**
		6,670,000	
		60.00%	
	10,000,000	4,002,000	14,002,000

Sales Denominator	**X Corp**	**Y Partnership**	**Total**
		16,666,000	
		60.00%	
	50,000,000	9,999,600	59,999,600

Michigan Apportionment Percentage		
	Numerator	14,002,000
	Denominator	59,999,600
	Apportionment %	23.34%

Taxable Income Computation		
	Apportionable Income	5,000,000
	Apportionment %	23.34%
	Michigan Apportioned Income	1,166,841

Practitioner Comment: Allocation Methodology for Corporate Owners of Non-Unitary Flow Through Entities and Planning Opportunities

Corporate owners of flow through entities that are not unitary with the corporation are allocated distributive shares of each flow through entity based on the flow through entity's separate apportionment factors. (Sec. 661(2), M.C.L.). This "allocation" approach differs from the more pure apportionment approach applicable to a unitary business structure. Because there is deemed to be no unitary relationship between a corporation that directly or indirectly owns 50% or less of the ownership interests of a flow through entity, a potential planning opportunity exists for corporate owners of flow through entities with apportionment factors that are different from the combined group's factor. In such cases, by structuring ownership of the flow through entity to 50% or less, the income of the flow through entity would be allocated to the corporate owner based on the flow through entity's lower apportionment factors.

Wayne D. Roberts, Varnum, LLP and Marjorie B. Gell, Western Michigan University Cooley Law School

---

Example of Apportionment of Income from Non-Unitary Flow Through Entity

Table 2

X Corp owns a 60% interest in the Y Partnership. X Corp is non-unitary with Y Partnership.

Taxable Income	X Corp	Y Partnership (distributive share)	Total
		5,000,000	
		60.00%	
	3,000,000	2,000,000	5,000,000

Sales Numerator	X Corp	Y Partnership
		6,670,000
		60.00%
	10,000,000	4,002,000

Sales Denominator	X Corp	Y Partnership
		16,666,000
		60.00%
	50,000,000	9,999,600

Michigan Apportionment Percentage	X Corp	Y Partnership
	20%	40%

Taxable Income Computation	X Corp	Y Partnership (distributive share)	Total
	600,000	800,000	1,400,000

• *Specific sourcing rules*

Tangible personal property. —Sales of tangible personal property are in Michigan if the property is shipped or delivered to a purchaser in Michigan. Property stored in transit for 60 days or more before receipt by the purchaser, or in the case of a dock sale not picked up for 60 days or more, is deemed to have come to rest at this ultimate destination. On the other hand, property stored in transit for fewer than 60 days before receipt by the purchaser, or in the case of a dock sale picked up before 60 days, is not deemed to have come to rest at this ultimate destination. (Sec. 206.665(1)(a), M.C.L.)

Practice Note: Throwback Rule

The corporate income tax does not have a "throwback" rule. (Michigan Department of Treasury, FAQs Nexus & Apportionment #3)

Practitioner Comment: No Throwback of Sales to Michigan Under the CIT, and Potential for Nowhere Sales

For taxpayers that qualify to apportion income, sales of tangible personal property to an out of state purchaser, even if not subject to taxation in the purchaser's state, are not "thrown back" and therefore are not included in the numerator of the Michigan sales apportionment factor. Michigan Department of Treasury, Frequently Asked Questions,

Corporate Income Tax, Nexus and Apportionment, Comment 3. Because a taxpayer does not need to actually file tax returns or pay tax in another state to qualify for apportionment, an opportunity make exist for "nowhere income" (i.e., sales that are not included in any state tax apportionment numerator).

Wayne D. Roberts, Varnum, LLP and Marjorie B. Gell, Western Michigan University Cooley Law School

---

Practitioner Comment: Throwback Inconsistencies Under CIT Versus Individual Income Tax

Under the CIT, there is no "throwback" of non-Michigan sales. Therefore, once a taxpayer establishes that it is subject to tax in another state (including a foreign country) all non-Michigan sales are generally eliminated from the sales factor numerator. *See* Sec. 206.661, M.C.L.). The CIT approach is consistent with the approach used under the prior MBT, but is in contrast to the approach applicable under the Michigan Individual Income Tax Act, which continues to apply a throwback rule. *See* Sec. 206.122(b), M.C.L.; MI-1040H Instructions. Therefore, unless business activities in another state exceed the protections afforded by PL 86-272, an individual taxpayer will not qualify for personal income tax apportionment. This is true because, for individual income tax purposes, a taxpayer can apportion only if business activities are taxable in another state (which can be accomplished by, for example, exceeding mere solicitation of sales of tangible personal property). This could impact the reporting of income taxed to an individual through a flow through entity that was previously not subject to throwback of sales under the MBT, but that now will need to apply and report throwback with respect to its flow through income.

Wayne D. Roberts, Varnum, LLP and Marjorie B. Gell, Western Michigan University Cooley Law School

---

Real property.—Receipts from the sale or lease of real property are in Michigan if the property is located in Michigan. (Sec. 206.665(1)(b), M.C.L.) Loan origination receipts, loan servicing fees, interest on loans, and gains from the sale of a loan secured by real property are sourced to Michigan if the property is located in Michigan, or more than 50% of the fair market value of the property is located in this state, or if more than 50% of the real property is not located in any one state, if the borrower is in Michigan. (Sec. 206.665(3), M.C.L.)

Practice Note: Location of Borrower

A borrower is considered located in Michigan if the borrower's billing address is in Michigan. (Sec. 206.665(22), M.C.L.)

Lease/use of property.—Receipts from the lease or rental of tangible personal property are Michigan sales to the extent that the property is used in Michigan, based on a fraction, the numerator of which is the number of days the property is located in Michigan during the lease period in the tax year and the denominator of which is the number of days of the property's physical location everywhere during all lease or rental periods in the tax year. If the physical location of the property during the lease or rental period is unknown or cannot be determined, the tangible personal property is considered used in the state in which the property was located at the time the lease or rental payer obtained possession. (Sec. 206.665(1)(c), M.C.L.)

Practice Note: Recordkeeping Requirements

To ensure that the proper amount of receipts from the lease or rental of property is apportioned to Michigan, taxpayers must keep detailed records, including the number of days during the tax year that the property was leased and its location.

Similarly, receipts from the lease or rental of property that is mobile transportation property are Michigan sales to the extent that the property is used in Michigan. The extent an aircraft will be deemed to be used in this state and the amount of receipts that is to be included in the numerator of this state's sales factor is determined by multiplying all the receipts from the lease or rental of the aircraft by a fraction, the numerator of the fraction is the number of landings of the aircraft in this state and the denominator of the fraction is the total number of landings of the aircraft. If the extent of the use of any transportation property within Michigan cannot be determined, then the receipts are in Michigan if the property has its principal base of operations in Michigan. (Sec. 206.665(1)(d), M.C.L.)

Royalties received for the use of intangible property, such as patents or franchises, are Michigan sales if the property is used in Michigan. If the property is used in more than one state, the income is apportioned to Michigan based on the proportion of the property's use in Michigan. If the portion of Michigan use of the intangible property cannot be determined, then the taxpayer must exclude the royalties from the sales factor numerator and denominator. (Sec. 206.665(1)(e), M.C.L.)

Performance of services.—All receipts from the performance of services are Michigan sales if the recipient of the services receives all of the benefit of the services in Michigan. However, if the recipient receives only some of the benefit of the services in Michigan, then the receipts are Michigan sales (*i.e.*, included in the sales factor numerator) to the extent that the recipient receives the benefit of the services in Michigan. Specific sourcing rules apply to securities brokerage services and certain services to a regulated investment company. (Sec. 206.665(2), M.C.L.) The recipient of the services may be someone other than the purchaser of the services. In addition, all the benefit of a service is received in Michigan if any of the following guidelines apply:

— The service relates to real property that is located entirely in Michigan.

— The service relates to tangible personal property that (a) is owned or leased by the purchaser and located in Michigan at the time that the service is received, or (b) is delivered to the purchaser or the purchaser's designee in Michigan.

— The service is received in Michigan and provided to a purchaser who is an individual physically present in Michigan at the time that the service is received.

— The service is received in Michigan and is in the nature of a personal service (such as consulting, training, or speaking) that is typically conducted or performed first-hand, on a direct, one-to-one or one-to-many basis.

— The service is provided to a purchaser that is engaged in a trade or business in Michigan and relates only to the trade or business of that purchaser in Michigan.

— The service relates to the use of intangible property such as custom computer software, licenses, designs, processes, patents, and copyrights, which is used entirely in Michigan.

If only a portion of the benefit of a service is received in Michigan, a taxpayer may use any reasonable method (consistently applied and supported by business records) to apportion the benefit between Michigan and one or more other states. (*RAB 2015-20*, Michigan Department of Treasury, October 16, 2015, CCH MICHIGAN TAX REPORTS, ¶402-012)

Practitioner Comment: Apportionment—Difference in Sourcing Methodologies for Sales Other than Sales of Tangible Personal Property

Sourcing methodologies for apportioning business income of corporations and pass through entities differ under Michigan law. The CIT, like Michigan's prior MBT, uses a single sale factor apportionment formula with market-based sourcing provisions, as well as the *Finnigan* rule in computing the sales factor for a unitary business group. (Sec. 206.665(2)(a), M.C.L.). While business income flowing through to members of a pass through entity is also apportioned using a single sales factor formula, the Michigan Income Tax Act applies a costs of performance methodology to business income that arises from sales other than sales of tangible personal property. Thus, for individual income tax purposes, a pass through entity's sales of services and receipts from intangible assets are sourced to Michigan only if more than fifty percent of the costs of the income producing activities are incurred in Michigan. Such sales are not sourced to the state in which the customer receives the benefit or uses the intangible asset. (Sec. 206.123, M.C.L.). This is an important distinction because sourcing methods can have a material impact on both the apportionment factor and overall tax liability.

Wayne D. Roberts, Varnum, LLP and Marjorie B. Gell, Western Michigan University Cooley Law School

---

Practice Note: Market Based Sourcing Rules

Like the Michigan business tax, the corporate income tax provisions utilize a "market-based" method of sourcing sales to Michigan, in which sales are sourced based on the location of the purchaser or where the good or service is used.

Practitioner Comment: Clarification on Sourcing Rules Based on Ultimate Destination

The CIT Act requires the apportionment of a taxpayer's tax base based on the sales factor, which is the total sales of the taxpayer in this State divided by the total sales of the taxpayer everywhere during the tax year. Sales sourced to Michigan include sales of tangible personal property that is shipped or delivered to any purchaser in Michigan based on the ultimate destination at the point that the property comes to rest, regardless of the free on board point or other conditions of the sales. A law enacted in 2012 confirms that (for MBT purposes), when determining the ultimate destination and when the property comes to rest, if the buyer does not identify the ultimate destination at the time of the transaction, property will be considered temporarily stored at that destination if it is stored for fewer than 60 days. See MCL 208.1305. Because the CIT sales sourcing rules are essentially the same as under the MBT, this legislation should provide guidance as to the CIT meaning of "ultimate destination."

Wayne D. Roberts, Varnum, LLP and Marjorie B. Gell, Western Michigan University Cooley Law School

---

Practitioner Comment: Sourcing Computer Software "Sales" Under the CIT

Under the CIT, a distinction is made between the sourcing of prewritten computer software and customized software. For purposes of sourcing sales from software under the CIT, the terminology included in the primary sourcing statute has been changed from referencing "computer software" to now reference specifically "*custom* computer software." (Sec. 206.665(1)(e), M.C.L.). As a consequence, while receipts from the sale of customized software are sourced based on where the software is used, receipts from the sale or use of *prewritten* computer software may now be sourced using the same provisions as used for tangible personal property and are based on the state to which software is shipped (not necessarily where the software is used). (Sec. 206.665(a)(1), M.C.L.). The Michigan Department of Treasury has not issued guidance on this issue, but if this differential approach is adopted, it would be a change from the MBT under which all receipts from the sale or use of computer software and other "intangible property" were attributed to the state where the intangible property was used.

Wayne D. Roberts, Varnum, LLP and Marjorie B. Gell, Western Michigan University Cooley Law School

---

Securities brokerage services: Receipts from securities brokerage services are sourced to Michigan on the basis of the location of the brokerage's customers. Receipts from securities brokerage services include the following:

—commissions on transactions;

—the spread earned on principal transactions in which the broker buys or sells from its account;

—total margin interest paid on behalf of brokerage accounts owned by the broker's customers; and

—fees and receipts of all kinds from the underwriting of securities.

If receipts from brokerage services can be associated with a particular customer, but it is impractical to associate the receipts with the customer's address, then the customer's address is presumed to be the address of the branch office that generates the transactions for the customer. (Sec. 206.665(2), M.C.L.)

Regulated investment companies: Sales of services that are derived from the sale of management, distribution, administration, or securities brokerage services to, or on behalf of, a Regulated Investment Company (RIC) or its beneficial owners are assigned to Michigan to the extent that the RIC shareholders are domiciled in Michigan. A separate computation must be made with respect to the receipts derived from each RIC. The total amount of sales attributable to Michigan is equal to the total receipts received by each RIC multiplied by a fraction, the numerator of which is the average of the sum of the beginning-of-year and end-of-year number of shares owned by the RIC shareholders domiciled in Michigan and the denominator of which is the average of the sum of the beginning-of-year and end-of-year number of shares owned by all shareholders. For purposes of the fraction, the year is the RIC's tax year that ends with or within the taxpayer's tax year. (Sec. 206.665(2), M.C.L.)

Unsecured loans.—Interest from a loan not secured by real property, gain from the sale of such loan, and loan servicing fees, are in Michigan if the borrower is located in Michigan. (Sec. 206.665(5), (6), and (9), M.C.L.)

Credit cards.—Receipts from credit card receivables, including interest, fees, and penalties from credit card receivables and receipts from fees charged to cardholders (such as annual fees), are in Michigan if the billing address of the cardholder is in Michigan. (Sec. 206.665(7), M.C.L.) Receipts from merchant discounts are in Michigan if the merchant's commercial domicile is in Michigan. (Sec. 206.665(8), M.C.L.)

Investment services.—Sales of securities and other assets from investment and trading activities, such as interest, dividends and gains, are sourced to Michigan if the person's customer is in Michigan or if the location of the person's customer cannot be determined then to the taxpayer's regular place of business within Michigan if the assets or the average value of the assets, depending on the assets involved, is assigned to taxpayer's regular place of business within Michigan. (Sec. 206.665(10), M.C.L.)

Telecommunications services.—In general, receipts from the sale of telecommunications services, including mobile services, are in Michigan if the customer's place of primary use of the service is in Michigan. "Place of primary use" is the customer's residential street address or primary business street address. For mobile services, the customer's address is the place of primary use only if it is within the provider's licensed service area. However, special rules apply to telecommunications service sold on an individual call-by-call basis, post-paid and pre-paid telecommunications services, private communication services, services with a channel termination in Michigan and at least two other states; billing and ancillary telecommunications services; network access fees or telecommunication sales for resale. (Sec. 206.665(13)-(19), M.C.L.)

Media.—Media receipts from sales by taxpayers whose business activities include television programming or live radio, as described in certain United States Department of Labor Standard Industrial Classification Codes (SIC Codes), are attributable to Michigan if the commercial domicile of the customer is in Michigan, and if the customer has a direct connection with the taxpayer pursuant to a contract under which the media receipts are derived. Media receipts from the sale of advertising to a customer who is commercially domiciled in Michigan, and who receives some of the benefit of the advertising sale in Michigan, are included in the numerator in proportion to the extent that the customer receives benefit from the advertising in Michigan. However, if the customer is a broadcaster, and the customer receives some of the benefit of the advertising in Michigan, then the media receipts are proportioned based on the ratio that the broadcaster's listening or viewing audience in Michigan bears to its total listening or viewing audience everywhere. (Sec. 206.665(20), M.C.L.)

Transportation services.—Generally receipts from transportation services rendered by a person subject to tax in another state are sourced to Michigan on the basis of the ratio of Michigan revenue miles over total revenue miles. In addition, special apportionment rules apply to the following transportation services:

—*Maritime transportation services:* 50% of receipts are sourced to Michigan if the services either originate or terminate in Michigan; 100% if the service both originates and terminates in Michigan.

—*Services involving the transport of both persons and property:* Receipts sourced separately determined on the basis of the total gross receipts for passenger miles and ton mile fractions, separately computed and individually weighted by the ratio of gross receipts from passenger transportation to total gross receipts from all transportation, and by the ratio of gross receipts from freight transportation to total gross receipts from all transportation, respectively.

—*Oil pipeline transportation services:* Receipts sourced on the basis of the ratio that the gross receipts for the Michigan barrel miles bear to the gross receipts for the total barrel miles transported by the person.

—*Gas pipeline transportation services:* Receipts sourced to Michigan on the basis of the ratio that the gross receipts for the 1,000 cubic feet miles transported in this state bear to the gross receipts for the 1,000 cubic feet miles transported by the person everywhere. (Sec. 206.665(11), M.C.L.)

All other receipts.—All other receipts not otherwise sourced are sourced based on where the benefit to the customer is received or, if that cannot be determined, to the customer's billing address. (Sec. 206.669, M.C.L.)

CORPORATE INCOME TAX
CHAPTER 15.4
CREDITS

¶1550 Overview

Law: Sec. 206.671, M.C.L. (CCH MICHIGAN TAX REPORTS, ¶12-001).

The corporate income tax contains only one credit.

CCH Practice Note: Michigan Business Tax Certificated Credits

Certain credits against the Michigan business tax are deemed "certificated" credits; if this is the case, taxpayers may choose to claim the credit and pay the MBT in lieu of paying the corporate income tax (see ¶1475, et. seq.).

Practitioner Comment: Creation of New Incentives Regime to Replace Tax Credits

Most business tax credits, including those for brownfield and historic preservation, were eliminated under the CIT. In lieu of tax credits, Michigan has adopted the Community Revitalization Program, which provides certain incentives for specified community investments ("Community Incentives"). These incentives are offered through the Michigan Strategic Fund. *See* Secs. 125.2090–125.2090d, M.C.L. By agreement with the Michigan Strategic Fund Board, investors can receive community revitalization grants or loans for as much as 25% of a project's eligible investment up to $10,000,000. The maximum amount of incentive loans is limited to $10,000,000, and the maximum amount of any grant is limited to $1,000,000. While both grants and loans may be combined on a single project, the total Community Incentives cannot exceed $10,000,000. Before entering into agreements with the Michigan Strategic Fund Board, applicants and investors should consider the federal tax consequences for structuring grants or loans including debt versus equity characteristics, potential cancellation of debt, partnership allocations and many other issues.

Wayne D. Roberts, Varnum, LLP and Marjorie B. Gell, Western Michigan University Cooley Law School

Practitioner Comment: Credits From "Closed" Tax Year May Be Carried Forward to Compute the Correct Tax Liability and Affect Tax Liabilities in Future "Open" Tax Years

In *Asahi Kasei Plastics North America, Inc. v. Dep't of Treasury*, Mich Ct App Docket No. 309240 (Jan. 29, 2013), the Michigan Court of Appeals affirmed a Michigan Court of Claims decision holding that non-refundable investment tax credits that, during an audit, were determined to have been generated in a tax year that was "closed" for purposes of obtaining a refund under Sec. 205.27a(2), M.C.L., could be carried forward—under the applicable ITC carryover statute set forth in Sec. 208.35a(4), M.C.L.—to an open tax year to compute the correct amount of net taxes due from the taxpayer in the tax year that was open for purposes of refund and assessment. The court rejected the Department of Treasury's argument that the carryover of non-refundable credits constituted a "refund" that was barred by the applicable statute of limitations. The Michigan holding in *Asahi Kasei* is consistent with parallel federal law as set forth in Rev. Rule 82-49, 1982-1 C.B. 5. Although this was a single business tax case, the reasoning of this "carryover" holding should be considered in connection with analyzing similar factual scenarios that may exist under income tax laws, along with both the MBT Act and the CIT Act.

Wayne D. Roberts, Varnum, LLP and Marjorie B. Gell, Western Michigan University Cooley Law School

¶1551 Small Business Credit

Laws: Sec. 206.671, M.C.L. (CCH Michigan Tax Reports, ¶12-142).

Effective January 1, 2012, taxpayers may claim a credit against the corporate income tax provided that their gross receipts do not exceed $20 million and their adjusted business income minus the loss adjustment does not exceed $1.3 million (subject to inflation). (Sec. 206.671(1), M.C.L.)

Adjusted business income.—Adjusted business income means business income with the following additions:

— compensation and directors' fees of a corporation's active shareholders and officers;

— a carryback or carryover of a net operating loss, to the extent deducted in determining federal taxable income; and

— a capital loss, to the extent deducted in determining federal taxable income.

(Sec. 206.671(10)(b), M.C.L.)

Loss adjustment.—The loss adjustment is the amount by which adjusted business income was less than zero in any of the five tax years immediately preceding the tax year for which eligibility for this credit is being determined. (Sec. 206.671(10)(f), M.C.L.)

• *Credit amount*

The credit equals the amount by which the corporate income tax exceeds 1.8% of the taxpayer's adjusted business income. (Sec. 206.671(4), M.C.L.)

• *Planning considerations*

Credit phaseout.—The credit is phased out based on a sliding scale for compensation or distributive shares of adjusted business income ranging from $160,000 to $180,000. For this purpose, the most-highly compensated person is used. (Sec. 206.671(1)(b), M.C.L.; Sec. 206.671(3), M.C.L.)

Disqualification.—Taxpayers are disqualified from receiving the credit if a person's compensation or a distributive share of adjusted business income exceeds $180,000. To determine if a unitary business group is disqualified, the amounts of all items paid or allocable by all persons included in the unitary business group to any one individual are combined. (Sec. 206.671(1)(a), (2)(b), M.C.L.)

Credit reduction.—If gross receipts exceed $19 million, the credit is reduced by a fraction. The fraction's numerator is the amount of gross receipts over $19 million, and the denominator is $1 million. (Sec. 206.671(5), M.C.L.)

CORPORATE INCOME TAX

CHAPTER 15.5

RETURNS, PAYMENTS, AND ADMINISRATION

¶1565 Returns and Payments

Laws: Secs. 206.683-691, M.C.L. (CCH MICHIGAN TAX REPORTS, ¶89-102)

Effective January 1, 2012, corporate income tax returns are required for taxpayers having allocated or apportioned gross receipts of $350,000 or more. However, the $350,000 threshold does not apply to insurance companies and financial organizations (see below). In general, returns are due, and any final tax liability paid, on or before the last day of the fourth month after the end of the tax year (*i.e.*, April 30 for calendar-year taxpayers). However, if the taxpayer's tax liability is less than or equal to $100, then the taxpayer does not need to file a return or pay the tax imposed. The flow-through entity's apportioned or allocated gross receipts is imputed to each of its members based upon the same percentage that each member's proportionate share of distributive income is to the total distributive income of the flow-through entity. (Sec. 206.685(1), M.C.L.)

With regard to partial tax years, if a taxpayer has apportioned or allocated gross receipts for a tax year of less than 12 months, the threshold amount of $350,000 is multiplied by a fraction, the numerator of which is the number of months in the tax year and the denominator of which is 12. (Sec. 206.685(2), M.C.L.)

At the option of the taxpayer, any Michigan business tax overpayments from the final return may be either refunded or carried forward and applied to the initial corporate income tax return. (Michigan Department of Treasury, FAQs Filing Requirements #10)

CCH Practice Note: Registration Not Required

Taxpayers registered for the Michigan business tax are automatically registered for the corporate income tax, provided that the taxpayer meets the definition of "taxpayer." (Michigan Department of Treasury, FAQs Filing Requirements #6)

• *Fiscal year taxpayers.*

If a taxpayer's tax year ends before December 31, 2012, then the taxpayer may compute the corporate income tax using one of these methods:

— compute the corporate income tax as if it were effective on the first day of the taxpayer's annual accounting period and then multiply the amount by a fraction, where the numerator is the number of months in the taxpayer's first tax year and the denominator is the number of months in the taxpayer's annual accounting period; or

— determine the corporate income tax base in the first tax year in accordance with an accounting method satisfactory to the department that reflects the actual corporate income tax base attributable to the period.

Michigan fiscal year taxpayers are required to use the same method of computing the corporate income tax for their first year as they used for the portion of the same tax year under the Michigan business tax. (Sec. 206.683, M.C.L.)

Practitioner Comment: Estimated Tax Payment vs Return Due Date Timing

Quarterly estimated tax payments are due for any taxpayer with an annual liability of more than $800. (Sec. 206.681(2), M.C.L.). Importantly, the first quarterly payment is due April 15 for a calendar year taxpayer, which is 15 days before the annual return is due. This incongruity, which is similar to the way the MBT operated, could create penalty exposure if there is an underpayment between the estimated payment due date and the time for filing the prior year return.

Wayne D. Roberts, Varnum, LLP and Marjorie B. Gell, Western Michigan University Cooley Law School

---

CCH Practice Note: Extension for Filing First Corporate Income Tax Return

Fiscal year taxpayers will be granted an automatic extension for their 2012 fiscal year annual CIT return or 2012 fiscal year annual MBT election return. Returns for fiscal years ending in 2012 will be due the same date as 2012 calendar year returns, which is April 30, 2013. (Michigan Department of Treasury, FAQs Filing Requirements #12)

• *Combined returns.*

Unitary business groups are required to file combined returns. (Sec. 206.691, M.C.L.)

• *Federal attachments.*

The Department may require taxpayers to submit copies of federal returns or portions of federal returns. (Sec. 206.687(1), M.C.L.)

• *Filing extensions.*

The Michigan Department of Treasury may, if the taxpayer applies and shows good cause, grant an extension. The extension does not apply to payment of the tax. (Sec. 206.685(2), M.C.L.)

CCH Practice Note: Application for Extension

According to a Michigan statute, if the taxpayer has a federal extension, the taxpayer may file a copy of the federal extension request, a tentative return, and tax payment to receive an automatic extension until the last day of the eighth month following the original due date (*i.e.*, December 31 for calendar-year taxpayers). (Sec. 206.685(3), M.C.L.)

• *Amended returns.*

Taxpayers must file an amended return within 120 days of the issuance of an IRS final determination. (Sec. 206.687(2), M.C.L.)

• *Information returns.*

At the request of the Department, taxpayers who are required to submit a federal information return of income paid to others are required at the same time to file the information with the Department, in form and content as prescribed by the Department, to the extent the information is applicable to residents of Michigan. (Sec. 206.689, M.C.L.)

• *Insurance company returns*

Insurance companies are subject to a gross direct premiums tax and must file annual tax returns before March 2 after the end of the tax year. The tax year for an insurance company is the calendar year. Automatic extensions are not available. (Sec. 206.643(3), M.C.L.)

• *Retaliatory tax statement*

Before March 1 of each year, each insurer liable for the retaliatory tax must file a statement with the Commissioner showing all data necessary for the computation of its tax due. Any additional tax owed for the preceding calendar year must accompany the statement. (Sec. 500.443(2), M.C.L.)

• *Financial institution franchise tax returns*

The financial franchise tax return is due on the last day of the fourth month after the financial institution's tax year end. For calendar year taxpayers, this is April 30. However, if the taxpayer's tax liability is less than or equal to $100, then the taxpayer does not need to file a return or pay the tax imposed. The same extension provision available to standard taxpayers applies to financial institutions as well. (Sec. 206.685, M.C.L.)

¶1566 Estimated Tax Returns and Payments

Laws: Sec. 206.681, M.C.L. (CCH MICHIGAN TAX REPORTS, ¶89-104)

Form: Form 4913, Corporate Income Tax (CIT) Quarterly Return.

Generally, a taxpayer who expects the corporate income tax liability to exceed $800 is required to file an estimated tax return and pay an estimated tax on a quarterly basis. (Sec. 206.681(1), M.C.L.) The estimated payments should equal (1) the estimated corporate income tax base for the quarter or (2) 25% of the estimated annual liability. Estimated payments for quarters other than the first quarter may have adjustments for overpayments or underpayments, if needed. Taxpayers subject to the corporate income tax, the gross premiums tax, and the franchise tax are required to make estimated tax payments. (Sec. 206.681(3), M.C.L.)

For a taxpayer that calculates and pays estimated payments for federal income tax purposes pursuant to IRC Sec. 6655(e), that taxpayer may use the same methodology as used to calculate the annualized income installment or the adjusted seasonal installment, whichever is used as the basis for the federal estimated payment, to calculate the required quarterly estimated payments. (Sec. 206.681(3), M.C.L.)

CCH Practice Note: Calculating Payments

Corporate income tax estimated payments cannot be based on the prior year's Michigan business tax liability. (Michigan Department of Treasury, FAQs Filing Requirements #14)

• *Due dates*

Calendar year taxpayers must file the quarterly estimated tax returns and pay the estimated tax by April 15, July 15, October 15, and January 15. For fiscal year taxpayers, returns are due on the corresponding date for the taxpayer's fiscal year end. (Sec. 206.681(2), M.C.L.) If filing monthly using Form 160, Combined Return for Michigan Taxes, and not making remittances by electronic funds transfer, monthly payments may be filed on the 20th day of the month. However, for taxpayers required to make remittances by electronic funds transfer or otherwise not using Form 160, corporate income tax estimates remain due on the 15th day of the month following the final month of the quarter. Regardless of the method chosen, the estimated tax for the quarter must also reasonably approximate the liability for the quarter. (Michigan Department of Treasury, FAQs Filing Requirements #3)

• *Estimates for short tax years*

The amount paid with each quarterly estimated return by a taxpayer filing an estimate for its first tax year of less than 12 months must be proportional to the number of payments to be made in the first tax year. However, no estimated tax payments are required for tax years of less than four months. (Sec. 206.681(5), M.C.L.)

• *Farmers and fishermen*

The special federal estimated tax provisions available to farmers and fishermen apply for corporate income tax purposes as well. (Sec. 206.681(8), M.C.L.)

• *Interest on underpayments*

Interest on underpayments will not be imposed if:

— the sum of the estimated payments equals at least 85% of the liability and the amount of each estimated payment reasonably approximates the tax liability incurred during the quarter for which the estimated payment was made; or

— for the 2013 tax year and beyond, if the preceding year's tax liability was $20,000 or less and if the taxpayer submitted four equal installments which equaled the immediately preceding tax year's tax liability.

(Sec. 206.681(3), M.C.L.)

¶1567 Combined Returns

Laws: Secs. 206.611, 206.691, M.C.L. (CCH MICHIGAN TAX REPORTS, ¶11-550)

Forms: 4891, Corporate Income Tax Annual Return; 4896, Unitary Business Group (UBG) Affiliates Excluded from the Return of Standard Taxpayers; 4897, Data on Unitary Business Group Members.

Effective January 1, 2012, unitary business groups are required to file combined returns for corporate income tax purposes. The combined return includes United States persons, but not foreign operating entities. (Sec. 206.691, M.C.L.)

• *Types of combined filing.* ***Elective combination.***—Applicable to tax years that begin after 2012, "affiliated groups" may elect to file water's edge combined returns. In general, the term "affiliated group" is defined as it is in IRC Sec. 1504, except that it includes all United States persons that are corporations, insurance companies, or financial institutions (other than a foreign operating entity) that are commonly owned, directly or indirectly, by any member of the affiliated group and other members of the group of which more than 50% of the ownership interest with voting rights or ownership interests that confer comparable rights is directly or indirectly owned by a common owner or owners. (Sec. 206.603(1), M.C.L.; Sec. 206.691(2), M.C.L.)

If this election is made, then the affiliated group files a combined return for 10 years, with the option to renew the election once for another 10 years. If the election renewal is not made immediately, then the election is not allowed in any of the next three tax years. The election is irrevocable and remains in effect for the time during which ownership requirements are met irrespective of whether the federal consolidated group to which the unitary business group belongs stops filing a federal consolidated return or whether the common parent changes due to a reverse acquisition or acquisition by a related person. (Sec. 206.691(2), M.C.L.)

Mandatory combination.—The water's edge method of combined reporting is mandatory and not elective for two or more corporations engaged in a unitary business conducted within and outside Michigan. (Sec. 206.691, M.C.L.)

Forced or discretionary combination.—The Michigan Department of Treasury does not have discretion or authority to force corporations to report the corporate income tax on a water's edge or world-wide combined basis. (Sec. 206.691, M.C.L.)

• *Unitary business group*

A unitary business group means a group of United States persons that are corporations, insurance companies, or financial institutions, other than a foreign operating entity, one of which owns or controls, directly or indirectly, more than 50% of the ownership interest with voting rights. In addition, the group must have business activities or operations which result in a flow of value between or among persons included in the group. Alternatively, the group must have business activities or operations that are integrated with, are dependent upon, or contribute to each other. Applicable to tax years that begin after 2012, "unitary business group" includes an affiliated group that makes the election to file as a unitary business group. (Sec. 206.611(6), M.C.L.)

CCH Practice Tip: The Control Test

The control test is satisfied when one taxpayer owns or controls, directly or indirectly, more than 50% of the ownership interests with voting (or comparable) rights of the other taxpayer(s). A taxpayer owns or controls more than 50% of the ownership interests with voting rights (or ownership interests that confer comparable rights to voting rights) of another taxpayer if that taxpayer owns or controls, directly or indirectly, (1) more than 50% of the total combined voting power of all ownership interests with voting (or comparable) rights or (2) more than 50% of the total value of all ownership interests with voting (or comparable) rights. (*Revenue Administrative Bulletin 2013-1*, Michigan Department of Treasury, January 7, 2013, ¶401-755)

In addition to meeting the control test, a group of taxpayers must meet one of two relationship tests. The two relationship tests are the flow of value test and the contribution/dependency test. (*Revenue Administrative Bulletin 2013-1*, Michigan Department of Treasury, January 7, 2013, ¶401-755)

An UBG is a group of persons that have business activities or operations that result in a flow of value between or among the persons in the group. Flow of value is established when members of the group demonstrate one or more of functional integration, centralized management, and economies of scale. An unitary business is functionally integrated, and the parts are mutually interdependent. Functional integration refers to transfers between, or pooling among, business activities that significantly affect the entities' operations. There is no requirement that a specific type exist (*i.e.*,. it may be horizontal or vertical). Centralized management is involvement or oversight by management in operational decisions. However, mere decentralization of day-to-day management responsibility and accountability will not preclude a finding that centralized management exists. Economies of scale are the relationship between business activities that result in a significant decrease in cost of operations or administrative functions for entities due to an increase in operational size. (*Revenue Administrative Bulletin 2013-1*, Michigan Department of Treasury, January 7, 2013, ¶401-755)

The contribution/dependency test determines if business activities are integrated with, dependent upon, or contribute to each other. If business activities contribute to income or the value of the whole enterprise, this indicates it is an unitary business. Also, if the facts indicate that the business activities are managed under one central system, there is evidence that the entities are dependent upon each other or that they contribute to each other and thus are an UBG. (*Revenue Administrative Bulletin 2013-1*, Michigan Department of Treasury, January 7, 2013, ¶401-755)

Practitioner Comment: Flow Through Entities and Unitary Business Groups

Under the CIT, certain businesses with a unitary relationship are required to file combined tax returns. (Sec. 206.691, M.C.L.). The unitary business group is a group of U.S. persons that are corporations, insurance companies, financial institutions, other than a foreign operating entity, or flow through entity, where the taxpayer owns or controls more than 50% of the ownership interest of the entity and has business activities that result in a flow of value between the persons in the group. (Sec. 206.611(6), M.C.L.); Sec. 206.663(1), M.C.L.). For a flow through entity that is unitary with the taxpayer, the taxpayer should include its proportionate share of income in its federal taxable income. In addition, the taxpayer should include its proportionate share of the sales numerator and denominator with the apportionment factors of the taxpayer's other unitary operations. For non-unitary flow through entities, (including those 50% owned or less than 50% owned by the corporation), distributive income is apportioned based on the flow-through entity's separate apportionment factors. (Sec. 206.611(2), M.C.L.; Sec. 206.663(1), M.C.L.).

Wayne D. Roberts, Varnum, LLP and Marjorie B. Gell, Western Michigan University Cooley Law School

---

• *U.S. person.* The definition under IRC Sec. 7701(a)(30) is adopted. (Sec. 206.611(7), M.C.L.)

• *Computation of tax*

Each United States person is treated as a single person. This means that all transactions between those persons included in the unitary business group are eliminated from the corporate income tax base and the sales factor apportionment formula. This includes any transactions attributable to insurance companies and financial organizations. Applicable to tax years that begin after 2013, for the purposes of determining exemptions, credits, and the filing threshold, all transactions between persons included in a unitary business group are eliminated. (Sec. 206.691, M.C.L.)

CCH Practice Tip: Short Tax Years

A person included in a unitary business group that joins or departs the group other than at the end of the person's federal tax year will have two short tax years. The first tax year will begin with the federal tax period and end on the date that the group is joined or departed from, and the second tax year will begin on the date the group is joined or departed from and end with the federal income tax period. (Sec. 206.611(4), M.C.L.)

Practitioner Comment: Treatment of Single Member LLCs Under the CIT vs. the MBT—No Separate Filing Requirement for a Disregarded Entity

Under the CIT, a person that is a disregarded entity for federal tax purposes, including a single member LLC, is not taxed at the entity level. (Sec. 206.611(5), M.C.L.; Sec. 206.623(1), M.C.L.). This is a change from Michigan's prior business taxes, including the MBT which generally required a single member LLC (as a "person") to file a separate return; *See Third Revised Notice to Taxpayers Regarding Federally Disregarded Entities and the Michigan Business Tax* (November 15, 2011); *See also Kmart Michigan Property Services LLC v Dep't of Treasury*, 283 Mich App 647 (2009) (772 NW2d 421 (2009) (holding that a single member limited liability company disregarded for federal tax purposes, was permitted to file an SBT return separate from its owner, contrary to administrative policy which required a federally disregarded single member LLC to be treated as a division of its owner).

Wayne D. Roberts, Varnum, LLP and Marjorie B. Gell, Western Michigan University Cooley Law School

---

¶1568 Withholding Laws

Laws: Sec. 206.703, M.C.L. (CCH MICHIGAN TAX REPORTS, ¶89-104)

A flow-through entity with business activity in Michigan that reasonably expects to accrue more than $200,000 in business income for the tax year, after allocation or apportionment to Michigan, must withhold on the distributive share of its partners or members that are corporations. This withholding is done at the CIT rate of 6%. The $200,000 threshold is determined at the flow-through entity level and is not a "per member" threshold. The entire amount of the flow-through entity's apportioned business income is included for purposes of this threshold, regardless of whether it is allocated to members that are corporations, other flow-through entities, or individuals. To apportion its business income for determining this threshold, the flow-through entity will use only its sales factor. The flow-through entity's sales factor is a fraction, the numerator of which is the total sales of the flow-through entity in Michigan during the tax year and the denominator of which is the total sales of the flow-through entity everywhere during the tax year. Withholding for each period is equal to 1/4 of the total withholding calculated on the distributive share of business income that is reasonably expected to accrue during the tax year of the flow-through entity. (Sec. 206.703(4), M.C.L.)

• *Exemptions*

A C corporation partner or member of a flow-through entity can elect to be exempt from withholding. (Sec. 206.703(16), M.C.L.) The C corporation must file an exemption certificate with both the flow-through entity and the Department. If an exemption certificate is received anytime within the tax year, the corporate partner/member is exempt from withholding for the entire tax year. (Michigan Department of Treasury. FAQs Withholding for Flow-Through Entities)

The flow-through entity is required to attach a copy of that exemption certificate to its Form 4918. (Sec. 206.703(16)(c), M.C.L.) The flow-through entity and its corporate owner are both required to retain a copy of the exemption certificate. (Sec. 206.703(16)(d), M.C.L.)

CCH Practice Note: Drafting a Withholding Exemption Certificate for Corporate Owners of Flow-Through Entities

The Department of Treasury does not provide an exemption certificate form. Any document created by the corporate member that meets the statutory requirements will be valid so long as it is signed by the corporate owner or someone on its behalf. The exemption certificate must state that the corporate member will: (1) file the returns required under the CIT; (2) pay the tax required under the CIT on the distributive share of the business income received from any flow-through entity in which the corporation is a member or in which the corporation has an ownership or beneficial interest, directly or indirectly through one or more other flow-through entities; and (3) submit to the taxing jurisdiction of Michigan for purposes of collection of the tax under the CIT (together with related interest and penalties under the Revenue Act) imposed on the corporation with respect to the distributive share of the business income of that corporation. (Sec. MCL 206.703(16)(a), M.C.L.; Michigan Department of Treasury, FAQs *Withholding for Flow-Through Entities*)

Practitioner Comment: Withholding Exemption Certificates for Corporate Owners of Flow-Through Entities Do Not Relieve Obligations to File Quarterly Estimated Tax Returns

As it was originally enacted, the CIT Act required that a flow-through entity withhold tax at the 6% CIT rate on distributive shares of corporate owners. In 2012, the CIT Act was amended (217 PA 212, adding Sec. 206.703(16), M.C.L.) to provide that a flow-through entity may not withhold tax on an owner corporation that provides an exemption certificate and meets certain statutory conditions. In addition, a flow-through entity may not withhold for a partner/member making an election to remain an MBT taxpayer. (217 PA 212, adding Sec. 206.703(18), M.C.L.) Corporate taxpayers that qualify for the exemption are cautioned that they are still responsible for any obligations to file quarterly estimated tax returns. (Sec. 206.681(1), M.C.L.) When an MBT election is in place for an LLC with a non-unitary corporate member, no withholding is required relative to such member. MCL 208.1500.

Wayne D. Roberts, Varnum, LLP and Marjorie B. Gell, Western Michigan University Cooley Law School

---

¶1569 Refunds

Laws: Sec. 205.27a, M.C.L. (CCH MICHIGAN TAX REPORTS, ¶89-224)

Overpayments of tax, erroneous or illegal assessments, and penalties are credited or refunded. Except as otherwise noted at ¶2402, claims for refund must be filed on or before the expiration of four years from the date set for filing the original return. If an annual return reflects overpayments or credits in excess of the tax, the statements to that effect on the return constitute a claim for refund. If the Department of Treasury agrees that the taxpayer's claim for refund is valid, the overpayment may be refunded or credited against any current or subsequent tax liability at the election of the taxpayer. Interest at the rate calculated for deficiencies will be added to the refund 45 days after the refund claim is filed or the due date of the return, whichever is later.

Practitioner Comment: Consider the Potential Personal Liability of Officers, Members, Managers and Partners for Unpaid Business Taxes, Including Taxes under the SBT, MBT, and CIT Acts

Michigan has one of the most expansive and punitive officer liability statutes in the country. Currently, any officer, manager, member or partner of a business (a corporation, limited liability company, limited liability partnership, partnership, or limited partnership) is potentially personally liable for any unpaid entity taxes administered by the Michigan Department of Treasury. This includes the Michigan SBT, MBT, CIT, sales, use or individual income taxes, regardless of whether the incidence of the tax is on the business, or was collected and held in trust for the state. (Sec. 205.27(a)(5), M.C.L.). And this is so whether or not the business has filed bankruptcy or dissolved, and whether or not the officer, member or partner has declared personal bankruptcy. *See Henderson, v. Dep't of Treasury*, Docket No 431375, Aug. 24, 2012, (citing *Quiroz v. Dep't of Treasury*, 472 BR 434 (ED Mich, 2011)).

It is important to note that the Department of Treasury takes the position that the original four-year statute of limitations on deficiency assessments protects only the business entity, and does not apply to personal liability assessments that may arise later once the original business entity assessment has become final. *See Livingstone v. Department of Treasury*, 169 Mich. App. 209, 214; 426 N.W.2d 184 (1988), *aff'd* 434 Mich. 771 (1990).

In a statutory amendment passed in 2014, MCL 205.27a(5), officer liability was materially reformed and limited to taxes collected and held in trust for the state (e.g., sales, use, tobacco, and payroll taxes). P.A.3 of 2014. This legislation also limits personal liability assessments to circumstances in which failure to remit was willful, and further limits assessment to situations in which the party being held responsible was in control of tax matters at the time the taxes at issue were incurred and the returns were due.

Wayne D. Roberts, Varnum, LLP and Marjorie B. Gell, Western Michigan University Cooley Law School

---

PART IV

SALES AND USE TAXES

CHAPTER 16

IMPOSITION OF TAX, BASIS, RATE

¶1601 Overview

(CCH Michigan Tax Reports, ¶60-010).

The sales tax is imposed upon the privilege of engaging in business as a retailer (¶1603, ¶1605). The use tax is imposed upon the use, storage, or consumption of tangible personal property in the state and upon certain specified services (¶1604, ¶1606). Local jurisdictions are not authorized to impose local sales and use taxes.

The sales tax is codified starting with Sec. 205.51, M.C.L., and the use tax is codified starting with Sec. 205.91, M.C.L. In addition to the state sales tax, there are a number of special purpose taxes, including privilege/equalization taxes (¶1604), the county lodging tax (¶1611), the stadium and convention facilities tax (¶1612), and the city utility users tax (¶1613).

Michigan voters approved S.J.R. S, Laws 1993, which amended the Michigan Constitution to increase the sales and use tax rate from 4% to 6%, effective May 1, 1994. Generally, 60% of the sales tax revenue from the 4% levy and all of the sales and use tax revenue from the additional 2% levy are dedicated to state school aid fund purposes.

Michigan is a member of the Streamlined Sales and Use Tax (SST) Agreement and enacted implementing legislation in 2004 (¶1602).

Exemptions from sales and use taxes are discussed in Chapter 17. Information on returns, payment, refunds, and administration of the taxes is discussed in Chapter 18.

¶1602 Streamlined Sales and Use Tax Agreement

Law: Secs. 205.59, 205.801-33, M.C.L. (CCH MICHIGAN TAX REPORTS, ¶60-096, ¶60-098).

The purpose of the Streamlined Sales and Use Tax (SST) Agreement is to simplify and modernize sales and use tax administration in the member states in order to substantially reduce the burden of tax compliance. The Agreement was developed by representatives of state governments, with input from local governments and the private sector. The Agreement went into effect on October 1, 2005, with a Governing Board made up of member states. The text of the Agreement can be found at http://www.streamlinedsalestax.org/uploads/downloads/Archive/SSUTA/SSUTA%20As%20Amended%20through%209-17-15.pdf.

Michigan is a full member of the Agreement with a seat on the Governing Board. It has enacted most of the provisions necessary to comply with the Agreement's requirements and these provisions currently are in effect. (Sec. 205.171, M.C.L. through Sec. 205.191, M.C.L.; Sec. 205.801, M.C.L. through Sec. 205.833, M.C.L.) As a full member, it may vote on amendments to or interpretations of the Agreement, and sellers registering under the SST system must collect and remit tax on sales into the state.

Outline of the Agreement.—A state that wishes to become a member of the Agreement must certify that its laws, rules, regulations, and policies are substantially compliant with each of the requirements of the Agreement. The requirements of the Agreement include the following:

— a central online registration system for all member states;

— an amnesty for uncollected or unpaid tax for sellers that register to collect tax, so long as they were not previously registered in the state;

— the use of new technology models for tax collection, including Certified Service Providers (CSPs);

— a monetary allowance for CSPs;

— relief from liability for collecting the incorrect amount of tax as a result of relying on data that each member state must provide in the form of a taxability matrix;

— state level administration of local sales and use taxes;

— a single state and local tax base in each state;

— adequate notice to sellers of changes in tax rates, the tax base, and jurisdictional boundaries;

— a single tax rate per taxing jurisdiction, with the exception that a state (but not a locality) may have a second rate on food and drugs;

— uniform, destination-based sourcing rule;

— direct pay authority for holders of permits;

— limitations on exemptions to make them simpler to administer;

— uniform returns and remittances;

— uniform rules for bad debt deductions;

— limitations on sales tax holidays;

— elimination of most caps and thresholds;

— a uniform rounding rule;

— customer refund procedures that limit a purchaser's ability to sue for a return of over-collected tax from the seller;

— uniform definitions, including uniform product definitions; and

— a "books-and-records" standard for certain bundled transactions.

Sourcing.—The Agreement requires that sales be sourced generally to the destination of the product sold, with a default to origin-based sourcing in the absence of that information. Michigan has adopted the destination-based sourcing requirements.

Taxability matrix.—States that are members of the Agreement must provide a taxability matrix indicating the state's tax treatment for clothing and clothing-related items, computer-related products, delivery and installation charges, food and food products, and healthcare products under the Agreement. Michigan's taxability matrix can be found at http://www.streamlinedsalestax.org/otm/. A seller or certified service provider is not liable for having charged and collected an incorrect amount of sales or use tax resulting from their reliance on erroneous data provided in the taxability matrix. (Sec. 205.819, M.C.L.; Sec. 205.809, M.C.L.)

Certificate of compliance.—States must file certificates of compliance with the Streamlined Sales Tax Governing Board in order to become members of the Agreement. The purpose of the certificate is to document compliance with the provisions of the Agreement and cite applicable statutes, rules, regulations, or other authorities evidencing that compliance. Topics covered in the certificate include definitions, sourcing, exemption certificates, bad debts, amnesty, and tax remittance. Michigan's certificate of compliance can be found at http://www.streamlinedsalestax.org/coc/.

Registration.—To register under the Agreement, sellers must go to https://www.sstregister.org/sellers. Sellers can also update previously submitted registration information at this website. The information provided will be sent to all of the full member states and to associate members for which the seller chooses to collect. When a seller registers under the Agreement, it must select the certified technology model it will be using (or it must select "Other" if it will not be using one of the certified models). The models are the following:

— Certified Service Provider (CSP), an agent certified under the Agreement to perform all the seller's sales and use tax functions.

— Certified Automated System (CAS), software certified under the Agreement to calculate the appropriate tax (for which the seller retains responsibility for remitting).

— Certified System (CS), a proprietary automated sales tax system certified under the Agreement.

Uniform exemption certificate.—The SST Governing Board has approved a uniform exemption certificate. Although full member states may continue to use their pre-existing exemption certificates, they must also accept the uniform certificate. Associate member and nonmember states may, but are not required to, accept the certificate.

Issue papers.—The Streamlined Sales Tax Governing Board has released several unofficial issue papers providing guidance on topics such as audit procedures, coupons and discounts, drop shipments, registration, return remittance, sourcing, and taxes affected by the Streamlined Sales and Use Tax Agreement. The issue papers can be found at http://www.streamlinedsalestax.org/index.php?page=issue-papers.

¶1603 Sales Tax Levied on Retailers

Law: Secs. 205.51, 205.52, 205.54d, 205.54m, 205.92, 205.95, M.C.L.; R205.108, R205.124, Mich. Admin. Code (CCH MICHIGAN TAX REPORTS, ¶60-020, 60-080, 60-110, 60-285, 60-310, 60-330, 60-645, 60-700, 60-720, 60-750, 61-110, 61-150, 61-180).

The rate of the Michigan sales tax is 6%. The 6% rate is comprised of a constitutionally authorized rate of 4% plus an additional tax of 2% to support school funding. The residential use of electricity, natural gas, or home heating fuel is exempt from the additional 2% sales and use tax rate and therefore, such fuels are subject to sales or use tax at the rate of 4%.

The sales tax is levied on the gross proceeds of all persons engaged in the business of making sales at retail by which ownership of tangible personal property is transferred for consideration.

CCH Comment: Place Where Possession/Title Transferred Controls

The Michigan Tax Tribunal has held that a taxpayer that purchased trucks from a Michigan truck dealer was not liable for Michigan sales tax on trucks manufactured in Florida, because although the sales contracts were executed in Michigan, the taxpayer actually took title and possession of the trucks in Florida. The MTT ruled that the fact that the tractor dealer was located in Michigan was not determinative as to the location of the sale. Under Michigan law, a "sale at retail" is a transaction by which the ownership of tangible personal property is transferred for consideration. Transfer of ownership is determined by transfer of title and possession. Accordingly, in this case a "sale at retail" did not occur because the taxpayer took title and possession of the trucks outside Michigan. (*Florida Leasco, LLC v. Michigan Department of Treasury,* Michigan Tax Tribunal, No. 264860, November 23, 2005, CCH MICHIGAN TAX REPORTS, ¶401-214)

Tax also applies to the following:

— the transmission and distribution of electricity to consumers or users for consumption or use rather than for resale;

— the sale or reauthorization of a prepaid telephone calling card or prepaid authorization number for telephone use rather than for resale; and

— a conditional sale, installment lease sale, or other transfer of property, if title is retained as security for the purchase but is intended to be transferred at a later date.

A taxpayer who engages in sales at retail and who also engages in other activities not subject to the sales tax is liable for sales tax on the taxpayer's entire activities, unless the taxpayer maintains separate records and books.

Incidence of tax: A merchant seller of tangible personal property, and not the buyer of the property, is the taxpayer of the Michigan sales tax (*Opinion of the Attorney General,* October 19, 1981; CCH MICHIGAN TAX REPORTS, ¶61-210.113).

CCH Advisory: Reporting of Imputed Sales Tax by Equipment Lessors

Sales tax must be imputed and reported by equipment leasing companies, even when the lessee is paying sales or use tax. (*Letter to Assessors and Equalization Directors,* Michigan State Tax Commission, October 3, 2007, CCH MICHIGAN TAX REPORTS, ¶401-331)

"Sale at retail" defined: "Sale at retail" means a sale, lease, or rental of tangible personal property for any purpose other than for resale, sublease, or subrent. The renting or leasing of property is a sale at retail unless the lessor pays the sales tax on the purchase price of the property when it is acquired. (Sec. 205.51(1)(b), M.C.L.; Sec. 205.95(4), M.C.L.) Sales at retail include conditional sales, installment lease sales, and other transfers of property when title is retained as security for the purchase price but is intended to be transferred later. (Sec. 205.52, M.C.L.) However, sales at retail do not include certain isolated transactions or commercial advertising elements. (Sec. 205.54d, M.C.L.)

"Incidental to service" test: An "incidental to service" test is used by the Department of Treasury to differentiate between sales of tangible personal property and sales of services, which are generally not subject to tax (*Revenue Administrative Bulletin 2004-3;* CCH MICHIGAN TAX REPORTS, ¶319-338). Under the "incidental to service" test, sales tax will not apply to transactions where the rendering of a service is the object of the transaction, even though tangible personal property is exchanged incidentally. The "incidental to service" test was adopted by the Michigan Supreme

Court in *Catalina Marketing Sales Corp. v. Department of Revenue*, 468 Mich. 869; 661 NW2d 230 (2004), CCH MICHIGAN TAX REPORTS, ¶401-085. Prior to the Court's decision in *Catalina*, the Department followed a "real object" test for purposes of determining the taxability of a transaction.

"Tangible personal property" defined: "Tangible personal property" means personal property that can be seen, weighed, measured, felt, or touched or that is in any other manner perceptible to the senses and includes electricity, water, gas, steam, and prewritten computer software. (Sec. 205.92(k), M.C.L.)

¶1604 Use Tax Imposed on Use of Tangible Personal Property and Taxable Services

Law: Secs. 205.54v, 205.92—205.93b, 205.93f, 205.94a, 205.95a, 205.97, 205.175, M.C.L.; R205.8, Mich. Admin. Code (CCH MICHIGAN TAX REPORTS, ¶60-020, 60-025, 60-110, 60-285, 60-460, 60-480, 60-520, 60-720, 61-210).

The rate of the Michigan use tax is 6%. The use tax is imposed on the privilege of using, storing, or consuming tangible personal property in the state. It complements the sales tax by protecting Michigan merchants from discrimination arising from the inability of the state to impose a sales tax on sales made outside Michigan to Michigan residents by out-of-state merchants.

Entering into a lease agreement in Michigan is not sufficient to impose the use tax if the leased property is actually used, stored, or consumed outside Michigan. (*Florida Leasco, LLC v. Michigan Department of Treasury*, Michigan Tax Tribunal, No. 264860, November 23, 2005, CCH MICHIGAN TAX REPORTS, ¶401-214) See ¶1603 for the definition of "tangible personal property."

However, property need not be physically present in order to be "used" in Michigan. A taxpayer that purchased a partial interest in an airplane and entered into a contractual agreement whereby the taxpayer and other airplane owners shared access to their planes was subject to Michigan use tax because the taxpayer exercised ownership rights over its plane in Michigan. The taxpayer did not use its own plane for transportation in Michigan. However, the taxpayer did use other planes in the fleet, and this use was pursuant to its contracts to share ownership rights over its own plane. The taxpayer exercised its rights of ownership by entering into agreements to give up part of its rights of control over the airplane. (*Fisher & Company, Inc. v. Department of Treasury*, Michigan Court of Appeals, No. 280476, January 29, 2009, CCH MICHIGAN TAX REPORTS, ¶401-407)

The amount of use tax due is based on the price of the property or service in question (see ¶1606).

No use tax is due if Michigan sales tax has been paid.

• *Presumption of taxability*

Personal property purchased outside Michigan and brought into Michigan within 90 days of the purchase date is considered as acquired for storage, use, or consumption in Michigan and is taxable. In addition, personal property (other than aircraft) purchased outside the state for personal, nonbusiness use will be presumed exempt if:

— the property was purchased by a person who was a nonresident at the time of purchase and who brought the property into the state more than 90 days after the date of purchase; or

— the property was purchased by a person who was a resident at the time of purchase and who brought the property into the state more than 360 days after the date of purchase.

CCH Note: Genesis of Use Tax Exemption Presumption

Prior to 2003, under applicable court precedent, property purchased outside Michigan and brought into Michigan after the passage of 90 days was still subject to tax absent an applicable exemption. (*Guardian Industries Corp. v. Department of Treasury,* (2000, Ct App) 243 Mich App 244, 621 NW2d 450; CCH MICHIGAN TAX REPORTS, ¶400-858). In *Guardian,* the Court of Appeals essentially held that the existence of a statutory presumption of taxability for items brought into the state within 90 days of purchase did not create an implied presumption that items brought into the state more than 90 days after purchase were exempt from tax. This led to undesirable results, causing Michigan residents to be taxed on items long after they had been purchased and put to use. Accordingly, the Michigan legislature enacted Act 27 (H.B. 4219), Laws 2003, which established the presumptions of exemption outlined above.

• *Use tax on services*

The use tax is also levied on the following services in the same manner as it is levied on tangible personal property:

— mobile wireless services where the customer's place of primary use is in Michigan, intrastate telecommunications services that both originate and terminate in this state, including intrastate private communications services, ancillary services, conference bridging service, 900 service, pay telephone service other than coin-operated telephone service, paging service, and value-added nonvoice data service, but excluding 800 service, coin-operated telephone service, fixed wireless service, prepaid calling service, telecommunications nonrecurring charges, and directory advertising proceeds;

— the furnishing of rooms or lodgings for one month or less by hotelkeepers, motel operators, and other persons furnishing accommodations to the public on a commercial basis;

— interstate telephone communications that either originate or terminate in Michigan and that are billed to a Michigan address or phone number by the provider either within or outside Michigan, including ancillary services, conference bridging service, 900 service, paging service, pay telephone service other than coin-operated telephone service, and value-added nonvoice data services, but excluding interstate private communications service, 800 service, coin-operated telephone service, fixed wireless service, prepaid calling service, telecommunications nonrecurring charges, and international telecommunications service;

— the laundering or cleaning of textiles (except textiles used by a restaurant or retail sales business) under a sale, rental, or service agreement with a term of at least five days;

— the transmission and distribution of electricity (other than sales for retail);

— for a manufacturer who affixes its product to real estate in state and maintains an inventory of its product that is available for sale to others by publication or price list, the direct production costs and indirect production costs of the product affixed to the real estate in state that are incident to and necessary for production or manufacturing operations or processes;

— for a manufacturer who affixes its product to real estate in state but does not maintain an inventory of its product available for sale to others or make its product available for sale to others by publication or price list, the sum of the materials cost of the property and the cost of labor to manufacture, fabricate, or assemble the property affixed to the real estate in state, excluding the cost of labor to cut, bend, assemble, or attach the property at the site to the real estate in state.

• *Use tax on Medicaid managed care organizations*

Medical services provided by Medicaid managed care organizations are subject to use tax. "Medical services" refers to services provided to Medicaid beneficiaries enrolled under Title XIX of the Social Security Act.

• *Use tax on motor vehicle dealerships*

A 2.5% use tax applies to motor vehicles held by a dealer for resale that are not otherwise exempt. An additional $30.00 per month is also imposed beginning with the month that the dealer uses the car or truck in a nonexempt manner. The Michigan Supreme Court has held that the "exemption" referred to applies to the motor vehicle dealership demonstration exemption, but not the resale exemption. (*Betten Auto Center, Inc. v. Department of Treasury*, 478 Mich. 864, 731 N.W.2d 424 (Mich SCt 2007), CCH MICHIGAN TAX REPORTS, ¶401-310)

• *Diesel fuel tax*

Interstate motor carriers are subject to a specific tax for the privilege of using or consuming diesel fuel in a qualified commercial motor vehicle in this state at a cents-per-gallon rate equal to 6% of the statewide average retail price of a gallon of self-serve diesel. This tax is collected under the International Fuel Tax Agreement (IFTA).

Motor carriers subject to this tax are entitled to a credit for 6% of the price of diesel fuel purchased in this state and used in a qualified commercial motor vehicle. This credit is claimed on the returns filed under the IFTA.

Beginning January 1, 2017, tax is imposed on interstate motor carriers for the privilege of using or consuming "motor fuel" and "alternative fuel" in the state as defined in the Motor Fuel Tax Act. Motor carriers subject to this tax are entitled to a credit for 6% of the price of motor fuel and alternative fuel purchased in this state and used in a qualified commercial motor vehicle. This credit is claimed on the returns filed under the IFTA.

• *Sourcing rules for telecommunication services*

Except as discussed below, telecommunication services sold on a call-by-call basis are sourced to each level of taxing jurisdiction where the call originates and terminates in that jurisdiction or each level of taxing jurisdiction where the call either originates or terminates and in which the service address is also located. Sales of telecommunications services that are not sold on a call-by-call basis are sourced to the customer's place of primary use.

A sale of post-paid calling service is sourced to the origination point of the telecommunications signal. The general sourcing rules apply to sales of prepaid calling services and prepaid wireless calling service. (Sec. 205.93c(3)(c), M.C.L.)

Michigan also adopts the provisions of the federal Mobile Telecommunications Sourcing Act (P.L. 106-252). Mobile telecommunications services are sourced to the customer's "primary place of use," which is the residential or primary business address of the customer and which must be located in the home service provider's licensed service area. The jurisdiction in which the primary place of use is located is the only jurisdiction that may tax the communications services, regardless of the customer's location when an actual call is placed or received.

A home service provider is responsible for obtaining and maintaining a record of the customer's place of primary use. In obtaining and maintaining the record, the home service provider may rely in good faith on information provided by a customer as to the customer's place of primary use and may treat the address used for a customer under a service contract or agreement in effect on August 1, 2002, as that customer's place of primary use for the remaining term of the service contract or agreement.

Additionally, if taxable and nontaxable mobile telecommunications services are bundled and sold for a single price, the home service provider is not required to separately state the charges on the bill if it maintains sufficient books and records to support the nontaxable portion of the charge. Although not part of the federal Act, the Michigan law extends the bundling provisions relating to mobile telecommunications to general intrastate and interstate telecommunications services.

• *Rentals*

The use tax also applies to rentals of tangible personal property if at the time of purchase by the lessor, the property leased or rented had not previously been subjected to Michigan sales or use tax or to another state's or to another state's political subdivision's sales and use tax at a rate of 6% or more.

• *Incidence of tax*

Although the use tax is a tax on the ultimate consumer, the law requires collection of the tax by licensed sellers. If a licensed seller fails to collect the tax, the seller becomes personally liable. However, the consumer remains liable for the tax until it has actually been collected by the state.

• *Definitions*

"Use" and "storage" defined: "Use" means the exercise of any right or power over tangible personal property incident to the ownership of the property, and includes any transfer of property in a transaction by which possession is given. "Storage" means any keeping or retention of property in the state for any purpose after the property loses its interstate character.

CCH Note: Distributions

Although the courts have held that a taxpayer that contracts with a common carrier to distribute catalogs into the state was not "using" the property in the state and therefore was not subject to the use tax (see *Sharper Image Corp v Dep't of Treasury*, 216 Mich App 698, 702; 550 NW2d 596 (1996)), distribution in the state is not automatically exempt. Rather, the real issue is whether the taxpayer is exercising control over the property. Consequently, in another appellate court case, the court found that the taxpayer was subject to use tax on telephone directories distributed by a third-party common carrier into Michigan, because the taxpayer maintained control and power over the property by dictating when and how the directories were to be distributed. (*Ameritech Publishing, Inc. v. Department of Treasury*, Michigan Court of Appeals, No. 276374, August 7, 2008, CCH MICHIGAN TAX REPORTS, ¶401-383).

"Purchase" defined: "Purchase" means acquired for a consideration, whether the acquisition involves a transfer of title or of possession, or both, or whether it involves a license to use or consume. The transfer may be absolute or conditional and effected by any means, and the price or rental may be in money or by way of exchange or barter. "Purchase" includes converting tangible personal property acquired for an exempt use to a use not exempt from the tax.

"Consumer" defined: "Consumer" means a person who, for consideration, acquires tangible personal property for storage, use, or other consumption in the state, whether acquired in person, through mail or catalog, over the Internet, or by other means. A consumer includes, but is not limited to, (i) a person who acquires tangible personal property if engaged in the business of constructing, altering, repairing, or improving the real estate of others and (ii) a person who converts tangible personal property or services that were exempt from sales or use tax to a use that is not exempt.

• *Nexus and duty to collect tax*

Out-of-state vendors: Although out-of-state vendors are required by statute to register with the Michigan Department of Treasury and to collect the use tax from

Michigan customers, federal constitutional law limits the extent to which Michigan can force registration of out-of-state vendors and require their collection of the tax. In its 1967 *National Bellas Hess* decision, 386 US 753, the U.S. Supreme Court ruled that an out-of-state vendor that does no more than communicate with customers in the state by mail or common carrier as part of an interstate business cannot be compelled to collect the state's use tax on sales made to the state's residents unless the vendor has retail outlets, solicitors, or property within the state.

The *Bellas Hess* decision rested on both Due Process Clause and Commerce Clause considerations. The position taken in *Bellas Hess* that physical presence is required to meet the requirements of the Commerce Clause was specifically reaffirmed by the High Court in *Quill Corp. v. North Dakota* (1992, US SCt), 112 SCt 1904. However, *Quill* overruled the *Bellas Hess* due process objections, holding that physical presence is not required by the Due Process Clause before a state can compel an out-of-state mail-order company to collect its use tax. With the *Bellas Hess* due process objection removed, the Court noted that Congress is now free to decide whether, when, and to what extent the states may burden out-of-state mail-order concerns with a duty to collect use taxes.

In *Sharper Image Corp. v. Department of Treasury* (1996, Ct App), 216 MichApp 698, 550 NW2d 596; CCH MICHIGAN TAX REPORTS, ¶400-554, the court held that a company that conducted business in Michigan through mail-order catalogs and also owned two retail stores in the state was not liable for use tax on its distribution of catalogs in the state from an out-of-state source. Although the catalog sales were taxable, the distribution of the catalogs was not a use in Michigan because the company's exercise of a right or power over the catalogs ended when the catalogs were delivered to the postal service in another state for mailing to Michigan. However, the court also held that separately-stated transportation charges for the delivery of goods were subject to Michigan use tax. Also, see discussion above of *Ameritech Publishing, Inc. v. Department of Treasury.*

CCH Note: Maintenance of Electronic Data and Processing of Orders on Servers in Michigan

In response to a CCH survey, the Department of Treasury has taken the position that maintenance of electronic data on a computer server located within Michigan creates sales and use tax collection responsibility for an out-of-state retailer with respect to sales of products delivered in Michigan. Furthermore, a selling company that has a representative in Michigan processing orders also has nexus with Michigan (*Response to CCH Survey on Nexus,* Michigan Department of Treasury, May 17, 2010; CCH MICHIGAN TAX REPORTS, ¶401-500).

• *Out-of-state seller liability to collect use tax*

Click-through nexus: A seller is presumed to be engaged in business in Michigan if the seller enters into an agreement with one or more residents under which the resident, for a commission or other consideration, directly or indirectly, refers potential customers, by a link on an Internet website, in-person oral presentation, or otherwise, to the seller. The presumption requires that the cumulative gross receipts from sales by the seller to customers in this state who are referred to the seller be greater than $10,000 during the immediately preceding 12 months and that the seller's total cumulative gross receipts from sales to customers in Michigan be greater than $50,000 during the immediately preceding 12 months.

The presumption may be rebutted by demonstrating that the persons with whom the seller had agreements did not engage in activities that were significantly associated with the seller's ability to establish or maintain a market in Michigan. The presumption would be considered rebutted by evidence of the following: (i) written agreements prohibiting all residents with an agreement with the seller from engaging in solicitation in Michigan on behalf of the seller and (ii) written statements from all residents with an agreement with the seller stating that the residents did not engage in any solicitation activities on behalf of the seller during the immediately preceding 12 months. An agreement where a seller purchases advertisements from a person in Michigan to be delivered via television, radio, print, the Internet, or any other medium is not an agreement that would lead to a presumption of nexus unless the revenue paid to the persons is commissions that are based on completed sales.

Affiliate Nexus: A seller is presumed to be engaged in business in Michigan if it or any other person, including an affiliated person, other than a common carrier, engages in the following activities:

— sells a similar line of products as the seller under the same or a similar business name;

— uses its employees, agents, independent contractors, or representatives to promote sales by the seller in Michigan;

— maintains an office, distribution facility, warehouse, storage place, or similar place of business in Michigan to facilitate the delivery of tangible personal property sold by the seller to customers in the state;

— uses, with the seller's knowledge or consent, trademarks, service marks, or trade names in the state that are the same or substantially similar to those used by the seller;

— delivers, installs, assembles, or performs maintenance or repair services for the seller's customers in Michigan;

— facilitates the seller's delivery of property to customers by allowing the seller's customers in the state to pick up tangible personal property sold by the seller at an office, distribution facility, warehouse, storage place, or similar place of business maintained by the person in the state;

— shares management, business systems, business practices, or employees with the seller, or, in the case of an affiliated person, engages in intercompany transactions related to the activities occurring with the seller to establish or maintain the seller's market in Michigan; or

— conducts any other activities in the state that are significantly associated with the seller's ability to establish and maintain a market in the state.

The presumption may be rebutted by demonstrating that activities of the other person or affiliated person were not significantly associated with the seller's ability to establish or maintain a market in Michigan.

An administrative bulletin specifies that an out-of-state seller must collect Michigan use tax when it:

— has one or more employees resident or temporarily present in Michigan engaging in any activity other than the limited contacts described below; an employee temporarily present in Michigan for two days will create nexus;

— owns, rents, leases, maintains, or has the right to use and uses tangible personal or real property that is permanently or temporarily physically located in Michigan;

— has employees who own, rent, lease, use, or maintain an office or other place of business in Michigan;

— has goods delivered to Michigan in vehicles the out-of-state seller owns, rents, leases, uses, or maintains or has goods delivered by a related party acting as a representative of the out-of-state seller;

— has agents, representatives, independent contractors, brokers, or others, who, acting on behalf of the out-of-state seller, own, rent, lease, use, or maintain an office or other place of business in Michigan, and this property is used in the representation of the out-of-state seller in Michigan; or

— has agents, representatives, independent contractors, brokers, or others who, acting on behalf of the out-of-state seller, are regularly and systematically present in Michigan conducting activities to establish or maintain the market for the out-of-state seller whether or not these individuals or organizations reside in Michigan.

Activities that establish or maintain the market for the out-of-state seller include, but are not limited to, the following: (a) soliciting sales; (b) making repairs or providing maintenance or service to property sold or to be sold; (c) collecting current or delinquent accounts, through assignment or otherwise, related to sales of tangible personal property or services; (d) delivering property sold to customers; (e) installing or supervising installation at or after shipment or delivery; (f) conducting training for employees, agents, representatives, independent contractors, brokers or others acting on the out-of-state seller's behalf, or for customers or potential customers; (g) providing customers any kind of technical assistance or service including, but not limited to, engineering assistance, design service, quality control, product inspections, or similar services; (h) investigating, handling, or otherwise assisting in resolving customer complaints; (i) providing consulting services; or (j) soliciting, negotiating, or entering into franchising, licensing, or similar agreements.

CCH Note: Solicitation by Representatives

Summary judgment should not have been granted in the taxpayer's favor where evidence was presented that suggested that the taxpayer engaged in sufficient business activity in Michigan to warrant the imposition of sales and use tax. The taxpayer was an out-of-state corporation that maintained no property or employees in Michigan during the period at issue. In support of its motion, the taxpayer submitted an affidavit stating that it had not solicited sales during the audit period. However, the taxpayer's responses to the state's nexus questionnaire advised that it solicited sales in Michigan between two and nine times per year. The nexus standard utilized by Michigan clearly stated that two contacts per year were sufficient to impose sales and use tax when the activity is the solicitation of sales. As a genuine issue of material fact was raised by the Department of Treasury's evidence, summary judgment should not have been granted. (*Barr Laboratories, Inc. v. Department of Treasury,* Michigan Court of Appeals, No. 291968, October 21, 2010; CCH MICHIGAN TAX REPORTS, ¶401-532).

Limited contacts: If an out-of-state seller is not conducting activities to establish or maintain a market in Michigan and its contacts in Michigan are limited to any of the following contacts, the contacts may generally be presumed not to create nexus:

— meeting with in-state suppliers of goods or services;

— in-state meetings with government representatives in their official capacity;

— attending occasional meetings (i.e., board meetings, retreats, seminars and conferences sponsored by others, etc.);

— holding recruiting or hiring events;

— advertising in the state through various media;

— renting customer lists to or from an in-state entity;

— attending a trade show at which no orders for goods are taken and no sales are made; or

— participating in a trade show at which no orders for goods are taken and no sales are made for less than 10 days cumulatively on an annual basis.

Once nexus is established by a seller for use tax collection purposes, nexus will exist for that seller from the date of contact forward for the remainder of that month and for the following 11 months. Either the seller or the Department of Treasury may submit proof that a longer or shorter period more reasonably reflects the sales that were proximately caused by the seller's in-state contacts under the facts and circumstances (*Revenue Administrative Bulletin 1999-1;* CCH MICHIGAN TAX REPORTS, ¶319-283).

¶1605 Basis of Sales Tax—"Gross Proceeds"

Law: Secs. 205.51, 205.51a, 205.52, 205.54i, 205.99a, M.C.L.; R205.22, R205.83, R205.112, R205.128, Mich. Admin. Code (CCH MICHIGAN TAX REPORTS, ¶60-020, 60-360, 61-110, 61-120, 61-130, 61-150, 61-170).

Sales tax liability is computed on the basis of "gross proceeds," or the sales price, which is the total amount of consideration, including cash, credit, property, and services, for which tangible personal property or services are sold, leased, or rented, valued in money, whether received in money or otherwise. Sales price includes:

— the seller's cost of the property sold;

— the cost of materials used, labor or service cost, interest, losses, costs of transportation to the seller, taxes (other than sales taxes) imposed on the seller, and any other expense of the seller;

— charges by the seller for any services necessary to complete the sale, other than separately stated tips or gratuities for the seller's employees or separately stated tangible personal property repair service charges;

— delivery charges incurred or to be incurred before the completion of the transfer of ownership of tangible personal property from the seller to the purchaser;

— installation charges incurred or to be incurred before the completion of the transfer of ownership of tangible personal property from the seller to the purchaser;

— credit for any trade-in (except for trade-in vehicles and watercraft); and

— consideration received by a seller from a third party as long as the following conditions are met: (i) the seller receives consideration from a party other than the purchaser and the consideration relates to a discount; (ii) the seller is obligated to pass the discount to the purchaser; (iii) the amount of the third party consideration is fixed and determinable by the seller at the time of the sale; and (iv) the purchaser identifies him/herself as a member of an organization entitled to a discount or presents documentation from a third party authorizing reimbursement or the third party discount is identified on the purchaser invoice or coupon.

The following are excluded from sales price:

— separately stated interest, financing, or carrying charges from credit extended on the sale of personal property or services;

— separately stated taxes legally imposed directly on the consumer;

— employee discounts that are reimbursed by a third party on sales of motor vehicles;

— separately stated credit for the agreed-upon value of a watercraft trade-in; and

— separately stated credit for the agreed-upon value of a motor vehicle or recreational vehicle trade-in up to a specified limit.

CCH Advisory: Separately Stated Entertainment Charges

Separately stated charges for entertainment that were included in drink prices at adult entertainment venues were subject to sales tax. The 50% entertainment charges could not be deducted from the beverage sale proceeds for sales tax purposes because the definition of "gross proceeds" did not contain an exclusion for entertainment charges or fees. (*Hamilton's Henry the VIII Lounge v. Department of Treasury*, Michigan Court of Appeals, Nos. 267537, 267538, 267539, and 267540, July 20, 2006, CCH MICHIGAN TAX REPORTS, ¶401-242)

Labor or service: Labor or service charges involved in maintenance and repair work on tangible personal property of others must be separately itemized and the tax applied only to the amount charged for the tangible personal property sold.

Delivery charges: A retailer is deemed to be simultaneously engaged in a separate, nontaxable delivery service if all of the following conditions are met prior to the transfer of ownership:

— the customer has the option to either pick up or have the merchandise delivered;

— the delivery service charge is separately negotiated and contracted for and is not a cost in calculating the merchandise price;

— the taxpayer's books and records separately identify the transactions used to determine the tax; and

— the delivery service shows a net profit.

Delivery charges are not taxable if they are incurred after the transfer of ownership (*Revenue Administrative Bulletin 2015-17;* CCH MICHIGAN TAX REPORTS, ¶402-006).

Delivery charges do not include the charges for delivery of direct mail if the charges are separately stated on an invoice or similar billing document given to the purchaser.

CCH Advisory: Allocation of Delivery Fees for Partially Exempt Property

Michigan sales and use tax statutes conform to the Streamlined Sales and Use Tax Agreement regarding how to calculate the amount of delivery charges included in *sales price* or *purchase price* if a shipment includes both exempt and taxable property. The Streamlined Sales and Use Tax Agreement allows allocation of delivery charges based on either the percentage of sales price of the taxable property to the total sales price of the shipment or the percentage of the weight of the taxable property to the total weight of the shipment.

• *Bad debts*

Bad debts may be deducted from gross proceeds to compute sales tax liability. The term "bad debt" means any portion of a debt related to a sale at retail for which gross proceeds are not otherwise deductible or excludable that is eligible to be claimed, or could be eligible to be claimed if the taxpayer kept accounts on an accrual basis, as a deduction pursuant to IRC Sec. 166. A bad debt does not include the following:

— interest, finance charges, or sales tax on the purchase price;

— uncollectible amounts on property that remains in the possession of the taxpayer until the full purchase price is paid;

— expenses incurred in attempting to collect any account receivable or any portion of the debt recovered;

— any accounts receivable that have been sold to and remain in the possession of a third party for collection; or

— repossessed property.

In computing the amount of tax levied under the sales tax law for the month, a taxpayer may deduct the amount of bad debts from the taxpayer's gross proceeds used for the computation of the tax. The amount of gross proceeds deducted must be charged off as uncollectible on the taxpayer's books and records and must be eligible to be deducted for federal income tax purposes, whether or not the taxpayer is actually required to file a federal income tax return.

Practice Note: Eligibility to Claim Bad Debt Deduction Clarified

A deduction for a bad debt for a seller is available exclusively to those persons with legal liability to remit the taxes on the transaction for which the bad debt is recognized for federal income tax purposes, effective October 1, 2007, and applicable retroactively for sales tax purposes applicable June 28, 1933, and for use tax purposes effective October 29, 1937. The clarification was enacted in response to a Michigan Court of Appeals decision in *Daimler Chrysler Service of North America, LLC v. Department of Treasury*, Michigan Court of Appeals, No. 264323, July 25, 2006, CCH MICHIGAN TAX REPORTS, ¶401-245, in which the court held that a finance company that financed sales of automobiles made by its affiliated dealerships was entitled to recover overpayments of Michigan sales tax under the state's bad debt statute.

However, after September 30, 2009, if a taxpayer who reported the tax and a lender execute and maintain a written election designating which party may claim the deduction, a claimant is entitled to a deduction or refund of the tax related to a sale at retail that was previously reported and paid if no deduction or refund was previously claimed or allowed on any portion of the account receivable and the account receivable has been found worthless and written off by the taxpayer that made the sale or by the lender after September 29, 2009. (Sec. 205.99a(6)(e), M.C.L.)

CCH Comment: Retailers that contracted with finance companies were not entitled to bad debt refund

The Michigan Court of Appeals has held that retailers that contracted with finance companies to issue private label credit cards were not entitled to claim refunds of sales tax based on the bad debt deduction provision because the retailers were fully compensated for the sales transactions, including the tax, pursuant to the reimbursement agreements with the finance companies. The consumers paid for the goods with funds from the credit card lenders, and, when the customers defaulted, the lenders wrote off these amounts as bad debts. The bad debt statute states that when the debt is paid by the consumer or another person, the taxpayer remains liable for remittance of the tax to the extent of the amount paid. Consequently, the payment of the bad debt by the third-party lenders did not entitle the retailers to a bad debt refund. Furthermore, the Legislature limited the availability of the deduction when it amended MCL 205.54i to allow a taxpayer and a lender to make an election designating which party may claim the deduction. The court expressly declined to follow *Home Depot USA, Inc. v. Department of Treasury*, Michigan Court of Appeals, No. 301341, May 24, 2012, CCH MICHIGAN TAX REPORTS, ¶401-679, which had permitted a retailer that had entered into private label credit card agreements with finance companies to claim a bad debt deduction, as the decision was unpublished and not binding precedent. (*Menard Inc. v. Department of Treasury*, Michigan Court of Appeals, No. 310399, September 12, 2013, CCH MICHIGAN TAX REPORTS, ¶401-819)

If a consumer or other person pays all or part of a bad debt with respect to which a taxpayer claimed a deduction, the taxpayer is liable for the amount of taxes deducted in connection with that portion of the debt for which payment is received and must remit these taxes in the taxpayer's next payment to the Department of Treasury. Any payments made on a bad debt or account are applied first proportionally to the taxable price of the property or service and the sales tax, and then to interest, service charges, and any other charges.

A seller's certified service provider may claim a credit or refund for a bad debt on behalf of the seller if the certified service provider credits or refunds the full amount of the bad debt deduction or refund to the seller. In situations where the books and records of the party claiming the bad debt allowance support an allocation of the bad debts among the states that are members of the Streamlined Sales and Use Tax Agreement (SSUTA) (see ¶1602), allocation is permitted.

CCH Advisory: Impact of SSUTA Implementing Legislation

Prior to the enactment of Michigan's SSUTA implementing legislation (¶1602), Michigan law required that the period of limitations for taking a bad debt deduction was to be measured from the return due date of the period in which the sale was made. SSUTA applies a longer limitation period based on when the debt is, or could be, written off for federal income tax purposes. SSUTA also allows deduction for debts that have been sold to a third party and then re-transferred back to the seller. The general four-year statute of limitations was previously applied from the return due date for the period within which the sale was made. Under SSUTA, the four-year statute of limitations begins with the return due date for the period within which the debt becomes worthless and is, or could be, written off for federal income tax purposes.

Example: A credit sale was made in August of 2004. The August 2004 return had a due date of September 15, 2004. The debt was found to be worthless and written off in December 2005. Prior to SSUTA, the bad debt had to be claimed (on an amended return for December 2005) no later than September 15, 2008. After SSUTA, the bad debt must be claimed (on an amended return for December 2004) no later than January 15, 2010, (the December 2005 return due date was January 15, 2006). (*Streamlined Sales and Use Tax Legislation,* Michigan Department of Treasury)

• *Discounts, rebates, and coupons*

Cash, trade, and quantity discounts to customers are deductible in arriving at the sales price that is taxable, however, rebates received by the retailer are included in gross proceeds. Instant rebates offered directly by the seller (without reimbursement by a third party) reduce the tax base. (R205.22, Rule 22, Mich. Admin. Code; CCH MICHIGAN TAX REPORTS, ¶65-043; *Revenue Administrative Bulletin 1995-6;* CCH MICHIGAN TAX REPORTS, ¶319-259).

A taxpayer may calculate a credit and seek a refund on sales taxes paid on motor vehicles subject to manufacturer rebate. The refund is 6% of the amount received by the taxpayer from the automobile manufacturer in reimbursement for a price reduction on the vehicle. The refund is only permitted if the following conditions are met: (i) the purchaser was not employed by the automobile manufacturer at the time of the discount, (ii) the taxpayer did not add sales tax to the part of the sales price received from the manufacturer when calculating the credit, and (iii) the refund would not be greater than the actual sales tax paid on that portion of the sales price received from the manufacturer. (R205.22, Rule 22, Mich. Admin. Code; CCH MICHIGAN TAX REPORTS, ¶65-043).

A revenue administrative bulletin gives examples of the application of discounts, coupons, and rebates to gross proceeds used to compute the sales tax (*Revenue Administrative Bulletin 1995-6;* CCH MICHIGAN TAX REPORTS, ¶319-259).

Motor vehicle refunds: Refunds, less an allowance for vehicle use, made for a motor vehicle that is returned under the Auto Lemon Law may be deducted from gross proceeds.

• *Taxes*

The Department of Treasury has issued a rule specifying which federal and state excise taxes may be deducted in computing the sales and use tax (R205.128, Rule 78, Mich. Admin. Code; CCH MICHIGAN TAX REPORTS, ¶65-253). Federal excise taxes on diesel and jet fuel are not allowed as deductions from the basis because the federal tax is assessed at the refiner, importer, or producer level (*Letter,* Department of Treasury, March 31, 1988; *Quarterly Tax Advisor;* CCH MICHIGAN TAX REPORTS, ¶201-424).

The federal excise tax on ChloroFluoroCarbons (CFCs) is a part of a CFC retailer's gross proceeds and is, therefore, subject to the sales and use tax (*Letter Ruling 90-22;* CCH MICHIGAN TAX REPORTS, ¶355-067).

"Gross proceeds" includes a tax paid on cigarettes or tobacco products at the time of purchase.

Documentary fees charged by a retailer in connection with the sale of a motor vehicle reflect part of the cost of the property sold and, therefore, must be included in gross proceeds (*Letter Ruling 90-20;* CCH MICHIGAN TAX REPORTS, ¶355-065).

¶1606 Basis of Use Tax—"Price"

Law: Secs. 205.92, 205.93, M.C.L.; R205.22, Mich. Admin. Code (CCH MICHIGAN TAX REPORTS, ¶60-330, 61-110).

The amount of use tax due is based on the price of the property or service in question. "Purchase price" or "price" means the total amount of consideration paid by the consumer to the seller, including cash, credit, property, and services, for which tangible personal property or services are sold, leased, or rented, valued in money, whether received in money or otherwise. Included in the measure of tax is:

— the seller's cost of the property sold;

— the cost of materials used, labor or service cost, interest, losses, costs of transportation to the seller, taxes (other than use taxes) imposed on the seller, and any other expense of the seller;

— charges by the seller for any services necessary to complete the sale, other than (1) separately stated tips or gratuities charged by the seller and (2) separately stated labor or service charges involved in maintenance and repair work on tangible personal property of others;

— delivery charges incurred or to be incurred before the completion of the transfer of ownership of tangible personal property from the seller to the purchaser;

— installation charges incurred or to be incurred before the completion of the transfer of ownership of tangible personal property from the seller to the purchaser;

— credit for any trade-in (except for trade-in vehicles and watercraft); and

— consideration received by a seller from a third party as long as the following conditions are met: (i) the seller receives consideration from a party other than the purchaser and the consideration relates to a discount; (ii) the seller is obligated to pass the discount to the purchaser; (iii) the amount of the third party consideration is fixed and determinable by the seller at the time of the sale; and (iv) the purchaser identifies him/herself as a member of an organization entitled to a discount or presents documentation from a third party authorizing reimbursement or the third party discount is identified on the purchaser invoice or coupon.

Practice Note: Manufacturer Leasing Its Product Allowed Choice of Tax Calculation

A Michigan court of appeal ruled that a company that manufactured gaming machines out-of-state and then leased them to Michigan casinos was allowed to either pay the applicable Michigan use tax on those machines based upon the price paid for the component parts or pay use tax on the rental receipts from leasing the machines to Michigan casinos. Where the equipment was manufactured was irrelevant. (*WMS Gaming, Inc. v. Department of Treasury*, Michigan Court of Appeals, No. 269114, February 27, 2007, MICHIGAN TAX REPORTS, ¶401-280)

Excluded from the measure of tax is:

— separately stated interest, financing, or carrying charges from credit extended on the sale of personal property or services;

— separately stated taxes legally imposed directly on the consumer; and

— employee discounts that are reimbursed by a third party on sales of motor vehicles.

— separately stated credit for the agreed-upon value of a watercraft trade-in;

— separately stated credit for the agreed-upon value of a motor vehicle or recreational vehicle trade-in up to a specified limit.

With respect to diesel fuel used by interstate motor carriers in a qualified commercial motor vehicle, the term "price" means the statewide average retail price of a gallon of self-serve diesel fuel as determined and certified quarterly by the Michigan Department of Transportation, rounded down to the nearest 0.1¢.

Practice Note: Reinstatement Fees Subject to Use Tax

Reinstatement fees received from customers under rental purchase agreements for exercising their right to reinstate a contract after a default were subject to Michigan use tax. The reinstatement fees were part of the *price* paid for the use and consumption of goods and were not paid for as a separate service. Although the tangible goods were available without paying the reinstatement fee (by entering into a new contract), the transaction was essentially and predominantly a rental or sale of goods. (*Continental Rental, Inc. v. Michigan Department of Treasury*, Michigan Tax Tribunal, No. 297569, April 28, 2005; CCH MICHIGAN TAX REPORTS, ¶401-154).

¶1607 Trade-Ins—Deduction Not Allowable

Law: Secs. 205.51, 205.61, 205.92, M.C.L.; R205.15, Mich. Admin. Code (CCH MICHIGAN TAX REPORTS, ¶61-140).

With the exception of watercraft and vehicle trade-ins, no deduction is allowed under either the sales or use tax for any credit allowed by the seller for a trade-in taken in exchange for part payment. The tax applies to the full selling price. The retail sale of used tangible personal property acquired by the seller by trade-in is taxable on the full selling price (R205.15, Rule 15, Mich. Admin. Code; CCH MICHIGAN TAX REPORTS, ¶65-029).

Credit for the agreed-upon value of a titled watercraft used as part payment of the purchase price of a new or used watercraft is excluded from the tax base so long as the agreed-upon value is separately stated on the invoice or bill of sale.

The agreed-upon value of a motor vehicle or recreational vehicle used as part payment of the purchase price of a new or used motor vehicle or a new or used recreational vehicle is excluded from the tax base. As of January 1, 2015, the maximum trade-in value is limited to $2,500, and each January thereafter, the allowable trade-in value increases by $500 unless Section 105D of the Social Welfare Act is repealed. Beginning January 1 of the year in which the trade-in value exceeds $14,000, there will no longer be a limit on the agreed-upon value of the trade-in vehicle. The agreed-upon value of the trade-in must be separately stated on the invoice or other similar document given to the purchaser.

In a taxable retail sale of motor vehicles where another motor vehicle is used as partial payment of the purchase price, the value of the motor vehicle used as partial payment is the value agreed to by the parties to the sale. A dealer that accepts a trade-in vehicle or watercraft with negative equity may not claim a deduction for any amount not attributed to the value of the trade-in vehicle or watercraft. (*Letter Ruling 2015-1*; CCH MICHIGAN TAX REPORTS, ¶401-974)

¶1608 Lease or Rental of Tangible Personal Property

Law: Secs. 205.94a, M.C.L (CCH MICHIGAN TAX REPORTS, ¶60-460).

No tax is levied on rental receipts if the tangible personal property rented or leased has previously been subjected to sales or use tax by Michigan or by another state or state's political subdivision when purchased by the lessor. However, Michigan sales or use tax will still be imposed to the extent the other state or locality's tax was less than Michigan's 6% sales and use tax rate.

¶1609 Private Sales of Vehicles, Aircraft, Snowmobiles, and Watercraft

Law: Sec. 205.93, 205.94bb, 205.179, 205.181, M.C.L.; R205.135, Mich. Admin. Code (CCH MICHIGAN TAX REPORTS, ¶60-570).

Both a use tax and a privilege tax (a streamlined sales and use equalization tax) applies to isolated transfers of vehicles (including off-road vehicles and mobile homes), aircraft, snowmobiles and watercraft, other than transfers to registered dealers for resale, by persons who do not transfer such vehicles in the ordinary course of business. The tax is collected by the Secretary of State prior to the transfer of any vehicle title or watercraft registration, except that the use tax on mobile homes is collected by the Department of Consumer and Industry Services. The tax on aircraft is paid directly to the Department of Treasury by the purchaser.

The use tax is imposed on the purchase price whereas the privilege/equalization tax is imposed on retail dollar value. A nonrefundable credit for use tax paid on purchase price may be used to totally or partially offset the equalization tax obligation.

All vehicles, aircraft, snowmobiles or watercraft brought into the state for registration purposes within 90 days from the date they were purchased are subject to use tax (R205.135, Rule 85, Mich. Admin. Code; CCH MICHIGAN TAX REPORTS, ¶65-267). The tax base for the equalization tax imposed on aircraft brought into the state is the value of the aircraft at the time it first enters this state. A nonrefundable credit for use tax paid on the purchase price may be used to totally or partially offset the equalization tax obligation.

The following transfers of vehicles, aircraft, snowmobiles, or watercraft are exempt:

— when the transferee is the spouse, parent, brother, sister, child, stepparent, stepchild, stepbrother, stepsister, grandparent, grandchild, legal ward, or a legally appointed guardian of the transferor;

— when the transferee is the father-in-law, mother-in-law, brother-in-law, sister-in-law, son-in-law, daughter-in-law, or grandparent-in-law of the transferor;

— when the transfer is a gift to a beneficiary in the administration of an estate;

— when the transferred property, which has once been subject to sales or use tax, is transferred in connection with the organization, reorganization, dissolution, or partial liquidation of a business and the beneficial ownership is not changed but vehicles purchased as part of the assets of a business are taxable; or

— when an insurance company acquires ownership of a late model distressed vehicle through payment of damages in response to a claim or when the person who owned the vehicle before the insurance company reacquires ownership from the company as part of the settlement of a claim.

¶1610 Financial Institutions

Law: R205.79, Mich. Admin. Code (CCH MICHIGAN TAX REPORTS, ¶60-370).

There are no specific statutory provisions on financial institutions, but a rule makes clear that sales and purchases by national banks are taxable (R205.79, Rule 29, Mich. Admin. Code; CCH MICHIGAN TAX REPORTS, ¶65-157), and Michigan has subjected national banks to the tax since 1969.

Under federal law a state is unable to subject to sales tax the following entities: Federal Home Loan Banks; Federal Reserve Banks; Federal National and Government National Mortgage Associations; Federal Financing Banks; Federal Intermediate Credit Banks; Production Credit Associations; or Federal Land Banks or Associations. Federal law also exempts federal credit unions.

¶1611 County Lodging Tax

Law: Secs. 141.861, 141.862, 207.623, 207.624, 141.882, 141.883, 141.872, 141.873, 141.1432, 141.1433, 141.1435, M.C.L. (CCH MICHIGAN TAX REPORTS, ¶ 60-480, 61-710).

A lodging tax may be levied by a county with a population of less than 600,000 and having a city of at least 40,000. The tax, not to exceed 5% of total charges for accommodations, is imposed on persons engaged in the business of providing rooms to transient guests for dwelling, lodging, or sleeping purposes. The county lodging tax is imposed in addition to other charges, fees, or taxes. (Sec. 141.866, M.C.L.)

A county that had a population of less than 600,000 and a city of at least 40,000 on the date it enacted the lodging tax may continue collecting the tax even if its county population later exceeds 600,000 or the city's population falls below 40,000.

Regional convention and tourism act.—A tourism and convention bureau may impose an excise tax on room charges in transient facilities within an assessment district for purposes of tourism and convention marketing and promotion. The excise tax will be imposed at a rate not exceeding 5%. An "assessment district" is composed of two or more adjoining municipalities. A "municipality," in turn, is defined as a county with a population greater than 80,000 and less than 115,000 that contains a city with a population exceeding 35,000 but less than 45,000, and that shares a border with a county that imposes a local accommodations tax pursuant to MCL 141.861. The assessment is imposed only on charges for occupancy of a room and excludes charges for food, beverages, use tax, and telephone service. An owner may pass along the cost of the assessment to its transient guests as long as it is disclosed on the bill. (Sec. 141.1432, 141.1433, 141.1435, M.C.L.)

An owner of a transient facility must remit the assessment to the bureau within 30 days after the end of each month, and within 30 days after the end of each calendar quarter, the owner must submit to the auditors of the bureau copies of its use tax returns for the prior quarter. An owner who is delinquent on payment of the assessment is subject to interest at a rate of 1.5% per month.

The excise tax becomes effective on the first day of the month following the expiration of the 40 day period after the marketing program notice has been mailed to owners of transient facilities within the assessment district. However, a referendum must be held if the director of the Michigan economic development corporation receives written requests within the 40 day period from either 40% of the owners or from owners representing 40% of the total number of rooms within the district.

State convention facility development act.—A tax is imposed on any person engaged in the business of providing accommodations to transient guests in a convention hotel, whether or not membership is required. For those convention hotels located within a qualified local governmental unit, a rate of 3% of the room charge is imposed for accommodations in a convention hotel with 81 to 160 rooms, and a rate of 6% of the room charge is imposed for accommodations in a convention hotel with more than 160 rooms. For convention hotels not located within a qualified local governmental unit, the tax is imposed at a rate of 1.5% of the room charge for accommodations in a convention hotel with 81 to 160 rooms, and a rate of 5% of the room charge for accommodations in a convention hotel with more than 160 rooms. (207.623, 207.624, M.C.L.)

Convention and tourism marketing act.—A convention and tourism bureau in a county with a population of over 1.5 million and designated contiguous counties may assess owners of transient facilities with 35 or more rooms up to 2% of room charges on stays of less than 30 consecutive days. Hospitals and nursing homes are exempt. (141.882, 141.883, M.C.L.)

Community convention and tourism act.—A convention or tourist bureau in a county with a population of less than 650,000 or in certain cities, villages, or townships within a county of less than 650,000 or a combination of both, may assess owners of transient facilities with ten or more rooms up to 5% of room charges. An owner of a building or combination of buildings with less than ten rooms may agree in writing to be subject to the assessment. College or school dormitories, hospitals, nursing homes, and facilities operated by organizations exempt from federal taxation are exempt. (141.872, 141.873, M.C.L.)

¶1612 Stadium and Convention Facilities Tax

Law: Secs. 207.751—207.757, M.C.L. (CCH MICHIGAN TAX REPORTS, ¶61-710).

Certain cities and counties are authorized, subject to voter approval, to impose excise taxes on food service establishments, rental cars, and accommodations to help finance professional sports, entertainment, or convention facilities or a professional baseball stadium. The rate of tax may not exceed 1% of gross receipts from the sale of food and beverages or charges for accommodations and 2% of gross receipts from car rentals.

¶1613 City Utility Users Tax

Law: Secs. 141.1155, 141.1163, 141.1164, M.C.L. (CCH MICHIGAN TAX REPORTS, ¶35-001).

Cities with a population of one million or more (Detroit) are authorized to impose a tax on users of telephone, gas, and electricity services. The rate may not exceed 5% of the utility bill. The tax is billed by the public utility or resale customer as part of the utility bill and remitted monthly to the taxing city. The constitutionality of the tax, whose sunset expiration date was retroactively extended, has been affirmed (*Taxpayers United for the Michigan Constitution, Inc. et al. v. City of Detroit* (1992, Ct App), 493 NW2d 463; CCH MICHIGAN TAX REPORTS, ¶400-235).

Public utility services provided in designated renaissance zones (see ¶204) to persons or corporations are exempt from the city utility users tax. A qualified start-up business (see ¶1126 and ¶1483) is exempt from the city utility users tax, provided that the business applies for an exemption by September 1 of each year, and the governing body of the city adopts a resolution approving the exemption in its last official meeting in September of any given year.

¶1614 Computation of Tax

Law: Sec. 205.73, M.C.L. (CCH MICHIGAN TAX REPORTS, ¶60-130).

Retailers must compute the tax to the third decimal place and round up to a whole cent when the third decimal place is greater than four, or down to a whole cent when the third decimal point is four or less.

¶1615 Sourcing Rules

Law: Sec. 205.110, M.C.L. (CCH MICHIGAN TAX REPORTS, ¶60-020, 60-460).

Sales are sourced generally to the destination of the product sold, with a default to origin-based sourcing in the absence of that information. See ¶1604 for the sourcing rules applicable to telecommunication services. The following general sourcing rules apply:

— when the product is received by the purchaser at a business location of the seller, the sale is sourced to that business location;

— when the product is not received by the purchaser at a business location of the seller, the sale is sourced to the location where receipt by the purchaser, or the purchaser's designated donee, occurs;

— if neither of the above applies, the sale is sourced to the location indicated by an address for the purchaser that is available from the business records of the seller that are maintained in the ordinary course of the seller's business when use of this address does not constitute bad faith;

— if none of the above apply, the sale is sourced to the location indicated by an address for the purchaser obtained during the consummation of the sale, including the address of a purchaser's payment instrument, if no other address is available, when use of this address does not constitute bad faith; or

— if none of the other rules apply, including the circumstance in which the seller is without sufficient information to apply the previous rules, then the location will be determined by the address from which tangible personal property was shipped, from which the digital good or the computer software delivered electronically was first available for transmission by the seller, or from which the service was provided.

• *Rentals and leases*

The following rules apply to sourcing of leases and rentals.

For a lease or rental that requires recurring periodic payments, the down payment and first periodic payment is sourced the same as a retail sale. Periodic payments made subsequent to the first payment are sourced to the primary property location for each period covered by the payment. The primary property location is as indicated by an address for the property provided by the lessee that is available to the lessor from its records maintained in the ordinary course of business, when use of this address does not constitute bad faith.

For the lease or rental of transportation equipment, the payments are sourced the same as a retail sale.

For a lease or rental of motor vehicles, trailers, semi-trailers, or aircraft that do not qualify as transportation equipment that requires recurring periodic payments, each periodic payment is sourced to the primary property location. The primary property location is as indicated by an address for the property provided by the lessee that is available to the lessor from its records maintained in the ordinary course of business, when use of this address does not constitute bad faith.

For a lease or rental that does not require recurring periodic payments, the payment is sourced the same as a retail sale.

These rules do not affect the imposition or computation of sales or use tax on leases or rentals based on a lump sum or accelerated basis, or on the acquisition of property for lease.

SALES AND USE TAXES

CHAPTER 17

EXEMPTIONS AND CREDITS

¶1701 In General

Various exemptions are provided from sales and use taxes. Some are provided by specific exemption provisions, while others are granted by provisions excluding certain transactions, etc., from the definition of "sale at retail" or other phrases. This chapter covers the major exemptions of general interest.

• *Apportionment of exemptions*

Property or services that are exempt from sales and use tax are exempt only to the extent that the property or services are used for statutorily exempt purposes. The exemption is limited to the percentage of exempt use to total use determined by a reasonable formula or method approved by the Department of Treasury.

Telecommunications property is exempt from sales and use tax only to the extent the property is used for statutorily exempt purposes. There is an irrebuttable presumption that 90% of total use is for exempt purposes.

CCH Comment: Legislative Intent of Apportionment

According to the Michigan Senate Fiscal Agency, the apportionment provisions are intended to clarify existing intent in the law that such exemptions be prorated between exempt and nonexempt uses. Telecommunications property is treated somewhat differently, however, because of the decision in *Michigan Bell Telephone Co.*, Michigan Court of Appeals, No. 192708, April 10, 1998; CCH MICHIGAN TAX REPORTS, ¶400-718. In that case, the court found that use tax did not have to be prorated among exempt and nonexempt uses of telecommunications equipment if a significant portion of the usage was for exempt purposes.

¶1702 Exemptions from Both the Sales and Use Taxes

The sales and use taxes contain many exemptions that are common to both. These exemptions, of three general types—exempt products, exempt transactions, and exempt purchasers—appear at ¶1703, ¶1704, and ¶1705.

Exemptions that apply to the sales tax only appear at ¶1706, and exemptions that apply to the use tax only appear at ¶1707.

¶1703 Exempt Products

Law: Secs. 205.51, 205.52(4), 205.54a, 205.54d, 205.54g, 205.54s, 205.54x, 205.94, 205.94d, 205.94k, 205.94n, 205.94u, M.C.L.; R205.127, R205.131, Mich. Admin. Code (CCH MICHIGAN TAX REPORTS, ¶60-240, 60-300, 60-390, 60-520, 60-550, 60-640, 60-740, 60-750, 61-110).

• *Property subject to Michigan sales tax*

A purchaser of tangible personal property in Michigan from a Michigan retailer bears the burden of proving entitlement to an exemption from use tax where the invoice does not list sales tax as a separate item. The exemption statute requires the payment of sales tax before the use tax exemption takes effect. (*Andrie, Inc. v. Dep't of Treasury*, Michigan Supreme Court, No. 145557, June 23, 2014).

Practitioner Comment: Michigan Use Tax Applicable To Certain Purchases From Michigan Vendors

In *Andrie, Inc. v. Dep't of Treasury*, 496 Mich. 161 (Mich 2014), the Michigan Supreme Court reversed, in part, a prior Michigan Court of Appeals decision and held that a retail purchaser is liable for Michigan use tax on purchases of tangible personal property unless it can substantiate that it either paid sales tax to a retailer, or that the sales tax was previously remitted by the seller. The Court in *Andrie* determined that because the sellers' invoices paid by the taxpayer did not specifically designate a charge for sales tax, the taxpayer could not otherwise prove that it was entitled to an exemption from use tax payments under an exclusion that is available when " . . . sales tax was due and paid on the retail sale to a consumer." MCL 205.94(1)(a). The Court noted that the burden of proving entitlement to the use tax exemption rests on the party asserting the exemption, and that if the retail seller does not admit that sales tax was collected or paid on a sale, the purchaser must show that sales tax was paid on the purchase before an exemption from the use tax is valid. Taxpayers seeking an exemption from Michigan use tax are advised to either obtain and retain invoices with separately stated sales tax, or as suggested by the Court in *Andrie*, seek affidavits from sellers that the sales tax has been remitted.

Wayne D. Roberts, Varnum, LLP and Marjorie B. Gell, Western Michigan University Cooley Law School

---

The following items are among those exempt from both the sales and the use tax:

• *Advertising*

A commercial advertising element is exempt if the element:

— is used to create or develop a print, radio, television or other advertisement;

— is discarded or returned to the provider after the advertising message is completed; and

— is custom-developed by the provider for the purchaser.

Generally, a "commercial advertising element" means a negative or positive photographic image, audiotape or videotape master, layout, manuscript, writing of copy, design, artwork, illustration, retouching, and mechanical or keyline instructions. However, the exemption does not apply to black and white or full color process separation elements and audiotape or videotape reproductions.

• *Aircraft and aircraft parts*

The sale of a new aircraft that is temporarily located in Michigan for the purpose of sale and prepurchase evaluation, customization, maintenance, improvement, or repair is exempt from sales and use taxes. The aircraft must leave Michigan within 15 days after the sale and the completion of the prepurchase evaluation, customization, maintenance, improvement, or repair related to the sale, whichever occurs later. Also, in order to qualify for the exemption, the aircraft must not be registered or based in Michigan prior to or after the sale and any prepurchase evaluation or customization related to the sale. (Sec. 205.54x(5), M.C.L.)

Sales and use tax also does not apply to parts or materials (excluding shop equipment or fuel) affixed or to be affixed to an aircraft not based or registered in Michigan. In order to qualify for this exemption, the aircraft must leave Michigan within 15 days after the sooner of the issuance of the final billing or authorized approval for final return to service, completion of the maintenance record entry, and completion of the test flight and ground test for inspection. Also, the aircraft must not have been based in this state or registered in this state before the parts or materials are affixed to the aircraft and the aircraft must not be based in this state or registered in this state after the parts or materials are affixed to the aircraft.

• *Bullion and coins*

Bullion and investment coins are exempt from sales and use tax.

• *Food*

Food for human consumption, except prepared food intended for immediate consumption, is exempt from tax. "Food for human consumption" means all food and drink items (including bottled water), intended primarily for human consumption, except for alcoholic beverages and tobacco. The term also includes live animals purchased with the intent to be slaughtered for human consumption.

Food or tangible personal property purchased under the federal food stamp program or meals sold by a person exempt from sales and use tax eligible to be purchased under the federal food stamp program are also exempt, as are fruit or vegetable seeds and fruit or vegetable plants if purchased at a place of business authorized to, or applying for authorization to accept food stamps. Deposits on returnable containers and cartons and cases for beverages are also exempt.

"Prepared food" means:

— food sold in a heated state or that is heated by the seller;

— two or more food ingredients mixed or combined by the seller for sale as a single item; or

— food sold with eating utensils provided by the seller, including knives, forks, spoons, glasses, cups, napkins, straws, or plates, but not including a container or packaging used to transport the food.

The following items are excluded from the definition of "prepared food" and are not taxable:

— food that is only cut, repackaged, or pasteurized by the seller;

— raw eggs, fish, meat, poultry, and foods containing items requiring cooking by the consumer in recommendations of the food code of the department of health and human services;

— food sold in an unheated state by weight or volume as a single item, without utensils; or

— bakery items sold without utensils.

(*Revenue Administrative Bulletin 2009-8;* CCH MICHIGAN TAX REPORTS, ¶401-456)

Food or drink heated or cooled mechanically, electrically, or by other artificial means to an average temperature above 75 degrees Fahrenheit or below 65 degrees Fahrenheit before sale and sold from a vending machine, except milk, nonalcoholic beverages in a sealed container, and fresh fruit, is subject to the tax. The tax on sales of food or drink from vending machines or mobile facilities selling both taxable and exempt items may be calculated by the vendor from either (1) actual proceeds from sales or (2) 45% of the proceeds from the sale of taxable and nontaxable items other than carbonated beverages.

Prepared meals provided free of charge or at a reduced rate to employees during work hours by a licensed food service establishment for the convenience of the employer are exempt from sales tax.

Practitioner Comment: Sales and Use Tax Does Not Apply to Bulk Sales of Ice Cream Products Made From a Cash-and-Carry Freezer in an Ice Cream Distributor Facility

In *Pars Ice Cream, Inc. v. Dep't of Treasury*, Mich Ct App Docket No. 305148 (Unpublished Aug. 14, 2012), the Michigan Court of Appeals affirmed the cancellation of a tax assessment that was made against an ice cream distributor to impose use tax on bulk sales of ice cream products, including ice cream bars, ice cream snacks, and miscellaneous ice cream novelty products. The Court of Appeals affirmed a Michigan tax tribunal decision that held these sales of ice cream were sales of food for human consumption that were not subject to tax. See *Pars Ice Cream, Inc. v. Dep't of Treasury*, Tax Tribunal Docket No. 332949 (June 28, 2011).

Wayne D. Roberts, Varnum, LLP and Marjorie B. Gell, Western Michigan University Cooley Law School

---

• *Prescription drugs*

The sale of drugs for human use that can only be legally dispensed by prescription and the sale of an over-the-counter drug for human use legally dispensed pursuant to a prescription, are exempt from tax, as is the sale of insulin for human use, and sales of oxygen for human use pursuant to a prescription. In addition, sales by hospitals of drugs and medicines furnished to patients and consumed on the premises are not taxable retail sales.

A drug company's distribution of prescription drug samples to licensed physicians was exempt from the use tax because the drug samples could not lawfully be dispensed to consumers without a prescription (*Syntax Laboratories, Inc. v. Department of Treasury* (1991, Ct App), 188 MichApp 383, 470 NW2d 665; CCH MICHIGAN TAX REPORTS [1989—1993 Transfer Binder], ¶400-120). The Department of Treasury has acquiesced in the *Syntax Laboratories, Inc.* decision (*Revenue Administrative Bulletin 1993-3;* CCH MICHIGAN TAX REPORTS, ¶319-229).

• *Medical devices*

Sales of prosthetic devices pursuant to a prescription, mobility enhancing equipment pursuant to a prescription, and durable medical equipment for home use pursuant to a prescription are exempt from sales and use tax.

• *Newspapers and periodicals*

The following types of newspapers and periodicals are exempt from sales and use taxes:

— newspapers and periodicals admitted as second-class mail matter or controlled circulation publications under present federal postal laws and regulations (cargo industry informational books did not qualify for use tax exemption as "controlled circulation publications" and were not eligible for the resale exemption, because they were received free of charge (*Fourth Seacoast Publishing Co. v. Department of Treasury*, MTT, April 22, 1992; CCH MICHIGAN TAX REPORTS, ¶400-200));

— newspapers and periodicals qualified to accept legal notices for publication in the state; and

— newspapers and periodicals of general circulation, if established not less than two years and published not less than once a week.

Sales of online newspapers and periodicals are also exempt from sales and use tax. The exemption extends to advertising supplements becoming a component part of a newspaper or periodical.

Advertising mailers of an out-of-state direct mail business operating a production facility in Michigan were held to be essentially a loose-leaf collection of advertising materials that did not qualify as a "periodical of general circulation" (*Advo-System, Inc.* (1990, Ct App), 465 NW2d 349; CCH MICHIGAN TAX REPORTS, ¶400-087). The court adopted the plain and ordinary meaning of the term "periodical" as a magazine or similar publication issued at regularly recurring intervals and rejected the use of the dictionary meaning that would have broadened the term to mean "a magazine or other publication that is issued at regularly recurring intervals."

All tangible personal property becoming a component part of newspapers and periodicals, such as paper and ink, is exempt.

Tangible personal property used or consumed in producing a newspaper published more than 14 times per year or a periodical published more than 14 times per year but not becoming a component part of the newspaper or periodical is subject to tax.

• *Films*

Copyrighted motion picture films are exempt from sales and use taxes. However, tangible personal property that is used or consumed but does not become a component part of a copyrighted motion picture film is subject to tax. When a theater sells tangible personal property to consumers, it must register and collect the tax.

• *Water*

Sales of water (1) through water mains or (2) by deliveries in bulk tanks in quantities of not less than 500 gallons are exempt from sales and use taxes. Sales of bottled water are also exempt. Sales of water delivered in any other manner are taxable, unless exempt under the categories of "industrial processing" or "agricultural producing" (R205.127, Rule 77, Mich. Admin. Code; CCH MICHIGAN TAX REPORTS, ¶65-251). The sale of equipment, tools, machinery, pipes, etc., for consumption or use in distributing and carrying water is taxable.

• *Commercial vessels*

Vessels of registered tonnage of 500 tons or more designed for commercial use are exempt from sales and use taxes if produced on special order of the purchaser. Bunker and galley fuel, provisions, supplies, maintenance, and repairs for the exclusive use of such vessels engaged in interstate commerce are also exempt.

Food sold for resale on vessels plying the Great Lakes is exempt if the vessel operator has a sales tax license and remits tax on all sales within the territorial waters of Michigan (R205.131, Rule 81, Mich. Admin. Code; CCH MICHIGAN TAX REPORTS, ¶65-259).

¶1704 Exempt Transactions or Uses

Law: Secs. 205.51, 205.52a, 205.54a, 205.54d, 205.54dd, 205.54g, 205.54j, 205.54k, 205.54m, 205.54t, 205.54y, 205.54bb, 205.92, 205.94, 205.94aa, 205.94h, 205.94i, 205.94*l*, 205.94n, 205.94o, 205.94w, 205.94y, 205.94z, M.C.L.; R205.8, R205.81, R205.91, Mich. Admin. Code (CCH MICHIGAN TAX REPORTS, ¶60-240, 60-310, 60-330, 60-340, 60-360, 60-390, 60-450, 60-530, 60-570, 60-620, 60-650, 60-740, 60-750, 61-020, 61-110).

The following types of transactions are among those exempt from both sales and use taxes.

• *Sales for resale*

Property purchased for purposes of resale is exempt from sales and use taxes. Sales for resale are sales of property not to be consumed or used by the immediate purchaser, but to be resold in the regular course of business by the purchaser.

A buyer who disposes of goods in any other manner than by resale becomes the final consumer. The seller is a consumer when (i) the seller removes goods from inventory for personal use or consumption, or in the conduct of the seller's business, and would be liable for use tax on the removed goods; or (ii) the seller converts tangible personal property acquired for an exempt use to a use not exempt from tax, and would be liable for use tax on the converted property. (R205.8, Rule 8, Mich. Admin. Code; CCH MICHIGAN TAX REPORTS, ¶65-015).

A seller may accept an exemption certificate in good faith if the seller receives a completed and signed exemption certificate from the buyer. A person who knowingly makes a sale for resale to a person not licensed under the sales or use tax acts is liable for tax on the sale. The good faith exemption certificate requirement does not apply to certain persons licensed by the Michigan Liquor Control Commission as a wholesaler for purposes of sales to another person licensed by the Commission or to sales by the Commission to authorized distribution agents to sell to licensed purchasers.

Property purchased for resale includes promotional merchandise transferred pursuant to a redemption offer to persons located outside Michigan.

• *Property in interstate or foreign commerce*

Although there is no specific provision in the sales tax act regarding interstate commerce, a rule of the Department of Treasury (R205.91, Rule 41, Mich. Admin. Code; CCH MICHIGAN TAX REPORTS, ¶65-181) provides that the tax does not apply to any sale of tangible personal property if the tax is prohibited by the U.S. Constitution or federal laws. The use tax act provides that use tax does not apply to the storage, use, or consumption of property that the state is prohibited from taxing under the U.S. Constitution, federal law, or the Michigan Constitution.

Another rule (R205.81, Rule 31, Mich. Admin. Code; CCH MICHIGAN TAX REPORTS, ¶65-161) provides that the tax does not apply to export sales if, as a necessary incident to the contract of sale, the exporter must and does deliver the goods to the purchaser at a foreign destination or places the goods in the hands of a common carrier consigned to the buyer at a foreign destination. However, the tax does apply to sales made by an importer in like manner and to the same extent as sales made by a retailer of domestic property.

Interstate carriers: See the discussion at ¶1705.

• *Aircraft*

Sales to a domestic air carrier of (a) an aircraft with a maximum certified takeoff weight of at least 6,000 pounds for use solely in the transport of air cargo and/or passengers, and (b) parts and materials, excluding shop equipment or fuel, affixed to such an aircraft, are exempt from sales and use tax. Sales to a person for subsequent lease to a domestic air carrier certified by the FAA under 14 C.F.R. 121, used solely for the regular transport of passengers are also exempt.

"Domestic air carrier" is limited to entities engaged in the commercial transport for hire of cargo or in the commercial transport of passengers as a business activity. The exemption applies only to commercial passenger aircraft used in regularly scheduled flights and not to chartered planes used to provide executive air charter services to a company's executives (*AeroGenesis, Inc.*, MTT, No. 258603, December 22, 1999; CCH MICHIGAN TAX REPORTS, ¶400-819).

• *Computers, computer software, and computer information services*

Different rules apply depending on the use of the computer equipment, the type of computer software, and the purpose of the transaction involving services.

Computers used in industrial processing: The following sales and uses of computer equipment are exempt:

— computers used in operating industrial processing equipment;

— equipment used in a computer-assisted manufacturing system;

— equipment used in a computer-assisted design engineering system integral to an industrial process;

— a sub-unit or electronic assembly that is a component in a computer-integrated industrial processing system;

— computer equipment used in connection with the computer-assisted production, storage, and transmission of data if the equipment would have been exempt had the data transfer been made using tapes, disks, CD-ROMS, or similar media by a company whose business includes publishing doctoral dissertations and information archiving, and that sells the majority of its products to nonprofit health, welfare, educational, cultural arts, charitable, or benevolent organizations; and

— equipment used in the production of computer software that is offered for general sale to the public or software modified or adapted to the user's needs or equipment by the seller, only if the software is available for sale from a seller of software on an as-is basis or as an end product without modification or adaptation.

Custom computer software: Sales of prewritten computer software are subject to sales and use taxes only if the software is available from a seller on an "as is" basis or as an end product without modification or adaptation. Specific charges for technical support or for adapting or modifying prewritten, standard, or canned computer software programs are not subject to sales or use tax if the charges are separately stated and identified. Retail sales of computer software that is originally designed for the exclusive use and needs of the purchaser are also not subject to sales tax.

Computer equipment used primarily for customizing software has been held not exempt from the sales and use taxes either as property used in industrial processing or as property purchased for resale (*Professional Guidance Systems,* MTT, May 11, 1992; CCH MICHIGAN TAX REPORTS, ¶400-221).

Practitioner Comment: Cloud Computing Services not subject to Sales or Use Tax

In two recent decisions, Michigan courts held that "cloud computing" –the remote access to computer systems of third party providers through the Internet –is a nontaxable sale. On October 27, 2015, in a published opinion, the Michigan Court of Appeals in *Auto-Owners Insurance Company v. Michigan Dep't. of Treasury,* No. 321505 (October 27, 2015), affirmed a Court of Claims decision that held that a taxpayer's remote access to a third party's technology infrastructure in order to retrieve data, process billing and payments, or access legal databases was not a sale subject to use tax. The Department took the position that such services, because they involved prewritten, non-customized software, were subject to sales and use tax. The Court disagreed, finding that these transactions did not qualify as the sale of prewritten software because the third-party providers did not surrender possession and control of the code to the taxpayer. In regards to transactions where prewritten software was installed onto the taxpayer's computers, the court applied the factors in *Catalina Marketing Sales Corp. v. Department of Treasury,* 470 Mich 13, 24-25; 678 NW2d 619 (2004), and concluded that the transfer of such property was incidental to the rendition of nontaxable professional services. In *Thomson Reuters, Inc. v. Department of Treasury,* Mich. Ct. App. Docket No. 313825 (May

13, 2014), the Michigan Court of Appeals, in an unpublished decision, reversed a ruling of the Court of Claims and found that under the "incidental to services" test, a taxpayer's sale of online legal research products was not subject to Michigan use tax because customers sought access to information, not underlying software, and any transfer of tangible personal property was incidental to the information service.

Wayne D. Roberts, Varnum, LLP and Marjorie B. Gell, Western Michigan University Cooley Law School

---

Computer information services: A company providing financial information services via computer equipment that it leased to its customers was liable for use tax on the receipts from the computer rentals. However, additional information services that were separate transactions from the rental of tangible personal property and separately billed were not subject to tax (*Letter Ruling 93-1;* CCH MICHIGAN TAX REPORTS, ¶355-081).

CCH Advisory: Treatment of Internet Transactions Clarified

In response to a CCH survey, the Michigan Department of Treasury has outlined the tax treatment for the following Internet transactions:

Digitized products: A computer program transferred electronically by a network, intranet, the Internet, or by any other electronic method is subject to Michigan sales and use taxes if the software being transferred is within the definition of canned software. Other products downloaded electronically, such as music, are not included in the definition of tangible personal property subject to sales and use tax.

Information services: On-line sales of information services that are electronically transmitted are not subject to sales and use tax if there is no transfer of tangible personal property.

(*Response to CCH Internet/Electronic Commerce Survey,* Department of Treasury, March 28, 2000; CCH MICHIGAN TAX REPORTS, ¶400-828).

• *Motor vehicles with special registration*

The tax on new vehicles purchased outside Michigan and delivered in Michigan by the manufacturer to a nonresident purchaser for removal out of state is reduced by the amount of use tax imposed and the amount of sales tax which would have been imposed by the state to which the vehicle is removed.

• *Vehicles given to qualified recipients*

Sales or use tax does not apply to the sale of or storage, use, or consumption of an eligible automobile provided to a qualified low-income recipient for employment related purposes by the Family Independence Agency or by a qualified organization. In addition, use tax does not apply to donations of motor vehicles to a regularly organized church or house of religious worship, or donations of motor vehicles from or through a church or house of religious worship to qualified recipients, if the church or house of religious worship received the motor vehicle with the intent that it be donated to a qualified recipient.

An individual is a *qualified recipient* if a church or house of religious worship certifies that:

— the individual receives, or is eligible to receive, public assistance under the Social Welfare Act or the individual has a total household income below 200% of the federal poverty guidelines; and

— the individual has a valid Michigan operator's or chauffeur's license.

• *Cars leased or loaned for school driving courses*

Sales or purchases of cars for the purpose of lending or leasing them to public or parochial schools offering courses in automobile driving are exempt from sales and use taxes; however, vehicles purchased by the schools must be certified for driver education and may not be reassigned for personal use of the schools' administrative personnel.

• *Motor vehicles used for demonstration purposes*

Property purchased for demonstration purposes is exempt from sales and use taxes. For dealers of new cars and trucks the exemption is determined by the number of new cars and trucks sold by dealers during the current calendar year or the immediate prior year without regard to specific make or style, as follows:

— 0 to 25, 2 exempt units;

— 26 to 100, 7 units;

— 101 to 500, 20 units;

— 501 or more, 25 units.

The use tax base of demonstration vehicles that exceed the number of such vehicles that qualify for the exemption is the purchase price of the car or truck times 2.5% plus $30, for every month that the vehicle is in the dealer's inventory, beginning with the month that the dealer uses the vehicle in a nonexempt manner.

CCH Advisory: Exemptions Not Available to Manufacturer

The Michigan Court of Appeals has held that an automotive manufacturer was improperly granted refunds of Michigan use tax on "program vehicles" used by its employees because the manufacturer did not purchase the vehicles and therefore did not qualify for the exemptions for property purchased for resale or for demonstration purposes. The taxpayer filed its claims for refund after the Michigan Court of Appeals ruled in *Betten Auto Center, Inc. v. Dept. of Treasury*, 272 Mich. App. 14, 723 N.W.2d 914, August 1, 2006, that vehicles that were used by the dealer on an interim basis before resale were still exempt as vehicles purchased for resale. The Michigan Legislature then amended the Use Tax Act to clarify that any use of property purchased for resale other than as passive inventory converts the property such that the use becomes taxable. The taxpayer did not qualify for exemption under either version of the use tax statute because it was a manufacturer; only vehicles purchased for resale or demonstration purposes are exempt. Also, the taxpayer did not qualify for the exemption for property purchased for demonstration purposes because it used the program vehicles for marketing and quality control as opposed to inducing retail sales from actual customers.

(*General Motors Corp. v. Department of Treasury*, Michigan Court of Appeals, No. 291947, October 28, 2010; CCH MICHIGAN TAX REPORTS, ¶401-536).

• *Railroad rolling stock*

Sales of railroad cars and other rolling stock, as well as fuel, equipment, and supplies used in railroad operations, are exempt from tax.

• *Agricultural equipment*

The sale of agricultural machinery capable of simultaneously harvesting grain and crops as well as biomass to a person engaged in a business enterprise is exempt from sales and use tax. Machinery used to harvest biomass is also exempt.

• *Air or water pollution control facilities*

Tangible personal property purchased and installed as a component part of an exempt air or water pollution control facility is exempt from sales and use taxes. Exemption certificates are issued to facilities by the State Tax Commission on the basis of a finding by the Director of Public Health that the facility is an air pollution control facility within the intent of the law or a finding by the Water Resources Commission that the facility is a water pollution control facility within the law's intent.

Air pollution control facilities do not include air conditioners or dust collectors used for the benefit of personnel.

• *Drop shipments*

Sales of property that are part of drop-shipment sales are exempt from sales and use tax if certain reporting requirements are met. Drop-shipment sales are those in which property is delivered to a purchaser in Michigan by a person (a manufacturer, for example) who has sold the property to another person not licensed in Michigan but possessing the equivalent of a resale exemption issued by another state (a wholesaler or retailer, for example).

• *Periodical advertising supplements*

Advertising supplements delivered directly to a newspaper or periodical by a person other than the advertiser or printed by the newspaper or periodical are exempt from sales and use taxes.

• *Concrete manufacturing*

Specially designed vehicles, along with parts, that are used to mix and agitate materials added at a plant or jobsite in the concrete manufacturing process are exempt from the sales and use taxes.

• *Qualified convention facilities*

Through January 1, 2016, tangible personal property for use in construction or renovation of a qualified convention facility under the Regional Convention Facility Authority Act is exempt from sales and use tax.

• *Energy fuels*

Electricity, gas, and home heating fuels for residential use are exempt from the additional 2% sales and use taxes (see ¶1603). The application of sales and use taxes to residential utilities is discussed in *Revenue Administrative Bulletin 94-08;* CCH MICHIGAN TAX REPORTS, ¶319-249.

Diesel fuel: Sales of diesel fuel to an interstate motor carrier for use in a qualified commercial motor vehicle are exempt from tax.

¶1705 Exempt Purchasers

Law: Secs. 205.51, 205.54a, 205.54h, 205.54m, 205.54o—205.54z, 205.54dd, 205.94, 205.94k, 205.94m, 205.94o, 205.94p, 205.94q, 205.94aa, M.C.L.; R205.51, R205.65, R205.79, Mich. Admin. Code (CCH MICHIGAN TAX REPORTS, ¶60-250, 60-285, 60-330, 60-420, 60-450, 60-510, 60-530, 60-580, 60-650, 60-720, 61-010).

Purchases by the following entities are exempt from sales and use taxes.

• *Federal and state governments*

Property purchased by the following are exempt from tax:

— the United States, its unincorporated agencies and instrumentalities, or any incorporated agency or instrumentality wholly owned by the United States or by a corporation wholly owned by the United States;

— the state of Michigan or its departments, institutions, or political subdivisions; and

— the American Red Cross and its chapters and branches.

Federal credit unions are exempt government instrumentalities (*U.S. v. Michigan* (1988, US CA-6), 851 F2d 803; CCH MICHIGAN TAX REPORTS, ¶60-370.33). Conversely, the Michigan Attorney General has taken the position that sales to state credit unions are subject to tax (*Opinion of the Attorney General,* No. 7062, October 4, 2000; CCH MICHIGAN TAX REPORTS, ¶400-856).

The Department of Treasury has explained the applicability of the tax to state-chartered credit unions. Essentially, state-chartered credit unions are exempt from a sales or use tax imposed directly on them, but are not exempt from the economic burden imposed directly on vendors or suppliers and passed on to the state-chartered credit union. Accordingly, such credit unions are only exempt when acting as a seller; when the state chartered credit union makes a purchase that is not otherwise exempt, the seller owes Michigan sales tax on the sale and may collect the tax from the credit union. However, because Michigan use tax is imposed directly on the purchaser, a state-chartered credit union would have no liability on purchases of tangible personal property in interstate transactions. Similarly, an out-of-state seller making a sale at retail to a state-chartered credit union in this type of situation would be relieved of any use tax collection obligation (*Legal Policy Determination 2003-2,* Michigan Department of Treasury, September 30, 2003, CCH MICHIGAN TAX REPORTS, ¶380-002).

In order to be exempt, sales to governments must be ordered on the prescribed government form or purchase order and must be paid for directly to the seller by warrant on government funds. If sales are made without the proper form being supplied in advance, credit may be allowed later for the tax payment upon receipt of the purchase order and warrant covering the sale (R205.79, Rule 29, Mich. Admin. Code; CCH MICHIGAN TAX REPORTS, ¶65-157).

• *Nonprofit institutions*

Sales not for resale to nonprofit schools, hospitals, homes for the care and maintenance of children or aged persons, nonprofit cultural arts institutions, and other health, welfare, educational, charitable, or benevolent institutions and agencies operated by an entity of government, by a regularly organized church, religious or fraternal organization, veterans' organization, or corporation incorporated under Michigan law are exempt from sales and use taxes. To qualify for the exemption the income from the operation of the institution must not inure to the benefit of any individuals or private shareholders and the entity's activities must be carried on for the benefit of the public at large and not limited to its members or any restricted group. The exemption also applies to sales not for resale to nonprofit organizations that are exempt from federal income tax under IRC Sec. 501(c)(3) or 501(c)(4).

Proof of exemption.—At the time the tangible personal property is transferred, the transferee must present one of two forms of proof of exemption for purchases that would otherwise be subject to sales tax. The acceptable forms of proof of exemption are (1) a valid exemption ruling letter signed by the Administrator of the Sales, Use, and Withholding Taxes Division, or (2) a signed statement, on a form approved by the department, stating that the property is to be used or consumed in connection with the operation of the organization, to carry out the purpose or purposes of the organization, or to raise funds or obtain resources necessary for the operation of the organization, that the organization qualifies as an exempt organization, and that the sales price of any single item of tangible personal property or vehicle purchased for purposes of raising funds or obtaining resources does not exceed $5,000.00, and a copy of the transferee's federal exemption letter. A copy of the federal exemption letter is not required if the organization is exempt from filing an application for exempt status with the IRS.

The exemption does not apply to sales of tangible personal property or vehicles licensed for use on public highways that are not primarily used to carry out the purposes of the tax-exempt organization or to raise funds or obtain resources necessary to carry out the purposes of the organization. The exemption for any single item of tangible personal property or vehicle used to raise funds is limited to a sales price not exceeding $5,000.

Sales and use taxes do not apply to property purchased by a person engaged in the business of constructing, altering, repairing, or improving real estate for others to the extent the property is affixed to and made a structural part of a nonprofit hospital or nonprofit housing entity.

• *Religious organizations*

Sales not for resale to regularly organized churches or houses of religious worship are exempt from sales and use taxes if paid for by the church from church funds, unless the property is to be used in activities that are mainly commercial enterprises. Licensed vehicles are taxable except vans or buses seating 10 or more that transport persons for religious purposes. Sales to organizations and societies of church members are taxable.

Tangible personal property that is to be affixed to or made a structural part of a sanctuary of a church or house of religious worship is exempt if purchased by a person engaged in constructing, repairing, or improving real estate for others.

Sales of tangible personal property, including sales of meals in a commercial activity, when conducted as a retail business for gain, benefit, or advantage, direct or indirect, are taxable and a sales tax license must be obtained.

If an exemption is claimed, the seller must retain an executed exemption certificate as part of his or her records (R205.65, Rule 15, Mich. Admin. Code; CCH MICHIGAN TAX REPORTS, ¶65-129).

• *Parent cooperative preschools*

Property sold to parent cooperative preschools is exempt from sales and use taxes.

• *Foreign diplomatic personnel*

Certain purchases by foreign diplomatic personnel, including the Taipei Economic and Cultural Representative Office (TECRO) in the United States, the Taipei Economic and Cultural Offices (TECOs), their designated employees and their qualifying dependents, are exempt when they make the purchase using an exemption card. The two types of exemption cards, personal and mission, each have one of two different levels of tax exemption. The level of exemption is denoted by the animal displayed on the card. Cards with an owl or an eagle exempt the bearer from state and local taxes, including sales tax, use tax, airport parking tax, and convention facility development tax. Cards with a buffalo or a deer require the purchase of a minimum amount of goods before an exemption is available. This type of card may also exclude a certain sector from exemption, such as hotel taxes. The tax exemption cards do not permit gasoline, vehicles, or utilities to be purchased exempt. Purchases of vehicles by diplomatic personnel must be cleared for tax exemption with a Motor Vehicle Tax-Exemption letter from the Office of Foreign Missions. If the exemption is denied, dealers should collect the tax that is normally imposed at the point of sale (*Revenue Administrative Bulletin 2015-13*, CCH MICHIGAN TAX REPORTS, ¶401-994).

• *Fundraising*

Fundraising sales by a school, church, hospital, parent cooperative preschool, or nonprofit organization are exempt from tax if the entity is issued an exemption letter ruling and has aggregate retail sales in the calendar year of less than $5,000. However, if sales in a calendar year are $5,000 or more, all sales are taxable. A tax-exempt organization affiliated with a school, church, hospital, or nonprofit organization that has been issued an exemption letter ruling is not considered a separate person for purposes of this exemption.

• *Agricultural producers*

Property sold to persons engaged in horticultural or agricultural production is exempt from sales and use taxes if used or consumed in the commercial production of horticultural or agricultural products for sale. Agricultural production means the commercial production for sale of crops, livestock, poultry and their products by persons regularly engaged in business as farmers, nurserymen, agriculturists, etc. The agricultural production exemption covers tangible personal property used in the direct gathering of fish by net, line, or otherwise by an owner-operator of a fishing enterprise, excluding a charter fishing business enterprise.

Agricultural land tile (defined as fired clay or perforated plastic tubing used as part of a subsurface drainage system), and subsurface irrigation pipe are exempt if used in the production of agricultural products as a business enterprise. Also exempt are portable grain bins used to shelter grain, if designed to be disassembled without significant damage to component parts. Grain drying equipment and natural or propane gas used to fuel that equipment for agricultural purposes are also exempt. Grain drying equipment may also qualify for an industrial processing exemption (see *"Industrial processors"* below).

CCH Comment: Testing Equipment Exempt

Equipment used by an agricultural cooperative to test milk before it could be commercially marketed was exempt from Michigan use tax under the exemption for property used in agricultural production. The quality control testing was a direct component of the agricultural production process because the cooperative was required to test the milk to ensure legally mandated standards were satisfied. (*Michigan Milk Producers Association* (2000 CtApp), 242 MichApp 486, 618 NW2d 917; CCH MICHIGAN TAX REPORTS, ¶400-861).

Transfers of fuel, clothing, or similar property for personal living or human consumption and property used to improve real estate or attached to and becoming a structural part of real estate are taxable.

The Department of Treasury has issued a rule specifically listing taxable and exempt sales to persons engaged in agricultural producing (R205.51, Rule 1, Mich. Admin. Code; CCH MICHIGAN TAX REPORTS, ¶65-101).

• *Industrial processors*

Property sold to manufacturers, processors, etc., for use or consumption in industrial processing is exempt from sales and use taxes. However, tangible personal property that is permanently affixed and becomes a structural part of real estate in Michigan; office furniture, office supplies, and administrative office equipment; and vehicles licensed and titled for use on public highways are taxable. Tax-exempt industrial processing equipment includes specially designed vehicles, and parts, that are used to mix and agitate materials added at a plant or jobsite in the concrete manufacturing process.

The industrial processing exemption from sales and use taxes also includes additional third-party servicers. The exemption applies to sales to the following entities:

— an industrial processor for use or consumption in industrial processing;

— a person, whether or not an industrial processor, if the tangible personal property is intended for ultimate use in and is used in industrial processing by an industrial processor;

— a person, whether or not an industrial processor, if the tangible personal property is used by that person to perform an industrial processing activity for an industrial processor; and

— a person, whether or not an industrial processor, if the tangible personal property is equipment used in computer assisted manufacturing, design, and engineering systems.

The exemption also includes research or experimental activity that is incident to the development, discovery, or modification of a product or a product related process, and includes activity necessary for a product to satisfy a government standard or to receive government approval. The exemption is limited to the percentage of exempt use to total use determined by a reasonable formula or method approved by the Department of Treasury.

"Industrial processing" does not include the receipt and storage of raw materials purchased or extracted by the user or consumer, the preparation of food and beverages by a retailer for retail sale, and services performed on property owned by others where the services do not transform, alter, or modify the property so as to place it in a different form, composition, or character.

An "industrial processor" is a person who performs the activity of converting or conditioning tangible personal property for ultimate sale at retail or use in the manufacturing of a product to be ultimately sold at retail or affixed to and made a structural part of real estate located in another state.

The Department of Treasury has released a bulletin providing 50 illustrative examples of various activities and properties that may or may not qualify for the exemption (*Revenue Administrative Bulletin 2000-4;* CCH MICHIGAN TAX REPORTS, ¶319-298).

The industrial processing exemption also applies to certain equipment used in sawmill operations. Exempt property includes front end loaders, forklifts, pettibone lifts, skidsters, multipurpose loaders, knuckle-boom log loaders, tractors, and log loaders used to unload logs from trucks at a saw mill site for processing at the site, and to load lumber onto trucks at a saw mill site for purposes of transportation from the site. (Sec. 205.94o, M.C.L.)

CCH Advisory: Industrial Processing Exemption

The industrial processing exemption does not apply to equipment used before processing begins or after processing ends. These principles are illustrated in a 1999 case involving recycling equipment.

The industrial processing exemption was allowed for a scrap and waste recycler's freon extraction equipment and cranes because they were used at the beginning of and during industrial processing of raw material. The extraction of freon from obsolete refrigerators was a fundamental step in recycling the refrigerators and, because the extraction occurred after processing began, the exemption applied. The cranes were exempt because they began the process of sorting piles made up of different kinds of various raw materials into piles of the same kinds of materials, thus transforming the physical composition of the piles of different kinds of materials.

The industrial processing equipment exemption did not apply to hoppers and rolloffs, because they were used in the receipt and storage of raw materials and not as part of the taxpayer's quality control process. Similarly, the exemption did not apply to radiation detection equipment because the equipment was used before processing began to inspect raw materials being delivered to the taxpayer's plant for radiation contamination, not as part of a product quality control process (*Louis Padnos Iron & Metal Co.*, MTT, No. 240432, March 31, 1999; CCH MICHIGAN TAX REPORTS, ¶400-777).

Practitioner Comment: Property Used in The Transmission and Distribution of Electricity Qualifies for The Industrial Processing Exemption

Tangible personal property used in the transmission and distribution phases of the electric system (i.e., property used outside the generating plants after the electricity is generated at high voltages) is simultaneously used for exempt "industrial processing" activities under MCL 205.94o(7)(a) and nonexempt "distribution" and "shipping" activities under MCL 205.94o(6)(b). *Detroit Edison Co v Dep't of Treasury*, Mich Sup Ct No 148753 (July 22, 2015). In these circumstances, the taxpayer is entitled to the industrial processing exemption based on the "percentage of exempt use to total use determined by a reasonable formula or method approved by the department [of Treasury]." MCL 205.94o(2). In *Detroit Edison*, the judgment of the Court of Appeals was affirmed in part and reversed in part, and the case was remanded to the Court of Claims for further proceedings to determine a "reasonable" apportionment between tax-exempt and taxable uses of the property at issue. With respect to "industrial processing," the Court specifically found that altering the voltage of electricity constitutes an industrial processing activity, and that electricity is not a final retail product until it reaches the customer's meter at the proper voltage level for the customer's use.

Wayne D. Roberts, Varnum, LLP and Marjorie B. Gell, Western Michigan University Cooley Law School

---

• *Extractive operators*

The sale of tangible personal property to an extractive operator for use or consumption in extractive operations is exempt. Extractive operations include the activity of taking or extracting for resale ore, oil, gas, coal, timber, stone, gravel, clay, minerals, or other natural resource material. An extractive operation begins when contact is made with the actual type of natural raw material product being recovered.

Extractive operations include all necessary processing operations before shipment from the place of extraction and all necessary processing operations and movement of the natural resource material until the point at which the natural raw product being recovered first comes to rest in finished goods inventory at the extraction site. Also, extractive operations include the actual production of oil, gas, brine, or other natural resource. Extractive operations for timber includes the transportation of timber from the extraction point to a place of temporary storage at the extraction site and transportation from temporary storage to a vehicle located at the extraction site for removal from the extraction site.

The exemption is limited to the percentage of exempt use to total use determined by a formula or method approved by the Department of the Treasury.

If an extractive operator sells any part of his product at retail, tax must be accounted for and remitted to the state.

• *Taxpayers subject to the minerals severance tax*

The sale of tangible personal property to taxpayers for use as or at mineral-producing property is exempt. The property is exempt only to the extent that it is used for exempt purposes. "Mineral-producing property" means real and personal property in Michigan that is part of a producing mine or utilized directly in association with a producing mine on a parcel on which the shaft, incline, or adit is located, or a parcel contiguous or appurtenant to a parcel on which the shaft, incline, or adit is located.

• *Contractors improving real estate*

Tangible personal property sold to contractors engaged in constructing, repairing, or improving the real estate of others is generally taxable (¶1603). However, such property is exempt if it becomes affixed and made a structural part of a sanctuary of a church or house of religious worship or the real estate of a nonprofit hospital or nonprofit housing. A contractor purchasing materials for an exempt use must give an exemption certificate to his or her supplier. An administrative bulletin discusses the application of sales and use taxes to the construction industry (*Revenue Administrative Bulletin 1999-2;* CCH MICHIGAN TAX REPORTS, ¶319-284).

Manufacturers/contractors that make their products available for sale may be entitled to the industrial processing exemption for property used or consumed in producing the product. Those that affix their products to the real estate of others but do not make products available for sale are not entitled to the exemption (*Revenue Administrative Bulletin 1993-5;* CCH MICHIGAN TAX REPORTS, ¶319-231).

Practitioner Comment: Distributor of Poles and Warning Sirens Subject to Use Tax as Consumer/Contractor Attaching Fixtures Annexed to Real Property of Public Utilities

In *West Shore Services, Inc. v. Department of Treasury*, Mich. Ct. App., Dkt. No. 321085, 07/21/2015 (unpublished), the Michigan Court of Appeals affirmed the Michigan Tax Tribunal's finding that poles, and sirens attached to the poles located in public right-of-ways, were subject to Michigan use tax as fixtures annexed to real property under MCL 205.91, *et seq.* Taxpayer West Shore Services, a distributor of outdoor weather warning sirens, contended that it was a retailer of sirens, not a contractor, and thus was not subject to use tax under the Michigan Use Tax Act. The Court, applying a three-part test from *Granger Land Dev Co v. Dep't of Treasury*, 286 Mich App 601, 610-611; 780 NW2d 611 (2009), found that (1) the property in question was physically and affirmatively annexed to real property, (2) the poles and sirens were "useful adjuncts" to the realty such that their application to the realty being used was appropriate, and (3) visible facts showed an intent that the poles and sirens be a permanent accession to the realty that would remain in place.

Wayne D. Roberts, Varnum, LLP and Marjorie B. Gell, Western Michigan University Cooley Law School

---

• *Licensed operators of commercial radio or television stations*

Tangible personal property sold to persons licensed to operate commercial radio or television stations is exempt from sales and use taxation if it is to be used as a component part of a completed film, tape, or recording produced for resale or transmission purposes. The exemption does not apply to property used in the receiving of programs for integration, property used in transmitting to or receiving from an artificial satellite, and vehicles licensed for use on public highways. A Department of Treasury bulletin provides lists of exempt items, taxable items, and items that can be either exempt or not, depending on their use (*Revenue Administrative Bulletin 1997-1;* CCH MICHIGAN TAX REPORTS, ¶319-271).

• *Intrastate telephone and telegraph companies*

Tangible personal property sold to intrastate telephone and telegraph companies used in providing taxable services is exempt from sales and use taxation. This exemption is limited to property located on the premises of the subscriber and the necessary exchange equipment.

Telecommunications property is exempt from sales and use tax only to the extent the property is used for exempt purposes provided in the statute (Secs. 205.54v and 205.94q, M.C.L.). There is an irrebuttable presumption that 90% of total use is for exempt purposes.

CCH Advisory: Telecommunications Companies Did Not Qualify for Industrial Processing Exemption

Purchases of electricity by telecommunications companies were not eligible for the industrial processing exemption because telecommunications signals are not tangible personal property. Industrial processing involves either (i) the modification of tangible personal property for ultimate sale at retail or (ii) the use of tangible personal property in manufacturing "a product to be ultimately sold at retail." In order to qualify for the exemption, a taxpayer must ultimately sell to consumers "tangible personal property." The taxpayers contended that telecommunications signals constitute tangible personal property as a modified form of electricity or the signals are tangible personal property in their own right. However, evidence showed that though such signals are electricity at some point in the transmission process, they are not electricity at every stage. The Court of Appeals concluded that "it is illogical to suggest that the word 'electricity' encompasses matter that is manifestly not electricity at various stages of its transmission."

Furthermore, the absence of "telecommunications signals" from MCL 205.51a(q) and the inclusion of other specific terms in the definition, indicates that the Legislature did not intend for telecommunications signals to fall within the definition of tangible personal property. The taxpayers also did not present any convincing evidence that telecommunications signals "can be seen, weighed, measured, felt, or touched, or [are] in any other manner perceptible to the senses."

(*MidAmerican Energy Company v. Department of Treasury*, Michigan Court of Appeals, No. 316902, December 4, 2014; CCH MICHIGAN TAX REPORTS, ¶401-947).

• *Interstate motor carriers*

Sales tax does not apply to a sale, rental, or lease of rolling stock to an interstate motor carrier if the rolling stock is used in interstate commerce. Use tax does not apply to the storage, use, or consumption of rolling stock used in interstate commerce and purchased, rented, or leased by an interstate motor carrier. "Rolling stock" includes parts or other tangible personal property affixed to or to be affixed to and directly used in the operation of a qualified truck or a trailer designed to be drawn behind a qualified truck. Equipment purchased and affixed to rolling stock after the sale of the rolling stock, which does not replace an original component of the rolling stock at the time of its purchase, does not qualify for exemption. The Michigan Department of Treasury has determined that "parts", within the definition of rolling stock, refer only to replacements for tangible personal property that were components of the qualified truck or trailer at the time of its purchase. (*Internal Policy Directive 2010-1*; CCH MICHIGAN TAX REPORTS, ¶401-512)

CCH Note: Determining Whether Rolling Stock Is Used in Interstate Commerce

The Department of Treasury has noted that rolling stock must be used in interstate commerce to qualify for the exemption. In determining whether an interstate motor carrier has used rolling stock in interstate commerce, the Department will consider whether the carrier intended to operate the rolling stock outside the state while engaged in the business of carrying persons or property for hire across state lines. If, for a given period, the carrier intended to use the rolling stock only in Michigan during the tax period, the exemption may not apply, even if the stock was held outside the state in the past.

The Department also will consider whether a carrier used a particular unit of rolling stock outside Michigan on at least one occasion during the tax period at issue. A single trip outside the state while engaged in the business of carrying persons or property for hire may suggest an intent on the part of the carrier to use the rolling stock in interstate commerce. Finally, the Department will consider whether a truck or trailer qualifying as rolling stock is licensed in Michigan only or is licensed for use in other states. The former would indicate that the stock would not meet the interstate commerce requirement (*Internal Policy Directive 2003-1*, Michigan Department of Treasury, September 30, 2003, MICHIGAN TAX REPORTS, ¶380-001).

However, it should be noted that a Michigan court of appeal held that taxpayers using rolling stock solely within Michigan during the relevant period were entitled to a use tax exemption for rolling stock used in interstate commerce. "Used in interstate commerce" was held to include the transport of goods moving in a continuous stream from one state to a destination in another state. The rolling stock therefore qualified for the exemption, despite staying within state lines, as it carried goods originating from or destined to locations outside of Michigan. (*Alvan Motor Freight, Inc. v. Department of Treasury*, Michigan Court of Appeals, No. 276511, September 23, 2008, MICHIGAN TAX REPORTS, ¶401-387)

• *Street railways*

Property of a street railway and its income and operations are exempt from all state and local taxes.

• *Industrial laundries*

Textiles, cleaning products, equipment, machinery, supplies, utilities, and other items sold or leased to an industrial laundry are exempt from sales and use taxes.

¶1706 Exemptions from Sales Tax Only

Law: Secs. 205.51, 205.54a, 205.54d, 205.54e, 205.54f, 205.54g, 205.92, 205.95, M.C.L.; R205.13, Mich. Admin. Code (CCH MICHIGAN TAX REPORTS, ¶60-020, 60-390, 60-460, 60-570, 60-590, 60-740, 60-760, 61-010).

The exemptions discussed below are among those limited to the sales tax.

• *Casual or isolated sales*

A sale made outside of the ordinary course of a seller's business is exempt from sales tax as an isolated transaction by a person not licensed or required to be licensed under the sales tax act, in which tangible personal property is offered for sale, sold, or transferred and delivered by the owner. However, if a person advertises or offers property for sale for the purpose of repeated sales, the person is considered to be regularly engaged in business and his or her sales are taxable, even though they may be few or infrequent (R205.13, Rule 13, Mich. Admin. Code; CCH MICHIGAN TAX REPORTS, ¶65-025).

• *Sales to students*

Food sold to bona fide enrolled students by schools or other nonprofit educational institutions is exempt from the sales tax. Also, textbooks sold by a public or nonpublic school to or for the use of students in any part of a kindergarten through twelfth grade program are exempt.

• *Sales to military*

The sale of tangible personal property (including motor vehicles) to a nonresident person actually serving in the U.S. Armed Forces who titles and registers the vehicle in the serviceperson's state of residence or domicile is exempt from sales tax. The statute requires a sworn statement from the purchaser's immediate commanding officer certifying that the purchaser is a member of the Armed Forces on active duty. The recorded domiciliary or home address of the purchaser must also be furnished.

• *Sales of property to be leased*

Sales of property to be rented or leased to others are exempt from sales tax if the rental or lease receipts will be subject to, or are specifically exempt from, use tax (¶1608).

¶1707 Exemptions from Use Tax Only

Law: Secs. 205.93, 205.94, 205.94j, 205.94k, 205.94bb, M.C.L. (CCH MICHIGAN TAX REPORTS, ¶60-020, 60-450, 60-460, 60-570, 60-720, 60-740).

The items discussed below are among those exempt from the use tax only.

• *Property subject to Michigan sales tax*

Property sold in Michigan on which Michigan sales tax has been paid is exempt from use tax.

• *Property of nonresident temporarily in state*

Property brought into Michigan by a nonresident for storage, use, or consumption while temporarily within the state is exempt from use tax, unless the property is used in Michigan in a nontransitory business activity for a period exceeding 15 days.

• *Property purchased for personal, nonbusiness uses*

Tangible personal property that is purchased outside the state and used solely for personal, nonbusiness purposes is exempt from use tax if the property was purchased by a person who was a nonresident at the time of purchase and was brought into the state more than 90 days after the date of purchase.

• *Property taxed in another state*

Property that has previously been subjected to a sales or use tax by another state, or a governmental unit within another state, equal to or in excess of the Michigan use tax, is exempt from the use tax, if the other state or local unit allows a similar exemption. If the other tax was less than the Michigan tax, Michigan use tax applies at a rate equal to the difference in the two tax rates.

• *Property affixed to out-of-state real estate*

Property purchased or manufactured by a taxpayer constructing, altering, repairing, or improving real estate is exempt if the property is affixed to and made a structural part of real estate located in another state. The exemption does not depend on whether sales or use tax was due and paid in the state in which the real estate is located.

• *Intrafamily and estate transfers*

Property transferred to a spouse, parent, brother, sister, child, stepparent, stepchild, stepbrother, stepsister, grandparent, grandchild, legal ward, or a legally appointed guardian of the transferor is exempt from use tax. Also exempt is property transferred as a gift to a beneficiary in the administration of an estate. Also exempt are transfers of vehicles, off-road vehicles, manufactured housing, aircraft, snowmobiles, or watercraft when the transferee or purchaser is the father-in-law, mother-in-law, brother-in-law, sister-in-law, son-in-law, daughter-in-law, or grandparent-in-law, of the transferor.

Practice Note: Form Over Substance

The exemption is only available if the title of the property is held in one of the specified relatives' names listed above. Consequently, the Michigan Tax Tribunal determined that a Michigan taxpayer was not exempt from use tax on five vehicles received through a judgment of divorce, because at the time of the transfer the vehicles were titled in the name of a dealership owned by the taxpayer's ex-husband and not in her husband's name. (*Meade v. Department of Bureau of Tax Policy*, Michigan Tax Tribunal, No. 329900, September 10, 2008, CCH MICHIGAN TAX REPORTS, ¶401-389).

• *Property purchased at less than $10 per month*

Property purchased outside Michigan for use in Michigan, for a purchase price or actual value not exceeding $10 in any calendar month, is exempt from Michigan use tax, if actual personal possession of the property is obtained outside Michigan.

• *Automobiles purchased outside Michigan by military personnel*

Automobiles purchased outside Michigan by Michigan residents who are in the military service are exempt if sales tax is paid in the state in which the automobile is purchased.

• *Purchases of businesses*

Property purchased as part of the sale or transfer of a business is not subject to use tax except for inventory or vehicles. Other sales and use tax exemptions may be applicable to inventory or vehicles. The sale of a business is exempt from sales tax as a casual or isolated sale (¶ 1706).

• *Rental receipts*

Rental receipts are exempt from use tax if the original sale was subject to the Michigan sales or use tax or was subject to another state's or locality's sales or use tax if the other jurisdiction's sales or use tax rate was 6% or more.

• *Motor vehicles*

Use tax does not apply to a motor vehicle acquired by a towing company from a police agency as satisfaction for towing and storage charges if the motor vehicle was impounded by the police agency or determined by the police agency to be an abandoned vehicle or an abandoned scrap vehicle.

Use tax is also not imposed when an insurance company acquires ownership of a late model distressed vehicle through payment of damages in response to a claim or if the person who owned the vehicle before the insurance company reacquires ownership from the company as part of the settlement of a claim.

• *Aircraft parts*

The use tax exemption for parts and materials, excluding shop equipment or fuel, affixed to aircraft owned or used by domestic air carriers is applicable to (1) aircraft that are used solely in the regularly scheduled transport of passengers, or (2) aircraft that have a maximum certificated takeoff weight of at least 6,000 pounds, are designed to have a maximum passenger seating configuration of more than 30 seats, and are used solely in the transport of passengers.

• *Prepaid calling cards/Internet access*

The use or consumption of intrastate or interstate telephone communications services by means of a prepaid telephone calling card, a prepaid authorization number for telephone use, or a charge for Internet access is exempt from use tax.

SALES AND USE TAXES

CHAPTER 18

RETURNS, PAYMENT, ADMINISTRATION

¶1801 Licensing and Registration

Law: Secs. 205.53, 205.105, 205.189, M.C.L.; R 205.1, R205.26, Mich. Admin. Code (CCH MICHIGAN TAX REPORTS, ¶61-240, 61-530).

The following discussion outlines the licensing and registration requirements for taxpayers making sales in Michigan.

• *Sales tax licenses*

A Michigan sales tax license must be obtained by every person selling tangible personal property at retail. Application for a license should be made at least six to eight weeks before commencing business, by submitting a completed Form 518, Registration for Michigan Taxes, to the Department of Treasury. A taxpayer is required to indicate on an application or renewal of a license whether the taxpayer is subject to the tobacco products tax. Sales tax licenses expire on September 30 each year (regardless of the date it was first issued) and must be renewed on the annual return.

Persons selling at retail at more than one location or place of business must obtain a license for each location. A sales tax license is not transferable from one owner to another. If a partner is added or dropped, or if a corporation is formed or dissolved, this constitutes a change in ownership requiring an application in the name of the new owner.

Exemption.—An entity engaged solely in industrial processing or agricultural production and that makes no sales at retail is not required to obtain a license.

• *Car sales by lessors*

The Michigan Department of Treasury has issued guidelines relating to the taxability of automobile sales. A company that leases automobiles is engaged in the business of making retail sales and must obtain a license when it sells or offers for sale a used vehicle after selling or offering for sale five or more used vehicles in the previous 12 months (*Revenue Administrative Bulletin 90-15;* CCH MICHIGAN TAX REPORTS, ¶319-171).

• *Use tax registration*

Persons engaged in the business of selling tangible personal property for storage, use, or other consumption in Michigan are required to register with the Department of Treasury. A rule issued by the Department (R205.26, Rule 26, Mich. Admin. Code; CCH MICHIGAN TAX REPORTS, ¶65-051) states that the following activities require registration:

— an out-of-state seller, not registered as a retailer under the general sales tax act, having nexus with Michigan;

— a business in Michigan buying tangible personal property from nonregistered sellers;

— a lessor of tangible personal property when rental receipts are taxable under the use tax act;

— a provider of intrastate telecommunication services having nexus with Michgan;

— a provider of interstate telecommunications services having nexus with Michigan;

— a provider of rental accommodations to the public; and

— a provider of laundering or textile cleaning service under a sale, rental, or service agreement with a term of at least five days having nexus with Michigan.

Persons licensed under the sales tax law are not required to register under the use tax law. A seller registered under the Streamlined Sales and Use Tax (SST) Act who is not otherwise required to register, is not required to register under the Michigan sales or use tax laws because of its registration under the SST.

• *Penalties for failure to obtain license or register*

The penalty for failure to obtain a sales tax license is a fine of not more than $1,000 and/or imprisonment for not more than 1 year. The penalty for failure to register under the use tax act is $25 for each day such failure to register continues after notice from the Department of Treasury.

• *Streamlined sales and use tax registration*

A seller, not otherwise obligated to register with the state, may voluntarily choose to register under the Streamlined Sales and Use Tax Agreement (see ¶1602). The seller may register online with the central on-line registration system or with the individual participating states. Once registered, the seller agrees to collect and remit sales and use taxes for all taxable sales in the participating state. The registration is voluntary and a seller registered under the Agreement may withdraw at anytime.

Registration under the Agreement does not in and of itself create nexus with Michigan for any taxes or fees.

¶1802 Returns and Payment of Tax

Law: Secs. 205.19, 205.23, 205.24, 205.53, 205.56, 205.56a, 205.58, 205.96, 205.98, 205.103, 205.821 M.C.L. (CCH MICHIGAN TAX REPORTS, ¶60-445, 60-500, 61-210, 61-220, 61-230, 61-250).

All persons making retail sales subject to sales tax must file sales tax returns. Use tax returns are due from sellers collecting use taxes from purchasers. Purchasers must file use tax returns if the tax was not paid to the seller at the time of purchase. Generally, on or before the 20th day of each month, a taxpayer must file a return and remit the tax due for the preceding month. However, taxpayers that collect large amounts of sales or use taxes are subject to a different remittance schedule. The Department of Treasury has prescribed quarterly or annual filing for certain taxpayers.

If a due date falls on a Saturday, Sunday, state holiday, or legal banking holiday, the tax is due on the next succeeding business day.

CCH Advisory: Consolidated Returns

A person engaging in the same type of business in two or more places must file a consolidated return covering all such business activities engaged in the state.

Forms: Taxpayers not required to file electronically complete Form 160 for combined reporting of Michigan sales and use taxes and the income tax withheld. (¶607)

• *Fuel retailers*

Purchasers or receivers of gasoline and diesel fuel must prepay a portion of the sales tax imposed on shipments from refiners at rates set monthly by the Department of Treasury. Prepayment is made to the refiner or terminal operator from whom the gasoline or diesel fuel is purchased or directly to the Department of Treasury when the gasoline or diesel fuel is purchased outside the state. Bad debts related to prepaid sales tax may be deducted when the debt becomes worthless.

• *Remittance*

The sales and use tax must be remitted to the Department of Treasury at the time of filing the return. The responsibility of remittance of both taxes normally rests with the vendor; however, the burden is transferred to the consumer in certain situations, such as when the consumer fails to pay the use tax to the seller. The obligation to collect and remit use tax extends to out-of-state vendors selling tangible personal property for storage, use, or consumption within Michigan if such vendors have engaged in activities within Michigan that constitute sufficient nexus. The Department of Treasury has been authorized to accept major credit cards, debit cards, or both for payment. The department may add a processing fee. However, the fee may not exceed the charges that the state incurs because of the use of the credit or debit card or both.

CCH Advisory: Seller Liability for Uncollected Use Tax

An out-of-state seller registered in Michigan was not liable for uncollected use taxes, because it exercised reasonable business care in attempting to collect the tax from its Michigan customers. Although sellers are required to collect use tax from their customers, such sellers are personally liable for uncollected taxes only if there is some fault on the part of the seller in failing to collect the tax. The ultimate burden of paying use tax was on the customer, and the seller liability provisions did not require a seller to become, in effect, a guarantor of its customers' use tax payments. The legislature intended that a seller be held liable for its consumers' use tax payments only if the seller acts wrongfully (*World Book, Inc.*, (1999 SCt) 222 MichApp 203, 564 NW2d 82; CCH MICHIGAN TAX REPORTS, ¶400-632).

Streamlined sales and use tax options.—Sellers that voluntarily register under the Streamlined Sales and Use Tax Agreement (¶1801) may choose one of four models for collecting and remitting sales and use taxes. Under Model 1, the seller uses a certified service provider to act as the seller's agent to perform all of the seller's sales and use tax collection functions other than the seller's obligation to remit sales or use tax on its own purchases. Under Model 2, the seller uses a certified automated system to perform part of the seller's sales and use tax collection functions, but the seller retains responsibility for remitting the tax. Model 3 allows a seller (including affiliated group of sellers) that has sales in at least 5 member states and total annual sales of at least $500 million to use a proprietary system that calculates the amount of tax due in each taxing jurisdiction. Alternatively, a seller may use any other system approved by the Department of Treasury.

Gasoline and diesel fuel tax prepayments.—Remittance of prepayments of gasoline and diesel fuel tax is made as follows: (1) 10th of the month for prepayments received after the 15th and before the end of the preceding month; and (2) the 25th of the month for prepayments received after the end of the preceding month and before the 16th of the current month.

• *Direct payment authorization*

The Department of Treasury may authorize a taxpayer to assume the obligation of self-accruing and remitting use tax on purchases or leases directly to the Department under a direct payment authorization. To receive authorization, the following conditions must be met:

— the authorization is to be used for the purchase or lease of tangible personal property or services;

— the authorization is necessary because it is either impractical to determine the manner in which the tangible personal property or services will be used or it will facilitate improved tax compliance; and

— the taxpayer requesting authorization maintains accurate and complete records in a form acceptable to the Department.

Direct payment authorization may be canceled without cause by the holder of an authorization letter or by the Department, provided there is 30 days advance written notice. However, authorization will be automatically canceled and written notice is not required if the holder fails to comply with the statutory or regulatory procedures.

Direct payment authorization may not be transferred or assigned to a third party or new business entity created in a corporate restructuring. If the holder of an authorization letter transfers a portion of business activity to a new business entity, the new business entity must have its own direct payment authorization and its own authorization number in effect within 60 days of the transfer. If a direct payment authorization letter is canceled or revoked, the taxpayer must immediately provide written notice of the cancellation or revocation to each vendor from whom the taxpayer has made a purchase or leased property or services using the authorization letter (*Revenue Administrative Bulletin 2000-3;* CCH MICHIGAN TAX REPORTS, ¶319-297).

• *Surety bond requirement*

When it is necessary to secure the collection of the sales tax, the Revenue Division may require a taxpayer to secure a surety bond in an amount not less than $1,000 nor more than $25,000, or to make a cash deposit in an amount to be determined by the Revenue Division to guarantee the payment of the tax, interest, and penalty and compliance with the sales tax law. The amount of the bond may be increased upon 30 days' written notice.

This surety bond or cash deposit requirement may also be required if a taxpayer (or the persons managing a corporation) has at any time failed to pay any tax, penalty, or interest, or if a taxpayer has attempted to evade a tax through a petition for bankruptcy.

• *Direct mail sourcing*

A purchaser of direct mail that is not a holder of a direct pay permit must provide to the seller, in conjunction with the purchase, either an exemption form or information to show the jurisdictions to which the direct mail is delivered to recipients.

Upon receipt of the exemption form, the seller is relieved of all obligations to collect, pay, or remit tax and the purchaser is obligated to pay or remit the applicable tax on a direct pay basis. An exemption form remains in effect for all future sales of direct mail by the seller to the purchaser until it is revoked in writing.

Upon receipt of information from the purchaser showing the jurisdictions to which the direct mail is delivered to recipients, the seller must collect the tax according to the delivery information provided by the purchaser. In the absence of bad faith, the seller is relieved of any further obligation to collect tax on any transaction for which the seller has collected tax pursuant to the delivery information provided by the purchaser.

If the purchaser of direct mail does not have a direct pay permit and does not provide the seller with either an exemption form or delivery information, the seller must source the sale to the location from which the tangible personal property was shipped.

A purchaser of direct mail that provides the seller with documentation of direct pay authority is not required to provide an exemption form or delivery information to the seller.

• *Accelerated electronic funds transfer*

A retailer or other business with sales and use tax liabilities of $720,000 or more in the prior calendar year must remit by electronic funds transfer, by the 20th of the month, an amount equal to 75% of its liability in the immediately preceding month or 75% of its liability for the same month in the preceding calendar year, whichever is less. Also due will be a reconciliation payment equal to the difference between the tax liability determined for the previous month and the amount of tax previously paid for that month.

CCH Advisory: Timely Receipt

To assure timely receipt, EFT payments must be initiated by 4:00 p.m. one business day prior to the due date. (*Change in Sales, Use, and Withholding Tax Due Dates,* Michigan Department of Treasury)

When a taxpayer's attempt to make a payment by EFT fails, there is an alternative method for making a same-day payment so as to avoid a penalty and interest. If the payment fails for a reason not related to the taxpayer's operations, such as a power failure, Act of God, or other similar circumstances determined by the Department of Treasury, payment will be considered timely if received on the next business day following the due date on which the reason for the failure is corrected. Written notice must be provided to the Department by the taxpayer describing and documenting the EFT failure. The notice must contain the name and account number of the taxpayer, the tax period involved, the specific taxes and amounts that were remitted late, and a description of the date, time, and manner that the failed EFT was initiated, as well as the reason it failed, and the date the failure was corrected. (*Internal Policy Directive 2004-6,* Michigan Department of Treasury, November 22, 2004, CCH MICHIGAN TAX REPORTS, ¶380-011)

• *Quarterly returns authorized for concrete and lumber businesses*

Businesses primarily engaged in either the sale of lumber and building materials, or precast concrete products or conduit or fitting products used in the collection, conveyance, or distribution of water or sewage who furnish real property improvement materials to an owner, contractor, subcontractor, repairperson, or consumer on a credit sale basis, have the option of filing quarterly sales tax reports for credit sales. Taxable sales and gross proceeds must be included in the first quarterly return due following the date of the credit sale, other than a credit card sale.

• *Penalties and interest*

Interest at the annual rate of prime plus 1% is charged on any deficiency of tax. Penalties for failure to file or pay the tax, deficiencies due to negligence, etc., are the same as those discussed under the income tax law (¶2404).

¶1803 Early-Payment Sales and Use Tax Discount

Law: Secs. 205.54, 205.94f, 205.823, M.C.L. (CCH MICHIGAN TAX REPORTS, ¶61-220).

Discounts are allowed to taxpayers that remit taxes on or before the due date. Generally, for payments made on or before the 12th day of the month, taxpayers may deduct a discount equal to 0.75% of the tax due at the rate of 4% for the preceding month, up to a maximum of $20,000, or a discount equal to the tax due at the rate of 4% on $150, whichever is greater. For payments made after the 12th day and on or before the 20th day of the month, taxpayers may deduct 0.5% of the tax due at the rate of 4% for the preceding month, up to a maximum of $15,000, or a discount equal to the tax due at the rate of 4% on $150, whichever is greater.

Sellers registered under the Streamlined Sales and Use Tax (SST) Agreement (¶1801) may claim the deduction if authorized to do so under the Agreement.

The early payment discount is prorated for sellers doing business for less than a month. The discount does not apply to the additional 2% tax (¶1603). No discount is given for payments made after the due date.

Practice Note: Discount for Large Retailers

A taxpayer that is required to remit sales or use tax by electronic funds transfer (¶1802) may deduct from its tax remittance 0.5% of the tax due at a rate of 4%, with no cap on the amount of the deduction.

Taxpayers that participate under the SST (see ¶1602) may be eligible for additional collection allowances.

¶1804 Records

Law: Secs. 205.52, 205.68, 205.104a, 205.104b (CCH MICHIGAN TAX REPORTS, ¶61-260, 61-420).

Persons liable for sales or use tax are required to keep an accurate and complete beginning and annual inventory, purchase records of additions to inventory, complete daily sales records, receipts, invoices, bills of lading, and all pertinent documents in a form required by the Department of Treasury.

A seller who claims exemption on certain sales must obtain identifying information of the purchaser and the reason for claiming the exemption at the time of the purchase or at a later date. If exemption is claimed by reason of a sale for resale, the sales tax license number of the purchaser must be obtained.

The required records must kept for four years. If inadequate records are kept, the Department may determine the amount of tax due the state from information available to it, whether obtained at the taxpayer's place of business or from any other source, and may assess the taxpayer for any deficiency, plus penalties.

- *Separate records required*

A person engaged in the business of making sales at retail and also engaged in another business or profession that is not taxable must keep books to show separately the transactions used in determining the sales tax. Failure to maintain separate books will result in the levy of sales tax on the entire gross proceeds of both businesses.

- *Vendor's tax liability*

A taxpayer who maintains the required records and who accepts an exemption certificate from a buyer in good faith is not liable for the collection of the unpaid tax after a finding that the sale did not qualify for exemption.

A valid sales tax exemption certificate includes a blanket exemption certificate that covers all exempt transfers between a buyer and a taxpayer for a period of four years or a shorter period agreed upon by the parties.

The good faith exemption certificate requirement does not apply to persons licensed by the liquor control commission as wholesalers for purposes of sales of alcoholic liquor to another person licensed by the commission or to the commission or a person certified by the commission as an authorized distribution agent for purposes of the sale and distribution of alcoholic liquor to a person licensed by the commission.

¶1805 Selling or Quitting Business

Law: Secs. 205.20, 205.101a, M.C.L. (CCH MICHIGAN TAX REPORTS, ¶61-470).

Any person liable for sales or use tax who sells the business or stock of goods or quits a business must file a final monthly return within 15 days of selling or quitting a business. The Michigan Supreme Court has held, however, that failure to file a final return does not render a taxpayer liable for sales and use taxes incurred by its successor (*Detroit Hilton Limited Partnership v. Department of Treasury* (1985, SCt), 422 Mich 422, 373 NW2d 586; CCH MICHIGAN TAX REPORTS, ¶61-470.30). Any successor to the business must withhold a sufficient amount of the purchase money to cover the amount of any tax, interest, and penalties due until the former owner provides a receipt from the Department of Treasury showing that all taxes have been paid or that no tax is due.

CCH Caution: Successor and Responsible Party Tax Liability

A purchaser or successor who fails to withhold taxes due from the purchase money will be personally liable for any taxes, interest, and penalties accrued and unpaid on the account of the former owner. However, the purchaser is not liable for such liabilities unless the Department files a lien for total tax liability at the register of deeds office in the county where the business is located.

In addition, for provisions governing the personal liability of responsible parties (*i.e.*, corporate officers and members, managers, or partners of flow-through entities), see ¶2403.

¶1806 Administration

Law: Secs. 205.13, 205.51, M.C.L. (CCH MICHIGAN TAX REPORTS, ¶60-030).

The Department of Treasury is charged with the administration of sales and use taxes.

The Taxpayer Bill of Rights, discussed at ¶702, applies to sales and use taxes.

¶1807 Assessment

Law: Secs. 205.20, 205.23, 205.24, 205.26, 205.27a, 205.829, M.C.L. (CCH MICHIGAN TAX REPORTS, ¶61-410, 61-420, 61-430, 61-520).

Sales and use taxes are generally self-assessing in that they are based on gross proceeds of sales of tangible personal property. However, if no return is filed or if an inaccurate amount of tax is returned, the Department of Treasury is authorized to assess the tax due. In the event of the taxpayer's failure to keep records (¶1804), or the maintenance of inaccurate records, the tax may be assessed on the basis of information available to the Department.

• *Audits*

Michigan allows managed audits of sales and use taxes in certain instances. Taxpayers seeking additional information about managed audits should contact the Department of Treasury Audit Discovery Division at (517) 636-4200. (E-mail from Michigan Department of Treasury, October 2009)

Offsets during audit.—In the course of an audit of Michigan taxes, a taxpayer has the right to claim credit amounts as an offset against debit amounts determined in the audit. In addition, a taxpayer that is the subject of a Michigan use tax audit of its purchases is entitled to offset the use tax liability determined in that audit by the amount of sales tax paid annually by it to a Michigan vendor, or use tax paid annually by it to a vendor located outside Michigan, on an amount of up to $5,000 in purchases. (Sec. 205.21b, M.C.L.)

• *Jeopardy assessment*

The Department may demand immediate payment of the tax due and the tax becomes immediately due and payable if the Department has reason to believe that a person liable for tax intends to leave the state, conceal his or her property, etc., in order to avoid payment of tax. However, if the person establishes that he or she will file a return and pay the tax, and if he or she is not in default in making any return or paying any tax due, the tax due will not become payable until the time fixed for usual payment.

• *Statute of limitations*

No deficiency, interest, or penalty may be assessed after the expiration of four years from the date set for filing of the return or from the date the return was filed, whichever is later, except that an unlicensed person is liable for all sales taxes due for the entire period during which the person has made sales at retail.

In cases involving fraud, the Department may assess the tax, plus penalties and interest, within two years after discovery of the fraud.

The statute of limitations will be extended in instances where the following time periods exceed the statute of limitations:

— the period pending the completion of an appeal of a final assessment;

— a period of 90 days after the issuance of a decision and order from an informal conference;

— a period of 90 days after the issuance of a court order resolving an appeal of a decision of the department in a case in which a final assessment was not issued prior to appeal; and

— for the period of an audit that started after September 30, 2014, and was conducted within a specified time frame established by law.

CCH Note: Commencement of appeal period

The Michigan Supreme Court has held that when a taxpayer has appointed a representative to receive copies of letters and notices relating to a dispute between the taxpayer and the Michigan Department of Treasury, the department must provide notice of a final assessment to the representative, pursuant to MCL 205.8, and to the taxpayer, pursuant to MCL 205.28. The provision to provide notice to the taxpayer representative is mandatory despite the greater specificity of MCL 205.28, which requires personal service or notice by certified mail, and applies to the department with equal force. Furthermore, satisfaction of both notice requirements must be completed before the assessment is deemed to have been issued, starting the appeal period. As the department delayed issuing notices to the taxpayers' representatives in the present cases, the running of the appeal periods was also delayed. The taxpayers' appeals were timely and the Tax Tribunal retained jurisdiction. The appeal period begins only when the department provides notice of a final assessment to the taxpayer via personal service or notice by certified mail and to the taxpayer representative. (*Fradco, Inc. v. Department of Treasury*, Michigan Supreme Court, Nos. 146333 and 146335, April 1, 2014; CCH MICHIGAN TAX REPORTS, ¶ 401-881)

• *Streamlined sales and use tax agreement amnesty program*

A seller will be granted amnesty for uncollected or unpaid sales or use taxes if the seller was not licensed in the state at any time during the 12-month period prior to Michigan's participation under the Agreement, the seller obtains a license within a 12-month period beginning on the date of Michigan's participation under the Agreement, and the seller is registered under the Agreement. See ¶1602 for information regarding the Agreement.

A seller may not receive amnesty for a tax:

— collected by the seller;

— remitted by the seller;

— that the seller is required to remit on the seller's purchases; or

— arising from a transaction that occurred within a time period that is under audit if the seller has received notice of the commencement of an audit and the audit has not been completed, including all administrative and judicial remedies in connection with the audit.

Amnesty granted to a seller applies to the time period during which a seller was not licensed and remains in effect if, for a period of three years, the seller remains registered under the Agreement and collects and remits the appropriate taxes.

Amnesty will not be allowed where a seller commits fraud or an intentional misrepresentation of a material fact.

In addition, a seller or certified service provider is not liable for having charged and collected an incorrect amount of sales or use tax resulting from their reliance on erroneous data provided in the taxability matrix provided for under the Agreement or by the Department.

¶1808 Refunds

Law: Secs. 205.30, 205.51(1), 205.56b, 205.60, 205.101, 205.182, 205.183, M.C.L.; R205.16, Mich. Admin. Code (CCH MICHIGAN TAX REPORTS, ¶61-610, 89-224, 60-570, 60-330).

Overpayments of tax or taxes that have been wrongfully collected may be credited against a subsequent tax or, at the request of the taxpayer, refunded. Interest at the rate calculated for deficiencies (¶2404) is paid beginning 45 days following the receipt of a tax return or a refund request, whichever occurs later. A taxpayer must claim a refund within four years from the date of filing the original return.

• *Refund to purchaser*

If a taxpayer or person liable for the collection of sales and use tax refunds all or a portion of the purchase price of returned tangible personal property or services, or provides a credit for such an amount, within the time period for returns stated in the refund policy or 180 days after the initial sale, whichever is sooner, the taxpayer or person liable for the tax collection must refund or provide a credit for the tax that was added to the amount of the purchase price that is refunded or credited. The seller or collector may claim a deduction from gross proceeds for credits or refunds given for returned goods.

CCH Note: Scope of returned goods credit

The Michigan Court of Appeals has held that a tire retailer was entitled to a returned goods sales tax credit on previously remitted sales tax because it conveyed cash refunds, including sales tax, to customers who returned damaged tires. The taxpayer's customers had the option of purchasing a certificate that entitled them to a full cash refund on irreparably damaged tires within three years of purchase. Though the department claimed that goods must be returned within a certain time frame and in the same condition as they were sold in order to qualify for a returned goods tax credit, the applicable statute, MCL 205.56b, contains no such requirements. (*Discount Tire Co. v. Department of Treasury*, Michigan Court of Appeals, No. 307038, November 6, 2012; CCH MICHIGAN TAX REPORTS,¶ 401-735; partially vacated by *Discount Tire Co. v. Department of Treasury*, Michigan Supreme Court, No. 146694, July 5, 2013)

A purchaser may not bring a cause of action against a seller for a refund or credit of overpaid taxes unless the purchaser provides the seller written notice that the purchaser requests the refund or credit containing the information necessary for the seller to determine the validity of the request. A cause of action may not be brought until 60 days after the day on which the seller receives the written notice.

In connection with a purchaser's request for over-collected taxes, a seller is presumed to have a reasonable business practice if, in the collection of sales and use taxes, the seller:

— uses either a provider or a system, including a proprietary system, that is certified by the Department of Treasury; and

— has remitted to the state all taxes collected less any deductions, credits, or allowances.

• *Refund procedures for motor vehicle dealers, manufacturers, and others*

To obtain more timely tax refunds, motor vehicle dealers or manufacturers should claim a sales tax credit on the Monthly-Quarterly Return Worksheet. This procedure applies when a motor vehicle is returned for a full refund of the purchase price, sales tax is improperly calculated, or a transaction is improperly subjected to tax. It also applies to certain refunds under manufacturer buy-back agreements mandated by the Michigan "lemon law" (*Revenue Administrative Bulletin 1995-9;* CCH MICHIGAN TAX REPORTS, ¶ 319-262).

• *Refund on sales taxes paid on motor vehicles subject to manufacturer rebate*

A taxpayer may calculate a credit and seek a refund on sales taxes paid on motor vehicles subject to manufacturer rebate. The refund will be 6% of the amount received by the taxpayer from the automobile manufacturer in reimbursement for a price reduction on the vehicle. The refund is only permitted if the purchaser was not employed by the automobile manufacturer at the time of the discount, the taxpayer did not add sales tax to the part of the sales price received from the manufacturer when calculating the credit, and the refund would not be greater than the actual sales tax paid on that portion of the sales price received from the manufacturer.

• *Refund for sales tax paid on earth-moving equipment core charge*

A taxpayer who paid sales tax on a core charge related to a recycling fee, deposit, or disposal fee for a component or part for heavy earth-moving equipment is eligible for a refund from the Department of Treasury equal to the amount of sales tax paid.

• *Refund of use taxes paid on hotel rooms*

A person who paid a use tax may obtain a refund from the Department of Treasury equal to 6% of an assessment imposed under the Convention and Tourism Marketing Act, the State Convention Facility Development Act, the Regional Tourism Marketing Act, or the Community Convention or Tourism Marketing Act that was added to charges for rooms or lodgings subject to use tax, but not to exceed the actual amount of use tax paid on those assessments.

• *Nonprofit organization refunds for auctioned items*

A nonprofit organization that sold an item at a charitable auction is allowed to claim a Michigan sales tax refund of 6% of the gross proceeds of the auctioned item in excess of the fair market value of that auctioned item. Alternatively, the nonprofit organization may choose to apply a credit to reduce its sales tax liability. The nonprofit organization may not seek a credit or refund for any portion of a qualified sale of an auctioned item for which sales tax was collected from the purchaser, unless the tax collected was refunded to the purchaser. In addition, the nonprofit organization must retain in its records certification of the fair market value supplied by the donor of an auctioned item on a form prescribed by the Department of Treasury.

¶1809 Advertising Absorption of Tax

Law: Sec. 205.73, M.C.L. (CCH MICHIGAN TAX REPORTS, ¶60-130).

Vendors are prohibited from advertising or holding out to the public in any way, directly or indirectly, that sales tax is not considered as an element in the price to the consumer. However, the law specifically states that nothing in the sales act is to be deemed to prohibit vendors reimbursing themselves by adding the tax to the sales price of the merchandise.

PART V

INHERITANCE, ESTATE, AND GENERATION-SKIPPING TRANSFER TAXES

CHAPTER 19

INHERITANCE, ESTATE, AND GENERATION-SKIPPING TRANSFER TAXES

¶ 1901 The Law

Michigan's Estate Tax is covered in Chapter 205, Secs. 205.201—205.256, Michigan Compiled Laws of 1979, as amended. Comprehensive coverage of estate and inheritance taxes is provided in Wolters Kluwer, CCH State Inheritance, Estate and Gift Tax Reporter. For more information go to CCHGroup.com or contact an account representative at 888-CCH-REPS (888-224-377).

PART VI

PROPERTY TAXES

CHAPTER 20

PROPERTY TAXES

¶2001 Scope of Chapter

Property taxes in Michigan are imposed on both real and personal property. Various statutory provisions limit the property tax rate for different taxing units. Except for the education tax, no state property tax is levied. Property taxes are levied and collected by the local jurisdictions based on information from taxpayers, except that certain public utility property is assessed by the State Tax Commission and collected by the state.

The purpose of this chapter is to give a general picture of the nature and application of the property tax and the manner of its administration. It is not intended to provide detailed coverage. It covers, generally, the questions of what property is subject to tax, the basis and rate of tax, and the requirements for filing returns and making payments.

¶2002 Imposition of Tax

Law: Secs. 211.1—211.6, 211.34c, 211.901—211.905, M.C.L. (CCH MICHIGAN TAX REPORTS, ¶20-105, ¶20-605).

The township and the city are the principal units in the assessment of property. The township and ward supervisors are designated as the assessing officials for all taxing bodies, except that, for villages or cities whose charters or acts of incorporation so provide, another assessing official may be designated.

On or before the first Monday in March in each year, the assessor is required to classify each item of assessable real and personal property for tax purposes. The following classifications pertain to assessable real property: agricultural; commercial; developmental; industrial; residential; and timber-cutover. The following classifications pertain to assessable personal property: agricultural; commercial; industrial; residential; and utility. If the total usage of a parcel of property includes more than one classification, the assessor is directed to determine the classification which most significantly influences the total valuation of the parcel. (Sec. 211.34c, M.C.L.)

• *State education tax*

A state education tax is levied on all taxable property. The tax is collected and distributed under the general property tax law provisions. (Sec. 211.901, M.C.L.—Sec. 201.905, M.C.L.)

¶2003 Property Subject to Tax

Law: Secs. 125.2120—125.2121c, 207.771—207.787, 211.1—211.14, 211.181, M.C.L. (CCH MICHIGAN TAX REPORTS, ¶20-105, ¶20-205, ¶20-275, ¶20-285, ¶20-310, ¶20-335).

All real and personal property within the jurisdiction of Michigan is taxable unless specifically exempted. Leasehold interests are specifically included in taxable property. Mobile homes located on taxable real property are taxable.

Generally, exempt real property leased by, or in the possession of, a private individual, association, or corporation and used in connection with a business conducted for profit is taxable to the person using the property, unless such property is used as a concession (see ¶2005).

Buildings or tangible personal property situated on the lands of another person or on exempt lands are assessed to the lessee as personal property separate from the land unless the value of the real property is also assessed to the lessee or owner of the buildings and improvements. Buildings and improvements located on leased real property will be taxed as real property to their owner if the value of the buildings or improvements is not otherwise included in the real property assessment. However, buildings and improvements on leased real property will not be treated as real property unless they would be treated as real property if they were located on real property owned by the taxpayer.

CCH Comment: Voters Approve Repeal of Tax on Industrial Equipment

Michigan voters have approved a shift in the state's use tax to local governments that triggers the repeal of personal property taxes on industrial equipment. Voters approved the measure 69.2% to 30.7% during the state's August 5, 2014, primary election, according to unofficial election results released by the Michigan Secretary of State. The shift in use tax revenue from 2015 through 2029 will fund a phaseout of the personal property tax on industrial equipment and replace it with the new state essential services assessment, which becomes effective January 1, 2016. Had the use tax shift not been approved, business exemptions to the tangible personal property tax were set to be repealed, as previously reported. (*Michigan Ballot Proposal 14-1*, as enacted by Act 80, S.B. 822, Laws 2014; *Unofficial Michigan Primary Election Results*, Michigan Secretary of State, August 5, 2014)

The shift in tax treatment for buildings and improvements on leased real property does not apply to buildings and improvements that are exempt as new personal property owned or leased by eligible businesses located in certain eligible districts. Exemptions for new personal property that were approved by the State Tax Commission before May 1, 1999, will be continued for the term authorized, and may not be restricted or impaired in any way during the term of the exemption, provided that the value of the real property is not assessed to the owner of the buildings and improvements.

• *Taxable situs*

Real property is assessed in the township or place where located. All tangible personal property, except as provided below, is assessed to the owner if known, in the local tax collecting unit where it is located on December 31. (Sec. 211.13, M.C.L.)

Guardians.—Property of minors under guardianship is assessed to the guardian by the local tax collecting unit in which the guardian resides. Tangible personal property of any other person under guardianship is assessed to the guardian by the local tax collecting unit in which the ward resides. (Sec. 211.14(3), M.C.L.)

Estates.—Until notice is given to the assessing officer that the estate has been distributed to the proper persons, tangible personal property of the estate of a deceased person is assessed by the local tax collecting unit and school district in which the deceased last resided. The tangible personal property of a decedent who was a Michigan nonresident is assessed by the local tax collecting unit in which the property is located. (Sec. 211.14(4), M.C.L.)

Trustees or agents.—A trustee or agent who has control of tangible personal property may be assessed for the property by the local tax collecting unit in which the trustee or agent resides. (Sec. 211.14(5), M.C.L.)

Nonresidents.—Tangible personal property of Michigan nonresidents is assessed in the local tax collecting unit in which the property is located to the persons having control of the premises where the property is located. If the property is in transit to another place in the state, it is assessed at its destination site. If the property is in transit to a place outside the state, it is assessed in Michigan at the place where it leaves the state. Property in transit is assessed to the owner or persons having control of the property. (Sec. 211.14(7), M.C.L.)

Daily rental property.—Daily rental property is assessed to the owner at the location of the rental business and not at the location where the property is located on tax day if the rental property is located in Michigan on tax day and the rental business is located in Michigan. (Sec. 211.8c, M.C.L.)

Leased personal property.—Qualified personal property made available by a qualified business for use by another person is assessable and taxable to the user, rather than to the qualified business. Generally, a "qualified business" is a for-profit business, including a unitary group, that obtains services from 30 or fewer employees or employees of independent contractors during a week selected at random each year by the State Tax Commission. "Qualified personal property" is property leased for a period of at least 1 year on which retail sales tax has been paid or liability accrued at the same time that a user acquires possession of the property, or on which sales tax would be payable if the property were not exempt from taxation. (Sec. 211.8a, M.C.L.)

A qualified business is required to file a statement regarding the use of qualified personal property not later than February 1 of the tax year with an assessor. Among other matters, the statement must include: (1) the name of the qualified business; (2) the user responsible for payment of the tax; (3) the type, location, purchase price, and date of acquisition of the property; and (4) a periodic-payments schedule. The user of the property must file a statement with an assessor by February 20. If a qualified business fails to comply with these requirements, the property is assessable and taxable to the person that makes it available, regardless of its character as qualified personal property. (Sec. 211.8a, M.C.L.)

• *Enterprise zones*

Owners of property located in an enterprise zone that was created after 1993 are subject to a specific annual tax (¶2005). A five-year exemption from property taxes applies to qualified businesses in enterprise zones. (Sec. 125.2120, M.C.L.)

Qualified residential facilities for which Neighborhood Enterprise Zone (NEZ) certificates are in effect are subject to an annual NEZ tax (CCH MICHIGAN TAX REPORTS, ¶20-170) instead of the general property taxes; however, the land on which the facilities are located is subject to general property taxes.

• *Taxes for school purposes*

Taxes that are levied for school operating purposes are not subject to the general requirement that the state legislature provide for the uniform general property taxation of real and tangible personal property in Michigan. (Sec. 3, Art. IX, Mich. Const.)

¶2004 Property Exempt

Law: Secs. 125.1415a, 125.1459, 207.551 *et seq.*, 207.606, 207.841—207.853, 211.7—211.7r, 211.7cc, 211.7dd, 211.7mm, 211.7nn, 211.7oo, 211.7pp, 211.7qq, 211.7ss, 211.9—211.9o, 380.1211, M.C.L. (CCH MICHIGAN TAX REPORTS, ¶20-105, ¶20-115, ¶20-145, ¶20-170, ¶20-180, ¶20-205, ¶20-215, ¶20-270, ¶20-275, ¶20-285, ¶20-405, ¶20-505, ¶20-510, ¶20-700).

The following principal exemptions are provided:

— property of the United States, public property belonging to Michigan, with exceptions, and property owned by, or being acquired pursuant to an installment purchase agreement by, a county, township, city, village or school district if used for public purposes; which includes preparing vacant land for resale for future economic development (*City of Mt. Pleasant v. State Tax Commission*, Michigan Supreme Court, No. 129453, 477 Mich. 50, 729 N.W.2d 833, March 28, 2007, CCH MICHIGAN TAX REPORTS, ¶401-292);

— intangible personal property (but this exemption does not affect the taxable status of computer software);

— personal property of Native Americans who are not Michigan citizens;

— real estate of nonprofit theaters, libraries, benevolent, charitable, educational or scientific institutions, certain nonprofit organizations devoted to fostering the development of literature, music, painting, or sculpture; see *Wexford Medical Group v. City of Cadillac*, Michigan Supreme Court, No. 127152, 474 Mich. 192, 713 N.W.2d 734, May 4, 2006, CCH MICHIGAN TAX REPORTS, ¶401-224 for the factors the Supreme Court has outlined to determine whether an entity qualifies as a charitable institution. The Michigan Supreme Court has ruled that the organization must actually occupy the property it owns in order to qualify for the exemption. Thus a nonprofit housing corporation was unable to claim an exemption for homes it owned and leased to low-income and disabled tenants in furtherance of its charitable purpose (*Liberty Hill Housing Corp. v. City of Livonia*, Michigan Supreme Court, No. 131531, April 2, 2008, CCH MICHIGAN TAX REPORTS, ¶401-359);

— memorial homes of world war veterans (Sec. 211.7p, M.C.L.);

— up to 480 acres of realty in the state of any Boy Scout or Girl Scout organization, YMCA, YWCA or 4-H clubs (Sec. 211.7q, M.C.L.);

— realty of clinics and hospitals (Sec. 211.7r, M.C.L.);

— personal property of libraries, charitable, educational and scientific institutions, charitable homes of such organizations operated for the aged and ill, patriotic and religious associations, Boy Scouts, Girl Scouts, 4-H clubs, Camp Fire Girls, YMCA, and YWCA; see *Wexford Medical Group v. City of Cadillac*, Michigan Supreme Court, No. 127152, 474 Mich. 192, 713 N.W.2d 734, May 4, 2006, CCH MICHIGAN TAX REPORTS, ¶401-224, for the factors the Supreme Court has outlined to determine whether an entity qualifies as a charitable institution;

— property owned by a nonprofit charitable institution or trust leased or loaned to a governmental entity provided certain conditions are met;

— health care facilities;

— churches and parsonages;

— cemeteries;

— principal residences of indigent individuals, disabled soldiers and sailors;

— nonprofit or government housing for use by elderly or disabled families;

— certain household property personal property does not have to be customarily owned and used by householders in order to be exempt (*Oryszczak*, Michigan Tax Tribunal, October 25, 1994; CCH MICHIGAN TAX REPORTS, ¶400-410), wearing apparel, and up to $500 in equalized value in personal business property and mechanics' tools;

— property actually being used in operations, other than food processing operations, and wood harvesting and farm implements held for sale by dealers for use in production; see ¶2005 for a discussion of the property recapture tax;

— deciduous and evergreen trees, shrubs, plants, bushes, and vines growing on land (greenhouses, however, on leased land were ruled ineligible for the exemption in *Dick & Don's Greenhouses, Inc. v. Comstock Township* (1982, Ct App), 112 MichApp 294, 315 NW2d 573; CCH MICHIGAN TAX REPORTS, ¶200-945);

— nursery stock seasonal protection unit, but not the land on which it is located;

— stored farm products intended for consumption as food;

— property in transit located in a public warehouse, dock, port facility or U.S. customs port of entry bonded warehouse;

— oil and gas rights and interests (see ¶2204 for the oil and gas severance tax);

— motor vehicles subject to specific taxes at the time of registration;

— aircraft and airports;

— personal property of banks, national banks, incorporated bank holding companies and trust companies organized under Michigan law, mortgages or other securities held by savings and loan associations, and personal property of credit unions;

— property of telegraph and telephone companies whose gross receipts within Michigan do not exceed $1,000 for the year ending December 31;

— special manufacturing tools, such as dies, jigs, fixtures, molds, patterns, gauges, etc., held for use, but not if the value of the tools is included in the valuation of inventory that is produced for sale;

— real and personal property of air pollution control facilities and real and personal property of water pollution control facilities; "facilities" mean machinery, equipment, structures, or any part or accessories of machinery, equipment, or structures, installed or acquired for the primary purpose of controlling or disposing of air pollution, but does not include test cells installed by automobile manufacturers to ensure that their vehicles and engines complied with certain federal environmental emissions standards because such equipment does not directly limit or curb the amount of pollution emitted (*DaimlerChrysler Corp. v. State Tax Commission*, Michigan Supreme Court, Nos. 133394, 133396, 133400-133402, 133403, 133404, 133405, 133406, July 30, 2008, CCH MICHIGAN TAX REPORTS, ¶401-381);

— real property leased or loaned to a school district for public school purposes;

— property owned and occupied by nonprofit religious or educational organizations;

— state fish hatcheries;

— public parks (the park must be open to all Michigan residents, see *Michigan State Tax Commission v. Grosse Pointe*, Michigan Court of Appeals, No. 257503, May 9, 2006, CCH MICHIGAN TAX REPORTS, ¶401-225), and any monument ground or armory belonging to a military organization;

— fire company equipment; fairs;

— principal residences of disabled soldiers and sailors;

— erosion and flood prevention structures;

— sugar from beets owned or held by processors;

— inventories ("inventory" includes (a) goods held for resale in the regular course of business, (b) raw materials, goods in process and finished goods of a manufacturing business, (c) materials and supplies including repair parts and fuel, but does not include personal property under lease or intended for lease or depreciable property, and (d) heavy earth-moving equipment subject to a lease of less than one year and principally intended for sale rather than lease);

— commercial forests (however commercial forests are subject to an in lieu tax discussed at ¶2005);

— personal property and real estate owned and occupied by a parent cooperative preschool if the property is used solely for operating a preschool education program;

— mass transportation system authorities;

— pensions;

— underground iron ore;

— computer software (a) not incorporated as a permanent component of a computer, equipment, or real estate and not commonly available separately, and (b) the cost of which is not included in the cost of the computer, equipment, or real property;

— gas tanks used for storing liquefied petroleum gas for residential or agricultural use;

— water conditioning systems used for residential dwellings;

— bottled water coolers available for lease or subject to an existing lease;

— personal property that is located in a federally designated rural enterprise community and is a component part of a natural gas distribution system until December 30, 2018;

— the real and personal property of a qualified start-up business (see ¶1126 and ¶1483) if the business applies for the exemption and the governing body of the local tax collection unit adopts a resolution approving the exemption. The exemption does not apply to special assessments, ad valorem property taxes levied for the payment of principal and interest on obligations approved by the electors or obligations pledging the unlimited taxing power of a local governmental unit, or certain enhancement millage or sinking fund taxes levied under the Revised School Code;

— until 2013, alternative energy personal property, including wind energy systems;

— biomass gasification systems, thermal depolymerization systems, methane digesters and methane digester electric generating systems, and machinery that is capable of simultaneously harvesting grain or other crops and biomass, as well as machinery used for the purpose of harvesting biomass; "biomass" means crop residue used to produce energy or agricultural crops grown specifically for the production of energy. (Sec. 211.9, M.C.L.);

— machinery used to install land tile or to install or implement soil and water conservation techniques when used on qualified agricultural property that is exempt from taxes levied for school operating purposes; if machinery is used to install land tile or to install or implement soil and water conservation techniques on property other than qualified agricultural property, the machinery is exempt only to the extent that it is used on qualified agricultural property. "Land tile" means fired clay or perforated plastic tubing that is used as part of a subsurface drainage system for land; "soil and water conservation techniques" means techniques for the conservation of soil and water described in the field office technical guide published by the Natural Resources Conservation Service of the U.S. Department of Agriculture. (Sec. 211.9, M.C.L.);

— the property of an innovations center that is located in a certified technology park and owned or used in the administration of the center by a qualified high-technology business;

— new construction on development property (for three years or until the new construction is no longer located on development property, whichever occurs first). "Development property" is real property on which a residential dwelling, condominium unit, or other residential structure is located, and the dwelling, unit, or structure meets all of the following conditions: (1) it is not occupied and has never been occupied; (2) it is available for sale; (3) it is not leased; and (4) it is not used for any business or commercial purpose. "New construction" means that term as defined in §211.34d, M.C.L., and refers to property not in existence on the immediately preceding tax day and not replacement construction. (Sec. 211.7ss, M.C.L.)

— beginning December 31, 2015, eligible manufacturing personal property that is qualified new personal property for which an exemption is properly claimed is exempt from local property taxes. "New personal property" means property that was initially placed in service in this state or outside of the state after December 31, 2012. "Eligible manufacturing personal property" means personal property that is predominantly used (i.e., more than 50%) in industrial processing or direct integrated support and located on occupied real property. The percentage of use is determined by multiplying the original cost of all personal property by the percentage of use in industrial processing or in direct integrated support, and dividing the resulting product of that calculation by the total original cost of all personal property located on that parcel of real property. The industrial processing use of personal property is based on the percentage of the industrial processing exemption the property is eligible for under the sales and use taxes. A person claiming a qualified new personal property exemption must file an affidavit with the local tax collecting unit by February 10 of the first year in which the person is claiming the exemption. (Sec. 211.9m, M.C.L.)

— beginning December 31, 2015, an exemption from local personal property taxes is allowed for qualified previously existing personal property for which an exemption has been properly claimed. "Qualified previously existing personal property" is eligible manufacturing personal property that has been subject to or exempt from the collection of taxes for the immediately preceding 10 years or would have been subject to or exempt from the collection of taxes if located in the state for the immediately preceding 10 years. "Eligible manufacturing personal property" means personal property that is predominantly used (i.e., more than 50%) in industrial processing or direct integrated support and located on occupied real property. A person may claim the exemption by filing an affidavit with the local tax collecting unit by February 10 of the first year in which the person is claiming the exemption. (Sec. 211.9n, M.C.L.)

— commercial and industrial personal property if the combined true cash value of all the property owned by, leased to, or in the possession of the owner or a related entity on December 31 of the immediately preceding year is less than $80,000 in the local tax collecting unit. A taxpayer may claim the exemption by filing an affidavit with the local tax collecting unit in which the property is located by February 10 in each tax year. (Sec. 211.9o, M.C.L.)

CCH Advisory: Exemptions for Business Personal Property

Industrial personal property is exempt from the 18-mill local school property tax and from the 6-mill state education tax, and commercial property is exempt from 12 mills of the 18-mill local school property tax. Personal property taxed under the industrial facilities tax is also exempt from the 6-mill state education tax and the 18-mill local school property tax. (Sec. 211.9k, Sec. 207.564, Sec. 207.564a, Sec. 380.1211, M.C.L.). Industrial personal property does not include a turbine powered by gas, steam, nuclear energy, coal, or oil whose primary purpose is the generation of electricity for sale. (Sec. 380.1211, M.C.L.)

Mineral-producing property: Any mineral-producing property that is subject to the minerals severance tax and any mineral located at an open mine is exempt from the collection of property taxes. The exemption does not apply to the surface property, rights in the surface property, surface improvements, or personal property at the open mine. (Sec. 211.7oo, M.C.L.; Sec. 211.7pp, M.C.L.; Sec. 211.7qq, M.C.L.) (see ¶2204)

Industrial facilities: Industrial facilities in municipal plant rehabilitation districts or industrial development districts may be exempt from tax but are subject to an in lieu industrial facilities tax and may be subject to an exemption application fee. (Sec. 207.561, M.C.L.) Commercial facilities in a commercial redevelopment district may be exempt from tax but are subject to an in lieu annual commercial facilities tax (¶2005).

Housing facilities: A federally financed housing project owned by a nonprofit housing corporation, consumer housing cooperative, or a limited dividend housing corporation is exempt from tax but is subject to an annual municipal service charge for public services in lieu of all taxes. (Sec. 125.1415a, M.C.L.)

Housing owned and operated by a limited dividend housing corporation for occupancy or use solely by elderly or disabled families is exempt from Michigan property taxation. A property owner must claim the exemption on a form prescribed by the Department of Treasury. Property that is used for occupancy or use solely by elderly or disabled families that is eligible for the exemption is not subject to forfeiture, foreclosure, and sale for delinquent taxes for any year in which the property is exempt. The Department of Treasury is allowed to deny an exemption. The department also has standing to appeal issues concerning the tax liability for exempt property in the Michigan Tax Tribunal and all courts of the state. The local tax assessor is required to notify the department, not just the owner, of the exemption's approval or disapproval. The owner of exempt property must notify the local tax collecting unit and the department of any change in the property that would affect the exemption. (Sec. 211.7d, M.C.L.)

The real and personal property of a charitable nonprofit housing organization is exempt from property tax if the property is used for a retail store operated by that organization and engaged exclusively in the sale of donated items suitable for residential housing purposes, the proceeds of which are used for the purposes of the organization. A "charitable nonprofit housing organization" is an organization that is not operated for profit and that is exempt from federal income tax under IRC §501(c)(3), the primary purpose of which is the construction or renovation of residential housing for conveyance to a low-income person. (Sec. 211.7mm, M.C.L.)

Supportive housing property is exempt from the tax levied by a local school district for school operating purposes to the extent provided under the revised school code, if an owner of the property claimed the exemption. An owner is required to rescind the claim of an exemption within 90 days after exempted property is no longer supportive housing property. Supportive housing property is real property certified as supportive housing property under an applicable statutory provision.

(Sec. 211.7nn, M.C.L.) In addition to other requirements, supportive housing property includes property owned by a nonprofit housing corporation. Supportive housing property must consist of, at most, six individual living units. An individual living unit cannot provide housing for more than six persons. (Sec. 125.1459, M.C.L.)

Multifamily housing facilities, not including land, may be exempt from tax. The increase in value of an existing facility that has been or is being converted to a multifamily housing facility may also be exempt. Such facilities are, however, subject to an annual commercial housing facilities tax. (Sec. 207.606, M.C.L.)

CCH Note: Housing Corporation Not Entitled to Charitable Institution Exemption

The Michigan Supreme Court has held that a nonprofit housing corporation was not entitled to a Michigan property tax charitable institution exemption on residential rental properties because the properties were leased to the low-income tenants, and thus, were not occupied by the corporation for purposes of the applicable exemption statute. (*Liberty Hill Housing Corp. v. City of Livonia*, Michigan Supreme Court, No. 131531, April 2, 2008, CCH MICHIGAN TAX REPORTS, ¶401-359)

Principal residences: Principal residences, qualified agricultural or forest property, supportive housing property, property occupied by a public school academy, and industrial personal property are exempt from the 18-mill tax for school operating purposes, except for the number of mills by which an exemption may be reduced for foundation allowance purposes. "Property occupied by a public school academy" means property occupied by a public school academy, urban high school academy, or school of excellence that is used exclusively for educational purposes. (Sec. 380.1211, M.C.L.)

A homeowner may retain a principal residence exemption after moving into a nursing home or assisted living facility if the homeowner manifests an intent to return to his or her home and satisfies certain conditions. (Sec. 211.7cc, M.C.L.)

A property owner may claim a principal residence exemption by filing an affidavit on or before June 1 for the immediately succeeding summer tax levy and all subsequent tax levies or on or before November 1 for the immediately succeeding winter tax levy and all subsequent tax levies. A special formula is used to calculate the taxable value of the principal residence portion of property used as a bed and breakfast. (Sec 211.7cc, M.C.L.)

Generally, a principal residence refers to that portion of a dwelling that is subject to ad valorem taxation and is owned and occupied as a principal residence by the owner of the dwelling or a tenant-stockholder in a cooperative housing corporation. Unoccupied residential property that adjoins a principal residence, cooperative housing property, certain life care facilities, certain portions of a dwelling or unit of an owner that are rented or leased, and all of a property owner's unoccupied timber-cutover property that is adjoining or contiguous to the owner's dwelling also may qualify as principal residences. Contiguity is not broken by a boundary between local tax collecting units, by a road, a right-of-way, or property purchased or taken under condemnation proceedings by a public utility for power transmission lines if the two parcels that are separated by the purchased or condemned property were a single parcel before the sale or condemnation. (Sec. 211.7dd, M.C.L.) See ¶2005 for a discussion of the agricultural property recapture tax.

Property may continue to qualify for a principal residence property tax exemption for three years after it is rented or leased to another person as a residence, if the owner of the dwelling or unit is absent while on active duty in the U.S. Armed Forces and the dwelling or unit otherwise qualifies as the owner's principal residence. The owner must file an affidavit with the assessor of the local tax collecting unit by May 1 attesting that it is his or her intent to occupy the dwelling or unit as a principal residence upon completion of active duty in the Armed Forces. (Sec. 211.7dd, M.C.L.)

In addition, a homeowner may retain an exemption for up to three years on property previously exempt as the homeowner's principal residence if the property is not occupied, is for sale, is not leased or available for lease, and is not used for any business or commercial purpose. A land contract vendor, bank, credit union, or other lending institution is allowed to retain the principal residence exemption as a result of a foreclosure or forfeiture of a recorded instrument or through deed or conveyance in lieu of a foreclosure or forfeiture on the property at the same percentage of exemption that the property previously had if the property is not occupied other than by the person who claimed the exemption immediately before the foreclosure or forfeiture, is for sale, is not leased to any person other than the person who claimed the exemption immediately preceding the foreclosure, and is not used for any business or commercial purpose. The homeowner must file a conditional rescission form on or before May 1 with the local tax collecting unit. A copy must be forwarded to the Department of Treasury. The owner or a land contract vendor, bank, credit union, or other lending institution is also required to verify annually to the local assessor on or before December 31 that the property is eligible for the special exemption. If the homeowner or a land contract vendor, bank, credit union, or other lending institution does not carry out an annual verification, the local assessor will deny the principal residence exemption on the property. (Sec 211.7cc, M.C.L.)

CCH Note: Property Title is Key

The principal residence exemption (aka homestead exemption) can only be claimed if the property is owned by an individual or a grantor trust. Thus, the exemption was denied to taxpayers who voluntarily and purposefully transferred title of the property to an LLC, which was created as part of a complex estate plan that included a trust. The trust was established on the same day that the LLC was organized and, under the LLC's operating agreement, the trust became the LLC's sole member. The property was never conveyed to the trust during the relevant time period and, therefore, the exemption was properly denied. (*Vanderwerp v. Charter Township of Plainfield,* Michigan Court of Appeals, No. 273112, April 22, 2008, CCH MICHIGAN TAX REPORTS, ¶401-363)

CCH Note: Property Needs Only to Be Unoccupied, Not Vacant

In order to qualify for the principal residence exemption (aka homestead exemption), taxpayers' property needed only to be "unoccupied," not "vacant." The Michigan Court of Appeals concluded that these two terms were not synonymous. The exemption provision did not require that contiguous property be vacant or completely devoid of any inanimate objects, contents, or structures to qualify for the principal residence exemption. Instead, the applicable statutory language merely required that the contiguous property be "unoccupied," which meant "without human occupants." The appellate court held that the Michigan Tax Tribunal misinterpreted the exemption provision and committed an error of law when it determined that the taxpayers' 10-acre parcel did not qualify for the principal residence exemption because it contained an abandoned, unimproved, and unused school building and, therefore, was not vacant. No part of the taxpayers' property or abandoned school building was used as a residence or dwelling, and no part of the property or school building had tenants or residents. (*Eldenbrady v. City of Albion,* Michigan Court of Appeals, No. 297735, October 4, 2011, CCH MICHIGAN TAX REPORTS, ¶401-605)

Taxpayers are required to file a rescission form issued by the Department of Treasury with the local tax collecting unit whenever the residence is no longer used a permanent residence. Failure to file such form will subject the taxpayer to back taxes and a penalty. (Sec. 211.7cc, M.C.L.) A Michigan court of appeal has held that filing a letter stating that the taxpayer no longer was residing at the residence was not sufficient to prevent the imposition of back taxes. (*Modzelewski v. Wayne County Treasurer*, Michigan Court of Appeals, No. 257619, March 23, 2006, CCH MICHIGAN TAX REPORTS, ¶401-216)

County treasurers or equalization directors, or assessors of local taxing units are allowed to deny a claim for a principal residence exemption for the current year and the immediately preceding three tax years if the official believes that the underlying property was not the principal residence of the claimant. In addition, a person is not entitled to a principal residence exemption if the person, or his or her spouse, claimed an exemption similar to the Michigan exemption on property owned in another state. This exception does not apply, however, if the person and his or her spouse file separate income tax returns. (Sec. 211.7cc, M.C.L.)

A process has been established by which property owners may file a request with the Michigan Department of Treasury for a property tax principal residence exemption for property owned and occupied by the owner in any year before the three immediately preceding tax years if the PRE was not on the tax roll due to a qualified error on the part of the local tax collecting unit, and the property owner owned and occupied the property within the applicable dates by which an affidavit for a PRE must be filed. A "qualified error" means the same as that term is defined in Sec. 211.53b, M.C.L. If the department approved the request and the exemption then results in an overpayment of tax by the property owner, the department must notify the treasurer of the local tax collecting unit, the county treasurer, and other affected officials. Local records must be corrected to account for the granting of the exemption consistent with procedures established by the department. (Sec. 211.7cc, M.C.L.)

• *Enterprise zone property*

A five-year exemption is available to qualified businesses in enterprise zones created after 1993. An in-lieu tax at a lower rate applies instead (¶2005). A credit is provided against some of the in-lieu taxes.

If an existing eligible business sells or leases exempt new personal property to an acquiring eligible business, the exemption continues for that acquiring eligible business for the duration of the time period specified in the local assessing district's resolution providing the original exemption. The exemption applies to the personal property being purchased or leased by the acquiring eligible business from the existing eligible business and to any new personal property purchased or leased by the acquiring business. The acquiring business is required to conduct business operations similar to those of the original eligible business at the same location. The exemption can continue in effect only if the governing body of the assessing district approves the continuation by adopting a resolution. (Sec. 211.9f, M.C.L.)

New personal property that is eligible manufacturing personal property that is exempt from local personal property taxes on December 31, 2012, remains exempt until the property otherwise becomes eligible for a new tax exemption. (Sec. 211.9f, M.C.L)

• *Renaissance zone property*

With certain exceptions, real and personal property located in a designated Renaissance Zone (RZ) (see ¶204) are exempt from property taxation. Personal property must generally be located in the RZ on tax day and for 50% or more of the immediately preceding tax year. However, personal property located in the RZ for less than 50% of the preceding year may still qualify for exemption if the property will be located in that RZ for not less than 50% of the tax year for which the exemption is claimed and if certain other conditions are satisfied. The RZ exemptions do not apply to special assessments, local levies for the payment of certain obligations, and local school district levies.

The RZ exemptions are available for residential rental property if the rental property is in substantial compliance with all applicable state and local zoning, building, and housing laws and the owner of the property files an affidavit to that effect before December 31 of the immediately preceding tax year or if the qualified local governmental unit in which the property is located determines that the property is in substantial compliance with all applicable state and local zoning, building, and housing laws, ordinances, and codes on December 31 of the immediately preceding tax year.

The exemptions do not apply to real and personal property owned or leased by a casino located in an RZ. A "casino" includes all property associated or affiliated with the operation of a casino, including parking lots, hotels, motels, or retail stores.

Relationship to other incentive programs: An enterprise zone business or industrial, commercial, or utility property located in an RZ is exempt from the specific property taxes levied on those businesses or properties (¶2003, ¶2005) except for special assessments and local levies. Similarly, a Neighborhood Enterprise Zone (NEZ) residential facility that is located in an RZ is exempt from the annual NEZ tax (¶2005).

In downtown development areas in which an RZ has also been designated, the initial assessed value of all taxable property in the area is reduced by the amount by which the current assessed value of the area was reduced in 1997 as a result of the RZ real and personal property tax exemptions, but in no case less than zero.

Except for special assessments and local levies, a technology park facility located in an RZ is exempt from the technology park facilities tax and certain industrial and commercial redevelopment facilities that are located in an RZ are exempt, respectively, from the industrial or commercial facilities tax (¶2005). Also, commercial forestland located in an RZ is exempt from the specific annual tax levied on lands approved as commercial forests.

The tax exemption allowed to certain lessees or users of otherwise tax-exempt property is extended to real property located in an RZ, except for the tax attributable to certain special assessments and local levies.

• *Alternative energy zones*

The board of the Michigan Strategic Fund may designate one renaissance zone as an alternative energy zone. The alternative energy zone must promote and increase the research, development, and manufacture of alternative energy technology as that term is defined in the Michigan Next Energy Authority Act. The zone has a duration not to exceed 20 years as determined by the board. Property located in the alternative energy zone that is classified as commercial real property and that the Michigan Next Energy Authority, with the concurrence of the assessor of the local tax collecting unit, determines is not used to directly promote and increase the research, development, and manufacture of alternative energy technology is not eligible for any exemption, deduction, or credit under the Michigan Renaissance Zone Act. Alternative energy zones are also allowed credits against the Michigan business tax (see ¶1488).

In addition, alternative energy personal property is exempt from Michigan property tax levied after 2002 and before 2013. For purposes of the exemption, "alternative energy personal property" means:

— an alternative energy system;

— an alternative energy vehicle;

— all of the personal property of an alternative energy technology business; or

— the personal property of a business that is not an alternative energy technology business that is used solely for the purposes of researching, developing, or manufacturing an alternative energy technology. (Sec. 207.822, M.C.L.)

To be eligible for the exemption, the property must be certified by the Michigan Next Energy Authority. Within 60 days after receipt of the certification, a local school district or local tax collecting unit may adopt a resolution to not exempt the property from certain local taxes. (Sec. 211.9i, M.C.L.)

• *Pharmaceutical renaissance zone*

The Board of the Michigan Strategic Fund may designate a pharmaceutical renaissance zone to promote the research, development, and manufacturing of pharmaceutical products of an eligible pharmaceutical company. The definition of "eligible pharmaceutical company" is the same as the definition of "eligible taxpayer" for purposes of the drug company research credit (see ¶1113).

• *Industrial facility district property*

Certified industrial facilities are exempt from real and personal property taxes and subject instead to the industrial facilities tax (¶2005). Certification is a tax incentive for new or improved facilities in areas in which facilities are obsolete. Plant rehabilitation districts and industrial development districts may be established by local governments if 50% or more of the State Equalized Valuation (SEV) of the industrial property in the district is obsolete. (Sec. 207.554, M.C.L.)

The certificate for a replacement or new facility is effective December 31 following the date of issuance, and the certificate for a speculative building is effective December 31 following the date it is being used as a manufacturing facility. Special provisions apply if the Commission determines that the cost of the facility exceeds $150 million of state equalized value. (Sec. 207.557a, M.C.L.) The certificate exempts a facility from real and personal property taxes for the period the certificate is in effect. Generally, a certificate remains in force for a period determined by the local governmental unit, ending on the December 31 following not more than 12 years (11 years in certain cases) after the completion of the facility. (Sec. 207.566, M.C.L.)

"Industrial property" includes land improvements, buildings, structures, and other real property, and machinery, equipment, furniture, and fixtures or any part or accessory whether completed or in the process of construction comprising an integrated whole, whose primary purpose and use are the engaging in activities specified in Sec. 207.552(7), M.C.L.

Also exempt from property taxation are those who would be taxed as lessees, users, occupants, or persons in possession of tax-exempt property. The exemption does not apply to the land on which the facility is located or the inventory of the facility.

• *Obsolete property*

A rehabilitated facility for which an obsolete property rehabilitation exemption certificate is in effect, but not the land on which the facility is located or most personal property, is exempt from general property tax, except for school operating taxes and the state education tax. However, these rehabilitated facilities are subject to the obsolete properties tax (¶2005).

The exemption lasts for a period of at least one year but not more than 12 years. No new exemptions may be granted after December 31, 2010, but an exemption then in effect may continue until the expiration of the exemption certificate.

• *Distressed area businesses*

An eligible local assessing district or the board of a Next Michigan Development Corporation that has an eligible local assessing district as a constituent member that contains a distressed area or distressed parcel may adopt a resolution to exempt from Michigan personal property tax all new property owned or leased by an eligible business located in one or more eligible districts or distressed parcels or an eligible Next Michigan business. A Next Michigan Development Corporation may adopt a resolution granting the personal property tax exemption only for new personal property located in a Next Michigan development district. "New personal property" means personal property that was not previously subject to tax or was not previously placed in service by an eligible business claiming an exemption and that is placed in service by an eligible district after a resolution is adopted by the eligible local assessing district or the board of a Next Michigan Development Corporation that has an eligible local assessing district as a constituent member, but excludes personal property located on real property owned by another, including buildings on leased land. An eligible business includes a business engaged primarily in manufacturing, mining, research and development, wholesale trade, office operations, or a business engaged primarily in the operation of a facility that is an authorized business eligible for the tax credits under the Michigan Economic Growth Authority (MEGA) Act (see ¶1112). Casinos, retail establishments, professional sports stadiums or portions of an eligible business used exclusively for retail sales are ineligible for the exemption. A "professional sports stadium" does not include a stadium in existence on June 6, 2000, that is not used by a professional sports team on the date of the adoption of a resolution granting a personal property tax exemption. For purposes of a Next Michigan Development Corporation, an "eligible business" means only an eligible Next Michigan business. (Sec. 211.9f, M.C.L.)

An "eligible district" means an enterprise zone, an industrial development district, a renaissance zone, a brownfield redevelopment zone, an empowerment zone, certain other specified districts and areas, or an area that contains an authorized business eligible for the tax credits under the Michigan Economic Growth Authority (MEGA) Act, or a Next Michigan Development district. If the Michigan State Tax Commission approves the adopted resolution, the exemption will take effect on the December 31 following the resolution. (Sec. 211.9f, M.C.L.)

• *Rehabilitated commercial property*

Certain rehabilitated commercial property in specially designated districts may receive a reduction of Michigan property taxes. Retail supermarkets, grocery stores, produce markets, or delicatessens in an underserved area are treated as qualified facilities for purposes of this reduction/abatement. A "qualified facility" also includes a building or a group of contiguous buildings, a portion of a building or group of contiguous buildings previously used for commercial or industrial purposes, obsolete industrial property, and vacant property that was commercial property within the immediately preceding 15 years. In addition, a "qualified facility" includes certain vacant property that is located in the city of Detroit and from which a previous structure has been demolished and on which commercial property is or will be newly constructed, provided that an application for a certificate had been filed with the city before July 1, 2010. A "qualified facility" also includes a hotel or motel that has additional meeting or convention space that is attached to a convention and trade center that is over 250,000 square feet in size and located in Oakland County. (Sec. 207.842, M.C.L.). See ¶2005 for more details.

• *Conservation organization property*

A Michigan property tax exemption is allowed for real property owned by a qualified conservation organization that was held for conservation purposes and that was open to all residents of the state for educational and recreational use. A "qualified conservation organization" is a nonprofit charitable institution or a charitable trust that meets all the following conditions:

— it is organized or established, as reflected in its articles of incorporation or trust documents, for the purpose of acquiring, maintaining, and protecting nature sanctuaries, nature preserves, and natural areas that predominantly contain natural habitat for fish, wildlife, and plants;

— it is required under its articles of incorporation, bylaws, or trust documents to hold in perpetuity property acquired for the purpose of maintaining and protecting nature sanctuaries, nature preserves, and natural areas in the state, unless the property is no longer suitable for that purpose or the sale of the property is approved by a majority vote of the members or trustees; and

— its articles of incorporation, bylaws, or trust documents prohibit any officer, shareholder, board member, employee, or trustee or one of their family members from benefiting from the sale of property acquired for maintaining and protecting nature sanctuaries, nature preserves, and natural areas. (Sec. 211.7o, M.C.L.)

• *Native American land*

A U.S. Court of Appeals has held that the state of Michigan and its local governments may not impose property tax on land that was allotted to Native Americans by treaty without an expression of "clear intention" by the U.S. Congress to allow such taxation (*United States, on behalf of the Saginaw Chippewa Indian Tribe v. Michigan,* U.S. Court of Appeals for the Sixth Circuit, Nos. 95-1574, 95-1575, 106 F.3d 130, January 22, 1997, pet. for cert. filed June 30, 1997, USSCt, Dkt 97-14; CCH MICHIGAN TAX REPORTS, ¶400-611). The U.S. Supreme Court vacated this decision on June 15, 1998, Dkt. No. 97-14. However, a subsequent court of appeal decision has held that the Michigan General Property Tax Act is not valid as applied to the lands held in fee simple by an Indian community or its members within the exterior boundaries of an Indian reservation (*Keweenaw Bay Indian v. Naftaly,* U.S. Court of Appeals for the Sixth Circuit, No. 05-1952, 452 F.3d 514, June 26, 2006, CCH MICHIGAN TAX REPORTS, ¶401-239, U.S. Supreme Court, Dkt. 06-429, petition for certiorari denied November 27, 2006).

CCH Note: Exemptions Inapplicable to Special Assessments

Lands exempt from real property tax are not also exempt from local special assessments made for police or fire protection services. With the exception of lands owned by the federal, state, or local governments, which are impliedly exempt, land benefited by township police and fire protection services is not exempt from special assessments levied to finance these services unless there is express statutory authority for the exemption (*Opinion* No. 7042, Michigan Attorney General, February 18, 2000; CCH MICHIGAN TAX REPORTS, ¶400-823).

¶2005 Basis and Rate of Tax

Law: Sec. 3, Art. IX, Mich. Const.; Sec. 6, Art. IX, Mich. Const.; Secs. 125.2120—125.2121c, 207.4—207.14, 207.561, 207.566a, 207.712, 207.774, 207.779, 211.8, 211.18, 211.27, 211.27a, 211.44, 211.181, 211.181a, 211.623, 211.624, 211.903, 324.51105, 324.51108, 324.51201, 324.51311, 380.625a, 380.705, 380.1211, 559.231, M.C.L. (CCH MICHIGAN TAX REPORTS, ¶20-115, ¶20-140, ¶20-170, ¶20-180, ¶20-245, ¶20-260, ¶20-270, ¶20-320, ¶20-330, ¶20-405, ¶20-610, ¶20-650, ¶20-700, ¶20-925).

Property is to be assessed at 50% of its true cash value. (Sec. 211.27a, M.C.L.) In valuing real property, the assessor must consider the advantages and disadvantages of location, quality of soil, quantity and value of standing timber, water power and privileges, mines, minerals, quarries and other valuable deposits known to be available. "Cash value" is defined as the usual selling price at the place where the property is located at the time of assessment—the price that could be obtained therefore at private sale, and not at forced or auction sale. (Sec. 211.27, M.C.L.)

Improvements to benefit a specific owner, such as those made to enhance business image, may not be capitalized to determine value if the improvements do not actually increase the potential selling price, the Michigan Supreme Court has ruled (*First Federal Savings and Loan Association of Flint v. City of Flint* (1982, SCt), 415 Mich 702, 329 NW2d 755; CCH MICHIGAN TAX REPORTS, ¶20-605.191).

The value of low-income housing tax credits under IRC Sec. 42 is includible in the true cash value of a low-income apartment complex. (*Huron Ridge, L.P. v. Township of Ypsilanti*, Michigan Court of Appeals, No. 263495, 275 Mich. App. 23, 737 N.W.2d 187, March 27, 2007, CCH MICHIGAN TAX REPORTS, ¶401-291)

In determining true cash value of land being farmed or otherwise put to an income-producing use, the assessor must consider the advantages and disadvantages of the economic income of farm structures and land. True cash value for assessment purposes may include closing expenses incurred in the sale of property rather than net proceeds to a hypothetical buyer (*Saginaw County et al. v. State Tax Commission* (1974, Ct App), 54 MichApp 160, 220 NW2d 706; CCH MICHIGAN TAX REPORTS, ¶200-548), but excludes increases in true cash value attributable to expenditures for normal repairs, replacement, and maintenance until the property is sold.

Property is taxed at the aggregate of county, township, municipal, school, and other district taxes. Generally, the Michigan Constitution limits the total amount of taxes on real and tangible personal property for all purposes in one year to 15 mills on each dollar of assessed valuation. However, qualified electors of a county may approve separate tax limitations for the county and its townships and school districts, the aggregate of which may not exceed 18 mills. A majority of qualified electors may increase the limitation to an aggregate not to exceed 50 mills on each dollar of valuation for a period not to exceed 20 years. (Sec. 6, Art. IX, Mich. Const.)

• *Public utilities*

The personal property and operating real property of public service companies subject to Chapter 207 (Taxation—Other Specific Taxes) are assessed by the state and are taxed at specific rates to be determined by the State Tax Commission; however, the real property of these companies that is not used in business operations remains subject to general property taxes and is assessed locally. (Sec. 207.4, M.C.L.)

The real and personal property having a situs in Michigan and used by the following companies in carrying on their business are subject to the specific tax assessed by the state on public utilities: railroad companies, union station and depot companies, telegraph companies, telephone companies, sleeping car companies, express companies, car loaning companies, stock car companies, refrigerator car companies and fast freight line companies, and all other companies owning, leasing, running, or operating any freight, stock, refrigerator, or any other cars not exclusively the property of any railroad company paying specific taxes upon its rolling stock, over or upon the line or lines of any railroad or railroads in Michigan. (Sec. 207.4, M.C.L.)

The property of other companies not listed above, including natural gas companies, electric light companies, telephone and telegraph companies and waterworks companies, is locally assessed and subject to general property taxes. (Sec. 211.8, M.C.L.)

In determining the true cash value of personal property owned by an electric utility cooperative, the assessor must consider the number of kilowatt hours of electricity sold per mile of distribution line compared to the average number of kilowatt hours of electricity sold per mile of distribution line for all electric utilities. (Sec. 211.27, M.C.L.)

• *Timber and commercial forestlands*

Timber cut from private forest reservations is taxed at 5% of the appraised valuation. (Sec. 324.51311, M.C.L.) Commercial forests are subject to a tax equal to $1.20 per acre. Effective January 1, 2012, the rate for timber cut from commercial reserves is increased 5¢ per acre and will be increased an additional 5¢ every five years thereafter. (Sec. 324.51105, M.C.L.) The tax is reduced by 15¢ per acre if the commercial forestland is subject to a sustainable conservation easement. (Sec. 324.51201, M.C.L.)

Property withdrawn from commercial forestland designation is subject to a withdrawal penalty. A forest owner may withdraw his or her land from the state's commercial forest program without paying the required withdrawal fee and penalty if the following conditions are met:

— evidence is submitted to the Department of Natural Resources (DNR) that the land met the legal requirements to be exempt from ad valorem property tax on tax day for the tax year in which the list application was submitted and approved and that the land would have met the legal requirements for exemption for each year that it was classified as commercial forest under the commercial forests provisions, if the land had not been classified as commercial forest under the commercial forests provisions;

— the application was submitted to the DNR by the same landowner who owned the land on tax day for the tax year in which the application was submitted and who submitted the application for commercial forest determination; and

— the landowner reimburses the state treasurer for the specific tax that was paid by the state treasurer to the county treasurer for each tax year that the land was classified as commercial forest under the commercial forests provisions. (Sec. 324.51108, M.C.L.)

The Department of Natural Resources is allowed to withdraw forestland from the classification as commercial forest if it had been acquired by a federally recognized Indian tribe and the associated property taxes subsequently were preempted under federal law. In this case, the withdrawal also is not subject to the withdrawal application fee or penalty. (Sec. 324.51108, M.C.L.)

In addition, a Michigan property recapture tax is imposed against qualified forest property that was converted by a change in use, and that no longer qualifies for a tax exemption. (Sec. 211.27a, M.C.L.)

CCH Comment: Deadline for Forestland Withdrawal Extended

Michigan has enacted legislation regarding property tax programs for forestland that extends the deadline for taxpayers to withdraw forestland from a classification of commercial forestland in order to enter the Qualified Forest Program. The legislation extends the deadline from June 11, 2014, to September 1, 2015. Prior to the deadline, taxpayers may move to the Qualified Forest Property Program without penalty, under certain conditions. (Act 146, S.B. 59, Laws 2014, effective June 4, 2014)

• *Low-grade iron ore*

The Michigan low-grade iron mining property tax equals the average annual production of low-grade iron ore in gross tons during the preceding five-year period multiplied by 1.1% of the mine value per gross ton. (Sec. 211.623, M.C.L.)

• *Trailer coaches*

The specific tax on trailer coaches in parks is $3 a month. (Sec. 125.1041, M.C.L.)

• *Condominiums*

Condominiums are assessed as individual units rather than by entire projects. Establishment as a condominium is determined by the status on tax day. (Sec. 559.231, M.C.L.)

• *Lessee-user tax*

Lessees and users of tax exempt real property that use the property in a business for profit are subject to tax in the same manner as if the lessees or users were the owners of the property. However, tax is not imposed on lessees or users of the following:

— federal realty for which payments are made in lieu of property taxes;

— real property of state-supported educational institutions;

— real property used as a concession at a public airport, park, market, or similar property;

— realty used in conjunction with a county, community, 4-H, or state fair or certain special events; and

— real property located in a Renaissance Zone, except for the tax attributable to certain special assessments and local levies. (Sec. 211.181, M.C.L.)

Qualified start-up businesses (see ¶1126 and ¶1483) are also exempt from the lessee-user tax, except for the part of the tax attributable to special assessments, debt millages, school enhancement millages, and school building sinking fund millages, provided certain requirements are met. To qualify for the exemption, the start-up business is required to file an affidavit on or before May 1 of any given year stating that the business qualified for the single business tax credit or Michigan Business Tax (MBT) credit for start-up businesses for the last year ending before that date, and permitting the Department of Treasury to release return information concerning that credit. To provide for the exemption, the local governing body, on or before its last meeting in May every year, must adopt a resolution approving the exemption. If the business has received an extension for filing its SBT or MBT return, it may claim the exemption after May 1, provided that the local governing body adopts a resolution approving the exemption for all qualified businesses applying for an extension.

Qualified start-up businesses may not receive the exemption from the lessee-user tax for more than a total of 5 tax years. In addition, an erroneously granted exemption must be corrected for the current tax year and the three immediately preceding tax years.

• *Neighborhood enterprise zone tax*

The Neighborhood Enterprise Zone (NEZ) tax levied on owners of residential property (although leased property located in a mixed use building is exempt if located in a qualified downtown rehabilitation district) located in an enterprise zone and exempted from general property taxes is computed as follows:

— on a new facility, the tax is determined each year by multiplying the state equalized valuation of the facility, not including the land, by one-half of the average rate of taxation imposed on all property on which property taxes were assessed as determined for the immediately preceding calendar year;

— on a rehabilitated facility, the tax is determined each year by multiplying the state equalized valuation of the facility, not including the land, for the tax year immediately preceding the effective date of the neighborhood enterprise zone certificate by the total mills imposed for general property tax purposes for the current year by all taxing units within which the rehabilitated facility is located; and

— on a homestead facility, the tax is the sum of the following: (1) one-half the number of mills levied for operating purposes by the local governmental unit in which the NEZ is located multiplied by the current taxable value of the homestead facility not including the land; (2) one-half the number of mills levied for operating purposes by the county in which the NEZ is located multiplied by the current taxable value of the homestead facility not including the land; and (3) the total number of mills collected under the general property tax provisions for the current year by all taxing jurisdictions within which the homestead facility is located excluding the number of mills levied for operating purposes by the local governmental unit and county in which the facility is located multiplied by the current taxable value of the homestead facility not including the land. (Sec. 207.779, M.C.L.)

In general, the law requires that an application for an NEZ certificate, which entitles the holder to an exemption for the underlying property, must be made before a building permit is issued for new construction or rehabilitation, but the law makes exceptions to this requirement for certain facilities. These exceptions are contained in Sec. 207.774(2), M.C.L.

Applications for a NEZ certificate for new or rehabilitated facilities are made to the State Tax Commission, whereas, applications for the homestead facility are made to the assessors of the local governmental units within which the homestead facilities are located.

• *Industrial facilities tax*

An industrial facilities tax is imposed in lieu of the general property tax on property for which an industrial facilities exemption certificate has been issued. The industrial facilities tax for a new facility or a speculative building for which an exemption certificate becomes effective after 1993 is determined by multiplying the state equalized value of the facility, less land and inventory, by the sum of one-half of the total mills levied for ad valorem taxes for that year by all taxing units within which the facility is located (other than mills levied for school operating purposes by local or intermediate school districts within which the facility is located or mills levied under the State Education Tax Act), plus one-half of the number of mills levied for school operating purposes in 1993. The State Treasurer may exclude one-half or all of the mills levied under the Education Tax Act from the calculation to reduce unemployment, promote economic growth, and increase capital investment in the state. (Sec. 207.564a, M.C.L.)

The amount of the tax for replacement facilities is determined by multiplying the total mills levied as property taxes for the year by all taxing units within which the facility is located by the state equalized valuation of the real and personal property of the obsolete industrial property for the tax year immediately preceding the effective date of the industrial facilities exemption certificate after deducting the state equalized valuation of the land and inventory. (Sec. 207.564, M.C.L.)

If an industrial facilities exemption certificate for a replacement facility, new facility, or speculative building becomes effective after 1995, for a period of time shorter than that generally allowed (normally, 12 years), the owner or lessee of the facility or building may apply for another certificate during the final year in which the original certificate is effective, or within 12 months after the certificate expires, or, as permitted by the local governmental unit, at any time in which the certificate is in effect. A local government's denial of the application may not be appealed. (Sec. 207.566a, M.C.L.)

Local governments may charge an application fee for industrial facilities exemption certificates. The fee may not exceed the lesser of the actual cost of processing the application or 2% of the total property taxes abated during the term that a certificate is in effect. (Sec. 207.555, M.C.L.)

Local governments may also impose an administrative fee on the collection of the industrial facilities tax. The fee, which is limited to 1% of the tax imposed, is calculated in the same manner and at the same rate as the administrative fee imposed by a local government on the collection of general property tax. As with the industrial facilities tax, the administrative fee is paid annually, at the same times, in the same installments, and to the same officer or officers as general property taxes and fees. (Sec. 207.561, M.C.L.)

Speculative buildings, new facilities, or replacement facilities of qualified start-up businesses (see ¶1126 and ¶1483) are exempt from the industrial facility tax, except for the part of the tax attributable to special assessments, debt millages, school enhancement millages, and school building sinking fund millages. The local tax collecting unit must adopt a resolution providing for the exemption under the same terms and conditions specified in the General Property Tax Act, and the exemption is effective for the tax year in which the resolution is adopted. The exemption may be received in nonconsecutive years, but is limited to a total of five tax years.

If a facility is subject to an industrial facilities exemption certificate or a technology park facilities exemption certificate or is certified as a qualified business on December 31, 2012, the portion of the facility that is eligible manufacturing personal property remains subject to the lower specific tax and exempt from local property taxes until the property otherwise becomes eligible for a new tax exemption. (Sec. 207.561a, M.C.L., Sec. 207.712a, M.C.L.)

• *Commercial facilities tax*

The commercial facilities tax is levied on the owner of a new, replacement, or restored facility that has been issued a commercial facilities exemption certificate. The tax on a restored facility is determined by multiplying the total mills levied for the year by all taxing units within which the facility is located by the state equalized valuation of the obsolete commercial property for the tax year immediately preceding the effective date of the exemption certificate after deducting the state equalized valuation of the land and other personal property not exempt from general property taxation. (Sec. 207.662, M.C.L.)

The tax on a new or replacement facility is determined by multiplying the state equalized valuation of the facility, less land and certain personal property, by the sum of one-half of the total mills levied as ad valorem taxes for that year by all taxing units within which the facility is located other than mills levied for school operating purposes by local or intermediate school districts or mills levied under the State Education Tax Act, plus one-half of the number of mills levied for school operating purposes in 1993. (Sec. 207.662, M.C.L.)

• *Obsolete property tax*

The obsolete properties tax is an in-lieu tax applicable to blighted, contaminated, or functionally obsolete property that has been granted a rehabilitation certificate (¶2004) and is based on the taxable value of the facility before rehabilitation and is payable at the same time and to the same officers as general property tax.

Upon application for an exemption from the obsolete properties tax by a qualified start-up business (see ¶1126 and ¶1483), the governing body of a local tax collecting unit may adopt a resolution to exempt a rehabilitated facility of the business from the collection of the tax. A qualified start-up business may receive the obsolete properties tax exemption for up to five nonconsecutive tax years. A qualified business that received the exemption is not exempt from special assessments, ad valorem property taxes levied for the payment of principal and interest on obligations approved by the electors or obligations pledging the unlimited taxing power of a local governmental unit, or certain enhancement millage or sinking fund taxes levied under the Revised School. (Sec. 125.2790, M.C.L.)

• *Agricultural property recapture tax*

An agricultural property recapture tax is imposed on qualified agricultural property if it is converted to a nonagricultural use. Property is converted by a change in use if, prior to a transfer of qualified agricultural property, the purchaser files a notice of intent to rescind the qualified agricultural property exemption with the local tax collecting unit. (Sec. 211.1002, M.C.L., Sec. 211.1003, M.C.L.)

The amount of the recapture tax is the benefit received on the property during the benefit period. This "benefit" is defined as the sum of the number of mills levied on the property in each year of the benefit period, multiplied by the difference in each year between the true cash taxable value of the property and the property's taxable value as determined with the annual assessment cap. The "benefit period" is defined as the period between the date of the first exempt transfer and the conversion by a change in use, not to exceed the seven years preceding the conversion by a change in use. (Sec. 211.1002, M.C.L.)

If recapture tax is imposed due to a change in use, the tax is the obligation of the person who owned the property at the time the property was converted by a change in use. If recapture tax is imposed because a purchaser files a notice of intent to rescind the qualified agricultural property exemption, the tax is the obligation of the person who owned the property prior to the transfer and the recapture tax is due when the instruments transferring the property are recorded with the register of deeds. (Sec. 211.1003, M.C.L.)

• *Conservation tax*

Counties are authorized to levy a real property tax of up to one mill for not more than 20 years and to remit the proceeds of the tax to a conservation district established in the county. Imposition of the tax must be approved by voters. (Sec. 46.22, M.C.L.)

• *Technology park facilities tax*

The technology park facilities tax is levied annually in lieu of the property tax on the owner or user of a facility covered by an exemption certificate. The tax is determined by multiplying the state equalized valuation of a facility, less land and inventory, by the sum of one-half of the total mills levied as ad valorem taxes for that year by all taxing units within which the facility is located, other than mills levied by local or intermediate school districts for school operating purposes or mills levied under the State Education Tax Act, plus one-half of the number of mills levied for school operating purposes in 1993. (Sec. 207.712, M.C.L.)

Facilities of a qualified start-up businesses (see ¶1126, ¶1483) that otherwise would be subject to the technology park facilities tax are exempt from the tax, except for the part of the tax attributable to special assessments, debt millages, school enhancement millages, and school building sinking fund millages. The local tax collecting unit must adopt a resolution providing for the exemption and the exemption is effective for the tax year in which the resolution is adopted. The exemption may be received in nonconsecutive years, but is limited to a total of five tax years. (Sec. 207.712, M.C.L.)

• *Education and school taxes*

State education tax: A state education tax is levied on all taxable property at the rate of 6 mills. (Sec. 211.903, M.C.L.)

Tax for school operating purposes: In order to receive school aid act funds, school district boards are required to levy taxes at a rate not to exceed 18 mills or the number of mills levied in 1993, whichever is less, for school operating purposes. (Sec. 380.1211, M.C.L.) Also, intermediate school districts may levy property taxes for operating purposes at a rate not to exceed 1.5 times the number of mills allocated to a district for those purposes in 1993. In addition, intermediate school districts may levy a regional enhancement property tax to enhance funding for local school district operating purposes at a rate not to exceed 3 mills, subject to voter approval. (Sec. 380.625a, M.C.L., Sec. 380.705, M.C.L.)

CCH Advisory: Exemptions for Business Personal Property

Industrial personal property is exempt from the 18-mill local school property tax and from the 6-mill state education tax, and commercial property is exempt from 12 mills of the 18-mill local school property tax. Personal property taxed under the industrial facilities tax is also exempt from the 6-mill state education tax and the 18-mill local school property tax. (Secs. 211.9k, 207.564, 207.564a, 380.211, M.C.L.)

• *Local administration fees*

Local property tax collecting units in Michigan may impose a property tax administration fee of not more than 1% of the total tax bill per parcel.

¶2006 Credits

Law: Secs. 207.13, 207.13b M.C.L. (CCH MICHIGAN TAX REPORTS, ¶20-905).

The only property tax credits allowed by Michigan apply to railroad companies and to public utilities for broadband investments. There is, however, a personal income tax and a Michigan business tax credit for property taxes paid (see ¶303 and ¶1482).

• *Railroad companies*

A railroad company is allowed a nonrefundable tax credit equal to 25% of the amount paid for maintenance or improvement of rights of way, including items, except depreciation, in the official maintenance-of-way and capital track accounts of the company in the state during the preceding calendar year. Generally, to qualify for the full 25% credit, a company must show that the highest priority of expenditures for the maintenance or improvement of rights of way has been given to rail lines handling hazardous materials, especially those located in urban or residential areas. (Sec. 207.13, M.C.L.)

Eligible companies that own, lease, run, or operate freight, stock, refrigerator, or other railcars subject to Michigan property tax are allowed a nonrefundable credit against Michigan property tax equal to one or more of the following: (1) the expenses incurred in Michigan during the preceding calendar year to maintain or improve an eligible company's qualified rolling stock; and (2) 75% of the expenses incurred in Michigan during the preceding calendar year for maintenance or improvement of rights of way, including those items, except depreciation, in the official maintenance-of-way and capital track accounts of the eligible company. (Sec. 207.13, M.C.L.)

The rolling stock may not be the exclusive property of a railroad company that pays property tax on its rolling stock. The sum of this credit and the existing railroad company credit may not exceed the taxpayer's property tax liability. (Sec. 207.13, M.C.L.)

"Eligible company" means railroad companies, union station and depot companies, sleeping car companies, express companies, car loaning companies, stock car companies, refrigerator car companies, fast freight line companies, and all other companies owning, leasing, running, or operating any freight, stock, refrigerator, or any other cars not the exclusive property of a railroad company paying taxes upon its rolling stock over or upon the line or lines of any railroad in Michigan. (Sec. 207.13, M.C.L.)

• *Public utilities—broadband investments*

A taxpayer is allowed a credit against the Michigan property tax imposed on public utilities for expenditures for eligible broadband investments. To receive the credit, the taxpayer must make expenditures to purchase and install eligible equipment. Eligible equipment is property placed in service in Michigan for the first time with information carrying capability in excess of 200 kilobits per second in both directions. (Sec. 207.13b, M.C.L.)

In general, the credit is equal to 6% of eligible expenditures incurred in the calendar year immediately preceding the tax year for which the credit is claimed. The credit may not exceed the greater of 12% of the taxpayer's tax liability for that year or 100% of the credit the taxpayer received in the immediately preceding tax year. (Sec. 207.13b, M.C.L.)

After the equipment credit described above is determined, the taxpayer is allowed a credit against the remaining property tax liability equal to the maintenance fee costs (see ¶2209), less the equipment credit. Excess credit amounts may not be refunded but may be carried forward until used up. (Sec. 207.13b, M.C.L.)

¶2007 Assessment Procedure and Equalization

Law: Sec. 3, Art. IX, Mich. Const.; Secs. 209.1—209.105, 211.27, 211.27a, 211.30c, 211.34, 211.34c, M.C.L. (CCH MICHIGAN TAX REPORTS, ¶20-605, ¶20-610, ¶20-620, ¶20-625, ¶20-630, ¶20-640, ¶20-645—¶20-720, ¶89-228).

Township supervisors and city assessors assess all property other than railroad, car, telegraph and telephone property, which is assessed by the State Tax Commission. Taxpayers are required to file annual reports listing their tangible personal property.

Property is generally assessed at 50% of its true cash value. Cash value is based on the selling price that could be obtained at a private sale. However, the purchase price paid in a transfer of property is not the presumptive true cash value of the property transferred. In determining the true cash value, an assessing officer must assess the property using the same valuation method used to value all other property of that same classification in the assessing jurisdiction. (Sec. 211.27, M.C.L.; Sec. 211.27a, M.C.L.)

For purposes of keeping local property taxes affordable for low-income families who buy homes from charitable organizations, the purchase price paid in a transfer of eligible nonprofit housing property from a charitable nonprofit housing organization to a low-income person that occurs after December 31, 2010, is the presumptive true cash value of the property transferred. In the year following the year in which the transfer takes place and each subsequent year, the taxable value of the eligible nonprofit housing property must be adjusted as provided in Sec. 211.27a, M.C.L. Under that provision, the taxable value of a parcel of property is the lesser of its current state equalized valuation or its taxable value in the preceding year minus any losses, multiplied by the lesser of 1.05 or the inflation rate, plus all additions. Upon a transfer of ownership, the property's taxable value for the year following the year of transfer is the property's state equalized valuation for the calendar year following the transfer. (Sec. 211.27(7), M.C.L.)

• *Equalization*

The Boards of Commissioners and the State Tax Commission must equalize separately each class of real property (¶2002) and taxable personal property in a township, city, or county by adding to or deducting from its valuation an amount that will produce a sum that represents the proportion of true cash value established by the legislature. (Sec. 209.4, M.C.L.)

A city or township whose state equalized valuation exceeds its assessed valuation by any amount must reduce its maximum millage rate so that property taxes do not exceed those that would have been levied on its assessed valuation. The millage reduction must permanently reduce the maximum rate authorized by law. The reduced maximum authorized rate must equal the product of the immediately preceding year's reduced maximum authorized rate multiplied by the current year's millage reduction fraction as adjusted for expired millage and for newly authorized millage.

The State Tax Commission sets the total assessed valuation for each county, rather than an assessment ratio. Occasionally a percentage increase is ordered for all property in the state in recognition of natural inflation. It is the duty of each County Board of Commissioners to spread the equalized values.

Constitutional limitation on valuation increases: The annual increase in the state equalized valuation of property is limited to the increase in the General Price Level in the immediately preceding year or 5%, whichever is less, until ownership of a parcel of property is transferred. When a transfer occurs, the parcel is reassessed at the applicable proportion of its current true cash value. (Sec. 3, Art. IX, Mich. Const.)

Practice Note: Transfers of Ownership Triggering Reassessment

A city was constitutionally permitted to partially uncap a nonprofit housing cooperative's Michigan property tax assessment based on transfers of a number of membership units because the transactions were transfers of ownership. The Michigan Constitution (Art. 9, Sec. 3) provided for a cap on the increase in the taxable value of each parcel of property until ownership of the parcel was transferred. When ownership was transferred, the parcel was to be assessed at the applicable proportion of current true cash value. When a member moved and a new member purchased a share of stock in the cooperative, there was a conveyance of a member's ownership interest in the cooperative. This event constituted a transfer of ownership, which triggered the uncapping of the taxable value of the property under the Michigan Constitution. (*New England Towne Houses Cooperative, Inc. v. Roseville*, Michigan Court of Appeals, No. 251577, February 24, 2005; CCH MICHIGAN TAX REPORTS, ¶401-141).

A statute provides a listing of certain types of transfers that will not trigger a reassessment. (Sec. 211.27a(7), M.C.L.) Among these exceptions to the transfer reassessment requirement is a transfer between legal entities if the entities involved are commonly controlled. A Department of Treasury administrative bulletin defines three categories of groups that can qualify as entities under common control: (1) parent-subsidiary entities under common control; (2) brother-sister entities under common control; and (3) a combination of entities under common control. The groups that qualify under these categories, however, have to be engaged in business or trade activities. (*Revenue Administrative Bulletin 1989-48*, Department of Treasury, May 31, 1989, CCH MICHIGAN TAX REPORTS, ¶201-591) A Michigan court of appeal applied the reasoning of RAB 1989-48, to deny the transfer of ownership for entities under common control when a trust transferred real property to a legal entity comprised of two members, each holding a 50% interest. The court reasoned that because a trust is not a legal entity engaged in business activity it could not qualify for the entities under common control exemption from the change of ownership reassessment. (*C & J Investments of Grayling, LLC v. City of Grayling*, Michigan Court of Appeals, No. 270989, November 13, 2007, CCH MICHIGAN TAX REPORTS, ¶401-335)

A transfer of ownership that results in uncapping includes transfers by will to a deceased owner's devisees or by intestate succession to a deceased owner's heirs. Title to a decedent's real property passes at the time of his or her death, whether by will or by intestate succession. However, the Michigan Attorney General has opined, if the land that passes at the time of death is subject to a conservation easement or is eligible for a federal charitable income tax deduction as a qualified conservation contribution, then the transfer of land, but not buildings or structures located on the land, is exempt from uncapping. In the case of a conservation easement or a deductible qualified conservation contribution that was created after the death of a property owner, the uncapping of the property's taxable value will not be avoided for the transfer that occurred at death. Further, qualified agricultural property is exempt from taxes levied for school operating purposes, and a transfer of such property is exempt from the uncapping of its taxable value. (*Opinion No. 7233*, Michigan Attorney General, June 16, 2009, CCH MICHIGAN TAX REPORTS, ¶401-429)

A revised case memo issued by the State Tax Commission discusses the Michigan Supreme Court's decision in *Klooster v. City of Charlevoix*, No. 140423, March 10, 2011,

CCH MICHIGAN TAX REPORTS, ¶401-572, regarding the interpretation of Code §211.27a(7)(h), M.C.L., and, specifically, which conveyances involving a joint tenancy are or are not transfers of ownership for local property tax assessment purposes. The Michigan Supreme Court found that the death of the only other joint tenant is a conveyance under the general property tax provisions and does not require a written instrument beyond the deed initially creating the joint tenancy. The memo provides the following conclusions on how to determine if a property should uncap. If a joint tenancy is created by an "original owner" and if the "original owner" or his or her spouse are also co-tenants in the joint tenancy, then the taxable value does not uncap. If a "successive" joint tenancy is created and an "original owner" or his or her spouse continue as co-tenants in the "successive" joint tenancy, then the taxable value does not uncap. If a joint tenancy is terminated by the death of an "original owner" or by the "original owner" making a conveyance, resulting in the ownership again being a sole ownership, and if the sole owner is an "initial joint tenant," then the taxable value does not uncap. If a joint tenancy is terminated by conveyance and the sole owner after the termination is an "initial joint tenant," then the taxable value does not uncap. (*STC Klooster Memo,* Michigan State Tax Commission, June 9, 2011, CCH MICHIGAN TAX REPORTS, ¶401-592)

Transfer of residential property to close relatives: Beginning December 31, 2013, for purposes of determining the taxable value of property, a transfer of ownership does not include a transfer of residential real property if the transferee is related to the transferor by blood or affinity to the first degree and the use of the residential real property does not change following the transfer. "Residential real property" is property classified as residential real property under Sec. 211.34c, M.C.L. (Sec. 211.27a(7)(s), M.C.L.)

Taxable value—Limitation on annual increase: The taxable value of a parcel of property is the lesser of the following:

— the property's taxable value in the immediately preceding year minus any losses, multiplied by the lesser of 1.05 or the inflation rate, plus all additions; or

— the property's current state equalized valuation. (Sec. 211.27a, M.C.L.)

A developer's installation of public service improvements on the real property are not considered "additions" exempt from the annual increase limitation. (*Toll Northville, LTD v. Township of Northville,* Michigan Supreme Court, No. 132466, February 5, 2008, CCH MICHIGAN TAX REPORTS, ¶401-354)

Reduced values: Generally, if a taxpayer has the assessed value or taxable value reduced as a result of a protest to a township board of review or if a taxpayer has the State Equalized Valuation (SEV), assessed value, or taxable value of property reduced pursuant to a final order of the Tax Tribunal, the assessor is required to use the reduced amount or reduced SEV as the basis for calculating the assessment in the immediately succeeding year. However, this duty is inapplicable to changes in assessment due to protests regarding claims of exemption. Also, the taxable value of property in a tax year immediately succeeding a transfer of ownership is the property's state equalized valuation in the year following the transfer. (Sec. 211.30c, M.C.L.)

Circuit court jurisdiction over State Tax Commission classification decisions: The Michigan Supreme Court has ruled that circuit courts have subject matter jurisdiction over appeals from State Tax Commission (STC) property classification decisions because they constitute final decisions that are quasi-judicial and affect private rights and, therefore, they fall within the ambit of Art. 6, §28, of the Michigan Constitution, which guarantees judicial review. The Legislature lacked the authority to abolish the right to judicial review by enacting a statute. As a consequence, the court declared the final sentence of Code Sec. 211.34c(6), M.C.L., unconstitutional because it denied appeal in the courts of STC classification decisions and the Legislature did not provide other means for judicial review of STC classification decisions. Further, nothing in the Tax Tribunal Act granted the Michigan Tax Tribunal jurisdiction over STC classification decisions. Aside from requiring a final quasi-judicial decision that affected private rights, Art. 6, § 28 provided that a decision must be subject to direct review by the courts "as provided by law." The Michigan Supreme Court held that the phrase "as provided by law" did not grant the Legislature the authority to circumvent the protections that the section guaranteed. If it did, those protections would lose their strength because the Legislature could render the entire provision as mere surplusage. See ¶2007. (*Midland Cogeneration Venture Limited Partnership v. Naftaly*, Michigan Supreme Court, Nos. 140814, 140817, 140818, 140819, 140820, 140821, 140822, 140823, and 140824, 489 Mich. 83, May 23, 2011, CCH MICHIGAN TAX REPORTS, ¶401-572)

¶2008 Returns and Payment

Law: Secs. 111.11, 125.1043, 207.6, 207.7, 207.8, 207.13, 207.14, 211.8a—211.8c, 211.18, 211.19, 211.44—211.46, 211.51, 211.78a, M.C.L. (CCH MICHIGAN TAX REPORTS, ¶20-260, ¶20-335, ¶20-645, ¶20-700, ¶89-102, ¶89-176, ¶89-204, ¶89-206).

Assessing officers are required to ascertain the taxable property of their assessing districts and the persons to whom it should be assessed. In order to make this determination, the assessing officer requires all persons having personal property in their possession to make returns. Returns are due on or before February 20 of each year. (Sec. 211.19, M.C.L.)

Reports of railroad, car, telegraph, and telephone companies are due between January 1 and March 31 if annual gross receipts exceed $1 million, and between January 1 and March 15 if annual gross receipts do not exceed $1 million. (Sec. 207.6, M.C.L.) Sleeping car company reports are due between January 1 and March 31. (Sec. 207.7, M.C.L.) Reports of trailer coach park owners are due on or before the fifth day of each month. (Sec. 125.1043, M.C.L.)

If the last day in a year that taxes are due and payable before being returned as delinquent is a Saturday, Sunday, or legal holiday, then the last day taxes are due and payable before being returned as delinquent is the next business day. Taxes levied in the preceding year that remain unpaid must be returned as delinquent on the next business day. (Sec. 211.78a, M.C.L.)

• *Payment of taxes*

General taxes, including township, county, and school taxes, are payable to township and city treasurers. Village taxes are collectible by the village treasurer according to his or her warrant. Township taxes are payable on or before February 14; village taxes on or before September 14; and fourth class city taxes are payable in two installments, January 10, and September 15.

County property taxes are due by September 15th.

Specific taxes on trailer coaches are payable by the park licensees to municipal treasurers within five days after each month.

Taxes on railroad, car, telegraph, and telephone property are payable to the State Treasurer on July 1.

Upon the receipt of the tax roll (on or before December 1), the township treasurer must proceed to collect the township, county, and school taxes. (Sec. 211.44(1), M.C.L.) The law provides for the township treasurer to remain in the office of the township treasurer from 9:00 a.m. to 5:00 p.m. on the following days: (1) at least one business day between December 25 and December 31, unless the township has an arrangement with a local financial institution to receive taxes on behalf of the township treasurer and to forward the payment to the township on the next business day; (2) the last day that taxes are due before becoming delinquent, and (3) for the collection of a summer tax levy, the last day taxes are due before interest is added. (Sec. 211.44(2), M.C.L.) Interest must be added to taxes collected after September 14 at the rate of 1% per month on delinquent property tax levies that became a lien in the same year. However, if September 14 is on a Saturday, Sunday, or legal holiday, the last day taxes are due and payable before interest is added is the next business day. Interest must then be added to taxes that remained unpaid on the following business day. (Sec. 211.44a, M.C.L.)

The statutory provision (Sec. 211.44, M.C.L.) authorizing addition of a 1% administration fee to taxes collected by township treasurers before February 14 was declared constitutional by the Michigan Supreme Court in *Rouge Parkway Associates et al. v. City of Wayne et al.* (1985, SCt), 423 Mich 411, 377 NW2d 748; CCH MICHIGAN TAX REPORTS, ¶201-209. The fee may also be imposed on taxes paid after February 14 and before March 1. There is an additional penalty of 3% on general taxes paid on or after February 14, and an administration fee of 4%, plus interest of 1% a month, is added on taxes collected on or after March 1.

Interest of 10% a year is added from July 1 to December 1 on taxes levied on a July roll unpaid by November 15. (Sec. 111.11, M.C.L.) Railroad, car, telegraph, and telephone company taxes bear interest at 1% a month from August 1 unless one-half of the taxes are paid before August 1, in which case the remaining taxes may be paid by December 1 without interest. (Sec. 207.14, M.C.L.) There is a penalty of $500 a day for failure to file an annual report. (Sec. 207.8, M.C.L.)

Qualified taxpayers may, until the later of September 15 or the time the summer property tax would otherwise become subject to a penalty for late payment, defer the summer taxes due to a city, village, or township until the following February 15 by filing notice of intent to defer July taxes with the treasurer of the local government unit. For purposes of this deferment, a "qualified taxpayer" is an eligible serviceperson, veteran, totally and permanently disabled person, paraplegic, quadriplegic, blind person, eligible surviving spouse, or a person who is 62 years old or older, or unremarried surviving spouses of persons who were 62 years of age or older at the time of death, whose total maximum household income for the prior tax year does not exceed $40,000. Property classified or used as agricultural real property may also claim a deferment of summer property taxes if the gross receipts of the agricultural or horticultural operations in the previous year or the average gross receipts in the previous three years are not less than the owner's household income for the previous year or the combined household incomes in the previous year of the individual members of a limited liability company or partners of a partnership that own the agricultural real property. A limited liability company or partners of the partnership may claim a deferment only if the individual members of the limited liability company or partners of the partnership qualified for a deferment before they formed the limited liability company or partnership. (Sec. 211.51, M.C.L.)

¶2009 Administration—Penalties, Refunds

Law: Secs. 205.28, 205.731 *et seq.*, 211.29—211.30c, 211.53a, M.C.L. (CCH MICHIGAN TAX REPORTS, ¶89-136, ¶89-202, ¶89-206, ¶89-208, ¶89-224, ¶89-234).

Failure to pay the tax on time or the nonpayment of any tax may cause the imposition of such penalties as addition of interest to the tax, seizure and sale of real and/or personal property, and suit by the township treasurer. However, interest could not be charged on an increased assessment of personal property taxes from the date of a Michigan Tax Tribunal decision until the due date of the tax bill (*Xerox Corp. v. Oakland County* (1991, Ct App), 191 MichApp 433, 478 NW2d 702; CCH MICHIGAN TAX REPORTS, ¶400-164).

CCH Comment: A Foreclosure Notice Requirement Discussed

The Michigan Supreme Court has ruled that a taxpayer's right to due process under the U.S. Constitution was satisfied by the mailing of tax delinquency and redemption notices to the taxpayer's address of record as required by the Michigan property tax statutes, even though the notices were sent to the taxpayer's former address and the notice of hearing was returned as undeliverable. The Department of Treasury was not obligated to undertake an investigation to see if a new address for the taxpayer could be located (*Smith v. Cliffs on the Bay Condominium Association,* Michigan Supreme Court, No. 111587, 463 Mich. 420, 617 N.W.2d 536, October 10, 2000; CCH MICHIGAN TAX REPORTS, ¶400-860).

However, in another case, the Supreme Court held that the notice was inadequate when there were two property owners and the Department only sent a notice to one of the taxpayers even though the Department was aware that there were two separate owners who had different mailing addresses. (*Sidun v. Wayne County Treasurer*, Michigan Supreme Court, No. 131905, July 2, 2008, CCH MICHIGAN TAX REPORTS, ¶401-377)

A taxpayer who pays excessive taxes due to a clerical error or mutual mistake of fact made by the assessor and the taxpayer may recover the excess so paid by suit commenced within three years from the date of payment. Alternatively, if the excess payment is due to clerical or mutual mistake and verified by the local assessing officer and approved by the board of review, the board of review may file an affidavit within 30 days relative to the error or mistake with the proper assessing officials. Then, a rebate of the overpayment is made. A correction may only be made by the board of review during the year in which the error was made or in the following year, unless the correction relates to the granting of a personal residence exemption. In instances involving a personal residence exemption, a correction may be made for the year in which the appeal is filed and the three immediate preceding years.

For a definition of "clerical error" or "mutual mistake of fact", see Sec. 211.53b(7).

CCH Note: Mutual Mistake of Fact

The Michigan Supreme Court has ruled that a mutual mistake of fact can arise as a result of a taxpayer's misreporting of information on a personal property statement. The personal property statements erroneously overstated the amount of the company's taxable property, including reporting the same property twice. Local tax assessors relied on the company's personal property statements as accurate when calculating the company's tax liability. This resulted in excessive assessments that were paid in full. The Supreme Court held that in such a situation both the taxpayer and assessors were operating under a mistake of fact as to the taxpayer's property subject to tax. (*Ford Motor Co. v. City of Woodhaven*, Michigan Supreme Court, Nos. 127422, 127423, 127424, 475 Mich. 425, 716 N.W.2d 247, June 28, 2006, CCH MICHIGAN TAX REPORTS, ¶401-240)

For assessments found by the Tax Tribunal to have been unlawful, interest is paid from the date of payment to the date of judgment, and the judgment will bear interest until the date of its payment. However, no interest is payable on interest unlawfully paid (see *Xerox Corp.* above).

• *Appeals to Tax Tribunal*

The Tax Tribunal has the exclusive and original jurisdiction regarding proceedings for direct review of a final decision, finding, ruling, determination or order of an agency relating to assessment, valuation, rates, special assessments, allocation or equalization under property tax laws. For purposes of appeal to the courts, the Tax Tribunal is the final administrative agency. However, except as noted below, the Tax Tribunal may not exercise jurisdiction unless a taxpayer protests the assessment to the applicable board of review, unless doing so can be shown to be futile (see, for example, *Primestar, Inc. v. Township of Niles,* Michigan Court of Appeals, Nos. 234855, 235147, 235148, and 235149, May 1, 2003, CCH MICHIGAN TAX REPORTS, ¶ 401-026).

Business property tax appeals may be brought directly to the Tax Tribunal without first appealing the assessment, valuation, or classification to the local Board of Review. (Sec. 205.735a, M.C.L.)

A taxpayer must file a petition with the Tax Tribunal by May 31 of the tax year involved in assessments involving commercial real property, industrial real property, developmental real property, commercial personal property, industrial personal property, or utility personal property. The filing deadline is July 31 for assessment disputes involving agricultural real property, residential real property, timber-cut-over real property, or agricultural personal property. In all other matters, the jurisdiction of the Tax Tribunal is invoked by filing a written petition within 60 days after the final decision, ruling, or determination. (Sec. 205.735a, M.C.L.)

• *Disclosure of information*

A person is permitted to disclose tax information if the disclosure is required for proper Michigan property tax administration purposes. A person who receives the information is prohibited from willfully disclosing it for any purpose other than for property tax administration purposes and is guilty of a felony for violating this prohibition. (Sec. 205.28, M.C.L.)

PART VII

MISCELLANEOUS TAXES

CHAPTER 21

EMPLOYMENT SECURITY TAX
(Unemployment Insurance)

¶2101 The Law

Michigan's Unemployment Insurance Tax is covered in the Michigan Employment Security Act. Comprehensive coverage of unemployment insurance is provided in Wolters Kluwer, CCH Unemployment/Social Security Reporter. For more information go to CCHGroup.com or contact an account representative at 888-CCH-REPS (888-224-7377).

MISCELLANEOUS TAXES

CHAPTER 22

OTHER STATE TAXES

¶2201 Scope of Chapter

This chapter outlines briefly the Michigan taxes not previously covered. Its purpose is to indicate who is subject to each tax, who is exempt, the basis and rate of the tax, report and payment requirements, and by whom the tax is administered.

The Taxpayer Bill of Rights, discussed at ¶702, applies to all taxes administered by the Department of Treasury.

¶2202 Alcoholic Beverage Taxes

Michigan's Alcoholic Beverage Tax is covered in MCL Chapter 436 Alcoholic Beverages. Current tax rates are:

— Beer . . . . $6.30 per barrel

— Wine (16% or less) and manufactured from grapes or fruits not grown in Michigan . . . . $0.135 per liter

— Wine (more than 16%) . . . . $0.20 per liter

— Spirits (off-premises) . . . . 8% base, plus 5.85%

— Spirits (on-premises) . . . . 8% base, plus 4.00%

— Mixed-spirit . . . . $0.48 per liter

Comprehensive coverage of taxation of alcohol, as well as licensing and distribution information is provided in Wolters Kluwer, CCH Liquor Control Law Reporter. For more information go to CCHGroup.com or contact an account representative at 888-CCH-REPS (888-224-7377).

¶2203 Motor Fuel Taxes

Law: Secs. 207.211 *et seq.*, 207.1001 *et seq.*, 207.1152, 259.203, 324.21508 *et seq.*, 324.71101 *et seq.*, M.C.L. (CCH MICHIGAN TAX REPORTS, ¶40-001—¶40-011).

The Michigan Motor Fuel Tax Act imposes a tax on gasoline, diesel motor fuel, and liquefied petroleum gas. In addition, separate laws impose taxes on aircraft fuel, motor carrier fuel, and recreational fuel. All refined petroleum products that are sold for resale or consumption in Michigan are also subject to an environmental protection regulatory fee. The tax imposed on gasoline is in lieu of all other taxes except for Michigan general sales and use tax. The tax imposed on diesel fuel is in lieu of all other taxes except for Michigan general sales and use tax and the motor carrier fuel tax.

Effective January 1, 2017, Michigan legislation enacted as part of a Road Funding Package makes changes to the Motor Fuel Tax Act by: (1) increasing the motor fuel and diesel fuel tax rates, (2) creating an annual adjustment to the rates, (3) applying the motor fuel tax to alternative fuels, (4) creating alternative fuel licenses, and (5) increasing penalties for the use of dyed diesel fuel. Additionally, the legislation makes complementary amendments to the Motor Carrier Fuel Tax Act. (Act 176 (H.B. 4738), Laws 2015, and Act 178 (H.B. 4616), Laws 2015)

Reciprocal agreement: Michigan is a member of the International Fuel Tax Agreement (IFTA). As a result, Michigan-based motor carriers file one combined fuel tax report with the state rather than a separate report for each jurisdiction in which they operate. If there is any conflict between the provisions of IFTA and the Michigan Motor Carrier Fuel Tax Act, the IFTA provisions will prevail. (Sec. 207.212a, M.C.L.)

Exemptions: The following motor fuel is exempt from tax:

— gasoline or diesel fuel sold directly by the supplier to the federal government, state government, or a political subdivision of the state for use in a motor vehicle owned and operated or leased and operated by the federal or state government or political subdivision;

— motor fuel sold directly by the supplier to a nonprofit, private, parochial, or denominational school, college, or university, and used in a school bus owned and operated or leased and operated by the educational institution that is used in the transportation of students;

— fuel for which proof of export is available in the form of a terminal-issued destination state shipping paper;

— gasoline removed from a pipeline or marine vessel by a taxable fuel registrant with the IRS as a fuel feedstock user;

— motor fuel sold by a supplier to a licensed end user who used the fuel for an exempt purpose;

— motor fuel sold for use in aircraft, but only if the purchaser paid the aircraft fuel tax, and was registered with the Department of Treasury;

— aviation fuel that is purchased to formulate Leaded Racing Fuel (LRF) (the exemption applies to the aviation fuel tax as well); and

— motor fuel acquired by the end user outside Michigan and brought into the state in the fuel supply tank of a motor vehicle that was not a commercial motor vehicle, but only if the fuel is retained within and consumed from that fuel supply tank. (Sec. 207.1030, M.C.L.)

Gasoline and diesel fuel used in the following watercraft is exempt from the recreational fuel tax:

— used for commercial fishing;

— used by the Boy Scouts;

— owned by the state or its political subdivisions or the federal government;

— used or owned by any railroad company or railroad car ferry company;

— used in trade, including a person's chief business or means of livelihood; or

— used in interstate or foreign commerce. (Sec. 324.71101, M.C.L.)

The motor carrier fuel tax does not apply to commercial motor vehicles owned and operated by the federal government, the state, and nonprofit schools. A public utility with more than 500,000 customers in Michigan is exempt from the environmental protection fee on petroleum used for the generation of steam or electricity. (Sec. 324.21508, M.C.L.)

Crankcase oils, old and contaminated hydraulic oils, and machining cutting oils that are collected and filtered in preparation for burning in commercial burners and that are not residual oils or middle distillates are not deemed refined petroleum products subject to the environmental protection fee (*Letter Ruling 89-64;* CCH MICHIGAN TAX REPORTS, ¶355-036).

The following persons or entities that paid the motor fuel tax may seek a refund:

— a person who used motor fuel for a nontaxable purpose (Sec. 207.1032, M.C.L.);

— an end user of motor fuel used for nonhighway purposes, except for motor fuel used in a snowmobile, off-road vehicle, or vessel (Sec. 207.1033, M.C.L.);

— a person who paid the tax on purchases that were tax-exempt (Sec. 207.1035, M.C.L.);

— a licensed exporter for tax paid on fuel, on which the tax had already been paid or accrued, and that was subsequently exported (Sec. 207.1036, M.C.L.);

— a person who exported from a bulk plant in a tank wagon to another state (Sec. 207.1037, M.C.L.);

— a licensed person registered with the federal government as an ultimate vendor, for state tax paid on kerosene sold tax-free through a blocked pump (Sec. 207.1037, M.C.L.);

— an end user of gasoline or leaded racing fuel used in an implement of husbandry or other nonhighway purposes not expressly exempt from tax, except for a snowmobile, off-road vehicle, or vessel (Sec. 207.1039, M.C.L.);

— a person who paid tax on fuel that was accidently contaminated, lost, or destroyed (Sec. 207.1040, M.C.L.);

— an end user of gasoline used in a passenger vehicle with a capacity of five or more that is operated under a license or permit to transport students (Sec. 207.1041, M.C.L.);

— an end user of diesel fuel used in a passenger vehicle with a capacity of 10 or more operated under a state certificate of authority or municipal license or permit and operated over regularly traveled routes (Sec. 207.1042, M.C.L.); and

— an end user operating a motor vehicle with a common fuel supply tank from which diesel fuel (effective January 1, 2017, motor fuel or alternative fuel) is used to both propel the vehicle and to operate attached equipment may seek a refund of 15% of the tax paid (Sec. 207.1045, M.C.L.).

In addition, a licensed retail diesel dealer may claim a deduction for taxes paid on sales of undyed diesel fuel in amounts of 100 gallons or less sold for nontaxable purposes. (Sec. 207.1038, M.C.L.) Also, a licensed exporter may claim a deduction for tax paid on motor fuel placed in storage in Michigan and subsequently exported by transport truck or tank wagon by or on behalf of a licensed exporter. (Sec. 207. 1043, M.C.L.)

Airlines are refunded 1½¢ per gallon if proof of scheduled interstate operations is provided within six months of purchase. (Sec. 259.203, M.C.L.)

Through 2016, Compressed Natural Gas (CNG) and Liquefied Natural Gas (LNG) are not subject to the motor fuel tax because CNG and LNG do not constitute gasoline, diesel fuel, or liquefied petroleum gas under the provisions of the tax. Both CNG and LNG are forms of natural gas, which is predominantly methane. The motor fuel tax is imposed on diesel fuel and gasoline on a "per gallon" basis, which is a unit of liquid measure, and the motor fuel tax does not provide for conversion of a substance in a gaseous state into a "gallon" for taxation purposes. Therefore, CNG and LNG do not constitute diesel fuel or gasoline (*Letter Ruling No. LR 2013-2,* Michigan Department of Treasury, May 29, 2013, CCH MICHIGAN TAX REPORTS, ¶401-801). Similarly, butane and propane also are not subject to the motor fuel tax on gasoline. If, however, either butane or propane is mixed or otherwise blended with a motor fuel, the butane or propane would be subject to the motor fuel tax (*Letter Ruling No. LR 2013-4,* Michigan Department of Treasury, September 12, 2013, CCH MICHIGAN TAX REPORTS, ¶401-820). However, effective January 1, 2017, the motor fuel tax is applied to all alternative fuels (based on the per-gallon energy equivalent to motor fuels). The rate is effective for alternative fuel commercial users beginning January 1, 2017, and for persons other than alternative fuel commercial users or alternative fuel dealers beginning January 1, 2018. (Sec. 207.1152, M.C.L.) "Alternative fuel" is defined as a gas, liquid, or other fuel that is capable of being used for the generation of power to propel a motor vehicle, including, but not limited to natural gas, compressed natural gas, liquefied natural gas, liquefied petroleum gas, hydrogen, hydrogen compressed natural gas, or hythane. The term does not include motor fuel, electricity, leaded racing fuel, or an excluded liquid. (Sec. 207.1151, M.C.L.; Sec. 207.1152, M.C.L.)

Basis and rate of tax: The rates of tax are:

— gasoline . . . . $0.19 per gallon

— diesel fuel, liquefied petroleum gas, and recreational fuel . . . . . $0.15 per gallon

— aircraft fuel . . . . $0.03 per gallon

Effective through December 31, 2016, in lieu of the $0.19 or $0.15 tax, a temporary $0.19 per gallon tax is imposed on gasoline that is at least 70% ethanol and a temporary $0.15 per gallon tax is imposed on diesel fuel that contains at least 5% biodiesel. (Sec. 207.1008, M.C.L.; Sec. 207.1152, M.C.L.; *Special Notice,* Michigan Department of Treasury, December 2007, CCH MICHIGAN TAX REPORTS, ¶401-531) Effective January 1, 2017, the tax rate on motor fuels (and alternative fuels) is increased from $0.19 per gallon to $0.263 per gallon, the tax rate on diesel fuel is increased from $0.15 cents per gallon to $0.263 per gallon. Beginning with the rate effective January 1, 2022, and January 1 of each year thereafter, the fuel tax rates will be adjusted based on the lesser of 5% or the inflation rate, rounding up to the nearest 1/10 of a cent. Beginning January 1, 2022, the Department must publish notice of the tax rate not later than 30 days before the effective date of the rate. (Sec. 207.1008, M.C.L.)

In computing the tax, a supplier may deduct 1.5% of the quantity of gasoline removed by the supplier to allow for the cost of remitting the tax.

An environmental protection regulatory fee of seven-eighths of a cent per gallon is imposed on all refined petroleum products sold for resale or consumption in Michigan. The fee is charged for capacity utilization of an underground storage tank system on a per gallon basis.

CCH Comment: E-Filing Required for 2015 IFTA Returns

International Fuel Tax Agreement (IFTA) tax returns must be electronically filed beginning in 2015. Therefore, the fourth quarter 2014 reporting period (due January 31, 2015) returns must be filed using Michigan's new electronic IFTA tax return processing system. Taxes may be paid by EFT Debit, EFT Credit, or bank check. (*IFTA Is Going Paperless,* Michigan Department of Treasury, July 2014)

Reports and payment: Motor fuel suppliers must file monthly reports with the Department of Treasury by the 20th of the month following the reporting period.

Licensed occasional importers, bonded importers, tank wagon operator-importers, exporters, transporters, licensed fuel vendors, and liquefied petroleum gas dealers must file quarterly reports by the 20th day of the month following the reporting period. The recreational fuel tax is paid in the same manner and at the same time as the motor fuel tax.

Motor carriers file quarterly statements by the last day of January, April, July, and October. Environmental protection regulatory fee reports for the first to the 15th of each month are due on the 25th of each month or the next business day thereafter; reports for the 16th to the last day of each month are due on the tenth or 11th of the following month. Tax payments must accompany the reports.

Administration: The taxes on motor fuel, recreational fuel, and aircraft fuel and the motor carrier fuel tax are administered by the Revenue Division of the Department of Treasury.

¶2204 Severance Taxes

Law: Secs. 205.301 *et seq.*, 211.781—211.791, M.C.L. (CCH MICHIGAN TAX REPORTS, ¶37-301 and following).

Oil and gas severance: The Michigan oil and gas severance tax, enacted in 1929 (Sec. 205.301, M.C.L. *et seq.*), is administered by the Michigan Department of the Treasury (Sec. 205.306, M.C.L.). The tax is a specific tax on oil or gas and is levied upon producers engaged in the business of severing oil and gas from the soil. (Sec. 205.301, M.C.L.) The tax is computed as of the time and place where production was severed or taken from the soil (Sec. 205.303(1), M.C.L.), *i.e.*, at the wellhead (*Revenue Administrative Bulletin 92-5*, CCH MICHIGAN TAX REPORTS, ¶319-218).

The severance tax is imposed on producers engaged in the business of severing oil or gas from the soil (Sec. 205.301, M.C.L.) but may be paid by a pipeline company, common carrier, or common purchaser on behalf of a producer. (Sec. 205.303, M.C.L.) "Oil" includes petroleum oil, mineral oil, or other oil taken from the earth. (Sec. 205.311, M.C.L.) "Gas" does not include methane gas extracted from a landfill. (Sec. 205.311, M.C.L.) A "producer" is a person who owns or is entitled to delivery of oil or gas or monetary proceeds from the sale of gas or oil as of the time of its production or severance (Sec. 205.312, M.C.L.); "producer" includes both working and royalty interest owners. (*Revenue Administrative Bulletin 89-16*, CCH MICHIGAN TAX REPORTS, ¶319-106; LR 83-30, Commissioner of Revenue, CCH MICHIGAN TAX REPORTS, ¶250-213)

The severance tax is imposed on the gross cash market value of the total production of a gas or oil well, computed as of the time and place it is taken from the soil, at the following rates:

— Oil 6.6%
— Gas 5.0%
— stripper well crude oil, crude oil from marginal properties 4.0%
— carbon dioxide secondary or enhanced recovery projects 4.0%

(Sec. 205.303, M.C.L.)

The owner of a brine disposal facility is not liable for severance tax on residual or skim oil that it separates from brine water and sells to purchasers of crude oil (*Letter Ruling 92-2;* CCH MICHIGAN TAX REPORTS, ¶355-080). The production, or proceeds therefrom, attributable to the state, the federal government or any political subdivisions thereof are exempt. (Sec. 205.303, M.C.L.) Methane gas extracted from a landfill is exempt from gas severance tax. (Sec. 205.311, M.C.L.) Oil and gas producers are exempt from the single business tax under the Severance Tax Act, which provides that the severance tax is "in lieu of all other taxes, state and local, upon oil and gas" (*Cowen v. Department of Treasury* (1994, Ct App), 204 Mich. App. 428; CCH MICHIGAN

TAX REPORTS, ¶400-323). The single business tax expired on December 31, 2007, and was replaced by the Michigan business tax. Oil and gas producers are generally not required to pay severance tax on income received from the hydrocarbons produced from devonian or antrim shale that qualifies for the federal nonconventional fuel credit and acquired through a royalty interest sold by the state. (Sec. 205.303, M.C.L.)

A taxpayer may receive a credit based upon the purchase of natural gas liquids that are injected into an oil well to assist in the removal of crude oil from the well. In this process the natural gas liquids become commingled with the existing heavy crude oil in the oil well resulting in a new and thinner crude oil product being severed from the soil. The credit is allowed against the severance tax and surveillance fee calculated on the newly severed commingled crude oil product for any severance tax and surveillance fees paid on the injected natural gas liquids. (*Internal Policy Directive 2005-5*, Michigan Department of Treasury, December 20, 2005; CCH MICHIGAN TAX REPORTS, ¶380-019)

Conservation (oil privilege) fee: A conservation (oil privilege) fee is levied at a rate not to exceed 1% of the gross cash market value on all gas and oil produced in Michigan. The fee is to be determined by the Department of Treasury annually on or before December 1. (Sec. 324.61524, M.C.L.) The fee amount is:

— 2015 . . . . 0.82%

— 2014 . . . . 0.92%

Nonferrous metallic minerals extraction severance: A nonferrous metallic minerals extraction severance tax is also levied on taxable minerals that a taxpayer extracts from the earth in the state or that a taxpayer beneficiates in the state. A mineral extracted from the earth in the state that is shipped outside the state for beneficiation outside the state is considered to have been sold by the taxpayer immediately before the shipment and is subject to the minerals severance tax. "Taxable mineral" refers to the first marketable mineral or mineral product sold or transferred by the taxpayer that is taxable under the new minerals severance tax. A taxable mineral also includes a mineral that has been sold or transferred by a taxpayer following beneficiation in the state and a mineral that is otherwise taxable under the new severance tax. A "mineral" is a naturally occurring solid substance that can be extracted from the earth in the state primarily for its nonferrous metallic mineral content for commercial, industrial, or construction purposes, but does not include low-grade iron ore or any property defined and taxed under the iron ore tax. "Beneficiation" means milling, processing, grinding, separating, concentrating, pelletizing, and other processes that are necessary to prepare nonferrous metallic mineral ore for sale or transfer. (Sec. 211.781—Sec. 211.791, M.C.L.)

The minerals severance tax is levied at the rate of:

— 2012 to current . . . . 2.75% of taxable mineral value

(Sec. 211.784, M.C.L.)

A taxpayer subject to the minerals severance tax is exempt from property taxes, income taxes, and sales and use taxes. (Sec. 211.784, M.C.L.) A taxpayer must pay the minerals severance tax to the local tax collecting unit on or before February 15 beginning in the calendar year immediately following the second year in which the department declares the property to be mineral-producing property. (Sec. 211.784, M.C.L.)

¶2205 Motor Vehicle Registration

Law: Secs. 257.216, 257.226, 257.801 *et seq.*, 259.77, 259.82, 259.86, 478.2, 478.7, 479.2, M.C.L.

A tax is levied on registrations of automobiles, motor homes, pickup trucks, and vans. The registration taxes applicable to the first registration are based upon the list price of the vehicle. (Sec. 257.801, M.C.L.)

¶2206 Tobacco Tax

Law: Sec. 205.421 *et seq.*, M.C.L. (CCH MICHIGAN TAX REPORTS, ¶55-001—¶55-010).

Persons subject to tax: A tax is imposed on the sale of all tobacco products. A license is required of any person who purchases, possesses, acquires for resale, or sells a tobacco product as a manufacturer, wholesaler, retailer, vending machine operator, importer, transportation company, or transporter.

Manufacturer: A "manufacturer" is a person who manufacturers or produces a tobacco product. A manufacturer also includes a person who operates or who permits any other person to operate a cigarette-making machine in Michigan for the purpose of producing, filling, rolling, dispensing, or otherwise generating cigarettes. A person who is a manufacturer constitutes a nonparticipating manufacturer in the Master Settlement Agreement. A person operating or otherwise using a machine or other mechanical device, other than a cigarette-making machine, to produce, fill, roll, dispense, or otherwise generate cigarettes is not considered a manufacturer so long as the cigarettes are produced or otherwise generated in that person's dwelling and for his or her self-consumption. (Sec. 205.422, M.C.L.)

Exemptions: There are no specific exemptions provided in the tobacco tax law.

Basis and rate of tax: The tax rate on cigarettes and other tobacco products is:

cigarettes	$0.10 per cigarette or $2.00 per pack of 20
cigars (less than $1.5625 each)	32% of wholesale price
premium cigars ($1.5625 or more each)	$0.50 per cigar
smokeless tobacco	32% of wholesale price
other tobacco products (non-cigarette tobacco)	32% of wholesale price

Wholesale price is the price charged by the manufacturer including the federal taxes before any discounts. (Sec. 205.427, M.C.L.)

Reports and payment: Monthly returns and payment of tax are due on or before the 20th of each month for the preceding month. Cigarette wholesalers and unclassified acquirers must affix a tax stamp on the bottom on each individual package of cigarettes to be sold within Michigan. A retailer or vending machine operator may not sell to the public an individual package of cigarettes without a tax stamp affixed. (Sec. 205.427, M.C.L.)

Penalties: The penalty on an unlicensed person who is in control or in possession of tobacco products in violation of the Michigan Tobacco Products Tax Act is 500% of the tax due. (Sec. 205.428, M.C.L.)

Indian tribe: An Indian tribe was required to pay the tobacco products tax on its sale of tobacco products to customers that were not members of the Indian community, because the legal incidence of the tax fell on the end consumer rather than on the community. (*Keweenaw Bay Indian Community v. Rising*, U.S. Court of Appeals for the Sixth Circuit, No. 05-2398, 477 F. 3d, 881, February 28, 2007, CCH MICHIGAN TAX REPORTS, ¶401-281)

• *Equity tax assessment*

A tobacco company that has chosen not to participate in the Master Settlement Agreement (nonparticipating manufacturer) must pay an equity assessment at the rate of 17.5 mills per cigarette or 35¢ for a pack of 20 cigarettes on all cigarettes sold in Michigan. A nonparticipating manufacturer is required to prepay the equity assessment by March 1 each year for all cigarettes that were anticipated to be sold in the current calendar year. The prepayment amount would be the greater of either (1) an amount determined by multiplying 17.5 mills times the number of cigarettes that the Department of Treasury reasonably determined that the nonparticipating manufacturer would sell in Michigan in the current calendar year or (2) $10,000. (Sec. 205.426d, M.C.L.)

A nonparticipating manufacturer must furnish any information reasonably necessary to determine the equity assessment prepayment amount. By February 15 of each year, the Department must notify the nonparticipating manufacturer of the amount of the prepayment due for the current year. The equity assessment must be collected and reconciled by April 15 of each year for cigarettes sold in the previous calendar year. The Department is required to credit a nonparticipating manufacturer with any prepayment it made for that year. (Sec. 205.426d, M.C.L.)

Administration: The tobacco tax is administered by the Department of Treasury.

The Department of Treasury is required to issue a request for proposal to acquire and use digital stamps that contain a unique nonrepeating code that can be read by a device that identifies the taxed product and also contains other security and enforcement features as determined by the department. (Sec. 205.425a, M.C.L.) Stamping agents are allowed to retain 0.5% of the tax due on cigarettes as compensation for equipment and technology upgrades that are necessitated by digital stamps. Stamping agents are also allowed to retain from monthly remittances, for 18 months, 5.55% of direct costs incurred for the initial purchase of eligible equipment. Furthermore, licensees are allowed to retain an amount equal to 1.5% of the total amount of the tax due on sales of untaxed cigarettes to Indian tribes. (Sec. 205.427, M.C.L.)

¶2207 Insurance Taxes

Law: Sec. 500.476a, M.C.L. (CCH MICHIGAN TAX REPORTS, ¶88-001 and following).

Foreign and alien insurers are potentially subject to a retaliatory tax. Beginning January 1, 2008, all insurance companies are subject to a gross direct premiums tax. For further discussion, see ¶1456 and ¶1515. Through 2007, insurance companies were subject to the former single business tax.

¶2208 Real Estate Transfer Tax

Law: Sec. 207.501 *et seq.*, 207.521 *et seq.*, M.C.L. (CCH MICHIGAN TAX REPORTS, ¶37-051).

Persons taxable: The tax is levied on the seller or grantor of the following instruments upon recording:

(1) contracts for the sale or exchange of real estate or any interest therein or any assignment or transfer thereof; and

(2) deeds or instruments of conveyance of real property or any interest therein, for a consideration. The tax also applies to instruments executed outside Michigan if the contract or transfer concerns property located within Michigan.

(Sec. 207.502, M.C.L.)

Exemptions: Some of the instruments exempt from tax are:

— transactions in which the value of the consideration is less than $100;

— transferring land located outside Michigan;

— writings given as security or any assignment or discharge thereof;

— evidencing leases, including oil and gas leases, or transfers of leases;

— evidencing interests assessable as personal property;

— evidencing the transfer of rights and interests in underground gas storage;

— land contracts whereby the legal title does not pass to the grantee until the total consideration specified in the contract has been paid;

— evidencing a transfer of mineral rights and interests;

— creating a joint tenancy between two or more persons if at least one of the persons already owns the property;

— transferring an interest in property pursuant to a foreclosure;

— conveying property or any interest in property to a receiver, administrator, or trustee in any bankruptcy or insolvency proceeding.

(Sec. 207.505, M.C.L.; Sec. 207.506, M.C.L.)

Rate and basis: The tax is levied at the rate of $0.55 on each $500 or fraction thereof of the total value in counties with populations of less than two million. In counties with a population of two million or more, the tax is levied at a rate of up to $0.75, as authorized by the county board of commissioners, for each $500 or fraction thereof of the total value. Value means the current or fair market worth in terms of legal monetary exchange at the time of the transfer. (Sec. 207.504, M.C.L.; Sec. 207.522, M.C.L.)

An additional state real estate transfer tax is imposed at the rate of $3.75 on each $500 or fraction thereof of the total value of the property being transferred. (Sec. 207.525, M.C.L.) The additional state real estate transfer tax is imposed on the seller or grantor of the same instruments as under the county real estate transfer tax. (Sec. 207.523, M.C.L.) Some of the instruments exempt for the additional state real estate transfer tax are:

— a transfer between any corporation and its stockholders or creditors, between any LLC and its members or creditors, between any partnership and its partners or creditors, or between a trust and its beneficiaries or creditors, when the transfer is to effectuate a dissolution and it is necessary to transfer the title of real property to the stockholders, members, partners, beneficiaries, or creditors;

— a transfer between any LLC and its members, or between any partnership and its partners, if the ownership interests in the LLC or partnership are held by the same people and in the same proportion as in the LLC or partnership before the transfer;

— a transfer of a controlling interest in an entity with an interest in real property if the transfer of the property would qualify for exemption if it had been accomplished by deed to the property between the people who were parties to the transfer; or

— a transfer in connection with the reorganization of an entity if the beneficial ownership is not changed.

(Sec. 207.526, M.C.L.)

An exemption from the additional state real estate transfer tax is also available for transfers of a principal residence if, on the date a parcel occupied as a principal residence is transferred by the owner, the property's state equalized value is less than or equal to the property's state equalized value on the date the owner purchased or acquired the property, and the property is sold for not more than its true cash value at the time of sale. (Sec. 207.526(t), M.C.L.)

Practitioner Comment: Real Estate Transfer Tax Refund Opportunity for Sellers of Principal Residences that have Depreciated in Value from Time of Acquisition

On July 9, 2015, in Gardner v. Department of Treasury, 498 Mich. 1 (2015), the Michigan Supreme Court, reversing the decision in the Michigan Court of Appeals, ruled that to be entitled to the transfer tax exemption available under MCL 207.526(u), a taxpayer needs only to show that (1) the property is the principal residence of the seller or transferor, (2) that it has an SEV at the time of conveyance that is less than or equal to the SEV at the time of acquisition, and (3) that it was sold or transferred for a price that is based on fair market value.

Wayne D. Roberts, Varnum LLP and Marjorie B. Gell, Western Michigan University Cooley Law School

---

Returns and payment: No returns are required. The tax, which is evidenced by affixing documentary stamps to the instrument or by use of a tax meter machine, is payable at the time of recording of the instrument. (Sec. 207.528, M.C.L.; Sec. 207.529, M.C.L.).

Administration: The tax is collected by the various county treasurers. The additional state real estate transfer tax is administered by the Department of Treasury. (Sec. 207.536, M.C.L.)

¶2209 Utilities Taxes

Law: Secs. 141.1152, 141.1162, 484.1401a, 484.1401b, 484.1401c, 484.3108, M.C.L. (CCH Michigan Tax Reports, ¶35-001, ¶80-110).

Telecommunication providers: The Metropolitan Extension Telecommunications Rights-of-Way Oversight Authority (METROWA) has exclusive authority to assess an annual maintenance fee on telecommunication providers that own telecommunication facilities in public rights-of-way within a metropolitan area. The fee is equal to 5¢ per linear foot. In certain cases, the fee may be reduced to provide nondiscriminatory compensation to municipalities for management of their rights-of-way. The fee requirement does not apply to educational institutions, electric and gas utilities, the state, counties, municipalities, and municipally owned utilities. (Sec. 484.3108, M.C.L.)

A provider of cable services in a metropolitan area is subject to a lower annual maintenance fee of 1¢ per linear foot of public right-of-way occupied by the provider's facilities within the metropolitan area. However, the cable provider may satisfy the fee requirement by certifying that the provider's aggregate investment in Michigan, since January 1, 1996, in facilities capable of providing broadband Internet transport access service exceeds the annual amount of the maintenance fee. (Sec. 484.3108, M.C.L.)

A provider must file an application for a permit and pay a one-time $500 application fee to each municipality whose boundaries include public rights-of-way for which access or use is sought by the provider. (Sec. 484.3108, M.C.L.)

Providers may take a credit against the utility property tax equal to the annual maintenance fees paid, less the equipment credit (see ¶2006). The maximum credit is the lesser of the following:

— the annual maintenance fee, less the amount of the equipment credit; or

— the amount that the annual maintenance fee, together with the provider's total service long run incremental cost of basic local exchange service, exceeds the provider's rates for basic local exchange service plus any additional charges of the provider used to recover its total service long run incremental cost for basic local exchange service. (Sec. 484.3108, M.C.L.)

Emergency 9-1-1 service charges: A state emergency 9-1-1 service charge and an optional county emergency 9-1-1 service charge are collected by each service provider from all service users, except for users of a prepaid wireless telecommunications service, within the geographical boundaries of the 9-1-1 service district. Each communication service supplier may retain 2% of the charge collected to cover costs for billing and collection. The amount of the state 9-1-1 charge must not be more than 25¢

or less than 15¢. The initial state charge was 19¢ per month per user. This rate was subject to annual adjustments for 2009 and 2010. Any adjustments to the state 9-1-1 charge after December 31, 2010, must be made by the Legislature. (Sec. 484.1401a, M.C.L., Sec. 484.1401b, M.C.L.)

In addition, each county may assess a monthly charge to service users, except for users of a prepaid wireless telecommunications service, by one of the following methods that will generate an amount of revenue not to exceed the amount necessary and reasonable to implement, maintain, and operate a 9-1-1 system in the county:

— up to $0.42 per month by resolution;

— up to $3.00 per month with the approval of county voters; or

— a combination of these methods, with a maximum county charge of $3.00 per month. (Sec. 484.1401b, M.C.L.)

A prepaid wireless 9-1-1 surcharge must be collected from prepaid wireless customers by retail sellers, rather than service suppliers. The prepaid wireless surcharge is set at 1.92% per retail transaction. Sellers are allowed to retain 2% of the prepaid wireless surcharge. The prepaid wireless surcharge must be remitted in the same manner as required for the sales tax. (Sec. 484.1401c, M.C.L.)

City utility users tax: The governing body of a city of 600,000 (Detroit) or more may adopt a uniform ordinance to levy a tax on utilities users at a rate of tax in increments of of 1%, but not to exceed 5%. The ordinance may be adopted at any time and its adoption becomes effective on the first day of any month following adoption of the ordinance. A village or a city under 600,000 population may not impose and collect a utility user's tax. The revenue generated from the tax is used exclusively to retain or hire police officers. (Sec. 141.1152, M.C.L.)

"Public utility services" are defined by ordinance to mean the providing, performing, or rendering of public service of a telephone, electric, steam, or gas nature, the rates or other charges for which are subjected to regulation by state public utility regulatory bodies, federal public utility or regulatory bodies or both, and the rendering of public service of an electric or gas nature by a government-owned facility. (Sec. 141.1162, M.C.L.)

PART VIII

LOCAL TAXES

CHAPTER 23

CITY INCOME TAXES

¶2301 Scope of Chapter

Michigan cities may impose income taxes by adopting a uniform ordinance prescribed by the legislature. The uniform ordinance sets rates, defines taxable income, gives requirements for returns, payment and collection, etc.

The purpose of this chapter is to give a general picture of the nature and application of the city income taxes and the manner of their administration. It is not intended to give detailed coverage of all aspects of the tax. It covers persons subject to tax, computation of income, exemptions, apportionment of income, withholding, returns, payment of tax, assessment and collection of tax, and taxpayer remedies.

¶2302 Uniform City Income Tax Ordinance Prescribed

Law: Secs. 141.502, 141.502a, 141.503, 205.13, M.C.L. (CCH MICHIGAN TAX REPORTS, ¶17-105).

A city may not impose a local excise tax on income unless the imposition of such a tax is approved by the qualified and registered electors of the city. Taxes already in effect on January 1, 1995, are not affected.

A city may impose an income tax only by adopting the Uniform City Income Tax Ordinance enacted by the legislature (Secs. 141.501—141.787, M.C.L.).

A city that imposes a city income tax may enter an agreement with the Michigan Department of Treasury under which the Department will administer, enforce, and collect the city income tax on behalf of the city.

¶2303 Cities That Have Adopted the Uniform Ordinance

(CCH MICHIGAN TAX REPORTS, ¶17-105).

The following cities have adopted the Uniform City Income Tax Ordinance:

City	Effective Date
Albion	January 1, 1972
Battle Creek	July 1, 1967
Big Rapids	January 1, 1970
Detroit	July 1, 1962
Flint	January 1, 1965
Grand Rapids	July 1, 1967
Grayling	July 1, 1972
Hamtramck	July 1, 1962
Highland Park	July 1, 1966
Hudson	January 1, 1971
Ionia	January 1, 1994
Jackson	January 1, 1970
Lansing	July 1, 1968
Lapeer	January 1, 1967
Muskegon	July 1, 1993
Muskegon Heights	January 1, 1990
Pontiac	January 1, 1968
Port Huron	January 1, 1969
Portland	January 1, 1984
Saginaw	July 1, 1965
Springfield	January 1, 1989
Walker	January 1, 1988

¶2304 Taxpayers and Rates

Law: Secs. 141.503, 141.605, 141.611, 141.627, M.C.L. (CCH MICHIGAN TAX REPORTS, ¶17-105).

The ordinance divides taxpayers into three classes: resident individuals, nonresident individuals, and corporations. Residents are taxed on all their income, regardless of its source and nonresidents are taxed only on income arising from sources within the city.

Generally, the tax rates are 1% for residents, 1% for corporations doing business in the city on that portion of their net profits attributable to business activity conducted within the city, and 0.5% for nonresidents. However, cities may adopt lower tax rates. If a lower rate is imposed, the rate on nonresident individuals may not exceed half of the rate on corporations and resident individuals.

As a larger city, Detroit has different tax rates. Beginning January 1, 2013 and beyond, the personal income tax rate is 2.4% on resident individuals and 1.2% on nonresident individuals. The tax rate is reduced to 2.2% on resident individuals and 1.1% on nonresident individuals beginning January 1 of the year (and beyond) immediately after the year that all bonds issued by the lighting authority have been paid. The tax rate on corporations is a maximum of 2%. (Sec. 141.503(2), M.C.L.)

"Doing business" means any activity conducted for gain or benefit, with the exception of certain types of solicitation for sales protected by P.L. 86-272.

An estate or trust is not taxable, except that it is treated as a nonresident individual to the extent its income derived from sources within the city is not includible in the return of a resident individual.

¶2305 Credit for Tax Paid Another City

Law: Sec. 141.665, M.C.L. (CCH MICHIGAN TAX REPORTS, ¶17-105).

Resident individuals who have income arising from a source outside the city are allowed a credit against the city income tax for amounts paid to another city as a tax on the same income. The credit may not exceed the amount that would be assessed on the same amount of income of a nonresident. The effect of this provision is to avoid taxation of the same income by two or more cities when an individual resides in one city and works in another city or has income-producing property in another city.

¶2306 Computation of Income

Law: Secs. 141.607, 141.612—141.614, 141.627, M.C.L. (CCH MICHIGAN TAX REPORTS, ¶17-105).

Resident individuals are taxed on the following types of income to the same extent and on the same basis that the income is taxable for federal purposes:

— salaries, bonuses, wages, commissions, and other compensation;

— net profits of an unincorporated business, profession, enterprise, undertaking, or other activity as a result of work done, services rendered, and other business activities, wherever conducted;

— dividends, interest, capital gains less capital losses, income from estates and trusts, and net profits from rentals of real and tangible personal property; and

— other income.

A resident individual must include income from estates and trusts in his or her income subject to tax without regard to the situs of the estate or trust.

Nonresident individuals are taxed on the following income to the same extent and on the same basis that the income is taxable for federal purposes:

— salaries, bonuses, wages, commissions, and other compensation for services rendered as an employee for work done or services performed in the city, except income received as a result of disability and after exhausting all vacation pay, holiday pay, and sick pay;

— net profits from an unincorporated business, profession, enterprise, or other activity as a result of work done, services rendered and other business activities conducted in the city; and

— capital gains less capital losses from sales of, and net profits from rentals of, real and tangible personal property located in the city.

However, certain types of payments or benefits are exempt (¶2307) and individuals are allowed to deduct personal exemptions and ordinary, necessary, and unreimbursed expenses paid in connection with services as an employee (¶2308).

CCH Tip: Early Retirement Payment Not Taxable

A lump-sum payment made to the taxpayer by his employer in exchange for the taxpayer's agreement to retire early was not subject to Detroit city income tax, because the payment did not qualify as compensation for work done or services rendered in Detroit. Although the employer received an economic benefit from the taxpayer's acceptance of the early retirement payment, the taxpayer's acceptance of the payment and the resulting economic benefit to the employer did not combine to constitute services performed in the city (*Wyckoff,* (1998 CtApp) 233 MichApp 220, 591 NW2d 71; CCH MICHIGAN TAX REPORTS, ¶400-760).

"Net profits" is defined as the net gain from the operation of a business, profession or enterprise, after provision for costs and expenses incurred in its conduct, as determined under the federal income tax law. Therefore, individuals having net profits from a business subject to tax, and corporations, whose taxable income is based on net profits, are allowed the same business deductions as are allowed under the federal law. However, the definition of "net profits" specifically provides that, while net operating losses and capital losses sustained after the effective date of the tax may be carried over to the same extent and on the same basis as under the federal law, they may not be carried back to prior years. Also, no deduction is allowed for federal or city taxes based on income.

For *corporations,* the tax applies to that portion of taxable net profits earned as a result of work done, services rendered, and other business activities conducted in the taxing city. "Taxable net profits" means federal taxable income, with certain exclusions and adjustments (¶2307, ¶2308).

¶2307 Exempt Income

Law: Sec. 141.632, M.C.L. (CCH MICHIGAN TAX REPORTS, ¶17-105).

The following items of income are exempt:

— gifts and bequests;

— interest from U.S., state or local obligations, and gains or losses from the sale of U.S. obligations;

— proceeds of insurance, annuities, pensions and retirement benefits (amounts received for personal injuries, sickness, or disability are excluded only to the extent provided under the federal law);

— military pay;

— welfare relief, unemployment benefits, workmen's compensation, and similar payments;

— amounts paid an employee as reimbursement for expenses necessarily and actually incurred by him or her in the actual performance of services and deductible as such by the employer;

— net profits of financial institutions and insurance companies;

— amounts received by charitable, religious, educational, and similar organizations that are exempt under federal law; and

— amounts received by unemployment or profit sharing trusts that are exempt under federal law.

¶2308 Personal Exemptions and Deductions

Law: Secs. 141.614, 141.631, 141.633, 141.634, 141.635, M.C.L. (CCH MICHIGAN TAX REPORTS, ¶17-105).

Individual taxpayers are allowed a minimum of $600 for each personal and dependency exemption. Additional exemptions may be allowed for taxpayers who are at least 65 years of age, blind, a paraplegic, quadriplegic, hemiplegic, or totally and permanently disabled, or deaf. In addition, exemptions may be granted for individuals with income below a specified threshold or for a person for whom another taxpayer is allowed a deduction.

Individual taxpayers are allowed the following deductions: (1) alimony, separate maintenance payments, and principal sums payable in installments to the extent includible in the spouse's income (a nonresident may deduct only that portion that his income taxable by the city bears to his total federal adjusted gross income); (2) moving expenses; (3) payments to a qualified retirement plan; and (4) payments to an individual retirement account.

Ordinary, necessary, reasonable, and unreimbursed expenses paid or incurred in connection with the performance of services as an employee may be deducted to the extent that the expenses are applicable to income taxable by the city. Deductible expenses are limited to following types (1) travel, meals, and lodging while away from home; (2) as an outside salesman; (3) transportation; and (4) if the reimbursement is included in total compensation reported.

If a corporation would be allowed a similar deduction under federal law, corporations may deduct income, war profits, and excess profits taxes imposed by a foreign country or possession of the U.S.

Individual residents of Renaissance Zones (RZ) in cities that impose a local income tax may claim deductions for earned income, capital gains, and lottery winnings. Corporations and unincorporated businesses and professions that are located in a RZ may deduct the portion of the company's paid compensation and average net book value of its business property in the RZ to the company's total value of its paid compensation and business property in the city. (¶204)

¶2309 Exempt Organizations

Law: Secs. 141.606, 141.632, M.C.L. (CCH MICHIGAN TAX REPORTS, ¶17-105).

The following are exempt:

— amounts received by charitable, religious, educational, and other similar nonprofit organizations that are exempt from the federal income tax;

— amounts received by supplemental unemployment benefit trusts or pension, profit sharing, and stock bonus trusts qualified and exempt under the federal income tax law; and

— net profits of a "financial institution," which is defined as a bank, industrial bank, trust company, building and loan or savings and loan association, credit union, safety and collateral deposit company, regulated investment company, and any other association, joint stock company or corporation at least 90% of whose assets consist of intangible personal property and at least 90% of whose gross income consists of dividends or interest or other charges resulting from the use of money or credit.

¶2310 Apportionment of Income

Law: Secs. 141.618—141.625, M.C.L. (CCH MICHIGAN TAX REPORTS, ¶17-105).

Apportionment methods are provided to determine the portion of taxable net income of a corporation subject to taxation by a city and to determine the portion of the distributive share of net profits of a nonresident owner of an unincorporated business that is attributable to the city. Separate accounting may be used if the taxpayer seeks and is granted permission to use this method or if the administrator requires use of this method.

If the separate accounting method is not allowed or required, the business allocation percentage method is prescribed. This method uses a three-factor formula of "in city" percentages of property, payroll, and sales and services. If a taxpayer's business involves activities other than sales of goods or services, he or she may request permission to substitute a different factor or to use another method. If the taxpayer or the administrator determines that the net profits attributable to the city cannot be equitably determined by separate accounting or the business percentage allocation method, another method approved by the administrator may be used.

¶2311 Withholding

Law: Secs. 141.651—141.661, 141.666, 141.760, 141.761, M.C.L. (CCH MICHIGAN TAX REPORTS, ¶17-105).

Every employer doing business or maintaining an establishment within the city is required to withhold the tax from wages paid employees. Withholding is not required, however, on reimbursements or on payments to domestic help or to independent contractors. The rate is set by ordinance (¶2304) on the income subject to tax after exemptions are subtracted.

Withholding may be determined either by a direct percentage computation or by referring to withholding tables issued by the cities.

Employers must file withholding returns on or before the last day of the month following the end of each calendar quarter and remit the amount of tax withheld, although individual cities may, by adopting alternative provisions of the Uniform Ordinance, require monthly payments by employers withholding more than $100 per month. An annual reconciliation return is required on or before the last day of February for the preceding calendar year. An employer within a city that has entered a contract with the Department of Treasury (¶2302) must file a return and pay taxes withheld for each calendar month on or before the 15th day of the month following the close of each calendar month; such payments are to be made by electronic funds transfer.

Similarly, if an employer within a city that has entered a contract with the Department of Treasury (¶2302) goes out of business or ceases to be an employer, withholding tax reconciliation forms and information return forms must be filed with the Department within 30 days after the employer ceases doing business or ceases being an employer.

Employees must file withholding certificates with their employer stating the number of exemptions claimed, the city of residence, the predominant place of employment, and the percentage of work done or services performed in the predominant place of employment.

Employers must file an information return for each employee from whom the city income tax has been withheld. The return must be on a copy of the federal Form W-2 or on a form furnished or approved by the city. A copy of the information return must be furnished to the employee.

¶2312 Returns and Payment

Law: Secs. 141.608, 141.616, 141.641—141.644, 141.646, 141.660—141.664a, 141.689, 205.19, M.C.L. (CCH MICHIGAN TAX REPORTS, ¶17-105).

Every corporation doing business in the city and every other person ("person" includes natural persons, partnerships, fiduciaries, associations, corporations, and other entities) having income taxable under the ordinance must file an annual return. Married couples may file joint returns (see below for rules affecting refunds to joint filers).

Returns are due on or before the last day of the fourth month following the end of the taxpayer's calendar or fiscal year. For a city that has entered into an agreement to have the Department of the Treasury administer and collect the city income tax, the annual return is due on or before the 15th day of the fourth month for the same calendar year, fiscal year, or other accounting period that has been accepted by the IRS for federal income tax purposes.

The Michigan Department of Treasury will process city of Detroit personal income tax returns, beginning with the 2015 tax year. Returns may be filed electronically. (*Press Release,* Michigan Department of Treasury, September 15, 2015)

Each person who anticipates receiving taxable income that is not subject to withholding must file a declaration of estimated tax on or before April 30 for calendar-year taxpayers and within four months after the beginning of each fiscal year for fiscal-year taxpayers. However, a declaration is not required if the total estimated tax, less credits, does not exceed $100 for individual or unincorporated entities or $250 for corporations. For a city that has entered a contract for the Department of the Treasury to administer and collect the city income tax, the declaration of estimated tax must be filed on or before April 15. The taxpayer must file an annual return with the Department on or before the 15th day of the fourth month of the following year.

Any balance of tax due must be paid at the time of filing the annual return. Estimated tax may be paid in full with the declaration or in four equal installments on or before the last day of the fourth, sixth, ninth, and 13th months after the beginning of the taxable year. For a city that has entered a contract for the Department of the Treasury to administer and collect the city income tax, the estimated tax *must* be paid in four equal installments as noted above.

For a city that has entered a contract for the Department of the Treasury to administer and collect the city income tax, if a taxpayer pays less than the sum of his or her declared city and state income tax liabilities and there is no indication how to allocate the payment between the two tax liabilities, the payment will first be applied against city income taxes. However, the taxpayer's designation of a payee on a payment is not a dispositive allocation of that payment.

An unincorporated business, profession, or activity owned by two or more persons must file an annual information return, setting forth its total net profits, the portion of net profits attributable to the city, each owner's distributive share of the net profits, and each nonresident's distributive share of the net profits attributable to the city. Employers must file an information return for each employee from whom the tax has been withheld and each employee subject to withholding.

Military personnel in combat zone: Military personnel assigned to a combat zone on the due date for filing a return, and their spouses, may delay filing and payment of Michigan income tax for 180 days after the period of service in the combat zone. The period includes the time of continuous hospitalization for injuries received during service in the combat zone. A taxpayer whose ability to pay income tax has been materially impaired by service in the military may defer payment of tax due before or during the period of service for up to six months after termination of such service without accrual of interest or penalty for nonpayment by invoking the Soldiers' and Sailors' Civil Relief Act and filing a written statement with the Collection Division of the Department of Treasury (*Revenue Administrative Bulletin 1991-2;* CCH MICHIGAN TAX REPORTS, ¶ 319-195).

Refund on joint return: If a claim for refund is reflected on a joint return, each taxpayer's share of the refund will be allocated according to each taxpayer's respective liabilities. If all or a portion of a refund is subject to interception to satisfy a liability of one or both spouses, the city or Department will notify the taxpayers by first-class mail that the nonobligated spouse may claim his or her share of the refund by filing a nonobligated spouse allocation form not more than 30 days after the date the notice was mailed. A nonobligated spouse allocation form will require the spouses to state their income and all adjustments to income and to allocate those amounts between the obligated and nonobligated spouse according to specified rules.

Successor and corporate officer liability: A person who sells a business or stock or goods or quits a business must file a final return within 15 days. The purchaser or succeeding purchasers who purchase a going or closed business or stock of goods must escrow sufficient money to cover the amount of taxes, interest, and penalties that may be due and unpaid until the former owner produces a receipt showing that the taxes due have been paid or a certificate stating that no taxes are due. If the successor fails to comply with the escrow requirements, it will be personally liable for the taxes, interest, and penalties of the former owner. Personal liability is limited to the fair market value of the business less any proceeds applied to balances due on secured interests that are superior to city tax liens.

If a corporation fails to file the required city income tax returns or to pay the tax due, any officers that have control or supervision of, or who are charged with the responsibility for, making the returns or payments are personally liable for the failure to file or pay. A signature on a return or payment of a tax is prima facie evidence of the officer's responsibility for making the return and payments. The dissolution of a corporation does not discharge an officer's liability for a prior failure of the corporation to make a return or pay a tax. The officer liability provisions described above apply to responsible parties of flow-through entities as well. See ¶ 2403 for details.

¶2313 Assessment, Collection, and Remedies

Law: Secs. 141.673, 141.683, 141.684, 141.687, 141.693, 141.694, M.C.L. (CCH MICHIGAN TAX REPORTS, ¶17-105).

If a city has entered an agreement for the Department of the Treasury to administer and collect the city's tax, the Department must send the taxpayer or employer a letter of inquiry stating the reason for the Department's opinion that the taxpayer or employer needs to furnish further information or owes taxes and explaining how to communicate with the Department to resolve any dispute. A letter of inquiry is not required if the taxpayer or employer files a return showing a tax due and fails to pay that tax, the deficiency resulted from an audit by the city or Department, or the taxpayer or employer admits that a tax is due.

If a dispute is not resolved within 30 days after the Department sends a letter of inquiry, or if a letter is not required, the Department must notify the taxpayer or employer of its intent to assess a tax. The notice must include the amount of tax owed, the reason for the deficiency, and a statement of the taxpayer's or employer's right to file a protest and to a hearing. A taxpayer or employer has 30 days after receipt of a proposed assessment or a notice of intent to assess within which to file a written protest with the administrator or Department.

If the administrator or Department finds that a person liable for tax intends to quickly depart from the city or remove property from the city to conceal himself or herself or property in the city, or to do any other act to render ineffectual collection of the tax, the administrator or Department may demand an immediate return and immediate payment of the tax by issuing a warrant or warrant-notice of levy.

Appeals: A taxpayer or employer may appeal a final assessment, denial, decision, or order of the income tax board of review to the Michigan Tax Tribunal within 60 days. Not more than 35 days after a final order by the Tax Tribunal, the taxpayer, employer, or other person must pay the taxes, interest, and penalty found to be due, and the city or Department must refund any amount found to have been overpaid.

A taxpayer, employer, other person, the city, or the Department may take an appeal by right from a decision of the Tax Tribunal to the court of appeals and may take a further appeal by leave to the Michigan Supreme Court in accordance with court rules.

An assessment is final, conclusive, and not subject to further challenge after 90 days after the issuance of the final assessment, decision, or order of the administrator or the Department. A refund of a tax, interest, or penalty paid pursuant to an assessment will not be allowed unless the aggrieved person has appealed the assessment as required by law.

Statute of limitations: Except in cases of fraud, failure to file a return or comply with withholding provisions, or a substantial omission of income, an additional assessment may not be made after four years from the date the return was due, including extensions, or from the date the return was filed, or the tax was paid, whichever is later. A claim for refund of taxes erroneously paid must be made within four years from the date the payment was made or the original final return was due, including extensions, whichever is later.

Interest and penalties: If a city has entered a contract for the Department of the Treasury to administer and collect the city income tax, a deficiency in the tax due or an estimated payment will be subject to a current monthly interest rate of 1% above the adjusted prime rate per annum from the time the tax or payment was due until paid.

If any part of a deficiency or an excessive credit claim is due to negligence, but without fraudulent intent, a penalty of $10 or 10% of the deficiency, whichever is greater, plus interest, will be imposed, unless the taxpayer can show reasonable cause, in which case the penalty may be waived. If any part of the deficiency or excessive credit claim is due to intentional disregard of the city tax ordinance, but without intent to defraud, a penalty of $25 or 25% of the deficiency, whichever is greater, plus interest, will be imposed. If the taxpayer successfully disputes this penalty, a negligence penalty may not be imposed. If any part of the deficiency or excessive credit claim is due to fraudulent intent to evade tax or to obtain a refund for a fraudulent claim, a penalty of 100% of the deficiency, plus interest, will be imposed.

PART IX

ADMINISTRATION AND PROCEDURE

CHAPTER 24

MICHIGAN ADMINISTRATION AND PROCEDURE

¶2401 Administrative Agencies

The Michigan Department of Treasury is the chief state tax administration agency in Michigan and administers and collects the bulk of the state revenue laws in the state. The agency can be contacted by:

Mailing Address
Department of Treasury
Lansing, MI 48922

Website
http://www.michigan.gov/taxes

Telephone
(517) 373-3200

The following is a description of other tax administrative bodies in Michigan:

State Tax Commission: This Commission has oversight and some appeal responsibilities with respect to the assessment of the property tax.

A new State Tax Commission was created within the Department of Treasury to supervise the administration of the property tax laws and assist and advise assessing officials. The new State Tax Commission consists of three members appointed by the governor, not more than two of whom can be members of the same political party. All of the authority, powers, duties, functions, responsibilities, records, personnel, property, and unexpended balances of appropriations, allocations, or other funds of the old State Tax Commission were transferred to the new State Tax Commission. (*Executive Order No. 2009-51*, October 29, 2009)

Secretary of State: The Secretary administers and collects the motor vehicle fees.

Department of Labor and Economic Growth: The Corporation Division of the *Bureau of Commercial Services* administers and collects the business corporation fees and the corporation annual report fee.

Liquor Control Commission: The *Liquor Control Commission* issues licenses for and administers and collects the alcoholic beverages tax.

Public Service Commission: The *Public Service Commission* administers and collects the motor carriers fee on cars and trucks.

Office of Financial and Insurance Services/State Treasurer: The *Office of Financial and Insurance Services* and the *State Treasurer* administer and collect the insurance companies tax.

Unemployment Insurance Agency: The *Unemployment Insurance Agency* administers and collects the unemployment tax.

Department of Natural Resources: The Department administers the emission fees for major emitting facilities and the air quality fees.

Local taxing officers: The local taxing officers administer and collect the convention facility development tax, forest lands tax, lodgings taxes, property taxes, and the realty transfer taxes.

¶2402 Refunds of Overpayments

Law: Secs. 205.23, 205.27a(2), 205.27a(6), 205.27a(7), 205.27a(12), 205.30, 205.30(2), 205.30a, 205.30a(5) and (6), 206.352, 206.473, M.C.L. (CCH MICHIGAN TAX REPORTS, ¶20-815, ¶89-224).

This section discusses the general rules on most state tax refunds.

• *Sources of refunds*

The Department of Treasury may refund or credit the following:

— any overpayment of taxes; or

— any taxes, together with penalties and interest, that are erroneously or unjustly assessed, excessive in amount, or wrongfully collected, provided the amount is $1 or more. (Sec. 205.30, M.C.L.)

• *Interest on refunds*

Interest is credited on all such refunds or credits at the same rate used when determining the interest due on tax deficiencies, commencing 45 days after the claim is filed or 45 days after the date established by law for the filing of a return, whichever is later (Sec. 205.30, M.C.L.; *Revenue Administrative Bulletin 1996-4;* CCH MICHIGAN TAX REPORTS, ¶319-266). Interest rates are announced periodically by the Department of Treasury (see ¶2404).

Additional interest must be paid on a personal income tax refund owed to an individual taxpayer if the refund is not paid within one of the following dates for the applicable tax year:

— May 1, for returns the Department received by March 1 of the applicable tax year;

— 60 days from the date the Department received the return, for returns received after March 1 of the applicable tax year.

The additional interest must be paid at a rate of 3% per annum, calculated from the time the tax was due and until the refund was paid, if all of the following conditions are met:

— the refund was due on an original return that was timely filed under the applicable income tax provision;

— the Department did not adjust the refund;

— the return was complete for processing purposes with no calculation errors and contained all required information prescribed by the Department;

— the taxpayer had complied with the Department's request, if any, for additional documentation or information within 30 days of the request;

— the refund was not subject to a suspension of the statute of limitations under Sec. 205.27a(3) or (4), M.C.L., except for an audit by the Department;

— no portion of the refund was subject to interception under Sec. 205.30a, M.C.L., for other liability of the taxpayer; and

— the amount to be refunded was more than $1. (Sec. 205.30, M.C.L.)

Beginning January 1, 2015, certain Michigan business tax refunds that are not paid within 90 days after the claim is approved or 90 days after the date established by law for filing the return, whichever is later, are eligible for an additional 3% interest. Required statutory conditions include: the refund is claimed on a timely-filed original return and the refund is not claimed by a unitary business group, among other things. (Sec. 205.30(6), M.C.L.)

• *Procedure*

A taxpayer claiming a refund or credit must file a petition for refund with the Department of Treasury. Generally, a refund claim is filed when a taxpayer gives the Department adequate notice of the claim within the applicable limitations period. A tax return commonly constitutes a valid refund claim if it reflects an overpayment of tax, or credits in excess of the tax due, and contains sufficient information for the Department to determine the amount of the refund. (Sec. 205.30, M.C.L.; *Revenue Administrative Bulletin 1996-4;* CCH MICHIGAN TAX REPORTS, ¶319-266)

Practice Note: Refund Claim

Interest on a refund claim commences 45 days from the date the taxpayer files a refund claim. The Michigan Supreme Court overruled an appellate decision that held that interest commences 45 days after the Department of Treasury sends a notice of overpayment after an audit, because the taxpayer did not file a refund claim on that date. Rather, the Supreme Court held that the 45 day period commenced when the taxpayer filed a claim for interest on the refund (*NSK Corporation v. Department of Treasury,* Michigan Supreme Court, No. 135997, May 30, 2008, CCH MICHIGAN TAX REPORTS, ¶401-371).

Practice Note: Filing of Refund Claim

The Michigan Supreme Court has clarified the required steps that a taxpayer must take in order to adequately file a "claim for refund" under the former single business tax and thus trigger the accrual of interest on a tax refund: under the applicable statute (M.C.L. § 205.30), the taxpayer must (1) pay the disputed tax, (2) make a claim or petition for a refund, and (3) file the claim or petition for refund. Although the claim or petition does not need to take any specific form, it must clearly demand, request or assert the right to a refund of the tax payments made to the Department of Treasury that the taxpayer asserts are not due. In order to file the claim or petition, the taxpayer must submit the claim to the department in a manner sufficient to provide the department with adequate notice of the taxpayer's claim. (*Ford Motor Company v. Department of Treasury*, Michigan Supreme Court, No. 146962, June 26, 2014, CCH MICHIGAN TAX REPORTS, ¶401-907).

Taxpayers may request that a refund be directly deposited with a financial institution of the taxpayer's choice. A request for direct deposit is made on forms prescribed by the Department.

• *Statute of limitations*

The general rule is that a refund claim must be filed within four years from the date set for filing the original return. (Sec. 205.27a(2), M.C.L.) However, a refund claim that is based on the laws or Constitution of the United States or the Michigan Constitution of 1963 must be filed within 90 days after the date set for filing the return. (Sec. 205.27a(6), M.C.L.)

The period to claim a refund is extended if a taxpayer obtains an extension of time to file the original return or if the refund claim period is otherwise extended by law (for example, for the period pending final determination of tax liability).

Practice Note: Suspension Period for Audits

Applicable to audit confirmation letters with a commencement date on or after January 1, 2009, the Department of Treasury has clarified the suspension period in situations in which an audit is conducted. In those instances in which an audit is conducted prior to the date the four year statute of limitations otherwise would have run, the limitations period is extended to a date one year after the conclusion of the audit or one year after the conclusion of an appeal if the audit is appealed, plus any days remaining from the four year limitations period that had not run prior to the audit commencement date. The running of the four year general statute of limitations recommences when the audit determination that was appealed has been finalized. Under this statutory authority, waivers are not required. (*Revenue Administrative Bulletin 2008-8*, CCH MICHIGAN TAX REPORTS, ¶401-398)

A taxpayer is not entitled to a refund once the time to challenge the assessment has expired. This prevents circumvention of the statutory limits for challenging an assessment, decision, or order by resort to the refund procedures (*Revenue Administrative Bulletin 1994-1*; CCH MICHIGAN TAX REPORTS, ¶319-242).

• *Effect of filing tax return*

Effective for all tax years that are open under the statute of limitations for all matters regarding the filing of a return, the filing of a tax return includes the filing of a combined, consolidated, or composite return whether or not any tax was paid and whether or not the taxpayer reported any amount in the tax line including zero. However, this does not affect a refund that is required by a final order of a court of competent jurisdiction for which all rights of appeal were exhausted or expired before May 1, 2012. (Sec. 205.27a(12), M.C.L.)

• *Application of refund to liabilities*

The Department of Treasury is authorized to apply any refunds against the following liabilities of the taxpayer (enumerated in the order of priority):

(1) any other tax liability of the taxpayer to the state;

(2) any nontax liability of the taxpayer to the state, including support payments, if the right to receive the payments has been assigned to the state and tax refund offset has been requested by the Office of Child Support;

(3) the following in the order of priority received: (a) support liability of the taxpayer other than as provided in (2) above; (b) a writ of garnishment or other valid court order; (c) a levy of the IRS to satisfy a liability of the taxpayer; or (d) a liability to repay certain unemployment benefits. (Sec. 205.30a(2), M.C.L.)

Any excess shall be refunded to the taxpayer or, at the taxpayer's request, credited against any current or subsequent tax liability. (Sec. 205.30(2), M.C.L.)

• *Joint taxpayers*

If the claim for refund stems from a joint tax return, the refund will be allocated to each joint taxpayer and the above rules of priority apply to each spouse's share. If a refund application applies to only one spouse (the "obligated spouse"), the Department must give notice of such fact to both spouses, and the nonobligated spouse must file a "nonobligated spouse allocation form" within 30 days from the date the notice was mailed, otherwise such spouse is barred from making any further claim. (Sec. 205.30a, M.C.L.)

¶2403 Tax Assessments

Law: Secs. 205.19(1), 205.21, 205.21(2), 205.23, 205.24, 205.25, 205.26, 205.27a(2), 205.27a(3), 205.27a(5), 205.28(1)(b), 205.30c, 208.80, M.C.L. (CCH MICHIGAN TAX REPORTS, ¶20-758, ¶89-108, ¶89-164 and follows).

Although most taxes are self-assessed, the Department of Treasury may audit the books and records of a taxpayer and assess taxes in the following cases:

— if a person fails or refuses to make a return or payment as required (Sec. 205.21, M.C.L.);

— if there is reason to believe that a return made or payment does not supply sufficient information for an accurate determination of the amount of tax due (Sec. 205.21, M.C.L.);

— if there is reason to believe, based upon an examination of a tax return, a payment, or an audit, that a taxpayer has not satisfied a tax liability or that a claim was excessive (Sec. 205.23, M.C.L.); or

— if a person fails or refuses to file a return or pay a tax within the time specified (Sec. 205.24, M.C.L.).

If as a result of an audit it is determined that a taxpayer is owed a refund, the Department must notify the taxpayer of the amount it believes is owed to the taxpayer as a result of the audit. The notice must inform the taxpayer of his or her appeal rights. (Sec. 205.21(3), M.C.L.) In addition, a taxpayer has the right to claim credit amounts as an offset against debit amounts determined in the audit. (Sec. 205.21b, M.C.L.)

Practitioner Comment: Michigan Statute Of Limitations Changes Related To Completion of An Audit: No Automatic Tolling Of The Statute For Certain Audits Commenced Between February 6, 2014 through September 30, 2014

Under MCL 205.21(6), for audits commenced after September 30, 2014 the department must complete fieldwork and provide a written preliminary audit determination for any period no later than one year after the general four-year statute of limitations period without regard to the extension provided for in section 27a(3).

A. Prior to 2014 Amendment

MCL 205.27a (3) Tolling Provision:

(3) The running of the statute of limitations is suspended for the following:

(a) The period pending a final determination of tax, including audit, conference, hearing, and litigation of the liability for federal income tax or a tax administered by the Department and for 1 year after that period.

B. Current Tolling Provision

MCL 205.27a (3):

(3) The running of the statute of limitations is suspended for the following if that period exceeds that described in subsection (2):

(a) The period pending a final determination of tax through audit, conference, hearing, and litigation of liability for federal income tax and 1 year after that period.

(b) The period for which the taxpayer and the State Treasurer have consented to in writing that the period be extended.

Summary: Under 2015 PA 3, the Department of Treasury employs a three-part approach:

1. Audits commenced prior to February 6, 2014:

Treasury follows the prior/repealed statutory provision pursuant to which the statute was tolled upon commencement of the audit

2. Audits commenced during the period February 6, 2014 – September 30, 2014:

There is no automatic tolling of the statute. Therefore, a portion of the 4-year audit period may have expired (shortened exposure period for taxpayer).

3. Audits commenced after September 30, 2014

The audit period is limited to 4 years from filing of the tax return, plus 1 additional year.

Comment: Consider whether the Department has a legal basis for approach No. 1 as the statutory provision supporting this approach has been repealed.

Wayne D. Roberts, Varnum, LLP and Marjorie B. Gell, Western Michigan University Cooley Law School

---

CCH Note: Treasury's Authority to Adjust Income

The Department of Treasury had the authority to adjust the amount of business income on the taxpayers' returns for single business tax (SBT) purposes because the deductions reported to arrive at business income were incorrect and unacceptable.

The starting point in calculating the SBT is business income, which is defined as federal taxable income. After determining that the taxpayers' federal taxable income was affected by a misallocation of employee compensation between subsidiaries, the Department adjusted the business income line of the taxpayers' SBT returns.

The Department had the express authority to audit Michigan tax returns, and that authority necessarily included the authority to assess the validity of the federal tax statements upon which the Michigan tax computations depended. (*Advanced Boring & Tool Co. et al.*, Michigan Court of Appeals, No. 220352, May 29, 2001 (unpublished opinion) CCH MICHIGAN TAX REPORTS, ¶400-890, affirming Michigan Tax Tribunal, Nos. 250302, 250303, 250304, and 250305, May 27, 1999; CCH MICHIGAN TAX REPORTS, ¶400-793).

• *Alteration or modification of federal tax liability*

If a taxpayer fails to notify the Department of any alteration in or modification of federal tax liability, the Department may assess the taxpayer for any tax due with interest and penalties within two years of discovery of the failure. (Sec. 205.27a, M.C.L.)

• *Liability for payment of tax*

Most Michigan taxes (other than property taxes) are self-assessed. Taxpayers are expected to voluntarily pay the proper amount of tax on the specified due dates.

Unless an extension of the tax payment deadline is obtained from the Department of Treasury, the tax becomes delinquent if it is not paid within the deadline.

Responsible party liability: Corporate officers and responsible parties of flow-through entities may be assessed upon failure of a corporate or flow-through entity to pay taxes due. (Sec. 205.27a, M.C.L.) This provision extends to all taxes administered under the Revenue Act and, thus, applies to the income tax withholding, sales and use taxes, tobacco products tax, and the motor fuel tax, among others. The single business tax, Michigan business tax, and corporate income tax are not subject to corporate officer liability. In the discussion that follows, the conditions for qualifying as a "responsible person" include the following: (i) the person is a current or former officer of the business, (ii) the officer controller, supervised, or was responsible for filing returns or making payment of taxes; (iii) the officer was an officer during the time period of default, and (iv) the officer willfully failed to file a return or pay the tax due.

The responsible party liability provision applies where the corporation fails to file the required return or pay the tax and a responsible party has control, supervision, or responsibility for the filing or payment. The signature of any responsible party on returns or negotiable instruments submitted in payment of taxes is rebuttable proof of responsibility for making returns or payment. Other evidentiary standards for responsible party liability as applied to corporate officers are set forth in *Revenue Administrative Bulletin 2015-23;* CCH MICHIGAN TAX REPORTS, ¶402-019, and in court and Tax Tribunal decisions.

Before assessing a responsible person as liable for a tax assessed to a business, the department must first assess a purchaser or succeeding purchaser of the business who is personally liable. However, the department may assess a responsible person notwithstanding the liability of a purchaser or succeeding purchaser if the purchaser or succeeding purchaser fails to pay the assessment within the later of two years after the assessment is issued against the business or 90 days after the assessment is issued against the successor.

Dissolution of the corporation or flow-through entity does not discharge the responsible party's liability. (Sec. 205.27a, M.C.L.) A responsible person may challenge an assessment to the same extent that the business could have when it was originally issued.

Practitioner Comment: Michigan "Officer Liability" Statute Applies Only to Taxes Collected and Held in Trust for the State, Including Sales, Use, Tobacco, and Payroll Taxes. For Assessments Prior to January 1, 2014, Consider Retroactive Application of PA 3 of 2014 for Assessments of Personal Liability of Officers, Members, Managers and Partners for Any Unpaid Business Taxes, Including Taxes under the SBT, MBT, and CIT Acts.

In a statutory amendment passed in 2014, MCL 205.27a(5), officer liability was materially reformed and limited to taxes collected and held in trust for the state (e.g., sales, use, tobacco, and payroll taxes). P.A. 3 of 2014. This legislation limits personal liability assessments to circumstances in which failure to remit was willful, and further limits assessment to situations in which the party being held responsible was in control of tax matters at the time the taxes at issue were incurred and the returns were due. The legislation also provides a 4-year statute of limitations on the assessment of responsible persons. The statute begins to run on the date the assessment is issued to the business in question. MCL 205.27a(5).

The provisions under PA 3 apply to assessments of "responsible persons" after December 31. 2013. However, the Michigan Supreme Court, in Shotwell v. Dep't of Treasury, 497 Mich. 977, 860 N.W.2d 623 (2015), affirmed the lower Court's finding that the provisions of PA 3 are retroactive, and apply to pre-January 1, 2014 assessments of officers, members, managers and partners for unpaid business taxes, including taxes under the SBT, MBT and CIT Acts. In addition, officer liability under MCL 205.27a(5) is limited to an officer who "controlled, supervised, or was responsible for filing returns or paying taxes during the relevant tax period," and personal liability does not extend to a de facto officer. Shotwell v. Dep't of Treasury, 305 Mich. App. 360, 369, 853 N.W.2d 414, 419 (2014).

Wayne D. Roberts, Varnum, LLP and Marjorie B. Gell, Western Michigan University Cooley Law School

---

Responsible party liability under bankruptcy: When a corporation or flow-through entity files a petition in bankruptcy, the Department will normally issue a responsible party liability assessment at about the same time a bankruptcy claim is filed through the Attorney General. This will place the responsible party on notice of a potential tax liability.

A pair of letter rulings issued by the Department of Treasury indicate that corporate officers may be assessed for the tax liability incurred by the corporation prior to the date bankruptcy proceedings were instituted (*Letter Rulings 85-30, 85-25;* CCH MICHIGAN TAX REPORTS, ¶250-262, ¶250-257). After instituting bankruptcy proceedings, a debtor in possession or a trustee in bankruptcy is liable for taxes. However, if the corporation remains the debtor in possession, or if a bankruptcy trustee has not been appointed, the corporate officer's personal liability for filing the return and paying the tax remains (*Revenue Administrative Bulletin 2015-23;* CCH MICHIGAN TAX REPORTS, ¶402-019).

In addition, a Michigan court of appeals found that a corporate officer was personally liable for unpaid SBT assessments levied against the corporation even though the corporate officer had been discharged of all his debts in a federal bankruptcy proceeding subsequent to the tax years at issue. The court found that the federal bankruptcy code did not discharge an individual debtor from any tax debt resulting from a failure to file a required return. (*Department of Treasury v. Coller,* Michigan Court of Appeals, No. 244344, March 9, 2004, CCH MICHIGAN TAX REPORTS, ¶401-072)

• *Payment methods*

All remittances of taxes must be made to the Department of Treasury payable to the state of Michigan by bank draft, check, cashier's check, certified check, money order, cash, or electronic funds transfer. However, the tax liability is not discharged until the negotiable instrument remitted has been honored. The department may also accept major credit cards, debit cards, or both for payment of taxes. The department may add a processing fee. However, the fee may not exceed the charges that the state incurs because of the use of the credit or debit card or both. (Sec. 205.19(1), M.C.L.)

• *Assessment procedure*

Letter of inquiry: If the Department of Treasury needs additional information to accurately determine tax due, the Department may send a taxpayer a letter of inquiry stating its reasons for believing that additional information is needed or that additional taxes are due. The letter must explain how a person may communicate with the Department to resolve the dispute. Letters of inquiry are not required when (1) a taxpayer files a return that shows tax due and fails to pay the tax, (2) a deficiency results from an audit, or (3) a taxpayer affirmatively admits that tax is due and owing. If a dispute is not resolved within 30 days of the letter of inquiry, the Department may give a taxpayer Notice of Intent to assess tax due. (Sec. 205.21(2), M.C.L.)

Notices: As a prerequisite to the issuance of a tax assessment, the Department, after determining the amount of tax due from a taxpayer, must notify the taxpayer of its intent to levy the tax and advise the taxpayer of his or her right to have an informal conference regarding the taxpayer's alleged liability. (Sec. 205.21(2), M.C.L.)

Informal conference: A taxpayer must exercise his or her option for an informal conference within 60 days after receipt of the notice. (Sec. 205.21(2), M.C.L.) Procedures and requirements for the informal conference are discussed at ¶2503. A hearing referee, who is an employee of the Department, will conduct such an informal conference, which is not on the record and does not involve sworn testimony.

Final assessment: After the conference, or if the taxpayer does not request an informal conference within 30 days, the Department will issue a written decision and order setting forth the reasons and authority for the assessment, which constitutes a final assessment from which an appeal may be made. (Sec. 205.21(2), M.C.L.) Appeals are discussed further beginning at ¶2501.

• *Injunction not available*

Proceedings for the assessment of a tax may not be enjoined under Michigan law (¶2501). (Sec. 205.28(1)(b), M.C.L.) A federal statute also prohibits federal district courts from issuing injunctions where there is a "plain, speedy, and efficient remedy" in state courts.

• *Jeopardy assessments*

The issuance of a jeopardy assessment consists of giving notice to a person liable for taxes demanding the filing of an immediate return and payment of the tax on the basis of findings justifying this extraordinary action. The Department may issue a jeopardy assessment in cases where there is reason to believe that a person liable for a tax intends to do the following:

— depart from the state or remove property from the state;

— conceal the person or the person's property in the state; or

— do any act tending to render wholly or partly ineffectual the proceedings to collect. (Sec. 205.26, M.C.L.)

A warrant or warrant-notice of levy may issue immediately upon the issuance of a jeopardy assessment. Thereupon, the tax becomes immediately due and payable, unless the person subject to the jeopardy assessment is not in default in making a return or paying a tax and satisfies the Department that the return will be filed and the tax paid on or before the time fixed for payment. (Sec. 205.26, M.C.L.)

Michigan has jeopardy assessment provisions specific to personal property taxes, the motor carrier fuel tax, and the uniform city income tax. These provisions are procedurally similar to the uniform provisions discussed above.

• *Payment of assessment*

Taxes for which a demand for payment has been made by the Department or its agent and for which proceedings have not been taken by the taxpayer to review the liability must be paid within 10 days after the demand. (Sec. 205.25, M.C.L.) In the case of jeopardy assessments, however, the assessment must be paid immediately. (Sec. 205.26, M.C.L.) If payment is not made, the procedures relating to collection of delinquent taxes become applicable.

Practitioner Comment: Taxpayer's Failure To Pre-Pay Interest That Accrued After Date Of Assessment Denied Jurisdiction To Appeal in the Michigan Court of Claims, But The Decision Was Reversed Legislatively

In *Coventry Health Care Inc. v Dep't of Treasury*, Mich Ct App No 31789 (October 16, 2014), the Department of Treasury issued a Notice of Additional Tax Due to the taxpayer on March 30, 2012. The notice provided that, if additional tax, penalty, and interest totaling $721,198.00 was not paid within 30 days, a Notice of Intent to Assess would be issued. The Department of Treasury subsequently issued a Notice of Intent to Assess which updated the interest bringing the total due to $746,952.07.

The taxpayer paid the amount of $721,198.00 from the original notice on June 28, 2012 which was 90 days after the issuance of the Notice of Additional tax Due. Coventry also filed a suit for tax refund in the Court of Claims on June 28, 2012. The Court of Claims held that it had no jurisdiction to hear the appeal because not all of the accrued interest was paid. On appeal, the Michigan Court of Appeals affirmed the trial court and held that Coventry Health Care did not "pay the tax, including any applicable penalties and interest" before it brought its appeal. The Court of Claims, therefore, did not have jurisdiction to hear the appeal. Although the appeal was filed within the 90-day appeal period, the pre-payment requirement was not satisfied.

In connection with the pre-payment requirement, taxpayers should note:

1) The Department accepts mailed payments as made on the date they are postmarked.

2) To comply with MCL 205.22(2), a taxpayer must determine the additional interest accrued from the date of the notice to the date of payment. The Department provides different methods to assist taxpayers in making these calculations including: (1) direct contact with the Department; (2) website interest calculator; and (3) publication of interest rates.

3) On June 16, 2015, Michigan enacted 2015 PA 79 (Enrolled SB 100) to amend MCL 205.22(2) to eliminate the requirement that, in an appeal of a tax case to the Court of Claims, a taxpayer must first pay the full amount of tax, penalty and interest at issue and seek a refund. This amendment becomes effective in early 2016, has prospective application, and will render the decision in Coventry no longer applicable. Taxpayers will no longer be required to pre-pay disputed amounts before they can appeal their tax cases to the Michigan Court of Claims.

Wayne D. Roberts, Varnum, LLP and Marjorie B. Gell, Western Michigan University Cooley Law School

---

• *Statute of limitations*

The period within which assessments may be issued is limited as follows:

In general—Four-year limitation: Deficient taxes, interest, or penalty may not be assessed after four years from the date the return was due for filing or was actually filed, whichever is later. However, a person who has failed to file a return is liable for all taxes due for the entire period for which the person would be subject to the taxes. (Sec. 205.27a, M.C.L.)

CCH Comment: 2014 Legislation Extends Statute of Limitations

Effective February 6, 2014, legislation was enacted that provided additional time periods for extending the four-year statute of limitations during which the Department of Treasury may assess a Michigan corporate income tax, personal income tax, sales and use tax, and miscellaneous tax deficiencies, interest, or penalties. The statute of limitations was extended in instances where the following time periods exceed the statute of limitations: (1) the period pending the completion of an appeal of a final assessment; (2) a period of 90 days after the issuance of a decision and order from an informal conference; (3) a period of 90 days after the issuance of a court order resolving an appeal of a decision of the department in a case in which a final assessment was not issued prior to appeal; and (4) for the period of an audit that started after September 30, 2014, and was conducted within a specified time frame established by law.

The legislation also struck references in the law to suspending the statute of limitations and instead provided that the statute of limitations was extended for the periods currently stipulated in the law as well as the additional time periods. The four-year statute of limitations also applies to taxpayers claiming refunds.

The legislation requires the department to provide a responsible person of a business with notice of any amount collected by the department from any other responsible person. The department may not assess a responsible person more than four years after the date of the assessment issued to a business. Before assessing a responsible person as liable for a tax assessed to a business, the department must first assess a purchaser or succeeding purchaser of the business who is personally liable. However, the department may assess a responsible person notwithstanding the liability of a purchaser or succeeding purchaser if the purchaser or succeeding purchaser fails to pay the assessment for sales and use taxes, tobacco products tax, motor fuel tax, motor carrier fuel tax, income tax withholding, and any other tax that a person is required to collect on behalf of a third person. A "responsible person" means an officer, member, manager of a manager-managed limited liability company, or partner for the business who controlled, supervised, or was responsible for the filing of returns or payment of any of the taxes during the time period of default and who, during the time period of default, willfully failed to file a return or pay the tax due. (Act 3, S.B. 337, Laws 2014, effective February 6, 2014)

Concealment of tax liability: A person subject to tax who fraudulently conceals all or part of the tax, or fails to notify the Department of any modification of federal tax liability, may be assessed up to two years after the discovery of the fraud or failure to notify, irrespective of the period from the date on which the tax liability accrued. The assessment may include penalties and interest computed from the date the tax liability originally occurred. (Sec. 205.27a, M.C.L.)

Suspension of statute of limitations: The running of the statute of limitations is suspended with respect to items that were the subject of an investigation as to the following periods:

— the period pending a final determination of tax, federal or state, including periods for audit, conference, hearing, and litigation, *and for one year* after that period; or

— a period that a taxpayer and the Department may consent to in writing. (Sec. 205.27a, M.C.L.)

A suspension other than by consent applies only to those items that were the subject of the federal or state audit, conference, hearing, or litigation (*Revenue Administrative Bulletin 1988-20;* CCH MICHIGAN TAX REPORTS, ¶319-049).

• *Voluntary disclosure agreement*

The Department of Treasury may enter into a voluntary disclosure agreement with a person who is a nonfiler and who (1) has a filing responsibility under nexus standards issued by the Department or enacted into law after December 31, 1997, or (2) has a reasonable basis to contest a liability for a tax or fee administered by the Department. In general, eligible taxpayers who have not been previously contacted by the Department may file returns and pay taxes and interest for a limited lookback period without imposition of penalties. (Sec. 205.30c, M.C.L.) A prior telephone contact by the Department, without more, may not be such a "prior contact" as would preclude a voluntary disclosure agreement. (*Waupaca Foundry v. Department of Treasury*, Michigan Tax Tribunal, No. 266585, July 3, 2001; CCH MICHIGAN TAX REPORTS, ¶400-906).

Potential relief offered in agreement: The following relief may be provided in a voluntary disclosure agreement:

— The Department will not assess any tax, delinquency, penalty, or interest covered under the agreement for any period before the "lookback period" (defined below) specified in the agreement.

— The Department will not assess any applicable discretionary or nondiscretionary penalties for the lookback period.

— The Department will provide complete confidentiality of the agreement and will agree not to disclose the agreement to any tax authorities of any state or governmental authority or to any person except as required by certain exchange of information agreements, including the federal International Fuel Tax Agreement. The Department will not exchange information with other states regarding the person unless the information is specifically requested by another state. (Sec. 205.30c, M.C.L.)

In addition, the Department will not bring a criminal action against a person for failure to report or to remit any tax covered by the agreement before or during the lookback period. (Sec. 205.30c, M.C.L.)

"Lookback period" defined: The "lookback period" in a voluntary disclosure agreement means one or more of the following:

— the most recent 48-month period or the first date the person subject to an agreement began doing business in Michigan if less than 48 months;

— for purposes of the former single business tax, the Michigan business tax, or the corporate income tax, the combined lookback period for all taxes covered under the agreement will be the four most recent completed fiscal or calendar years over a 48-month period or the first date the person began doing business in Michigan if less than 48 months;

— the most recent 36-month period or the first date the person began doing business in this state if less than 36 months, if tax returns filed in another state for a tax based on net income that included sales in the numerator of the apportionment formula that now must be included in the numerator of the apportionment formula under the former single business tax, the Michigan business tax, or the corporate income tax, and those sales increased the net tax liability payable to that state; and

— if there is doubt as to liability for the tax during the lookback period, another period as determined by the Department to be in the best interest of Michigan and to preserve equitable and fair administration of taxes. (Sec. 205.30c, M.C.L.)

Requirements for entering agreement: To be eligible for a voluntary disclosure agreement, a person must be a "nonfiler," *i.e.,* a person who has never filed a return for the particular tax being disclosed, and must meet all of the following requirements:

— has had no previous contact by the Department regarding a tax covered by the agreement;

— has had no notification of an impending audit by the Department;

— is not currently under audit by the Department or under a state or local governmental investigation regarding a tax covered by the agreement;

— is not currently the subject of a civil action or a criminal prosecution involving any tax covered by the agreement;

— has agreed to register, file returns, and pay all taxes due for all periods after the lookback period;

— has agreed to pay all taxes due for the lookback period, plus statutory interest, within the period of time and in the manner specified in the agreement;

— has agreed to file returns and worksheets for the lookback period as specified in the agreement; and

— has agreed not to file a protest or seek a refund of tax paid to Michigan for the lookback period on the basis of the issues disclosed in the agreement. (Sec. 205.30c, M.C.L.)

Agreement conditions: A voluntary disclosure agreement is effective when signed and returned to the Department. The Department will only provide the relief specified in the executed agreement. Any verbal or written communication by the Department before the effective date of the agreement will not afford any penalty waiver, limited lookback period, or other benefit. (Sec. 205.30c, M.C.L.)

A material misrepresentation of fact by an applicant relating to the applicant's current activity in Michigan nullifies an agreement. A change in the activities or operations of a person after the effective date of the agreement is not a material misrepresentation of fact and will not affect the agreement's validity. (Sec. 205.30c, M.C.L.)

The Department may audit any of the taxes covered by the agreement within the lookback period or in any prior period if, in the Department's opinion, an audit of a prior period is necessary to determine the person's tax liability for the tax periods within the lookback period or to determine another person's tax liability. (Sec. 205.30c, M.C.L.)

Any tax collected or withheld from another person by an applicant must be remitted to the Department without respect to whether it was collected during or before the lookback period. (Sec. 205.30c, M.C.L.)

• *Agreement with Indian tribes*

The Department of Treasury is authorized to enter into tax agreements with the 12 federally recognized Indian tribes in Michigan to ensure uniform enforcement of state tax laws. Agreements must specify the applicability of a state tax on a tribe, its members, and any person conducting business with the tribe, as well as the duration of the agreement, termination provisions, administration, collection, enforcement, disclosure or information, dispute resolution, sharing of the tax revenue, and a provision making the agreement binding on all members of the tribe. (Sec. 205.30c, M.C.L.)

¶2404 Penalties and Interest

Law: Secs. 205.19(3), 205.23(2)—(5), 205.24(2)—(6), 205.25, 205.27(1)—(5), 205.27a(5), 205.28(2), 205.30(1), 205.30a(7), 205.31, 205.737, M.C.L.; R205.1012, R205.1013, Mich. Admin. Code (CCH MICHIGAN TAX REPORTS, ¶20-752, ¶20-770, ¶20-906, ¶89-202—¶89-210, ¶89-234).

Waiver of penalty: The Department of Treasury has authority to waive penalties in appropriate circumstances. In addition, certain civil and criminal penalties may be waived pursuant to a voluntary disclosure agreement.

If a taxpayer does not satisfy a tax liability or makes an excessive claim for refund as a result of reliance on erroneous current written information provided by the Department, the Department is required to waive all criminal and civil penalties for failing or refusing to file a return, for failing to pay a tax, or for making an excessive claim for refund, provided that the taxpayer makes a written request for waiver, files a return or an amended return, and makes full payment of tax and interest.

The Department will waive penalties for negligent tax deficiencies, excessive claims for credit, or for failure to file a return or pay a tax due if reasonable cause is established. Rules 12 and 13 of the Bill of Rights provide examples of what constitutes "reasonable cause" for waiver of the penalties (R205.1012, R205.1013, Mich. Admin. Code).

Civil Penalties

The penalties are due and payable after notice and conference (see ¶2501 for the appeal procedures). In all cases, interest, as set forth below under "Interest on Deficiencies and Overpayments," is also imposed.

• ***Deficiency taxes determined after examination of the return, payment or audit***

— *If there is negligence without intent to defraud:* $10 or 10% of the deficiency, whichever is greater. If a taxpayer subject to the *negligence* standard demonstrates to the satisfaction of the Department of Treasury that a deficiency or excess claim for credit was due to reasonable cause, the Department must waive the penalty. (Sec. 205.23(3), M.C.L.)

— *If there is intentional disregard of the law or rules promulgated by the Department of Treasury, but without intent to defraud:* $25 or 25% of the deficiency, whichever is greater. However, if a taxpayer subject to the *intentional disregard* standard successfully disputes a penalty under its provisions, the Department of Treasury may not impose the penalty prescribed by Sec. 205.23(3), the *negligence* standard, to any tax otherwise due. (Sec. 205.23(4), M.C.L.)

— *If there is fraudulent intent to evade a tax or obtain a refund, or a fraudulent claim:* 100% of the deficiency. (Sec. 205.23(5), M.C.L.)

Certain deficiency situations occur in spite of the taxpayer's good faith effort to comply with tax laws. Generally, no penalty is imposed in such cases. Examples of "no penalty" situations are cited in *Revenue Administrative Bulletin 2005-3;* CCH MICHIGAN TAX REPORTS, ¶319-342 (replacing *Revenue Administrative Bulletin 1995-4;* CCH MICHIGAN TAX REPORTS, ¶319-257).

The Department has also defined "negligence," "intentional disregard," and "fraud" for purposes of the above penalties in the above-cited bulletin.

CCH Note: Court of Appeals Interprets Intentional Disregard Standard

A Michigan court of appeals held that despite the Treasury Department's statements in *Administrative Bulletin 1995-4,* the personal income tax law does not place the burden of proof on the taxpayer to dispute the Department's finding of an intentional disregard of the law and does not provide that an assessment is prima facie correct. In addition, the court held that the governing statute authorizes the penalty for the intentional disregard of a law or rule only, and not for the intentional disregard of instructions. (*Wisne v. Department of Treasury,* Michigan Court of Appeals, No. 270633, May 20, 2008, CCH MICHIGAN TAX REPORTS, ¶401-369)

"Negligence" is the lack of due care in failing to do what a reasonable and ordinarily prudent person would have done under the particular circumstances. If a taxpayer fails to file a return in accordance with instructions, negligence is presumed. (R205.1012, Mich. Admin. Code)

There is "intentional disregard" when a person knowingly and wilfully disregards the laws, rules, and instructions published and/or administered by the Department without the intent to commit a fraud or evade payment of tax.

"Fraud" occurs when a person knowingly and willfully acts in a manner to commit fraud, such as failing or refusing to file a return; filing a false return, with the intent to evade payment of tax or part of a tax; claiming a false refund or a false credit; or aiding, abetting, or assisting another in an attempt to commit the aforementioned violations. However, the mere failure to file a tax return is not enough to sustain a fraud charge without some overt act showing intention to defraud.

The bulletin noted above lists examples or indicators of fraud, intentional disregard, or negligence.

• ***Failure to file return or pay tax on time***

Tax-due return: $10 or 5% of the tax, whichever is greater, if the violation is for not more than one month, with an additional 5% penalty for each month or fraction thereof of continuing violation, up to a maximum of 50%. If it is shown that the failure was due to reasonable cause and not to wilful neglect, the penalty may be waived at the Department's discretion. (Sec. 205.24, M.C.L.)

A 5% penalty is imposed if the failure to file was for not more than two months, with an additional 5% for each additional month, up to a maximum of 25%. (Sec. 205.24, M.C.L.)

Information return or report: $10 per day for each day for each separate failure or refusal, up to a maximum of $400. (Sec. 205.24, M.C.L.)

• ***Failure to remit withheld income tax payments***

A separate penalty applies to certain taxpayers that fail or refuse to remit withheld personal income tax payments as prescribed by law. A penalty of 0.167% of the tax due is added for each day that the failure continues or the tax and penalty are not paid, up to a maximum of 25% of the tax due. (Sec. 205.24, M.C.L.)

• ***Estimated tax payments***

If a taxpayer fails to pay a personal income tax estimated tax payment, a penalty may not be imposed if the taxpayer was not required to make estimated tax payments in the immediately preceding tax year. (Sec. 205.24, M.C.L.)

• ***Failure or refusal to surrender property subject to levy***

In addition to the personal liability imposed for failure or refusal to surrender property subject to levy, a penalty equal to 50% of the amount recoverable is imposed. This amount is not creditable against the liability for the collection of which the levy was made. (Sec. 205.23, M.C.L.)

• ***False statement by a nonobligated spouse***

A person who knowingly makes a false statement on a nonobligated spouse allocation form is liable for a penalty of $25 or 25% of the excessive claim, whichever is greater, in addition to other penalties that may be imposed. (Sec. 205.30a, M.C.L.)

• ***Payment of tax by a nonnegotiable remittance***

For using a nonnegotiable instrument as tax payment, a penalty equal to 25% of the tax due may be added, in addition to other penalties that may be imposed. (Sec. 205.19, M.C.L.)

• ***Frivolous protests***

If a taxpayer attempts to avoid or delay payment of a tax by raising claims that are not valid on their face or have repeatedly been found to be nonmeritorious in prior litigation, a penalty of $25 or 25% of the tax due, whichever is greater, see *Internal Policy Directive 2008-3*, Michigan Department of Treasury, November 14, 2008, CCH MICHIGAN TAX REPORTS, ¶401-394.

Criminal Penalties

The Attorney General and the prosecuting attorney of each county have concurrent power to enforce criminal penalties for tax violations.

• ***Prohibited acts***

The following prohibited acts are subject to criminal penalties:

— failure or refusal to make a return or payment within the time specified;

— making a false or fraudulent return or payment or false statement in a return or payment;

— making or permitting to be made a false return or payment or false statement in a return or payment, or a false claim for credit or refund; and

— aiding, abetting, or assisting another in an attempt to evade the payment of all or part of a tax or to file a false claim for credit. (Sec. 205.27, M.C.L.)

• ***Felonies***

The following felony actions are punishable by a fine of not more than $5,000 and/or imprisonment for not more than five years:

— any violation of the prohibited acts enumerated above with intent to defraud or evade or assist in defrauding or evading (Sec. 205.27, M.C.L.); and

— any violation of the restrictions against compromising or reducing taxes or against disclosing confidential tax information; if the unauthorized disclosure of confidential information is committed by a state employee, that person shall be discharged from employment upon conviction. (Sec. 205.28, M.C.L.)

• *Misdemeanors*

Any violation of tax law other than the specified prohibited acts constitutes a misdemeanor, punishable by fine of not more than $1,000, or imprisonment for not more than one year, or both. (Sec. 205.27, M.C.L.)

• *Perjury*

A person who knowingly swears to or verifies a false or fraudulent return, a false or fraudulent payment, or a return or payment containing a false or fraudulent statement with intent to aid, abet, or assist in defrauding the state is guilty of perjury. The penalty for perjury will be imposed in addition to the felony penalty. (Sec. 205.27, M.C.L.)

Interest on Deficiencies and Overpayments

Deficiency interest is charged at 1% above the adjusted prime rate charged by banks from the time payment was due until paid. The rate is administratively determined twice a year by the Department of Treasury. (Sec. 205.23, M.C.L.) Interest rates announced periodically by the Department of Treasury for use when determining the interest due on tax deficiencies are equally applicable to the interest payable on certain overpayments of tax. (Sec. 205.30, M.C.L.)

• *"Adjusted prime rate charged by banks" defined*

"Adjusted prime rate charged by banks" means the average predominant prime rate quoted by not less than three commercial banks to large businesses, as determined by the Department of Treasury, during the six-month periods ending March 31 (which becomes effective July 1) and September 30 (which becomes effective January 1). (Sec. 205.23, M.C.L.)

• *Interest rates*

The actual interest rates on deficiencies and overpayments are periodically announced by the Department of Treasury in a Revenue Administrative Bulletin.

Recent interest rates are as follows:

— 2015 (Jul – Dec) 4.25%
— 2015 (Jan – Jun) 4.25%
— 2014 (Jul – Dec) 4.25%

• *Example of how rates are applied*

Taxpayer A, who files on a calendar year basis, filed an MI-1040 return for 2005 showing tax due of $1,500. If the tax is not paid until January 1, 2014, the amount of interest calculated due from April 17, 2006, to December 31, 2013, is as follows:

Period		Calculation	Interest
April 17, 2006	June 30, 2006	74 days × .0001973 × $1,500 =	$ 21.90
July 1, 2006	December 31, 2006	184 days × .0002245 × $1,500 =	61.96
January 1, 2007	June 30, 2007	181 days × .0002493 × $1,500 =	67.68
July 1, 2007	December 31, 2007	184 days × .0002534 × $1,500 =	69.94
January 1, 2008	June 30, 2008	182 days × .0002514 × $1,500 =	68.63
July 1, 2008	December 31, 2008	184 days × .0002151 × $1,500 =	59.37
January 1, 2009	June 30, 2009	181 days × .0001644 × $1,500 =	44.63
July 1, 2009	December 31, 2009	184 days × .0001288 × $1,500 =	35.55
January 1, 2010	June 30, 2010	181 days × .0001164 × $1,500 =	31.60
July 1, 2010	December 31, 2010	184 days × .0001164 × $1,500 =	32.13
January 1, 2011	June 30, 2011	181 days × .0001164 × $1,500 =	31.60
July 1, 2011	December 31, 2011	184 days × .0001164 × $1,500 =	32.13
January 1, 2012	June 30, 2012	182 days × .0001161 × $1,500 =	31.70
July 1, 2012	December 31, 2012	184 days × .0001161 × $1,500 =	32.04
January 1, 2013	June 30, 2013	181 days × .0001164 × $1,500 =	31.60
July 1, 2013	December 31, 2013	184 days × .0001164 × $1,500 =	32.13
			$684.59

• *MTT interest rates*

An amount determined by the Tax Tribunal to have been unlawfully paid or underpaid bears interest from the date of payment to the date of judgment, and the judgment bears interest to the date of its payment. Interest accrues at one percentage point above the adjusted prime rate. "Adjusted prime rate" means the average predominant prime rate quoted by at least three commercial banks to large businesses, as determined by the Department of Treasury. The adjusted prime rate is based on the average prime rate charged by at least three commercial banks during the six-month periods ending on March 31 and September 30. One percentage point is added to the adjusted prime rate and the resulting sum is divided by 12 to establish the current monthly interest rate. The resulting current monthly interest rate that is based on the six-month period ending March 31 becomes effective on the following July 1, and the resulting current monthly interest rate that is based on the six-month period ending September 30 becomes effective on January 1 of the following year. (Sec. 205.737, M.C.L.) The MTT has exclusive jurisdiction over property tax matters and concurrent jurisdiction with the court of claims over matters involving Michigan state taxes (¶2505).

For the period July 1, 2015, through December 31, 2015, the interest rate applicable to amounts of Michigan tax determined by the Tax Tribunal to be unlawfully paid or underpaid is 4.25%.

ADMINISTRATION AND PROCEDURE

CHAPTER 25

TAXPAYER REMEDIES

¶2501 Overview

Law: Secs. 15.261—15.275, 24.271—24.287, 24.301—24.306, 205.4, 205.5, 205.6a, 205.7, 205.21(2), 205.22, 205.28(1)(b), 205.30c, 205.701—205.779, 600.202—600.251, 600.301—600.321, 600.6401—600.6475, M.C.L.; R205.1001—R205.1013, Mich. Admin. Code (CCH MICHIGAN TAX REPORTS, ¶20-902—¶20-906, ¶89-222—¶89-240).

Generally, a taxpayer may obtain relief through an informal administrative review upon timely request (60 days) when the taxpayer receives notice of intent with respect to a proposed state tax assessment. A subsequent assessment, decision, or order of the Department of Treasury may be appealed to the Michigan Tax Tribunal (a quasi-judicial agency) within 35 days (beginning 91 days after adjournment of the 2015 session, an appeal to the Tax Tribunal may be made within 60 days after the final decision) or the Michigan Court of Claims within 90 days if paid under protest, then to the Michigan Court of Appeals, and finally the Michigan Supreme Court. Further review may also be sought from the U.S. Supreme Court in appropriate cases.

• *Injunction not available*

Proceedings for the assessment or collection of a tax may not be enjoined under state law. A federal statute (28 U.S.C. §1341) also prohibits federal district courts from issuing injunctions for the assessment, levy, or collection of any tax under state law where there is a "plain, speedy, and efficient" remedy available in state courts.

• *Declaratory judgment not available*

A taxpayer cannot make use of an action for declaratory judgment to challenge the validity or applicability of a letter ruling. A taxpayer who feels aggrieved by such a ruling must use the remedial procedures discussed in the following paragraphs.

• *Burden of proof*

The burden of proof on appeal is with the taxpayer to prove that an assessment is unwarranted.

CCH Advisory: Reliance on Department Bulletins and Rulings

A taxpayer may rely on a bulletin or letter ruling issued by the Department of Treasury after September 30, 2006, for Michigan tax purposes and will not be penalized for that reliance until the bulletin or letter ruling is revoked in writing. (Sec. 205.6a, M.C.L.)

• *Refund of overpaid, erroneous, or illegal taxes*

The general rules for seeking refund of overpaid, erroneous, or illegal taxes are discussed at ¶2402.

• *Statutes relating to taxpayer remedies*

Remedial hearings and appeals are governed by a number of Michigan statutes, namely:

— The Administrative Procedures Act of 1969: "Procedures in Contested Cases" and "Judicial Review." This is discussed above.

— The Revenue Act (Act 122, Laws 1941): "Appeal Procedure;" the Tax Tribunal Act, together with the Tax Tribunal Rules; and the Court of Claims Act and Court of Claims Rules. These are discussed in the following paragraphs.

— The Open Meetings Act.

— The Revised Judicature Act of 1961: Michigan Court of Appeals and Michigan Supreme Court, together with the rules of practice of the respective judicial bodies.

• *Voluntary disclosure agreement*

The Department of Treasury may enter into a voluntary disclosure agreement that allows a nonfiler to file returns and pay taxes and interest for a limited lookback period (generally, three or four years) without imposition of penalties for that period. See ¶2403 for details.

CCH Comment: New Offer-in-Compromise Program Created for 2015

Michigan enacted legislation regarding the settlement of unpaid tax liabilities that creates an offer-in-compromise program. The legislation mandates that the program begin on January 1, 2015, and requires the Michigan Department of Treasury to issue guidelines to taxpayers and department employees by December 18, 2014. To be eligible under the new offer-in-compromise program, there must be a doubt as to liability, doubt as to collectibility, or the taxpayer must have been granted a related tax compromise under the federal offer-in-compromise program. Features of the program are set to include: a required payment of $100 or 20% of the offer made (whichever is greater) at the time an offer is submitted; a prohibition against levying against property to collect a tax liability while a compromise is pending; publication of a public report on a granted offer-in-compromise; an independent administrative review process; revocation of compromise under certain conditions, such as an intent to mislead in obtaining a compromise or a failure to meet terms of a compromise; and offer rejections that are final and not subject to appeal. (Act 240, H.B. 4003, Laws 2014, effective June 21, 2014)

• *Taxpayer Bill of Rights*

The Michigan Department of Treasury has adopted a series of rules known as the Taxpayer Bill of Rights (R205.1001—R205.1013, Mich. Admin. Code; CCH MICHIGAN TAX REPORTS, ¶89-700—89-700*l*). The rules address standards for treatment of the public, confidentiality of information, representation before the Department, informal conferences, and the negligence and failure to file a return or pay the tax owed penalties (discussed at ¶2404).

Informal conferences: A taxpayer is entitled to an informal conference on the question of liability for an assessment, provided that the taxpayer (1) serves written notice upon the Department within 60 days after receiving a notice of intent to assess, (2) remits the uncontested portion of the liability, and (3) provides a statement of the contested amounts and an explanation of the dispute. As discussed at ¶2503, an informal conference is also available to contest a credit audit or a refund denial.

Purpose of informal conference: The purpose of an informal conference is to informally discuss the positions of the parties, narrow the subjects at issue, and present arguments that enable a conferee to make written recommendations to the Department. The Department may accept or reject the recommendations in a written decision and order. After a written decision is issued, a notice of final assessment must be sent to the taxpayer, advising the taxpayer of his or her right to appeal. *An informal conference does not constitute a contested case proceeding and is not subject to the Administrative Procedures Act.*

Time, place, and manner of informal conference: The Department must set a mutually agreed upon or reasonable time and place for the conference. Generally, informal conferences will be scheduled throughout the year during regular business hours. The Department must provide written notice of the time and place of the conference by certified mail not less than 20 days before the date of the conference. A conference may also be based upon written statements or be conducted by telecommunications under certain circumstances. Sound recordings are authorized, but a formal record of a conference is not made.

Confidentiality of information: Except as otherwise provided by law, Department of Treasury employees may not disclose information obtained in connection with the administration of a tax, including audit and tax collection criteria, to any person except an affected taxpayer and his or her representative. Access to confidential data is restricted to Department employees who have a need to know the information to perform their duties. Similarly, private contractors are strictly prohibited from disclosing taxpayer information to third parties.

Confidential information may be disclosed (1) to adjudicate a taxpayer's tax liability, (2) to properly administer the laws in Michigan, (3) to facilitate the investigation or enforcement of support obligations, (4) to assist local, state, or federal agencies in the administration of the criminal laws, or (5) because of reciprocal agreements with the U.S. Department of Treasury, taxing officials of other states, or other Michigan departments or local governmental units. Under certain circumstances, the disclosure of casino receipts and taxes is allowed as well.

Absent these circumstances, a third party must furnish appropriate authorization from a taxpayer before confidential information may be disclosed. A taxpayer may name only one representative for a single dispute. A taxpayer's conduct may constitute express or implied authorization to the Department to disclose confidential information.

Treatment of public by Department staff: Employees of the Michigan Department of Treasury must avoid the appearance of impropriety in their conduct. Among other matters, improper conduct includes the failure to properly report possible conflicts of interest, the falsification of records, the misuse of confidential information, and the participation in business transactions for financial gain that take advantage of an employee's official position. The Department is required to monitor its employees' conduct with the public.

¶2502 General Provisions for Contesting Agency Determinations

Law: Secs. 24.203, 24.271—24.287, 24.301—24.306, 205.745, M.C.L.; R205.3101—R205.3802, R792.10201—R792.10289, Mich. Admin. Code (CCH MICHIGAN TAX REPORTS, ¶20-904, ¶20-906, ¶89-228, ¶89-232, ¶89-234, ¶89-238).

This paragraph discusses the provisions relating to "contested cases" as applicable to agencies in general and the judicial review of the decisions and orders arising from such cases.

• *Contested cases before Department of Treasury*

The Department of Treasury has adopted rules governing the appeal of contested cases (R205.3101—R205.3802, Mich. Admin. Code; CCH MICHIGAN TAX REPORTS, ¶89-992a—¶89-992hhh). The following eight subjects are addressed in the rules: General Provisions; Commencement of Appeal Proceeding; Pleadings, Motion Practice, and Intervention; Joint and Consolidated Proceedings; Prehearing Conferences; Conduct of Hearings; Decisions; and Remand Proceedings. These rules do not apply to state taxes that are assessed by the Department.

• *Contested cases before Michigan Tax Tribunal*

The provisions on contested cases in the Administrative Procedures Act, the Tax Tribunal Act and the Michigan Administrative Procedures Act are applicable to tax-related cases pending before the Michigan Tax Tribunal where an applicable Tax Tribunal rule does not exist. Most contested case provisions are covered by specific Tax Tribunal rules. Pursuant to the Tax Tribunal Act and the Michigan Administrative Procedures Act, the Tribunal has promulgated its administrative rules of practice and procedure (R792.10201—R792.10289, Mich. Admin. Code; CCH MICHIGAN TAX REPORTS, ¶89-990—¶89-990qq).

A "contested case" is a proceeding in which a determination of the legal rights, duties, or privileges of a named party is required by law to be made by an agency after an opportunity for an evidentiary hearing. (Sec. 24.203, M.C.L.)

Hearings: Parties to a contested case are entitled to a hearing after notice. Failure of a party to appear after proper notice will not bar the agency from proceeding with the hearing. Oral and written arguments are permitted at the hearing. Hearings are presided over by one or more members of the agency, a person appointed by statute, or hearing officers appointed by the agency. (Sec. 24.271, M.C.L.)

Discovery: Subpoenas may be issued by an agency if authorized to do so. Testimony under oath, certification of official acts, and depositions may be taken. The rules of evidence in nonjury civil cases in a circuit court are followed as far as practicable. (Sec. 24.273, M.C.L.; Sec. 24.274, M.C.L.; Sec. 24.275, M.C.L.)

Final decisions and orders: Final decisions and orders must be in writing or stated in the record, issued within a reasonable time, and based exclusively on the evidence and on matters officially noticed. (Sec. 24.285, M.C.L.)

Rehearings: Rehearings are allowed when the record of testimony at the hearing is inadequate for purposes of judicial review. (Sec. 24.287, M.C.L.)

• *Judicial review*

The provisions on judicial review of contested cases in the Administrative Procedures Act are considered generally not to apply to appeals from a tax assessment, although there are reported appellate decisions that refer to or rely upon these provisions. The provisions of the Revenue Act, the Court of Claims Act, and the Tax Tribunal Act govern the timing and procedure of appeals in these tax cases. (*Letter to CCH,* Department of Treasury, October 17, 1989)

Exhaustion of remedies: Exhaustion of administrative remedies is a prerequisite for judicial review of a contested case; however, the filing of a motion for rehearing or reconsideration is not required unless agency rules require it. Preliminary agency action or ruling is not immediately reviewable, unless a court determines that review of the agency's final decision would not provide an adequate remedy. (Sec. 24.301, M.C.L.)

Additional evidence: A court may order the taking of additional evidence before the agency under the following circumstances:

— timely application is made to the court for presentation of additional evidence; and

— an inadequate record was made at the agency's initial hearing; or

— the additional evidence is material and there are good reasons for failing to record or present such evidence in earlier proceedings. (Sec. 24.305, M.C.L.)

Review of contested cases: Judicial review of a final decision or order in a contested case shall be by any applicable special statutory review proceeding specified by law. Otherwise, it is governed by the Administrative Procedures Act, which requires the filing of a petition for review within 60 days from date of mailing notice of the agency's final decision. Filing of the petition does not stay enforcement of the agency action, although the court may on its own initiative grant a stay. (Sec. 24.304, M.C.L.)

¶2503 Informal Conference

Law: Sec. 205.21(2) and (3), M.C.L. (CCH MICHIGAN TAX REPORTS, ¶20-906, ¶89-230).

Taxpayers may request an informal conference to contest a notice of intent to assess tax due, a credit audit, or a refund denial (see ¶2403 under "Assessment procedure" and ¶2501 under "Taxpayer Bill of Rights"). The request must be filed within 60 days of receiving the assessment notice, credit audit, or refund denial. To seek a conference to protest an assessment notice, a taxpayer must prepay the uncontested portion of the liability. The taxpayer's request must include the taxpayer's statement of contested amount and an explanation of the dispute. Alternatively, a taxpayer may pay the contested amount and convert the contest of the assessment to a claim for refund. (Secs. 205.21, 205.21A, M.C.L.)

Upon receipt of the taxpayer's written notice, the Department is required to set a *mutually agreed upon or reasonable* time and place for the informal conference and give the taxpayer at least 20 days' reasonable written notice of the conference. Written notice of the conference must specify an intent to assess tax due and the type of tax and tax year at issue in a case. An informal conference is subject to the rules governing informal conferences as promulgated by the Department in accordance with the Administrative Procedures Act of 1969, Act No. 306 of 1969, but is not governed by the act itself. A taxpayer may appear or be represented by any person at a conference. With advance notice and at a party's own expense, an audio recording of the conference may be made. (Sec. 205.21(2)(d), M.C.L.)

After an informal conference, the Department must render a written decision, setting forth reasons and authority, limited to the subject matter of the conference as included in the notice. If a taxpayer does not protest a notice of intent to assess tax due within the time provided, the Department may assess the tax due. A final notice of assessment must include a statement advising a taxpayer of the right to appeal. (Sec. 205.21(2)(d), M.C.L.) See also ¶2501.

A taxpayer's request for an informal conference is considered denied if the Department of Treasury fails to issue an order and determination within 180 days of the taxpayer's notice. In cases where the request is denied in such a manner, the taxpayer may still appeal the contested issues. (Sec. 205.21(2)(d), M.C.L.)

Frivolous protests or those intended to delay or impede the administration of taxes are subject to penalties (¶2404).

¶2505 Tax Tribunal Jurisdiction and Powers

Law: Secs. 205.10, 205.20, 205.22, 205.721, 205.731, 205.732, 205.736, 205.774, 205.779, M.C.L. (CCH MICHIGAN TAX REPORTS, ¶20-906, ¶89-234).

The Michigan Tax Tribunal (MTT) is a quasi-judicial agency composed of seven members appointed by the Governor, with the advice and consent of the Senate. It is considered part of the Department of Treasury for administrative purposes only. (Sec. 205.721, M.C.L.)

• *Historical background*

This historical background is provided because some cases cited in this *Guidebook* may make reference to agencies that have since been replaced by the MTT. Prior to the creation of the MTT in 1973, a taxpayer could appeal to the circuit court after paying the tax, or to the State Board of Tax Appeals (BTA) or the Corporation Tax Appeal Board (CTAB) without paying the tax.

• *Procedures subject to appeal*

The following state tax circumstances may be appealed:

— a proceeding for direct review of a final decision, finding, ruling, determination, or order of an agency relative to assessment, valuation, rates, special assessments, allocation, or equalization, under property tax laws (Sec. 205.731, M.C.L.);

— a proceeding for refund or redetermination of a tax under the property tax laws (Sec. 205.731, M.C.L.);

— an appeal to the MTT authorized by any other tax statute, principally the Department of Revenue Act (Sec. 205.731, M.C.L.);

— a final determination of a tax deficiency;

— the denial of a claim for refund;

— the recovery of taxes paid under protest; or

— any other decision of the Department of Treasury, such as denial of tax-exempt status. (RAB 94-1, Department of Treasury, ¶319-242)

• *Tribunal's jurisdiction*

The MTT has jurisdiction over disputes concerning all taxes, unless otherwise provided by specific authority in a taxing statute administered by the Department of Treasury. The MTT shares with the Court of Claims the appellate jurisdiction over disputes involving Michigan taxes. (Sec. 205.22, M.C.L.)

The right to sue any agency for refund of any taxes other than by proceedings before the Tax Tribunal is abolished after September 30, 1974. It is not necessary that the payment of an erroneous tax or unlawful tax be made under protest in order to seek a refund by a proceeding before the Tax Tribunal. (Sec. 205.774, M.C.L.)

CCH Note: Tribunal Had Jurisdiction Over Garbage Tax

The Michigan Tax Tribunal (MTT) had exclusive jurisdiction over a city's garbage tax levied on commercial and industrial property located in the city because the tax was based on the taxable value of real property and, therefore, was authorized under property tax laws. Even if the garbage tax was considered a general tax rather than a special assessment, jurisdiction was proper in the MTT under the statutory provision that set forth the MTT's jurisdiction. This provision stipulated that the MTT had original and exclusive jurisdiction over a proceeding for a refund or redetermination of a tax levied under the property tax laws of the state. (*Parker v. City of Detroit,* Michigan Court of Appeals, No. 282427, April 23, 2009, CCH MICHIGAN TAX REPORTS, ¶401-418)

• *Powers of MTT*

The MTT has power to:

— affirm, revise, modify, or remand a final decision or order of an agency;

— order payment or refund of taxes;

— grant other relief or issue writs;

— promulgate rules consistent with the Administrative Procedures Act;

— mediate a proceeding before the tribunal; and

— certify mediators to facilitate claims in the court of claims and in the tribunal. (Sec. 205.732, M.C.L.)

• *Mediation*

Appeals to the MTT may be resolved through mediation provided that both parties consent to mediation, agree on a mediator and the MTT issues an order designating the proceeding for mediation. The mediator does not have authoritative decision-making power to resolve a dispute in mediation. If an agreement is reached, the MTT will accept the agreement if it comports with the MTT's requirements.

¶2506 Appeal Procedures

Law: Sec. 205.22(1)—(3), 205.8, 205.28, 205.701—205.779, 205.725, 205.735, 205.736, 205.744, 205.745, 205.751, 205.752, 205.752(2), M.C.L. (CCH MICHIGAN TAX REPORTS, ¶20-906, ¶89-234).

Currently, tax disputes involving property tax must be appealed to the MTT while other state taxes may be appealed to the MTT or to the Michigan Court of Claims.

Appeals to the Michigan Tax Tribunal (MTT) would be governed principally by Sec. 205.22, M.C.L., in conjunction with the Tax Tribunal Act and the rules promulgated by the MTT. Although certain provisions of the Tax Tribunal Act were originally intended to apply only to property taxes, they are now applicable to nonproperty tax cases by reason of the broadening of the MTT's jurisdiction.

• *Written petition*

Practitioner Comment: Department of Treasury Required to Provide Notice to Designated Representative (Power of Attorney) Before Limitations Period For Filing an Appeal Begins to Run

In two combined cases, *SMK v. Dep't of Treasury*, 495 Mich. 104, , 845 N.W.2d 81, (2014) and *Fradco, Inc. v. Dep't of Treasury*, (Docket Number, Apr. 1, 2014). the Michigan Supreme Court affirmed two lower court rulings and held that the Department of Treasury is required to send a Notice of Final Assessment to a taxpayer's designated representative before the 35-day appeal period set forth in Sec. 205.22(1), M.C.L. begins to run. (Note: beginning 91 days after adjournment of the 2015 session, an appeal to the Tax Tribunal may be made within 60 days after the final decision) In both cases, the taxpayer, pursuant to Sec. 205.8, M.C.L., designated an authorized representative by filing a Michigan Power of Attorney form with the department. The department conducted a sales tax audit and assessed additional sales taxes against each taxpayer. However, while the department reportedly sent a copy of the Notice of Final Assessment to the taxpayer's address, which would satisfy the basic notice requirement set forth in Sec. 205.28(1)(a), M.C.L., no copy of the Notice of Final Assessment was sent to the taxpayer's authorized representative (as required by Sec. 205.8, M.C.L.). The taxpayers in each case appealed the final assessments when the authorized representative ultimately received a copy of the final assessment, but these appeals were filed more than 35 days after the original final assessment was sent to the taxpayer's address.

Wayne D. Roberts, Varnum, LLP and Marjorie B. Gell, Western Michigan University Cooley Law School

---

• *Prerequisites to appeal*

The uncontested portion of the state tax assessment, decision, or order must be paid as a prerequisite to appeal. All property taxes must be paid before the MTT issues its decision in an appeal. (Sec. 205.22(1), M.C.L.)

The appellate court held that a personal income taxpayer's due process rights were not violated by the statute that required prepayment of the uncontested portion of the tax assessment. The court noted that a promise to pay the debt or partial payment were not sufficient to satisfy the statute. The court determined that the tax scheme satisfied due process requirements because the taxpayer was afforded a meaningful opportunity to be heard and the state had a legitimate interest in the prompt payment of taxes such that it could condition the hearing on the prepayment of uncontested taxes. (*Anderson v. Department of Treasury,* Michigan Court of Appeals, No. 303470, August 9, 2012, CCH MICHIGAN TAX REPORTS, ¶401-700)

Practitioner Comment: Reinstatement of Appeal Rights Where Taxpayer's Authorized Representative Not Properly Notified

In a Notice released in October 2015, the Michigan Department of Treasury announced that in all cases where (1) a request for an informal conference, (2) an appeal to the Tax Tribunal, or (3) an appeal to the Court of Claims have been denied as untimely because the Department failed to provide the taxpayer's representative with a copy of the relevant notice or letter, the Department will not consider that the time period for requesting a conference or appeal has begun, and on request will reinstate a taxpayer's appeal rights. See the Michigan Department of Treasury's *Notice Appeal Extension When Taxpayer's Representative Was or is Not Provided the Required Copy of a Letter or Notice* (October 2015). While the Notice does not make reference to the statute of limitations, presumably this Notice will apply solely to open tax years.

Wayne D. Roberts, Varnum LLP and Marjorie B. Gell, Western Michigan University Cooley Law School

---

• *Open meetings required*

Provisions of the Open Meetings Act (Secs. 15.261—15.275, M.C.L.) requiring that meetings be open to the public are applicable to MTT sessions.

• *De novo proceedings*

Proceedings before the MTT are original, independent, and *de novo.* (Sec. 205.735, M.C.L.; Sec. 205.735a(2), M.C.L.)

The MTT may issue subpoenas for the testimony of witnesses and the production of books, records, and other evidence. The chairman may require any state or local government unit to make available books, records, documents, information, and assistance to the MTT. (Sec. 205.736, M.C.L.)

Practitioner Comment: Leaseholders of Commercial Property are "Parties of Interest" and Eligible for Streamlined Tax Appeals under MCL 205.735a

In *Spartan Stores, Inc. and Family Fare, LLC v. City of Grand Rapids,* the Michigan Court of Appeals reversed the Tax Tribunal's finding that a leaseholder of commercial property was not a "party of interest" for purposes of MCL 205.735a.

Under MCL 205.735a, a "party in interest" in a tax assessment dispute involving certain types of commercial, industrial, or developmental property can bypass the board of review and appeal directly to the Tax Tribunal. The Michigan Court of Appeals agreed with petitioner Family Fare, LLC that as a leaseholder of commercial property, it was a party in interest entitled to appeal a tax assessment directly to the Tax Tribunal. However, the Court found that petitioner Spartan Stores, Inc., parent company of Family Fare, LLC, was not a party in interest because it did not own the property, nor was it a party to the lease. As a holder of a mere financial interest in the property, Spartan Stores, Inc. was not permitted to protest the assessment under MCL 205.735a.

Wayne D. Roberts, Varnum LLP and Marjorie B. Gell, Western Michigan University Cooley Law School

---

• *Intervention or impleading*

The MTT may allow any governmental unit that receives tax funds from the taxpayer to be impleaded. In the case of the Small Claims Division of the MTT, it must be shown that the intervenor has material monetary interest in the case that is not likely to be presented by the parties. (Sec. 205.744, M.C.L.)

• *Decisions or orders*

Final decisions and orders of the MTT must be in writing or stated in the record, issued within a reasonable time, and based on evidence admitted during the proceedings. (Sec. 205.751, M.C.L.) Such decision or order is conclusive on all parties unless reversed, remanded, or modified on appeal. (Sec. 205.752, M.C.L.) A decision or order may be entered upon written consent of the parties filed in the proceeding or stated in the record. Such order or decision is not appealable and has like effect as an order or decision in a contested hearing. (Sec. 205.745, M.C.L.)

• *Rehearings*

Rehearings may be allowed upon written motion within 20 days after the entry of the decision or order. A decision or order may be amended or vacated after the rehearing. (Sec. 205.752(2), M.C.L.)

• *Failure to appeal—Defective appeals*

If an assessment, decision, or order of the Department is not appealed, such assessment, decision, or order becomes final and is not reviewable by mandamus, appeal, or any other form of indirect or collateral attack. (Sec. 205.22(4), M.C.L.)

A taxpayer may not circumvent the time limit for challenging an assessment, decision, or order by resorting to the refund procedure. Once the time to challenge an assessment has expired, a taxpayer is no longer entitled to a refund.

• *Corporate officer liability*

Personal liability of corporate officers for unpaid corporate taxes does not arise until after the corporation has concluded its pursuit of appellate remedies. Thus, issuance of an Intent to Assess an officer prior to the conclusion of the corporation's appeal is premature. However, an officer assessed for a corporate tax debt which has become final as to the corporation cannot contest the basis for the assessment to the corporation (*Revenue Administrative Bulletin 1989-38,* CCH MICHIGAN TAX REPORTS, ¶319-128).

Officer liability provisions include responsible parties of flow-through entities, such as limited liability companies and partnerships. For details, see ¶2403.

• *Informal settlement conferences*

A petitioner or a local property tax collecting unit may request an informal settlement conference after a petition is filed in the residential property and small claims division of the Tax Tribunal. The request must be made before a hearing has been scheduled. The party requesting an informal settlement conference must submit a written request to the other party and file a copy with the residential property and small claims division. The local tax collecting unit must hold an informal settlement conference within 60 days after a request is made. An informal settlement conference must be held telephonically or at the offices of the local tax collecting unit. (Sec. 205.762b, M.C.L.)

¶2507 Appeals to State Courts Generally

The Michigan Court of Claims is an alternative avenue whereby assessments, decisions, or orders of the Department of Treasury may be appealed. Decisions of the MTT or the Court of Claims may be appealed to the Michigan Court of Appeals. Decisions of the Court of Appeals may be raised for review to the Michigan Supreme Court.

¶2508 Appeal to Court of Claims

Law: Secs. 205.22(1), 205.22(2), 600.6401 to 600.6475, 600.6419, 600.6440, M.C.L. (CCH MICHIGAN TAX REPORTS, ¶20-906, ¶89-236).

A disputed assessment, decision, or order may be appealed to the Michigan Court of Claims, instead of to the MTT, within 90 days after the assessment, decision, or order, if the assessment in question is paid under written protest. Procedural rules applicable are set forth in the Court of Claims Act and Court of Claims Rules. (Sec. 205.22(1), (2), M.C.L.)

• *Jurisdiction*

The Michigan Court of Claims has jurisdiction over claims and demands against the state or any of its departments or officers and over counterclaims by the latter against the claimant. All actions initiated in the Michigan Court of Claims must be filed in the Michigan Court of Appeals. (Sec. 600.6419) However, a claimant who has an adequate remedy in the federal courts is barred from filing a claim in the Court of Claims. (Sec. 600.6440, M.C.L.)

• *No payment prerequisite to appeal*

Under legislation enacted on June 16, 2015 and effective 91 days after adjournment sine die of the 2015 Regular Session of the Michigan Legislature taxpayers, will no longer have to first pay the tax, including any applicable penalties and interest, under protest and claim a refund before appealing to the Michigan Court of Claims. Until the effective day of the legislation, taxpayers must first pay the tax before appealing to the Court of Claims.

Practitioner Comment: Michigan Taxpayers Now Have A Right To Appeal Non-Property Tax Disputes to The Michigan Courts with Prepayment of Tax

Effective in late March 2016, or early April 2016 (91 days after adjournment sine die of the 2015 Regular Session of the Michigan Legislature), taxpayers will no longer be required to pre-pay disputed tax assessments before appealing to the Michigan Court of Claims. On June 16, 2015, Governor Rick Snyder signed into law enrolled SB 100, which will eliminate the requirement that taxpayers pay all tax, penalties, and interest before they can have their tax appeals heard by a court of law. This new law opens Michigan's court system to all Michigan taxpayers, and guarantees that taxpayers have their "day in court" before they are required to pay tax assessments. Prior to the enactment of enrolled SB 100, taxpayers had two options to appeal a non-property tax assessment, order, or decision that was adverse to them: they could appeal the case to the Michigan Tax Tribunal without paying amounts that were in dispute; or they could appeal the case to the Michigan Court of Claims, but only after paying all amounts of taxes, penalties, and interest assessed, including amounts that were being contested.

Wayne D. Roberts, Varnum LLP and Marjorie B. Gell, Western Michigan University Cooley Law School

---

¶2509 Appeal to Court of Appeals

Law: Secs. 205.22(1), 205.22(3), 205.753, M.C.L. (CCH MICHIGAN TAX REPORTS, ¶20-906, ¶89-236).

A decision of the MTT or the Court of Claims may be appealed to the Court of Appeals as a matter of right. (Sec. 205.22(3), M.C.L.) Appeals, which must be taken on the record made before the MTT or the Court of Claims, are made in accordance with court rules after the entry of a final decision or order or after denial of a motion for rehearing. (Sec. 205.753, M.C.L.)

¶2510 Appeal to Supreme Court

Law: Sec. 205.22(1), 205.22(3), M.C.L. (CCH MICHIGAN TAX REPORTS, ¶20-906, ¶89-236).

A decision of the Court of Appeals may be further appealed to the Michigan Supreme Court only by application for leave to appeal. (Sec. 205.22(3), M.C.L.)

¶2511 Federal Court Actions

Tax disputes involving the United States Constitution or federal statutes may also be brought in federal courts. This right to bring federal suit is limited by the Tax Injunction Act, the fundamental principle of comity and the doctrine of abstention.

• *Tax Injunction Act*

A federal statute (28 U.S.C. § 1341) prohibits injunctions in federal district courts against assessment, levy, or collection of any state tax when there is a "plain, speedy, and efficient remedy" in state courts. This principle set forth in the statute has evolved into the federal abstention doctrine as it has been amplified by case law, including these U.S. Supreme Court cases: In *Railroad Commission v. Pullman Co.* ((1941, US SCt), 312 US 496, 61 SCt 643), the Court called for abstention when interpretation of state statutes in state forums might in and of itself eliminate constitutional questions; in *Younger v. Harris* ((1971, US SCt), 401 US 37, 91 SCt 746), the Court held that abstention was proper in deference to a state's interest in ongoing proceedings in its own forums and in deference to the state judiciary's power to consider constitutional claims.

A provision of the Railroad Revitalization and Regulatory Act (the "4-R Act") that gives federal courts jurisdiction to prevent violations of the prohibition against taxes that discriminate against rail carriers was held to be an express exception to the Tax Injunction Act and it authorizes a federal court to prevent or terminate a violation of the 4-R Act (*National R.R. Passenger Corp. v. California State Board of Equalization* (1986) 652 FSupp 923).

• *"Plain, speedy, and efficient remedy" construed*

There is plain, speedy, and efficient remedy within the context of the Tax Injunction Act if the state remedy provides the taxpayer with a full hearing and judicial determination at which the taxpayer may raise any and all constitutional objections to the tax (*Rosewell v. LaSalle National Bank* (1981, US SCt), 450 US 503, 101 SCt 1221). It is not required that the state remedy be the best available or even equal to or better than the remedy available in the federal courts (*Rodriguez v. Steirheim* (1979), 465 FSupp 1191) or that it be the best and most convenient remedy.

• *Principle of comity*

Although the federal Tax Injunction Act codified the principles of comity, the U.S. Supreme Court has stated that the passage of the Tax Injunction Act did not restrict the preexisting principles of comity. In a case brought as a civil action for deprivation of rights under 42 U.S.C. § 1983 by Missouri taxpayers claiming damages from alleged unequal property valuation, the U.S. Supreme Court held the federal suit to be barred by the principle of comity (*Fair Assessment in Real Estate Association, Inc., et al. v. McNary et al.* (1981, US SCt), 454 US 100, 102 SCt 177).

• *Criteria for exercising federal jurisdiction*

The criteria for accepting jurisdiction by federal courts has been set forth in *In the Matter of Levy* (1978, US SCt), 439 US 920, 99 SCt 301, as follows:

— there are no unsettled questions of state law that affect federal claims;

— present state proceedings would not be interrupted by exercise of federal jurisdiction; and

— the most important questions of law presented by the suit are federal, not state, questions.

ADMINISTRATION AND PROCEDURE

CHAPTER 26

MICHIGAN RESOURCES

Bureau of Revenue

Michigan Department of Treasury
Treasury Building
430 West Allegan Street
Lansing, Michigan 48922
Phone: (517) 373-3200
Fax: (517) 373-4023
Corporate income tax information: (517) 636-6925
Individual income tax information: (517) 636-4486
Income tax refund status: (517) 636-4486
Single Business Tax; Michigan Business Tax: (517) 636-6925
Business tax registration: (517) 636-6925; Fax: (517) 636-4520
Cigarette/Tobacco tax: (517) 636-4630; Fax: (517) 636-4631
Email: treas_TobaccoTaxes@michigan.gov
Collections: (517) 636-5265; Fax: (517) 636-5245
Homestead Exemption: (517) 636-4486
Legislative Liaison: (517) 373-3223
Motor Fuel, Severance Tax: (517) 636-4600; Fax: (517) 636-4593
Email: TreasMotFuel@michigan.gov
Sales, Use and Withholding Taxes: (517) 636-6925
Tax Clearance: (517) 636-5260
Unclaimed Property: (517) 636-5320; Fax: (517) 322-5986
Tax Fraud Hotline: (517) 636-4157
Email: ReportTaxFraud@Michigan.gov

Field offices

The Michigan Department of Treasury has the following field offices that are open to the public and provide limited assistance to taxpayers:

Detroit

Cadillac Place, 1st Floor
3060 W. Grand Boulevard
Detroit, MI 48202-6060
Audit Division phone number: 313-456-4340
Audit Division fax: 313-456-4311

Collection Division phone number: 313-456-4340
Collection Division fax: 313-456-4272

Escanaba

State Office Building, Second Floor
305 Ludington Street
Escanaba, MI 49829
Audit Division phone number: (906) 786-6334
Audit Division fax: (906) 786-4959
Collection Division phone number: (906) 786-6339
Collection Division fax: (906) 786-4959

Flint

State Office Building, 7th Floor
125 E. Union Street
Flint, MI 48502
Audit Division phone number: (810) 760-2782
Audit Division fax: (810) 760-2014
Collection Division phone number: (810) 760-2782
Collection Division fax: (810) 760-2787

Grand Rapids

State Office Building
350 Ottawa Street NW
Grand Rapids, MI 49503
Audit Division phone number: (616) 356-0300
Audit Division fax: (616) 356-0642
Collection Division phone number: (616) 356-0300
Collection Division fax: (616) 356-0439

Saginaw

State Office Building
411-I E. Genesee Street
Saginaw, MI 48607
Audit Division phone number: (586) 997-6618
Audit Division fax: (989) 758-1419

Sterling Heights

41300 Dequindre, Ste. 200
Sterling Heights, MI 48314
Phone number: (586) 997-0801
Fax: (586) 997-1502

Traverse City

701 S. Elmwood Avenue, 4th Floor
Traverse City, MI 49684

Audit Division phone number: (231) 922-5230

Audit Division fax: (231) 922-5243

Collection Division phone number: (231) 922-5244

Collection Division fax: (231) 922-5246

Property Tax Division: (231) 922-5247

The telephone numbers for the county equalization departments are as follows:

Alcona County—(517) 724-6223.

Alger County—(906) 387-2567.

Allegan County—(616) 673-0230.

Alpena County—(517) 356-1943.

Antrim County—(231) 533-6320.

Arenac County—(517) 846-6246.

Baraga County—(906) 524-7331.

Barry County—(616) 948-4821.

Bay County—(517) 895-4075.

Benzie County—(616) 882-0014.

Berrien County—(616) 983-7111.

Branch County—(517) 279-4312.

Calhoun County—(269) 781-0700; Battle Creek (269) 966-3369; Treasurer's Office (269) 781-0807.

Cass County—(616) 445-4442.

Charlevoix County—(231) 547-7230.

Cheboygan County—(616) 627-8810.

Chippewa County—(906) 635-6307.

Clare County—(517) 539-7894.

Clinton County—(517) 224-5170.

Crawford County—(517) 348-2841.

Delta County—(906) 789-5109.

Dickinson County—(906) 774-2515.

Eaton County—(517) 543-7500 ext. 236.

Emmet County—(231) 348-1708.

Genesee County—(810) 257-3017. n.

Gladwin County—(517) 426-9327.

Gogebic County—(906) 663-4414.

Grand Traverse County—(616) 922-4772.

Gratiot County—(517) 875-5203.

Hillsdale County—(517) 439-9166.

Houghton County—(906) 482-0250.

Huron County—(517) 269-6497.

Ingham County—(517) 676-7212; www.ingham.org.

Ionia County—(616) 527-5376.

Iosco County—(517) 362-5801.

Iron County—(906) 875-6502.

Isabella County—(517) 772-0911.

Jackson County—(517) 788-4388.

Kalamazoo County—(616) 383-8960; www.kalcounty.com/equalization/equalreport.htm.

Kalkaska County—(231) 258-3340.

Kent County—(616) 632-7520; (616) 632-7542; www.accesskent.com; Grand Rapid's Treasurer (616) 456-3020.

Keweenaw County—(906) 337-3471.

Lake County—(616) 745-2723.

Lapeer County—(810) 667-0228.

Leelanau County—(616) 256-9823.

Lenawee County—(517) 264-4522.

Livingston County—(517) 546-4182.

Luce County—(906) 293-5611.

Mackinac County—(906) 643-7313.

Macomb County—Mt. Clemens (586) 469-5260; Sterling Heights (586) 446-2340 (ext. 180); St. Clair Shores (586) 445-5212 (ext. 355); Warren (586) 574-4500 (ext. 4532).

Manistee County—(231) 723-1572.

Marquette County—(906) 225-8405.

Mason County—(231) 845-6288.

Mecosta County—(231) 592-0108.

Menominee County—(906) 863-2683.

Midland County—(517) 832-6844.

Missaukee County—(616) 839-2702.

Monroe County—(734) 240-7235.

Montcalm County—(517) 831-7492.

Montmorency County—(517) 785-3411.

Muskegon County—(616) 724-6386.

Newaygo County—(231) 689-7242.

Oakland County—Pontiac, MI 48341; (248) 858-1000; Royal Oak (248) 246-3000.

Oceana County—(231) 873-4609.

Ogemaw County—(517) 345-0328.

Ontonagon County—(906) 884-2765.

Osceola County—(231) 832-6122.

Oscoda County—(517) 826-1103.

Otsego County—(517) 732-6484.

Ottawa County—(616) 738-4826.

Presque Isle County—(517) 734-3810.

Roscommon County—(517) 275-8121.

Saginaw County—(517) 790-5260; www.saginawcounty.com.

St. Clair County—(810) 989-6920.

St. Joseph County—(616) 467-5550.

Sanilac County—(810) 648-2955.

Schoolcraft County—300 Walnut, Room 207, Manistique, MI 49854; (906) 341-3677.

Shiawassee County—(517) 743-2263.

Tuscola County—(517) 672-3830.

Van Buren County—(616) 657-8234.

Washtenaw County—(734) 994-2511.

Wayne County—, Detroit, (313) 224-6219; (313) 224-2342; Detroit (313) 224-3035; www.ci.detroit.mi.us.

Wexford County—(231) 779-9474.

PART X

DOING BUSINESS IN MICHIGAN

CHAPTER 27

BUSINESS FORMATION AND QUALIFICATION

¶2701 Overview

Michigan's business law provides for the formation, operation, combination, and dissolution, etc., of for-profit corporations and other business entities (such as limited liability companies (LLCs) and the assorted partnership formats). The state, whether by statute, regulation, or other administrative action, also imposes various service fees in connection with the above aspects of a business entity's lifecycle. The Michigan Department of Licensing and Regulatory Affairs (LARA) administers these diverse business law and service fee provisions. (See http://www.michigan.gov/lara)

These fees, which are generally payable to the Michigan Department of Licensing and Regulatory Affairs, are in the nature of public compensation for either a state-granted privilege, such as the right to transact business in the state, or for a specified administrative service. These fees also serve to enforce compliance with all of the state's applicable statutory, regulatory, and administrative business provisions.

General business formation and operation information, as well as fee information in connection with the activities noted above, are more specifically addressed at ¶2702 Domestic Business Entities, and also at ¶2703 Foreign Business Entities.

The concept of "doing business" in Michigan is briefly introduced, as well.

Finally, for additional, state-provided resources on business choice of entity, formation, and operation in Michigan, see http://www.michigan.gov/lara/0,4601,7-154-35299_61343_35413---,00.html.

¶2702 Domestic Business Entities

Law: Secs. 449.1—449.373, 450.1101—450.2099, 450.4101—450.5200, M.C.L. (CCH MICHIGAN TAX REPORTS, ¶1-105).

Michigan has several business-related enactments addressing the formation, operation, combination, and dissolution, etc. of for-profit domestic corporations and other domestic business entities. These corporate, limited liability company (LLC), and assorted partnership enactments provide significant information regarding the internal operations of a corporation, LLC, partnership, or other business entity, such as ownership rights, voting rules, director/manager obligations, and bylaw/agreement contents, etc. These enactments also address the service fees that are applicable to the various interactions between the state and the above domestic business entities. Business law resources and the location of applicable fee information are specifically noted below.

• *Corporate entities*

Michigan's general corporation law provisions addressing domestic corporations are found within the Michigan Business Corporation Act (Chapter 450 Corporations, Business Corporation Act; Act 284 of 1972, Chapter 1 to Chapter 10 (Sec. 450.1101, M.C.L. to Sec. 450.2099, M.C.L.)).

All parties desiring to incorporate a for-profit domestic corporation in Michigan, that is, a corporation created under the laws of the state, must execute and file articles of incorporation with the Michigan Department of Licensing and Regulatory Affairs (LARA). Among other items, such articles generally provide the name of the corporation, the number of shares that the corporation may issue, the address of the corporation's registered office in the state, and the name of its registered agent authorized to receive the service of process.

The Michigan Department of Licensing and Regulatory Affairs (LARA) imposes and collects a service fee for this filing and for issuing a certificate of incorporation. The department also charges other related fees for assorted corporate filing activities. Such fees are generally payable at the time that the requisite documents are filed. For additional, specific information on these fees and the amounts due, see http://www.michigan.gov/lara/0,4601,7-154-35299_61343_35413---,00.html.

• *Other business entities*

In addition to forming and operating as a domestic corporation, among other choices, a business taxpayer can choose to form and operate as either a domestic LLC or as one of the varied domestic partnership formats. The noncorporate business entity choices are briefly addressed below.

LLCs.—Michigan's general LLC law provisions addressing domestic LLCs are found within the Michigan Limited Liability Company Act (Chapter 450 Corporations, Business Corporation Act); Act 23 of 1993; Article 1 to Article 11 (Sec. 450.4101, M.C.L. to Sec. 450.5200, M.C.L.).

All parties desiring to organize a for-profit domestic LLC in Michigan, that is, an LLC created under the laws of the state, must execute and file articles of organization with the Michigan Department of Licensing and Regulatory Affairs (LARA). Among other items, such articles generally provide the name of the LLC, the address of the initial designated office, the name and address of the initial agent for service of process, and the name and address of each organizer.

The Michigan Department of Licensing and Regulatory Affairs (LARA) imposes and collects a service fee for this filing and for issuing a certificate of organization. The department also charges other related fees for assorted LLC filing activities. Such fees are generally payable at the time that the requisite documents are filed. For additional, specific information on these fees and the amounts due, see http://www.michigan.gov/lara/0,4601,7-154-35299_61343_35413_35429---,00.html.

Partnerships.—Michigan's general partnership law provisions addressing domestic partnerships are found within the Michigan Uniform Partnership Act (Chapter 449 Partnerships); Act 72 of 1917; (Sec. 449.1, M.C.L. to Sec. 449.373, M.C.L.).

The Michigan Department of Licensing and Regulatory Affairs (LARA) imposes and collects a service fee for certain filings and for the issuance of specified instruments. Such fees are generally payable at the time that the requisite documents are filed. For additional, specific information on these fees and the amounts due, see http://www.michigan.gov/lara/0,4601,7-154-35299_61343_35413---,00.html.

¶2703 Foreign Business Entities

Law: Secs. 449.1—449.373, 450.1101—450.2099, 450.4101—450.5200, M.C.L. (CCH MICHIGAN TAX REPORTS, ¶1-110).

Michigan has several business-related enactments addressing the qualification and operation of for-profit foreign corporations and other foreign business entities. These corporate, limited liability company (LLC), and assorted partnership enactments provide significant information regarding the internal operations of a corporation, LLC, partnership, or other business entity, such as ownership rights, voting rules, director/manager obligations, and bylaw/agreement contents, etc. These enactments also address the service fees that are applicable to the various interactions between the state and the above foreign business entities. Business law resources and the location of applicable fee information are specifically noted below.

• *Corporate entities*

Michigan's general corporation law provisions addressing foreign corporations are found within the Michigan Business Corporation Act (Chapter 450 Corporations, Business Corporation Act); Act 284 of 1972, Chapter 1 to Chapter 10 (Sec. 450.1101, M.C.L. to Sec. 450.2099, M.C.L.).

In the same manner that the incorporation of a domestic corporation and its ability to do business in Michigan is a privilege to be conferred only by law and upon such conditions and payments as the state sees fit, the exercise of the corporate franchise in Michigan and the transaction of business in the state by a business entity created and incorporated elsewhere is a privilege upon which conditions may be imposed and for which fees may be charged. No foreign corporation may engage in any business in Michigan until all applicable fees have been paid and the entity has procured a certificate of authority from the Michigan Department of Licensing and Regulatory Affairs (LARA) to transact business in the state.

Upon the issuance of a certificate of authority by the Michigan Department of Licensing and Regulatory Affairs (LARA), the foreign corporation possesses rights, privileges, duties, and restrictions comparable to those of a domestic corporation incorporated in the state.

A party desiring to qualify a foreign corporation in Michigan must apply for a certificate of authority from the Michigan Department of Licensing and Regulatory Affairs (LARA). Among other items, such an application must generally provide the name of the corporation, the place of incorporation, the address of its principal office, the number of shares that the corporation may issue, the address of the foreign corporation's registered office in the state, and the name of its registered agent authorized to receive the service of process.

A foreign corporation that transacts business in the state without a certificate of authority is liable to the state for the years or parts thereof during which it engaged in business without a certificate of authority. The charge will be an amount equal to all fees that would have been imposed upon the corporation had it applied for and received a certificate of authority and filed all of the required reports, plus all penalties for the failure to pay the fees. The state's Attorney General will bring proceedings to recover all amounts due to the state.

The Michigan Department of Licensing and Regulatory Affairs (LARA) imposes and collects a service fee for reviewing the application for, and issuing, a certificate of authority to a foreign corporation to "do business" (see below) in the state. The department also charges other related fees for assorted corporate filing activities. Such fees are generally payable at the time that the requisite documents are filed. For additional, specific information on these fees and the amounts due, see http://www.michigan.gov/lara/0,4601,7-154-35299_61343_35413_35426-120069--,00.html.

• *Other business entities*

In addition to operating as a foreign corporation, among other choices, a business taxpayer can choose to operate as either a foreign LLC or as one of the varied foreign partnership formats. The noncorporate business entity choices are briefly addressed below.

LLCs.—Michigan's general LLC law provisions addressing foreign LLCs are found within the Michigan Limited Liability Company Act (Chapter 450 Corporations, Business Corporation Act); Act 23 of 1993; Article 1 to Article 11 (Sec. 450.4101, M.C.L. to Sec. 450.5200, M.C.L.).

All parties desiring to qualify a for-profit foreign LLC in Michigan must present the LLC's articles of organization and apply for a certificate of authority from the Michigan Department of Licensing and Regulatory Affairs (LARA). Among other items, the articles of organization generally provide the name of the LLC, the address of the initial designated office, the name and address of the initial agent for the service of process, and the name and address of each organizer.

The Michigan Department of Licensing and Regulatory Affairs (LARA) imposes and collects a service fee for reviewing the application for, and issuing, the certificate of authority. The department also charges other related fees for assorted LLC filing activities. Such fees are generally payable at the time that the requisite documents are filed. For additional, specific information on these fees and the amounts due, see http://www.michigan.gov/lara/0,4601,7-154-35299_61343_35413_35429---,00.html.

Partnerships.—Michigan's general partnership law provisions addressing foreign partnerships are found within the Michigan Uniform Partnership Act (Chapter 449 Partnerships); Act 72 of 1917; (Sec. 449.1, M.C.L. to Sec. 449.373, M.C.L.).

The Michigan Department of Licensing and Regulatory Affairs (LARA) imposes and collects a service fee for certain filings and for the issuance of specified instruments. Such fees are generally payable at the time that the requisite documents are filed. For additional, specific information on these fees and the amounts due, see http://www.michigan.gov/lara/0,4601,7-154-35299_61343_35413---,00.html.

• *Doing business*

"Doing business," as far as a foreign business entity is concerned, refers to a link or connection that the entity establishes by its business operations or activities in a state. Whether a foreign business entity is doing business in a state is important in at least three areas of the law:

(1) whether the entity has subjected itself to a state's laws on qualification to transact business in the state,

(2) whether the entity is subject to the state's taxing power, and

(3) whether the entity is amenable to suit in the state.

The concept of "doing business", however, is not similarly defined in these three areas.

For additional, more specific information on this topic in the income taxation context, see CCH MICHIGAN TAX REPORTS, ¶10-075 Nexus—P.L. 86-272—Doing Business in State, and, in the sales and use tax context, see CCH MICHIGAN TAX REPORTS, ¶60-025 Nexus—Doing Business in Michigan.

PART XI

UNCLAIMED PROPERTY

CHAPTER 28

UNCLAIMED PROPERTY

¶2801 Unclaimed Property

"Escheat" is the vesting in the state of title to unclaimed property.

Michigan enacted a Uniform Unclaimed Property Act (Act 29, Public Acts 1995) effective on January 1, 1996, that became the primary law governing unclaimed property. (Sec. 567.221, M.C.L.) The law is essentially patterned after the Uniform Unclaimed Property Act of 1981. In addition, the following laws also deal with escheat of property:

(1) the older laws on Lost and Unclaimed Property (Chapter 434, Michigan Compiled Laws). These laws, which actually cover lost, unclaimed, abandoned and stolen property, have not been invalidated by the Uniform Unclaimed Property Act and are still in the books (Sec. 567.262, M.C.L.); and

(2) the law on escheats (Chapter 567, Michigan Compiled Laws). This law applies to the escheat of property left behind by a person who dies intestate with no heirs or by a person missing for the required statutory period.

CCH Comment: Potential federal/state conflict

Escheat is an area of potential federal/state conflict. A federal statute may preempt state escheat provisions, as for instance Sec. 514(a) of the Employee Retirement Income Security Act of 1974 (ERISA). Pursuant to this provision, the Department of Labor has been of the opinion that funds of missing participants in a qualified employee benefit plan must stay in the plan despite a Texas escheat provision because ERISA preempts application of the Texas escheat laws with respect to such funds. (Advisory Opinion 94-41A, Department of Labor, Pension and Welfare Benefit Administration, Dec. 7, 1994) However, some states have challenged the federal position on this and similar narrowly delineated situations. Thus, practitioners are advised that a specific situation where federal and state policy cross on the issue of escheat may, at this time, be an area of unsettled law.

In the case of federal tax refunds, IRC Sec. 6408 disallows refunds if the refund would escheat to a state.

Michigan Uniform Unclaimed Property Act

The Michigan State Treasurer is the administrator of the Uniform Unclaimed Property Act and acts as custodian of the property on behalf of the owner. Every business or government agency holding unclaimed property belonging to someone whose last known address is in Michigan must report. If the holder is incorporated in Michigan and the owner's address is unknown, then the holder must report those properties to Michigan. Two conditions are necessary for escheat to take place: (1) the property must be abandoned, and (2) there must be some basis for the state taking custody of the property.

• *"Abandoned" property*

Generally, all tangible or intangible personal property that is held, issued, or owing in the ordinary course of a holder's business and has remained unclaimed by the owner for more than three years after it became payable or distributable is presumed abandoned. (Sec. 567.223, M.C.L.) Other presumptive periods for abandonment apply to certain types of property, as discussed below.

• *Presumptions of abandonment*

Actual abandonment of property may be proved at any time, but since unclaimed property is usually held under circumstances in which ownership of the property is unknown or uncertain, Michigan provides the following presumptive periods for abandonment:

One-year property

Unpaid wages . . . . 1 year
Utility deposits . . . . 1 year
Property from a dissolved business association . . . . 1 year
Refunds ordered by a state court or agency . . . . 1 year
Property held by a court, governmental agency, public corporation or public authority . . . . 1 year

Three-year property

Uncashed checks or drafts . . . . 3 years
Inactive bank accounts . . . . 3 years
Certain specialized bank deposits . . . . 3 years
Safe deposit box or repository . . . . 3 years
Unclaimed funds held by a life insurance company . . . . 3 years
Property held by fiduciary . . . . 3 years
Gift certificate or credit memo . . . . 3 years
Funds held under prepaid funeral contract funding act . . . . 3 years
Money orders . . . . 3 years
Automatic reinvestment plans . . . . 3 years
Stocks and dividends or other distributions . . . . 3 years

Fifteen-year property

Traveler's checks . . . . 15 years

Unpaid wages.—Unpaid wages which have remained unclaimed by the owner for more than one year after becoming payable are presumed abandoned. (Sec. 567.236, M.C.L.)

Utility deposits.—Deposits or advances made to secure payment for utility services that remain unclaimed for more than one year after termination of the service are presumed abandoned. (Sec. 567.229, M.C.L.)

Property from a dissolved business association.—Property that is distributable in the course of the dissolution of a business association and that remains unclaimed more than one year after the date of final distribution is presumed abandoned. (Sec. 567.232, M.C.L.)

Refunds ordered by a state court or agency.—Funds that a business association has been ordered to refund that remain unclaimed by the owner for more than one year after becoming payable are presumed abandoned. (Sec. 567.230, M.C.L.) In order to obtain a refund, Form MI 3277 Claim for Refund of Unclaimed Property must be filed. Use Form MI 3165 Michigan Holder Request for Refund to request a refund of unclaimed property that was reported to the state of Michigan in error.

Property held by a court, governmental agency, public corporation or public authority.—Property held for the owner by these entities is presumed abandoned if it remains unclaimed for more than one year after becoming payable or distributable. (Sec. 567.234, M.C.L.)

Uncashed checks or drafts.—Any sum payable on a check, draft or similar financial instrument (except money orders or traveler's checks), including a cashier's check and a certified check, on which a banking or financial organization is directly liable which has been outstanding for more than three years after it was payable (or after its issuance, if an instrument payable on demand) is presumed abandoned, unless within the three-year period the owner has communicated with the bank or otherwise indicated an interest. (Sec. 567.226, M.C.L.)

Inactive bank accounts.—Any demand, savings, or matured time deposit, and any sum paid toward the purchase of an interest in a banking or financial organization, is presumed abandoned after three years, unless within the three-year period the owner has increased or decreased the balance of his account, established another relationship with the bank, communicated in writing with the bank, or otherwise indicated interest concerning the property. Certain specialized bank accounts are also subject to a three-year dormancy period. (Sec. 567.227, M.C.L.)

Safe deposit box or repository.—All property held in a safe deposit box or repository in Michigan in the ordinary course of the holder's business, and proceeds from the sale of such property, that remains unclaimed by the owner for more than three years from the date the rental period expired is presumed abandoned. (Sec. 567.237, M.C.L.)

An owner is required to file Form MI 3167 Inventory of Safe Deposit Box Contents and attach a copy of the list of contents to Form MI 2011 Holder Transmittal for Report of Unclaimed Property along with Form MI 1223 Annual Report of Unclaimed Cash and Safe Deposit Boxes or a diskette when it is reported to the state of Michigan.

Unclaimed funds held by life insurance companies.—Funds held under any life or endowment insurance policy or annuity contract that has matured are presumed abandoned if unclaimed for more than three years after the funds became due and payable. However, where the insured has attained, or would have attained if he were living, the limiting age under the mortality table on which the reserve is based, the dormancy period of the fund is two years. (Sec. 567.228, M.C.L.)

Unclaimed property in conjunction with demutualization of insurance company.—Unclaimed property payable or distributable in conjunction with the demutualization of an insurance company is presumed abandoned after two years. The term "demutualization" means the payment of consideration for the relinquishment of a mutual membership interest in a mutual insurance company, regardless if undertaken in conjunction with a plan of demutualization, liquidation, merger, or other form of reorganization. (Sec. 567.228b, M.C.L.)

Property held by fiduciary.—Property held in a fiduciary capacity for the benefit of another person is presumed abandoned after three years from the time it became payable or distributable, unless within the three-year period the owner increased or decreased the principal, accepted payment of principal or income, communicated concerning the property, or otherwise indicated an interest therein. (Sec. 567.233, M.C.L.)

Gift certificate, gift card, or credit memo.—A gift certificate, gift card, or credit memo is presumed abandoned if either of the following apply:

(1) the certificate, card, or memo is not claimed or used for a period of three years after becoming payable or distributable; or

(2) the certificate, card, or memo is used or claimed one or more times without exhausting its full value, but subsequently is not claimed or used for an uninterrupted period of three years.

A gift certificate or gift card is considered to have been claimed or used if there is any transaction processing activity on the certificate or card, including redeeming, refunding, or adding value to it. Any activity initiated by the card issuer, including assessing inactivity fees or similar service fees, does not constitute transaction processing activity. In the case of a gift certificate or gift card, the owner is presumed to be a gift recipient of the certificate or card, and the amount presumed abandoned is the price paid by the purchaser for the gift certificate or gift card, less the total of any purchases or fees assessed against it. Gift certificates that are issued by retailers are not considered abandoned property. (Sec. 567.235, M.C.L.) The state does not have a separate treatment for gift cards. (*Telephone Conversation with the Michigan Department of Treasury in response to CCH Survey on Treatment of Gift Cards as Unclaimed Property*, February 27, 2004, ¶401-083)

Funds held under a prepaid funeral contract.—Funds held by a provider of a prepaid funeral contract are presumed abandoned after they remain unclaimed for three years after the death of the beneficiary (or the owner of the contract, if no beneficiary has been designated). The unclaimed funds may be held by a provider under a contract governed by the 1986 law (Sec. 328.211 to Sec. 328.235, M.C.L.) or pursuant to the 1954 law (Sec. 328.201 to Sec. 328.204). (Sec. 567.228a, M.C.L.)

Stock, share, or other intangible ownership interest.—Any stock, share, or other intangible ownership interest in a business association is presumed abandoned if the owner of the interest did not claim a dividend or other distribution for over three years, and the association did not know of the owner's location. In addition, the abandonment of stock enrolled in an automatic reinvestment plan is presumed abandoned if the owner had not communicated with the business association for at least three years, and at least three years had elapsed since the owner's location became unknown to the business association. (Sec. 567.231a, M.C.L.)

All available owner information must be filed on Form MI 3164 Report of Unclaimed Shares of Stock/Mutual Funds. Form MI 3164 must be attached to Form MI 2011 Holder Transmittal for Report of Unclaimed Property.

Money orders.—Any sum payable on a money order or similar written instrument other than a third-party bank check that has been outstanding for more than three years after its issuance is presumed abandoned, unless within the three-year period the owner has communicated in writing with the issuer or otherwise indicated an interest. (Sec. 567.225, M.C.L.)

Traveler's checks.—Any sum payable on a traveler's check that has been outstanding for more than 15 years after its issuance is presumed abandoned, unless within the 15-year period the owner has communicated in writing with the issuer or otherwise indicated an interest. (Sec. 567.225, M.C.L.)

Certain specialized deposits in a financial institution.—The following types of deposits are presumed abandoned after three years of dormancy:

(1) any bank deposit that is automatically renewable;

(2) a trust deposit with respect to which the trustor did not specify the terms of the trust other than the identity of the beneficiary (Sec. 487.702, M.C.L.); and

(3) an account established under the Michigan Uniform Gifts to Minors Act. (Sec. 554.451 to Sec. 554.461, M.C.L.)

(Sec. 567.227, M.C.L.)

• *Business-to-business exemption*

Michigan has a business-to-business exemption from the provisions of the Uniform Disposition of Unclaimed Property Act. Except with respect to property in a demand, savings, or matured time deposit with a banking or financial organization or property held in a safe deposit box or other safekeeping repository, the exemption applies to any credit balances, overpayments, deposits, refunds, discounts, rebates, credit memos, or unidentified remittances created on or after April 1, 2009, and issued, held, due, or owing in any transaction between two or more associations. The exemption does not apply to outstanding checks, drafts, or other similar instruments. An "association" means a business association, a public corporation, or any other commercial entity, including a sole proprietorship. (Sec. 567.257a, M.C.L.)

• *Unclaimed property inquiry*

A claimant must file Form MI 3433 Unclaimed Property Inquiry providing property owner information and listing all former addresses used by the property owner.

• *Basis for taking custody of the property*

In addition to satisfying a presumptive period of abandonment, the state must have some basis for taking custody of the property. The nexus may consist of any of the following:

(1) the records of the holder showing that the last known address of the apparent owner or person entitled to the property is in Michigan, or in another state that does not provide for escheat or whose escheat law does not apply to the property and the holder is domiciled in Michigan or is a Michigan government agency;

(2) if the holder's records do not indicate the owner's last known address, a showing that the last known address of the person entitled to the property is in Michigan or that the holder is domiciled in Michigan or is a government entity in Michigan;

(3) if the apparent owner's last known address as shown on the holder's records is in a foreign nation, a showing that the holder is domiciled in Michigan, or is a Michigan government agency; or

(4) if the last known address of the apparent owner or person entitled to the property is unknown, or in another state that does not provide for escheat or whose escheat law does not apply to the property, and the holder's domicile is another state that does not provide for escheat or whose escheat law does not apply to the property, a showing that the transaction out of which the property arose occurred in Michigan.

(Sec. 567.224, M.C.L.)

Michigan Law on Lost and Unclaimed Property.—The Uniform Unclaimed Property Act (UUPA) does not apply to unclaimed, lost or abandoned property that is the subject of another Michigan statute that specifies who becomes the owner of the property. (Sec. 567.262, M.C.L.) Thus, the following older laws relating to unclaimed, lost or abandoned property, which were not repealed by UUPA, are still in place. Lost, unclaimed, or abandoned personal property in the custody of departments, boards, or institutions of the state of Michigan may be disposed of if it remains unclaimed after six months. (Sec. 434.153, M.C.L.) The property typically consists of items lost or abandoned by the owners in state owned or leased property such as hospitals, prisons, state offices, etc. (Sec. 434.151, M.C.L.) If they are determined to have intrinsic or commercial value, a list is forwarded to the Commissioner of State Police, who may decide to include them in one of the sales events held from time to time for stolen property. (Sec. 434.155, M.C.L.) Those without intrinsic or commercial value are donated or destroyed. (Sec. 434.156, M.C.L.)

Stolen property recovered by county or local law enforcement officers, or abandoned property discovered by them, may be disposed of if it remains unclaimed for six months after its recovery or discovery. (Sec. 434.171, M.C.L.; Sec. 434.181, M.C.L.) The property is sold by law enforcement officers after obtaining approval from the appropriate administrative authority (county board of supervisors, village council, or township board of trustees). (Sec. 434.173, M.C.L.; Sec. 434.183, M.C.L.) If the property is an abandoned or stolen bicycle, the county or local law enforcement agency may request authority from the appropriate administrative authority (county board of commissioners, local governing body) to donate the bicycle to a state-licensed charitable organization. (Sec. 434.171, M.C.L.; Sec. 434.181, M.C.L.)

Lost property found by private individuals.—Michigan's finder's law (Sec. 434.21 to Sec. 434.29, M.C.L.) is briefly noted here, but strictly does not belong to a discussion of escheats. Most property falling under this statute defaults to the finder if the owner cannot be found. If the finder cannot be found or does not want the property, the property may be retained by the law enforcement agency or donated to charity.

• *Obligations of holder of unclaimed property*

Report filing.—Under the Unclaimed Property Act, a holder of abandoned property with a value of $50.00 or more (except traveler's checks and money orders, to which the qualifying amount does not apply) must file a verified annual report containing information concerning the property required by the State Treasurer. For years ending after 2011, the report is due on or before July 1 of each year for the period ending on the preceding March 31. The Treasurer has discretion to authorize an extension of the filing date based on a written request filed before the expiration of the due date. (Sec. 567.238, M.C.L.) Form MI 1223 Annual Report of Unclaimed Cash and Safe Deposit Boxes must be accompanied by Form MI 2011 Holder Transmittal for Report of Unclaimed Property.

The Michigan Department of Treasury has prepared a manual to help organizations file unclaimed property reports. It does not address legal issues relating to unclaimed property, nor does it describe all types of property that must be reported. However, it does provide instructions for reporting the most common types of unclaimed property. (*Manual for Reporting Unclaimed Property*)

Negative reporting.—Under the Michigan Unclaimed Property Act, entities having no unclaimed property to report under the act do not need to file a zero or negative report. (*Manual for Reporting Unclaimed Property*, Michigan Department of Treasury, Unlciamed Property Division, revised April 2015)

Written notice.—Under the Unclaimed Property Act, not less than 60 days or more than 365 days before filing the annual report, the holder of property presumed abandoned must send written notice to the apparent owner at his or her last known address advising him or her of the fact that he holds such property. (Sec. 567.238, M.C.L.)

Publication in newspaper.—Under the Unclaimed Property Act, the Department of Treasury is required to publish twice yearly in a newspaper of statewide circulation, the Department's website address and the number of unclaimed properties added to the website. The website is required to list the owners of unclaimed property. (Sec. 567.239, M.C.L.)

Delivery.—Under the Unclaimed Property Act, the abandoned property must be paid or delivered to the Treasurer simultaneously with the filing of the report. (Sec. 567.240, M.C.L.) Where property consists of stock, a duplicate certificate or other evidence of ownership may be delivered if the holder does not issue certificates of ownership. In general, the payment or delivery of the property to the Treasurer relieves the holder of all liability to the extent of the value of the property paid or delivered for any claim existing or which may arise with respect to the property. (Sec. 567.241, M.C.L.)

Required time periods.—The period during which the Treasurer may begin an action or proceeding under the Unclaimed Property Act with respect to any duty of a holder of records of transactions between two or more associations is limited to five years rather than 10 years after the duty arose. The period during which a holder of records of transactions between two or more associations is required to maintain a record of the name and last known address of the owner is also limited to five years rather than 10 years after the property becomes reportable. (Sec. 567.250, M.C.L.; Sec. 567.252, M.C.L.)

Penalties.—Under the Unclaimed Property Act, the late payment or delivery of property is subject to an interest penalty (adjusted prime rate plus one percent) from the date the property should have been paid or delivered to the date of its actual payment or delivery. The penalty for willfully failing to render a report or to perform other required duties is a fine of not more than $100 per day of violation, to a maximum of $5,000. Willfully failing to pay or deliver property to the Treasurer is subject to a civil penalty of 25% of the value of the property that should have been paid or delivered. In addition, a person who willfully refuses after written demand by the Treasurer to pay or deliver property is guilty of a misdemeanor punishable by a fine, imprisonment, or both. (Sec. 567.255, M.C.L.)

Appeal process.—Effective March 1, 2015, a process is enacted by which holders of property may contest a determination of unclaimed property liability and appeal to the state circuit court. A holder of unclaimed property that receives an examination determination may contest it within 90 days by either bringing an action in circuit court or filing a request for reconsideration with the administrator. (Sec. 567.251a, M.C.L.)

• *Records auditing*

The auditing standards and processes for uniform unclaimed property records examinations include the following requirements:

— any examination of a person's records by the state treasurer or his or her agents must be performed in accordance with generally accepted auditing standards to the extent applicable to unclaimed property examinations;

— a person who has been audited or whose records have been examined must be given a complete copy of the audit report;

— the work performed, the property types reviewed, any estimation techniques employed, calculations showing the potential amount of property due, a statement of findings, and all other correspondence must be specified in detail;

— the state treasurer or agents must be allowed to determine the amount of any abandoned or unclaimed property due and owing based on a reasonable method of estimation consistent with the auditing standards, if the person being examined does not have substantially complete records; and

— the state treasurer must file a request for rule-making with the Office of Regulatory Reinvention to initiate rules on auditing standards. (Sec. 567.251, M.C.L.)

If a person filed all required reports and maintained substantially complete records, all of the following apply:

— the examination must include a review of the person's books and records;

— the examination must not be based on an estimate;

— the administrator or his or her agents must consider all evidence presented by the holder to remediate the findings. (Sec. 567.251, M.C.L.)

"Substantially complete records" means at least 90% of the records necessary for unclaimed property examination purposes as defined under the principles of internal controls. Substantially complete records are not meant to be an absolute measurement of all available records. (Sec. 567.251, M.C.L.)

• *Recovery of escheated property*

Under the Unclaimed Property Act.—A person claiming an interest in any property paid or delivered as abandoned property under the Uniform Disposition Act may file a claim with the Treasurer, who must consider such claim within 90 days after it is filed. (Sec. 567.245, M.C.L.) If the claimant is another state, the claim must satisfy certain requirements that establish a reasonable basis for the state's claim. (Sec. 567.246, M.C.L.)

A person aggrieved by a decision of the Treasurer or whose claim was not acted upon within 90 days after the filing date may, within 90 days after the decision of the Treasurer or 180 days after filing the claim not acted upon, commence an action in the circuit court to establish the claim against the Treasurer. (Sec. 567.247, M.C.L.)

Under the Escheat Law.—Claims for redemption of escheated property are made with the Treasurer. (Sec. 567.259, M.C.L.)

• *Administrator*

The Michigan Unclaimed Property Law is administered by the Department of Treasury, Unclaimed Property Division, P.O. Box 30756, Lansing, MI 48909. Phone: (517) 636-6940; Fax: (517) 322-5986.

The Michigan Escheat Law is administered jointly by the State Attorney General and the State Treasurer. (Sec. 567.259, M.C.L.)

LAW AND RULE LOCATOR

This finding list shows where all sections of Michigan compiled laws and administrative rules referred to in the *Guidebook* are discussed.

LAW

RULES

TOPICAL INDEX

References are to paragraph (¶) numbers.

A

E

J

L

M

N

R